Facing the Gods

This is the first history of epiphany as both a phenomenon and a cultural discourse within the Graeco-Roman world. It explores divine manifestations and their representations both in art and in literary, historical and epigraphic accounts. The cultural analysis of epiphany is set within a historical framework that examines its development from the archaic period to the Roman Empire. In particular, a surprisingly large number of the images that have survived from antiquity are not only religious but epiphanically charged. Verity Platt argues that the enduring potential for divine incursions into mortal experience provides a reliable cognitive structure that supports both ancient religion and mythology. At the same time, Graeco-Roman culture exhibits a sophisticated awareness of the difficulties in apprehending deity and representing divine presence, and of the potential for the man-made sign to lead the worshipper back to an unmediated epiphanic encounter.

VERITY PLATT is Associate Professor in the departments of Classics and Art History at Cornell University, having previously taught at the universities of Exeter and Chicago. Her research interests include attitudes to the sacred image in antiquity, ancient theories of representation, the relationship between image and text, and Roman wall-painting and funerary art. This is her first book.

GREEK CULTURE IN THE ROMAN WORLD

Editors

Susan E. Alcock
Brown University

Jaś Elsner
Corpus Christi College, Oxford

Simon Goldhill
University of Cambridge

The Greek culture of the Roman Empire offers a rich field of study. Extraordinary insights can be gained into processes of multicultural contact and exchange, political and ideological conflict, and the creativity of a changing, polyglot empire. During this period, many fundamental elements of Western society were being set in place: from the rise of Christianity, to an influential system of education, to long-lived artistic canons. This series is the first to focus on the response of Greek culture to its Roman imperial setting as a significant phenomenon in its own right. To this end, it will publish original and innovative research in the art, archaeology, epigraphy, history, philosophy, religion, and literature of the empire, with an emphasis on Greek material.

Titles in series:

Facing the Gods

Epiphany and Representation in Graeco-Roman Art, Literature and Religion

VERITY PLATT

CAMBRIDGE
UNIVERSITY PRESS

University Printing House, Cambridge CB2 8BS, United Kingdom

Cambridge University Press is part of the University of Cambridge.

It furthers the University's mission by disseminating knowledge in the pursuit of education, learning and research at the highest international levels of excellence.

www.cambridge.org
Information on this title: www.cambridge.org/9781316619193

© Verity Platt 2011

First published 2011
3rd printing 2012
First paperback edition 2016

A catalogue record for this publication is available from the British Library

Library of Congress Cataloguing in Publication data
Platt, Verity J. (Verity Jane), 1977–
Facing the gods : epiphany and representation in Graeco-Roman art, literature, and religion / Verity Platt.
    p.   cm. – (Greek culture in the Roman world)
Includes bibliographical references and index
ISBN 978-0-521-86171-7 Hardback
1. Rome – Religion.   2. Greece – Religion.   3. Epiphany in art.
4. Rome – Civilization.   5. Greece – Civilization.   I. Title
BL810.P53   2011
292–dc22   2011012624

ISBN 978-0-521-86171-7 Hardback
ISBN 978-1-316-61919-3 Paperback

To my parents,
Jane and Richard Platt,
with love and thanks.

Colours are all muddled up
and the image is entangled
with the thing
and the eyes burn.

Saadi Youssef, *Poetry*

He believed that it was for the man of letters to record these
epiphanies with extreme care, seeing that they themselves
are the most delicate and evanescent of moments.

James Joyce, *Stephen Hero*

Contents

Illustrations

Acknowledgements

As it was for Leto, so this book's birth pangs were a test of endurance. Yet although the result may be less than divine, I lacked neither a veritable pantheon of supporters, nor many a place to call my Delos. My deepest thanks are due to Jaś Elsner, who oversaw the project from its inception as a doctoral thesis to its final publication. His imagination, intellectual generosity, patience and kindness of spirit ensured that it is considerably better in its final form than it would otherwise have been. Richard Neer has a gift for asking questions that open doors to the most productive avenues of thought, and was a most supportive colleague throughout the process of revision. Among those who provided very helpful feedback on the manuscript, Robin Osborne was a vital source of advice and encouragement, while Simon Goldhill's constructive responses always made me think anew, and John Ma shared his formidable knowledge of Hellenistic epigraphy. As my DPhil examiners, Richard Gordon and Chris Pelling gave me invaluable advice on how best to develop the project. Michael Squire and Milette Gaifman helped me think through many of the most knotty issues this book addresses, and continue to be a source of inspiration and encouragement, reminding me of the broader art historical and theological traditions with which our work is in dialogue. Georgia Petridou generously shared her encyclopaedic knowledge of epiphany in Greek religion, which was invaluable to me in writing the early chapters of this book.

This project would not have been possible without the support of several institutions. In Oxford, Christ Church supported my doctoral studies with a generous Senior Scholarship and welcomed me back as a visiting scholar in 2005–6. From 2003 to 2005 the Stevenson Junior Research Fellowship at University College gave me valuable breathing space in which to develop my thesis into book form, and in 2006–7 I spent a productive year of leave as a visiting fellow in the friendly and inspiring community of Corpus Christi College. This leave was generously granted by the University of Chicago. I am particularly grateful to my Chicago colleagues in the departments of Art History and Classics, especially Marty Ward and Joel Snyder, who have been outstandingly supportive department chairs in Art History, and Sarah Nooter, who kindly proofread my Greek. Many others generously shared their forth-coming work, helped me think through ideas, directed me to references or lent me books: my warm thanks are due to Clifford Ando, Emily Barag-wanath, Shadi Bartsch, Ruth Bielfeldt, Barbara Borg, Ewen Bowie, Alan Bowman, Alain Bresson, Emma Bridges, Matei Candea, Robin Cormack, Martine Cuypers, Janet Downie, Chris Faraone, David Fearn, Jane Fineron, Martin Henig, Sarah Iles Johnston, Julia Kindt, Nektaria Klapaki, Renée Koch Piettre, Barbara Kowalzig, Aden Kumler, Rosemary McEvoy, Zahra Newby, John North, Mark Payne, Ivana Petrovic, Alexia Petsalis-Diomidis, Jim Porter, Antonia Ruppel, Jeffrey Rusten, Ian Rutherford, Richard Ruther-ford, Rolf Schneider, Bert Smith, Alex Stevens, Jeremy Tanner, Katherine Taylor, Caroline Vout, Tim Whitmarsh and Rebecca Zorach. Thank you, too, to the Chicago students who helped me refine many of the ideas in this book during seminars on the aesthetics of the sacred in antiquity, especially Nicola Cronin, Mia Khimm, Vivienne Hana Kim (who was also a stellar research assistant), Ann Patnaude, Angele Rosenberg and Jie Shi. At Cambridge University Press, Michael Sharp has been extraordinarily patient and generous with his time; I am particularly grateful to him for his help in sourcing images, and to Liz Davey, Liz Hanlon and Merle Read for their superb editorial support.

Among the many friends who have shared ideas and given encourage-ment, I would like to thank Stephen Bernard, Alice Harlan, Felicity James, Jacob Mackey, Jessica Mayberry, Caroline Petit, Melissa Terras and Rachel Zayer (who also provided invaluable help with the bibliography). This book would never have epiphanised at all if not for the enduring love, support and good humour of my parents, Jane and Richard Platt, my sister Belinda, and brother, Theo, and especially my husband, Roger Moseley, whose kindness and understanding provided the calm seas and gentle breeze that finally brought me to dry land.

Note on the text

Faced with the classicist's familiar dilemma over dating and nomenclature, I have used BCE/CE rather than BC/AD for dates, and have retained the familiar Latin forms of Greek names, except in Chapter 8, where (with the exception of Selene), I have used the Roman rather than Greek names of deities portrayed in Roman funerary art. Any abbreviations in the main text that are not listed on pp. xvi–xviii employ the conventions of Liddell and Scott's *Greek–English Lexicon* (LSJ). Translations are my own, unless otherwise stated.

The second half of Chapter 4 is reworked from my article 'Evasive Epiphanies in Ekphrastic Epigram', published in *Ramus* 31 (2002: 33–50). Chapter 7 is an extended and revised version of 'Virtual Visions: *Phantasia* and the Perception of the Divine in *The Life of Apollonius of Tyana*', published in E. Bowie and J. Elsner (eds.), *Philostratus* (Cambridge, 2009: 131–54). I am grateful to Aureal Publications and Cambridge University Press for their permission to reuse this material.

Abbreviations

AA	*Archäologischer Anzeiger*
A&A	*Antike und Abendland. Beiträge zum Verständnis der Griechen und Römer und ihres Nachlebens*
AION	*Annali dell'Istituto universitario orientale di Napoli*
AJA	*American Journal of Archaeology*
AJPh	*American Journal of Philology*
ANRW	*Aufstieg und Niedergang der römischen Welt*
AntC	*L'Antiquité classique*
Anth. Pal.	*Anthologia Palatina*
Anth. Plan.	*Anthologia Planudea*
AntK	*Antike Kunst*
ArchEph	*Αρχαιολογική Ἐφημερίς*
ARV²	Beazley J. D. *Attic Red-Figure Vase-Painters.* Oxford, 1963
ASR	*Die antiken Sarkophagreliefs.* Berlin
AthMitt	*Mitteilungen des Deutschen Archäologischen Instituts, Athenische Abteilung*
BABesch	*Bulletin Antieke Beschaving. Annual Papers on Classical Archaeology*
BCH	*Bulletin de correspondance hellénique*
BICS	*Bulletin of the Institute of Classical Studies, University of London*
BMMA	*Bulletin of the Metropolitan Museum of Art*
BSA	*Annual of the British School at Athens*
Carm. Epigr.	Buecheler, F. and A. Riese (eds.). *Anthologia Latina sive Poesis Latinae Supplementum. Pars Posterior: Carmina Epigraphica. Fasciculus II.* Leipzig, 1897
Carm. Sep.	Kholodniak, I. I. (ed.). *Carmina Sepulcralia Latina.* St Petersburg, 1897
CEG	Hansen, P. A. *Carmina Epigraphica Graeca.* 2 vols. Berlin, 1983–9
CIA	*Corpus Inscriptionum Atticarum*
CIL	*Corpus Inscriptionum Latinarum*
CJ	*Classical Journal*
ClAnt	*Classical Antiquity*
CPh	*Classical Philology*
CRAI	*Comptes rendus de l'Académie des inscriptions et belles-lettres*

CQ	*Classical Quarterly*
CW	*Classical World*
DK	Diels, H. (ed.). *Die Fragmente der Vorsokratiker.* 6th edn. Rev. W. Kranz. 3 vols. Berlin, 1952
EA	*Epigraphica Anatolica*
EG	Kaibel, G. *Epigrammata Graeca.* Berlin, 1878
EL	*Études de lettres*
GP 1965	Gow, A. S. F. and D. L. Page. *The Greek Anthology: Hellenistic Epigrams.* 2 vols. Cambridge, 1965
GP 1968	Gow, A. S. F. and D. L. Page. *The Greek Anthology. The Garland of Philip and Some Contemporary Epigrams.* 2 vols. Cambridge, 1968
GRBS	*Greek, Roman and Byzantine Studies*
FD	*Fouilles de Delphes*
FGrH	Jacoby, F. (ed.). *Die Fragmente der griechischen Historiker.* Berlin and Leiden, 1923–62
HSCP	*Harvard Studies in Classical Philology*
I. Iasos	(*IK* 28.1–2) Blümel, W. *Die Inschriften von Iasos.* 2 vols. Bonn, 1985
I. Knidos	(*IK* 41) Blümel, W. *Die Inschriften von Knidos.* Bonn, 1992
I. Mylasa	(*IK* 34–5) Blümel, W. *Die Inschriften von Mylasa.* 2 vols. Bonn, 1987–8
I. Stratonikeia	(*IK* 21, 22.1, 22.2) Şahin, M. Ç. *Die Inschriften von Stratonikeia.* 3 vols. Bonn, 1981, 1982, 1990
ICS	*Illinois Classical Studies*
IG	*Inscriptiones Graecae. Consilio et Auctoritate Academiae Scientiarum Berolinensis et Brandenburgensis Editae.* Berlin, 1873–
IK	*Inschriften griechischer Städte aus Kleinasien.* Bonn, 1972–
Inschr. Perg.	Fraenkel, M. *Die Inschriften von Pergamon.* Altertümer von Pergamon 8. 2 vols. Berlin, 1890–5
IOSPE	Latyschev, V. V. *Inscriptiones Antiquae Orae Septentrionalis Ponti Euxini.* St Petersburg, 1916
IstMitt	*Istanbuler Mitteilungen*
IvM	Kern, O. *Die Inschriften von Magnesia am Maeander.* Berlin, 1900
JDAI	*Jahrbuch des Deutschen Archäologischen Instituts*
JHS	*Journal of Hellenic Studies*
JRA	*Journal of Roman Archaeology*
JRH	*Journal of Religious History*
JRS	*Journal of Roman Studies*
KA	Kassel, R. and C. Austin. *Poetae Comici Graeci.* Berlin, 1983–

KRS	Kirk, G. S., J. E. Raven and M. Schofield. *The Presocratic Philosophers. A Critical History with a Selection of Texts.* 2nd edn. Cambridge, 1983
LBW	Le Bas, P. and W.-H. Waddington. *Voyage archéologique en Grèce et en Asie Mineure.* 3 vols. Paris, 1851–70
LIMC	*Lexicon Iconographicum Mythologiae Classicae.* Zurich, 1981–99
LSAM	Sokolowski, F. *Lois sacrées de l'Asie Mineure.* Paris, 1955
Mansi	Mansi, J. D. *Sacrorum Conciliorum Nova et Amplissima Collectio.* 31 vols. Florence and Venice, 1759–98
MD	*Materiali e discussioni per l'analisi dei testi classici*
MÉFRA	*Mélanges de l'École française de Rome. Antiquité*
MH	*Museum Helveticum*
NTS	*New Testament Studies*
OGIS	Dittenberger, W. *Orientis Graeci Inscriptiones Selectae. Supplementum Sylloges Inscriptionum Graecarum.* 2 vols. Leipzig, 1903–5
PCPS	*Proceedings of the Cambridge Philological Society*
PMG	Page, D. L. *Poetae Melici Graeci.* Oxford, 1962
PPM	*Pompei. Pitture e mosaici.* Rome, 1990–2003
QUCC	*Quaderni urbinati di cultura classica*
RA	*Revue archéologique*
RAC	*Rivista di archeologia cristiana*
RCCM	*Rivista di cultura classica e medioevale*
RE	Pauly, A., G. Wissowa *et al. Realencyclopädie der classischen Altertumswissenschaft.* Stuttgart, 1894–1980
REA	*Revue des études anciennes*
RhM	*Rheinisches Museum für Philologie*
RIA	*Rivista dell'Istituto nazionale d'archeologia e storia dell'arte*
RM	*Mitteilungen des Deutschen Archäologischen Instituts, Römische Abteilung*
RRC	Crawford, M. H. *Roman Republican Coinage.* Cambridge, 1974
RSP	*Rivista di studi pompeiani*
Sammelbuch	*Sammelbuch griechischer Urkunden aus Ägypten.* Strasburg
SB	Shackleton Bailey, D. R. *Anthologia Latina.* Stuttgart, 1982
SEG	*Supplementum Epigraphicum Graecum*
Syll.³	Dittenberger, W. *Sylloge Inscriptionum Graecarum.* 4 vols. 3rd edn. Leipzig, 1960
SyllClass	*Syllecta Classica*
TAPA	*Transactions of the American Philological Association*
ZPE	*Zeitschrift für Papyrologie und Epigraphik*

Introduction

Ἀφροδίτην ἐλεφαντίνην ἐν ἁπαλοῖς μυρρινῶσιν ᾄδουσιν ἁπαλαὶ κόραι. διδάσκαλος αὐτὰς ἄγει σοφὴ καὶ οὐδὲ ἔξωρος. ἐφιζάνει γάρ τις ὥρα καὶ ῥυτίδι πρώτῃ, γήρως μὲν τὸ ὑπόσεμνον ἕλκουσα, τούτῳ δ᾽ αὖ κεραννῦσα τὸ σῳζόμενον τῆς ἀκμῆς. καὶ τὸ μὲν σχῆμα τῆς Ἀφροδίτης Αἰδοῦς, γυμνὴ καὶ εὐσχήμων, ἡ δὲ ὕλη συνθήκη μεμυκότος ἐλέφαντος. ἀλλ᾽ οὐ βούλεται γεγράφθαι δοκεῖν ἡ θεός, ἔκκειται δὲ οἷα λαβέσθαι.

βούλει λόγου τι ἐπιλείβωμεν τῷ βωμῷ; λιβανωτοῦ γὰρ ἱκανῶς ἔχει καὶ κασίας καὶ σμύρνης, δοκεῖ δέ μοι καὶ Σαπφοῦς τι ἀναπνεῖν. ἐπαινετέα τοίνυν ἡ σοφία τῆς γραφῆς, πρῶτον μὲν ὅτι τὰς ἀγαπωμένας λίθους περιβαλοῦσα οὐκ ἐκ τῶν χρωμάτων αὐτὰς ἐμιμήσατο, ἀλλ᾽ ἐκ τοῦ φωτός, οἷον ὀφθαλμῷ κέντρον τὴν διαύγειαν αὐταῖς ἐνθεῖσα, εἶτα ὅτι καὶ τοῦ ὕμνου παρέχει ἀκούειν. ᾄδουσι γὰρ αἱ παῖδες, ᾄδουσι, καὶ ἡ διδάσκαλος ὑποβλέπει τὴν ἀπᾴδουσαν κροτοῦσα τὰς χεῖρας καὶ ἐς τὸ μέλος ἱκανῶς ἐμβιβάζουσα.

Aphrodite, made of ivory, delicate maidens are hymning in delicate myrtle groves. The chorister who leads them is skilled in her art, and not yet past her youth; for a certain beauty rests even on her first wrinkle, which, though it brings with it the gravity of age, yet tempers this with what remains of her prime. The type of the goddess is that of Aphrodite goddess of Modesty, naked and graceful, and the material is ivory, closely joined. However, the goddess is unwilling to seem painted, but she stands out as though one could take hold of her.

Do you wish us to pour a libation of discourse on the altar? For of frankincense and cinnamon and myrrh it has enough already, and it seems to me to give out also a fragrance as of Sappho. Accordingly the artistry of the painting must be praised, first, because the artist, in making the border of precious stones, has used not colours but light to depict them, putting a radiance in them like the pupil in an eye, and, secondly, because he even makes us hear the hymn. For the maidens are singing, are singing, and the chorister frowns at one who is off key, clapping her hands and trying earnestly to bring her into tune.

Philostratus, *Imagines* 2.1–3[1]

---

[1] Transl. from Arthur Fairbanks's Loeb Classical Library edition, 1969 (with some modifications).

A statue, a song, a scent: the stage is set for Aphrodite. A libation of *logos* – composed by her singing worshippers, by the painter, by the narrator of the ekphrasis, by Philostratus himself – is poured in expectation of her presence. But where is the goddess? In an infinite recession of registers, she stands as an ivory image, depicted within a painting, described within a text. This Aphrodite, here in her guise as a goddess of Modesty (*aidōs*), is surely beyond our grasp. Ivory, medium of duplicity (and the gate through which false dreams pass), signals the statue's capacity to tempt and deceive, even as its flesh-like tones and organic warmth recall the wish fulfilment granted to Pygmalion (whose living doll, in Ovid's *Metamorphoses*, was also made of ivory).[2] And yet, despite the veil of representation that stands between reader and goddess, Aphrodite 'does not want to seem painted'; she is 'set forth' or 'projected' (ἔκκειται) from the screen of discourse, willing herself to be 'seized', even 'possessed' (λαβέσθαι) by the viewer. Is it not strange to impute motives to the image in this way, to refer to it as 'the goddess' (ἡ θεός), rather than 'the statue'? What does it (she?) want?[3]

She wants, Philostratus suggests, to be experienced as an epiphany.

Here, in the programmatic introduction to his second book of ekphraseis, Philostratus gives form to an abiding tension that exists between art and the sacred (and, indeed, at the heart of representation itself): what does it mean to make the gods present through acts of human creativity? How can images be experienced as divine, when their material, their facture, their framing are so clearly dependent upon cultural artifice? When, as in the opening words of the ekphrasis, deity must be inevitably coupled with statue, Aphrodite with ivory (Ἀφροδίτην ἐλεφαντίνην), in a necessary symbiosis of form and matter? The text generates a double affect akin to the play of 'absorption and erudition' that accompanies the viewing of any naturalistic image, giving form to the viewer's simultaneous desire for the image to be 'real' and recognition of its status as a man-made object.[4] In this sense the ivory

---

[2] *Met.* 10.243–97: see Rosati (1983), Elsner (1991, 2007: 113–31), Sharrock (1991a, 1991b), Hardie (2002: 173–226), Salzman-Mitchell (2008) and, on the fantasy of living statues, K. Gross (1992: esp. 69–75) and my discussion of agalmatophilia in Chapter 4, 183–8. Clement of Alexandria (*Protrepticus* 4.57.2) and Arnobius (*Adv. Nat.* 6.22) tell us that Pygmalion actually fell in love with an ivory statue of Aphrodite. On deception in the *Imagines*, see McCombie (2002), R. Webb (2006b) and Squire (2009: 416–27). Philostratus mentions the gates of dreams at 1.27.3, alluding to *Od.* 19.563–7, on which see Amory (1966) and Cox Miller (1994: 14–17), with my discussion in Chapter 6, 253–4.

[3] On the concept of 'what pictures want', see W. J. T. Mitchell (1994).

[4] On the relationship between 'absorption and erudition' in the *Imagines*, see Newby (2009), whose helpful phrase reappears throughout this book. On the desire to collapse distinctions between image and prototype in practices of viewing, see Freedberg (1989) and Maniura and Shepherd (2006).

Aphrodite occupies a perfect position as the lure between books 1 and 2 of the *Imagines*, an embodiment of art's sensuous promise and the inevitable experience of thwarted desire that accompanies any act of beholding (or reading).[5] The goddess's palpable presence draws us in, only to be revealed as a play of mirrors; the shuttling between Ἀφροδίτην and ἐλεφαντίνην, or goddess and image, is a programmatic expression of the continual shifting between wonder and wisdom (*thauma* and *sophia*) generated by the text's educated exegete, whose word-pictures express now emotional involvement with the painting's content, now detached commentary on the *technē*, or skill, of the painter.[6]

Yet there is more at stake in this particular ekphrasis, signified by the elaborate ritual frame that shapes our mental picture (or *phantasia*) of Aphrodite.[7] For although the goddess exists as a statue within a painting within a text, the epiphanic manoeuvre by which this ontological hierarchy is collapsed is generated by a hymn. Aphrodite is made present and palpable for the reader through a series of embedded textual performances prompted by the ekphrastic fireworks of the sophist, who conjures up the hymnic invocation directed by the female choir-mistress (the *didaskalos*) within the text. Together, these enact a libation of *logos*, a verbal offering that through its synaesthetic potency stands for (is literally *redolent* of) the fragrant offerings poured upon the altar in the painting, and which, through a sensuous form of intertextuality, 'breathes forth a scent of Sappho' (Σαπφοῦς τι ἀναπνεῖν).[8] Sappho it was who, as a *didaskalos* of maidens similar to those described in the painting, invoked Aphrodite in her famous hymn as 'enthroned in many colours' (ποικιλόθρονα) and 'weaver of wiles' (δολόπλοκε), begging her to facilitate the fulfilment of her desire for an elusive love-object.[9] In this way Philostratus indirectly invokes Aphrodite

---

[5] On the structure of the *Imagines*, see G. Anderson (1986: 265–6), Elsner (1995: 37–9, 2000a) and Braginskaya and Leonov (2006). On ekphrasis, see my discussion in Chapter 4, with bibliography.

[6] On the significance of *paideia* in the *Imagines*, see Maffei (1991) and Elsner (1995: 21–39). The important of *technē* is twice made clear in the proem to book 1, where it is used to refer to proportion (1) and the use of colour (3).

[7] On the relationship between epiphany, representation and *phantasia*, see my discussion in Chapters 5 and 7, esp. 320–9, on Philostratus' *Life of Apollonius of Tyana*. On *phantasia* in the *Imagines*, see Elsner (1995: 37–8), Abbondanza (2001), Thein (2002) and Squire (2009: 340–2).

[8] Cf. Libanius on the offering of a 'feast of *logoi*' to Artemis as the crowning event of celebrations in honour of her cult, in a letter to Bacchius of Tarsus, *c.* 362 CE (83 Norman, with Goldhill, 2006: 118–19). On synaesthetic effects in the *Imagines*, see Manieri (1999) and R. Webb (2006b: 120–2).

[9] Sappho fr. 1, lines 1–2; cf. *Imagines* 2.1.3, where Philostratus describes the maidens as 'honey-voiced (μελίφωνοι), to use a charming expression of Sappho', evoking fr. 71.6, μελλιχόφων[ος, 'soft-voiced'. On the role of Aphrodite in the hymn, see A. Cameron (1939),

as a goddess of painting (and writing, for *graphein* refers to both), alluding to epithets that would, of course, be entirely appropriate for a collection of ekphraseis in which painted and rhetorical 'colours' are woven together in an increasingly dazzling examination of the playful elusiveness of both prototypes within images, and images within texts.[10] Through this play of allusion and description, the ekphrasis becomes itself a form of worship.

By pointing to Sappho's *Hymn to Aphrodite* (itself placed first within the collection of her poems known to antiquity), Philostratus facilitates a form of indirect epiphany, diverting us to an ancient prayer in which the goddess was indeed presented as animate and present, speaking and smiling to and through her female devotee(s).[11] His ekphrasis closes with the maidens singing of Aphrodite's birth: 'By looking upward they indicate that she is from Heaven (Ouranos), and by slightly moving their upturned hands they show that she has come from the sea, and their smile is an intimation of the sea's calm (τὸ μειδίαμα δὲ αὐτῶν γαλήνης ἐστὶν αἴνιγμα).' Their use of aetiological myth to narrate the goddess's original epiphany prompts a smile (μειδίαμα) that echoes Sappho's description of Aphrodite 'smiling with an immortal countenance' (μειδιαίσαισ᾽ ἀθανάτῳ προσώπῳ), uniting the goddess with her worshippers through gesture and performance.[12] The ekphrasis suggests that when experienced within the context of *ritual* – when the song can actually be *heard* – text and image can generate a 'real' experience of the divine. Crucially, however, such encounters can be facilitated only through the most exquisite human

Page (1955: 12–19) and West (1970), who play down the poem's epiphanic aspects; Bowra (1961: 198–205), on the hymn as a private prayer; Saake (1972: 55–60); Stanley (1976); Carson (1996); Greene (1996a: 243–6); Hutchinson (2001: 159–60); Winkler (2002: 42–53) and Nagy (2007: 25–8). On the reception of Sappho in antiquity, see Reynolds (2002: 67–74). Philostratus' implicit comparison of Sappho to the female *didaskalos* with her maiden pupils also offers a female paradigm of the homoerotic pedagogic relationship between the sophist and *pais* established in book 1, on which see Elsner (2004: 173–7).

[10] On Sappho's use of the epithet *poikilothronos*, see Scheid and Svenbro (1996: 53–60). On colour in the *Imagines*, see Dubel (2009); on the correspondences Philostratus suggests between visual and rhetorical techniques, see Conan (1987), Beall (1993), Cassin (1995: 493–512) and R. Webb (2006b). On the use of γράφειν to mean both 'to paint' and 'to write', see Lissarrague (1992), Boeder (1996: 149–65), Neer (1998) and Squire (2009: 147–8, 347–8, on *Imagines* 2.18.3; 421–2, on *Imagines* 1.31.1, 3).

[11] On the programmatic positioning of Sappho fr. 1 within collections of her works formed during the Hellenistic period, see Winkler (2002: 42–3).

[12] Fr. 1, line 14. Compare *H. Hom.* 5.3, which describes Aphrodite as 'always smiling' (αἰεὶ μειδιάει): see Boedeker (1974: 23–6, 32–5) on Aphrodite's Homeric epithet φιλομμειδής, and on the *Homeric Hymn to Aphrodite*, my discussion in Chapter 1, 63–72. On the ritual orchestration of myth in archaic and classical choral poetry and the mutually reinforcing relationship between belief and practice in Greek religion, see Kowalzig (2007).

technē: the ivory must be 'closely joined' (συνθήκη); the choristers must sing 'in tune' (ἐς τὸ μέλος). In this sense *thauma* and *sophia*, or absorption and erudition, need not be mutually contradictory. Indeed, it is only through such co-ordinations of wisdom and skill – through the acquisition and demonstration of *paideia* – that the divine might actually be apprehended. It is significant in this sense that the final phrase of the ekphrasis describes the maidens' smiles as an *ainigma* of the sea's calm at Aphrodite's birth, a verbo-visual 'riddle' that by intimating divine epiphany nevertheless reasserts its resistance to all but the most subtly calibrated invocations of presence.[13]

Nowhere is this careful equilibrium between mortal skill and divine radiance more palpable than in Philostratus' description of the precious or 'cherished' gems (τὰς ἀγαπωμένας λίθους) that have been 'cast around' the painting (περιβαλοῦσα), presumably as a kind of frame.[14] On one hand, the *technē* required to manipulate base pigments into transparent, gleaming stones is presented as a sign of the painter's *sophia* – his technical wisdom. On the other hand, the suggestion that he has painted with light itself (ἐκ τοῦ φωτός) to generate a radiance (διαύγειαν) that transforms the jewels into shining eyes takes us beyond the boundaries of representation, shifting into a revelatory mode. In their dazzling indeterminacy, the gem-eyes are akin to the iridescence of Athena's epiphany at *Imagines* 2.27.3, when she springs fully formed from the head of Zeus: 'As for the material of her panoply (τὴν δὲ ὕλην τῆς πανοπλίας), no one could guess it; for as many as are the colours of the rainbow, which changes its light now to one hue and now to another, so many are the colours of her armour'.[15] Likewise the embroidered flowers on the garments of Aphrodite's *korai* at 2.1.3 'are miraculous

---

[13] Compare 1.6.3, where the allegorical significance of the Erotes' play is described as a 'beautiful riddle' (καλὸν τὸ αἴνιγμα). Significantly, 2.1 makes visible an Aphrodite who is present but unseen at 1.6.7, signified only by offerings in a rural shrine: 'Do you look, please, at Aphrodite (σὺ δέ μοι τὴν Ἀφροδίτην βλέπε). But where is she and in what part of the orchard yonder? . . . Be sure that Aphrodite is there, where the Nymphs, I doubt not (οἶμαι), have established a shrine to her.' The pointed contrast in 2.1, which makes 'Aphrodite' the very first word of book 2, draws attention to the increased emphasis on the sacred in the second book of the *Imagines*, with its focus on divine epiphany and its corresponding rituals in 2.1, 2.16 (Palaemon) and 2.27 (the birth of Athena). I am grateful to Jaś Elsner for sharing with me an unpublished piece on Philostratus' use of religion in these ekphraseis.

[14] This is the interpretation of περιβαλοῦσα suggested by Fairbanks, following Benndorf and Schenkel (1893). It does not, however, preclude the idea that the gems are 'scattered around' Aphrodite's shrine as votive offerings. On the dedication of gem collections, or *dactyliothecae* in temples, see Pliny *HN* 37.11 and Suetonius *Divus Iulius* 47.

[15] On this and parallel descriptions of divine materials at 1.10.3 (Amphion's chlamys), 1.16.4 (Pasiphae's iridescent tunic) and 2.2.2 (Achilles' chlamys), see Dubel (2009: 317).

[literally *daemonic*] imitations' (δαιμονίως ἐκμεμίμηται).[16] When experienced as divine or daemonic, matter (*hulē*) has the power to confound conventional categories of material, colour and description altogether, just as at 2.1.1 Aphrodite resists her status as a painted statue and wriggles out of conventional iconographic schemata, being simultaneously 'modest' and 'naked' (note the juxtaposition of Αἰδοῦς, γυμνή).[17] The gem-studded frame that surrounds her, and points to the ekphrasis' status as a frame for the book itself, is simultaneously matter and light, a painted *ainigma* that demonstrates the artist's skill while pointing to the divinity of its depicted content.

As one might expect, the programmatic ekphrasis of *Imagines* 2.1 foregrounds the act of looking. But in line with Philostratus' increased emphasis on the sacred in book 2, the visual operations he traces within the text continually push beyond the conventional limitations of human artistry in order to suggest that the object of the gaze *looks back*.[18] In this respect the all-seeing gems encourage us to read anew the dancing *korai* of the opening paragraph: are they maidens, or, in a pun on an alternative meaning of κόρη ('pupil'), might they too be eyes?[19] Surrounded by all-seeing gems and dancing 'eyes', the statue of Aphrodite cannot but be imbued with a subjectivity of her own, viewed as a sentient being who 'does not want to seem painted', but to engage directly with her worshippers beyond the frame. In this way, Philostratus not only highlights a cultural predilection to attribute agency to anthropomorphic divine forms, but also demonstrates how a complex

---

[16] Fairbanks translates 'are represented with wonderful truth'. Compare 2.34, the final ekphrasis in the collection where the Horai are described, in a wonderful echo of 2.1, as being depicted 'with miraculous skill' (δαιμονίου τέχνης): see Elsner (2000c).

[17] On *hulē* as matter itself ('that from which [things] are generated', as opposed to 'wood'), see Arist. *Metaph.* 1032a17, and in late antique theology, Finney (1994: 47–53). Philostratus may imply here that Aphrodite is represented in the *Pudica* pose, with her arms concealing her breasts and pudenda, yet as the juxtaposition of Αἰδοῦς and γυμνή suggests, such a simultaneous revelation and concealment of the goddess's body is itself a form of visual paradox. On the problems inherent in making Aphrodite visually and corporeally accessible to her mortal viewers, see my discussion of Praxiteles' Aphrodite of Knidos in Chapter 4.

[18] See above, n. 14, and on objects that look back, Elkins (1996: 46–85).

[19] See LSJ s.v. κόρη, citing Pl. *Alc.* 1.132e–133a: 'Have you observed that the face of the person who looks into another's eye is shown in the optic confronting him, as in a mirror, and we call this the pupil (ὃ δὴ καὶ κόρην καλοῦμεν) for in it is an image (εἴδωλον) of the person looking?' (translation from W. R. M. Lamb, *Plato*, vol. viii Loeb Classical Library, 1955). Cf. the proem to *Imagines* 1, where Philostratus specifically claims that 'the varying nature of bright eyes the plastic artist does not bring out at all in his work; but the "grey eye", the "blue eye", the "black eye" are known to painting' (καὶ αὐγὰς ὀμμάτων ὁποῖαί εἰσιν ὁ πλαστικὸς μέν τις ἥκιστα ἐργάζεται, χαροπὸν δὲ ὄμμα καὶ γλαυκὸν καὶ μέλαν γραφικὴ οἶδε, proem 2): see Newby (2009: 325).

interweaving of ritual performance, synaesthetic effect and iconographic, literary and mythological know-how might generate *enargeia*, 'clarity' or 'vividness', in the (mind's) eye of his viewer-readers.[20] In short, he reveals to us the mechanics of epiphany – the cultural codes of representation, performance and reception by which the gods might be made present and accessible to mortal perception. In doing so, he also demonstrates the high level of self-consciousness with which the relationship between epiphany and cultural practice was explored, celebrated and problematised in the literature of imperial Greece (or as he himself termed it, the 'Second Sophistic').[21] For Philostratus was well aware that in order to come face to face with the divine, one must – as the title of this book suggests – supply the very face one seeks.

I start with Philostratus because, as Charly Clerc long ago observed, it is in the prose literature of the second and third centuries CE that we find our most sustained, sophisticated theorisation of the relationship between Greek gods and their images.[22] Texts such as the *Imagines* and Philostratus' works on more overtly sacred themes, such as the *Heroicus* and the *Life of Apollonius of Tyana*, repeatedly draw attention to the idea that within Greek culture, epiphany (by which I mean the manifestation of deities to mortals) inspired, and was in turn inspired by, practices of visual and literary representation, generating a mutually reinforcing bond that operated within both identifiably sacred contexts and the cultural imagination at large.[23] In examining this relationship, Philostratus and his contemporaries repeatedly highlight the hermeneutic challenges raised by the notion of unmediated access to beings who are by definition invisible and incorporeal, and the difficulty of conveying such experiences through human modes of expression. For example, even a supposed 'first-hand' account of epiphanic autopsy, such as that supplied by Aelius Aristides in his *Sacred Tales* (which relate his experiences of incubation in the sanctuary of Asclepius at Pergamon), is filtered through a complex process of rhetorically self-conscious

---

[20] On *enargeia* in the *Imagines*, see R. Webb (2006b), and in Second Sophistic literature more broadly, my discussion in Chapter 5, with further bibliography. On the attribution of agency and interiority to sacred images, see Gell (1998: 134–6).

[21] *Lives of the Sophists* 481. For a discussion of the term and its potential drawbacks as a description of the period's literature, see Goldhill's introduction to his 2001 edited volume, esp. 14–15, and Whitmarsh (2001b: 42–4), with my discussion in Chapter 5, 215–18.

[22] Clerc (1915).

[23] Graf (2004a: 1122) defines epiphany (and the Greek term ἐπιφάνεια) as 'the manifestation of a deity in a spontaneous vision, or during an actual ritual process, as well as in stories'. On the unity of the Elder Philostratus' œuvre, see Lannoy (1997) and Elsner (2009a).

narration.[24] Despite the inevitably aporetic nature of much epiphanic discourse, however, these authors repeatedly advance modes of reading and viewing that offer the possibility of crossing the gap between human artifice and divine reality – between 'ivory' and 'Aphrodite'.

Crucially, for Philostratus, as for Dio Chrysostom, Pausanias, Aelius Aristides and Plutarch, any attempt to access divinity in the present is heavily dependent upon the cultural conventions of the past. Just as Aphrodite's maidens must invoke her presence by telling the story of her birth (her first epiphany, itself a programmatic demonstration of her divine identity), so Philostratus' attempt to render Aphrodite present through language in the *Imagines* must draw upon the hymnic invocations made by his literary predecessor Sappho. Such a concern for the cultural conditions of divine presence (and equally, its absence) is therefore inseparable from the broader motivation of Second Sophistic thinkers to recover and preserve their religious and cultural history; their sense of 'secondariness' is inevitably dependent upon what came before.[25] In this sense, the model of epiphany they advance is dependent upon a particularly Hellenic form of *paideia*, which looks to sacred tradition in order to emphasise continuity with the living religious culture of the present. So it is that while Part II of this book concentrates upon the relationship between epiphany and representation in the Second Sophistic, Part I addresses some of the religious, artistic and literary practices that characterised epiphanic discourse in archaic, classical and Hellenistic Greece, providing the necessary cultural background for a proper understanding of epiphany in the Greek culture of the Roman Empire. Even so, we shall see that in many cases, the intense interest in the phenomenon displayed by later Greek writers entails that much of our evidence for its earlier history is filtered through imperial texts. In order to understand the various epiphanic strategies employed by archaic and classical cult statues, for example (as I do in Chapter 2), it is necessary to perform a kind of textual archaeology, sifting between competing strata of evidence while bearing in mind the interpretative idiosyncrasies and ideological commitments of the author at hand. We might call it the 'curse of Pausanias' that the Narnia of Greek religion is often only accessible through the wardrobe of later tradition. Yet as much recent scholarship has

---

[24] See my discussion in Chapter 6, 260–6, 288–90, together with Pearcy (1988), S. Harrison (2000–1), Petsalis-Diomidis (2006b), Downie (2008a) and Holmes (2008).

[25] On the attempts of Second Sophistic authors to re-enter or 'animate' the past, see Bowie (1970), Swain (1996: 65–100), Schmitz (1997, 1999), J. Connolly (2001), Whitmarsh (2001b: 26–9, 41–89) and R. Webb (2006a), with my discussion in Chapter 5.

demonstrated, Pausanias and his colleagues have a great deal to offer the historian of antiquity in their own right.[26]

Until recently the role played by epiphany in Greek culture received rather limited scholarly attention; for decades the standard reference work for historians of Greek religion has been Friedrich Pfister's attempt to catalogue a definitive typology of human–divine encounters in an encyclopaedia entry of 1924.[27] Yet several recent doctoral theses, conferences and ensuing publications have suggested that the cognitive and hermeneutic dilemmas raised by epiphany are of particular interest to contemporary scholars.[28] The vanguard has been led by cultural historians of the French school inspired by Jean-Pierre Vernant's structuralist approach to religious *mentalité*, such as Renée Koch Piettre, together with classical philologists excited by the potential for deconstructive readings of the modalities of divine presence and the aporetic nature of epiphanic language in literary texts.[29] Epiphany

---

[26] On attitudes to Greek religion in Second Sophistic literature, see most notably Elsner (1997a, 2001b), Lightfoot (2003), Aitken and Maclean (2004), Galli (2004), Goldhill (2006), Rutherford (2009), Whitmarsh (2009), and, on Pausanias in particular, Elsner (1992, 1994, 1995: 125–55, 2007: 29–66), the papers gathered together in Bingen (1996) and Alcock *et al.* (2001), Hutton (2005b) and Pirenne-Delforge (2008).

[27] Pfister (1924), where he distinguishes between epic, mythic, legendary, cultic and Christian epiphanies; see also Pax (1955), who focuses upon cross-cultural similarities between Greek, Indo-Iranian, Egyptian, Babylonian and Christian models of epiphany, Lührmann (1975), who emphasises their soteriological function, Lane Fox (1986: 102–67), who traces the cultural history of Greco-Roman epiphany against the background of religious change in late antiquity, Versnel (1987), on the vexing question of what ancient viewers actually saw in their visions of the gods, and, for helpful summaries of epiphany's role in Greek religion, Cancik (1990) and Graf (2004a).

[28] Doctoral theses include Stevens (2002) and Turkeltaub (2003), on Homeric epiphany, Platt (2004), on which the present volume is based, and Petridou (2006, to appear in book form with Oxford University Press), which offers a comprehensive survey of the evidence for epiphanic experience in literary and epigraphic sources, together with an analysis of their role in Greek cult and significance for cultural and political identity. Conferences in America and the UK have led to a special edition of *Illinois Classical Studies* on the role of epiphany in Greek religion from Minoan Crete to early Christianity (2004), and a forthcoming volume edited by Petridou and Platt (in press) which foregrounds the special hermeneutic challenges raised by epiphany in Graeco-Roman literature, art and philosophy.

[29] In an unpublished doctoral thesis Koch Piettre (1996) explores the semiotics of epiphany across a range of literary and philosophical texts of the archaic and classical periods with particular reference, following Vernant, to the body of the divine: see also Veyne (1987), Koch Piettre (1999, 2001, 2005), Jaillard (2007: 69–98) and Belayche (in press). The European research project *FIGVRA. La représentation du divin dans les mondes grec et romain* (directed by Nicole Belayche) is also sure to yield interesting work on epiphany. On literary epiphanies, see in particular Pucci (1998, 2002) and Bierl (2004), on Homeric epiphany; Wildberg (1999–2000, 2002) and Sourvinou-Inwood (2003), on Greek drama; Hunter (1986, 1992), Henrichs (1993a), Vestrheim (2002) and I. Petrovic (2007), on Hellenistic poetry; and Feeney (1991:

is a subject, after all, with a long literary pedigree and a powerful (albeit more secular) resonance in modernist fiction.[30]

Classicists have shown less interest, however, in the *visuality* of Graeco-Roman epiphany – the practices of viewing, and thinking about viewing, that informed and reflected the ways in which invisible gods were made visible to their worshippers.[31] Admittedly, not all epiphanies are 'visions': from the shouts of encouragement heard at the battle of Salamis to Zeus' thunderclaps and Hecate's howling hounds at Stratonikeia, epiphanies can be sonic (and even olfactory) as well as visual.[32] Manifestations of divinity often involve significant crossover between the categories of 'vision' (*opsis*) and 'miracle' (*aretē*), and have much in common with other forms of sacred semiosis, including oracles and portents.[33] Yet insofar as manifestations of divinity can only gain significance through human perception (or *aisthēsis*),

75–7, 1998: 104–7), on epiphany in Hellenistic epic and Latin literature. For a sophisticated deconstructive reading of the epistemological dilemmas and elusive language intrinsic to scenes of epiphany in the Homeric epics, see Stevens (2002, in press). On epiphany in the Greek novel, see T. Hägg (2002), and, in Apuleius' *Metamorphoses*, Elsner (2007: 289–302).

[30] On James Joyce's adaptation of divine epiphany (most notably in *Stephen Hero* and *A Portrait of the Artist as Young Man*), to refer to 'a sudden . . . manifestation, whether in the vulgarity of speech or of gesture or in a memorable phrase of the mind itself' (Joyce, 1963: 216), which enables the thinker to access a kind of inner vision or mental clarity, see Hendry (1963), Bea (1971) and Bowen (1979). On epiphany in Romantic and modernist literature more generally, see Langbaum (1983), Nichols (1987), Bidney (1997) and Tigges (1999) with Maltby (2002 on moments of vision in the post-modern novel. For a subtle analysis of the appropriation and transformation of pagan epiphany by modern Greek poets such as Cavafy, Sefaris and Sikelianos, see Klapaki (2005, in press).

[31] Notable exceptions are Gordon (1979: 10–11, discussed in Chapter 2, 78), Gladigow (1985–6, 1990), van Straten (1992a, a brief abstract), Platt (2002), Elsner (2007: 289–302), Gaifman (2008b, in press) and Klöckner (2009). The role played by epiphany in religious modes of viewing is briefly acknowledged by Donohue (1997: 44–5) and Steiner (2001: 95–104), while the related difficulties of representing the divine in image form are explored by Frontisi-Ducroux (1986, 1988, 1991) and Vernant (1990b, 1991: 27–49, 151–63). On epiphany in Minoan visual culture, see Matz (1958), R. Hägg (1986) and C. D. Cain (2001). On visuality as a 'cultural system' distinct from the mechanism of vision, concerned with both historical techniques of viewing and reflection upon the act of viewing, see Foster (1988) and Nelson (2000), with Levin (1997), on the historicity of vision.

[32] Salamis: Herodotus 8.84.2. Stratonikeia: *I. Stratonikeia* 10, on which see Belayche (in press) and my discussion in Chapter 3, 157. On sonic epiphanies, see Versnel (1987: 50–1) and Wiseman (in press).

[33] On the relationship between epiphany and aretalogy, see Lührmann (1975), who takes the extreme position of denying that *epiphaneiai* ever refer to personal appearances, rather than miraculous demonstrations of power, and Versnel (1987), who surveys the range of strategies, from full anthropomorphic manifestations to meteorological phenomena, by which divine presence was experienced in antiquity. Petridou (2006: 62–76) emphasises the popularity of what she terms *pars pro toto* epiphanies, in which attributes or symbols of the gods are experienced metonymically as manifestations of the gods themselves. On parallels between epiphanies and oracles, see my discussion in Chapter 1, 54–5.

the visual sense tends to predominate in Greek epiphanic discourse, as the ocular profusion of Philostratus' ekphrasis strikingly demonstrates. In Greek thought, it is the eyes, rather than the ears, that give access to truth: as Aristotle claimed, 'we prefer sight (τὸ ὁρᾶν), generally speaking, to all the other senses. The reason of this is that of all the senses, sight best helps us to know things (γνωρίζειν), and reveals (δηλοῖ) many distinctions'.[34] In both literal and metaphorical terms, vision and knowledge are fundamentally intertwined through the vocabulary of *theōria*.[35] Yet, as Ian Rutherford has shown, *theōria* ('going to see', or 'spectating') has its roots firmly in religious tradition, referring first to expeditions made by state envoys to the great panhellenic festivals and, by the imperial period, to more individual forms of pilgrimage.[36] Sacred sights and sacred sites were thus deeply connected in ancient models of viewing, even more so through the false (but telling) etymology by which *theōria* and *theatēs* ('spectator') were related to *theos* ('god').[37]

In his survey of pre-modern attitudes to sight, Martin Jay points to the truism that 'the Greek gods were visibly manifest to humankind, which was encouraged to depict them in plastic form'.[38] But why was the idea of seeing and representing the gods so important in Hellenic culture? In the great monotheistic religions, by contrast, any attempt to make divinity visible must negotiate the abiding influence of the Second Commandment and the wrath of a deity who, while happy to be heard, jealously

---

[34] Arist. *Metaph.* 980a (translation from Hugh Tredennick's Loeb Classical Library edition, 1956); see J. I. Porter (1997). Contrast Plato *Timaeus* 61d–68e, where vision is employed as a metaphor for 'seeing' with the mind, in contrast to the illusionism of sense perception. As Jay (1993: 28–9) comments, however, Plato's ambiguous attitude to sight nevertheless contributed to 'the elevating of the status of the visual in Western culture. For if vision could be construed as either the allegedly pure sight of perfect and immobile forms with the "eye of the mind" or as the impure but immediately experienced sight of the actual eyes, when one of these alternatives was under attack, the other could still be accounted the noblest of the senses'.

[35] On the dominance of sight in Greek theories of perception and knowledge, see Gosling (1973: 120–39), Jonas (1982: 135–52), Jay (1993: 21–31) and Bartsch (2006: 15–17, 42–7). On *theōria* as a philosophical metaphor, see Nightingale (2001, 2004), with my discussion in Chapter 1, 59–60.

[36] See Rutherford (1995, 2000), Montiglio (2005: 118–79) and, on the importance of 'seeing the gods' in ancient traditions of pilgrimage, Elsner and Rutherford (2005). *Theōria* is discussed in more detail in Chapters 1, 59–60, 5, 251–2, and 7, 296–7.

[37] On the relationship between *theōros/theōria* and *theos/theion* (denied by Philodemus *De musica* 4.40–col. 5.12), see Plutarch *De musica* 27 (τὸ θεωρεῖν... ἀπὸ τοῦ θεοῦ τὴν προσηγορίαν ἔλαβεν) and Alexander of Aphrodisias' commentary on Aristotle's *Prior Analytics* 1 (Wallies 3, 20: τὸ γὰρ θεωρεῖν καὶ ἀπ' αὐτοῦ τοῦ ὀνόματος δῆλον ὡς ἔστι περὶ τὴν τῶν θείων ὄψιν τε καὶ γνῶσιν), with Rausch (1982: 13–17), Heidegger (1997: 44) and McNeil (1999: 252–66).

[38] Jay (1993: 23).

guards his prerogative to remain unseen.[39] The partial and fleeting nature of Old Testament epiphany – the burning bush, the pillar of cloud, the 'back parts' of God – is in this sense inseparable from the prohibition of images and the fear of idolatry.[40] Greek tradition frequently acknowledges the idea that gods should not, or cannot, be seen (consider the myths of Zeus and Semele, or Artemis and Actaeon), but the concept of a hidden god stands at one extreme of a spectrum that covers all possible degrees of visibility, from mortal disguise to full revelation.[41] Without a definitive source of textual authority, Greek polytheism functioned as a fluid system characterised by variety and multiplicity, with strong local traditions and highly specific taxonomies of divinity.[42] The visual and narrative tools developed for correctly identifying and distinguishing between different divine beings were therefore essential for the system's efficacy. Gods and heroes needed to be visible to their worshippers in part because the acts of visualising, categorising and representing their bodies, costumes and attributes were necessary components in the celebration of their respective spheres of influence.

Epiphanies played a crucial role within this system by providing *cognitive reliability*, not only for the gods' existence, but also for the traditions of representation by which they were known to their worshippers. As we shall see, Greek literature is riddled with examples in which gods appear to their viewer-worshippers in the form of their images, while depictions of encounters between gods and mortals in the visual arts often maintain, like Philostratus' ekphrasis of Aphrodite, a careful ambiguity between cult statue and living deity.[43] Likewise, sacred images are often authenticated by narratives of epiphanic autopsy, which confirm the bond between object and divine prototype by claiming that the artist's work was inspired by

---

[39] Exodus 20.4–6. See Finney (1994: 15–17), Mettinger (1995: 13–17), Belting (1996: 7–8), Besançon (2000: 63–108), Kessler (2000: 31–52) and my discussion in Chapter 2, 102, n. 90.

[40] Burning bush (Exodus 3.2–5); pillar of cloud (Deuteronomy 31.15, Exodus 33.9–10); smoke and fire (Exodus 19); God's back (Exodus 33.21–3). Besançon (2000: 70) defines these epiphanies as 'the sign of a presence; they are not Presence itself. On the relationship between epiphany and representation in Christianity, see below.

[41] See Versnel (1987). On mythological explorations of the dangers of seeing the gods, see Buxton (1980), Platt (2002) and my discussion of Callimachus' *Hymn to Athena* in Chapter 4, with bibliography.

[42] See, e.g., Burkert (1985b: 119–89, 216–25), Vernant (1988: 101–19, 1991: 195–206), Sourvinou-Inwood (1991: 147–88), Koch Piettre (1996: esp. 35–8), Parker (2005) and Bremmer and Erskine (2009). On evidence for sacred texts (*hieroi logoi*, or *hierai bibloi*) in antiquity and the sacred function of the written word, see Henrichs (2003).

[43] On gods appearing in the form of their images, see esp. Chapter 6, on dream visions.

a vision.[44] This circular relationship between vision and representation is produced by – and inseparable from – a deep commitment to the cult of images and a ready belief in the propensity of divine beings to manifest their presence before human eyes. Yet it also exists alongside a sophisticated cultural discourse on the status and power of the image, and a profound anxiety (demonstrated most famously in Plato's *Republic*) about its truth value.[45] To this end, visual and textual artefacts seldom treat the relationship between epiphany and representation as unproblematic; rather, they acknowledge and even celebrate the enduring problems of cognition, interpretation and mediation that are intrinsic to each phenomenon.

The problems raised by this close alliance between divine manifestation and human artifice are strikingly illustrated by a passage in Plutarch's *Life of Aratus*, the Hellenistic general of Sicyon. Highlighting the role played by epiphany in Greek military history, Plutarch relates how, in 241 BCE, Aetolian allies of Antigonas Gonatas invaded the Peloponnese from the north and took possession of the town of Pellene in eastern Achaea, only to be accosted by Aratus and his allies in the Achaean League:[46]

In the midst of this confusion, one of the captive women, daughter of Epigethes, a man of distinction, and herself conspicuous for her beauty and stateliness of person (αὐτὴ δὲ κάλλει καὶ μεγέθει σώματος εὐπρεπής), chanced to be sitting in the sanctuary of Artemis, where she had been placed by the captain of a picked corps, who had seized her for his prize and set his three-crested helmet upon her head. But suddenly she ran forth to view the tumult (2), and as she stood in front of the gate of the sanctuary and looked down upon the combatants from on high, with the three-crested helmet on her head, she seemed to the citizens themselves a vision of more than human majesty (θέαμα σεμνότερον ἢ κατ' ἄνθρωπον ἐφάνη), while the enemy thought they saw an apparition from heaven (φάσμα θεῖον) and were struck with amazement and terror (φρίκην ἐνέβαλε καὶ θάμβος), so that not a man of them thought of defending himself.[47]

While *Imagines* 2.1 demonstrates how divine presence might be consciously invoked through acts of worship, Plutarch here alludes to the other side

---

[44] See Chapters 5, 224–8, and 7, 321–5, on the epiphanic inspiration behind Phidias' chryselephantine statues of Zeus and Athena; Chapter 3, 167, on Parrhasius' vision of Heracles; Chapter 5, 225, on evidence for the trope in Pausanias; and Chapter 6, 266–75, on artists' dream visions of deities.

[45] See, e.g., *Republic* 596b–598d, with Else (1958), Nehamas (1982), C. Osborne (1987), Janaway (1995), Halliwell (2002: 37–71) and my discussion in Chapter 2, 119–23.

[46] Cf. Plutarch *Life of Agis* 13.5–15. On the historical background to this event, see Walbank (1933: esp. 182–4), W. H. Porter (1937: esp. l–lii) and Scholten (2000: 123–7).

[47] *Life of Aratus* 32.1–2. Translation from Bernadotte Perrin's Loeb Classical Library edition, 1926 (Plutarch's *Lives*, vol. XI).

of the epiphanic coin – the sudden appearance of deities at moments of great crisis.[48] Yet even in the midst of battle, he suggests, it is a human act of simulation that serendipitously (and erroneously) generates epiphanic experience, for 'Artemis' is rendered visible by means of the mimetic potential of anthropomorphism. Seeing a young woman possessed of great beauty and stature (the hallmark of deities in Homeric epiphanies), the Aetolians readily identify her as a goddess when she appears as a *dea ex machina* in front of the sanctuary of Artemis Soteria wearing a crested helmet, the customary attribute of goddesses dressed for battle.[49] As she looks down from the city's acropolis, the daughter of Epigethes is viewed as Artemis Soteria herself, come to rescue her loyal worshippers in a battle epiphany typical of both Homeric epic and Hellenistic military tradition.[50] The identification of the girl as Artemis depends upon her viewers' familiarity with a long-established iconography, and their reaction of 'shuddering' (*phrikē*) and 'terror' (*thambos*) is deeply culturally engrained.[51] Yet although divine presence is suggested by a familiar form, the daughter of Epigethes nevertheless possesses an ambiguous ontological status: are the Aetolians simply mistaken in viewing her as a sacred apparition (a *phasma theion*)? Or is Artemis actually working through her mortal avatar, generating an epiphany that may be simulated, but is no less 'real'? It is significant, in this regard, that the girl is not named – rather, she acts as a mere cipher for the deity whose presence she channels upon the city walls.

The appearance of gods in battle was a long-established trope in Greek antiquity and played a particularly high profile in the tumultuous decades of the third century BCE, as preserved in numerous epigraphic and literary records.[52] For Artemis Soteria to appear in defence of the Achaeans at Pellene in 241 would have been perfectly in line with the salvific epiphanies of Apollo and local heroes at Delphi in 279, after which their repulsion of invading Gauls from the sanctuary was commemorated in a festival also

---

[48] On the relationship between 'internally' and 'externally' generated epiphanies, see Chapter 1, 54–6. On crisis epiphanies, see Petridou (2006: 96–160, in press b).

[49] On the role played by 'beauty and stature' (*kallos kai megethos*) in Homeric epiphany (e.g., *H. Hom.* 2.275–9, 5.171–5), see my discussion in Chapter 1, 63–5. On the sanctuary of Artemis Soteria at Pellene, see also Paus. 7.27.3.

[50] Literary and epigraphic sources for battle epiphanies are gathered by Pritchett (1979: 11–46) and discussed by Speyer (1980), Chaniotis (2005: 143–65) and Petridou (2006: 97–117); see also my discussion in Chapter 3. On saviour gods and civic security, see also Kearns (1990).

[51] Compare the use of φρίκη and φρίττω as a response to epiphany in Philostratus *Imagines* 2.27.1 (Athena) and *Heroicus* 6.3 (Homeric heroes), discussed in Chapter 5, 248–9.

[52] See above, n. 32.

known as the Soteria.[53] Indeed, it is in an inscription related to this event that we find our first extant use of the Greek substantive noun *epiphaneia* to refer to a manifestation of divine power.[54] Plutarch, however, chooses to emphasise how a fortuitous alignment of occasion and gesture could allow a mortal woman to be *mistaken* for a goddess. In this way he alludes to a venerable historiographic tradition, placing the daughter of Epigethes in a long line of staged epiphanies that stretch back to the Athenian tyrant Peisistratus' triumphant return to Athens in 556/5 BCE accompanied by Phye, a similarly tall, beautiful woman dressed as Athena; Herodotus was famously aghast at the fact that she had only to dress in armour and ride in a chariot to deceive the so-called 'cleverest of the Greeks'.[55] It is telling that the faux-epiphany at Pellene is included as an effective military device in Polyaenus' second century CE collection of *Stratagems*, where he identifies the girl as a priestess of Athena, 'the most beautiful and tallest of the young women' (ἡ καλλίστη καὶ μεγίστη τῶν παρθένων) and claims that 'when the Aetolians saw the armored young woman come out of the temple of Athena and imagined that Athena herself (αὐτὴν τὴν Ἀθηνᾶν) had come as an ally to the Pellenaeans, they retreated'.[56]

Like Herodotus' Phye, the daughter of Epigethes reveals the dangers of an anthropomorphic system that continually blurs the boundaries between

[53] On the influence of the epiphany at Delphi (itself an echo of an earlier epiphany of local heroes who repulsed the Persians in 480 BCE, reported by Herodotus 8.38–9) and the festival of the Soteria, see my discussion in Chapter 3, 154–8, with bibliography.

[54] *Syll.*³ 398, translated by Bagnall and Derow (2004: no. 17) and Austin (2006: no. 60). On the etymology, use and meaning of the term, see Pfister (1924: 277–8), Pax (1955: 9–13), van Straten (1976: 26), Versnel (1987), Koch Piettre (1996: 396–8) and Petridou (2006: 10–11), with my discussion in Chapter 3, 149–51.

[55] Herodotus 1.60. The bibliography on this passage is vast, but on the issue of epiphany and performance in particular, see Connor (1987: 42–7), Sinos (1993), Kavoulaki (1999), T. Harrison (2000: 90–2), Koch Piettre (in press) and Petridou (in press b). Significantly Phye's name, φυή, means 'noble stature', and is applied to extraordinary mortals in the Homeric poems when, as the object of others' gaze, they embody high status and godlike beauty, such as the dead Hector admired by the Trojans (*Il.* 22.370), Menelaus and Odysseus during Helen's *teichoskopia* from the walls of Troy (*Il.* 3.208), and Nausicaa, compared to Artemis by Odysseus (*Od.* 6.152). In the *Homeric Hymn to Aphrodite*, the goddess uses it of Trojans beloved by the gods such as Anchises and Ganymede, who she claims are 'most godlike in beauty and stature' (*H. Hom.* 5.200–1: ἀγχίθεοι δὲ μάλιστα καταθνητῶν ἀνθρώπων / αἰεὶ ἀφ'ὑμετέρης γενεῆς εἶδός τε φυήν τε). Phye's name therefore expresses a kind of interstitial status between the human and divine.

[56] *Stratēgika* 8.59: translation from Krentz and Wheeler (1994: 2.837). For parallel examples of epiphanic simulation in the *Stratagems*, see 1.41 and 2.31, both Spartan exempla in which troops are deceived by staged epiphanies of the Dioscuri. On Polyaenus' use of false epiphany as a military device, see Krentz and Wheeler (1994: ix–xvi), Petridou (2006: 135–45) and Platt (in press a).

divine and human form. Yet if Plutarch, like Herodotus before him, demonstrates a degree of cynicism about the simulation of epiphany by mortal actors, this is not simply because of a secular rationalism that rejected the possibility of divine manifestation altogether (for both report 'real' epiphanies elsewhere).[57] Rather, it is a response to the continual slippage between presentation and representation that characterised Greek religious practice, and the difficulty of distinguishing between real and mediated presence. Phye and the daughter of Epigethes are able to simulate divine presence convincingly because the familiar formulae that make epiphanies verifiable (height, beauty, costume, attributes) also provide the very recipe for their imitation. In line with the mode of enquiry expected of historiography, Plutarch and Polyaenus, like Herodotus before them, choose to interpret such acts as a form of deceptive (if unpremeditated) performance – a mere mimesis of divinity. Yet distinctions between epiphany and its mortal simulation were not always so clearly drawn. It is telling that Polyaenus describes Athena's imposter at Pellene as the goddess's *priestess*, echoing parallel Greek traditions in which cult personnel donned the dress and attributes of the deities they served.[58] Pausanias, for example, describes a festival of Artemis Laphria at Patrae in which the priestess of the goddess arrived epiphanically in a chariot drawn by deer.[59] The cultural and theological implications of

---

[57] For epiphanies in Herodotus, see 6.105–6 (Pan to Philippides, discussed in Chapter 1, 55–6), 6.117 (Epizelus at Marathon) and 8.38–9 (Phylacus and Autonous at Delphi, discussed in Chapter 3, 155–6). On epiphanies and other forms of divine presence in the *Histories*, see Sinos (1993: 86), Henrichs (1999: 236), T. Harrison (2000: 82–92, with bibliography) and Graf (2004b: 115–18). Although Harrison argues that most Herodotean epiphanies are geographically, chronologically or narratalogically distanced (to Egypt, the distant past or hearsay), that of Pan is an example of epiphany's mark upon the landscape of a 'rationalised' centre of Hellenic culture, while those at Marathon and Delphi provided an influential model for the expression of Hellenic identity in subsequent Greek battle narratives. Plutarch includes a great number of epiphanies in the *Lives*, including those of Athena at Athens in *Pericles* 13.13 and at Ilion in *Lucullus* 10.34; on the uneasy alliance between myth, history and epiphany in the *Lives*, see Pelling (2002: 171–95) and Platt (in press a). On Plutarch's theology, see Brenk (1977, 1987), Valgiglio (1988), Swain (1989, 1996: 151–61), García Valdés (1994), I. Gallo (1996) and Pérez Jiménez and Casadesús Bordoy (2001).

[58] On priestly impersonation of the divine, see Back (1883), Burkert (1985a: 97), Hamilton (1985: 55), Tanner (2006: 57–60), Connelly (2007: 104–15) and Petridou (2006: 31–9, on 'enacted epiphanies', and in press b). On the complex relations between goddesses and their mortal 'doubles' (often their priestesses), see Lyons (1996: 134–70). The topos is later exploited in the Greek novel (e.g., Chariton *Callirhoe* 1.1.16, 1.14.1, 2.2.6, 2.3.5–6, 3.2.17, 3.9.1; Xenophon *Ephesiaca* 1.2.7, 1.12.1; Heliodorus *Aethiopica* 1.2.1, 1.7.2), on which see Connor (1987: 44) and T. Hägg (2002).

[59] Paus. 7.18.12, discussed by Frazer (1898 *ad loc.*), Piccaluga (1980), Sinos (1993: 83–4) and Goldhill (2006: 135–48). Cf. Paus. 7.24.4, on the priest of Zeus in his Boyhood (Zeus Pais) at Aigion, who was selected from the most beautiful boys in the polis; 9.10.4, on the priest of Ismenian Apollo at Thebes, 'a boy of noble family, who is himself both handsome and strong',

such events reveal the practical role played by mimesis in religious practice. Within the ritual context of the festival procession, the woman is both priestess and goddess – not a substitute for Artemis, but, in phenomenological terms, Artemis herself. In this sense, the festival at Patrae is parallel to the ritual procession in which Phye accompanied Peisistratus, or the appearance of the daughter of Epigethes in the mêlée of battle at Pellene; all three occasions provide a cultural context in which divine presence is desired, invoked and even expected by mortal worshippers.[60] In such contexts, what is the ontological status of ritual performance? When should impersonation of a deity be understood as a masquerade or a stratagem, and when should it be understood as an epiphany?

The questions raised by epiphanic performance are many, and have important implications for the role of ritual in Greek theatre, the status of gods on stage, the identity of Dionysus as a particularly epiphanic deity, and the relationship between religion and spectacle.[61] This book, however, focuses on a parallel, but rather different, strategy by which gods were made present for their viewers in antiquity – that of the sacred image. Significantly, Plutarch introduces this as a third possibility in his account of the events

---

who took the title *Daphnaphoros* ('the laurel bearer') and wore a laurel wreath; and 9.22.1, on the Tanagran festival of Hermes the Ram-Bearer, when 'whichever of the youths is judged to be the most handsome goes round the walls . . . carrying a lamb on his shoulders', re-enacting Hermes' first epiphany in the city, when he averted a plague by doing the same. Significantly, at Tanagra there is also an *agalma* of Hermes Kriophoros attributed to the sculptor Calamis, so that Hermes is made present and visible as both a ritual actor and an image. On the fluid relationship between epiphany, human avatar and statue, see below. Unless otherwise stated, all translations from Pausanias' *Periēgēsis* are from W. H. S. Jones's Loeb Classical Library edition, 1926.

[60] On the sacred quality of processions and their relationship to performance in Greek culture, see Kavoulaki (1999). For Gernet (1981: 299–301), Peisistratus' procession is associated with political triumph and marriage ritual; for Boardman (1972: 60–2), it echoes the apotheosis of Heracles, a web of associations developed in Gloria Ferrari (1994–95); for Connor (1987), Peisistratus presents himself in a more restrained manner, as Athena's protégé. Blok (2000) and Hedreen (2004: 48) argue that Phye's appearance does not parallel a festival of Athena's arrival, but a triumphant procession in which the victor is accompanied home by a deity after securing divine guidance or a period of exile (such as the return of Hephaistos to Olympus escorted by Dionysus). Petridou (2006: 144–5; in press b) sees the procession as a staged Katagogia festival of 'divine return'. As Connor (1987: 43) has pointed out, however, 'No single "explanation", no minimalist aetiology, can catch the richness and multivalence of the event.' On the multiple plays of meaning and ontological status generated by ritual processions, see Beard (2003), on the Roman triumph.

[61] On epiphany and Greek drama, see especially Sourvinou-Inwood (2003: 459–511), with Pucci (1994), on Sophocles; Seaford (1996: 195–203, 236; in press), Segal (1997: 223–42) and Wildberg (1999–2000, 2002), on Euripides; Bierl (2001), on Aristophanes; Otto (1965), Henrichs (1993b) and Larson (2007: 126–43), on Dionysus; and Mastronarde (1990), Easterling (1993), Wiles (2007: 231–60) and Koch Piettre (in press), on epiphany and theatricality.

at Pellene: were the Aetolians repelled by a 'real' epiphany of Artemis, by a mortal woman in the guise of Artemis, or, as he finally suggests, by the goddess's statue?

But the Pellenaeans themselves tell us that the image of the goddess (τὸ βρέτας τῆς θεοῦ) usually stands untouched, and that when it is removed by the priestess and carried forth from the temple, no man looks upon it, but all turn their gaze away (ἀποτρέπεσθαι); for not only to mankind is it a grievous and terrible sight (ὅραμα φρικτὸν εἶναι καὶ χαλεπόν), but trees also past which it may be carried, become barren and cast their fruit. (3) This image, then, they say, the priestess carried forth from the temple at this time, and by ever turning it in the faces (ἀντιπρόσωπον) of the Aetolians robbed them of their senses and took away their reason.

Plutarch makes clear that epiphany generated by human performance is a simulation of divine presence in which, despite the Aetolians' confusion, woman and goddess each possess a discrete identity. His description of the effect generated by Artemis' statue, however, blurs the distinction between deity and representation more thoroughly, so that beholding the ancient *bretas* is presented as akin to beholding the very goddess.[62] Moreover, the statue's potency is not just subjectively felt by its mortal viewers, but has an observable impact on the natural world, withering the trees past which it is carried.[63] While Epigethes' daughter's mediation of divine presence invites the gaze of her mortal viewers, projecting a glorious (if terrifying) vision of superhuman beauty, the statue of Artemis Soteria reveals a darker side to epiphany. As a 'grievous sight' (ὅραμα φρικτόν), the image is 'terrible' or 'difficult' to look upon (χαλεπόν), robbing the senses of those forced to face it directly (ἀντιπρόσωπον); in causing its mortal viewers to 'turn their gaze away' (ἀποτρέπεσθαι), it is literally apotropaic.[64] Plutarch's language here echoes the poet's claim in the *Homeric Hymn to Demeter* that 'It is difficult (χαλεποί) for mortals to look upon the gods' – difficult in that the gods are hard to see, possessed of multiple forms and disguises, or given to partial and fleeting signs of their presence, but also difficult in that unmediated perception of godhead can damage and even destroy those

---

[62] On the importance of this mode of viewing in Greek religious tradition, see Gordon (1979: esp. 10–11), Elsner (2007: 30–2, 43–5), and my discussion in Chapter 2, with further bibliography.

[63] On nature as a more 'innocent' viewer of images in ancient narratives of animals beholding artworks, see W. J. T. Mitchell (1994: 329–44).

[64] On Greek apotropaism, see Frontisi-Ducroux (1988), Vernant (1991: 111–50, 207–9), Faraone (1992), Wilk (2000: 145–81), Steiner (2001: 172–81, esp. 178) and Mack (2002). For sacred objects that provoke insanity or blindness when viewed without appropriate ritual preparation, see also Paus. 7.9.6–9 and Plutarch *Moralia* 309f–310a.

caught unawares.[65] The tension between the salvific and destructive impact of divine manifestation is reflected in Artemis' statue, which invites the viewer's gaze (the Aetolians are compelled to look) and simultaneously repels and confounds its beholders. Significantly, while the reader is given several clues about the appearance of the daughter of Epigethes, Plutarch does not describe the image at all, merely its unnerving effect.[66] Indeed, his use of the term *bretas* evokes an ancient, even aniconic form of image that does not function as a simulation of divine form so much as a denotation of divine presence.[67] In this way he signals the limits of both language and representation when faced with divine power; just as Philostratus stops short of describing Aphrodite herself in *Imagines* 2.1, referring the reader instead to Sappho's hymnic invocation, Plutarch talks *around* epiphany, leaving a 'signalled absence' within his text.[68]

The Pellenaean *bretas* does not, therefore, simply 'represent' Artemis Soteria in mimetic terms; rather, when ritually deployed by the goddess's priestess for the protection of her city, it is activated as a material agent of salvation. This, Plutarch tells us, is the explanation of events passed down by 'the Pellenaeans themselves', demonstrating both their ability to employ the sacred image strategically for their own political and military ends, and their faith in the goddess's enchantment of the object, positing a perfect union of divine and human agency. In this way the image of Artemis at Pellene functions as a paradigmatic *palladion*, a talisman which, by denoting the presence of a divine guardian, guarantees the protection of a settlement from external forces.[69] Plutarch's narrative echoes the role of the original Palladion at Troy, and anticipates the use of icons for the same purpose in later Christian tradition, such as the Mandylion of Edessa and Marian icons such as the Hodegetria at Constantinople.[70]

By juxtaposing the apotropaic effect of Artemis' statue at Pellene with a tale of simulated epiphanic performance, however, Plutarch relates the

---

[65] *H. Hom.* 2.111: χαλεποὶ δὲ θεοὶ θνητοῖσιν ὁρᾶσθαι; cf. *Od.* 13.312–13. On the *Homeric Hymns* and the difficulties and dangers of perceiving the divine in the Homeric poems, see my discussion in Chapter 1, 57–9.

[66] Cf. Steiner (2001: 107).

[67] On the significance of the term *bretas*, often associated with antiquity and great potency, see Scheer (2000: 24–33) and my discussion in Chapter 2, n. 80.

[68] Cf. Paus. 8.37.9, with Elsner (1992: 22–7) and my discussion in Chapter 5, 223–4.

[69] On the epiphanic connotations of *palladia* in antiquity, see my discussion in Chapter 2, 92–100, and on Greek talismanic statues in general, Faraone (1992).

[70] On the Byzantine use of *palladia* and their continuity with Graeco-Roman practice, see Cormack (1985: 124–5, 159), Beckwith (1993: 86–92), Belting (1996: 36–41, 75–7), Pentcheva (2006) and Ando (2008: 149–97).

concept of the talisman to far larger questions about the phenomenology of sacred modes of representation. By entwining goddess, woman and image in a trio of visionary phenomena, he foregrounds the role of mediation in the apprehension of the divine, and the very real influence that cultural artefacts can have upon human behaviour. He thus explores the *fluid* relationship that exists in Greek culture between the categories of deity, human body and material object, employing the *bretas* of Artemis to demonstrate how sacred images negotiate the relationship between divine presence and absence, between material object and transcendent deity, and between ontological status and phenomenological effect. In this sense, he is just one of a succession of Greek thinkers concerned to reconcile ritual modes of viewing (in which the distinction between image and deity is frequently suppressed) with a recognition of the human acts of invention, imitation and materialisation that drive the creation and display of such objects. Like Philostratus, Plutarch responds to an ongoing cognitive dilemma prompted by a strained relationship between analytical and devotional attitudes towards religious modes of signification – a desire to view the image *qua* image, and yet to acknowledge its sacred status and epiphanic potential. Indeed, we shall see that in many ways Greek culture was actually dependent upon such ontological instability for its efficacy as a religious system.

How, as modern readers, are we to understand this nexus of ideas – particularly when *our* concept of epiphany is not only filtered through secular appropriation of the term in twentieth-century fiction, but also influenced by the visionary traditions of Christian monotheism, not least the feast of Epiphany itself? First, we must remember that, in antiquity, explorations of the tension between divine manifestation and representation rarely spring from an explicit notion of idolatry or iconoclasm, such as Tertullian's anxiety about the pagan urge to 'confuse stones with gods'.[71] In Christian tradition the very possibility of Christ's representation is dependent upon a notion of incarnation that does not apply to Graeco-Roman polytheism. Although scholars have identified common patterns in pagan and Christian narratives of revelation, in contrast to members of the Graeco-Roman pantheon, Christ's form can be visualised and envisioned because of his very corporeality, most dramatically emphasised in the tactile epiphany offered to (but not

---

[71] Tertullian *Apologeticum* 22, discussed by Belting (1996: 37). On evidence for iconoclastic attitudes in Plato, see C. Osborne (1987) and Janaway (1995), and more generally on negative attitudes towards the sacred image in Greek thought, see Clerc (1915: 89–123) and Barasch (1992: 49–62).

necessarily taken by) Doubting Thomas.[72] By extension, Christ's material representation is acceptable to some because, as the Byzantine iconophiles argued, he was himself the 'image' of God, as the Word made Flesh.[73] While God the Father is the ultimate *deus absconditus*, resistant to both epiphany and its representation (with notable exceptions), Christ's potential visibility is foreshadowed and legitimised by his first epiphany – his appearance to the Magi as a mortal child, in an event still celebrated on 6 January – and his baptism, transfiguration, death and resurrection.[74] The concept of a familiar and accessible Jesus was made possible by the Christological debates that have shaped belief and practice throughout church history, particularly the doctrine of the Trinity, which explicitly theorises the distinction between transcendent Father and incarnate Son.[75] The issues of Christ's divine or mortal status, his visibility to mortal worshippers, and his depiction in image form thus all hinge upon a theological tradition focused upon correct interpretation of a master-text and the desire to define religious orthodoxy.[76]

[72] For contrasts and parallels between pagan and Christian epiphany, see Pax (1955), with Nock (1957), Lührmann (1975), Theissen (1983), Lane Fox (1986: 375–418), Brenk (1994), Frenschkowski (1995 and 1997), Weaver (2004) and J. B. F. Miller (2007: 21–39), although, as Margaret Mitchell comments (2004: 186), 'literary studies of early Christian "epiphanies" have a hard time ever getting out of the starting-gate of definitional issues'. On the issue of tactile proof in the story of Doubting Thomas (John 20.24–9) and the conflicting interpretations of its textual lacunae, see most recently Most (2005, with bibliography).

[73] John 1.14, Colossians 1.15 ('the image of the invisible God'), as used by John of Damascus (e.g., *On the Divine Images* 2.5) and Germanos (Mansi 13.101BC, 188CD): see Pelikan (1990: 81–4), Belting (1996: 7), K. Parry (1996: 70–80), Besançon (2000: 115–23), Kessler (2000: 35–7), C. Barber (2002: 69–77) and Giakalis (2005: 133–6).

[74] See Botte (1932), Bradshaw (1992: 202–4) and Kyrtatas (2004), who points out that although Epiphany refers to the visitation of the Magi in the Christian West, in the Orthodox East, the feast celebrates Christ's epiphany as the Son of God and the revelation of the Trinity on the occasion of his baptism, while for Armenian Christians, Epiphany is also a celebration of the Annunciation and Nativity. On the relationship between the feast of Epiphany and earlier pagan epiphanic festivals, see Nock (1972: vol. i, 391) and Lane Fox (1986: 116), citing Epiphanius *Panarion* 51.22.10. While the terms 'epiphany' and 'theophany' do not appear in the Gospels, in other New Testament texts *epiphaneia* and its cognates are used to refer to both the First Coming (2 Timothy 1.10; Titus 2.11, 3.4) and Second Coming (2 Thessalonians 2.8; 1 Timothy 6.14; 2 Timothy 4.1, 8; Titus 2.13) of Jesus: see Kyrtatas (2004: 207). On tensions between the lexical range of *epiphaneia* in early Church literature (on which see Pax, 1955, and Lau, 1996) and the broader revelatory phenomena of the Gospels – described as 'epiphanic' by scholars such as Pfister (1924: 321–3), Dibelius (1935: 266–86) and Bultmann (1963: 290) – see M. Mitchell (2004: 183–7).

[75] On the relationship between Christology and visual representation, see P. Henry (1977), von Schönborn (1994) and C. Barber (2002).

[76] On the notion of *Buchreligion*, see Lang (1990), and on differences between Judeo-Christian and Greek polytheistic approaches to the authority of sacred texts, Henrichs (2003: esp. 240–2).

Despite these differences, one might argue that Christian narratives appropriated, subverted and transformed Greek religious traditions in ways that were fundamental both to the forging of a distinctive group identity and successful evangelism within the Hellenised world of antiquity; as Margaret Mitchell has pointed out, the Gospel's account of Christ's entry to Jerusalem and the Crucifixion is in many ways a conscious *inversion* of Greek epiphanic conventions.[77] In the light of Plutarch's account of events at Pellene, one might also consider the episode in the Acts of the Apostles in which, following a healing miracle, the people of Lystra mistakenly identify Barnabas and Paul as Zeus and Hermes and attempt to perform sacrifices in their honour, claiming, 'The gods have come down to us in the likeness of men!'[78] This erroneous epiphany is pointedly used as a pedagogical example of the difference between a polytheistic propensity to see divine presence in any human indication of extraordinary stature or achievement, and Christianity's emphasis upon a 'living God' (θεὸν ζῶντα) who communicates through both natural signs such as 'rain from heaven and crops in their seasons' and the active testimony of his human followers, rather than a veil of anthropomorphic disguise.[79]

In contrast to Christianity's scriptural mission to shape and determine a normative faith, Graeco-Roman polytheism was neither a religion of the book, nor committed to defining a commonly held credo. In this sense, although the relationship between gods and material bodies was continually explored (and self-consciously problematised) in antiquity, it was not vigorously contested in theological debates that formed the basis of religious identity. The Philostratean and Plutarchan examples discussed above, however, demonstrate that despite the lack of explicit doctrinal debate in the

---

[77] M. Mitchell (2004: 192–4), focusing on the use of irony in the Gospel of Mark, such as the 'secret epiphany' of Christ's baptism (1.10–11), the mock epiphanic procession into Jerusalem (11.11), the parodic crown of thorns, purple robes and *proskynesis* (15.16–19), the missed epiphany of the Crucifixion itself (15.33–9) and the epiphany *in absentia* at Christ's tomb (16.8).

[78] Acts 14.8–18 (14.11: οἱ θεοὶ ὁμοιωθέντες ἀνθρώποις κατέβησαν πρὸς ἡμᾶς), recalling Jupiter and Mercury's appearance to Baucis and Philemon in Ov. *Met.* 8.618–724. On this passage, see Versnel (1987), on its use of pagan epiphanic conventions; Breytenbach (1993), Gill and Winter (1994: 81–6) and Gempf (1995), on the Greco-Roman context; L. H. Martin (1995), Fournier (1997), Bechard (2000: esp. 279–354), on the influence of the Phrygian flood myths; Wordelmann (2003) and Weaver (2004: 6–10), on the influence of Greek theoxenic epiphany narratives; Kauppi (2006: 64–82), on the role of sacrifice; and J. B. F. Miller (2007: 222–3, n. 191).

[79] On the use of epiphany to 'introduce and advance the gospel mission' (283) in the Acts and the text's reworking of pagan models (particularly Dionysiac 'liberation miracles'), see Weaver (2004).

Graeco-Roman tradition, there nevertheless existed a highly evolved cultural discourse about the manifestation of deities to their human worshippers, and the mediating role played by representation in both the formation and communication of such epiphanies. It is such a discourse that forms the subject of this book, which argues that although we do not find a sustained philosophical discussion of epiphany in antiquity, the range and sophistication of texts and images that celebrate, interrogate or problematise the appearance of deities to human worshippers prove that it was a major cultural preoccupation.[80] Moreover, just as Christian epiphanic conventions exist in a complicated yet necessary relationship with pagan tradition, so the self-conscious, even playful treatment of epiphany we find in Greek imperial authors such as Plutarch exists in an informed and complex dialogue with the epiphanic conventions and concerns of earlier Hellenic culture.

In his treatise *On the Nature of the Gods*, Cicero relates a tale associated with the Greek poet Simonides. Asked by the Sicilian tyrant Hieron to 'inquire into the being and nature of god', Simonides is said to have asked for a day to think. 'Next day, when Hiero repeated the question, he asked for two days, and so went on several times multiplying the number by two; and when Hieron in surprise asked why he did so, he replied, "Because the longer I deliberate, the more obscure the matter seems to me".'[81] For Anne Carson, the Simonides narrative offers 'a sort of concrete poem of man's relations with the Godhead ... What we see enacted in the interchange with Hieron is the properly invisible nature of divinity, receding out of our grasp down the lengthening corridor of time and into the darkness at the back of the painting.'[82] Indeed, 'the darkness at the back of the painting' is where epiphany inevitably leads the intrepid scholar, for as much as this book is about revelation, it is also about the continual *aporia* that accompanies the hermeneutics of the sacred. To claim to have had the last word on epiphany

---

[80] Important (but fragmentary) exceptions are examined by Koch Piettre (1996: 490–622) and include Plato's discussion of 'visible' and 'invisible' gods in *Laws* 931a; Balbus' use of epiphany as a Stoic proof for the existence of the gods in Cicero's *De natura deorum* 2.6; and Democritean and Epicurean attempts to explain the existence of divine *eidola* (e.g., Sextus Empiricus *Math.* 9.19 = DK 68 B166 and 9.25, Epicurus *Epistle to Menoeceus* 123, Philodemus *De piet.* 1888–92 Obbink, and Lucretius *De rerum natura* 5.1169–71), on which see Koch Piettre (1996: 556–622), Obbink (2002) and Mackey (in press). On the use of epiphanic *language* in philosophical literature, particularly Plato's appropriation of the terminology of pilgrimage (*theōria*) into his theory of Forms, see Nightingale (2001, 2004, 2005), and my discussion in Chapter 1, 59–60.

[81] *De natura deorum* 1.60.

[82] Carson (1999: 61), with her translation of Cicero.

would be to do violence to a subject that is by its very nature resistant to the conventional interpretative manoeuvres of classical scholarship. This book is therefore offered in a rather apophatic spirit, in the hope that others will both engage in a productive dialogue with the arguments put forth and address the representational complexities of epiphany in genres and contexts that, owing to the tyrannies of time and space, I have been unable to cover.

Although my text follows a linear chronology, the retrospective nature of Second Sophistic approaches to epiphany and the significance of epiphanic modes of representation within the visual language of classicism mean that certain problems and motifs recur in different periods, contexts and media throughout the book. Chapter 1 introduces the particular cognitive and hermeneutic challenges that Greek formulations of epiphany posed by examining cultural artefacts from archaic and classical Greece: votive reliefs from fourth-century Attica and a selection of *Homeric Hymns*. Despite obvious differences in date and medium, both seek to frame and describe encounters between humans and their gods in order to establish a relationship between their mortal and immortal audiences, while demonstrating a subtle awareness of the limits of human modes of representation. For votive dedications, as for hymnic *prooimia*, aesthetic decisions about form and content had important theological implications, and we shall see that epiphany functions as both an artistic goal (the communication of divine presence) and as a powerful tool for exploring the elusive nature of deity.

These themes are further unpacked in Chapter 2, which moves from objects that frame divine encounter to those that function as the focus of ritual, and therefore as embodiments or 'markers' of divine presence. It has often been noted that cult images purported to engender an experience of epiphany for their viewer-worshippers, particularly the colossal, gleaming chryselephantine statues of Phidias, which in their beauty and magnitude echoed the manifestations of gods in the *Homeric Hymns*. Yet Greek culture recognised the epiphanic quality of such images, while retaining a profound ambivalence about their sanctity that was closely related to their overt display of material wealth and human skill, or *technē*. In fact, the Phidian images stood at one end of a spectrum of image types that shaped experience of the divine in strikingly different ways: whether aniconic markers, rough-hewn *xoana* or highly naturalistic statues, each negotiated the relationship between divine prototype, human artist and physical matter by employing subtly different representational or denotative strategies. Among these, the combination of epiphanic simulation and spectacular *technē* embodied by the Phidian statues meant that they continued to dominate debates about image worship and the epiphanic potential of representation throughout antiquity: they are summoned into play by the Hellenistic cult images of the Peloponnese discussed in Chapter 3, the urbane ekphrastic epigrams discussed in Chapter 4, the self-consciously Hellenising rhetoric of Dio Chrysostom discussed in Chapter 5, and the grand set-piece defence of Greek anthropomorphism in book 6 of Philostratus' *Life of Apollonius of Tyana*, discussed in Chapter 7.

Chapters 3 and 4 explore how the sophisticated thematics of vision and representation already established within Greek artistic and literary modes influenced the great flowering of epiphanic culture in the Hellenistic period, when *epiphaneia* is first attested as a substantive noun in civic inscriptions and *Epiphanēs* was adopted as a royal title. Chapter 3 demonstrates how the notion of 'making manifest' dominated sculptural production (such as the cult images of Damophon or the Great Altar of Pergamon), as well as the self-representation of kings and the religious and civic 'peer polity interaction' of the Greek cities. In each case a desire to witness divine presence (or to appropriate its dynamics for ideological ends) reconciles an interest in new sources of authority and expression with a strong need for continuity with the Greek past. Claims to epiphanic presence in a specific location act as both a testament to divine favour in the present and a sign of historical significance, so while the visual language of Phidias provides a form of epiphanic 'citation' for an *agalmatopoios* such as Damophon, enhancing the sanctity of the temples he adorns, so historical records of manifestation in cities and sanctuaries such as Magnesia-on-the-Maeander or the Lindian sanctuary of Athena facilitate their claims to venerability (and, by implication, autonomy and inviolability). In both cases we can see that principles of self-conscious artistry or scholarship traditionally associated with a Hellenistic move away from the sacred are actually closely allied to religious practice and experience, from the celebration of festivals to the setting up of images and inscriptions. Chapter 4 moves away from material evidence to elite literary contexts, exploring how a similarly productive tension between the aesthetic, the intellectual and the sacred is at work within both the literary hymns of Callimachus and the corpus of ekphrastic epigrams based upon cult statues (such as Praxiteles' Aphrodite of Knidos). While both genres are divorced from their original contexts – whether performative or epigraphic – their engagement with the epiphanic potential and failure of representation is heavily indebted to the theological complexities already at play within the images and rituals they appropriate for literary (and meta-literary) ends. In this way, they demonstrate how the cognitive and hermeneutic challenges posed by epiphany formed a vital element of the Greek cultural imagination which would be highly influential upon the model of *paideia* advanced in the Second Sophistic.

Part II examines the close alliance of piety and *paideia* in the Greek prose literature of the imperial period and the role played by epiphany in the development of a self-conscious Hellenism conceived in response to Roman *imperium*. Chapter 5 explores how for Dio Chrysostom, and later Pausanias and Philostratus, traditional Greek image-worship offered a means of testifying to the vibrancy of a living religious culture while celebrating the artistic achievements of their predecessors through the demonstration of a sophisticated sense of visuality. In the Second Sophistic the tension between present encounter and historical citation that characterised Hellenistic models of epiphany becomes allied to a more coherent cultural agenda, expressed in the encyclopaedic project of Pausanias' *Description of Greece*, in which epiphany provides an essential means of imbuing the materiality of cult with an enduring numinosity. In Philostratus' *Heroicus*, this investment in the 'stones of Hellas' supports an extended epiphanic ekphrasis, whereby encounter with the heroes of Greece's glorious past is facilitated by a form of literary archaeology (allied to a virtual pilgrimage) that allows venerable texts such as the Homeric poems to be radically dismembered and experienced anew. Chapter 6 examines how this cultural investment in encounter with the divine is concentrated in narratives of dream epiphany, in which the ontologically ambiguous realm of oneiric experience provides a means of collapsing the distinction between gods and their images. For Pausanias, the mutually reinforcing relationship between dream visions and cult statues allows him to emphasise continuity between experiences of divine presence and the sacred landscape; for Aelius Aristides, slippage between gods and their statues in dream visions unites disembodied deity and physical matter, offering a means of reconciling his experience of Asclepius with the limitations imposed by his ailing body; for Artemidorus, the equivalence of dream vision and sacred image fits within a broader matrix of correspondences that allow him to relate each individual's oneiric experience to his waking world.

In navigating the relationship between epiphany and representation, then, Second Sophistic authors also navigated their own cultural, intellectual and religious identities. Nowhere is this more vividly expressed than Philostratus' biography of Apollonius of Tyana. In narrating the adventures of this first-century CE 'holy man', Philostratus explores a panorama of religious and philosophical themes in celebration of the ultimate Greek sage. Chapter 7 focuses on Apollonius' meeting with the Ethiopian gymnosophists in book 6, during which he is forced to defend traditional forms of Hellenic anthropomorphism. In an extended *apologia* Apollonius develops a theory of *phantasia* (or 'viewing with imagination') that manages to defend Greek image-worship from internal philosophical challenges derived from the Platonic theory of mimesis, while also outlining a theory of viewing that allies Greek models of epiphany to philosophical *paideia*. In doing so, however, Apollonius also points the way to a more allegorical or symbolic mode of visualising the divine that obviates the need for images altogether, pointing to an uneasy tension between traditional anthropomorphism and third-century attitudes to the sacred that anticipates late antique transformations of the relationship between vision and representation.

While Part II focuses upon the philosophical and literary concerns of Second Sophistic prose authors, Part III examines how the relationship between epiphany, representation and *paideia* is addressed in contemporary visual culture. Significantly, the most extensive body of surviving evidence for representations of epiphany in the second and third centuries CE comes from the funerary sphere – specifically the mythological scenes depicting encounters between deities and mortals identified with the deceased that were so popular on sarcophagi commissioned in metropolitan Rome. Chapter 8 therefore examines how the tensions between vision and memory, presence and absence, so characteristic of Second Sophistic nostalgia (and so firmly established in the classicising visual tradition) are appropriated and reconfigured in the context of the tomb. Epiphany and death, it turns out, each form a powerful metaphor for the other. In their resistance to representation – and their fragile offer of hope – both have the capacity to inspire the most profound and enduring feats of creativity.

PART I

1 | Framing epiphany in art and text

Greek votive reliefs: an exercise in visual theology

A group of worshippers processes through a sanctuary of Asclepius bringing votive offerings to dedicate to the god, perhaps to invoke his healing powers, or to give thanks for a return to health or an escape from fatal illness. What do they expect, or hope, to see? Such a ritual is depicted in Figure 1.1, a fourth-century BCE votive relief from the Asclepieion on the Athenian Acropolis.[1] The relief commemorates an act of dedication, establishing and perpetuating a relationship of mutual gratitude between the god and his mortal devotees. As a representation of the act of offering, it is also an offering in itself – an *anathēma* intended to please and honour the god through its skilled workmanship and charming detail, and to enhance the status of its dedicants. As such, it provides a model of ritual behaviour for its viewers to imitate, functioning as a 'mediating mechanism' through which worshippers might negotiate their relationship with both Asclepius and their broader community.[2]

The scene is structured as a ritual act of viewing, in which devotees approach a cult statue group displayed within its sacred frame of temple and *temenos*.[3] Yet, significantly, the divine figures with whom the mortals come face to face are not actually represented as statues.[4] Though subtly distanced by their large size and architectural setting within a high *naiskos*, they are not displayed on bases, nor differentiated by a contrast in style or medium. Instead they are rendered with the same sense of three-dimensional naturalism and flowing drapery as their worshippers, who thus seem to

---

[1] Athens NM 1377; see Neumann (1979: 51), Ridgway (1983: 196–7; 1997: 197) and Kaltsas (2002: 215, no. 442, with earlier bibliography). On general dedicatory practices in the Athenian Asclepieion, see Aleshire (1989).

[2] Day (2000: 43).

[3] On the depiction of architectural elements in Greek votive reliefs, see Karouzou (1979), Neumann (1979: 78–9) and Ridgway (1983).

[4] On the representational devices used in archaic and classical Greek art to distinguish representations of statues from gods, and the often ambiguous status of deities depicted in vase-paintings, see Schefold (1937), Bielefeld (1954–5), Alroth (1992) and my discussion in Chapter 2, 93–6, 114–22, with further bibliography.

Figure 1.1 Votive relief from the sanctuary of Asclepius, Athens, mid fourth century BCE

confront Asclepius himself, towering between the fluted columns of his high temple porch, accompanied by his daughter Hygieia and seated wife Epione.

How were visitors to the sanctuary meant to interpret an image like this? By depicting the scene's sacred context in such detail, and yet eschewing any overt signifiers of 'representation' in its rendering of the divine figures, the relief constitutes a powerful statement about the nature of ritual experience. Read literally, it suggests that human acts of worship are balanced by a corresponding bestowal of divine presence – that within the network of reciprocity so characteristic of Greek religious practice, the divine goodwill generated by a dedication or sacrifice is rewarded with an epiphany, a 'becoming visible' of immortal form to mortal eyes.[5] The reciprocal acts of offering and epiphany are confirmed by the meeting of gazes that structures the horizontal movement of the relief, grounding human–divine relations in a mutual act of sense perception and a mirroring of bodies, facilitated by the uniform naturalism of the relief's sculptural style. In this particular example, the epiphanic aspect of the confrontation is even more powerfully stressed by the projection of the high *naiskos* into the viewer's space, bursting out of the relief's frontal plane.

In depicting an epiphanic encounter between gods and their worshippers, Figure 1.1 highlights a number of issues relevant to the perception and representation of deities in Greek culture. The relief provides a visual field for exploring the relationship between mortals and immortals, establishing the spatio-temporal conditions in which the divine can be apprehended. In doing so, it also raises questions about how such relations can be depicted and communicated, reflecting and shaping the physical and conceptual framing devices that influenced ritual activity and modes of viewing within the sanctuary. Most strikingly, the naturalistic style by which epiphany is rendered blurs the boundaries between image and reality, establishing a set of expectations about the ways in which cult statues mediate relations between worshipper and god. This effect is explicitly contrasted with alternative modes of representation employed on each side of the relief which, though still pertaining to the divine, engage the viewer's attention in very different ways. On the left stands a *peplophoros* figure with a *polos* hat and two torches; on the right, a bearded herm – both in very shallow relief

---

[5] On reciprocity in Greek religion, see Mauss (1950), van Straten (1981), Grottanelli (1989–90), J. M. Bremer (1998) and Parker (1998); on the role of epiphany within reciprocal relations, see Day (2000: 47–51). For comparable examples of epiphanic representation in votive reliefs depicting dedications to Athena, see Palagia (1995); for a parallel example from the Amphiareion at Oropos, see Petsalis-Diomidis (2006a: 208–9).

Figure 1.2 Left side of Figure 1.1, depicting   **Figure 1.3** Right side of Figure
a *peplophoros* with two torches   1.1, depicting a bearded herm

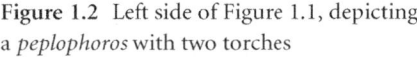

(Figures 1.2–3).[6] The iconography of these images is debated: the *peplophoros* is now commonly identified as Hecate, though the figure shares iconography with Artemis, Demeter and Kore, all of whom are represented holding torches in fifth-century vase-paintings and reliefs;[7] the herm may depict Hermes or Dionysus.[8]

The stylistic contrast between the images depicted on the frame and the forms of the deities within is particularly striking in the light of the central scene's naturalistic rendering. The *kore*-like hieratic pose, stiff linear folds,

---

[6] See Svoronos (1908: vol. I, pl. 48). On the pictorial effects achieved by the layering of relief planes and (now lost) painted detail, see Ridgway (1983; 1997: 195–200).

[7] Hecate: *LIMC* s.v. Hekate, no. 50; see E. Simon (1985: 280) and Kaltsas (2002: 215). Demeter, Kore or Artemis: see Svoronos (1908: vol. I, 294–8).

[8] Dionysus: Svoronos (1908: vol. I, 294), a suggestion ignored by later scholars, who simply refer to it as a 'herm' (e.g., Ridgway, 1983: 197; Kaltsas, 2002: 215). Archaising herms of Dionysus are less common than those of Hermes in the fifth and fourth centuries BCE and, unlike Figure 1.3, are often distinguished by long locks of hair or an ivy crown; see *LIMC* s.v. Dionysos, nos. 161–87.

tightly bound curls and long corkscrew locks of the *peplophoros*, and the schematically carved beard of the herm, employ subtly archaising effects quite unlike the rounded forms and softly flowing drapery of the figures within the structure of *naiskos* and stoa. The combination of archaising and naturalistic elements on these lateral reliefs echoes the stylistic details of two commonly reproduced iconographic types that date back to the late fifth century BCE, associated with Hermes Propylaios ('before the gates') and Hecate Dadophoros ('the torchbearer').[9] During this period, both deities were honoured with archaising statues attributed to Alcamenes, which were displayed on the south-west corner of the Acropolis: the Hecate Epipyrgidia, standing on the bastion of the Temple of Athena Nike, her three forms dressed in pseudo-archaic *peploi* and *poloi*, and the Hermes Propylaios, a herm located on the approach to the Acropolis' Periclean Propylaea with an archaising hair and beard on a classically modelled head.[10] Both deities are associated with entrances and boundaries, and, positioned by the sacred gateway, functioned as divine guardians of the Acropolis' threshold, their stylised appearance conferring an ancient and apotropaic power that was repeated in the form of archaising herms and *hekataia* all over the Greek world.[11]

Whether or not we interpret the lateral reliefs of Figures 1.2–3 as specific sculptural references, the juxtaposition of the two deities certainly suggests that *peplophoros* and herm draw upon the iconography of Athens' sacred landscape, relating the votive dedications and ritual practices of the Asclepieion to Athenian threshold guardian deities.[12] Their presence on the frame of a votive relief makes sense in the light of each deity's function as

[9] *LIMC* s.v. Hermes, nos. 42–65; *LIMC* s.v. Hekate, nos. 1–95.

[10] Paus. 1.22.8, 2.30.2, discussed by A. Stewart (1990: vol. I, 164–5). On the Hecate Epipyrgidia (also called Artemis Hecate), see Kraus (1960: 85–101), E. B. Harrison (1965: 86–107), E. Simon (1985), Fullerton (1986) and Brahms (1994: 159–61); on the Hermes Propylaios, see E. B. Harrison (1965: 122–4), Willers (1967) and Brahms (1994: 113–33); on archaisation, see also Havelock (1965). Several later inscriptions from the Acropolis are dedicated to both Hecate and Hermes, e.g., *CIA* 1.5, 2.208 (Farnell, 1896: vol. II, 599 n. 15). On Hecate's worship in Athens and associations with Hermes, see von Rudloff (1999: 34–7, 61–74, 80–2). On herms in Greek religious and domestic contexts, see Rückert (1998).

[11] On guardian deities, see Faraone (1992: 7–9) and on herms, Vernant (2006: 157–61). A base for a *hekataion* stood in the Asclepieion itself, while Hecate also received dedications at Epidaurus (Kraus, 1960: 169). Herms of Hermes Propylaios were also found within the healing sanctuary of Amphiaraos at Oropos and the *prothyron* of the Eleusinion in Athens (E. B. Harrison, 1965: 121–2); Thucydides tells us that Attic herms were placed 'at the doorways of private houses and in sanctuaries' (6.27.1); on Hecate's role as Propylaia and her apotropaic aspect, see von Rudloff (1999: 92–7); on the association between archaism and apotropaism, see Steiner (2001: 92).

[12] This also applies if we follow Svoronos in identifying the herm as a *bärtigen Dionysos* (above, n. 8): the sanctuary of Dionysus was positioned next to the Asclepieion at the south foot of the Acropolis, suggesting that the herm defined the shared boundary of the two *temenoi*; likewise,

an intermediary between human and divine, Hermes as messenger, Hecate as 'a vital factor in the success of human endeavor', frequently called upon in prayer.[13] The archaising forms and creation of pictorial effects through incision and shallow carving combine with the herm's nature as a sculpted object to indicate a clear contrast in representational status from the centrally depicted deities. This becomes dramatically apparent when the relief is viewed from the right, its planes bisected so that the variations in depth and style can be viewed simultaneously. Unseen by the viewers within the image, the lightly carved *peplophoros* and herm are external to the epiphanic tableau held within its central composition. The herm's semi-iconic nature introduces a form of sacred image radically different in conception and function to the fully anthropomorphic naturalism of the deities within.[14] While Asclepius and his consorts seem to operate within the three-dimensional space of their sanctuary as fully realised bodies, any hint of their sculptural status suppressed in accordance with contemporary votive convention, the architectonic form, triple base and lateral handles of the herm emphatically signal its materiality. Whereas the side reliefs' archaising and semi-iconic elements draw upon the denotative or symbolic functions of sacred images, indicating a clearly defined sphere of 'representation' and temporal alterity, the central scene employs naturalistic forms to suggest that here and now, within the space of the sanctuary, human and divine exist within a conterminous ontological sphere in which divinity is fully manifest. Theological concerns with the difference between 'presence' and 'representation' are thus explored through the subtle employment of contrasting stylistic signifiers.[15]

Yet an important question remains. Can we really interpret the relief's central scene so literally? Does it suggest that the Asclepian family are *actually* present – and visible – within the temple to acknowledge the offerings of their devotees? Or should we say that they are *symbolically* present during ritual performance, in the form of their sculpted images, or in the minds of their worshippers? Does the relief's rendition of divine presence depict a 'real' aspect of religious experience, or does it employ the artistic

---

Svoronos tentatively associates the *peplophoros* with the sanctuary of Ge Kourotrophos and Demeter Chloë, also on the slopes of the Acropolis (Paus. 1.22.3).

[13] Marquadt (1981: 244), on Hesiod *Theogony* 411–52; see also R. Osborne (1985: 53–4).

[14] On the iconicity and alterity of herms, see R. Osborne (1985) and Frontisi-Ducroux (1991: 213–20).

[15] On use of the term 'theology' in relation to pre-Christian Greek poetics, see Pucci (2002); on the relationship between theology and composition in Greek temple sculpture, see R. Osborne (2009).

conventions of naturalistic anthropomorphism in order to give visual form to an abstract notion of divine favour?[16] Significantly, the relief denies us a definitive answer. Although Asclepius and his consorts are not portrayed as statues, but as living deities, the iconography employed to make them recognisable for visitors to the sanctuary is – and must be – precisely the same as that employed for their artistic representation.[17] The relief may blur the distinction between statue and 'real' deity within its ritual and pictorial frame, yet it is still dependent upon the sculptural tradition that it seems to disavow. In this sense, it functions as a 'multi-stable image', allowing the viewer to shuttle between different modes of interpretation: it is both literal *and* symbolic, both god *and* image.[18]

To understand why the relief equivocates between these two visual strategies, we must recognise its role within the context of ritual practice. In contrast to the frontality of the lateral figures (who are distanced by virtue of their representational status), Asclepius is almost completely hidden from the external viewer of the image and is only viewed directly by the devotees within. By holding the epiphanic gaze within its internal narrative and declining to display the god directly to the onlooker, the relief defers the actual moment of encounter. Rather than giving us access to the epiphany experienced by the dedicants, it suggests by example the practical means by which Asclepius might be apprehended, a strategy confirmed by the effect that is generated if one attempts to look 'inside' the *naiskos* by viewing from the right: while the cultic group becomes visible in all its three-dimensionality, and the viewer 'joins' the worshippers processing towards the god, the herm stands in the way, a liminal reminder of the ritual and topographical framing necessary for such encounters with deity.

Through these structural devices, the relief stages a presentation of divine form to its internal worshippers, while re-presenting the god and his consorts to a broader group of external viewers. The latter may only see the god in image form, yet for those who have entered the ritual system of reciprocity, such representations have effaced their status as mere objects and 'become' the divine beings they embody. In this way, the relief functions as

---

[16] As argued by van Straten (1992a); see also van Straten (1993).

[17] See van Straten (1976: 14–15), Alroth (1992: 45) and Tanner (2006: 85 n. 197). On the iconography of Asclepius and his family, see Edelstein and Edelstein (1945: vol. II, 214–31) and *LIMC* s.v. Asklepios; on the cult image in the Athenian Asclepieion (its statue type as yet unidentified), see Aleshire (1991: 43–4).

[18] On multi-stable images, see W. J. T. Mitchell (1994: 45–57, 74–6). For further examples of ambiguous depictions of the divine in narrative representations of epiphany, see Gaifman (in press).

its own verification: the very similarity between the deities and their images confirms the authenticity of the worshippers' experience of divine felicity, and therefore the piety of their dedication. By directly associating this ambiguous epiphany with the act of dedication, the relief thus encourages active ritual response – a proliferation of further dedications that will, by implication, take the dedicant within the realm of representation framed by the architectural devices of temple and stoa, and thence to the privileged position of an internal viewer. In this sense, its treatment of the ritual is both narrative and proleptic: while depicting a dedication and epiphany that have – implicitly – already taken place, it also looks forward to future dedications and epiphanies.[19] Moreover, as an offering in itself, designed to delight the god into attendance, the relief also depicts the very event it is designed to bring about, playing a dynamic role within the sacred economy of reciprocity through its simultaneous representation and invocation of divine presence.[20]

Votive reliefs such as Figure 1.1 celebrate the potential for epiphanic experience within the context of a particular space and activity. In its topographical context in the sanctuary of Asclepius, the epiphanic aspect of this particular example echoes and supports the ritual activities of the god's cult, including the practice of incubation, in which the god appeared in the dreams of his worshippers to heal and give medical advice.[21] But commemorations of epiphany are not unique to the cult of Asclepius, nor to votive reliefs: they are found throughout the sacred landscape of Greece, in relation to a broad range of deities. Indeed, one of our first extant inscribed records of Greek epiphanic experience also comes from the Acropolis, but is dedicated to Athena – a fourth-century stele set up by a woman called Meneia to commemorate a vision of the goddess' *aretē*.[22] Just as the votive relief prevaricates between literal and symbolic modes in its presentation of epiphanic experience in the cult of Asclepius, so Meneia's inscription is markedly imprecise in celebrating her apprehension of Athena, simply

---

[19] On votive reliefs' perpetuation of the act of offering, see Klöckner (2006).

[20] On the ritual charging of votive objects, see Day (2000) and Elsner (2007: 42–3); on ritual as spectacle, see Jameson (1999). On the sculptural deferment of epiphanic encounter in relation to ritual experience on the Acropolis, see R. Osborne (1989: 100–1).

[21] On incubation, see Deubner (1899), Edelstein and Edelstein (1945), van Straten (1976), Graf (1992) and Wacht (1998). Dream epiphanies are discussed more extensively in Chapter 6.

[22] Ἀθηνάαι Μένεια ἀνέθηκεν ὄψιν ἰδοῦσα ἀρετὴν τῆς θεοῦ. Syll.³ 3.1151 = *IG* 2². 4326, discussed by Kiefer (1929: 21–2), Longo (1969: 23–4, no. 67), Grandjean (1975: 1 n. 7), van Straten (1981: 77), Veyne (1987: 390), Versnel (1990: 191) and Henrichs (1999: 245). For another vision-inspired dedication to Athena on the Acropolis (associated with her epiphany and healing powers as Athena Hygieia), see Plutarch *Pericles* 13.13.

stating 'Meneia set this up to Athena having seen a vision of the goddess's *aretē*'. The language used may emphasise the visual quality of her experience (it is referred to as an *opsis*, 'vision') yet refrains from giving us any details. Indeed, the brevity of the inscription creates an ambiguity whereby *opsis* could refer either to the vision Meneia has experienced, or to the material record set up upon the Acropolis – the *opsis* generated by the stele itself.[23] *Aretē*, often translated as 'manifest power', could in this period mean anything from an actual vision of Athena to the exhibition of a divine 'sign', an act of healing or the granting of a prayer.[24] Did Meneia therefore behold Athena herself, or witness the goddess's workings in the world? Can we, indeed, distinguish between the two?

By representing – and yet underdetermining – forms of divine manifestation within ritual contexts, artefacts like these exhibit theology in action. While retaining an important degree of ambiguity about the ontological status or precise details of epiphanic experience, they explore the visual and verbal means by which the gods' favour can be apprehended and communicated through material markers of divine presence. The variety of visual formulae through which sculptors and their patrons chose to denote such relations between mortal and divine in votive reliefs suggests a considered process of composition. For example, many reliefs from the Athenian Asclepieion and other sacred sites in Attica place an altar between worshippers and deity (Figure 1.4).[25] This serves as a material marker of both the locus and occasion of communication between the two, commemorating the reciprocal acts of dedicatory sacrifice and divine attendance. Yet like contrasts in scale between humans and gods, it also functions as a marker of distance and difference: while Asclepius and Hygieia are still represented in potentially epiphanic terms as anthropomorphic bodies in high relief, the altar suggests a more symbolic means of apprehending divinity, through the mediatory power of a non-figurative cultic object.[26] A contemporary relief

---

[23] I am grateful to Michael Squire for this point. For examples of the use of *opsis* in dream inscriptions, see the appendix to van Straten (1976: 23, no. 5). The term seems to be more common in fourth-century BCE epigraphy, prior to the coinage and widespread adoption of *epiphaneia* in the Hellenistic period; see Chapter 3, 149–51.

[24] On this broader significance of *aretē*, as against its more specific meaning as 'miracle', see Grandjean (1975: 2–5). On the double meaning of 'apparition' and 'miracle' ascribed to both *aretē* and *epiphaneia*, see Versnel (1987 and 1990: 191 n. 321).

[25] Athens NM 1338; discussed by Kaltsas (2002: 141, no. 269). Compare Athens NM 1431, a votive relief from the Piraeus of Zeus Meilichios seated behind an altar approached by three worshippers; Kaltsas (2002: 213, no. 435, mid fourth century BCE).

[26] On altars in the cult of Asclepius, see Petropoulou (1991); on the representation of altars in other artistic media, Cassimatis (1991); on the complex and varied roles played by altars as cultic objects, Gaifman (2005: 197–9).

Figure 1.4 Votive relief of worshipper approaching the altar of Asclepius and Hygieia
from the sanctuary of Asclepius, Athens, 420–410 BCE

from Aegina combines a similar ritual composition with a representational
strategy that underdetermines divine presence still further (Figure 1.5).[27]
A group of worshippers approaches an altar in order to make a libation,
bringing with them a sacrificial goose and deer; in the background, a torch-
holding goddess (usually identified as Hecate) is incised in very shallow
relief on a recessed plane.[28] Here, the high stepped altar itself serves as the

[27] See E. Simon (1985: 279–80), who links the image of Hecate here with her Aeginetan cult
image, a wooden sculpture attributed to Myron, and Kaltsas (2002: 142, no. 273).

[28] This relief is also included under the entry for Artemis at *LIMC* s.v. Artemis, no. 733, and
LIMC s.v. Hekate, no. 51. It is worth noting that Pausanias tells us Hecate was worshipped
with particular enthusiasm on Aegina (2.30.2), where she was the object of a mystery cult
(G. Hirschfeld 1894, *RE* vol. I, 964 s.v. Aigina; Farnell, 1896: vol. II, 505, 551). On syncretism
between Artemis and Hecate, see Farnell (1896: vol. II, 509–19), Krestou (1953–4) and von
Rudloff (1999: 67–74, esp. 69), on relations between Artemis, Hecate and the Aeginetan deity
Aphaia.

Figure 1.5 Votive relief of worshippers approaching altar (of Hecate or Artemis) found at Palaiochora, Aegina, late fifth or early fourth century BCE

visual focus of the composition. In contrast, the physicality of the goddess's ritual presence is decidedly ambiguous; faintly incised rather than three-dimensionally sculpted, she is seemingly unseen by her worshippers. It is left to the viewer to follow the relief's ritual cue by imaginatively 'fleshing out' the divinity whose presence the object simultaneously suggests and invokes.

The variety of sculptural strategies employed to denote divine presence on these reliefs has traditionally been understood according to formalist art historical criteria – the development of three-dimensional and pictorial effects under the influence of contemporary painting.[29] Yet if we seek to understand their form in relation to their votive function and ritual context, we must accept that the rendering of divinity is in each case also theological. As a body of images, classical reliefs present us with a taxonomy of representational formulae in which the relationship between gods and their devotees is expressed through subtle variations in style, composition and level of relief that together signify varying degrees of epiphanic presence. By drawing attention to the range of choices available, such compositions simultaneously highlight and question the ontological status of the

---

[29] E.g., Ridgway (1983; 1997: 195–200).

divinities they depict. The popularity of different formulae varies according to deity, cult practice and local tradition. Asclepius' 'embodied' presence in Attic reliefs, for example, is an expression of his close relationship with the human body, as both healer and deified mortal, and corresponds to his frequent epiphanies to worshippers at Athens and his related healing sanctuary at Epidaurus.[30] In contrast, Hecate's ghostly presence on the Aegina relief may reflect Pausanias' statement that she was the object of a mystery cult on the island, suggesting that her 'embodied' epiphany was only visible – and therefore representable – to the initiated.[31] Yet as the contrasts between Figures 1.1 and 1.4 demonstrate, we also find great variety in the standard compositional structure of worshipper(s) approaching deity within single cultic locations, suggesting an active, self-conscious process of differentiation by sculptors and their patrons which does not map straightforwardly onto individual deity or cult practice.[32] While the visible, three-dimensional rendering of Asclepian epiphanies may be expressive of his sphere of authority and related ritual activity, the compositional devices used to explore his relationship with his mortal worshippers are not unique to healing cults. We find a similar structure and emphatic corporeality in votive reliefs from the sanctuary of Artemis at Brauron, where close relations between worshipper and goddess were expressed through her supervision of rites of passage.[33] Likewise, votive reliefs dedicated to the kindly Nymphs demonstrate the deities' close relationship with their worshippers (particularly the so-called *nympholeptoi*) through epiphanic compositions located within the Attic caves where they were worshipped.[34]

The relationship between the style, composition and ritual function of classical reliefs has provoked a range of responses. For Jeremy Tanner, their naturalism and compositional structure allows them to function as

---

[30] Herzog (1931), Edelstein and Edelstein (1945: vol. ii, 83–4), Longo (1969: 63–75), LiDonnici (1995).

[31] See above, n. 28. This connection between incised form and mystery cult is drawn by E. Simon (1985: 280).

[32] The variety of representational formulae employed in a single cultic location is sensitively illustrated in relation to the Amphiareion at Oropos by Petsalis-Diomidis (2006a).

[33] E.g., Brauron Museum 1151–3; see Giuman (1999: 48–52). On Artemis' relationship with her worshippers in Attic social and civic life, see Kahil (1983), Calame (2001: 91–100) and Tanner (2006: 74–6).

[34] E.g., Athens NM 4465 (Kaltsas, 2002: 213, no. 434), a mid-fourth-century BCE relief from the Cave of the Nymphs on Mount Penteli. On reliefs dedicated to the Nymphs and Pan, see Feubel (1935), Fuchs (1962), van Straten (1976: 1–2, 19–20), C. M. Edwards (1985), Ridgway (1997: 197–8), Larson (2001: 226–67) and Gaifman (2008b). On the visionary sensibilities of *nympholeptoi* such as Archedemos, companion of the Nymphs at Vari, see Himmelmann-Wildschütz (1957), Connor (1988) and Larson (2001: 13–20).

'expressive symbols' of relations between deities and their worshippers, rather than 'cognitive' statements about the nature and appearance of the gods, while the iconography of the deities depicted both draws upon and magnifies the 'aura' of the cult image, preparing the viewer for an epiphanic encounter with the statue within by contributing to its ritual framing.[35] This interpretation is certainly compatible with the dedicatory function and contextual display of such votives. Most importantly, it underlines their status as ideological artefacts expressive of civic identity and the greater accessibility of 'new' deities such as Asclepius with the development of Athenian democracy (for these are a predominantly Attic phenomenon).[36] As the Acropolis Meneia inscription confirms, it is precisely in this period that epiphanic experience began to be explicitly recorded and displayed in epigraphic media as well as votive reliefs. While the accessibility of civic deities such as Athena and the rise of private cults such as those of Asclepius, Pan and the Nymphs influenced the increased prominence of epiphany within the material record, the visual language of naturalism and the 'epigraphic habit' of the democratic polis provided the visual and verbal devices by which encounters with the divine could be commemorated by ordinary individuals.[37] The epiphanic compositions that characterise fourth-century Attic Asclepius reliefs, for instance, coincide with the growing reputation of his cult at Epidaurus, where inscribed narratives of the god's ritual appearance during incubation expressly publicised the frequency and efficacy of the god's *aretai* to the sanctuary's visitors.[38]

However, Tanner's emphasis on the 'expressive' function of epiphanic votive reliefs does not fully explain their active exploration and juxtaposition of *different* modes for denoting divine presence. Nor does it explain the urge to do so in such expressly visionary terms. For the symbolic significance of these compositions is always in tension with the emphatic visual power of the encounters they present. While they may anticipate the epiphanic viewing of a cult statue, they simultaneously raise the possibility of an encounter with deity itself, of the god's existence and visible manifestation independently of the material form of its representation. The ontological

---

[35] Tanner (2006: 85–7) also discusses how, for mid-twentieth-century German scholars such as Himmelmann ([1959]1998) and Hausmann (1960: 34–7, 52–3), the profile compositions and contrasts in scale indicated religious decline and an increasing distance between man and god.

[36] See Garland (1992: esp. 116–35, on Asclepius), Clinton (1994) and A. Connolly (1998).

[37] I borrow the phrase 'epigraphic habit' from MacMullen (1982). On epiphanic inscriptions, see Chapter 3, 147–69.

[38] See above, n. 30. Cf. Strabo's comment that the Epidaurian sanctuary's fame was due to both the 'visible presence' (τὴν ἐπιφάνειαν) of Asclepius and 'the votive tablets (τῶν ἀνακειμένων πινάκων) on which his cures have been inscribed' (8.6.15).

Figure 1.6 Votive relief of Archinos from the sanctuary of Amphiaraos, Oropos, first half of the fourth century BCE

ambiguity of the divinities depicted thus pushes beyond a mere 'expression' of relations between worshipper and god to point to the *cognitive* value of ritual activity, specifically the role of visual experience within religious practice.

A rich example of artistic engagement with the cognitive and representational challenges set by epiphany comes from a healing sanctuary associated with the deified hero Amphiaraos (Figure 1.6) in the Attic town of Oropos.[39] This relief explicitly draws upon the iconography of incubation, depicting a multiple narrative of the god's manifestation within the oneiric realm and his direct impact, through medical intervention, upon the worshipper's body. The events are located within a frame designed to look like a

[39] Athens NM 3369: Kaltsas (2002: 209–10, no. 425). See Hausmann (1948: 38–60), van Straten (1976: 3–4), Bravo (2004: 69–70) and Petsalis-Diomidis (2006a: esp. 209–10). On the Amphiareion at Oropos, see Karidas (1968) and Androutsopoulos (1972).

pillared colonnade, a formal echo of the stoa within the sanctuary in which the incubants would sleep. On the far right a dedicator in the costume of an Athenian citizen stands in an attitude of prayer, either requesting help from, or giving thanks to, the hero. In the plane behind, a man lies asleep while a sacred snake (a familiar feature of many hero cults, especially that of Asclepius) licks his right shoulder. To the left a man with an identical costume and hairstyle is depicted standing before the anthropomorphic form of Amphiaraos himself (also dressed in citizen garb), who carries out a medical procedure upon the same shoulder. In the background a votive *pinax* in shallow relief locates the scene within the Amphiareion, acting as a reminder of the commemorative function of the object itself.[40] This reflexive reference to its own material presence emphasises the object's role in transforming an ephemeral experience of divinity into a permanent, visible memorial of the god's impact upon the physical world. In this way the relief declares its own contribution to the numinous qualities of the sanctuary it adorns and its influence upon subsequent pilgrim-worshippers.

Together the multiple scenes within the relief denote divine presence in different spheres of religious experience. On the left we see the oneiric manifestation of the hero in anthropomorphic form, which conforms to his iconography in other media (including, perhaps, his cult image within the sanctuary) and emphasises his civic unity with the worshipper. To the centre right we encounter a highly ambiguous image in the form of the snake, which could be interpreted as either an animal sacred to Amphiaraos, or his manifestation in theriomorphic form.[41] Both representations mark the miraculous impact of divinity upon the worshipper's body, while pointing to the manifold means by which such effects can be experienced and understood.[42] In this way they question the relationship between the ontological status of epiphany (i.e., the level of experience on which divinity is apprehended) and its phenomenological reception (i.e., the visual power of

---

[40] The reflexive nature of the votive object, pointing to its existence within a series of dedications, is often suggested in reliefs of the period by the depiction of a small relief or *pinax* within the architectural setting of temple or precinct; see van Straten (1976: 4 n. 41; 1992b: 255–60).

[41] On 'reptilian epiphanies', see Petridou (2006: 81–6). On snakes in healing cult, see Küster (1913: 133–7), Edelstein and Edelstein (1945: vol. II, 227–31), Hausmann (1948: 157–8), Schouten (1967), van Straten (1976: 8) and Mitropoulou (1977: 183–201); on snakes as signs of heroic status more generally, see Salapata (1997: 250–2) and Bravo (2004: 71–2). On the bearded and bare-chested cult image of Amphiaraos at Oropos, see Petsalis-Diomidis (2006a: 216).

[42] A parallel account of simultaneous snake-healing and anthropomorphic dream-vision is narrated in the Epidaurian miracle inscriptions, A 113–19; see Herzog (1931: 14, no. 17); Edelstein and Edelstein (1945: vol. I, no. 233.17), discussed by van Straten (1976: 4) and LiDonnici (1995: 97 [A17]).

the experience itself). While the theriomorphic marker of divine presence may be more 'real', for the snake is physically 'present' in the sanctuary, it is not directly viewed by the sleeping worshipper, whose 'conscious' meeting with the hero in anthropomorphic guise takes place within the dream world.[43] This visual separation of 'conscious' and 'physical' experience is underlined by the composition of the relief, which foregrounds Archinos' oneiric meeting with Amphiaraos and renders the dream figures in a larger scale and higher relief. The status of the actual rite of incubation, recessed within the composition by its more shallow modelling, is compromised. As a miraculous narrative of divine power and agency does it represent what 'actually' happened, or a further layer of oneiric experience?

Significantly, we are offered no explicit indicator that the three mortals in the relief represent the same individual. The inscription beneath simply reads 'Archinos set this up to Amphiaraos'.[44] Are we to read the scenes from right to left, as a narrative of Archinos' experience within the Amphiareion? If the relief is meant to depict different facets of a single experience, then surely the left and middle scenes should be read as happening simultaneously, but at different levels of cognition. Or does the relief indicate in more general terms the manifold ways in which encounters with Amphiaraos might be conceived of and understood, by one or many individuals? Some meet the god in dreams as a magnified reflection of human form (his citizen dress expressing shared cultural ideals), some in the form of a theriomorphic avatar, and others through the process of visiting a sanctuary and sharing in the practice of pilgrim viewing. By juxtaposing these diverse experiences within a single frame, this strategy of multiplicity emphasises both sameness and difference, intimacy and distance, between god and mortal, pointing to the *subjectivity* of sacred vision and thereby evading any straightforward relationship between the god and his material representation.

As in other votive reliefs of the period, this multiplicity of representation draws attention to the challenges presented by epiphany as a religious phenomenon, highlighting and problematising the means by which divine presence might be explained, visualised and communicated. By depicting the god in different guises and registers, the relief blurs the division between the metaphorical and literal, the symbolic and the real. That the very nature of vision is fundamental to the relief's conception, execution and display

---

[43] For examples from Athens and Rhamnous where the dreamer is depicted as awake, see van Straten (1976: 3).

[44] Ἀρχῖνος Ἀμφιαράω ἀνέθηκεν (*IG* 2². 4394). On the performative value of self-representation in Greek ritual contexts, both visual and verbal, see Day (2000).

is suggested by the prominent eyes carved into its upper frame, as if above the antefixes of the stoa's roof. These have been interpreted as apotropaic, intended to avert the evil eye from the goodwill conferred upon the dedicator by his miraculous cure.[45] Yet it is surely significant that of all the elements that make up this complex object, the eyes and the internal *pinax* are the only details facing directly out of the image, meeting the gaze of the external viewer. If the relief encourages a meditation upon the nature of vision itself, and its role within traditions of pilgrimage and miraculous healing, then the eyes play an important role in that they *look back*.[46] They emphasise that any act of ritual viewing is itself observed and acknowledged by the numinous powers present within the sacred space the relief adorns. In their disembodied, abstracted position on the object's edge, they also nod to a form of epiphanic confrontation that is unrepresentable within the iconic formulae of the relief itself, suggesting that, despite its multiple strategies of depiction, it is by no means exhaustive in its presentation of divine form, but leaves open a crucial space in which the apprehension of divinity lies beyond the image, in the ritual preparation and subjective experience of each individual visitor to the sanctuary.

In their enactment of a kind of visual theology, fourth-century votive reliefs are emblematic of two abiding preoccupations within Greek religious art. First, they illustrate the mutually reinforcing relationship between deities and their visual representations. On one hand, depictions of the forms that gods take in dream visions and other kinds of epiphanic confrontation necessarily conform to the same iconography as their statues and other visual media such as painting and relief sculpture, for how else would they be recognisable? On the other hand, images themselves have the potential to be viewed as epiphanic embodiments of the deities they represent. They can simultaneously symbolise and *constitute* divine presence.[47] This prevarication characterises the experience of representation in a broad sense. We can compare it to Wollheim's identification of a characteristic twofoldness or 'seeing in', whereby the viewer of a work of art moves between an apprehension of the entity 'in' the image (i.e., the deity) and an awareness of the image's created nature, its status as an object (i.e.,

---

[45] Kaltsas (2002: 209) and Petsalis-Diomidis (2006a: 209). On possible Egyptian influence, see Mitropoulou (1977: 35–40).

[46] On the dynamics of seeing and being seen in relation to the epiphanic, see Vernant (1991: 141–50).

[47] The Greek propensity to view images of the gods as epiphanic embodiments of the gods themselves in ritual contexts has been well documented; see Chapter 2 for a more extensive discussion, with bibliography.

a statue).[48] As we shall see in subsequent chapters, this twofold effect is a
defining feature of naturalism, which intensifies an object's power simultaneously to demand complicity in its illusionary powers and appreciation of
the artist's skill. It is also characteristic of theatrical performance, whereby
an audience has the choice to suspend or maintain disbelief in the dramatic
illusion presented by the actors.[49] The display of artistic objects and dramatic pageantry were, of course, intrinsic elements of religious activity in
antiquity, but in the sphere of the sacred the process of 'seeing in' relied on an
additional set of cultural assumptions about the authenticity of divine forms
that was closely bound to a belief in visionary experience. Wollheim points
out that 'representational-seeing' is characterised by standards of 'correct-
ness', derived 'from the intention of the maker of the representation' and
related to the viewer's familiarity with the prototype on which the image is
based.[50] But representations of divine beings raise a special set of problems,
for their prototypes are, by nature, incorporeal, elusive and inaccessible.
The authenticity and religious efficacy of sacred iconography, therefore,
were for many ancient thinkers dependent upon the gods' ability to render themselves visible independently of their material representations –
on the authority of epiphany as a seemingly *unmediated* visual encounter
with divinity. A ritual commitment to perceiving sacred images in epiphanic
terms reflected a state of cultural immersion that was fundamental to sacred
modes of viewing.[51] For although visions were themselves mental representations, dependent upon pre-existing forms generated through cultural
activities such as poetry and image-making, they provided what we might
call 'cognitive reliability' for the traditional forms of the mythical panoply.
The reciprocal relationship between images and epiphanies thus provided
an essential binding element within the representational system of Greek
religion.

Second, however, these votive reliefs demonstrate how a ready engagement with the phenomenological verities of the divine in Greek culture

---

[48] Wollheim (1980: 205–29), applied to ancient art by Neer (1995) and Steiner (2001: 19–22). The
twofoldness of 'seeing in' is contrasted with 'seeing as', an apprehension of the object 'as' the
thing it represents without recognition of its artefactual nature.

[49] Compare the tension between 'absorption' and 'theatricality' as theorised by Fried (1980). On
parallel effects in ancient drama, see Bain (1975 and 1987) and Goldhill (1996 and 1999). One
might also consider Herodotus' tale at 1.60 of Peisistratus' 'divine' escort Phye/Athena along
such lines: see Connor (1987: 42–7), Sinos (1993), Day (2000: 41–2), T. Harrison (2000: 90–2)
and Koch Piettre (in press). On the sacred quality of processions and their relationship to
performance in Greek culture, see Kavoulaki (1999) and Hedreen (2004).

[50] Wollheim (1980: 205).

[51] See Elsner (2007: 11–26). On 'ritual commitment', see Humphrey and Laidlaw (1994: 97–100).

existed side by side – and in constant dialogue – with an experimental, conceptualising approach to the possibilities offered by different strategies of representation, so generating a rich tradition of cultural commentary, both visual and literary, upon ritual and artistic means of apprehending the gods. Figures 1.1–1.6 may privilege the visual language of classical naturalism and the traditional iconographical formulae of anthropomorphism, but even within this precise stylistic remit, each relief finds multiple ways of depicting divine form and denoting its presence within sacred space. When these two preoccupations influence the design, display and ritual efficacy of objects such as votive dedications, the images thereby produced testify to the metaphysical reality of the sacred and the potential for its visible manifestation to mortal eyes, but they also exhibit an awareness of the *difficulties* of interpreting, recording and responding to such contact with the divine.[52]

Recent scholarship has sought to draw distinctions between these approaches to the image in Graeco-Roman culture, expressing the tensions between the two as contrasting modes of visuality, such as the 'ritual' and 'naturalistic', 'sacred' and 'aesthetic', or 'popular' and 'intellectual'.[53] Yet in wrenching apart these two forms of engagement with the visual and secularising the self-referential or intellectual aspects of image-making and viewing, we risk overidentifying with the latter, while bracketing the former in a separate category labelled 'religion'.[54] Quite apart from the many problems raised by this anachronistic separation of sacred and secular, the hermeneutic challenges posed by epiphany suggest that even *within* the sphere of the sacred, a belief in the power of the image to 'make present' and efface its own identity qua image did not preclude reflexive examination of its ritual, material, and representational status and function.[55] Aesthetic choices – concerned with aspects of composition, iconography and stylistic details such as three-dimensionality, degree of naturalism and relative scale – are also theological ones. Each visual detail selected by artist and/or patron actively negotiates the relationship between god and human in ways that play a dynamic role in the construction of religious experience.

---

[52] On the limits of figurative representation in Greek religious art, see Frontisi-Ducroux (1986, 1988) and Gaifman (2005).

[53] On 'ritual' and 'naturalistic' or 'aesthetic' modes, see Elsner (2000b), who also expresses the contrast in terms of 'Medieval' and 'Renaissance' forms of visuality (46), but points out that the two modes were by no means mutually exclusive in antiquity (62); see also Elsner (1996b: esp. 515–17, 529–30). On the 'sacred' (or 'fetishistic') and 'aesthetic', see Tanner (2006: 45–54). On the fallacy of distinguishing between the religious and aesthetic in any culture but the post-Enlightenment West, see Gell (1998: 97).

[54] Cf. Humphreys (2004: 1–3).   [55] See Goody (1977: 25) and Humphrey and Laidlaw (1994: 60).

An awareness of this process did not necessarily lessen the numinosity of the images thereby created. Greek viewer-worshippers were fully aware, for instance, of the materiality of cult statues (the use of wood, stone, ivory or precious metals was actually of paramount importance), but they were rarely impious enough to think them 'just' statues.[56] Indeed, a continual shuttling between 'ritual' and 'aesthetic' modes of viewing was integral to both religious practice and broader cultural trends concerned with the visualisation and perception of the divine. And while the riddles posed by the circular relationship between vision and depiction were explored by the most sophisticated intellectual circles, they also posed very real practical concerns for commissioners, artists and viewers of the finest and most humble images. What do the gods look like? How, and to what extent, can they be seen and experienced? And how can knowledge of divine forms be verified, recorded and transmitted correctly and convincingly? As we shall see, the connections between vision, belief, knowledge and representation are negotiated in multiple and nuanced ways throughout Greek culture. They are where the abstract and material coincide in ways that are fundamental to religious, literary and artistic practice.

The semiotics of epiphany in early Greek culture

Μουσάων Ἑλικωνιάδων ἀρχώμεθ᾽ ἀείδειν,
αἵ θ᾽ Ἑλικῶνος ἔχουσιν ὄρος μέγα τε ζάθεόν τε
. . .
ἔνθεν ἀπορνύμεναι κεκαλυμμέναι ἠέρι πολλῷ
ἐννύχιαι στεῖχον περικαλλέα ὄσσαν ἱεῖσαι
. . .
αἵ νύ ποθ᾽ Ἡσίοδον καλὴν ἐδίδαξαν ἀοιδήν,
ἄρνας ποιμαίνονθ᾽ Ἑλικῶνος ὕπο ζαθέοιο.
τόνδε δέ με πρώτιστα θεαὶ πρὸς μῦθον ἔειπον,
Μοῦσαι Ὀλυμπιάδες, κοῦραι Διὸς αἰγιόχοιο.
"ποιμένες ἄγραυλοι, κάκ᾽ ἐλέγχεα, γαστέρες οἶον,
ἴδμεν ψεύδεα πολλὰ λέγειν ἐτύμοισιν ὁμοῖα,
ἴδμεν δ᾽ εὖτ᾽ ἐθέλωμεν ἀληθέα γηρύσασθαι."
ὡς ἔφασαν κοῦραι μεγάλου Διὸς ἀρτιέπειαι,
καί μοι σκῆπτρον ἔδον δάφνης ἐριθηλέος ὄζον

---

[56] On this dual attitude to religious images, see Gell (1998: 118–26). On their materiality, see Chapter 2.

δρέψασαι, θηητόν. ἐνέπνευσαν δέ μοι αὐδὴν
θέσπιν, ἵνα κλείοιμι τά τ᾽ ἐσσόμενα πρό τ᾽ ἐόντα,
καί μ᾽ ἐκέλονθ᾽ ὑμνεῖν μακάρων γένος αἰὲν ἐόντων,
σφᾶς δ᾽ αὐτὰς πρῶτόν τε καὶ ὕστατον αἰὲν ἀείδειν.

Let us begin to sing from the Heliconian Muses, who possess the great and holy mountain of Helicon...

Starting out from there, shrouded in thick invisibility, by night they walk, sending forth their very beautiful voice...

One time, they taught Hesiod beautiful song while he was pasturing lambs under holy Helicon. And this speech the goddesses spoke first of all to me, the Olympian Muses, the daughters of aegis-holding Zeus: 'Field-dwelling shepherds, ignoble disgraces, mere bellies; we know how to say many false things similar to genuine ones, but we know, when we wish, how to proclaim true things.' So spoke great Zeus' ready-speaking daughters, and they plucked a staff, a branch of luxuriant laurel, a marvel, and gave it to me; and they breathed a divine voice into me, so that I might glorify what will be and what was before, and they commanded me to sing of the race of the blessed ones who always are, but always to sing of themselves first and last.[57]

The sophisticated edifice of the ancient Greek pantheon, with its care-fully woven genealogies and highly codified areas of divine expertise, was dependent upon a complex system of divine bodies. Herodotus influen-tially attributed this to the vividly anthropomorphic narratives of Homer and Hesiod, 'who taught the Greeks of the descent of the gods, and gave to all their several names, and honours, and arts, and declared their outward forms (*eidea*)'.[58] From long-armed Zeus to fleet-footed Iris, each deity's significance was defined and supported by a complex system of epithets and activities grounded in gender, age, form and attributes, each of which contributed towards defining his or her identity and sphere of influence within the polytheistic system. To know and worship a divinity was thus to engage with the nature and significance of his or her body.[59] However, Herodotus' aetiology of the Hellenic pantheon expresses a conundrum

[57] Hesiod, *Theogony* 1–2, 9–10, 22–34. All Hesiodic text and translations are taken from Glenn Most's Loeb Classical Library edition, 2006.

[58] Herodotus 2.53 (translation from A. D. Godley's Loeb Classical Library edition, 1920). On the influence of Homeric and Hesiodic concepts of the divine, see Vlastos (1970: 97–102), Burkert (1985b), Dietrich (1985–6), Nagy (1990a: 44–7), Most (1999: 336–46) and Price (1999: 6–7); on more ancient Near Eastern anthropomorphic influences, see Burkert (1985a: 182).

[59] On the corporeality of the Greek gods, see Burkert (1985a: 182–9), Vernant (1991) and Koch Piettre (1996: 35–43).

probed by philosophers from Xenophanes onwards – the idea that divine *eidea*, while conceived of as immortal bodies unconstrained by the limits of space, matter and time, are nevertheless constrained by the human imagination, set in the physical, social experience of their mortal worshippers.[60] Knowledge and understanding of divine forms are essential for efficacious religious practice. Yet Herodotus and other Greek thinkers were aware that such forms must necessarily be mediated through culturally engendered devices, such as mythical narratives and visual representations. The verb the historian uses to define such practice is *sēmainein*, to 'signify' or 'interpret'.[61] Just as cult and votive images constitute some of the practical means by which artists negotiated this relationship, so Greek literature, from its very beginnings, was concerned with the problem of how the gods can be known and apprehended by humans, and of the poet's responsibility for shaping his audience's beliefs and expectations.

In the proem to his *Theogony*, a hexameter poem dated to the late eighth or early seventh century BCE that presents a systematic account of the Greek gods and their origins, Hesiod narrates an encounter with the Muses of Mount Helicon which stands as an ur-text for programmatic, first-person epiphanic narratives in Greek literature.[62] It demonstrates how epiphany provided a potent – and highly influential – device by which to claim privileged knowledge and authority, yet also explores the necessary limitations placed on human access to the divine.[63] Significantly, the Muses who legitimate Hesiod's narrative go abroad by night, 'shrouded in thick invisibility' (κεκαλυμμέναι ἠέρι πολλῷ, 9); it is they, not the poet, who decide when 'to proclaim true things' (ἀληθέα γηρύσασθαι, 28), and when to speak 'false things similar to genuine ones' (ψεύδεα . . . ἐτύμοισιν ὁμοῖα, 27). Despite his claims to a 'divine voice' (αὐδὴν / θέσπιν, 31–2), Hesiod portrays himself as subject to the capriciousness of divine revelation. As he says, all human representation of the divine – all song 'of the race of the

---

[60] On Xenophanes' problematisation of anthropomorphism (DK B14–16), see Jaeger (1947: 47–8), Kirk *et al.* (1983: 167–72), Lesher (1992: 85–94) and K. A. Morgan (2000: 47–53).

[61] 2.53: see Gould (1985: 22–4), Nagy (1990b: 215–49), Manetti (1993: 16–17) and Hartog (1999: 193). Cf. Heraclitus fr. 22 DK B93, discussed by Manetti (1993: 16–19) and Kindt (2006: 37).

[62] Hesiod, proem to the *Theogony*, 1–34: see Koch Piettre (1996: 167–76). On the problems of language and representation associated with Hesiod's proem, see Pucci (1977: 1–44), Arthur (1983), Giovanni Ferrari (1988), Lincoln (1999: 3–18, 23–5) and Stoddard (2004: 60–97; 2005); for a summary of scholarly approaches with bibliography, see Katz and Volk (2000: 122–3).

[63] On the poetic influence of Hesiod's *Dichterweihe* – demonstrated, for example, by Archilochus (*SEG* 15.517, the Mnesiepes inscription, which relates the poetic initiation of Archilochus following an epiphany of the Muses) and Callimachus *Aitia* fr. 1.23–32 – see Kambylis (1963, 1965), Murray (1981) and Nagy (1990a: 49). On the authority conferred by the Muses, see Bowie (1993) and Nagy (1996).

blessed ones' – must begin and end with the Muses, agents of representation who may transmit knowledge of the divine directly to mortals, but who cannot be relied upon to do so with clarity or truth.[64] In order to claim validity, human creativity must be framed by divine modes of transmission, but this framing device exposes a fundamental gap between divine truth and its expression in human terms, which can only be bridged at immortal whim.[65] Indeed, Hesiod carefully leaves open the question of whether this gap can ever be bridged at all.

In evoking – and then problematising – epiphany's revelatory potential, the semiotic complexities of Hesiod's proem pose a dilemma intrinsic to the relationship between divinity and mortal creativity in Greek culture. That is, humans can only know the gods by means of representations (whether conceptual, verbal or visual), yet in order to be compelling and trustworthy, these representations must derive their value and authority from a perceived potentiality for direct engagement with the divine.[66] While acknowledging the obstacles that hinder the representation of epiphany, artists and poets must thus also hold out the possibility of surpassing them. For this reason, we must be careful not to deconstruct the ineffability of divine *alētheia* too far. Hesiod's Muses do not provide 'an imitation of that which is forever absent' in a Derridean sense, so much as express the *difficulty* of transmitting such knowledge clearly and correctly.[67] Their statement actually accords better with the logic of apophatic religious thought. By stating what god is not, and acknowledging the impossibility of capturing the divine in terms of human *logos*, it is, paradoxically, possible to reach a better understanding of what god is – a premise that is essential for the more 'kataphatic', orthodox assertions about the nature of the gods that Hesiod's proem serves to introduce.[68]

---

[64] See Pucci (1977: 2) and Detienne (1996: 22–5, 84–6). Compare *Il.* 2.485–6, where it is stated that the Muses alone are beholders or witnesses of the events the poet narrates, and Pindar *Paean* 6.1–6, 51–3, where poetic wisdom inspired by the Muses is compared to oracular consultation dependent upon divine revelation (Kurke, 2005: 104, 115–16). On the role of the Muses in archaic Greek culture, see Detienne (1996: 39–52) and Murray (2004).

[65] Thalmann (1984: 149) and Collins (1999). Compare Xenophanes' declaration that 'It is for god to *know* the truth, but for men to *believe* it', reported by Arius Didymus and Varro, DK 21 A24; see Lesher (1999: 226). For Manetti (1993: 15), 'The sign is the instrument of mediation between the total knowledge of the gods and the more limited knowledge of humankind'.

[66] See Thalmann (1984: 147–50), Detienne (1996: 45, 85) and Vernant (2006: 116–21) on the relationship between memory, truth and vision in the *Theogony* proem.

[67] Pucci (1977: 16), critiqued by Giovanni Ferrari (1988) and Collins (1999).

[68] On the place of 'negative theology' in ancient philosophy and the interdependency of apophatic and kataphatic approaches to the divine, see Armstrong (1979) and Kenney (1993). On the role of 'unknowability' in Greek religion, see Rudhardt (1992: 103–6) and T. Harrison (2006: 138–9).

Crucially, the Muses' challenge does not preclude the possibility of success. Like the votive reliefs discussed above, it paradoxically draws upon the tantalising promise of representation to eclipse its own denotative qualities and allow an encounter with the *thing itself,* to make the absent present. Epiphany in this sense has a transformative power: it allows Hesiod to move from being a shepherd trapped in mortal ignorance ('mere bellies', 26), to being a seer, literally 'inspired' or 'breathed into' by the Muses (ἐνέπνευσαν δέ μοι, 31).[69] In the verses that follow, the 'divine voice' of poetic inspiration is proven to be dependent upon both privileged access to the gods and the exercise of artistic skill and vivid expression – the qualities of *technē* and *enargeia.*[70] It is fundamental to the bardic enterprise, and indeed to all religious art, that these need not be mutually exclusive.

Hesiod's 'musings' on the tension between epiphany and poetic inspiration demonstrate a sophisticated literary self-consciousness, yet, as a comment upon the relationship between humans and their gods, they must be understood alongside contemporary religious acts and expectations. Within a religious system dependent upon forms of cultural mediation, indications of supernatural activity such as miracles, manifestations, oracles and portents played a vital role: worshippers were invited to apprehend such *sēmata* as direct communication from the gods.[71] Epiphany holds a special place within this category of divine signs as a form of unmediated encounter which, unlike oracular pronouncements or omens, can be experienced and understood independently of preordained systems of specialist interpretation.[72] Indeed, epiphany functions as the cognitive device by which such systems can be proven valid. That the potential for

---

[69] Svenbro (1976: 50–9); Ford (1992: 172–97, esp. 195): 'The poet's "divine human voice" is not an oxymoron or a ventriloquism but an epiphany: divine knowledge appears in sound and presents to human senses a world not otherwise apparent . . . in it the human account of the past and the divine perspective upon it, as far as they can, appear together on earth'. Note Katz and Volk (2000), who offer a new interpretation of the significance of *gastēr* in archaic poetry.

[70] On the relationship between divine inspiration and human *technē* in early Greek poetry, see Murray (1981); on the double meaning of *enargēs* as 'vividly present' (in archaic contexts) and its later appropriation as a rhetorical technique for 'bringing vividly before the eyes' through words, see Calame (1991) and Hartog (1999). On *enargeia* and epiphany, see Koch Piettre (2005) and my discussion in Chapter 5.

[71] On the significance of the term *sēma* in archaic Greek diction and its relationship to cognitive processes of *noēsis* ('perception' and 'understanding') and phenomena of affective signification, see Nagy (1983) and Prier (1989: 108–12).

[72] On the difference between epiphanies and oracles as forms of contact with the divine, see Hartog (1999: 188–90), who maps the difference onto the move from *mythos* to *logos* between Homer and Herodotus, ignoring the continuity of evidence for epiphany in Greek culture. On the semiological processes required by oracles and divination and their social and religious function, see Parker (1985), C. Morgan (1990), Manetti (1993: 14–35), Maurizio (1993: esp. 98–137; 1997), Potter (1994: 4–57), Bowden (2005) and Kindt (2006).

immediate visionary perception of a deity's *eidos* was an important element of Greek religious thought is suggested by the frequency with which epiphanies occur within poetic and historiographical narratives, where they are closely related to both the establishment of cults and festivals and moments of crisis or change.[73] Votive reliefs and inscriptions such as those from the Athenian Asclepieion testify to the potential for divine encounter within a ritual framework, characterised by carefully controlled systems of invocation, praise and dedication. But this is only one side of the epiphanic coin. As forms of divine communication that often bypass established structures of worship and interpretation, epiphanies also occur *outside* conventional human space and experience, and are witnessed independently of traditional religious locations and rituals. Hesiod's hillside vision of the Muses while shepherding his lambs, for example, presents us with a *locus classicus* of epiphanic experience that is echoed in numerous visionary narratives, such as Pan's alleged epiphany to the lonely long-distance runner Philippides in the Arcadian hills before the battle of Marathon.[74]

The sudden, uncanny and often disturbing nature of such experiences requires immediate acknowledgement and active response, an integration of the foreign or unusual into traditional beliefs and practices.[75] The Athenian reaction to Pan's confrontational epiphany, for example (Philippides is to 'tell the Athenians that they neglected him although he was well-disposed towards them'), was to found a cave sanctuary beneath the Acropolis and to honour the god with annual sacrifices and torch-races.[76] In this way the manifestation of a divine power external to identifiably civic

---

[73] On epiphany and crisis, see Petridou (2006: 96–160).

[74] Herodotus 6.105. See Drexler (1893), Haldane (1968), Pritchett (1979: 6–7, 23–5), Versnel (1987: 49–50), Borgeaud (1988: 133–62, esp. 243 n. 3), Garland (1992: 47–63), T. Harrison (2000: 82–92, with further bibliography), and Hornblower (2007: 143–4). On the intermediate nature of the pastoral zone in which epiphanies often take place, see Segal (1974), Arthur (1983: 101), Rudhardt (1996) and Petridou (in press a).

[75] As discussed, with some cynicism, in Plato's *Laws* 10.909e–910a: 'It is customary for all women especially, and for sick folk everywhere, and those in peril and distress . . . to dedicate whatever happens to be at hand at the moment, and to vow sacrifices and promise the founding of shrines to gods and demigods and children of gods; and through terrors caused by waking visions or by dreams (ἔν τε φάσμασιν ἐγρηγορότας διὰ φόβους καὶ ἐν ὀνείροις), and in like manner as they recall many visions (ὄψεις πολλάς) and try to provide remedies for each of them, they are wont to found altars and shrines, and to fill with them every house and every village, and open places too, and every spot which was the scene of such experiences' (translation R. G. Bury, Loeb Classical Library edition, 1961). On dangerous epiphanies, see Pfister (1924: 320–1) and on the importance of being ritually prepared for the viewing of the divine, Frontisi-Ducroux (1975: 110–11). On sacrifice as a traditional response to epiphany, see Dickie (2004: 177–8) and Stevens (in press).

[76] Translation from Parker (1996: 163), who discusses the introduction of Pan's cult to Athens in the early fifth century BCE (163–8). On the cave of Pan beneath the Athenian Acropolis, see Travlos (1971: 91–4, 417–21).

or sacred space is acknowledged and commemorated within the ritual and geographical boundaries of state religion.[77] Thus while epiphanies might *seem* to bypass acts of cultural representation, causing potential rupture, their subsequent integration into the system, through ritual responses such as sacrifice, dedication and the foundation of cults and festivals, actually serves to reinforce it. For this reason epiphanies are often retrospectively associated with unusual or troubling events, as a means of explaining and absorbing oddities and inconsistencies into the social fabric through the soothing power of charter myths. This is particularly the case for the introduction of new cults, such as those of Dionysus, Pan and Asclepius, where epiphanies of the god provide a divinely generated aetiological force for the absorption of a deity perceived as foreign or 'other' into pre-existing religious structures.[78]

Epiphany's role within the conventions of Greek religion is thus to confirm and reinforce relationships between inside and outside, mortal and immortal. Manifestations of the gods offer the potential for a seemingly direct sensory experience of divine *eidea* – a moment in which mortal bodies can apprehend immortal bodies, whether it be through sound, scent or, most commonly, sight. It is in this sense that they provide 'cognitive reliability' for the forms of the gods preserved and transmitted by more conventional representational devices, such as cult images and mythical narratives. In all cases, however, it is necessary that the impulse behind epiphanies is attributed not to human imagination, but to the gods themselves. In the vocabulary of archaic Greek experience, an epiphany functions as the ultimate form of *thauma*, a 'wonder', in which divine presence, or *eidos*, is asserted in profoundly physical terms and experienced phenomenologically as a sensory extravaganza, generated by 'appearing' (*phainesthai*) rather than 'seeming' (*dokein*), that comes from outside or elsewhere (the 'other/that' rather than the 'this') and has a powerful, often transformative effect upon its witnesses and their surroundings.[79] In the Homeric poems epiphanies are repeatedly expressed in the vocabulary of *enargeia*,

---

[77] Yet see Borgeaud (1988: 151) on the otherness of this sacred location: 'In the heart of the town (in the *astu*), a wild spot has been found for him.'

[78] Parker (1996: 186). On Asclepius, see above, n. 36. On Dionysus as *der kommende Gott* and his status as the perennial outsider, see Otto (1965: 74–85), Massenzio (1969), Detienne (1986, 1989: 12–13), Henrichs (1993b) and Seaford (2006: 39–48). For other vision-inspired foundations of Pan cults, see Paus. 2.32.6 (Pan Luterios at Troezen) and, in a literary context, Menander's *Dyscolos* and Longus 2.23.4: Borgeaud (1988: 256 n. 164).

[79] Prier (1989: 41–117, esp. 56–64, 84–101), with Koch Piettre (1996: 121–3) and Neer (2010: 57–66).

experience of a god's 'full unmediated presence'.[80] The intense immediacy of such unsought experiences serves to validate and reinforce ritually generated means of encountering the divine, and so affirms traditional religious practice and belief.

However, the concept of divine agency that gives epiphany meaning and force within conventional religious frameworks also makes it problematic. For while ritual activity is generated by mortal worshippers, set about with carefully defined rules, boundaries and preparations, epiphany – by its very nature – knows no such constraints. Knowledge and comprehension of divine form may be essential for correct religious practice, yet the gods exercise a capricious control over the revelation of their bodies. From Athena's multiple disguises in the *Odyssey* to Semele's fatal experience of Zeus' godhead, the question of how and to what extent deities might manifest themselves to humans posed a profound and inspirational challenge for the Greek imagination.[81] The limitations of epiphanic experience form one of the major themes of divine–mortal interaction in Homeric epic, a poetic space in which gods freely mingle with men, but even heroes must admit, as Odysseus to Athena, that 'it is hard, goddess, for a mortal man to know you when he meets you, however wise he may be, for you take what shape you will'.[82] While the gods might choose when, where and how they make themselves manifest, the onus is on humans to read correctly the *sēmata* of divine appearance.

In this sense the complexities of the Greek anthropomorphic system mean that no encounter with divinity can transcend the need for interpretation entirely. As many epiphanic narratives suggest, the visual manifestation of a god, often signified by the use of *phainesthai* or *enargēs*, requires a corresponding process of perception and recognition – *noēsis* and *anagnōrisis* – from its mortal witnesses.[83] This is a complex semiological process in which

---

[80] See, e.g., *Il.* 20.131: χαλεποὶ δὲ θεοὶ φαίνεσθαι ἐναργεῖς ('For dangerous are the gods when they appear in manifest form'), with Koch Piettre (1996: 124–35) and Hartog (1999: 188–9). All translations of the *Iliad* are from the A. T. Murray and W. F. Wyatt Loeb Classical Library edition, 1999.

[81] On Semele, see Cook (1914–40: vol. ii, 22–9), Buxton (1980: 34–5) and Vernant (1991: 41–6). Pausanias claims that 'even now' the Thebans allow no one to step into the building identified as Semele's bridal chamber (9.12.3).

[82] *Od.* 13.312–13. All translations of the *Odyssey* are from A. T. Murray and G. E. Dimock's Loeb Classical Library edition, 1995. The problematics of Homeric epiphany are discussed at length by Koch Piettre (1996: 44–155) and Stevens (2002, in press). See also D. Bremer (1975), Dietrich (1983, 1994), Burkert (1997: 21), Pucci (1998: 69–96), Fernández Contreras (1999), Hartog (1999: 188–9), Koch Piettre (2001: 215–23), Turkeltaub (2003) and Bierl (2004).

[83] E.g., *Il.* 1.199–200, *Od.* 1.322–3, 16.159–64. On the recognition and decoding of signs in archaic Greece, see Nagy (1983); on the relationship between *phainesthai* and *noēsis*, Prier

the relevant divinity must be correctly identified by recourse to the numerous *sēmata* of form and attribute that distinguish each individual god from the pantheon. But proper cognitive response to an epiphany also necessitates the understanding that, although each divine *sēma* may function as a 'sign', it also constitutes the *thing itself*, for what makes an epiphany 'epiphanic' is that the categories of sign and referent inexorably coalesce.[84] Thus we find that, in many cases, the moment of epiphany is marked by the god's statement '*I am*...'[85] Such a declaration of identity emphasises the immediacy of the encounter – this is *the god himself* – but it also hints at the human difficulty of correctly identifying and distinguishing divine *eidea* from the panoply of characteristics, attributes and shifting forms that make up the mythical pantheon.[86]

This challenging act of simultaneous recognition and interpretation characterises many epiphanic encounters in Homeric epic, in which a deity's powerful presence is acknowledged but nevertheless presents a hermeneutic challenge to mortal viewers, their response often proving demonstrative of their level of piety, intellect and heroism.[87] In *Iliad* 13 the Lesser Ajax confidently asserts 'Plain to be known are the gods', yet he identifies Poseidon (disguised as the prophet Calchas) by 'the signs he left of feet and of legs as he went from us': it is the character of his *ichnia* or 'footprints' – the vestigial *sēmata* of the god's presence – that enables Ajax's *anagnōrisis*.[88] Feet can leave traces of their presence, of course (and Poseidon was known for the beauty of his feet), but why legs (or shins)? The curious phrase

---

(1989: 56–7). On Aristotle's use of *anagnorisis* in relation to the *Odyssey* (*Politics* 1459b13–16) and related terms in Homeric Greek, see Prier (1989: 210–14).

[84] On this synthetic function and unmediated quality of the *sēma* in archaic Greece, see Prier (1989: esp. 200–1).

[85] E.g., *Il.* 2.26, 24.173, 24.460; *Od.* 11.252, 20.47; see D. Bremer (1975: 2–3). The convention is also employed in epiphanic scenes in Attic drama. In Euripides' *Hippolytus*, for example, each goddess identifies herself when she appears on the *theologeion*: at line 2, Aphrodite claims 'I am called the goddess Cypris'; at line 1285 Artemis declares 'It is I, Artemis, Leto's daughter, who address you'. See also Aristophanes *Ploutos* 78 and relevant discussion by Richardson (1974: 243–9) and W. J. Slater (1988).

[86] See Henrichs (1993b: 15–17), on this dilemma.

[87] See Pucci (1998: 69): 'The appearance of the god is managed through a representation of his physical presence that is always weak and arbitrary.'

[88] *Il.* 13.71–2: ἴχνια γὰρ μετόπισθε ποδῶν ἠδὲ κνημάων / ῥεῖ' ἔγνων ἀπιόντος. ἀρίγνωτοι δὲ θεοί περ. As Walter Burkert has commented (1985a: 186), 'A god is a god in that he reveals himself; but the epiphany of anthropomorphic gods could never be spoken of in anything but a very *vestigial* sense' (my italics); see also Burkert (2004: 3). Ajax's statement here is in stark contrast to more nuanced comments on the difficulties of identifying divine form found elsewhere in the Homeric poems and demonstrates a lack of religious sensibility that may foreshadow his impious rape of Cassandra (see Heubeck *et al.* 1988, on *Od.* 1.325–7, and Janko, 1992, *ad loc.*). On the complexities of Homeric epiphany in this passage, see Vernant (1991: 43), Koch Piettre (1996: 53–62) and, in relation to *Il.* 15.488–93, Stevens (in press).

troubled Homeric scholars in antiquity, who suggested replacing *ichnia* with *ithmata* ('movements'), a reference to the god's gait, but it can also be understood as an authentic application of a customary Homeric formula, a redundant expression for 'feet'.[89] Perhaps the strangeness is deliberate: the awkwardness with which Ajax explains his identification of Poseidon expresses the difficulty of describing divine form and communicating the immediacy of epiphany. The poet is forced to twist the conventions of poetic diction in order to convey the ineffable, readily exposing the limitations of language (as much as, elsewhere, he delights in its possibilities). If it is so difficult to describe or represent the gods, can it *really* be as easy as Ajax claims to identify them? What, after all, do the *ichnia* of Poseidon's feet actually look like? The passage raises an important problem associated with the transmission of epiphanic experience. The point at which Ajax must explain or communicate his apprehension of Poseidon is also the point at which the presentation of divine form must become re-presentation, when divine *alētheia* must cross the gap (presided over by Hesiod's Muses) to poetic narrative or artistic representation, and the ineffable nature of divine body must be constrained within the arbitrary conventions of human formulae. For an epiphany to have meaning, it must be commemorated and communicated through language or visual form, but in that very act the immediacy of divine *eidos* is lost. Much of Greek art and literature is concerned, as we shall see, with the question of how to get it back.

Epiphany thus constitutes a complex exercise in hermeneutics, concerned with the relationship between sense-perception and conceptual knowledge – with the question *how do I know what I see?* In this sense, it sheds its own revelatory light upon the design and operation of the gods within Greek culture, for although such beings are entirely socially constituted (and frequently acknowledged as being so), they are by definition assigned a power and significance that passes far beyond the boundaries of human knowledge and experience.[90] As a hermeneutic exercise, however, epiphany also functions as a religious expression of the epistemological project that drove much Greek philosophy and, by the fourth century BCE, found its most

---

[89] Janko (1992), *ad loc.*, with reference to the scholion of Didymus in Erbse (1969–88: vol. III, 413). For a similar problem, see Pucci (1998: 75) on alternative ancient readings of the Muses' epiphany to Hesiod at *Theogony* 31: such uncertainty 'is unavoidable once the tradition introduces divine intervention without actually describing its appearance'. One might argue that the reluctance to describe such intervention is in fact a topos of epiphanic narrative; see below on the *Homeric Hymns*.

[90] See, e.g., Lesher (1992: 228–31) on Xenophanes' attitudes to divine *sapheneia*, a 'godlike synoptic view of "all things"' to which mortals can never have access (231).

influential examination in the works of Plato.[91] Like the Platonic Forms, the gods stand as ultimate beings in a metaphysical realist system in which the most pressing question is not whether they exist at all, but, first, how they can be known and, second, how such knowledge can be correctly transmitted without sacrificing cognitive immediacy to the distancing effects of representation.[92] It is telling that epiphany's negotiation of the relationship between vision and knowledge provided Plato and his contemporaries with an influential paradigm for philosophical practice itself. As Andrea Nightingale has so eloquently demonstrated, the 'spectator theory of knowledge' that characterises fourth-century philosophy is modelled upon the concept of *theōria*, the tradition of 'going to see' a god, usually in the context of a festival, that typified state and personal pilgrimage in Greek culture.[93] Religious and secular epistemological practices are thus closely bound by their privileging of visual – and visionary – means of gaining access to transcendent truths. Both are also beset by an anxiety about the cognitive reliability of the knowledge thereby gained. Plato's objections to mimesis both spring from and contribute to a broader concern about the relationship between metaphysical beings and their more accessible material exemplars that finds its sacred parallel in the tension between vision and representation. This relationship is shifting and never entirely resolved: epiphany may be dependent upon the power and influence of representation (in the form of mental impressions, verbal narratives or visual images), but crucially – for both religious and philosophical means of knowledge acquisition – it simultaneously disavows and transcends the very concept. For all its aporetic potential, epiphany is primarily concerned with *presentation*.

'What god is this?' Hymnic guides to epiphanic viewing

One of the most potent sites of engagement between sacred modes of representation and the problematic nature of epiphany in Greek culture is the

---

[91] See, e.g., the epiphanic language employed by Parmenides (KRS Fr. 1 = Sextus *Adversus mathematicos* 7.3) in his Hesiodic apprehension of the goddess who reveals 'true knowledge' (*alētheia*): Jaeger (1947: 90–108), Kirk *et al.* (1983: 242–4), Cordero (1990) and Detienne (1996: 36–8, 130–4). On Plato's theology, see Gerson (1990: 33–81).

[92] On metaphysical realism, see Burnyeat (1982) and Rockmore (2004: 18–44, esp. 26): 'the Greek [philosophical] tradition . . . consists of a series of variations on the Platonic claim to know the real'.

[93] Nightingale (2001, 2004: esp. 40–71, 2005). On the religious significance of *theōria* and its relationship to pilgrimage, see Rutherford (1995, 2000) and Montiglio (2005: 118–79), and, on its sociopolitical significance, Goldhill (1999: 5–8).

literary hymn, a poetic act designed to invoke divine presence in preparation for a performance of epic poetry, often as part of a religious festival celebrated within the sanctuary of the relevant divinity.[94] The conventions of hymnic diction and performance mark a transition from secular to sacred behaviour and expectations, and constitute a ritual act.[95] Appropriately, texts such as the proem of Hesiod's *Theogony* and the poems gathered as the *Homeric Hymns* (mostly dated to the seventh and sixth centuries BCE) function as *prooimia*, 'preludes', that frame and introduce the epiphanic encounters of the mythopoetic realm.[96] In providing both ritual and literary preparation for their mortal audience, hymns elucidate a deity's identity and sphere of influence through the use of mythological narratives, so underlining the performance's status as a celebration of his or her power.[97] In this sense they function like votive offerings, *agalmata* designed to 'delight' the god into honouring a space and occasion with his or her presence and *charis*.[98] Accordingly they demonstrate a high degree of poetic and aesthetic self-consciousness. The beauty and sophistication of the hymn – its own qualities of *charis* – are essential for its efficacy as both a sacred device and a

[94] E.g., *H. Hom.* 2, *To Demeter*, which has strong associations with Eleusis (Richardson, 1974: 5–30), *H. Hom.* 3, *To Apollo*, which refers to festivals at both Delos and Delphi (Parker, 1991: 1; West, 2003: 10) and *H. Hom.* 4, *To Hermes*, which has been associated with Olympia (West 2003: 13–14). On the difficulty of determining the performative context of the *Homeric Hymns*, see Aloni (1980), Herter (1981), Clay (1989: 6–7), who controversially associates them with the symposium, and Parker (1991: 1), who claims that 'the normal context of performance is likely to have been a festival, the obvious occasion in archaic Greece both for rhapsodic contests and for the recitation of independent narrative hymns'. On ritual (as opposed to Homeric narrative) hymns in antiquity, see J. M. Bremer (1981) and Bremer and Furley (2001).

[95] See Depew (2000) and Bremer and Furley (2001: 1–64), who emphasise the difficulty of distinguishing between sacred and secular in much Greek poetry, but claim the distinguishing feature of hymn is the direct address of the gods with the 'goal of incurring divine goodwill' (3), functioning as 'the verbally articulated complement to expressive action in religious worship' (4). On the process of 'ritualisation' as enacted by hymns and choral lyrics in archaic Greece, see Kurke (2005).

[96] On the proem to the *Theogony* as a hymn, see West (1966: 150–1) and Thalmann (1984: 134–8). On hymns as *prooimia*, see Richardson (1974: 3–4), Lenz (1975: 278–86), Aloni (1980), J. M. Bremer (1981), Janko (1981), Parker (1991), Calame (1995) and Furley (1995). The length of some *Homeric Hymns* suggests they may have also stood as independent poems in their own right; see Allen *et al.* (1936: xciv–xcv). On the dating of the *Hymns*, see Janko (1982).

[97] Clay (1989). On the complex relationship between Greek poetic texts and ritual performance, see Kurke (2005).

[98] On the hymn as an *agalma*, see especially Depew (2000), with Furley (1995: 32–6), Pulleyn (1997: 49–50) and Bremer and Furley (2001: vol. I, 3–7). On the role of *charis* in Greek religion, see Grottanelli (1989–90), MacLachlan (1993), Day (1994), Calame (1995) and Pulleyn (1997: esp. 39–55). As Parker (1998: 108–9) points out, the term is notoriously difficult to translate, meaning both 'charm, delight' and that which causes it, as well as suggesting notions of gratitude and reciprocity.

legitimisation of the mythical narrative that will follow.[99] Hymns therefore have a dual function that relates closely to the ambiguous role of epiphanic representations in Greek religion, such as the votive reliefs discussed above: they are designed to *make epiphany happen*, calling upon the god to be present, whilst simultaneously providing their audience with a sophisticated *representation* (in narrative form) of divine activity that prefigures the subsequent epic performance.[100] As performative texts in which the poet is highly aware of his responsibility both to invoke and represent immortal *eidea* for his mortal audience and divine addressee, the *Homeric Hymns* present us with some of the most vivid and challenging narratives of divine manifestation in Greek literature.

Epic poetry presents a world in which gods mix with heroes, a lost golden age accessible only through mythical narrative.[101] As frames or transitional aids to this lost heroic world, the *Homeric Hymns* explore encounters between gods and 'ordinary people': the royal women who experience Demeter's epiphanies at Eleusis (*H. Hom.* 2); the Tyrsenian pirates who attempt to kidnap Dionysus (*H. Hom.* 7); the storm-tossed sailors who invoke the aid of the Dioscuri (*H. Hom.* 33).[102] Even the *Hymn to Aphrodite*, which narrates the goddess's seductive epiphany to the Trojan shepherd Anchises, concentrates on her mortal lover's fear and vulnerability, rather than on his heroic status.[103] Each hymn focuses through its mortal witnesses so that the audience too is drawn into the epiphanic narrative, presented

---

[99] Furley (1995). On hymnic invocation as legitimising the poet's ensuing Homeric narrative, see de Jong (1987: 46–9).

[100] On the call for divine presence in cletic hymns, see J. M. Bremer (1981: 194–5) and Bierl (2001: 140–50; 2004: 44); on the performative nature of hymnic language, see Koch Piettre (2001: 220–1).

[101] This is not to simplify the complex hermeneutics of epiphany within the Homeric poems themselves. As Pucci (1998) has so eloquently demonstrated, epiphany has the power to rupture the 'seamless whole' of divine–mortal relations in the Homeric world in ways that can seem more withholding and problematic than epiphanies within the hymnic narratives (79); yet the hymnic epiphanies are, I would argue, far more problematic in their revelation of divine *eidos* than Pucci would like to imply (69–70).

[102] See Lenz (1975: 9–22), Sowa (1984: 241) and Parker (1991: 2–3). All text, translations (with some modifications) and numeration of the *Homeric Hymns* are taken from Martin West's Loeb Classical Library edition, 2003.

[103] The suggestion that the *Hymn to Aphrodite* was a more secular text, associated with the ancestry of the 'Aeneadae' of the Troad (see Reinhardt, 1956; Faulkner, 2008, with bibliography), complicates this hymn's religious, social and geographical associations, but has been rejected by many scholars in favour of a concentration on the unbridgeable gap between mortal and divine; see Segal (1974), van der Ben (1980, 1986: esp. 12, 21–2), P. Smith (1981a, 1981b), Clay (1989: 166–70) and Turkeltaub (2003: 75–8), with a reassessment of the argument by Faulkner (2008). On erotic epiphanies and sexual relations between gods and mortals in Greek culture, see Petridou (in press a). On the hymn's exploration of Aphrodite's role within the Olympian hierarchy, see Frangeskou (1995).

with a series of *sēmata* constituting the dangers and delights of divine encounter, which demand acknowledgement and interpretation. As texts concerned with the aetiology of divine authority and religious tradition, hymns repeatedly employ epiphanic narratives in which the *eidea* of the relevant deity are first made manifest – whether through the god's birth, acquisition of powers and arrival on Olympus (as in the hymns to Apollo, Hermes and Pan);[104] through his or her first arrival among humans (the *Hymn to Dionysus*); or through revelations of divine form that prompt the foundation of cultic institutions (the *Hymn to Demeter*). Often many such narratives are combined in the same hymn (such as in those to Apollo and Hermes).

The hymn's function as a bridge between the mythic and the everyday, the sacred and profane, is reflected in its narrative structures, for such foundation myths are repeatedly concerned with the act of incorporating a divinity into specific cultural practices and geographical locations, of *bringing the deity in*, marking a transition from dangerous, unsought and misunderstood encounter to that which is ritually prepared for – and correctly recognised – by mortal worshippers. In this sense, the hymn performs the difficult balancing act of incorporating the god into mortal space and activity, acculturating his or her divine *eidea* through acts of representation, while simultaneously recognising the god's power to transcend the limitations of sanctuary, human body and material form.[105] The difficulties confronting human comprehension of divine *eidea* are therefore central to the hymn's concerns.

The fraught process of interpreting and acculturating the *sēmata* of divine appearance is enacted at length in two of the most prominent hymns to have come down to us: the *Hymn to Demeter* and the *Hymn to Aphrodite*. Each dramatises the corporeal and existential gap between mortal and divine in moments of disturbing epiphany, when goddesses previously disguised as humans during seemingly benign encounters suddenly and terrifyingly reveal the form and stature (*eidos kai megethos*) of their divine nature.[106] Each goddess's Olympian status is initially veiled: Aphrodite appears 'like an unmarried girl in stature and form' so as not to frighten Anchises;[107] in her guise as an old woman, Demeter goes unrecognised by the daughters of Keleos, for, as the poet states, 'Gods are hard for mortals to

---

[104] On birth in the *Hymn to Apollo*, see Clay (1989: 28–9) and Bakker (2002a). On the *Hymn to Hermes*, see Jaillard (2007).

[105] See Vernant (1991), on the paradoxical nature of divine bodies.

[106] See Loraux (1991), Koch Piettre (1996: 291–306), Steiner (2001: 95–7) and Turkeltaub (2003: 51–90).

[107] *H. Hom.* 5.82: παρθένῳ ἀδμήτῃ μέγεθος καὶ εἶδος ὁμοίη.

see'.[108] Nevertheless, each goddess's divinity is suggested by hints of superior dignity and loveliness; the moment of epiphany is anticipated by the 'wonder' or *thauma* with which she is first beheld by the hymn's mortal witnesses, and each divinity is addressed as being 'like a goddess'.[109]

With their divine *eidos* partially veiled, the goddesses enter the private domestic space of their mortal witnesses and engage with them at a very physical, intimate level. They take them as lovers, as Aphrodite does Anchises, or nurse their children, as Demeter tends Metaneira's infant Demophon 'in her fragrant bosom and immortal arms'.[110] In each case, however, an unnerving revelation of divine form and disruption of intimacy is prompted by a sense of misunderstanding or difference that opens up between mortal and god – grim reminders of the chasm that yawns between the human and the divine. Metaneira interrupts Demeter's attempt to immortalise her child, and so unwittingly condemns him to 'death and mortality'; Anchises' postcoital slumber marks his vulnerability to the 'terrible sorrow' of Aphrodite's desire for a mortal lover, and foreshadows the 'hostile, merciless old age' that is his inevitable lot.[111] As the climax of an anthropomorphic narrative exploring the potential for divine–mortal interaction, the moment of epiphany in each hymn marks a point of contrast and rupture between god and human, which is expressed through the exceptional characteristics of divine bodies and the paralysis or mutism of their mortal counterparts. The poet emphasises a dramatic growth in each goddess's size (*megethos*), accompanied by a wondrous beauty (*kallos*), fragrance and searing luminosity.[112] At Demeter's epiphany we

---

[108] *H. Hom.* 2.111: χαλεποὶ δὲ θεοὶ θνητοῖσιν ὁρᾶσθαι. Demeter is described at 94 as 'disguising her *eidos*'. Compare *Od.* 13.312–13 (mentioned above, n. 82) and 16.161, where, after a partial epiphany of Athena, Odysseus states to Telemachus that 'It is not at all the case that the gods appear in manifest form to all' (οὐ γάρ πως πάντεσσι θεοὶ φαίνονται ἐναργεῖς); discussed by Sowa (1984: 238–9), Stevens (2002), Turkeltaub (2003: 242–80) and Bierl (2004).

[109] *H. Hom.* 5.154: γύναι εἰκυῖα θεῇσιν; 159: δὴ γὰρ θεοείκελός ἐσσι. Compare the helmsman's uneasy sense of the god's strangeness in the *Hymn to Dionysus* (*H. Hom.* 7.17–24, discussed below). For an epic parallel to epiphany's production of *thauma*, see Achilles' response to Athena at *Il.* 1.199.

[110] *H. Hom.* 2.231–2: θυώδεϊ δέξατο κόλπῳ / χερσίν τ' ἀθανάτοισι.

[111] *H. Hom.* 2.262: νῦν δ' οὐκ ἔσθ' ὥς κεν θάνατον καὶ κῆρας ἀλύξαι, 5.198–9: οὕνεκά μ' αἰνόν / ἔσχεν ἄχος, and 2.244–5: νῦν δέ σε μὲν τάχα γῆρας ὁμοίιον ἀμφικαλύψει / νηλειές. Cf. Hesiod *Theogony* 26. On the condemnation of mortal helplessness as a traditional element of divine self-revelation, see Richardson (1974: 243–4, and on parallels between the epiphanic language of the two hymns, 42–3). On notions of mortality in the *Hymn to Aphrodite*, see P. Smith (1981b).

[112] *H. Hom.* 2.275–9, 5.171–5. On the characteristic details of such epiphanies, see Pfister (1924: 314–15) and Richardson (1974: 252–6).

are told that 'a radiance shone afar from her immortal body' (278–9), creating an almost oxymoronic contrast between her flesh (χροός) and her divinity (ἀθανάτοιο); similarly, 'a divine beauty' shines from Aphrodite's cheeks.[113] Furthermore, just as the radiance of divine form transcends the earthbound matter of mortal flesh, pouring from it as if a physical emanation, so its size bursts beyond the confines of human space.[114] Despite the ease with which each goddess has entered the domestic realm of the hymn's protagonists – Keleos' palace, Anchises' hut – the physical frame of the narrative's location cannot sustain the force or dimensions of her true *eidos* once it is revealed. After seducing Anchises, Aphrodite rises from his fur-strewn bed and stands before him, her head reaching 'to the sturdy rafter'.[115] In Demeter's first partial epiphany to Metaneira, at her arrival, her head 'reached to the rafter, and she filled the doorway with divine radiance'; in the second, at her departure, 'the sturdy house was filled with a brilliance as of lightning' (280).[116] In each case the intensity and magnitude of divine form destabilise the reassuring solidity of the human domestic structures that frame the encounter. In contrast, human responses to epiphany are defined by corporeal deficiency: they cannot withstand the visual intensity projected by divine form and must hide their faces in fear, as Anchises, or, in a response characteristic of the effects of *thauma*, are struck dumb, as Metaneira, who is so overcome that she forgets her baby and leaves him lying distressed on the floor (282–3).[117]

The image of a goddess in the doorway cast a long shadow over the ancient cultural imagination.[118] It is striking and memorable because it expresses the impossibility of framing and holding divine form within the dimensions of human space – the incursion of the divine into the domestic sphere has something of the effect of a bull in a china shop.[119] In the immediate context of the hymn, the image of a deity pausing upon the threshold also reflects the poem's function as a performative act designed to bring the god into

[113] *H. Hom.* 2.278–9: τῆλε δὲ φέγγος ἀπὸ χροὸς ἀθανάτοιο / λάμπε θεᾶς, 5.174–5: κάλλος δὲ παρειάων ἀπέλαμπεν / ἄμβροτον.

[114] Richardson (1974: 253).   [115] *H. Hom.* 5.173–4: εὐποιήτου <δὲ> μελάθρου / κῦρε κάρη.

[116] *H. Hom.* 2.188–9: καί ῥα μελάθρου / κῦρε κάρη, πλῆσεν δὲ θύρας σέλαος θείοιο, 5.280: αὐγῆς δ' ἐμπλήσθη πυκινὸς δόμος ἀστεροπῆς ὥς.

[117] *H. Hom.* 5.182: τάρβησέν τε καὶ ὄσσε παρακλιδὸν ἔτραπεν ἄλλη, 2.282–3: δηρὸν δ' ἄφθογγος γένετο χρόνον, οὐδέ τι παιδός / μνήσατο τηλυγέτοιο ἀπὸ δαπέδου ἀνελέσθαι.

[118] E.g., Catullus 68.70–2. Compare reliefs and vase-paintings in which gods frequently 'burst through' the boundaries of formal framing devices, discussed in Chapter Two, 89–90.

[119] Compare Dionysus' epiphanic bursting of domestic frameworks and literal destruction of the house of Pentheus in the *Bacchae* 585–603, discussed by Seaford (in press); see also Steiner (2001: 85).

the audience's domain. Just as the *Hymn to Aphrodite* traces the goddess's movement from Olympus through the liminal pastoral zone of Mount Ida and thence to Anchises' hut, foreshadowing the birth of her descendant Aeneas in the Trojan court, so the *Hymn to Demeter* traces Demeter's journey from Olympus to Eleusis in search of her daughter Persephone, and commemorates the subsequent foundation of her temple and the Eleusinian mysteries. Each hymn charts the goddess's transition from the divine to the human realm and the means by which the presence of the gods can be marked and memorialised by those who witness it, whether through the spawning of heroic lineages or through the establishment of religious institutions. Hymnic epiphanies – which often take place at highly charged moments of arrival and departure – mark these nodes of transition by exploring the precise instances at which the worlds of mortal and immortal collide. While these moments of confrontation pose practical, ethical and interpretative difficulties for their mortal witnesses, the concluding injunction, common to many hymnic narratives, to found a temple, altar or festival in the god's honour finally serves to frame and domesticate the divinity in an appropriate ritual manner. In the *Hymn to the Dioscuri*, the brother gods' epiphany to storm-tossed sailors at sea is set firmly within a ritual context. Invoked with the correct sacrificial honours aboard the ship's deck, the 'beautiful signs' (σήματα καλά, 33.16) of the gods' airborne manifestations are salvific, rather than dangerous: 'The sailors rejoice at the sight, and their misery and stress are ended'.[120] In some cases the acculturation of epiphany is demonstrated by the creation of images, representations of the divinity which, like the hymn itself, can provide a safe mediatory object through which the deity can be viewed, recognised and honoured: as Zeus concludes in Hymn 1, *To Dionysus*, 'they will set up many *agalmata* in his shrines'.[121]

In narrating apprehensions of immortal *eidos*, the Homeric Hymns present their audience with a guide to viewing the divine. The central *argumentum* or *pars epica* of each poem is concerned with the establishment of definitive *eidea* through narratives of birth, the acquisition of powers or

---

[120] *H. Hom.* 33.16–17: οἱ δὲ ἰδόντες / γήθησαν, παύσαντο δ᾽ ὀϊζυροῖο πόνοιο. Here I am at odds with Clay (1989: 27), who claims that 'Each divine manifestation resembles every other . . . each single epiphany of the Dioscuri may be a single event, but is simultaneously identical to all other epiphanies.' Rather, the hymns repeatedly emphasise that divine self-revelation is capriciously shifting and polysemic. In this sense, there is a clear difference between the randomness of unsought epiphanies and those invoked through ritual, which call upon a pre-established set of divine *sēmata*.

[121] Section D, line 1: καί οἱ ἀναστήσουσιν ἀγάλματα πόλλ᾽ ἐνὶ νηοῖς.

aetiological epiphanies in which humans learn to read correctly the *sēmata* of divine presence and recognise the special qualities of divine bodies.[122] Yet in fixing divine *eidea* within the minds of their audience, hymns also testify to their multiplicity and boundlessness, thematising the hermeneutic challenges that epiphanic encounters pose. While customary *sēmata* of epiphany such as an expansion of *megethos*, emanation of light and wonderful fragrance are repeated from hymn to hymn, so too is the metamorphic potential of divine form. In particular the *Hymn to Apollo* and *Hymn to Dionysus* stress the shifting nature of each god's *eidos* and the difficulties confronting mortal witnesses in safely reaching *anagnōrisis*. The latter tells how Dionysus 'appeared' (ἐφάνη, 2) on the seashore – another liminal space full of epiphanic potential.[123] At first he presents himself 'in the likeness (ἐοικώς, 3) of a youth in first manhood', his hair flowing round his shoulders in the manner of a kouros statue. Like Demeter and Aphrodite, the beauty of his anthropomorphic disguise hints at his divine status.[124] But just as the kouros formula could be employed for representations of both gods and young men, so the youth is easily mistaken for nobility and kidnapped by pirates eager for a fat ransom. Even the helmsman, who recognises the mysterious youth's divine status, cannot correctly identify him: 'This is either Zeus, or silverbow Apollo, or Poseidon!' he claims.[125] The god's subsequent transformation from kouros into a lion, roaring in the bows of the ship, performs a shift in *eidos* that moves beyond the anthropomorphic to the theriomorphic, a terrifying reminder that the mirroring of human form that allowed the Greeks to feel close to their gods could be an all-too-comfortable illusion.[126] In a further subversion of epiphanic expectations, Dionysus simultaneously creates 'a shaggy-maned bear' that rears up in fury amidships, a doubling of the manifestation which the poet describes as σήματα φαίνων – literally 'making signs appear' (46).[127]

---

[122] On the tripartite division of the hymn into *invocatio – pars epica – precatio*, see J. M. Bremer (1981), who terms the central part *argumentum*.

[123] On seashore epiphanies and interstitial spaces, see Petridou (in press a). On epiphany in the *Homeric Hymn to Dionysus*, see Koch Piettre (1996: 263–9) and Turkeltaub (2003: 109–16).

[124] Compare *H. Hom.* 3.449–50, in which Apollo appears on the shore of Crisa 'in the likeness of a sturdy yeoman in his first prime, his hair falling over his broad shoulders', and is greeted by the leader of the Cretans as 'not at all like a mortal in body and stature, but like the immortal gods' (464–5).

[125] *H. Hom.* 7.19–20: ἢ γὰρ Ζεὺς ὅδε γ᾽ ἐστὶν ἢ ἀργυρότοξος Ἀπόλλων / ἠὲ Ποσειδάων.

[126] See Gould (1985: 28–9). On the destructive and metamorphic influence of Dionysiac epiphany, see Seaford (in press).

[127] Compare *Il.* 2.353, 4.381, 9.236 and *Od.* 21.413, where Zeus is described as *sēmata phainōn*, discussed by Prier (1989: 64): 'The "other/that" is the "symbol maker" and lies at the source of symbolic, phenomenological appearance.'

This dramatic demonstration of power thoroughly destabilises the fixity of divine form and identity: what is god, and what is a *sēma* of the god? The scarcely adequate response to such a semiotic crisis is for Dionysus' mortal witnesses to surrender their own fixity of form: the dissenters are transformed into dolphins, and only then does the god finally claim 'I am Dionysus' (56). By extending the theme of divine mutability to the mortal witnesses of Dionysus' manifestation, the hymn thus dramatically illustrates epiphany's transformative effect upon the viewer. Confronted with the force and caprice of divine revelation, human *eidos* is what turns out to be malleable and impermanent.[128]

The continual movement of divinities between bodies in the Homeric poems begs the question of what divine *eidea* actually constitute. On this the poets fall silent. While the *Homeric Hymns* dramatise the intensity and potential dangers of divine encounter, when they move from narrative to description and attempt to convey what their mortal protagonists see, they reach the edges of language. In some cases they suppress the details of visual appearance altogether. Though they may convey a general impression of size, beauty and radiance (as in the hymns to Demeter and Aphrodite), description of the deity's actual body is withheld, and the audience is diverted instead to the materiality of substances that serve to conceal form. Demeter 'holds a veil before her face', when she first sits down in the house of Keleos (197). Aphrodite arouses wonder, or *thauma*, in Anchises, not just through her 'size and stature', but also through a 'dress brighter than firelight', bright bracelets and earrings, and necklaces that 'shine like the moon' (86–90).[129] When her mortal lover undresses her, the hymn teasingly describes how each garment is progressively removed, until . . . silence. The moment of revelation and the moment of sexual union (which, in the realm of Aphrodite, are arguably the same thing) are passed over swiftly.[130] The hymn's lingering description of Aphrodite's garments instead employs the traditions of Homeric ekphrasis, concentrating on the miraculous workmanship of her dress and jewellery (160–5), which are themselves a *thauma idesthai* (90). By a process of synecdoche the poet merges the shining qualities of precious metals with the radiance of Aphrodite's body in such a way

---

[128] Cf. *Il.* 1.199–200, with Pucci (1998: 74), Stevens (2002) and Turkeltaub (2005).

[129] On the 'aesthetics of radiance' in Greek culture, see Prier (1989: 50–6), Parisinou (2000), Steiner (2001: 97–8), and Neer (2010).

[130] On the *Hymn to Aphrodite's* anticipation of romantic formulae, see Bickerman (1976); on the workings of *erōs* in the hymn, see H. Parry (1986).

that the material and divine are inexorably blurred.[131] Yet at the heart of the epiphanic experience, all that the hymn can convey is a state of ignorance: we are simply told that the mortal Anchises 'by divine will and destiny lay with the immortal goddess, *without knowing clearly*'.[132] When he awakes from sleep to his moment of *anagnōrisis*, the goddess is once more dressed. Though her searing beauty is conveyed by only her 'neck and lovely eyes' (181), Anchises must hide his face even from this partial revelation of her form. In return he receives a lecture on his own mortality.

While some hymns resort to silence at the moment of encounter, others seek diversion through the language of (re)semblance. Just as, in English, we must ask what something looks *like* in order to create a visual impression, so the hymns repeatedly describe divine forms in terms of beings other than themselves. Deities repeatedly appear 'in the likeness of' something else: Apollo appears 'in the likeness of a dolphin' (δελφῖνι ἐοικώς, 3.400), then 'in the form of a star' (ἀστέρι εἰδόμενος, 441), then 'in the form of a strong man' (ἀνέρι εἰδόμενος αἰζηῷ, 449).[133] As the last of these he addresses the Cretans chosen to tend his sanctuary at Delphi with the words 'I am Zeus' son, I declare myself Apollo' (480).[134] Yet there is no assurance that the shifting signifier of the kouros with which the hymn ends is his definitive *eidos*, simply that it is the form by which he chooses to communicate with men most efficiently (and therefore the iconography most suitable for human representations of the god).[135] The hymn's prevarication on this matter recalls Odysseus' statement that Athena is difficult to see because she is 'like all things' (παντὶ ἐΐσκεις).[136] Such passages imply that, like Hesiod's Muses, the gods have an inexhaustible mimetic power which they draw upon in order to insert themselves into the matrix of human experience. As guides to

---

[131] On the thaumatic qualities ascribed to wrought objects such as clothing and jewellery and the realm of representation more generally in archaic language, see Prier (1989: 94–7). On the epiphanic aspects of Aphrodite's toilette, see Koch Piettre (1996: 282–91).

[132] *H. Hom.* 5.166–7: ὃ δ' ἔπειτα θεῶν ἰότητι καὶ αἴσῃ / ἀθανάτῃ παρέλεκτο θεᾷ βροτός, οὐ σάφα εἰδώς (translation with author's modification).

[133] LSJ s.v. εἴδομαι: when used with the dative in archaic poetry, this verb is understood to mean 'to take the appearance of' or 'to make oneself like' a thing, e.g., *Il.* 2.791, when Iris 'made her voice like that of Polites': εἴσατο δὲ φθογγὴν... Πολίτῃ. See D. Bremer (1975: 2–5), Versnel (1987: 45), Koch Piettre (1996: 239–41) and Turkeltaub (2003: 101–6).

[134] εἰμὶ δ' ἐγὼ Διὸς υἱός, Ἀπόλλων δ' εὔχομαι εἶναι.

[135] Cf. Pucci (1998: 69–70) and Bierl (2004: 47–8) on Athena's epiphany in 'the form of a woman (ἤϊκτο γυναικί), beautiful and tall, and skilled in glorious handwork' at *Od.* 13.288–9; see Buxton (2004: 142–3) and Stevens (in press) on the difficulty of distinguishing between metamorphosis and metaphor in Homeric narratives of epiphany.

[136] *Od.* 13.313.

the relationship between human and divine, hymns record and negotiate the various *eidea* favoured by different deities in their dealings with the mortal sphere. On one hand, they seek to secure a taxonomy of divine bodies, as part of their attempt to define the sphere of authority presided over by each member of the pantheon; on the other hand, they leave open a crucial interpretive space in which the degree of revelation and choice of form is left entirely to the deity invoked. Like cletic hymns, which summon the god through a sequence of distinct names and epithets, the shape-shifting of the *Homeric Hymns* makes serial allusions to specificity of form and identity as a means of acknowledging the multiplicity of divine nature.[137] Just as deities transcend the boundaries of human space – as Demeter in Metaneira's doorway – so they transcend the boundaries of physical form. If gods are really 'like all things', then any encounter with a seemingly 'definitive' *eidos* can, in truth, constitute only a partial revelation of godhead; in order to celebrate a divinity's power with appropriate piety, the hymn must therefore acknowledge the limitations of its own representational devices.

That hymns function as celebrations of the gods' elusive mimetic powers is suggested by the passage that closes the Delian section of the *Hymn to Apollo*. One of the great 'wonders' or *thaumata* in the island sanctuary is a chorus of handmaidens who sing hymns to Apollo, Artemis and Leto, but can also 'imitate the tongues of all men and their clattering speech: each man would say that he himself was singing, so made fast [to the object of imitation] is their sweet song'.[138] As intermediaries between human and divine, who mirror the divine chorus of Apollo's Muses on Olympus, the maidens are, like Hesiod's Muses, agents of representation: they represent both gods and humans to themselves as if in a mirror, to the extent that their

---

[137] Compare lines 19–29 of the *Hymn to Apollo*, where the poet expresses bewilderment at the endless variety of themes appropriate for his hymn; see A. M. Miller (1979: 184–5). Buxton (2004: 150) comments that in the world of the Homeric epics, where humans are so frequently 'godlike', 'the gods' power to change shapes is one of the qualities which actually does distinguish immortals from mortals'.

[138] *H. Hom.* 3.162–4: πάντων δ᾽ ἀνθρώπων φωνὰς καὶ κρεμβαλιαστὺν / μιμεῖσθ᾽ ἴσασιν. φαίη δέ κεν αὐτὸς ἕκαστος / φθέγγεσθ᾽. οὕτω σφιν καλὴ συνάρηρεν ἀοιδή. Translation adapted from A. M. Miller (1986: 59–60). Bing (1993: 194–6) argues convincingly that the *mega thauma* of the Delian chorus does not refer to different dialects (as assumed by N. K. Miller, 1986: 59), but to wondrous mimetic powers akin to those of Helen in *Od.* 4.278–9. On the mimetic function of hymns, see Bremer and Furley (2001: vol. I, 16–17); on the praise of the Delian maidens as a miniature hymn in itself, see A. M. Miller (1979: 182) and Lonsdale (1995); on the hymn's function as a *mnēma*, see Depew (2000: 71–2); on the maidens' 'epic' combination of hymnic praise and mythical narrative, see Bakker (2002a: 71–3); on cultic song and choral performance on Delos, see Kowalzig (2007: 56–128, esp. 65–8).

mortal audience perceives a total coalescence of model and copy.[139] The term the hymn's poet uses to define this relationship – συνάρηρεν – is derived from the language of craft and literally means 'made fast' or 'hammered together'.[140] It introduces a concept of imitation that does not necessarily imply deception or distance in a Platonic sense (that would come later), but, within the sacred context of Apollo's sanctuary, like Hesiod's epiphanic encounter on Helicon, argues for a fusion of sign and referent that absorbs and transforms the viewer or listener to the extent that he or she temporarily transcends the limitations of mortal form and understanding.[141] This form of imitation-as-coalescence closes the gap between model and copy through a principle of *homoiosis*, or identification, and echoes the uncanny blending of *sēma* and god that constitutes the experience of divine epiphany within hymnic narrative.[142] It is an enactment, in human terms, of the god's power to be 'like' something other than himself (a kouros, a lion), yet simultaneously to 'be' (Apollo, Dionysus).

While the handmaidens are expressive of the hymn's poetic qualities,[143] they also function as a metaphor for the poem's power both to represent the god in communicable terms (to say what he is 'like') and to invoke his presence at the occasion of the hymn's performance.[144] The distance necessitated by 'imitation' is essential to allow space for the god to choose the means of his becoming present; yet the hymnic narrative's efficacy as a charming *agalma* depends upon being as 'made fast', or closely fitted, to its model as possible.[145] As a sacred text, the hymn draws upon representation's uncanny power to suggest simultaneous presence and absence in order to convey the fact that, although gods may be 'here', framed and shaped by human structures of worship, they are also 'everywhere'. The hymn's poetics do not, therefore, rely upon a simple concept of art's power to make

---

[139] Nagy (1990b: 375–7) goes so far as to identify the Delian maidens as Muses local to Delos itself; for Calame (2001: 104–10), they represent a permanent professional chorus. On the hymn's exploration of the poetics of mimesis, see N. K. Miller (1986: 57–60) and Nagy (1990b: 43–4, 375–6).

[140] Listed as a *varia lectio* by LSJ under συναράσσω. On archaic poetry's reflexive play upon its own status as a product of craft, see Svenbro (1976: 139–212), Scheid and Svenbro (1996: 111–30) and Neer (1995: 119–20).

[141] Cf. Vernant (2006: 115–38) and Murray (2004: 366), on memory and inspiration, and the imagery of the magnet in Plato's *Ion* 533d–e.

[142] On this pre-Platonic concept of imitation as identification, see Vernant (1991: 165–6).

[143] Clay (1989: 4) and Calame (2001: 75–6).

[144] On the poetics of divine presence in the *Hymn to Apollo*, see Thalmann (1984: 152) and Bakker (2002a). On the deictic quality of hymnic poetry, see Depew (2000).

[145] Compare the use of συνθήκη to describe the ivory statue of Aphrodite in Philostratus *Imagines* 2.1.1, discussed in the Introduction, 4–5.

the absent present; rather, they employ strategies of vivid narration and description – of *enargeia* – which project a sense of divine presence in specific terms, while acknowledging the necessary insufficiency of a model of presence that must speak to the specificity of human experience. Epiphanic narratives within the hymnic genre are thus an effective means of fulfilling the hymn's invocatory function, while also expressing the potential dangers and responsibilities that divine presence incurs. By recognising the limitations inherent in mortal encounters with the divine, the poet seeks the grace of divine favour, so neutralising the potential hubris of his invocatory enterprise; he brings the deity in – to human practices of ritual and representation – while acknowledging the great unknown sphere of the without. The aporetic quality of epiphanic narrative – its propensity to diversion and reticence – is, in this sense, an essential element of the hymn's politics of praise.

Framing the sacred: epiphany and ritualisation

At first glance the votive reliefs discussed earlier in this chapter are far removed from the *Homeric Hymns* in terms of medium, period and context. The hymns draw upon the archaic terminology of sight and appearance, evoking a world of *thaumata* generated by a Homeric representational system based in myth, centred on privileged *aristoi* and expressed through poetic formulae. Attic reliefs, on the other hand, derive their representational schemata from the ritual experiences of their patrons and viewers, emphasise close relations between deities and members of the democratic citizenry, and are dependent upon the mimetic potential of naturalism. Yet insofar as they are part of an ongoing religious culture in which relations with the divine are maintained through practices of invocation, dedication and ritual viewing, *Homeric Hymns* and classical votive reliefs demonstrate functional, structural and representational similarities that shed important light on cultural formulations of epiphany in the Greek world.

Significantly, both media are charged with framing experiences of divine encounter. In their role as *prooimia*, hymns introduce the epiphanic narratives of heroic epic; in more conventional cultic contexts, they accompany the worship of deities at festivals, where they have an invocatory function, charming their divine addressee into witnessing rhapsodic or choral displays, acknowledging receipt of sacrifices and dedications, or attending ritual processions, such as those celebrating a deity's arrival in a city, like the

Katagogia of Dionysus in Asia Minor and the Anthesteria in Athens, which paralleled the seventh Homeric hymn, *To Dionysus*, in its enactment of the god's epiphany on board a ship.[146] By describing the god's appearance in narratives of birth, divine arrival, demonstrations of power and manifestations to mortal worshippers, the hymn is designed to induce the god's attendance at its own performance; the poem's successful fulfilment of this expectation is demonstrated by the greeting χαῖρε which so often signals the text's completion.[147] In this sense, hymnic performance functions as a spatio-temporal frame, defining the move from secular to sacred modes of action and experience, accompanying the god's arrival in song, procession or dance and establishing the circumstances of ritual engagement that it serves to introduce.[148]

While the hymn accomplishes its simultaneous act of invocation and representation through poetic performance, votive reliefs do so through visual depictions of divine encounter which anticipate experiences of divine presence within a specific sacred space. Displayed within the *temenos* of the deity they celebrate, such objects also formed part of the ritual experience of *theōria* – the practice of 'going to see' a god – and prepared visitors for their own encounters with deity by drawing upon the visual authority of the cult image that served as the divinity's ultimate embodiment. Like hymns, votive reliefs also served as representations of divine presence intended to delight their divine addressee into a reciprocal relationship of *charis*, perpetuating the blessings conferred in the epiphanies they record through an act of permanent commemoration – the establishment of a physical *mnēma* that parallels the hymn's continuous activation of divine presence through repeated performance. Indeed, hymns themselves, from the fourth century BCE, were also turned into material artefacts through the act of inscription: several later hymns survive in the epigraphic record, including a paean to Apollo and Asclepius at Epidaurus by a local aristocrat called Isyllos, which celebrates Asclepius' birth and juxtaposes it with a personal epiphanic miracle narrative that parallels both the collections of inscribed *aretai* displayed within the sanctuary by the god's priests and the scenes of

---

[146] On parallels between the hymn and festival, see Burkert (1985a: 166); on the epiphanic aspects of Dionysiac processions, see Hedreen (2004) and Parker (2005: 302). For hymns celebrating the epiphanic arrival of a deity see also Callimachus' *Hymn to Athena* and the Athenians' hymn to Demetrius Poliorcetes, discussed in Chapters 3, 143–6, and 4, 175–80.

[147] E.g., *H. Hom.* 3.545, 4.579, 5.292, 6.19. On hymns' sympathetic inducement of divine presence, see Furley (1995: 36); on the *Hymn to Apollo* and on the function of *chaire*, Bergren (1982) and Depew (2000: 74–5).

[148] The hymn's dynamic contribution to this process is explored in relation to Pindar's sixth paean by Kurke (2005).

incubation recorded in votive reliefs.[149] Through word and image, hymns and reliefs both perform acts of remembering, which record and (re)activate epiphanic encounters located within the realm of mythical narrative or the ritual experiences of listeners and viewers.[150] In doing so, they help to structure their audience's engagement with the sacred, presenting narratives or representations of divine encounter within the spatial and temporal frames of religious activity that are designed to mirror, anticipate and shape encounter itself. Like Hesiod's *Theogony*, they celebrate 'what will be and what was before'.[151]

By simultaneously mirroring and anticipating their audience's experience of divine presence, hymns and votive dedications both partake in what Catherine Bell has termed a process of 'ritualisation'. Both constitute ritual acts that locate or draw their authority from external sources (the epiphanic agency of the divine), yet are actually responsible for creating the very cosmic order and presupposition of divine presence that they draw upon, helping to generate a sacred environment which, 'constructed and reconstructed by the actions of the social agents within it, provides an experience of the objective reality of the subjective schemes that have created it'.[152] By recounting narratives of divine birth and the acquisition of powers, hymns confer those powers upon the deity they celebrate, and in defining divine identity, generate the very being whose presence they invoke. Similarly, visual narratives of divine encounter in votive reliefs draw upon the iconography of deities as perceived in visions or viewed epiphanically in the form of cult images, and, in doing so, enhance the authority of such forms within the imaginations of their viewer-worshippers. Once internalised, these forms shape subsequent visionary experiences, where deities are frequently described as appearing in the form of their images.[153] This process is enacted by and upon the bodies of religious actors themselves, in the sensual experience of epiphany through dance, song and ritual viewing, and – in the case of healing cults – through the miraculous impact of visionary experience in rites of incubation.

---

[149] On the Epidaurian hymn of Isyllos (*IG* 4².128.64–77), see Garland (1992: 16), Depew (2000: 64), Bremer and Furley (2001: vol. I, 227–40, vol. II, 180–92, with bibliography) and Kolde (2003). On inscribed hymns, see Herington (1985: 201–3) and Depew (2000: 76–7, 262 n. 91).

[150] On the power of memory to 'make present', see Bakker (2002a: 70–3) and Vernant (2006: 116–17).

[151] *Theogony* 32: τά τ᾽ ἐσσόμενα πρό τ᾽ ἐόντα.

[152] Bell (1992: 141). For an application of ritualisation theory to Greek religious culture, see Kurke (2005).

[153] This phenomenon is discussed more extensively in Chapter 6.

For Bell (influenced by Althusser and Bourdieu), the power of such subjective schemes to construct objective 'realities' and invest them with sacred
authority constitutes 'a redundantly circular . . . chain of associations' which
is founded upon a fundamental process of 'misrecognition'.[154] It is certainly
the case that the relationship between epiphany, ritual and representation
constitutes a coherent, mutually reinforcing system characterised by circular
deferment, in which practice 'does not see the production process that constitutes the "object"'.[155] But it is also a system that incorporates a multitude
of tensions, looks to competing sources of knowledge and influence, and
demonstrates a high level of self-consciousness.[156] What is striking about
Greek hymns and votive reliefs is not the extent to which they subscribe to
or reinforce dominant conventions about the nature and appearance of the
gods, so much as their active exploration of the *different* ways in which gods
can be embodied, seen and represented. Each medium exhibits an interest in both the plurality and unrepresentability of divine *eidos*, employing
poetic or visual formulae that signal its potentially metamorphic and elusive
nature. Thus while they function as guides to viewing the divine, framing
and anticipating epiphanic encounter, hymns and reliefs also draw attention
to the complexities and limitations of their representational systems.

This tendency towards ambiguity is due in part to the multifaceted nature
of Greek religious culture – the result of a polytheistic system incorporating
many different traditions, with a high degree of local variation. But it is
also due to the cognitive dilemmas introduced by the theme of epiphany
itself. In seeking reliability about the nature of the gods through narrative
or representational devices of divine manifestation and its human apprehension, texts and images must also (to be convincing) acknowledge and
communicate the elusive, ambiguous nature of such experiences. In this
sense, ambiguity is a 'strategic' device unconsciously employed to maintain
the system's potency.[157] Bell's theoretical model thus applies convincingly
to the workings of epiphany from the point of view of a detached observer
operating outside the realm of ancient discourse. Yet in order to understand
better the representational issues at stake for religious actors within their

---

[154] Bell (1992: 140); Bourdieu (1977) and Althusser and Balibar (1979).   [155] Bell (1992: 87).

[156] On ritual self-consciousness within sophisticated religious contexts (and for a response to
Bell), see Humphrey and Laidlaw (1994).

[157] Bell (1992: 109). Compare Maurizio (1997), Bowden (2005: 49–51) and Kindt (2006) on
the ambiguity and polysemy of oracular discourse, especially Maurizio (331): 'Tellers of
oracular tales were interested in how oracles were divine utterances which eluded human
comprehension because of their tropic nature. That is, they were interested in the interstices of
language, its capacity to hold multiple meanings that can make manifest the presence of the
divine breaking in on the human world.'

cultural context, we must appreciate, first and foremost, that subjectively constructed objective authorities (i.e., the gods) are ascribed an agency that is fundamental to the efficacy of the cultural artefacts that celebrate them. As the anthropologist Alfred Gell has argued, the important factor is that 'people believe that the causal arrow is orientated in the other way'.[158] For internal religious actors, divine agency is not constructed by and through cultural acts (although it may be engaged by them); rather, it is located *outside* the perceived realm of cultural representation.[159] Although Greek thinkers such as Herodotus exhibited an awareness of the constructed nature of divine *eidea*, the gods' 'actual' existence as signified entities beyond the realm of discourse was rarely in doubt. It is by virtue of their perceived external and ontologically prior status that such authorities are set about with anxieties about the potential for human access.

In this sense the pleasures and problems of cognition are built into Greek religion's unperceived structures of 'misrecognition'. Sacred texts and images draw attention to the limitations or ambiguities of representation's 'enargeic' or epiphanic potential as part of their engagement in an active ritual and theological process. While they make assertions about the nature of the divine, they move between signifiers of divine presence, highlighting the play of multiple *sēmata* that characterises the modalities of divine appearance in ways that leave a crucial interpretative space. In framing epiphany, such religious artefacts facilitate communication between internal social actors and external metaphysical beings, even as they problematise it. Whether in the ritual moment that follows the hanging χαῖρε of a hymn's close, or the oneiric encounter with deity generated by incubation, this space allows the god to interpolate him- or herself into the subjective experience of the viewer, reader or listener.

---

[158] Gell (1998: 25).

[159] One might also acknowledge in this respect the idea that ritualised acts themselves are perceived as 'given' and external to religious actors; see Humphrey and Laidlaw (1994: 5, 89).

2 | Material epiphany: encountering the divine in cult images

'Ωργεῖος Πολύκλειτος ὁ καὶ μόνος ὄμμασιν Ἥρην
  ἀθρήσας καὶ ὅσην εἶδε τυπωσάμενος,
θνητοῖς κάλλος ἔδειξεν, ὅσον θέμις. αἱ δ' ὑπὸ κόλποις
  ἄγνωστοι μορφαὶ Ζηνὶ φυλασσόμεθα.

Polyclitus the Argive, who alone saw Hera with his eyes
And moulded as much as he saw of her, has shown her beauty to
Mortals, as far as is lawful. We, the
Unknown shapes beneath the folds, are reserved for Zeus.[1]

The hymns and reliefs discussed in Chapter 1 exemplify how images and texts could reflect and shape experiences of the divine in Greek culture. Each posits various means by which a deity might be visualised, recognised and worshipped, yet simultaneously defers the moment of encounter. By framing and anticipating, rather than acting as the actual embodiment of divine form, each medium provides a narrative *re*-presentation of epiphany, rather than functioning as a presentational device in its own right. When performed at festivals or set up within sanctuaries, hymns and *anathēmata* such as votive reliefs formed part of the process of *theōria*. Yet the epiphanic climax of such events, and the most insistent, direct and powerful means of experiencing divine encounter, was by viewing a physical image that served as the object of cult, usually a statue displayed in a prominent position within a temple.[2] In such cases, representation served neither to frame divinity, nor as a mere 'symbolic actualisation' of immortal form, but as a living embodiment of the divine, inhabiting the same space as the

---

[1] *Anth. Plan.* 216 = GP 1968: Parmenion 14. Translation from Gow and Page (1968: vol. 1, 297).

[2] On the difficulties of defining the category of 'cult image' in the absence of a specific ancient term, and the importance of ritual practice and epiphanic viewing to an understanding of their function, see Donohue (1997). The absence of precise terminology does not mean that the category did not exist, however, and the moniker 'cult image' (or *Kultbild*) still has significant heuristic value for modern scholars, as demonstrated by Nick (2002) in her examination of the Athena Parthenos. I use the terms 'cult image' and 'temple statue' throughout this chapter to refer to images that served as the primary object of ritual activity and/or veneration within temple sanctuaries, though not without an awareness of the slippage that can occur between 'cult' and 'votive' statues (on which see Nick, 2002: 77–88).

viewer-worshipper.[3] To view a cult image was to encounter a being who *looked back.*

Since Richard Gordon drew attention to the theological implications of the 'ambiguous status of the art object' in his seminal 1979 article 'The Real and the Imaginary', the equivalence of 'god' and 'image' in ritual contexts has become something of a commonplace in classical studies.[4] It has often been pointed out that, in ancient Greek, temple statues were frequently referred to as 'the deity' rather than 'an image of [x]'; this 'failure to distinguish between god and statue at the linguistic level' is found in a huge variety of texts, from the Trojan statue of Athena in the *Iliad*, which is referred to as 'Athena' herself, to passages in Attic drama and even historiography that refer to Phidias' Athena as 'the Parthenos' or 'the goddess'.[5] Much important work has been done on the rituals of washing, dressing, feeding and display that served to animate cult objects and thereby collapse the distinction between image and deity.[6] Jeremy Tanner has described the ritual, architectural and kinaesthetic sensory strategies used to create heightened moments of religious significance surrounding the revelation of cult statues – climactic occasions that were structured by the religious calendar and set about with strict regulations concerning access and display.[7] These moments of coalescence between image and god vividly illustrate Geertz's assertion that 'In ritual the world as lived and the world as imagined, fused under the agency of a single set of symbolic forms, turns out to be the same world'.[8]

The cultural reception of this phenomenon in antiquity was by no means straightforward, however. It was repeatedly teased apart, problematised or reinforced in different media, genres, periods and contexts. The epigram attributed to Parmenion that stands as this chapter's epigraph offers a delightfully provocative way into such a representational Gordion knot.

---

[3] 'Symbolic actualisation': Vernant (1991: 152).

[4] Gordon (1979: esp. 10–11), followed by Gladigow (1985–6), Versnel (1987: 46–7), Vernant (1991: 27–49), Schnapp (1994), Donohue (1997: 44–5), Koch Piettre (2001), Lapatin (2001: 5–6, 55), Steiner (2001: 99–104), Tanner (2006: 48) and Elsner (2007: 30–2, 43–5); the fusion between image and prototype in contexts of sacred viewing is explored in a cross-cultural context by Freedberg (1989: 27–40).

[5] Gordon (1979: 8): *Il.* 6.263–311; Aristophanes *Birds* 667–70, *Knights* 1168–70 (discussed by Lapatin, 2001: 64); Thucydides 2.13.5 (discussed by Tanner, 2001: 262–3; 2006: 48 n. 63). On the dispute over the Parthenos' status as a 'cult image' and relationship to the archaic image of Athena Polias, see below.

[6] E.g., Gladigow (1985–6), Scheer (2000: 54–66) and Bettinetti (2001: 137–60).

[7] Tanner (2006: 45–8). On temple access, see Corbett (1970) and, in relation to ritual and moral impurity, Dickie (2002); on the importance of ritual and physical framing devices for investing cult images with interiority, and thus agency, see Gell (1998: 134–6).

[8] Geertz (1973: 112–13).

Figure 2.1 Roman copy of Polyclitus' fifth-century BCE cult image of Hera from the Argive Heraion

Preserved in the first-century BCE *Garland of Philip*, it negotiates the epiphanic authority of the chryselephantine statue of Hera in the Argive Heraion, attributed in antiquity to the fifth-century sculptor Polyclitus and known to us from a handful of Roman copies (Figure 2.1).[9] Although it typifies sophisticated Hellenistic games with the ekphrastic potential of

---

[9] See A. Stewart (1990: vol. I, 263–6) and Lapatin (2001: 101–5), including discussion of the sculpture's disputed authorship; the late fifth-century date of the temple has led many scholars to attribute the Hera to a shadowy Polyclitus II. Copies (originally surmounted with portraits of Roman *matronae*, hence the addition of a *stola*) – Boston example, discovered in second/third-century CE Roman baths at Vasciano, near Todi, Umbria (MFA 03.749): Comstock and Vermeule (1976: 95 no. 148), Vermeule and Comstock (1988: 111), Linfert (1990: 254 figs. 114 and 117) and Lapatin (2001: 102 fig. 205); example in private collection (previously at Wilton House): Christie's auction catalogue, 3 July 1961, no. 140, and Lapatin (2001: 102 fig. 206).

religious art (which I examine in detail in Chapter 4), the epigram draws upon a nexus of ideas that are fundamental to post-archaic responses to the sacred image, focusing on the naturalistic divine forms of the fifth century BCE in its exploration of the relationship between vision, representation and artistry. In common with numerous texts relating to Polyclitus' contemporary Phidias, the poet credits the sculptor with an epiphanic perception of divinity that, owing to his creative skill, is transmitted via the statue to the viewer (and, via the poet's verbal evocation of the image, to the reader of the epigram).[10] Yet this praise of the statue's power to produce a sense of epiphanic encounter for its viewers is compromised in the second half of the poem. First, Parmenion raises the concept of divine law, or *themis*, questioning the limits of the artist's revelatory endeavour. To what extent should divine bodies, especially those of rather prudish goddesses, be revealed by and to human viewers? Here the poet implies, with a wink, that Polyclitus (who was held to have a particular sense of decorum among ancient artists) has exercised restraint in his representation of the queen of the gods. The only voyeur allowed in *this* situation is Zeus himself, and the goddess's most intimate parts – her *agnostoi morphai* – must otherwise remain unseen. Like the ekphrasis of Aphrodite's body in her *Homeric Hymn*, the epiphany that the sculptor transmits is necessarily incomplete, provoking a frisson between the image's revelation and concealment of divinity.[11]

Parmenion thus praises the epiphanic authority of Hera's cult image only to undermine it with a sophistic twist related to its materiality, pointing to the notion of absence that accompanies any act of mimetic representation. The quip would have been enhanced for readers familiar with the statue by the knowledge that, being chryselephantine, it was hollow – so lending another dimension to the concept of Hera's 'hollow parts'. Since the goddess's ivory flesh and golden drapery were moulded onto a wooden armature, there would, in fact, have been no 'unknown forms beneath the folds [of her dress]' at all, just mere void, or absence of form.[12] This contradiction was a familiar one in antiquity: Phidias' chryselephantine image of Zeus at Olympia was customarily referred to as an epiphanic embodiment

---

[10] *Anth. Plan.* 81 (attributed to Philip; see also Chapter 4, 204); Cicero *Orator* 2.8–9. On Phidias' visionary sensibilities, see also Quint. *Inst.* 12.10.9, Seneca *Controversiae* 8.2, Dio Chrysostom 12.70–1 and Philostr. *VA* 6.13, with Pollitt (1974: 52, 83) and my discussion in Chapters 5, 224–35, and 7, 322–7. Strabo (8.6.10) claims that Polyclitus' Argive sculptures (including the Hera and a statue of Hebe, assigned to Naukydes by Pausanias, 2.17.4–5) are 'the most beautiful in the world in terms of skill (τέχνῃ), but inferior to those by Phidias in expense and size (πολυτελείᾳ δὲ καὶ μεγέθει)'.

[11] See Chapter 1, 68–9.

[12] On the framework and hollow core of chryselephantine statues, see Lapatin (2001: 70–3).

of the god himself, yet ancient viewers were nevertheless troubled by the statue's materiality, and particularly its hollow interior. Lucian twice claims that the statue was inhabited by mice and rats who 'conducted their civic business' inside it.[13]

However, herein lies Parmenion's deliciously outrageous conceit. For the final word of the poem, φυλασσόμεθα, reveals with its use of the first person plural that those very 'unknown forms' constitute the poetic voice itself. Hera's hidden – hollow – parts are elements of female divine form that are necessarily inaccessible to mortal experience, never explicitly depicted in ancient statuary, and defined by void. Yet they are, paradoxically, the component that is made most present by the poem.[14] The poet thus undermines the visual authority of the image by alluding to its necessary partial nature, only to transform the absence at the statue's core into its most epiphanic feature. For despite their hollow nature, Hera's *agnostoi morphai* can only conceptually exist by virtue of the representational act that surrounds and defines them.

In the context of ekphrastic epigram, this unnerving come-on is exploited to express the power of verbal forms to communicate what the visual cannot, and is part of the ongoing tension between image and text that gives the genre such verve. But the conceit also taps into a far broader set of questions raised by the tradition of anthropomorphism, concerning both the potential and limitations of representation. In an echo of the play between presence and absence that is generated by the image itself, Parmenion sets two modes of viewing in perpetual counterpoint, juxtaposing apprehension of the statue as 'Hera' with recognition of its artefactual nature. While the former reflects a ritual commitment to view the statue in epiphanic terms (and thus a form of iconophilia), the latter suggests the poet's self-conscious detachment from the image's religious context and pose of arch rationalism (so veering towards a more iconophobic questioning of the image's sanctity).[15]

Parmenion's intellectual play with Polyclitus' Hera is rooted in responses to naturalism, the problematisation of mimesis in Platonic philosophy, and the self-conscious poetics of Hellenistic ekphrasis. Yet we should not be too quick to map the distinction he elucidates between divinity and materiality onto a forced contrast between the sacred and secular. As with the votive

---

[13] Lucian *Gallus* 24, *Jupiter Tragoedus* 8. Lucian's conceit was later exploited in a critique of pagan idolatry by Arnobius (*Adversus nationes* 6.16): 'O that you could enter the hollow interior (*medias introire pendigines*) of some statue!' (trans. McCracken, 1949). On the epiphanic qualities of Phidias' statue see below.

[14] On the non-representation of female pudenda in ancient statuary, see Chapter 4, 199–201.

[15] On the 'rationalisation' of responses to art in the Hellenistic period, see Tanner (2006: 212–34).

reliefs discussed in Chapter 1, the separation of 'religious' and 'aesthetic' responses to sacred images imposes a false dichotomy, ignoring the theological issues that are implicit in both their design and perception, and the potential for change, tension and critical engagement within the framework of religious thought and practice. Although cult images commanded a visual authority that encouraged their epiphanic reception, this very authority prompted a degree of anxiety that cannot simply be bracketed within the concerns of elite intellectuals such as Parmenion, but is also reflected, for example, in popular narratives of the discovery, creation or effects of viewing such objects.[16] The tension actually springs from a paradox that is negotiated by *all* sacred images in Greek culture – between their phenomenological effect (when they are experienced as a form of epiphany) and their ontological status (that is, their material and representational nature, their existence as *objects*). In what did the 'sacred' status of cult images reside? How could objects created by mortal craftsmanship out of materials such as wood, stone and metal be divine? How authentic was the form that each image took? And if the image really 'was' the deity, then how should it be viewed and treated by his or her worshippers?

   This chapter explores how such questions were formulated in relation to a range of cult image-types in Greek antiquity and elucidates the diverse strategies that were employed by Greek craftsmen, religious personnel and viewer-worshippers in order to evoke the epiphanic within sacred space. For the relationship between divinity, materiality and artistry was negotiated by a broad variety of cultic objects within Greek visual culture – from aniconic and semi-iconic forms such as herms to fully anthropomorphic statues.[17] It was also a guiding element in the choice of medium. These formal and material means of denoting divine presence were often accompanied by narratives (frequently aetiological in nature) that influenced their display and reception, defining the relationship between god and image in various and ingenious ways in order to determine (or problematise) each object's ritual efficacy and epiphanic force. As we shall see, these stories cluster most abundantly around the more naturalistic temple statues of the classical period

---

[16] Much of the textual evidence for such narratives is transmitted by later texts, such as Pausanias' *Description of Greece*, where they express concerns about the nature of sacred visuality that are specific to the so-called 'Second Sophistic'; these aspects will be considered within their cultural context in Chapter 5. For now, I must succumb to the familiar temptation (*pace* Donohue, 1997) to extract such evidence in service of a broader argument about the function of cult images in earlier religious tradition, relying upon Pausanias' powers of observation as a *theōros* and immersion within a living exegetical culture practised within Hellenic sanctuaries, on which see C. P. Jones (2001a).

[17] See Gaifman (2005: 1–6).

because they embody the conflict in a highly beguiling but complex manner, demanding complicity in their mimetic illusionism while simultaneously calling for appreciation of the artist's skill. On one hand, naturalism fulfilled the epiphanic imperative implicit in the linguistic fusion of cult image and deity: it brought divine form before the eyes of the viewer with an *enargeia* comparable to the vivid anthropomorphism of the Homeric poems, ascribing a corporeal specificity to each deity that was expressed in every aspect of his or her body, and suggesting a formal continuity between the realms of human and divine.[18] It thus allowed for easy slippage between 'image' and 'epiphany', because representations of gods could match their 'real' appearances (the principle of *cognitive reliability*). On the other hand, naturalism's privileging of mimetic representational strategies drew attention to the role of human *technē* in the representation of divine *eidea*, and suggested a gap between man-made image and divine prototype, so prompting a degree of what we might call *cognitive dissonance*. This conflict between cognitive reliability (provided by epiphany) and cognitive dissonance (generated by artistry and mimesis) lies behind the conceit formulated in Parmenion's epigram on Polyclitus' Hera; it also provided a conceptual axis around which responses to sacred images pivoted throughout post-classical antiquity.

Parthenos and Polias: multiple epiphanic strategies within Greek sacred space

Polyclitus' chryselephantine statue of Hera was not the only cult image that stood within the goddess's Argive temple. Indeed, Pausanias tells us that the fifth-century sculpture was displayed alongside a small *agalma* of the goddess made of pear wood, which he describes as ἀρχαιότατον – 'most ancient'.[19] Whereas the large gold and ivory statue was attributed to a famous sculptor, the smaller wooden object beside it was not associated with a named artist, but was said to have been brought to Argos from Tiryns, where the image was originally dedicated by Peirasus, son of the mythical Argive founder Argus.[20] Its origins thus lay in the shady realms of distant history – a history that was visually communicated by the object's humble medium and ancient appearance. Together with the wooden images

---

[18] On epiphanic viewing as a driving force in the development of naturalism, see Tanner (2006: 67–92).

[19] Paus. 2.17.5.

[20] Paus. 2.17.5; Plutarch *De Daedalis Plataeensibus* = *Moralia* fr. 158 Sandbach 1969.

of Athena Polias, Hera on Samos, Apollo on Delos and Athena at Lindos, the ancient Argive Hera was said by Callimachus and Plutarch to be one of the oldest cult images in Greece.[21] The uneasy juxtaposition of contrasting origins, materials, techniques, styles and scale in the Argive temple must have made a striking impression on ancient visitors, and raises many questions about the appearance and function of Greek cult images. If such objects are 'epiphanic', how does each type of image evoke divine presence for its viewer-worshippers? Which acts as the focus of ritual activity? How do they interact? And, perhaps most crucially, where is the deity?

The doubling of sacred images in the Argive Heraion was not, of course, an isolated occurrence in Greek culture. During the first half of the fifth century, a monumental acrolithic sculpture of gilded wood and marble was commissioned for the Temple of Athena Aphaia on Aegina, probably funded by spoils from the battles of Salamis.[22] The commission demonstrated a growing interest in the potential of composite techniques to project a sense of divine radiance and, if the sculptures from the temple's east pediment are anything to go by, a readiness to harness the visual effects of naturalism in the representation of immortal form.[23] Significantly, epigraphic and archaeological evidence suggests that the pseudo-chryselephantine statue supplemented a smaller ivory image that had formed the focus of Aphaia's cult prior to the building of the new temple.[24] Likewise at some point in the fifth century a marble statue of Artemis attributed to Praxiteles supplemented her archaic cult image at Brauron, which (in an echo of the Argive Hera's mythical origins) had supposedly been brought from Tauris by Iphigenia.[25]

The most high-profile doubling of images in a Greek sanctuary, however, was on the Athenian Acropolis, where from 437 BCE Phidias' chryselephantine statue of Athena (subsequently titled the 'Parthenos')

---

[21] Plutarch *De Daedalis Plataeensibus* = *Moralia* fr. 158 Sandbach 1969 = Callimachus fr. 100 Pfeiffer. Cf. Philostr. *VA* 3.14, who lists the oldest images of the gods (τὰ ... ἀρχαιότατα) as the Athena Polias, Apollo on Delos, Dionysus 'in the Marshes' and the Apollo of Amyclae. See also Romano (1980: 18).

[22] Lapatin (2001: 55–6, 61).

[23] On the use of 'Severe' and 'Classical' styles as a conscious choice rather than due to mere chronology at Aegina, see A. Stewart (2008).

[24] The base of the earlier statue and cuttings for the base of the later statue survive: see Lapatin (2001: 61–2 and fig. 112). Evidence for the archaic cult image comes from a sixth-century inscription referring to an ἐλέφας ('ivory') of the goddess (*IG* 4.1580): see Lapatin (2001: 56).

[25] Paus. 1.23.7, discussed by Romano (1980: 83–93); see also Paus. 2.19.3, on the 'contemporary' *agalma* attributed to Attalus (an otherwise unknown sculptor) and ancient wooden *xoanon* in the Argive sanctuary of Apollo Lycius. On the coexistence of two cult images within the same sanctuary, see Romano (1980: 3, 87–9), A. Stewart (1990: vol. I, 44, 137), Donohue (1997: 37, 43), Lapatin (2001: 78, 101), Steiner (2001: 82, 93, 102–4) and Nick (2002: 89–99), with further examples.

supplemented the ancient olive-wood image of Athena (known by Pausanias' time, at least, as the 'Polias').[26] Whereas at Argos, Aegina and Brauron the two sacred objects seem to have stood together in each sanctuary's temple, at Athens each image stood within its own architectural complex; from the 420s the Polias was displayed in the Erechtheion, while the Parthenos was housed in the structure that eventually drew its title from the statue itself – the Parthenon.[27] Many questions raised by this doubling of images at Athens are particular to local cultic activity, and the specific social, political and economic circumstances in which the Periclean building programme was conceived.[28] Yet such parallel evidence from Aegina, Argos and Brauron suggests that the coexistence of the Parthenos and Polias on the Acropolis was also part of a broader phenomenon within Greek religious practice. In the absence of any surviving images, the rich cultural reception of both statues means that literary and visual responses provide a wealth of evidence for exploring the relationship between epiphany, divinity and materiality in a specific sacred location. The Parthenos and Polias exemplify some of the diverse strategies by which different image-types might project or denote divine presence, and demonstrate the ways in which such multiple means of evoking the divine might interact within a single sanctuary. In what follows, I examine the problems raised by such a juxtaposition and, in particular, the cognitive dissonance generated by Phidian modes of representation. The tension such practices generate between divinity and materiality has had a profound influence upon responses to the Athena Parthenos, both in antiquity and in modern scholarship. Yet I shall also argue that it is inherent in the design of the image itself, where it is embodied in the figure of Pandora positioned on the statue's base. This reference to divine craftsmanship beneath the very statue, combined with the variety of epiphanic strategies employed on the Acropolis, allows us to unpack the straightforward assumption that temple statues were viewed as 'gods themselves' in antiquity. Rather, it suggests a self-consciousness about the practice that does not necessarily lessen each image's numinosity, but illustrates an active theological engagement with the many-stranded process of representing and apprehending divine form.

---

[26] Paus. 1.26.6. On the ambiguous relationship between the Parthenos and Polias, see Herington (1955, esp. 6–15); on the patchy evidence for each statue's title, Preisshofen (1984), Schmaltz (1997), Lapatin (2001: 78) and Nick (2002: 1–7).

[27] See Herington (1955: 36–7), who also draws a parallel with the sanctuary of Dionysus on the south side of the Acropolis, where an archaic temple housing the ancient image of Dionysus Eleuthereus was supplemented in the late fifth century by a temple containing a large chryselephantine statue by Alcamenes.

[28] See most recently Hurwit (2004) and Kallet (2005).

Figure 2.2 Phidias' statue of Olympian Zeus: artist's impression

Epiphany in the Phidian mode

Instant Fish
by Phidias!
Add water
and they swim.[29]

Together with the chryselephantine statue of Zeus at Olympia (*c.* 430), also attributed to Phidias, the Athena Parthenos was one of the best-known and frequently reproduced sacred images in Greco-Roman culture.[30] Both sculptures were destroyed in late antiquity, but have been reconstructed numerous times on the basis of ancient copies in other media and descriptions in literary texts (Figures 2.2 and 2.3).[31] Repeated responses suggest that

[29] From Peter Porter's 1972 collection *After Martial*, 7 (a translation of Martial 3.35: 'artis
       Phidiacae toreuma clarum / pisces aspicis: adde aquam, natabunt').
[30] See Lapatin (2001: 61–95, with bibliography; 2005).
[31] See Leipen (1971), Flynn (1997) and below, n. 37.

Figure 2.3 Reconstruction of Phidias' Athena Parthenos

they stood for viewers throughout antiquity as the quintessential material manifestation of deity, passing into the cultural imagination as archetypal embodiments of the divinities they represented – the perfect expression of Homeric anthropomorphism.[32] Milette Gaifman has demonstrated that many representations of Athena in classical vases and sculpted reliefs borrowed the iconography of the Parthenos to signify 'Athena herself', both in mythical narratives and symbolic scenes such as those found on Attic document reliefs, in which the goddess (and sometimes her attendant Nike) crowns the recipients of civic honours (Figure 2.4).[33] The conflation of

---

[32] See Strabo 8.3.30, Polybius 30.10.6, Dio 12 *passim*, Valerius Maximus *Memorabilia* 8.14.6, Plutarch *Aemilius Paullus* 28.2 and Macrobius *Saturnalia* 5.13.23.

[33] Gaifman (2006); see also Ridgway (1981: 161–7), Lawton (1995: 40–5) and Lapatin (2001: 3, figs. 155–7). Vase-painting: see a red-figure column krater attributed to the Hephaistos Painter,

Figure 2.4 Cast of an honorary decree from the Athenian Acropolis depicting Athena Parthenos, *c.* 375–350 BCE

goddess and statue in such contexts demonstrates not only how Athena's image rapidly took on an iconic status by virtue of its repeated evocation, but also how it was literally enlivened or animated within the minds of her viewers, becoming, in Schefold's term, a *lebende Statue*.[34] Within the Athenian imagination, Athena *was* the Parthenos. Thus while the statue itself projected a sense of epiphanic presence for its viewers upon the Acropolis, its broader cultural reception served to magnify its status and thereby enhanced the aura of the original, to the extent that, centuries later, the Second Sophistic orator Aelius Aristides could claim (in language borrowed straight from the *Homeric Hymns*) that Athena had appeared to him in a dream 'with her aegis and the beauty and magnitude (καὶ τὸ κάλλος καὶ τὸ

dated 430–420 BCE, which depicts Ajax and Achilles playing dice attended by Athena in the form of the Parthenos, complete with winged Nike: Berlin, Staatliche Museen inv. V.I. 3199, *ARV²* 1114, 9; see Schefold (1937: 31, fig. 1) and Gaifman (2006: 264–7, fig. 1). For document reliefs depicting Athena Parthenos, see Lawton (1995: nos. 16, Athens EM 6899; 30, Athens NM 1474; 65, Athens EM 6615; 106, location unknown, cast in Bonn; 132, Athens NM 2985; and 164, Berlin, Staatliche Museen, Antikensammlung K 104).

[34] Schefold (1937: 33 – 'Das Kultbild ist der lebendige Gott selbst, und das Leben ist von göttlichen Kräften durchgestaltet' – and 58–67); see also Alroth (1992: 10).

μέγεθος) and the whole form of the Athena of Phidias in Athens'.[35] Likewise for Dio Chrysostom, the Phidian Zeus was a 'wondrous sight' (θέαμα), the visual equivalent of the Iliadic Zeus, while Pausanias relates that 'the god himself bore witness' to Phidias' *technē* by hurling a lightning-bolt at the statue's completion.[36] The images were thus ascribed an epiphanic potential that made an indelible impression on cultural formulations of each deity, spilling beyond the sanctuaries of Olympia and the Athenian Acropolis throughout the Hellenised world, carried by literary references and multiple evocations in other media.[37]

In many ways the Phidian statues were a logical outcome of earlier Greek practice. Their frontality and (as far as we can tell from copies in other media) slight archaising qualities marked them out as conservative in style, evoking the sanctity associated with older image-types.[38] Yet these stylistic features were combined with an enhanced naturalism of form, facilitated by the flesh-like quality of large expanses of ivory and the gleam of gold, glass and precious jewels, in order to simulate epiphany itself.[39] Their spectacular size, wealth and radiance did not evoke divinity by symbolic means, but actually sought to *reproduce* divine encounter, projecting the immediacy of immortal *eidos* by drawing upon the models of epiphany we find in the *Homeric Hymns*, where deities are spectacularly big, beautiful and shining, bursting the boundaries of the human frames within which they appear. Like Aphrodite and Demeter at their hymnic moments of self-revelation, the Olympian Zeus famously appeared too small for the architectural space in which he was housed, so that, in Strabo's memorable words, 'if he arose and stood erect he would unroof the temple'.[40] This idea finds visual expression

---

[35] *Hieroi Logoi* 2.41, translation Behr (1981), discussed in Chapter 6, 261–3.

[36] Dio 12.25–6, 49–52; Paus. 5.11.9: both passages are discussed further in Chapter 5, 224–35. For a literal 'animation' of the Phidian Zeus in our own period, see the 1997 Disney film *Hercules*, in which the young hero goes for some paternal advice to the Olympian temple, where his father's statue comes to life – a delightful touch in a visually sophisticated film designed and supervised by Gerald Scarfe.

[37] Over 200 representations of the Parthenos survive: see Leipen (1971), Prag (1972, 1984), Lapatin (1996; 2001: 66, with bibliography), Nick (2002: 177–205) and Gaifman (2006). On the Olympian Zeus, see Schrader (1941), Liegle (1952), Richter (1966), Conticello *et al.* (1987) and Lapatin (2001: 80, with bibliography). For literary references, see Overbeck (1868: nos. 645–90) and Lapatin (2001: 154–92).

[38] On the stylistic conservatism of the Phidian images and continuity with archaic practices, see Lapatin (2001: 67) and Neer (2010: 100–3).

[39] See Gordon (1979: 13–14), Donohue (1997: 44–5) and Steiner (2001: 100–2). On 'golden' gods and 'golden' statues, see A. Stewart (1990: vol. I, 36), Ridgway (2005: 113) and Lapatin (2005: 270).

[40] Strabo 8.3.30: ἐὰν ὀρθὸς γένηται διαναστάς, ἀποστεγάσειν τὸν νεών (translation from H. L. Jones's *Loeb Classical Library* edition, 1927). Gordon (1979: 14) comments, 'I take it that

in Attic document reliefs depicting Athena Parthenos as an animated deity (such as Figure 2.4), where not only does she tower above her internal audience, but also her helmet repeatedly pierces through the upper frame of the relief, as if to demonstrate the difficulty of constraining divine form within human space. Each statue thus generated an intense experience of *thauma* that was fuelled by archaic tradition, yet by virtue of scale, splendour and holistic visual effect stood in dramatic contrast to earlier forms.

How, then, did the Phidian images' projection of epiphanic plenitude relate to their emphatic materiality? In numerous epigraphic and literary sources dated to the classical period (such as the Acropolis inventory tablets), the Athena Parthenos is referred to as an *agalma*, a 'delightful object'.[41] Originally applied to votive dedications and cult images alike, the term was derived from the verb ἀγάλλειν – 'to adorn' or 'to honour' – and denoted an object whose sacred, material and aesthetic value was inseparable from its dynamic role within ritual, whether as a dedication intended to charm a deity into presence, or a cult image functioning as the focus of such activity.[42] As Louis Gernet famously argued in his essay 'The Mythical Idea of Value in Greece', the *agalma* projected a glorious radiance that pertained to the immortal sphere, but was also closely bound to the material significance of precious objects, simultaneously encompassing the notion of things mysteriously alive and the splendid, 'thaumastic' effects of superior craftsmanship.[43] Like the description of Aphrodite's clothing in her *Homeric Hymn*, it conflated the shining qualities of precious metals with the luminosity of the divine, combining the effects of *enargeia* and *technē* in a compelling fusion of the material and the sacred that embodied 'a singular notion of value, one in which the "aesthetic element" predominates'.[44] Significantly, the term does not specifically denote an object's representational function, but instead refers to the web of reciprocal relations between worshipper and deity in which it is embedded: the *agalma*'s function was primarily to delight, not to depict. In this way, it could invoke divine

---

Pheidias incorporated a deliberate allusion to the puzzle over the gods' ability to transcend human polarities into his design: Zeus is in the temple, but also not – he does not "fit".'

[41] E.g., *IG* 1³. 457.4–5, *IG* 2². 1407.5–6, 1443.10, 1468.6–7, 1477.12–14 (see D. Harris, 1995: 130–1); Thucydides 2.13.5. For further examples, see Herington (1955: 7) and Lapatin (2001: 63 n. 22).

[42] On the use and significance of *agalma*, see Scheer (2000: 8–18), Bettinetti (2001: 27–37) and Nick (2002: 12–15). See also Tanner (2001: 264) on the semantic relationship between *agalma* and *gelao* ('to smile' or 'to laugh') and *aglaos* ('shining' or 'splendid').

[43] Gernet (1981: 73–111), reassessed by von Reden (1999). On the significance of radiance, wonder and skill for archaic concepts of the image in general, see Neer (2010).

[44] Gernet (1981: 103).

presence through its material and aesthetic qualities without *necessarily* acting as an embodiment of divine form.

The use of *agalma* in relation to the Athena Parthenos is appropriate, for in many ways the image stood as the ultimate manifestation of the concept – the perfect fusion of precious medium, skilful artistry and divinity. It also reflects a gradual restriction in usage, whereby from the fifth century BCE *agalma* was increasingly applied to denote temple statues serving as the object of cult, rather than a more extensive range of objects that also encompassed votive dedications.[45] In its traditional sense, however, the broader application of *agalma* allowed for a certain ambiguity about the statue's actual status. For although the Parthenos may have stood as the ultimate embodiment of Athena for her viewers, she was not an official focus of cult practice on the Acropolis; the Parthenon seems to have had no priesthood, nor any altar.[46] Instead, she seems to have functioned in ritual terms more like a magnificent votive offering, a simultaneous invocation and representation of the polis' patron goddess, whose epiphanic authority lay predominantly in *being seen*.[47] She still functioned as an object of veneration in a broader sense and indeed inspired a powerful religiosity in many of her viewers, as numerous ancient responses attest, while evidence for an ivory-inlaid table within the Parthenon's cella suggests that she may also have received votive offerings.[48] Official ritual activity on the Acropolis, however, was primarily focused upon an object that employed a radically different set of epiphanic strategies – the ancient olive-wood image of Athena Polias.[49]

---

[45] See A. Stewart (1990: vol. I, 45), Scheer (2000: 17–18) and Bettinetti (2001: 35) on restriction in meaning in the classical period, so that *agalma* came to signify a statue of a deity in the round, which usually stood within a temple as the focus of cult practice. This shift meant that by Pausanias' time *agalma* could be used of any sculpture modern scholars would label a 'cult image', including semi-iconic forms such as the Athena Polias (called an *agalma* at 1.26.6). On *agalmata* and other archaic image-types, see Dietrich (1985–6).

[46] Herington (1955: 8–9, 28–9).

[47] On the Parthenos as a votive offering, see Herington (1955: 37–8), Leipen (1971: 17) and Lapatin (2005: 282), with Kroll (1979) on the frieze as a votive relief. Nick (2002), however, argues convincingly that scholarly distinction between the categories of cult image and votive offering distorts the evidence, and that the Parthenos was definitely a *Kultbild* (see esp. 119–32); more recently Gaifman (2006: 260, 271) has suggested that the Parthenos was an 'instrumental emblem' of the cult of Athena Polias, if not its actual focus.

[48] On veneration of the Parthenos, see Donohue (1997: 43–4). The table in the Parthenon is mentioned in the Acropolis inventories, e.g., *IG* 2². 1421.112: see D. Harris (1995: 93). On its potential significance for the statue's status, see J. M. Mansfield (1985: 232 n. 19), Ridgway (1992: 135), Nick (2002: 208) and Lapatin (2005: 284).

[49] On evidence for the Polias, see Jahn and Michaelis (1901: 68–9) and Kroll (1982, with bibliography). On the relationship between the two statues, see Ridgway (1989).

Epiphanic alternatives 1: the *xoanon*

Housed in the Erechtheion from *c.* 420 BCE but of unknown date and origin, the Polias' appearance is shrouded in mystery. Reconstructions have ranged from the aniconic, consisting of a small, plank-like piece of wood, to the fully figurative, based on the detail that the image wore a diadem and held out a phiale.[50] Scholars have disputed whether it was a striding figure or whether it was seated.[51] It may even have changed form during its lifetime, acquiring a more figurative shape and attributes such a helmet and *gorgoneion* in the sixth century BCE.[52] Whatever its appearance, the Polias, not the Parthenos, formed the focus of the city's predominant festival, the Panathenaia, when the image was ritually dressed in a magnificent woven peplos, as well as rites such as the Plynteria, in which it may have been ritually bathed.[53]

The Polias belongs to a class of wooden divine images, many invested with great antiquity, that are categorised by later authors such as Pausanias and Plutarch under the term *xoanon*.[54] Although the identification of this category was influenced by a supposed etymological association with ξύλον, 'wood', *xoanon* actually derives from the verb ξέω, 'to smooth or polish by scraping', and so draws attention to the worked nature of the object's medium.[55] In contrast to the term *agalma*, both the false etymology *xulon* (which alludes to the *xoanon*'s materiality) and the true etymology *xeō* (which alludes to its facture) draw attention to the object's substance

---

[50] Aniconic form is suggested by Tertullian *Apologia* 16.3.8: in accordance with his rejection of idolatry, he describes the 'Attic Pallas' as 'a rough pole and unformed piece of wood without shape' ('sine effigie rudi palo et informi ligno prostant'). On figurative form, see below. Evidence for the Polias' attributes comes from the Erechtheion's fourth-century inventory tablets, *IG* 2². 1424, 11–16; 1425, 307–12; 1426, 4–8; 1428, 142–6; 1429, 42–7; 1424a, 362–6.

[51] Striding Athena: Jahn (1866), Farnell (1896: vol. I, 334–7), Frazer (1898: vol. II, 341), Petersen (1907: 40–60); seated Athena: Furtwängler (1884–90), Frickenhaus (1908), Herington (1955: 22–6). The arguments are summarised by Kroll (1982); see also J. M. Mansfield (1985: 135–88) and Alroth (1989: 48–54).

[52] As suggested by Kroll (1982: 73–4), who argues that the Polias consisted of an aniconic 'nucleus' forming a standing image, which was anthropomorphised by sixth-century figurative additions attributed to the sculptor Endoios.

[53] On the Panathenaia and Plynteria, see Deubner (1932: 17–35), Herington (1955: 30–4), J. M. Mansfield (1985: 277–96, 371–8, 424–33), Neils (1992), N. Robertson (1996b) and Parker (2005: 226, 253–68, 478).

[54] E.g., Plutarch *De Daedalis Plataeensibus* = *Moralia* fr. 158 Sandbach 1969, on the Athena Polias. See Donohue (1988: 133–8, on Plutarch, and 140–9, on *xoanon* in Pausanias). See also Bennett (1917a, 1917b), Pritchett (1998: 204–94; 1999: 168–79) and Bettinetti (2001: 48–52).

[55] On *xulon*, see Donohue (1988: 12); on *xeō*, see W. H. Gross (1967), Donohue (1988: 28–9, on the association between *xeō* and craft, and 31: in classical Greek the term *xoanon* 'is associated not with subject but with process – with the artistic technique of objects, that is to say, and not with their identity') and A. Stewart (1990: vol. I, 37).

rather than its ritual function. *Xoana* seem to have ranged in form from semi-iconic, rough-hewn poles or planks surmounted with worked heads and limbs to naturalistic images of high workmanship, and are often less than life-size in scale.[56] Although predominantly anthropomorphic in conception and execution, the *xoanon*'s status and sanctity did not necessarily reside in an ability to suppress its object status by force of a resemblance to or simulation of divine form. Instead, such images were invested with a talismanic status that was visually expressed through their material and schematic properties and, especially for later viewers, their perceived antiquity.[57] This was often related to their mythical origin.[58]

A typical example of this blend of schematic form and mythical status was the Trojan Palladion, which is represented in fifth-century vase-paintings as a statue with the static posture of an archaic kore, supplemented by a helmet and shield and brandishing a spear (Figures 2.5 and 2.6).[59] The Palladion functioned as the ur-type of such images in the Greek imagination and was laid claim to by many sanctuaries, which stated that their own *xoanon* was the original object, stolen from Troy by Diomedes, in an attempt to appropriate its presumed protective properties.[60] The frequency with which the image

---

[56] Although Donohue points out that Pausanias uses *xoanon* for some images that are clearly post-archaic and possibly naturalistic (e.g., 2.30.2, the *xoanon* of Hecate on Aegina, attributed to Myron), he most frequently qualifies the term with *archaion*, 'ancient' (e.g., 1.23.7, 1.33.1, 1.38.8, 2.2.3, 2.10.1, 2.12.1, 3.13.9, 3.15.7, 3.17.5, 7.25.13, 7.26.6, 8.5.8, 8.31.5–6, 9.11.4), and several times associates *xoana* with the styles attributed to Daedalus (2.4.5, 8.35.2, 8.53.7–8, 9.3.1–9, 9.11.4, 9.40.3–4) and the Pelasgians (3.20.5): see S. P. Morris (1992: 243–4). Meiggs (1982: 302) suggests that when *xoanon* is used for post-archaic images by Pausanias it is because they are acrolithic statues with a wooden core.

[57] See Paus. 2.4.5, who comments that the works of Daedalus (which he terms *xoana*) 'are distinguished by some divine quality inside them (*ti entheon*)'. On this passage, see J. L. Porter (2001: 70–1), Steiner (2001: 102–3 n. 92) and Elsner (2006: 71, 85).

[58] E.g., the *xoanon* of Artemis Orthia at Sparta, supposedly brought from Tauris by Orestes and Iphigenia (Paus. 3.16.7–11). On the talismanic power of early cult images, see Faraone (1992).

[59] See Havelock (1965: 333–4), Matheson (1986), Connelly (1993), Oenbrink (1997: 34–72) and Nick (2002: 30–3), with *LIMC* s.v. Aias II nos. 16–108, Athena nos. 67–117 and Diomedes nos. 23–40. Figure 2.5: Attic red-figure amphora attributed to the Tyszkiewicz Painter, Stockholm, Medelhavsmuseet 1963.1, Beazley *ARV*² 1643, early fifth century; see Alroth (1992: 20) and *LIMC* s.v. Athena, no. 103. Figure 2.6: Attic red-figure calyx krater attributed to the Altamura Painter, Boston, MFA 59.176, Beazley *ARV*² 590, 11, second quarter of the fifth century; see *LIMC* s.v. Athena, no. 87, and Matheson (1986: 105), on the statue's frontality. In many earlier examples the Palladion matches the iconography of Athena Promachos, stepping forward with one leg and raising her spear-bearing arm: see Shapiro (1989: 36–7) and Connelly (1993: 102–3), who relates the type to the Athena in the gigantomachy pediment of the Old Athena Temple on the Acropolis. On the Palladion in general, see Ziehen and Lippold (1949).

[60] E.g., Athens (Paus. 1.28.8–9, on the homicide court ἐπὶ Παλλαδίῳ), Argos (Paus. 2.23.5) and Sparta (Plutarch *Quaestiones Graecae* 48 = *Moralia* 302e–d): see Faraone (1992: 7). On Greek Palladion shrines, see N. Robertson (1996a: esp. 430–8; 2001); on later claims to the Trojan Palladion in Rome and Constantinople, see Ando (2008: 149–97).

Figure 2.5 Diomedes seizes the Palladion: detail of Attic red-figure vase attributed to the Tyszkiewicz Painter, early fifth century BCE

is depicted on fifth-century Attic vases suggests a special interest in the Palladion's function as a talismanic denotation of Athena; it must have had special resonance in the goddess's favoured polis, where the Polias fulfilled a similar function.[61] Significantly, while the Palladion was epiphanically

---

[61] See, e.g., Plutarch *Themistocles* 10, on the statue's importance during the Persian invasion, discussed by Kroll (1982: 65), who argues it was taken aboard an Athenian vessel for safekeeping, and J. M. Mansfield (1985: 135–6), who argues it was essential that the statue remained on the Acropolis. Athens laid claim to the Palladion itself, of course (above, n. 60), which may have been identified with an ancient statue displayed in the late fifth-century Ilissos Temple: see Burkert (1990), Krumme (1993) and N. Robertson (1996a: 392–8; 2001: 38–40, 48–50, with caution). Significantly, however, the section of the temple's frieze depicting a scene of assault parallel to that of Cassandra includes a small column or statue base but *no image*: see Picón (1978: 64–6).

Figure 2.6 Cassandra seeks asylum at the Trojan statue of Athena: detail of Attic red-figure calyx krater attributed to the Altamura Painter, *c.* 465 BCE

referred to as Athena herself in the *Iliad*, and is generally depicted in black-figure vase-paintings as an active embodiment of Athena rather than a static image, from the fifth century its identity in the Greek visual imagination centred on its materiality, portability and status as an *object*.[62] Its depiction

[62] On the difference between archaic and classical representations of the Cassandra myth, see Schefold (1937: 41), Davreux (1942: 140–1), Matheson (1986: 103–7), Shapiro (1989: 36–7), Connelly (1993: 90–109, esp. 101), on the statue's relationship to Athena, and M. J. Anderson (1997a: 199–202). On the portability of cult statuettes, see Gladigow (1985–6: 118–19) and Vernant (1983: 305); on the exchange value and cultural capital ascribed to portable *agalmata* in archaic culture, see Gernet (1981) and Tanner (2006: 55–67).

in red-figure narrative scenes relating to Diomedes' theft and the rape of Cassandra suggests that the Palladion's sanctity did not lie in its ability to generate epiphanic encounter so much as its mythical aetiology and powers of guardianship.[63] As a talisman or locus of asylum, its agency lay precisely in its accessible physicality. This is visibly demonstrated by its size. In Attic vase-paintings the object's dimensions shift in accordance with the narrative requirements of the scene at hand: in scenes of its theft by Diomedes (where it has to be easily portable) it is generally portrayed as a miniature statuette (Figure 2.5); in scenes of Cassandra's rape (where it has to stand as a locus of asylum and visual contrast to Cassandra's fleshy vulnerability) it is depicted as a kore statue, closer to life-size (Figure 2.6). The fact that in both these scenes the object fatally fails to fulfil its function as a talisman suggests a certain self-conscious anxiety about the Palladion's relationship to divine presence, which is unsurprising, one might argue, in the years following Athens' sack by the Persians.[64] The goddess is conceived of as operating independently of her image, and its identity as 'Athena herself' is by no means guaranteed. The object thus operates, in Steiner's formulation, by 'metonymic rather than similarity-based relations'; it acts as a symbolic *marker* rather than a mimetic *depiction* of divinity.[65]

If objects such as the Palladion did not evoke a sense of the epiphanic through the divine radiance attributed to naturalistic forms or precious metals, how, then, did they function? Significantly, the Trojan Palladion is regarded by numerous authors in antiquity as διοπετές, literally 'fallen from Zeus';[66] Burkert even derives the term 'palladion' from πάλλειν, 'to hurl'.[67] Rather than being given an epiphanic appearance, the object is invested with a form of origin-myth which takes the form of a narrative of epiphanic *arrival*. These were applied to numerous *xoanon*-type images in

---

[63] The identification of the Athena statue at which Cassandra seeks refuge as the Palladion is complicated, of course, by the image's supposed theft by Diomedes. Were there in fact *two* statues of Athena at Troy? The internal contradictions of the mythic cycle do not, however, preclude the talismanic function of each image; if Cassandra's image is not *the* Palladion, then it is certainly treated as *a* palladion. On this problem, see Moret (1975: vol. I, 87–97), Shapiro (1989: 36 n. 147) and N. Robertson (1996a: 431–4).

[64] On the influence of historical events on the shifting form of the Palladion, see Connelly (1993: 88–9, 108–9, 120–3), who, however, emphasises the object's authority rather than its potential failure. On the Ilioupersis in Athens, see Gloria Ferrari (2000).

[65] Steiner (2001: 92).

[66] Acts 19.35, on the Artemis of Ephesus; numerous authors regard the Trojan Palladion as *diopetes* (e.g., Apollodorus *Biblio* 3.12.3): see Romano (1980: 352–3), Gernet (1981: 80–1, 90–1), Burkert (1985a: 167), Faraone (1992: 4–5), Pritchett (1998: 99–118), Bettinetti (2001: 71–6, 90) and Steiner (2001: 104–5, n. 98).

[67] Burkert (2004: 12–14).

antiquity, including the Athena Polias, the Artemis of Ephesus and the image of Dionysus Cadmus at Thebes (which all supposedly fell from heaven), and the cult images of Dionysus at Methymna, Heracles at Erythrae and Hermes Perpheraios at Ainos (which were recovered from the sea by fishermen).[68] Like the mythical origins of the ancient image of Hera at Argos, or Artemis at Brauron, the *aition* embeds history in the image itself. It also allows the object to mediate between inside and outside sacred space, reconciling the relationship between the internal ritual activation of material images and the external agency of the divine by attributing an external origin to the object. Its arrival from 'elsewhere' asserts the gods' power to materialise their own presence within the physical world by echoing narrative patterns associated with divine manifestation. Pausanias' narrative of the discovery of the image of Dionysus Phallen by fishermen at Methymna, for example, echoes the circumstances of the god's initial manifestation in the seventh *Homeric Hymn*, in which he suddenly appears on the seashore and cannot be identified by his mortal viewers; like the helmsman in the hymn, the fishermen only know that there is *to theion* – 'something of the divine' – in the strange object that appears in their nets.[69] In the case of the cult image of Heracles at Erythrae, tales of the image's unexpected arrival from Tyre on a wooden raft are combined with a dream vision instructing the local fishermen to drag the raft ashore using a rope woven from the women's hair. The object's emphatic materiality is thus almost literally entwined with the bodies of its worshippers, establishing a determinedly physical relationship between viewer, object and deity that is directed and supported by an external authority evinced through visionary experience.[70]

Despite evidence for sculpted details (and therefore mortal workmanship) on these figures, the miraculous circumstances of their discovery suppress the responsibility of any mortal creator, and explain any divergence

---

[68] On the Athena Polias, see Paus. 1.26.6; on Artemis of Ephesus, Acts 19.35; on Dionysus Cadmus, Paus. 9.12.4. Euripides attributes the same origin to the *agalma* of Tauric Artemis (*Iphigenia in Tauris* 977). On Dionysus of Methymna, see Paus. 10.19.3; on Heracles of Erythrai, Paus. 7.5.5–9; on Hermes Perpheraios, Callimachus *Iambus* 7 = fr. 197 Pfeiffer with I. Petrovic (2010). Such examples are discussed by Bettinetti (2001: 91–9), Steiner (2001: 82–4) and Tanner (2006: 55–7). On the recovery of precious objects from the sea, see also Gernet (1981: 85–8, 90–2). Consider also the stone which Rhea gives to Cronus as a substitute for the infant Zeus in Hesiod's *Theogony* 485–98, subsequently set up by the god as a *sēma* at Delphi: see Neer (2010: 58–9).

[69] Paus. 10.19.3, with Vernant (1991: 154). On Dionysus *Phallen*, see Frontisi-Ducroux (1991: 193–201). On the *Homeric Hymn to Dionysus*, see Chapter 1, 67–8.

[70] On the relationship between dream visions and cult images in Pausanias, see Chapter 6, 266–75.

from anthropomorphic Hellenic conventions.[71] Each object functions as an *acheiropoiēton* (to borrow a term from Byzantine debates over sacred modes of representation): its epiphanic quality does not primarily reside in its appearance so much as its status as an image 'not made by human hands'.[72] Epiphanic arrival narratives thus stand as a structural opposite to the narratives of vision-inspired creativity that cluster around classical sculptors such as Phidias and Polyclitus.[73] Each functions as a direct response to material form: epiphanic origin myths are ascribed to supposedly 'primitive' images (whether aniconic or semi-iconic) in order to ascribe divinity to unconventional or humble objects, while artists' visions are associated with the creation of images of great skill and, usually, high naturalism, as a means of counteracting the distancing effects generated by both mortal artistry and mimesis.

There is, however, a tension between the aetiology of images such as the Palladion and the Polias, which locates their sanctity in epiphanic origins, and the etymology of the term *xoanon* applied to them by later authors, which emphasises their materiality. This is less problematic, perhaps, if one considers that divinity can also imbue the very substance of which they are made.[74] The Athena Polias was famously made of olive wood, its epiphanic arrival in Athens thus symbolic of the goddess's great gift to her favourite polis.[75] The sacred qualities of such wood are confirmed by the Damia and Auxesia episode related by Herodotus, in which the material is specifically procured for the creation of the goddesses' cult images at Epidaurus because

---

[71] Pausanias describes the Dionysus of Methymna as 'outlandish, and unlike the normal figures of Greek gods' (10.19.3); the Heracles of Erythrae is 'absolutely Egyptian' (7.5.5). Evidence for the sculptor Endoios' creation of the Athena Polias comes only from a corrupt text of Athenagoras (*For the Christians* 17); no other extant sources refer to a mortal artist in connection with the image, though certain attributes such as the *gorgoneion* may have been added in the late sixth century (see Romano, 1980: 44–5; Kroll, 1982, and Keesling, 2003: 156–7). The Hermes Perpheraios discussed in Callimachus' *Iambus* 7 is an exception, although its attribution to Epeios, the creator of the Trojan Horse, locates its origins firmly in the mythic past: see Chapter 4, n. 18.

[72] See also Paus. 1.36.2 for statues of Pan on Salamis 'made each by itself' (Πανὸς δὲ ὡς ἕκαστον ἔτυχε ξόανα πεποιημένα), with, e.g., E. *IT* 87–8, 977–8 (on the *agalma* of Artemis supposedly brought by Iphigenia from Tauris to Greece) and Acts 19.35 (on the Artemis of Ephesus). On Byzantine *acheiropoiēta*, see Kitzinger (1954: 112–15), Grabar (1984: 33–40), Cormack (1997: 98–100, 115–28) and Wolf (2002), and on evidence for pagan *acheiropoiēta*, Clerc (1915: 10–31) and Burkert (1985a: 91 n. 94). On the denial of artistic agency in relation to sacred objects in antiquity, see Tanner (2006: 48–50).

[73] On artists' visions of the divine, see Tanner (2006: 50) and Chapter 6, 266–75.

[74] Romano (1980: 359–61), Bettinetti (2001: 65–70). On the 'medium as the message' in archaic and classical sculpture, see Neer (2010: 73–4).

[75] Romano (1980: 44). On the relationship between cult images and trees, see Bettinetti (2001: 107–36).

Athenian olive trees are regarded as the 'holiest' (ἱρωτάτας) of their kind.[76] Pausanias tells us that Aphrodite was worshipped by the Hermos river in the form of a living myrtle tree, a wood whose aphrodisiac qualities were fundamentally entwined with the goddess's status as an embodiment of desire, while, at Sparta, Asclepius' image was made of *agnus castus*, a plant well known for its healing properties.[77] Likewise, we hear from Athenaeus that, on Naxos, images of Dionysus were made of fig and vine wood, depending on the character of his cultic epithet; the use of the latter is associated, unsurprisingly, with his identity as Baccheus.[78] Elsewhere, the material employed was representative not of a deity's particular sphere of authority, but of his or her immortal status. The images of Ismenian Apollo at Thebes, Artemis at Orchomenos and, perhaps, the archaic *xoanon* of Artemis at Ephesus were made of cedarwood; Vitruvius tell us this was on account of its 'everlasting' qualities (*propter aeternitatem*) – most appropriate for a 'deathless' deity.[79] In all these examples a god's identity and sphere of activity are not primarily conveyed by the object's appearance (unlike the gold, bronze, ivory and marble employed in more spectacular cult images), but by the innate qualities of its often humble medium. In this way deity is instantiated through natural, living forms that often bypass the processes of mortal facture and representation altogether. It is striking in this regard how many of the terms employed for ancient cult objects play down the depictive potential of the image, in contrast to terms more commonly employed for statues of mortals, such as *andrias*, which derives from ἀνήρ ('man') and, from the

---

[76] Herodotus 5.82, discussed most recently by Haubold (2007). On evidence for wooden statues, see Meiggs (1982: 300–24).

[77] Paus. 5.13.7, 3.14.7. He also tells us that the image of Artemis Soteria in Laconia was made of myrtle (3.22.12), perhaps in recognition of the goddess's association with *parthenoi* on the brink of marriage, although see Steiner (2001: 85), who argues that myrtle actually has 'antaphrodisiac qualities', and so embodied Artemis' virginal status; as Detienne (1994: 63) points out, however, myrtle was also used as a euphemism for female pudenda, 'the ultimate expression of . . . seductive attraction'. For further examples of specific wood types in Pausanias, see 2.17.5 (the *agalma* of Hera at Samos, made from wild pear-tree), 6.18.7, 8.17.2 and 9.3.4. On Pausanias' treatment of trees in the *Description of Greece*, see Birge (1994). On the use of plants within sanctuaries to enhance 'expressive and sensory responsiveness' to cult images, see Tanner (2006: 47–8).

[78] Athenaeus 3.78. See also the scholion to Apollonius' *Argonautika* 1.1117 (Wendel, 1935: *loc. cit.*), which reports that a certain *xoanon* of the Mother of the Gods 'is made of a grapevine, because the grapevine is in like way sacred to Rhea' (translation from Donohue, 1988: 249, no. 26).

[79] Apollo: Paus. 9.10.2; Artemis at Orchomenos: Paus. 8.13.2; at Ephesus: Vitruvius 2.9.13 (noted by Romano, 1980: 236). See also Lapatin (2001: 70) on the qualities of cypress wood, used for two archaic figures at Acragas and the interior 'mast' of the Athena Parthenos on account of its sweet scent and durability (Dio Chrysostom 12.49, Plin. *HN* 16.212).

fifth century, *eikōn* (literally 'a likeness'), both of which explicitly signal the image's representational function by alluding to its prototype.[80]

Epiphanic alternatives 2: aniconism

The tendency to emphasise ritual function or material denotation rather than figurative resemblance in the terminology of archaic cult images finds its logical extension in the use of so-called 'aniconic' objects as the focus of ritual. These can take many forms, from unwrought stones to distinctive shapes such as pyramids and stelae inscribed with the names of divinities.[81] Traditional art historical narratives (following the lead of Pausanias and other Greek authors) have associated aniconism with either early, 'primitive' cult practice or the influence of the Near East.[82] However, recent work on Greek material religion has emphasised that such objects were worshipped synchronically with more figurative forms throughout antiquity, and, rather than constituting a response to exotic foreign influences, were usually firmly embedded within the traditions of local cult practice.[83] The non-representational nature of aniconic forms might seem radically 'other' when compared with the post-Phidian tradition of naturalistic cult statues, for fifth-century innovations in the rendering of divine form introduce a mimetic function that is not explicitly employed by more schematic types of image. Yet when considered alongside image types evoked by the terms *xoanon* (and in its earlier meaning, the *agalma*), we can see that aniconic objects partake in a similar negotiation of the relationship between material object and divine presence. As Gell has argued, all forms of 'idol', whether

---

[80] On the use of *andrias* and *eikōn* for images of mortals in Herodotus, Thucydides and Xenophon, see Scheer (2000: 14–16, with some exceptions). In this regard it is worth pointing out that *bretas*, a term often used in tragic poetry for images of gods, is only derived from *brotos* ('mortal') in much later texts seeking to distinguish between the usage of *bretas* and *agalma* through false etymologies (e.g., Clement *Protrepticus* 4.40 P): see Donohue (1988: 25 n. 62, on the term's non-Indo-European origin, and 45, 169, 171, 203 on the false etymology). Its original meaning is probably more closely associated with concepts of antiquity and potency (i.e., its talismanic rather than representational status): see Scheer (2000: 24–33).

[81] Unwrought stones: Eros at Thespiae (Paus. 9.27.1); pyramid: Apollo Karinos at Megara (Paus. 1.44.2), Zeus Meilichios at Sicyon (Paus. 2.9.6); stelae: cult of the nymphs in Arcadia (Rhomaios, 1911; Gaifman, 2005: 25–6, 216–26). For further examples, see Frazer (1898: vol. IV, 154–5), Metzler (1985–6), Donohue (1988: 195–205, 219–30), Gladigow (1988), Pritchett (1998: 143–7), Steiner (2001: 80–9) and Gaifman (2005, 2008b).

[82] E.g., Paus. 7.22.4: 'At a more remote period all the Greeks alike worshipped uncarved stones (*argoi lithoi*) instead of images (*agalmata*) of the gods.'

[83] See Gaifman (2005: esp. 7–14; 2008b).

iconic or not, function neither as 'depictions' nor 'portraits', but as 'artefactual *bodies*'; they do not seek to project an illusionistic sense of epiphanic confrontation with divine form, but rather to indicate a deity's spatio-temporal presence.[84] In particular, aniconic objects function as the focus of ritual practice, while simultaneously providing a conceptual space for the viewer-worshipper to imagine divine form for him- or herself. They may indicate certain properties such as number (as expressed by a triple stele of the Nymphs in Arcadia),[85] or even shape (such as the rounded conical stone associated with Aphrodite at Paphos).[86] Yet they retain a determined ambiguity as to the form, size or attributes that their relevant deities might take. In this way they circumvent the dominance of anthropomorphism, and acknowledge the necessarily partial nature of material representation. They may precipitate ritual encounter within the space of the sanctuary, yet they simultaneously allow for the shifting, manifold nature of divinity, giving space to an external model of epiphany in which agency rests principally with the gods themselves, who, as the Homeric poems make clear, might take whatever form they choose when making their presence manifest to mortal worshippers.

While references to rough-hewn *xoana* and *acheiropoiēta* hint at a material form of aniconism (which may, indeed, have characterised the Athena Polias), we find a more extreme aniconic alternative at Olympia, where there seems to have been no image or material denotation of the god at all prior to Phidias' fifth-century statue.[87] Like the sanctuary of Zeus on Mount Hymettos, where there was no special object to denote the god, the primary focus of ritual in the Olympian sanctuary was an ash altar.[88] We find here a *de facto* form of 'empty-space aniconism' that stands as the extreme alternative to the hyper-embodied images of classical naturalism.[89] It is not surprising, perhaps, that so many cults dedicated to Zeus chose to denote his presence by aniconic means; as ruler of all, god of the sky and embodiment of fate, Zeus was closest in conception to the God of the Old Testament, in which the impossibility of seeing deity face to face

---

[84] Gell (1998: 98, italics in orginal; see also 26).   [85] Gaifman (2005: 223–4).

[86] On the conical stone discovered in the sanctuary of Aphrodite at Old Paphos and now in the Cyprus Museum, see Dikaois (1961: 89–90), Maier (1979: 228, pl. 34.1) and Sophocleous (1985: 5–8, pl. 1.1).

[87] See Romano (1980: 147), Ridgway (2005: 112).

[88] On the ash altar, Paus. 5.13.8–11. On Hymettos, see Langdon (1976: 1–8) and Gaifman (2005: 1–3), though note Cook (1914–40: vol. I, 121; vol. II, 897 n. 5) mentions a later statue. On the altars at Olympia, see Elsner (2001b: 8–18; 2007: 13–17, with bibliography).

[89] On 'empty-space' aniconism, see Mettinger (1995: esp. 19) and Gaifman (2005: 170–5). On the difference between '*de facto*' and 'programmatic' aniconism, see Mettinger (1995: 18).

Figure 2.7 Coin of Olba, *c.* first century CE. Obverse: the Olban throne of Zeus; reverse: thunderbolt and inscription *Olbeōn*, 'Of the Olbans'

and the prohibition of graven images are directly related to the complex demands of monotheism.[90] The inherent polytheism of Greek culture never produced a theorised form of iconoclasm, despite the objections of some thinkers – notably Xenophanes – to the representation of the divine.[91] Yet it is noteworthy that although Homer's Zeus is highly anthropomorphised, he never appears directly to the mortal protagonists of the epics (unlike the other Olympians), and maintains a tension between forceful exhibition of power and corporeal elusiveness that serves to accentuate his authority.[92]

This 'Jovian' tension between anthropomorphised form and withheld epiphany finds an effective material counterpart in objects such as the empty thrones that formed the focus of ritual activity in various sanctuaries of Zeus, including his cult at Cilician Olba, modern Ura/Uğuralanı (Figure 2.7).[93]

---

[90] E.g., Exodus 20.2–6, Deuteronomy 4.15–18, Psalm 115.3–8, Isaiah 44.9–20, Jeremiah 10.3–5: see L. W. Barnard (1974), Dietrich (1985–6: 172–3), Halbertal and Margalit (1992), Chisholm (1995), Mettinger (1995: 13–17, with bibliography), Poorthuis (2003) and the essays collected in Barton (2007). See also Herodotus 1.131.1–2, on the association between Persian aniconism and the worship of Zeus as god of the sky, discussed by Donohue (1988: 90–2) and Lightfoot (2003: 452–3).

[91] See Chapter 1, 51–2.

[92] The Homeric scholion states at *Il.* 13.18b that, unlike Poseidon, Zeus never descends to earth, nor undergoes any metamorphosis: see Petridou (2006: 251–3), who nevertheless points out that on a cultic level the god is more 'mobile', taking part in numerous theoxenic rites as Zeus Philios; see also Koch Piettre (1996: 70–1). Mastronarde (2005: 322) concurs that Zeus was rarely represented on the dramatic stage, either. On the problematisation of Zeus' epiphany in the *Iliad*, see Stevens (in press).

[93] On the epiphanic quality of the empty throne, see also Koch Piettre (2001: 212–13).

Founded with a new, Greek-style temple in the Hellenistic period, the Olban cult nevertheless maintained an important continuity with the pre-Greek cult of a local weather-god (associated with the Hittite deity Tarku), and exists in line with a long tradition of empty thrones in Near Eastern tradition.[94] But it also found several parallels in Greece itself, where rock-cut thrones of Zeus survive at a number of sites (including the island of Chalke, off the west coast of Rhodes) and are particularly associated with mountain cults.[95] The combination of iconic throne and empty space generates a powerful sense of potential anthropomorphic presence. Though perhaps periodically activated in ritual performances, in which a priest might symbolically 'become' the god, the throne as object has the ongoing potential both to receive Zeus 'himself', and to generate epiphany within the mind of the viewer-worshipper.[96] Like the hymns and reliefs discussed in Chapter 1, the empty throne provides a clearly defined space for the god to interpolate himself in a seemingly unmediated fashion into the subjective experience of the viewer. By withholding a *representation* of divine form, the throne paradoxically makes it more present, while simultaneously alluding to the god's ability to transcend the limitations of sanctuary, human body and physical medium. In this sense it is like Polyclitus' Hera turned inside out: the potentially epiphanic void is located outside the image, rather than within it. Yet unlike the Hera, or Phidias' chryselephantine image of Zeus enthroned at Olympia, the throne provides a lesser degree of iconographic specificity, and thus demands the creative application of the viewer's religious knowledge. Other images of Zeus might influence the form of divine presence each viewer-worshipper projects into the space provided, but the ultimate *eidos* of the god remains fluid and

[94] On empty thrones in the Near East (often associated with the goddess Astarte), see Metzger (1985), Philonenko (1993), Mettinger (1995: 100–3) and Gaifman (2008a); Lucian refers to a throne at the sanctuary of the Syrian Goddess in Hierapolis that was reserved for the sun, but devoid of an image (*On the Syrian Goddess* 34; see Lightfoot, 2003: 449–55; Elsner, 2007: 249). On Zeus' cult at Olba, see Magie (1950: vol. II, 1143–4, with bibliography), and Staffieri (1976).

[95] See Gaifman (2005: 193–5). On mountains as 'thrones' of Zeus in Greek culture, see Cook (1914–40: vol. I, 124–48, fig. 94). On a double hilltop throne inscribed with the names of Zeus and Hecate (*Inscriptiones Insularum Maris Aegaei* vol. I, no. 958) on Chalke, see Cook (1914–40: vol. I, 141–2) and Gaifman (2005: 187–93). See also Paus. 2.36.1, with Elderkin (1937: 429), who argues that the original name of Mount Cuckoo near Halice, sacred to Zeus, which Pausanias gives as *Thornax* (Θόρνακος), was actually *Thronax*, 'throne'. On divine thrones in early Greek culture, see Jung (1982).

[96] As suggested by Cook (1914–40: vol. I, 125). On priestly epiphanies in ritual performance, see my Introduction, 13–17. This blurring of priest and deity must have had particular resonance at Olba, which during its independence prior to the establishment of Roman rule in the late first century CE was governed by priest-kings of the cult of Zeus: see Strabo 14.5.10, with Hill (1899).

undetermined.[97] On a Cilician coin commemorating the Olban cult
(Figure 2.7), the throne is juxtaposed with the god's thunderbolt, the divine
sēma by which he was most frequently apprehended (as Zeus Kataibates).[98]
The presence of the 'seen' and 'unseen' deity at Olba is thus publicised by
a potent combination of iconic, aniconic and symbolic form that acknowledges and celebrates the multiple, shifting means by which divinity can be
experienced.[99]

In the light of Zeus' Olban throne, it is significant that the term *hedos*,
or 'seat', is applied to many Greek cult images, including the Athena Polias
and the archaic statue of Artemis at Brauron.[100] *Hedos* is used for a variety
of iconographic types and does not necessarily imply that the statue is in
a seated pose; rather, whereas *agalma* and *xoanon* evoke the artefactual,
created nature of sacred images (as do terms such as *hidruma* and *kolossos*),
hedos refers to their function as 'vessels' or 'receptacles' of divine presence,
periodically – and always potentially – activated by deity.[101] The *hedos* makes
concrete the idea that sacred images operate as a kind of frame; they provide
a physical object to act as a 'container' for divinity, and even indicate the
form the god might take. Yet by indicating the possibility of absence and
mobility, the concept of the image as seat also expresses the idea that divinity
operates beyond the framework of ritual and representation that constitutes
his or her worship in a specific location. In this way it gives visual form to the

---

[97] In this sense, the throne offers a combination of potential corporeality and empty space that in
its Olban context engages in interesting ways with the cult's Greco-Anatolian syncretism.

[98] Dated to the first century CE, bronze, 24 mm; SNG Levante 645 (Collection of Dr Edoardo
Levante). Published in connection with an online auction at http://www.wildwinds.com/
coins/greece/cilicia/olba/SNGLev'645.jpg. For coins from the same series dated to the late
first century BCE, see Hill (1899: 203; 1900: 119.1, pl. 21.7) and Staffieri (1978: no. 1,
figs. II.1–2, with further references). On Olban coinage in general, see Hill (1899) and Staffieri
(1978).

[99] On the contrast between deities 'seen' in cosmic phenomena and those accessible only in
image form, see Plato *Laws* 931a, discussed by Gaifman (2005: 15–16).

[100] Romano (1980: 47–8, on the Athena Polias, and 86–9, on the *hedos* of Artemis at Brauron);
Scheer (2000: 21–3, 120–3).

[101] It is used for the Athena Polias and Parthenos, for example, both of which were standing
figures: see Kroll (1982), Burkert (1985a: 89), Shapiro (1989: 25), Bettinetti (2001: 52–4) and
Lapatin (2001: 61 n. 5). On the statue as vessel, see Faraone (1992: 18–35, 94–223), Steiner
(2001: 79–134) and Neer (2010: 109–21). *Hidruma*, used for temples and statues alike, derives
from the verb ἵδρυμαι – 'to found' or 'set up' – and associates the physical panoply of cult with
the practical processes of its establishment: see LSJ s.v. ἵδρυμα and Aeschylus *Persae* 811, with
Brunel (1953), Malkin (1991), Bettinetti (2001: 54–63) and Nick (2002: 24). *Kolossos*, a term
applied to archaic images such as kouroi and korai, derives from the word for 'column' and
evokes the image's cylindrical nature and wooden origins: see Roux (1960), Ridgway (1977:
23), Vernant (1983: 305–20), A. Stewart (1990: vol. I, 44), Nick (2002: 16) and Neer (2010:
110).

process of negotiation by which different categories of cult image mediate between materiality and divinity, ritual activation and external agency.

Reconciling form and function on the Athenian Acropolis

This brief survey of different image-types employed to negotiate the relationship between worshipper and deity, materiality and divinity, within Greek sanctuaries sheds light on the radically different strategies by which the Parthenos and Polias evoked their goddess's presence in Athens. While Phidias' Athena may have been more epiphanic in appearance and effect, for example, the Polias was epiphanic in origin: as Pausanias records, it had 'fallen from heaven' (πεσεῖν ἐκ τοῦ οὐρανοῦ).[102] While the Parthenos employed materials chosen for their value and visual splendour, the Polias consisted of a widely available type of wood chosen because it embodied Athena's mythical and practical relationship to her favoured polis. Finally (and perhaps most significantly), while the Parthenos sprang epiphanically into the cultural imagination as an authentic visual embodiment of the goddess, the Polias continued to be the recipient of honours and the focus of rituals such as the Panathenaic peplos ceremony, which invested the image with epiphanic status by 'animating' it through rituals of *kosmēsis*.[103]

As Romano has pointed out, such rites and their accompanying processions 'relate principally but not exclusively to early cult images, especially wooden ones', partly because they are so closely bound to their portability.[104] The sanctuary of Dionysus at Athens, for example, housed both the archaic image of Dionysus Eleuthereus, which was carried in procession during the Dionysia, and a chryselephantine statue of the god attributed to the fifth-century sculptor Alcamenes, which remained firmly in place within its temple.[105] Such juxtapositions generated a contrast between a fully kinaesthetic engagement with the object and a more concentrated emphasis upon the process of viewing.[106] It is unclear how cultic activity was affected in the Aeginetan and Argive sanctuaries, where the old and new images of each goddess were displayed together, but on the Acropolis, at least, the housing of the Parthenos and Polias in separate temples (the Parthenon and Erechtheion respectively) generated a gap between visual effect and ritual

---

[102] Paus. 1.26.6.   [103] See E. J. W. Barber (1992).   [104] Romano (1988: 127–8).

[105] Herington (1955: 36–7). On the role and identity of cult images in Athenian Dionysiac festivals, see Romano (1980: 70–8).

[106] Vernant (1991: 158–9), Steiner (2001: 103).

treatment that has troubled generations of ancient historians. Historically, this has not affected responses to the Phidian Zeus at Olympia, perhaps because the pre-Phidian alternative of aniconic absence was so effectively superseded by the classical statue, whose sanctity has been recognised and celebrated by both ancient viewers and modern scholars.[107] On the Athenian Acropolis, however, the continued presence of the Polias demanded a more complex response. Scholars have accordingly sought to categorise the Parthenos as an 'offering' rather than a cult image, to describe the Parthenon as a 'treasury' rather than a temple, and to associate Phidian naturalism with more secular modes of representation that were less 'divine' than the rough-hewn idols of old.[108] While indebted to post-Reformation suspicions of idolatry, such interpretations also take their lead from post-classical responses to chryselephantine cult statues, such as Pausanias' comment that there is *ti entheon* – 'something divinely inspired' – about ancient *xoana*, or Porphyry's claim, anachronistically attributed to Aeschylus, that archaic *agalmata*, 'although simply made, are considered divine (*theia*), while the new ones provoke *thauma* through their elaborate workmanship, but give less impression of godhead'.[109]

One could argue, however, that the frequency with which old and new temple statues were juxtaposed in Greek sanctuaries indicates that the practice was less problematic for fifth- and fourth-century viewers than it was for imperial and late antique authors (or contemporary scholars) seeking authentic religiosity in a 'primitive' Hellenic past.[110] To concentrate on the responses of Pausanias or Porphyry is to ignore the sanctity conferred upon the Phidian images in their immediate context, their widespread replication in other media, and the strong association engendered between image and deity in their viewers' imaginations. While the Polias might have functioned as the actual focus of priestly, sacrificial and ritual activity on the Acropolis,

---

[107] This is not to rule out the significance of the Olympian ash altar as an alternative (aniconic) site of deity, however. On the epiphanic qualities of the Phidian Zeus as expressed in Dio's *Twelfth 'Olympian' Oration*, see Chapter 5, 224–35.

[108] See, e.g., Herington (1955), who regards classical chryselephantine images as 'a superfluous creation' (36), and frames his book by quoting Pausanias' emphasis upon the Polias as the 'holiest' (ἁγιώτατον) object upon the Acropolis (1.26.6), and, more recently, A. Stewart (1990: vol. I, 45). For a critique of such attitudes, see Donohue (1997: 37–8) and Nick (2002: esp. 1–7). On the Parthenon as a treasury (with no priesthood or altar), see Hurwit (2004: 156, 163–5). On the Parthenos as a votive, see above, n. 47.

[109] Paus. 2.4.5: see above, n. 57; see also 1.26.6, where he claims the Polias is 'the most holy symbol' (τὸ δὲ ἁγιώτατον) of Athens. Porphyry *De abstinentia* 2.18 = Aesch. T114 Radt, discussed by Donohue (1988: 136) and Steiner (2001: 103). On the Lutheran logic of Western art history, see Koerner (2004) and Squire (2009: 15–89).

[110] See Donohue (1988: 121–50) and, on Second Sophistic attitudes to the sacred past, Part II.

the entire architectural complex surrounding the Parthenos encouraged the new image's reception in epiphanic terms. Like earlier Greek temples, the Parthenon's external decoration provided a physical and conceptual frame that established the deity's sphere of authority, and enhanced the ritually generated epiphanic encounter that awaited within by alluding to the manifestation of divine power without.[111] In keeping with the epiphanic narratives that clustered around festivals and cult images, it located divine presence in mythical origins – Athena's contest with Poseidon for supremacy in Athens on the west pediment, and her birth on Olympus on the east.[112] Such narrative framing served to collapse the gap between the human and divine spheres and, like the *Homeric Hymns*, anticipated the goddess's radiant epiphany with narratives of her first 'arrival' and acquisition of powers.[113]

Moreover, the Panathenaic procession depicted on the Parthenon's frieze surrounded the Parthenos with a depiction of the very ritual associated with the Polias.[114] If the ancient olive-wood statue served as the practical focus of sacred activity, then the Parthenos visually embodied its desired result. And while the Parthenon alluded to the primary ritual associated with the Erechtheion, the Erechtheion itself visually directed its viewers straight back to the Parthenon by means of the sculpted *parthenoi* on its south porch.[115] This relationship was also established for visitors to the Acropolis on the west face of each building, for the myth of Athena's struggle with Poseidon on the Parthenon's west pediment referred to each deity's original gift to Athens – the ancient olive-tree growing in the precinct to the west of the Erechtheion, known as the sanctuary of Pandrosus, and the marks

[111] Compare the pedimental depiction of divine power in the midst of mythic battles such as the gigantomachy in the west pediment at Delphi (*c.* 510), the Trojanomachies in both pediments of the Temple of Athena Aphaia at Aegina (*c.* 490–475) and the centauromachy in the west pediment at Olympia (*c.* 470–457), or the reference to divine *theophania* in Apollo's arrival at Delphi, in the east pediment of his Delphic temple, and the metopes depicting his return from the Hyperboreans in the north porch of the Temple of Apollo at Bassae (*c.* 420). On epiphanic narratives in architectural sculpture, see A. Stewart (1990: vol. i, 86–9), Marszal (1998, on the Old Athena Temple at Athens), R. Osborne (2009) and Neer (2010: 92–9).

[112] Compare the role of Zeus in the Pelops narrative depicted in the east pediment at Olympia and the *theophania* of Apollo in the east pediment at Delphi. On the Parthenon pediments, see E. Berger (1974) on the east pediment and Palagia (1993: esp. 27–30, on the central figures; 2005).

[113] On the screen or frame as a 'microcosm' and mediating mechanism within sacred space, see Grimes (2006: 87–99). The birth of Athena was actually celebrated in her *Homeric Hymn* (1.7–16), which has strong associations with Athens: see Palagia (2005: 235).

[114] *Pace* Connelly (1996)! For defence of the traditional interpretation of the Parthenon frieze as an allusion to the Great Panathenaia, see E. B. Harrison (1996b) and Neils (2005b).

[115] On relations between the two structures, see Hurwit (1999: 174; 2005: 28).

supposedly left by Poseidon's trident in its north porch.[116] The pedimental sculpture thus exploited the epiphanic potential of naturalism in order to (re)present a foundation epiphany that had taken place upon the Acropolis itself, while the olive tree and trident marks served as its physical marker or *sēma*; Pausanias refers to the olive tree, in particular, as the μαρτύριον or 'testimony' of the goddess's regard for Attica.[117] The two structures were thus inextricably bound by their diverse but complementary means of celebrating the cult of Athena on the Acropolis. So were the images they housed. Each functioned in fundamentally different ways – the Polias as a metonymic sign of divine presence, the Parthenos as a mimetic likeness of divine form. But *together* they covered multiple strategies by which divinity might be rendered. Like diverse evocations of divine form and identity in Homeric and cletic hymns, the juxtaposition of contrasting representational modes did not measure the relative sanctity of different image-types, but rather acknowledged the many and shifting ways in which immortal *eidea* could be invoked and experienced.

In producing a representational experience of epiphany rather than generating it by metonymic strategies, however, the Parthenos offered an epiphanic plenitude that risked falling victim to its own success. For the very means by which Athena was made 'present' for her viewers were the conspicuous product of extreme wealth and technical sophistication associated with identifiable, mortal individuals. While the concept of the *agalma* maintained a balance between (immortal) form and (material) content by highlighting the object's ritual, rather than representational, function, the mimetic experience of *thauma* generated by colossal chryselephantine images pushed the familiar tension between the object's divine and artefactual nature to extremes. This is reflected in the stories that cluster around their most prominent creator.[118] On one hand Phidias was credited with an epiphanic perception of the divine (a response which locates the image's authority in the cognitive reliability provided by visionary experience). On the other hand, he was regarded as a cheat and a thief, who hubristically included his own crypto-portrait on Athena's shield, and assisted Pericles in the theft of gold from the statue (an expression of cognitive dissonance generated by tension between the Parthenos' status and effect).[119] The image

[116] Herodotus 8.55, Paus. 1.26.5, 27.2. See Hurwit (1999: 203–4), Boardman (2002: 109–10) and Palagia (2005: 243).

[117] Paus. 1.27.2.

[118] On ancient sources for Phidias (and his relationship with Pericles), see Overbeck (1868: nos. 618–807) and A. Stewart (1990: vol. I, 257–63, with bibliography).

[119] Self-portrait: Pseudo-Aristotle *De mundo* 6 (= 399b–400a), Cic. *Tusc.* 1.15.34, Valerius Maximus 8.14.6, Apuleius *De mundo* 32, Plutarch *Pericles* 31.4; the conceit is interestingly

was thus set about with controversies that revolved around two problematic areas: the size and value of its raw materials, and the less than pious behaviour of its creator and commissioner. Phidias, in particular, rapidly acquired a notoriety within the historical record to rival that of the mythical artist Daedalus, who had long served within the Greek imagination as a model for exploring the limits of mortal skill and ambition, but, in keeping with an enhanced interest in artistic *technē*, acquired a new prominence in fifth-century Athens.[120]

Our earliest source for the claim that Phidias was charged for embezzlement of the Parthenos' gold or ivory, condemned to exile and subsequently put to death by the Eleans is Philochorus, a Hellenistic historian of Attica quoted in the scholion to Aristophanes' *Peace*.[121] In keeping with many Phidian tales, these claims belong to a post-classical tradition rooted in a Hellenistic preoccupation with the practice of portraiture and the artist as a cultural figure.[122] So although many scholars have attempted to date the sculptor's trial and construct a precise curriculum vitae of his activities (nefarious or not) in Athens and Olympia, it is perhaps more productive to treat the details of his biography as products of the cultural imagination.[123] As Lefkowitz has shown, ancient *bioi* are often rooted in the nature and reception of their subjects' works, reflecting a fundamentally ambivalent attitude to extraordinary achievement; while hard facts about Phidias may be small in number, his reputation is nevertheless revealing of attitudes to creators of sacred images, or *agalmatopoioi*, in antiquity.[124] One might argue accordingly that Hellenistic controversies associated with statues such as the

---

attributed to Daedalus in Ampelius *Liber memorialis* 8.1; see Preisshofen (1979) and Steiner (2001: 269). Embezzlement and trial: scholion to Aristophanes' *Clouds* 859.2 and *Peace* 605 (quoting Philochorus = *FGrH* 328 F121), Diodorus Siculus 12.39–40, Seneca *Controversiae* 8.2, Plutarch *Pericles* 31.2–3, Suidas s.v. Pheidias; see Donnay (1968), Wesenberg (1985) and A. Stewart (1990: vol. I, 257–8). On Phidias' visionary abilities, see above, n. 10; on the same topos as applied to Praxiteles' cult image of Aphrodite of Knidos, see Chapter 4.

[120] See Frontisi-Ducroux (1975), Gordon (1979): 8–9, S. P. Morris (1992) and Spivey (1996: 56–60). The story of Daedalus may even have featured on some of the lost south metopes of the Parthenon itself: see M. Robertson (1979).

[121] Scholion to *Peace* 605 = *FGrH* 328 F121. See Jacoby's commentary *ad loc.* and A. Stewart (1990: vol. I, 258–9).

[122] See Tanner (2006: 205–34) and my discussion in Chapters 3 and 4.

[123] For attempts to recover the historical figure of Phidias, see, e.g., E. B. Harrison (1996a) and Spivey (1996: 152–71), critiqued by Hurwit (1997). On the Hellenistic origin of such tales, see Preisshofen (1979); on their later visual reception, see, e.g., E. B. Harrison (1981).

[124] Lefkowitz (1981). It is striking how similar Phidias' life story is in structure to those of his contemporary playwrights Aeschylus and Euripides, whose biographies follow a common tragic pattern, identified by Lefkowitz (93–7) as 'versatility', 'accomplishments', 'isolation, exile' and 'violent death'. On mythic patterns characteristic of artists' biographies, see Kris and Kurz (1979).

Parthenos are perversions of ideas already implicit in their contemporary reception – an expression of latent anxiety over the statue's materiality and the cultural shift that had taken place in the production and display of sacred art in the fifth century. Here the prominence of the Parthenos, rather than Olympian Zeus, in the tradition is telling, for such anxiety must have been partly generated by the Athenian political and financial decision-making processes that led to the statue's commission. The democratic arena in which Pericles' programme for the Acropolis was conceived opened up a procedure that had been previously downplayed or consigned to the mythic past, thereby thrusting the new image's master craftsman into the spotlight.[125] Pausanias identifies the sculptors behind some earlier Greek cult images; Endoios is even credited with the addition of figurative elements to the semi-iconic Athena Polias in the late sixth century – a sign, perhaps, of a growing desire for a more 'mimetic' depiction of the city's patron goddess.[126] But these are shadowy figures compared with Phidias, who both was named on a bronze stele displayed upon the Acropolis and, so Pausanias records, signed his name on the base of the Olympian Zeus.[127]

Combined with the enhanced public prominence of the image's creator was the double status of the Parthenos herself. For not only was she the ultimate embodiment of Athena, but she was also part of the Athenian Treasury – a symbol and more importantly, perhaps, a functional component of the polis' financial capital.[128] The tension between these two identities is vividly demonstrated by Thucydides when reporting Pericles' account of Athenian resources during the Peloponnesian War: in addition to temple treasures, he claims that, in dire straits, 'they could even use the

[125] Lapatin (2001: 55). On public scrutiny of religious art in democratic Athens, see Tanner (2001: 272; 2006: 146): 'Public discussion and evaluation of the artist's work played a central role in the organisation of the production process and significantly informed the transformative reconstruction of artists' identities, role and agency'. On public accounts concerning the Parthenos' gold and ivory, see Donnay (1967) and Eddy (1977).

[126] E.g., the Cretan sculptors Dipoinos and Skyllia (credited with *sphyrelaton* images at Sicyon and ebony *agalmata* of the Dioscuri and their families at Argos, 2.22.5, 5.17.1) and the late sixth-century sculptors Endoios (creator of the chryselephantine *agalma* of Athena Alea at Tegea, 8.46.4) and Canachus (credited with the chryselephantine *agalma* of Aphrodite at Sicyon, 2.10.4–5). See Raubitschek (1942), A. Stewart (1990: vol. I, 115, 122–3, 242–3, 248–9) and Lapatin (2001: 43, 56). On Endoios' contribution to the Polias see above, n. 52.

[127] Paus. 5.10.2: Φειδίας Χαρμίδου υἱὸς Ἀθηναῖος μ᾿ἐποίησε ('Phidias son of Charmides, an Athenian, made me'). On the stele, see Plutarch *Pericles* 13.14; although the date of the Olympian inscription is unclear, Lapatin (2001: 63 n. 21) suggests that the Athenian inscription was the bronze stele mentioned in Acropolis inventories dated to the early fourth century (*IG* 2². 1407, 5–6; 1410, 7; 1443, 10–11; 1468, 7; 1477).

[128] See Donnay (1967), Eddy (1977), Kallet-Marx (1989) and Lapatin (2001: 64–6, with bibliography), on the cost and financing of the Parthenos.

gold that coated the goddess herself (αὐτῆς τῆς θεοῦ); for the *agalma* displayed forty talents of pure gold that was all removable'.[129] Here linguistic fusion of deity and image ('the goddess herself') is entwined with a reference to the Parthenos' purely fiscal value, whereby the gold of her drapery and attributes served both a representational and economic function.[130] While his language strikingly demonstrates the uneasy relationship between divinity and materiality negotiated by *any* statue (for all *agalmata* were, to some extent, symbols of their sanctuary's wealth), it also indicates how the Phidian image intensified this paradox to such a degree that it became a major factor in the Parthenos' cultural reception. We find a similar sense of contradiction (pushed for humorous effect) in Aristophanic comedy: in *Birds*, Peisetairos comments on the sexy nightingale Procne, 'What a lot of gold she's wearing, just like Parthenos! (ὥσπερ παρθένος)', punning on the name of the statue and the 'young maiden' Procne represents, while alluding to its material wealth.[131] In the light of such contemporary responses, one could argue that the relationship the Parthenos negotiated between removable gold and divine status was so jarring that it was in many ways inevitable that her creator would be charged (either within his lifetime or by history) with avarice and impiety.

There is a degree, however, to which the Parthenos herself bore witness to the contradiction she embodied between materiality and mortal artistry, on one hand, and divinity and epiphanic effect, on the other. It lies in the narrative of Pandora's genesis by the gods depicted upon the statue's base, which has traditionally been a source of much anxiety for the Parthenon's interpreters.[132] Why is such a negative myth portrayed at the heart of such a celebratory ensemble?[133] For Steiner, the act of divine creativity 'clamorously

---

[129] 2.13.5. While the removability of the Parthenos' gold is given short shrift by Lapatin (2001: 65), its mention by Thucydides in a near-contemporary source (and attribution to Pericles) testifies to the imaginative potency of the very idea, on which see Gordon (1979: 24). The concept emerges again in the troubled year 295/4, when the Parthenos' gold was supposedly removed by the tyrant Lachares in order to pay his mercenaries: see Paus. 1.25.7, *POxy.* 17.2082 = *FGrH* 257a and Demetrios II 1 KA, who claims in his comedy *Areopagites* that 'Lachares made Athena naked' (Mikalson, 1998: 91).

[130] The claim is echoed by Plutarch *De vitando aere alieno* 2 and *Pericles* 31.2–3 (where it is directly related to the charge of embezzlement).

[131] *Birds* 667–70; compare *Knights* 1168–70, on the size of Athena's ivory hands. The Parthenos' materiality and the role of Phidias as craftsman are also exploited for rhetorical effect in the disputed Platonic dialogue *Hippias Major* 290 a–d.

[132] Pandora's position on the base is mentioned by Pausanias (1.24.7) and Pliny (*HN* 36.19), who uses the Greek term *genesis*. For a summary of interpretations, see Leipen (1971: 24–7, with proposals for reconstructions), Lapatin (2001: 67; 2005: 268–9) and Hurwit (2004: 151–3).

[133] A question posed by Loraux (1993: 114–15), Hurwit (1995), who sees Pandora as an 'anti-Athena' expressing Athenian notions of patriarchy, and Connelly (1996: 72–6), who

calls attention to the act of craftsmanship, and in so doing reminds the viewer of its own status as a work of art created by a mortal's hands'.[134] But Pandora also represents something more subtle and, indeed, more important for the image's efficacy as an *agalma*. It is characteristic for large chryselephantine or acrolithic cult images to be adorned with subsidiary iconography, which offsets each statue's mimetic specificity and enhances its visual splendour by providing symbolic narratives that allude to the deity's cosmic status and broader sphere of authority.[135] In this sense Pandora offers a narrative which, positioned directly in front of the viewer on the Parthenos' base, polices his or her engagement with the image. Significantly, she is presented in Hesiod's *Theogony* and *Works and Days* (in language parallel to the *Homeric Hymns*) as a false epiphany.[136] With 'a face like the immortal goddesses (ἀθανάτης δὲ θεῆς εἰς ὦπα ἐίσκειν)' she is a *thauma idesthai* who, like Aphrodite to Anchises, appears among men in the guise of a young maiden, adorned with finely worked garments and jewellery.[137] Her wonderful crown, wrought by Hephaestus with creatures 'like living beings with voices' (ζωοῖσιν ἐοικότα φωνήεσσιν) 'breathed beauty on all' (χάρις δ᾽ ἐπὶ πᾶσιν ἄητο), just like Demeter at the moment of her epiphany to Metaneira.[138] Although she is a 'likeness' (ἴκελον) of a *parthenos*, she is also a *parthenos* herself; 'unbearable for mortals' to look upon, she renders them 'helpless' (ἀμήχανον).[139]

Whether or not the statue's viewers were familiar with the Hesiodic text, Pandora stands in telling counterpoint to Athena, her birth on the statue's base an echo of the goddess's birth on the Parthenon's east pediment. She is an epiphanic (though mortal) *parthenos* generated by divine

interprets the scene as a representation of apotheosis related to a beneficent 'gift-giving' Attic Pandora, rather than the Hesiodic version.

[134] Steiner (2001: 104); see also Hurwit (1995: 183). On the Pandora myth as an allegory for the role of *technē* in Periclean Athens, see Pollitt (1990b).

[135] See, e.g., Paus. 5.11.1–9, on the iconography surrounding the Olympian Zeus, and 3.18.10–16, on the throne of Apollo at Amyclae. Significantly, the creation of Pandora on the Parthenos' base was matched at Olympia by the birth of Aphrodite from the sea on the base of Phidias' Zeus (Paus. 5.11.8), and the birth of Erechthonius on the base of Alcamenes' cult images of Hephaestus and Athena in the Hephaesteion (in which autochthony is presented as the epiphanic 'arrival' of the first Athenian): see E. B. Harrison (1977) and Hurwit (1995: 178 n. 24).

[136] *Theogony* 570–89, *Works and Days* 60–80. See West (1966: 305–8), Vernant (2006: 42–3; 1990a: 183–201) and Loraux (1993: 72–110), who comments on familiarity with the passage in classical Athens (73).

[137] *Works and Days* 62; cf. *Il.* 3.158, on Helen. θαῦμα ἰδέσθαι: *Theogony* 575, 581; θαῦμα: *Theogony* 588, *H. Hom.* 5.81–90; see also goddesses dressing at *Od.* 5.230–2, 10.543–5, and *Il.* 14.178–87, as noted by West (1966: 327), who also notes a parallel between Pandora's and Aphrodite's reception by mortals at *Theogony* 588–9 and the *Homeric Hymn to Aphrodite* 6.14–18.

[138] *Theogony* 583–4. Compare *H. Hom.* 2.276 (περί τ᾽ ἀμφί τε κάλλος ἄητο).

[139] *Works and Days* 71, *Theogony* 572, 589.

technē, who frames – even supports – the epiphanic (divine) *parthenos* gen-erated by human *technē* who towers above. Craftsmanship, of course, fell under Athena's purview; in Hesiod's narrative, it is she who dresses Pandora and teaches her *erga* (specifically 'intricate weaving', πολυδαίδαλον ἱστόν), and her prominence in the narrative on the statue's base must have been crucial.[140] As a sculpted woman (or, in Hesiod's words, a 'sheer deception' – δόλον αἰπύν) Pandora stands as a reminder that, however 'many intricate works' (δαίδαλα πολλά) are wrought by mortal skill, the gods have a far greater mimetic power which, when ignored or flouted (as by Prometheus), has the potential to work 'evil' (κακόν) for mankind in return.[141] Pan-dora's presence thus provides acknowledgement of the fact that, whatever man might achieve through his own powers of mimesis, the gods can do better. Like the *gorgoneion* on Athena's aegis above, she has an apotropaic function; she is a warning built into the statue's very foundation.[142] Most importantly, she acts as a pressure valve which, by paying homage to the superiority of divine mimesis, allows the mortal image its full technical, material and epiphanic *thauma* without overtly risking the dangers of hubris. In this way she demonstrates a specifically tragic sense of the limits of human endeavour that finds numerous parallels in contemporary Athenian culture.

In accounting for the cultural and sacred status of the Phidian images, scholars often fall into two camps: they may stress either the self-conscious artistry involved in their design and production, or the sense of epiphanic plenitude they generated for contemporary viewers.[143] Donohue, for exam-ple, reacts to academic de-sanctification of the Parthenos with the declara-tion that 'We must accept that the images were deemed successful. There are no grounds for thinking that the Greeks had anything less than per-fect confidence in their ability to render the appearance of the gods – that is to say, in the mimetic enterprise.'[144] Yet, as Pandora's presence on the Parthenos' base suggests, this conflict does not have to be a case of scholarly

---

[140] *Works and Days* 63–4, 76, *Theogony* 573–5; see West (1978: 158–9). For Athena's proposed position, see Leipen (1971: 25), and on supervision of the birth by the Parthenos herself, Loraux (1993: 80).

[141] *Theogony* 589, 581, 570. Note that *dolos* is also used of Hephaestus' trap at *Od.* 8.276 and Hermes' powers of deception in his *Homeric Hymn* (*H. Hom.* 4.66); in Hesiod's *Works and Days*, Pandora's ability to deceive is specifically the gift of Hermes (66–8).

[142] Pandora's apotropaism must have been enhanced, if reconstructions of the scene are correct, by her static frontality in the relief's centre, flanked by active profile gods: see Leipen (1971: 24) and Hurwit (1995: 177–8).

[143] For the former, see, e.g., A. Stewart (1990: vol. I, 45); for the latter, Donohue (1997).

[144] Donohue (1997: 44).

position. Rather, it deconstructs and simplifies a tension that was already subtly mediated by the images themselves, whereby an awareness of the mimetic process *coexisted* with an appreciation of its presentational potential: each statue's success as a *theama*, or 'wondrous sight', was inherently dependent upon the self-conscious *technē* of its creator, rather than inhibited by it. This inherent ambiguity proved remarkably seductive to ancient viewers. On one hand, the Phidian style generated divine forms that were replicated as physical and mental representations throughout post-classical antiquity – cultural 'memes' that influenced the design of cult images (creating a new visual orthodoxy in late classical and Hellenistic Greek sanctuaries), and even shaped epiphanic experience itself.[145] On the other hand, the marked tension they embodied between phenomenological effect and ontological status prompted complex ways of viewing that profoundly influenced the theorisation of epiphany and its relationship to representation; in Hellenistic, Roman and Greek imperial literature, the Phidian cult images would repeatedly act as foci for questions about the origins and authenticity of divine *eidea*.

Epiphany and the theology of naturalism

Although Phidias' statues of Zeus and Athena seem to have incorporated a certain hieratic formality of style, so maintaining an important sense of continuity with the archaic past, the epiphanic force generated by their simulation of divine form simultaneously anticipated the mimetic effects produced by more fully naturalistic images such as Polyclitus' Argive Hera and, ultimately, late classical marble statues such as Praxiteles' Aphrodite of Knidos (which is discussed in Chapter 4). Fifth-century religious art may have provided a formal model for representations of the divine – a visual language of epiphany. Yet, from its inception, this tradition was accompanied by a vigorous negotiation of the relationship between image and deity, in which the epiphanic potential of naturalism was both indulged and interrogated. While the Trojan Palladion had long offered an opportunity for visual explorations of the status and authority of sacred images (as I discussed above), from the mid fifth century BCE we begin to find repeated depictions of scenes in which a statue of a deity is pointedly juxtaposed with

---

[145] Lapatin (2001: 96–119). On the influence of Phidian forms on Hellenistic cult images, see Chapter 3, 126–30.

a 'real' divine presence.[146] In this way the relationship between epiphany and representation is highlighted and implicitly problematised.

While juxtapositions of image and deity are found on numerous south Italian red-figure vases, we also find them in monumental form in mainland Greece, most strikingly on the internal frieze of the Temple of Apollo at Bassae, dated *c.* 410–400 BCE.[147] On the east section of the frieze two Lapith women trying to escape the assault of an aggressive centaur flank an archaising statue of a goddess, identified by Madigan as Artemis (Figure 2.8).[148] As in classical vase-paintings of Cassandra and the Trojan Athena, the women's soft, fleshy, naturalistically rendered bodies contrast with the smaller scale and rigid frontal stance of the statue (whose tightly curled ringlets echo the schematic hairstyles of archaic statuary), while their dramatic gestures serve to heighten the object's impassivity.[149] And yet, while viewers of Cassandra's predicament are all too familiar with its tragic outcome, the frieze at Bassae seems to tell a different story.[150] For while the statue itself may seem to 'fail' to protect its worshippers, the narrative extends to the north section of the frieze, where the viewer encounters the salvific epiphany of Apollo and Artemis themselves, bursting onto the scene in a deer-drawn chariot to avenge the sacrilege perpetrated by the forces of barbarianism (Figure 2.9).[151] Whereas Athena's revenge is only foreshadowed in scenes

---

[146] The first documented example of this juxtaposition is the Polygnotos Iliupersis vase in the Getty Museum (79.AE.198), dated 440–435 BCE and discussed by Matheson (1986), in which an archaising Palladion is juxtaposed with a naturalistic depiction of Athena herself. Significantly, the label AΘENA is positioned between the heads of the two figures, precluding any ontological differentiation between image and goddess.

[147] On south Italian examples, see Moret (1975: vol. I, 9–28, 69–97), Connelly (1993: 115–16 n. 102) and below, 120–2. On the Bassae frieze the definitive work is Madigan (1992), whose arrangement I follow here, with Cooper (1992–6) on the temple itself. For alternative arrangements of the relief slabs, see Dinsmoor (1956), Hofkes-Brukker and Mallwitz (1975), a summary of different arrangements by Madigan (1992: 39) and the Corbetts' arrangement in the British Museum, supported by Jenkins and Williams (1993).

[148] Madigan (1992: 80–1). The identification is dependent on evidence for the worship of Artemis and her counterpart Ortheia at Bassae (see Cooper, 1992–6: vol. I, 64–5), rather than any formal qualities of the statue itself, which is parallel in dress and pose to many images of the Trojan Palladion; see Havelock (1965: 333–4), with comparanda. Brahms (1994: 182) suggests that the statue draws upon the archaising form of Artemis Hecate.

[149] For the emphasis on Cassandra's eroticised form in classical vase-paintings, see Connelly (1993: 116–17).

[150] On Cassandra's fate, see Davreux (1942: 3–87). Madigan (1992: 80–1) argues somewhat unconvincingly that the statue at Bassae is not on a base, but is being carried by the woman to the right, whom he identifies as the priestess of Artemis Ortheia, who is protectively cloaking the image with her peplos rather than clutching it in supplication.

[151] Madigan (1992: 81–2), who with Cooper places the epiphany scene (slab 523) adjacent to the central axis of the north frieze (opposite the central figure of Heracles on the south), and the statue scene (slab 524) as the second slab from the south end. Dinsmoor (1956) had the two

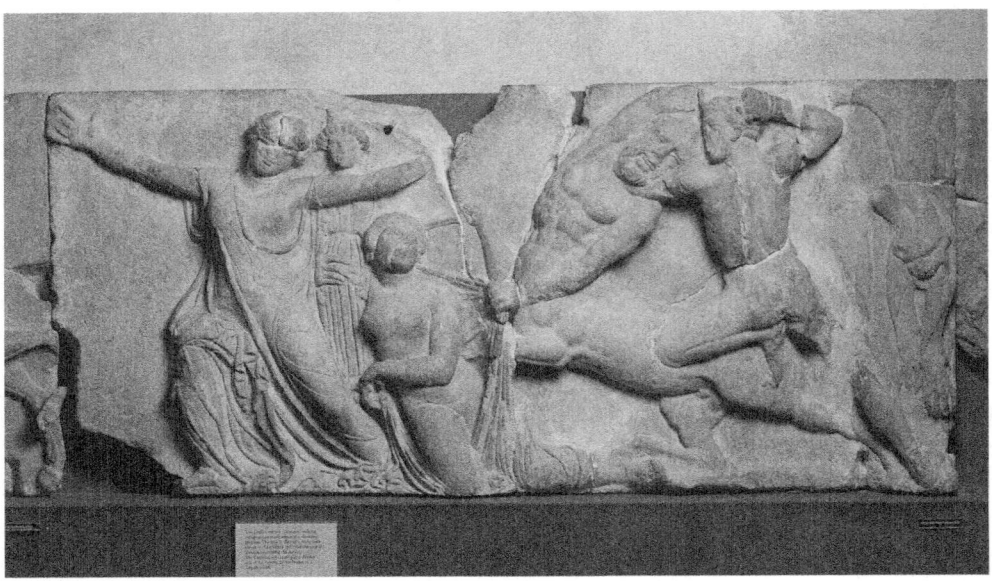

Figure 2.8 Section of the centauromachy frieze from the Temple of Apollo at Bassae depicting women claiming asylum at cult image, *c.* 400 BCE

Figure 2.9 Section of the centauromachy frieze from the Temple of Apollo at Bassae depicting the arrival of Apollo and Artemis, *c.* 400 BCE

of Cassandra's violation, the Bassae frieze collapses sacrilege and vengeance into the same narrative sequence. In contrast to the static, archaising object that provides a focus for ritual activity, the swift motion, flowing drapery and naturalistic bodies of Apollo and Artemis define them as active agents who inhabit the same ontological realm as the living figures of the frieze. In this way contemporary modes of depicting divine form are constructed as 'natural' (in contrast to the schematic strategies of earlier forms), suggesting a totalising correspondence of sign and referent that is implicitly contiguous with the realm of the mortal viewer.[152] Significantly, if we follow Cooper and Madigan's organisation of the internal frieze, the epiphanic arrival scene was placed directly behind the metopes of the temple's pronaos, which depicted Apollo Kitharoidos and his entourage returning from the land of the Hyperboreans – another significant epiphanic moment in the god's mythic cycle.[153] These external and internal epiphanies thus flanked the temple's actual entrance, signifying the building's status as the dwelling of the god to whom it was dedicated, and reflecting his dual identity as both joyous patron of music and vengeful Far-Shooter.[154]

However, while the fluid forms of Apollo and Artemis demonstrate an enormous confidence in naturalism's potential to present the 'gods themselves' to their mortal viewers, they do not function as mere replacements for the archaising *xoanon*. First, the liminal position of the epiphanic arrival scenes draws attention to the reliefs' status as subsidiary decorative devices adorning the entrance to the temple, rather than the focus of ritual activity. While Apollo and Artemis may demand to be *viewed* as if they are epiphanically present, they are not actually *treated* as such in the context of cult practice. Second, the salvific role the deities play within the centauromachy requires their depiction in profile: in order to engage convincingly with the

---

slabs meet at the north-east corner of the temple, juxtaposing image and epiphany more explicitly. The Corbetts' arrangement in the British Museum also places slab 523 (the epiphany) in the east corner of the north frieze, but positions slab 524 (the statue) as the third slab from the south end in the east frieze.

[152] On the fraught relationship between 'nature' and 'convention' in responses to classical modes of representation, see most recently Tanner (2006: 67–9). I do not here deny the socially constructed nature of the conventions employed in fifth- and fourth-century Greek art in favour of an essentialising theory of naturalism; my point is that contemporary stylistic modes are constructed as contiguous to the realm of the viewer in a way that is explicitly contrasted with earlier forms.

[153] See Madigan (1992: 16–28, on the pronaos; 9–15, on the metopes of the opisthodomos, which depicted the rape of the Leucippidae). For a literary parallel to Apollo's musical advent, see the *Homeric Hymn to Apollo* 3.182–206.

[154] See Madigan (1992: 90): 'On the frieze the god draws his bow, the stringed instrument of death; on the metope he plays his kithara, the stringed instrument of order and life'.

events depicted and assert their divine authority, they must remain locked within the narrative and physical framework of the frieze itself. Such narrative coherence is fundamental to naturalism, and is echoed in *Daseinsbilder* (profile depictions of gods pouring libations or engaging in other isolated activities, which were popular from the fifth century BCE) or the narrative absorption of fourth-century sculptures such as Praxiteles' *Aphrodite of Knidos* (*c.* 340) and *Apollo Sauroktonos*.[155] These compositional devices reject traditional hieratic frontality in order to construct a scenario that renders the deity's presence plausible: but in doing so they transform the viewer into a voyeur, thereby precluding any direct engagement with divinity itself.[156] The epiphanic plenitude offered by naturalism thus has the paradoxical effect of reinforcing the very distinction between image and deity that it seeks to collapse.

If the Bassae frieze does offer a direct engagement with the divine, then it is to be found in the archaising image that, in contrast to the profile forms of Apollo and Artemis, looks out of the narrative frame directly into the temple's inner space. Connelly comments that the frontal form of the Trojan Athena in fifth-century vase-paintings of the Cassandra myth 'denies even the slightest visual interaction between statue and suppliant', emphasising the goddess's distance.[157] This may be so within the narrative logic of the myth, yet the frontality of such represented statues is precisely what allows them to reach beyond their narrative frames in order to meet the gaze of the external viewer. We might compare the Asclepieion relief discussed in Chapter 1, in which a frontally depicted, archaising herm functions as a liminal and ritual framing device mediating access to an encounter with the naturalistic profile form of Asclepius within. At Bassae the statue's impassivity to its Lapith suppliants is precisely the formal device that enables its relationship with viewers within the temple itself; in contrast, the active agency of Apollo and Artemis allows them to be 'present' within the frieze,

---

[155] On *Daseinsbilder*, see Himmelmann (1998: 115–38), who argues that this shift emphasises distance between the spheres of worshipper and self-sufficient deity (in line with the rationalising force of the 'Greek Revolution'), playing down the tension between epiphany and representation such images produce through the motif of voyeuristically observed presence. For a rethinking of *Daseinsbilder* as a form of reflexivity, signalling the origin of ritual in the divine realm, see Patton (2009). On the narrative absorption of free-standing classical statues of deities, see A. Stewart (1990: vol. i, 176–9) and Ridgway (1997: 263).

[156] See Elsner (2006), who argues that 'The very naturalism of these figures – the fact that they have been designed to stand the way real people stand – denies our gaze' (78), and that the shift from archaic 'gaze' to naturalistic 'glance' in the fifth century 'can as much be read as a series of losses as they were a series of gains' (70).

[157] Connelly (1993: 115).

yet prohibits any direct relationship with the external viewer and thereby reinforces their status as representations. Each form's status as a presentation or re-presentation thus shifts according to whether one performs a narrative reading of the frieze or seeks direct encounter. One stylistic mode is not necessarily more sacred than the other, but both work together; indeed, it is arguable that Apollo and Artemis are only epiphanically present within the frieze *because* of the sanctity invested in the statue by its Lapith viewers.[158]

The combination of archaic and naturalistic forms at Bassae echoes the combination of ancient *xoanon* and chryselephantine *agalma* recorded in numerous classical sanctuaries, from Aegina and Argos to the Athenian Acropolis. Like the votive reliefs discussed in Chapter 1, the frieze employs formal contrasts in order to probe the epiphanic potential of naturalism, and its implication for images stylistically identified as 'antique'. In this way archaic cult-statues are established as material markers of divine presence that mediate between god and worshipper when activated through ritual, but are nevertheless ontologically distinct from the deities they signify. Naturalistic forms, by contrast, have no specific ritual function and are seen to elide their status as images in order to constitute 'gods themselves'. Together, the two modes offer a guide to viewing the diverse divine *sēmata* a worshipper might find within or upon a classical temple, generating a play of presence and absence, reality and representation, in which godhead can be apprehended not only in multiple images, but also on multiple ontological planes.

The slippage between 'god' and 'image' engendered by naturalism is by no means straightforward, however. For while archaising forms make only a limited claim to representational authority, parading their status as man-made objects, the epiphanic status of the Apollo and Artemis at Bassae rests on a principle of precise congruence between god and image. The correlation this suggests between epiphany and representation is

---

[158] Unfortunately our evidence for a cult image of Apollo at Bassae is flimsy at best. Pausanias mentions a 12-foot bronze statue of Apollo Epikourios, which was taken from Bassae to Megalopolis when the city was founded in 370/69 BCE (8.41.7), though Cooper (1992–6: vol. I, 70), argues that this was *not* the cult image, but was instead a large votive dedication that stood outside the temple. Fragments of a large marble acrolithic statue of a seated Apollo Kitharoidos were discovered within the temple cella in 1812, but these seem to be of later Hellenistic or Roman date. Madigan (1993: 116–17) suggests that the acrolith replaced an archaic cult image which he identifies as the ivory Apollo in the Forum of Augustus, removed from Bassae as a symbol of the victory at Actium, as happened to the ivory statue of Athena Alea at Tegea (Paus. 8.46.1). Conversely, it has been suggested that the Bassae temple's cult image was actually its central Corinthian column, a provocative nod to aniconism that would further enrich the interaction of different divine forms in the temple's sculptural scheme: see Cooper (1992–6: vol. I, 305–24) and Tzortzi (2000: 42).

Figure 2.10 Fragment of a calyx krater depicting Apollo and his cult image, 400–385
BCE

tempered by the cognitive dissonance prompted by the relationship of *likeness* this establishes. In this sense the relief is an *eikōn* or *mimēma* of divine
form, a notion that introduces a crucial gap between image and prototype, destabilising the very principle of congruence that gives the scene its
epiphanic force.[159] The representational and cognitive dilemmas this paradox raises are illustrated by a number of late classical vase-paintings from
southern Italy which juxtapose naturalistically rendered gods with naturalistic statues.[160] In a fourth-century calyx krater fragment, for example, the
god Apollo, depicted with lyre and laurel wreath and labelled ΑΠΟΛΛ…,
sits juxtaposed with a Doric temple, its doors opened to reveal a standing
statue of Apollo within, holding a bow and phiale (Figure 2.10).[161] The

---

[159] On the significance of *eikōn*, see Saïd (1987), Koonce (1988), Vernant (1990a; 1991: 164–85),
Halliwell (2002: 182–4) and Tanner (2006: 106–8).

[160] On cult statues in Italian vase-paintings, see Schneider-Herrmann (1972: esp. 31–6), on
Apollo, Schauenburg (1977) and Oenbrink (1997: esp. 116–36).

[161] Amsterdam, Allard Pierson Museum 2579, from Taranto, attributed to the Painter of the Birth
of Dionysus. Fragments show that the vase also depicted Artemis (to the right of the seated
Apollo) and, on the other side, Dionysus with a maenad and silen. See *LIMC* s.v. Apollo, no.
428, pl. 216, with Schneider-Herrmann (1972: 31–4), Trendall and Cambitoglou (1966:
686–8; 1978: vol. i, 34, 36, no. 10, pl. 9.2), Alroth (1992: 39–40) and Oenbrink (1997: 126–7,
no. D7, pl. 34a–c).

scene invites a 'compare and contrast' exercise, in which the figures' shared identity as 'Apollo' (with smoothly modelled torsos, long flowing hair and clean-shaven, youthful features) is fragmented by their divergent pose and attributes. As at Bassae, the peaceful Apollo Kitharoidos outside the temple is juxtaposed with the Lord of the Bow within. The major contrast between the two figures, however, lies in the rendering of their flesh. For while the seated Apollo has been painted according to classic red-figure technique (thus corresponding to the realm of the 'real' within the vase's depictive space), the Apollo within the temple has been covered with a gold wash, subtle brown shading and white highlights in order to give the effect of a bronze statue, and thus a man-made representation.[162]

The stylistic similarity and yet material and ontological contrast between the two Apollos thus present the viewer with a doubleness of form that prompts serious theological reflection on the status and function of the image. Where, ultimately, is the god? Does the labelling of the seated Apollo, rather than his image, imply that only the external figure 'is' the god, suggesting a clear ontological hierarchy? Or, conversely, is Apollo only 'present' on the vase because he is made present by his gleaming statue? It is perhaps significant in this regard that the seated god does not acknowledge his representation, but is lost in his own music-making, as if casually observed rather than self-consciously manifest. Does the seated Apollo then occupy the same space as the temple, or does he exist in an entirely separate sphere, 'invisible' within the scene itself and yet visible to the external viewer? Should the similarities between the two Apollos inspire confidence in the veracity of the cult image? Or do their iconographic differences, combined with the scene's separation of 'god' and 'statue', imply that the relationship between the two is arbitrary? Such dilemmas raise the question of how, in fact, we are to understand the gap between image and prototype that naturalism necessarily establishes, even as it makes its claim to mimetic truth. The scene constitutes a visual exploration of the principle of cognitive reliability, in which any claim for the truth of established divine forms is tempered by the depictive status of the image as a whole: for even the 'real' Apollo is only a painted god, and thus subject to the constraints of material production.

Scenes such as Figure 2.10 may call attention to the familiar Platonic problem of mimesis, but they do not simply expose the statue's status as

---

[162] Schneider-Herrmann (1972: 31) likens the bronze Apollo to the Phidian-style Kassel type, dated *c.* 440 BCE, known in Roman copies and imitated in Tarentine terracottas of the second half of the fifth century BCE.

an inferior 'copy' of its divine original.[163] Rather, the visual correspondence they draw between god and image prompts a continual renegotiation of the relationship between the two. On one hand, the viewer is trapped in a hermeneutic circle, unable to escape the realm of constructed discourse (a form of cognitive dissonance). On the other hand, this implicit acknowledgement of the mimetic dilemma acts to reinforce the theological importance of epiphany itself as a means of ratifying established divine form (thereby offering cognitive reliability). It is arguable that by rejecting metonymic modes of indicating divine presence in favour of epiphanic simulation, mimetic naturalism actually made epiphany *more* necessary as a cultural, religious and aesthetic phenomenon. In this sense it is not surprising that encounters with the divine would play such an important role in the reception of classical cult images from the Hellenistic period onwards, whether to suggest that artists based their images on actual visions (as in Parmenion's epigram on Polyclitus' Hera), or that gods appeared in the form of their images (as in the appearance of Athena Parthenos to Aelius Aristides). In such cases, the externally generated appearance of a deity corresponding to his or her image serves to validate the internal representational system so crucial to Greek religious practice.

The bond between gods and their cult statues is, like epiphany itself, continually shifting and elusive. Ritual treatment, form and terminology can tell us much about the diverse formulations of this relationship in Greek culture. Most importantly, they reveal how an active and self-conscious engagement with the ontological and theological problems raised by the mutual dependence of epiphany and representation was fundamental to religious art and its visual and literary reception. While Gordon is right to stress the 'ambiguous status of the art object', it is important to emphasise that the ritual model of image *as* epiphany (in which viewing a cult image was akin to an encounter with the deity it represented) existed alongside other epiphanic models. The Palladion and *acheiropoiēton* traditions, for example, located divinity in both epiphanic origin myths and an emphatic materiality of the sacred, while aniconic traditions emphasised the role of the object as a marker or vessel of potential presence, in which divine form is left open to both viewer imagination and divine agency. In each of these formulations, the inherent sanctity of the object stands in tension with the independent existence (and multiple forms and identities) of the deity it signifies. The partial or metonymic quality of so many sacred image-types is thus an implicit acknowledgement of the limitations of matter and

---

[163] See, e.g., *Republic* 596b–598d, with Else (1958), Nehamas (1982) and Halliwell (2002: 37–71).

human skill when faced with the diverse and elusive nature of divine form. Naturalistic images, however, make a claim for epiphanic plentitude and corporeal precision that can potentially disrupt the delicate balancing act performed by other categories of sacred object. By simultaneously collapsing and reinforcing the distinction between 'god' and 'representation', they quickened the relationship between divinity, human skill and materiality in ways that would have a far-reaching effect upon post-classical engagements with the sacred image.

3 | Epiphany and authority in Hellenistic Greece

The years between the death of Alexander in 323 BCE and Rome's definitive conquest of the Mediterranean at Actium in 31 saw shifts in cultural and political attitudes to divine manifestation that have important implications for the relationship this book traces between epiphany and representation. While the expansion of the Hellenised world and the rise of kingship introduced new elements into traditional religious practice (not least the foundation of ruler cults), the ritual infrastructure of the old Greek poleis remained largely unchanged; despite the scholarly cliché that this was a period of religious 'decline', there is a wealth of evidence for the continued vitality of civic, as well as personal, religion.[1] We see in Hellenistic culture a productive tension between conservatism and innovation, in which the archaic and classical Greek past is treated on one hand as a venerable source of identity and authority, and on the other as a toolbox for creative acts of transformation and modernisation. Across the shifting sands of the Hellenistic Mediterranean, epiphanies provided a means of both accessing the religiosity of the past and bypassing established sources of authority in order to legitimise the new. Their proliferation in the cultural record is typified by the adoption and widespread use of the substantive noun *epiphaneia* to refer to manifestations of divine presence in epigraphic texts from the third century onwards, while a number of Ptolemaic and Seleucid kings adopted the title *Epiphanēs*, 'the Manifest', as part of their political self-legitimation.[2]

This chapter examines just some of the diverse ways in which manifestations of divine presence were strategically generated, recorded or alluded to in Hellenistic culture, concentrating on a handful of visual and epigraphic examples. It is by no means comprehensive in its treatment of what was a profoundly complex and widespread phenomenon, but instead continues to explore the more precise relationships between vision and representation,

---

[1] See L. Robert (1966), van Straten (1993), Graf (1995), Mikalson (1998) and Potter (2003). For the 'decline' argument, see Festugière (1954: 9–18) and Gehrke (1990: 185–92), with bibliography. On ruler cult, see below.

[2] See below, with bibliography.

divinity and artistry, that formed the focus of Chapters 1 and 2. In particular I wish to question how the epiphanic models provided by earlier artistic, literary and religious practice functioned in traditional Greek cities during a period of rapid political change, and how such cultural *sēmata* were reformulated for new contexts, media and audiences. Chapter 4 continues to explore these themes in relation to Hellenistic literary culture, focusing on the relationship between epiphany and cult images in ekphrastic epigram.

Epiphany and artistry in the Hellenistic Peloponnese: the case of Damophon

One of the most provocative engagements between the epiphanic models of classical Greek art and the contemporary concerns of Hellenistic cities can be traced in the Peloponnese, near ancient Megalopolis in Arcadia. At some point in the early second century, four acrolithic cult images were commissioned for the sanctuary of a local fertility goddess named Despoina ('the Mistress') at Lykosoura, not far from Bassae.[3] These are attributed to the sculptor Damophon, who seems to have been active between 214 and 182 BCE, creating at least twelve cult statues or statue groups in the Peloponnese and beyond.[4] The Lykosoura group can be reconstructed with some confidence thanks to a coin from Megalopolis and a detailed account in Pausanias' *Description of Greece* (Figure 3.1).[5] Within a small Doric temple a

[3] On the cult of Despoina, see Stiglitz (1967: 30–50) and Jost (1985: 172–8, 326–37). On the temple, see Tomlinson (1963), who dates it *c.* 175–150. On the sculptures, see Dickins and Kourouniotis (1906–7) and Dickins (1910–11), Becatti (1940: 40–6), A. Stewart (1979: 57; 1990: 94–6), Pollitt (1986: 165–6), Moreno (1994: 504–18), H.-U. Cain (1995: 124–5), Faulstich (1997: 163–8), Damaskos (1999: 58–71) and Kaltsas (2002: 279–81); on evidence for Damophon's output elsewhere in the Peloponnese, see Themelis (1993, 1994, 1996), Torelli (1998), Damaskos (1999: 44–58) and Luraghi (2008: 278–85, with bibliography). On the identity of Despoina, whose 'real' name was kept secret, see Loucas-Durie (1991), who identifies her as Artemis.

[4] I take these dates from Themelis (1994: 24–30; 1996: 170–2), who, like Dickins (1905–6), places Damophon's activity early in the second century during the independence of Messene, prior to its capitulation to the Achaean League (though see Luraghi, 2008: 284–5, for a later date of 170–150 and Torelli, 1998, for an earlier date of 275–200). The Lykosoura sculptures (and thus Damophon's sculptural output) were controversially dated to the Hadrianic period by Lévy owing to the discovery of Hadrianic coins under the statue group, but these are now thought to have been deposited after repairs were made to the images following an earthquake: see Lévy (1967), retracted in Lévy and Marcadé (1972: 986, 1003), with Habicht (1985: 47–57), Pollitt (1986: 312 n. 2), A. Stewart (1990: vol. I, 94–5) and Themelis (1996: 167).

[5] Athens Numismatic Museum, Julia Domna on obverse; see *LIMC* s.v. Anytos no. 2, Dickins (1910–11) and Themelis (1996: 167). On Pausanias' account (at 8.37.3–4) of the Lykosoura sculptures in its Second Sophistic context, see my discussion in Chapter 5, 220–3.

Figure 3.1 Reverse of a coin of Megalopolis depicting the statue group from the Temple of Despoina, Lykosoura, 193–217 CE

broad, 8 m long podium supported two centrally seated marble sculptures – Demeter (Figure 3.2), on the left, and her daughter Despoina (who was associated with Persephone in Arcadia) on the right – flanked by standing figures of Artemis (who was known locally as Demeter's daughter) and the Titan Anytus, Despoina's childhood guardian, or *kourotrophos* (Figures 3.3–4). Enthroned in the half-light of the temple, the statues towered as high as 5.7 m, robed in dark polychrome drapery.[6]

Study of the fragments has traditionally been dominated by stylistic analysis – an attempt to define Damophon's artistic influences and contribution to the sculptural trends of the second century. The consensus is that he combines the monumental, idealising forms of Phidian classicism with the softer modelling of fourth-century Praxitelean goddess iconography, adding a few impressionistic touches in the hairstyles that are more typical of a Hellenistic interest in movement and expression.[7] Scholarly tussles have thus

---

[6] See A. Stewart (1990: 94), on the dark blue curtain behind the throne, the deep purple-red of Despoina's veil and Demeter's black chiton (which echoes her black-draped semi-theriomorphic image at Phigaleia, described by Pausanias (8.42.4–5). On Anytus, see Loucas-Durie (1989).

[7] See Themelis (1996: 157–9, 163), where he identifies a similar eclecticism of style in Damophon's surviving sculptures from the Asclepieion at Messene, described by Pausanias at 4.31.10.

Figure 3.2 Head of Demeter from the Temple of Despoina, Lykosoura, early second century BCE

Figure 3.3 Head of Artemis from the Temple of Despoina, Lykosoura, early second century BCE

Figure 3.4 Head of Anytus from the Temple of Despoina, Lykosoura, early second century BCE

ensued between those who dismiss the sculptures as second-rate examples of a long-established Peloponnesian tradition derived from classical models,[8] and those who see Damophon as one of the first neoclassicists, performing an innovative, self-conscious exercise in stylistic synthesis and allusion that functions as a conservative reaction to the excesses of the Pergamene baroque.[9]

In placing Damophon's sculptures within a neat narrative of stylistic development, however, this secularising mode of analysis ignores the context in which they would have been viewed, and thus neglects the immediate phenomenological authority and religious significance of their visual allusions. Epigraphic evidence from the site makes clear that access to the sanctuary was carefully controlled, with elaborate sacred laws concerning

[8] E.g., R. R. R. Smith (1991: 240–1): 'Damophon was not a revivalist reinventing a style that had since disappeared.... It was simply the continuing sculptural manner for cult statues in mainland Greece'.

[9] E.g., Becatti (1940: 45–6), A. Stewart (1979: 57, a view considerably revised in his sensitive reading of the statues in 1990: 94–6) and Pollitt (1986: 165–6).

Figure 3.5 Fragment of Despoina's robe, from the Temple of Despoina, Lykosoura, early second century BCE

the dress, offerings and even child-bearing status of those who entered, while Despoina's veil was adorned with symbolic attributes that made subtle allusions to her sacred rites and local identity as 'Mistress of Animals' (Figure 3.5).[10] For worshippers initiated into her cult, Damophon's skill as an artist would have lain in his ability to harness different illusionistic strategies, inspired by a variety of stylistic modes, to project a sense of authoritative divine presence within the temple. Significantly, Pausanias tells

---

[10] *IG* 5.2.514, with Voutiras (1999) and *SEG* 49.446. See Dickins (1906–7: 392–5), Kouroniotis (1912: 155–8), Wace (1934), A. Stewart (1990: 95), Loucas and Loucas (1994), H.-U. Cain (1995: 125) and Jost (2003: 157–9; 2005: 98–100).

us that Damophon was commissioned to repair Phidias' chryselephantine statue of Zeus at Olympia following an earthquake in 183 BCE.[11] Certainly, the solid, hieratic form of the Phidian cult image can be traced in the Lykosoura group; like the Olympian statue, the sturdy, seated figures of Demeter and Despoina filled the space they inhabit, possessing an incipient movement that implied they might stand up and break through the roof of the temple (as Strabo said of Phidias' Zeus).[12] Further, the rounded profiles and emphasis on the major axes of the face look to Attic fifth-century models – Pausanias compared them to Agorakritos' (now lost) statue of the Athenian Mother Goddess – while their emphatic corporeality is appropriately reminiscent of the 'Demeter' and 'Kore' figures of the Parthenon's east pediment.[13]

This traditional impulse, however, is blended with more softly modulated forms that borrow the epiphanic language of fourth-century goddess iconography, especially in the faces of Artemis and Demeter, which combine idealising features with gentle expressions and sensually rendered flesh. Here we need not claim, with R. R. R. Smith, that the Praxitelean modelling of Artemis' face is a 'formless' appropriation of such modes, or, with Andrew Stewart, that Damophon's eclectic style gives the impression of 'a hollow and purely external rhetoric'.[14] Rather, we might argue that the fluid plasticity of the white marble faces, arms and feet creates a highly naturalised impression of feminine corporeality that must have contrasted dramatically with the dark, draped forms of laps and torsos.[15] Together with each figure's piercing inlaid eyes, this soft fleshiness enhanced the statue group's eerie projection of epiphanic presence and generated a sense of intimate encounter that would have been heightened by the small space of the temple. The slightly asymmetrical positioning of Artemis' eyes energises her features, while the semi-parted lips and delicately flared nostrils hint at breath, endowing the sculpture with a sense of life by suggesting – in a term commonly found in Hellenistic epigram – that her image is *empnoos*.[16] This sense of animation

---

[11] Paus. 4.31.6: see Dinsmoor (1941) and Lapatin (2001: 83, 86). Interestingly, Dickins (1905–6: 134–5) publishes an early second-century herm carved with a relief trident from Megalopolis which is dedicated by one Damophon to Poseidon Asphaleios (the 'Steadfast'), who was associated with earthquakes (*IG* 5.2.454).

[12] Strabo 8.3.30, discussed in Chapter 2, 89–90. On Damophon's Phidian grandeur, see A. Stewart (1990: vol. I, 45).

[13] Paus. 8.37.3; Agorakritos' period of activity is dated to the 440s and 430s BCE. See Dickins (1906–7: 396–7), A. Stewart (1979: 57; 1990: 94–5, 169) and Pollitt (1986: 165).

[14] R. R. R. Smith (1991: 241); A. Stewart (1979: 57), citing Becatti (1940: 43).

[15] A. Stewart (1990: 94–5).

[16] The term can be translated variously as 'having breath', 'alive' or 'animated'. See, e.g., *Anth. Pal.* 9.715.2, 740.3, 741.4, 742.4, 793.2, *Anth. Plan.* 30.

is enhanced by the more 'baroque' elements that have been identified in the figures, such as the slight torsion of Demeter's and Artemis' bodies and the Titan's deep-set eyes and writhing locks of hair.[17] Their very currency imparts the figures with a sense of contemporaneity that vitalises their more conservative aspects for Hellenistic viewer-worshippers; past and present are brought together in a way that derives venerability from traditional forms while generating a sense of fresh encounter through the dynamic techniques of the new.[18] Damophon's stylistic eclecticism is thus driven by a theological impulse that is entirely related to the demands of its immediate sacred context, while at the same time exhibiting features characteristic of the allusive cultural play so commonly defined as 'Hellenistic'.[19] In this way his careful selection of stylistic elements effectively mobilised the visual language of epiphany in order to make Despoina and her divine companions present for their worshippers within the sanctuary.

That Damophon was considered particularly successful in this enterprise is demonstrated by a second-century inscription from Messene, probably set up after the artist's death, which preserves a series of civic decrees in his honour.[20] Inscribed on a fluted column over three metres high discovered within the Messenian Asclepieion, the text provides evidence for the activities of 'Damophon son of Philip' not only in the Peloponnese (including Lykosoura), but as far afield as the Ionian islands of Leukas and Kephallenia and the Cycladic islands of Kythnos and Melos.[21] The people of Kythnos, in

---

[17] For a justification of the use of the anachronistic term 'baroque' to define these features in Hellenistic sculpture, see A. Stewart (1993: 133–7).

[18] Cf. Themelis (1996: 180), on the Lykosoura sculptures, and Kousser (2005), on the significance of a neoclassical and Hellenistic synthesis of styles for the Aphrodite of Melos: 'The end result was a visually compelling work that appeared deeply rooted in the past but also vividly contemporary' (238). On stylistic retrospection, see Fullerton (2003).

[19] E.g., Pollitt (1986: 14–16), Gelzer (1993: 144–7), Fantuzzi and Hunter (2004: esp. 1–17), Bing and Bruss (2007: 373–517) and Gutzwiller (2007: 168–78).

[20] See Themelis (1994, 1996: 168–78) and *SEG* 39.380, 40.364 and 48.488. Inscribed dedications by Damophon and his relatives have also been found at Lykosoura itself (*IG* 5.2.539 and 540), Messene (*IG* 5.1.1443) and Megalopolis (*IG* 5.2.454, above, n. 11), where Pausanias tells us he made a cult group of Demeter and Kore Soteira, accompanied by two female statues identified as either Athena and Artemis or (less likely) the daughters of Damophon, plus an acrolithic Aphrodite and a wooden Hermes (8.31.1, 5). On a posthumous date of *c.* 150 for the Messenian inscription, see Matthaiou's edition of *IG* 9.².1.4. 1475. On the phenomenon of *Ehrentafeln* (epigraphic monuments that collect multiple decrees in honour of an individual into one inscription), see Ma (2007: 212); on the uniformity of civic decrees across the Hellenistic world, see Billows (2003: 197).

[21] The decrees are from the cities of Lykosoura (*SEG* 41.332; see Themelis, 1996: 169–74, and my discussion below), Kythnos (*SEG* 49.423; see Themelis, 1996: 176–8), Krane on Kephallenia (*IG* 9².1.4.1583, *SEG* 51.467), Leukas (*IG* 9².1.4.1475, *SEG* 51.466); see Themelis, 1996: 174–6), Oiantheia (Themelis, 2003), Melos and Gerenia (both unpublished). Height given by Damaskos (1999: 45–6).

particular, praise Damophon for his virtuous character, goodwill to the city and *theosebeia*, or 'reverent attitude towards the gods' (102–3). How is this manifested? By a statue he has made for the Kythnian sanctuary of Aphrodite (presumably of the goddess herself), which is 'most excellently fashioned by his skill' (ἐ]τεχνωσέν τε κα[ὶ] ἄριστον) and set in place under his personal supervision (106–7).[22] Likewise, the people of Leukas praise Damophon for employing all the *technai* at his command to create an *agalma* of Aphrodite Limenarchis for her sanctuary that is 'worthy of both goddess and polis' (τὸ ἄγαλμα] ἄξι|ον τᾶς τε θεοῦ καὶ τᾶ[ς πόλιος, 12–13). Both cities heap numerous honours upon the sculptor, granting him the titles of *euergetēs* (benefactor) and *proxenos* (status as their official local representative) and, in the case of Kythnos, *asylia* (inviolability).[23] In both decrees the language of artistic skill (*technē*) is explicitly related to Damophon's religious and civic sensibilities, implying that the stylistic synthesis he employed as an *agalmatopoios* satisfied ritual, political and aesthetic expectations with particular efficacy.

In this sense Damophon may not have been vastly different from the *agalmatopoioi* throughout the Greek world who fulfilled commissions for large-scale cult images in Phidias' wake.[24] What is most striking about the decrees, however, is the evidence they provide for not just the commissioning of new cult images by traditional Greek poleis in the second century, but also the development of an epigraphic language through which to draw attention to the creative act itself. The allusion to both *technē* and *theosebeia* explicitly encourages the viewer-worshipper to combine his or her sense of encounter with the deity represented with an evaluative judgement of the artist's work, in which sculptural skill, iconography and presentation are dependent on a sense of what is appropriate for, or 'worthy of', the god. Significantly, each decree was inscribed in both the collective document at Messene (which was also adorned by Damophon's *agalmata*), and the individual sanctuary to which it referred. Each text, then, functioned as both an honour to the artist and a guide to viewing his works *in situ*.

In contrast to literary engagements with the concept of the *agalmatopoios* (which I explore in Chapter 4), these epigraphic texts do not overtly

---

[22] Themelis (1996) interprets the decree to refer to a statue of Aphrodite, and identified fragments of a standing, semi-nude cult statue discovered close to her sanctuary on Kythnos.

[23] On the language of benefaction in the Hellenistic period, see Gauthier (1985) and Ma (1999: 179–214); on *proxeny* see Walbank (1982: 148–9), Gauthier (1985: 129–48), Herman (1987: 130–42) and Austin (2006: 104); on *asylia* and Hellenistic civic decrees, see Rigsby (1996) and my discussion below, 151–4.

[24] On these, see Faulstich (1997: 43–104) and Lapatin (2001: 96–121).

problematise the relationship between cult images and their makers. Nor do they suppress the artist's role in the production of sacred images, unlike the concepts of the *xoanon* or *palladion* that I traced in Chapter 2. On the contrary, they reveal a culture in which ritual modes of viewing and practices of connoisseurship coexist, and awareness of an artist's identity and working methods is considered to enhance the status and religiosity of his creations.[25] That such a clear emphasis on the coexistence of *technē* and *theosebeia* is possible in the Hellenistic world is due to both a greater self-consciousness about modes of viewing (eagerly documented in recent scholarship), and the inherently nostalgic nature of religious modes of representation.[26] If Phidias and his contemporaries had defined an epiphanic visual language for classical Greece, then its continuous appropriation and adaptation by subsequent generations acted to validate this mode and to wrap its epiphanic authority in skeins of cultural allusion. The conjuring of divine presence by means of visual representation was thus simultaneously an act of visual quotation and adaptation; to quote correctly rested on a piety that necessarily looked to earlier models that had gained cognitive reliability as 'true' forms of the deities they depicted. In this respect it is no accident that Damophon was also chosen to repair Phidias' statue of Zeus at Olympia, which functioned as the most authoritative embodiment of godhead in the post-classical Greek world.

The epiphanic authority of Hellenistic *agalmatopoioi* may have rested in their technical ability and familiarity with the works of the past, but, perhaps more crucially, it was also dependent on the recognition of such pious applications of skill by patrons and viewers. The display of Damophon's honorific decrees in the sanctuaries he adorned, for instance, suggests that the reading of each text was considered an important component of each statue's viewing. The inscription itself acted within the sanctuary as a physical testimony to the ritual and aesthetic efficacy of its most holy *agalmata*.[27] Damophon's epiphanic creations are thus rendered inseparable from Damophon himself, and the civic machinery in which he was invested as citizen and craftsman. The symbiotic relationship between artist and cult image is further ramified by the decrees of Leukas and Lykosoura, which each proclaim that the

---

[25] Compare the viewing of sacred images *in situ* by ordinary worshippers in Herodas 4 and Theocritus 15, in which religious sensibilities intersect with 'connoisseurial' comments on votive objects: see Goldhill (1994).

[26] See, e.g., Goldhill (1994), Chaniotis (1997), G. Zanker (2004, with Elsner, 2005), Tanner (2006: 205–76), Newby (2007b) and my discussion in Chapter 4, with further bibliography.

[27] On the symbolic display of civic decrees in sacred contexts, and the status of the inscription itself as an inscribed performance, see R. Osborne (1999), on classical Athens.

honours paid to the sculptor are to be inscribed together with a bronze portrait (εἰκόνι χαλκέαι) of Damophon, to be set up in the sanctuaries of Aphrodite Limenarchis and Despoina respectively.[28] In this way, a mimetic *eikōn*, or 'likeness', of the artist would have been juxtaposed with the divine *agalmata* he himself had created, making Damophon visibly present within each sanctuary as both an eternal viewer of his own works and himself a focus of *theōria*.[29] This emphasis on the artist's visibility is made most explicit in the Lykosoura decree. After praising Damophon for waiving a large part of his fee for the creation of the Despoina group and for making a statue of Artemis Hagemone for the same sanctuary (1–21), the text then lists the honours heaped upon him by the city in return for his largesse (21–46).[30] The sculptor is proclaimed a *euergetēs*, granted *proxeny* and *asylia* for himself and his sons, and awarded a crown, a public eulogy and proclamation to various local games. Most strikingly, the inscription and bronze portrait testifying to these honours are to be set up in the sanctuary of Despoina ἐν τῶι ἐπιφανεστάτωι τόπωι, in 'a site of the *highest visibility*' (35–6, 46).[31] At Messene (where the inscribed catalogue of decrees was actually found) the artist's presence may have been accentuated still further, if Petros Themelis is correct in identifying a heroon close to the Asclepieion as Damophon's actual tomb.[32] Here, in the artist's home city, we find a literal *sēma* of his body that trumps the mere *eikones* of Leukas and Lykosoura by investing him with nigh-heroic honours.[33]

---

[28] Leukas (*IG* 9².1.4.1475): εἰκόνι χαλκ[έαι, 22. Lykosoura (*SEG* 41.332): εἰκόνι χαλκέαι, 33, 43. On the display of portraits in Hellenistic sanctuaries and their religious significance, see Krumeich (2007).

[29] See Damaskos (1999: 305–9) on the different uses of *agalma* and *eikōn* in the Hellenistic period.

[30] On the high sums of money (3,546 silver tetradrachms) involved in this transaction and their political significance, see Themelis (1996: 169–71). On the increasing significance of individual financial participation in cult activity in the Hellenistic period, see Mikalson (2006: 215–16). On the function of portraits within the reciprocal honours system of the Greek polis, see Höghammar (1993), Wörrle (1995), P. Zanker (1995b: 40–89, with R. R. R. Smith, 1999; 1995b), Ma (2006, 2007) and Platt (2007b).

[31] The inscription to be displayed with Damophon's portrait reads: Ἁ [πόλις ἁ Λυκουρα]|σίων ἀνέθηκε Δαμ[οφῶντα Φιλίππου Μεσ]|σάνιον τόν τοῦ τε ἱε[ροῦ καὶ τᾶς πόλιος εὐερ]|γέταν [..]αρύσαντ[..] ἀεὶ ἐν τῶι ἀγῶνι τῶν | Νεμέων καὶ Λυκαίων καὶ [- - - Μεσ]|σανίων Ἰθωμαίων [- - - - - - - - -] | τῶν Λυκουρασίων [- - - Δαμοφῶντα Φιλίππου] | Μεσσάνιον εἰκόνι χαλκέαι καὶ εἶναι [πρό]|ξενον καὶ εὐεργέταν, στᾶσαι δὲ τὰν εἰ|κόνα ἐν Λυκοσούραι ἐν τῶι ἱερῶι τᾶς Δεσ|ποίνας ἐν τῶι ἐπιφανεστάτωι τόπωι (*SEG* 41.332, 36–46).

[32] Themelis (1996: 168–9), on the basis of the discovery of fragments of the inscribed column in this area. Boehringer (2001: 278), Fröhlich (2007: 108–10) and Luraghi (2008: 284) all express some dissatisfaction with this hypothesis, however.

[33] On *sēma* as both 'tomb' and 'sign', see Svenbro (1993: 17–18).

The politics of *epiphanēs*: making manifest in Hellenistic Greece

The juxtaposed *sēmata* of artist and deity at these cultic locations and the use of the curious phrase *epiphanestatos topos* at Lykosoura typify Hellenistic attitudes to the semiotics of the sacred in three significant ways: they highlight the cultural contribution of the artist; they demonstrate an intensified interest in the language of manifestation; and, implicitly, they point to the religious and political capital offered by the semiotics of epiphany to Hellenistic cities and their rulers. Each of these can be related to broader trends we see elsewhere in the Greek *oikoumenē*.

First, Damophon's visual and epigraphic prominence demonstrates a desire on the part of civic institutions to emphasise the artist's role in the construction, preservation and enhancement of a sanctuary's sacred status. This positive attitude to the sculptor's contribution is most interesting at a time when Phidias' reputation as an embezzler was being enshrined in the historiographic record by Atthidographers such as Philochorus (who was writing in the third century BCE).[34] While Phidias' name certainly seems to have been inscribed on or near his chryselephantine images at Athens and Olympia, the only mention of his portrait is related to the scandalous notion that he concealed his own features within the Amazonomachy on the Parthenos' shield.[35] At first glance, these attitudes to Damophon and Phidias might seem mutually contradictory, the former a product of ritual modes of viewing preserved in an epigraphic medium (and unattested in any literary sources except Pausanias), the latter expressed in historiographical texts produced by an intellectual elite. Yet a heightened anxiety about Phidias' reputation as the ultimate *agalmotopoios* is understandable in the light of fifth-century influence over Hellenistic visualisations of the divine: Phidias' piety (and therefore authority) is questioned precisely because he was held responsible for the epiphanic neoclassicism with which so many deities were subsequently 'made present' for Hellenistic viewer-worshippers by contemporary artists such as Damophon. Both attitudes demonstrate a self-consciousness about the act of viewing a sacred image that goes hand in hand with what Hans-Ulrich Cain has identified as an emphasis on the *museale*, or 'Museum-style', presentation of Hellenistic cult statues, according to which large, ornate creations were displayed in small but highly decorated

---

[34] Scholion to *Peace* 605 = *FGrH* 328 F121: see Chapter 2, n. 121.
[35] Pseudo-Aristotle *De mundo* 6 (= 399b–400a), Cic. *Tusc.* 1.15.34, Valerius Maximus 8.14.6, Apuleius *De mundo* 32, Plutarch *Pericles* 31.4: see Chapter 2, n. 119.

cultic shrines (as we see at Lykosoura), commanding the viewer's attention in naturalistic, narrative-driven compositions that echoed the theatrical staging of divine presence in religious festivals.[36] To this we should add the nostalgic force of neoclassicism, which invested contemporary images with sacred authority (thus generating a sense of immediate encounter with the divine), while encouraging a sense of historicity that complicated the viewing process by inserting allusions to mortal creativity between god and worshipper.

This blend of epiphanic quotation (itself an oxymoron) and artistic prominence is not confined to Hellenistic *agalmata*, but is also found in other media such as relief sculpture. For example, scholars have often commented on the classicising elements that are incorporated into the wild 'baroque' of the gigantomachy frieze from the Great Altar at Pergamon (which is roughly contemporary with the works of Damophon).[37] This is particularly notable on the faces of the gods, whose impassive expressions and rounded proportions look to fifth-century forms, harnessing the iconography of *sophrosunē*, or 'self-control', in order to convey divine detachment from the passions that govern their enemies.[38] As at Lykosoura, these retrospective stylistic elements are transposed into a new cultural idiom that makes emphatic use of contemporary styles and techniques. While the frieze's neoclassicisms have been justifiably related to the Attalids' desire to establish cultural authority for their young kingdom by looking to the dominant models of the Greek mainland (especially Athens), it is important to remember the function of the structure they adorn.[39] If the Pergamon Altar (as current thinking concurs) is indeed an altar rather than

---

[36] See H.-U. Cain (1995: esp. 123–4) on the Asclepieion at Messene, where Damophon's sculptures were displayed in a series of open rooms on the west side of the *temenos* (on which see also Themelis, 1996). On theatricality in Hellenistic civic and religious life, see also Pollitt (1986: 4–7), Coleman (1996), Chaniotis (1997) and I. Petrovic (2007: 124–7).

[37] On the Pergamene baroque as a 'historically conscious style', see A. Stewart (1993). On the altar's date, see most recently A. Stewart (2000), who reviews the various arguments, and Queyrel (2005: 123–5). Pottery from the site gives us a *terminus post quem* of 185–170 BCE, while the earliest securely dated dedication was set up by 149/8. It was therefore probably commissioned under Eumenes II (r. 197–158), and possibly dedicated (perhaps still incomplete) under Attalos II (r. 158–138). See Callaghan (1981), M. Kunze (1990) and Schmidt (1990) for the argument that it was commissioned following defeat of the Macedonians in 168 and the Celts in 166; see Hoepfner (1996) for an earlier date following the Peace of Apameia in 188.

[38] See Pollitt (1986: 105), who compares the small mouth and circular head of the figure identified as Nyx (on the north frieze) with the Parthenon sculptures, and A. Stewart (1993: 162), who suggests the contrast between classicising gods and baroque giants emphasises 'the horror and quasi-Manichaean dualism of the conflict'.

[39] On Pergamon's lack of cultural authority, see A. Stewart (1993: 166) and Gruen (2000).

a heroon, then, like a cult statue, it was also the focus of ritual activity related to the gods.[40] The classicising forms of the Olympians and their allies on the frieze thus garner their visual and theological force from the *sacred* authority of their models, which is inseparable from their status as avatars of Greece's cultural flowering in the fifth century.

This union of religious and cultural concerns is demonstrated by the well-known section of the altar's east frieze depicting Zeus and Athena (Figures 3.6–7). Springing apart from each other in a dramatic pair of diagonal forces, the gods most strikingly recall the central composition of the west pediment of the Parthenon, in which Athena and Poseidon battled it out for the status of Athens' patron deity.[41] At Pergamon, Athena is paired with her father against the forces of hubris and barbarianism represented by the snaky-legged giants that rear between them, but the compositional allusion makes a pointed reference not only to a central myth of divine patronage in Greece's cultural centre, but also to an architectural framing device that is explicitly epiphanic in its desire to locate the gods within the sacred space of the Acropolis. At Athens, Poseidon and Athena would have been the first pair of deities encountered by any ritual procession to the Parthenon; at Pergamon, Zeus and Athena faced the city walls in such a way that they would have been the first deities encountered when approaching the altar's enclosure from the city or sanctuary of Athena. If Max Fränkel was right in arguing that the altar was dedicated to Zeus and Athena Nikephoros, then the classicising quotation is doubly epiphanic, for the structure was designed to define a space in which sacrifice could, indeed, make these deities present for the kings and people of Pergamon.[42] Significantly, the Nikephoria festival celebrated in Athena's honour at Pergamon seems to have been founded in response to an epiphany of the goddess in battle, while an inscription of 135 BCE relates Attalos II's foundation of a cult

---

[40] For the heroon argument, see Stähler (1978) and P. Webb (1998), dismissed by A. Stewart (2000: 35); for the altar argument, Linfert (1995: 140). On the difficulty of identifying the structure's function, see A. Stewart (2000: 32–3), who points out that the term *ara* employed by Ampelius (*Liber memorialis* 8.14) can also refer to hero shrines and honorific monuments.

[41] On the Parthenon's west pediment, see Brommer (1979: 39–44); on the Pergamene allusion, see Pollitt (1986: 105), A. Stewart (1993: 165) and Queyrel (2005: 157–60). On the epiphanic significance of the Parthenon pediments, see Chapter 2, 107.

[42] See *Inschr. Perg.* 1.69 with Fränkel *loc. cit.* The fragmentary nature of the dedicatory inscription has also led to suggestions that the altar was dedicated to Zeus alone, all the gods, Telephos, Agatha Tyche or Apollonis, mother of Eumenes and Attalos: see A. Stewart (2000: 34–9, with bibliography), who argues for a dedication to Zeus and Athena Nikephoros on the basis of dedications from the site, the proximity of the sanctuary of Athena and the prominent position of both deities in the east frieze. Queyrel (2005: 112–22) surveys the evidence and concludes that the altar was dedicated to the Twelve Gods and the divinised Eumenes II.

Figure 3.6 Section depicting Zeus from the east gigantomachy frieze of the Great Altar of Pergamon, first half of the second century BCE

Figure 3.7 Section depicting Athena from the east gigantomachy frieze of the Great Altar of Pergamon, first half of the second century BCE

of Zeus Sabazios in the sanctuary of Athena Nikephoros in response to the god's repeated *epiphaneiai*.[43] Neither of these events needs be directly related to the altar's foundation, yet the commemoration of both deities' manifestations in aid of their city establishes their divine patronage in terms that, like the gigantomachy frieze, echo the mythico-epiphanic traditions of cities such as Athens and mark the gods' presence within the Pergamene here and now.

The use of retrospective epiphanic citation is not the only parallel we find between the Pergamon altar and the sanctuary of Despoina at Lykosoura, for both sites also employ epigraphy in order to stress the contribution of the artist. On the Great Altar, the names, patronymics and cities of the sculptors who executed the frieze were displayed on the socle below their very works, while the identities of the deities within the frieze were inscribed on the entablature above, with those of the giants on the moulding below.[44] Together, these epigraphic texts provided a guide to viewing the figures with which they were juxtaposed, encouraging recognition of both the sacred knowledge that had influenced their design, and the skill that had facilitated their execution.[45] Significantly, the sculptors' ethnics tell us that while many were local, some also came from the production centres of Athens and Rhodes, standing in a long line of craftsmen trained in the venerable traditions of religious sculpture. The presence of their names makes a claim for the cultural authority of Pergamon itself as inheritor of this tradition, while the combination of stylistic allusion and learned labelling of gods and giants demonstrates the innovative religiosity of the city and its royal benefactors.[46] Again, *technē* and *theosebeia* are presented as mutually reinforcing. Knowledge of the gods in the present requires a fluency in the visual language of the past; in order to maintain cognitive

[43] Athena Nikephoros: see Segre (1948: 117). The victory may have been that over Philip V of Macedon in 201 BCE, or Prusias of Bithynia in 183. Zeus Sabazios: *OGIS* 331.51–2 (*Inschr. Perg.* 248.51–2): ἐκρίναμεν διὰ τὰς ἐξ αὐτοῦ | γενομένας ἐπιφανείας συγκαθιερῶσαι τῆι Νικηφόρωι Ἀθηναῖ. See also *Inschr. Perg.* 247.II.1–4, in which Attalos II prescribes sacrifices to Zeus Tropaios in response to an *epiphaneia* that seems to be connected to Attalos' victories over the Galatian Tolistoagians in 278/7. On the use of *epiphaneia* in such inscriptions, see below.

[44] On the names (*Inschr. Perg.* 70–85 with Fränkel *loc. cit.*), see Thimmer (1946), A. Stewart (1993: 159–60, 168), who relates the artists' epigraphic prominence to overt signs of facture (such as tool marks) on the frieze itself, and Queyrel (2005: 109–11).

[45] On the allegorical 'programme' structuring the frieze, see E. Simon (1975), who relates it to genealogies in Hesiod's *Theogony* arranged by the guiding hand of the Stoic Krates of Mallos, Pfanner (1979), who argues for a geographical arrangement, with the Olympians on the east, and Pollitt (1986: 109), R. R. R. Smith (1991: 164) and A. Stewart (1993: 158), who suggest the Stoic Kleanthes' lost epic poem *On Giants* as a possible source.

[46] On labelling in Hellenistic art, see Newby (2007b), on the Archelaos relief.

reliability, divine form is necessarily mediated by the guiding hand of a skilful craftsman. For this reason, Pergamon's artists, too, find themselves in an *epiphanestatos topos* within the sacred site they have adorned.

This brings us to my second point about Hellenistic semiotics of the sacred – their relationship to a keen interest in the language of manifestation, or visibility, in contemporary culture. What does *epiphanestatos topos* mean? And how is it connected to the notion of epiphany as a visible manifestation of the divine? In the Lykosoura decree the adjective *epiphanēs* is used to suggest 'visible' in a literal sense, referring to the position of Damophon's portrait within the sanctuary, rather than the epiphanic quality of the site itself. It is therefore in line with earlier Greek usage of the term, where *epiphanēs* can be used to mean 'appearing', 'in full view', 'conspicuous' and thus 'notable'.[47] Renée Koch Piettre has shown that *epiphanēs* was traditionally used in either a passive sense, to mean 'that which is laid open to view' (often found in geographical and medical texts), or applied in an active sense to 'dazzling', 'illustrious' and therefore exceptional individuals.[48] The term is employed with increasing frequency in the epigraphic and literary record from the third century BCE, particularly in its superlative form.[49] To be 'manifest' was considered an honour of the highest order, especially within the euergetic system of the Greek polis.[50] At Lykosoura it is explicitly related to Damophon's skill and experience as an *agalmatopoios* and his generosity to the city and sanctuary, reflecting his dynamic engagement in public life.[51] The emphatic focus on visibility in the Lykosoura decree also demonstrates the degree to which cult images and high-profile sacred commissions could function as a form of civic self-representation.[52] Whereas

---

[47] LSJ s.v. ἐπιφανής.

[48] Koch Piettre (1996: 392–3). On *epiphanēs* in geographical and medical texts, see also Pax (1955: 13–14), and examples at Diodorus Siculus 2.30.3 and Galen *De venae sectione adversus Erasistratum*, vol. XI, p. 184, 11 Kühn. For *epiphanēs* as 'illustrious', see, e.g., Herodotus 2.89 and Thucydides 2.43. For Diodorus Siculus, the pyramids are 'among the Seven Most Illustrious Works' (ἐν τοῖς ἑπτὰ τοῖς ἐπιφανεστάτοις ἔργοις), i.e., the Seven Wonders of the World (1.63.2).

[49] See, from hundreds of examples, *OGIS* 227.16 (also Welles, 1934: no. 22.16), dated *c*. 246 BCE, in which Seleukos II promises to raise the city of Miletus to 'a more illustrious state' (εἰς ἐπιφανεστέραν διάθεσιν ἀγαγεῖν), and *OGIS* 224.24–5 (also Welles, 1934: no. 36.24–5), dated *c*. 204 BCE, in which Antiochos III asks that letters detailing the cult of his wife Laodice be displayed 'in the most visible locations' (ἐν τοῖς ἐπιφανεστάτοις | τόποις). On the broad application of *epiphanēs* in such contexts, see Price (1984a: 87).

[50] See Billows (2003: 211–13).

[51] On Damophon's wealth and high social status in Messene and its neighbouring cities, see Themelis (1996: 184–5).

[52] See Lapatin (2001: 114, 119), on polis competition through the commissioning of chryselephantine cult statues, and H.-U. Cain (1995), on the ideological significance of cult statues for Hellenistic city-states.

the display of artists' names and origins at Pergamon served to advance the cultural and political interests of the Attalid kings, local pride in Damophon and his works in the Peloponnese reflected the ideological agenda of traditional cities on the Greek mainland, as they jostled for independence and influence amid the shifting alliances of the Aetolian and Achaean Leagues, under the threatening shadows of Macedon and Rome.[53] In both regions local political concerns and traditional religious practices and expectations unite as a driving force behind the commission, display and reception of such objects.

The phrase *epiphanestatos topos* therefore combines both the literal and metaphorical significance of *epiphanēs*. While it is used in practical terms to refer to the prime location of Damophon's portrait, it also conveys the illustrious nature of the *eikōn* awarded in his honour, perpetuating his own status as an *epiphanēs* individual within the Hellenistic Peloponnese (and, implicitly, the illustrious nature of the cities that commissioned him to represent their patron deities). Furthermore, epigraphic use of the term has an inherently reflexive quality: to draw attention to the portrait's visibility through the inscription of the phrase itself invests the text with a prominent visibility of its own. For while the inscription is a material record of both the artist's contribution and the city's capacity to award him honours, its very physical permanence means that it also functions as an honour itself.[54] This self-conscious concern with visible illustriousness, projected into public space by means of the traditional machinery of image and inscription, reflects the significance of *epiphanēs* in a broader context. For in addition to its topographic and honorific applications, *epiphanēs* was both employed as an epithet by Hellenistic kings and applied to the manifest divine. Together these uses of the term demonstrate a continuum of interest

[53] On the decree as a 'cardinal form of polis self-expression', see Ma (2003a: 81). The immediate political relevance of Damophon's high status in Messenia and Arcadia depends on the dates assigned to him. Themelis (1996: 167–71) sees his works as expressive of Messenian conservatism and nostalgia during its brief period of independence before it was forced to join the Achaean League in 182 BCE. Torelli (1998: 478–9) claims that Damophon's activities in cities of the Achaean League suggest he was part of a pro-Achaean faction in Messene during the late third century, while Luraghi (2008: 285) emphasises his links to cities of the Aetolian League such as Oinatheia and Krane, and concurs with Müth (2007: 183–5), who dates Damophon's Messenian sculptures to the period of peace between the leagues after 182 and prior to the Achaean War against Rome in 146. On the political identity of Arcadia in this period, see Pretzler (2005), who mentions similar local honours awarded to Polybius, who came from Megalopolis (Polybius 39.3.3–5.6, Paus. 8.30.8–9, 8.37.2, 8.44.5, 8.48.8).

[54] See Ma (1999: 184; 2007: 219): 'Inscription, both in the form of the formula on the statue base and the extended honorific decree, does not only embed an image within a constraining social context, but also functions as a story about this process of embedding.' Cf. Corbeille (2006), on the visibility of inscribed text in Rome.

in the language of manifestation and its strategic potential that complicates any straightforward contrast between the sacred and secular, practical and metaphorical.

The title *Epiphanēs*, as adopted by Ptolemy V (204–180), Antiochos IV (175–164), Antiochus VI (145–142) and Seleukos VI (96–95), had contemporary influence precisely because it looked both to the honours system of the traditional polis (the praise of 'illustrious' individuals) and the superhuman powers of the divine.[55] Most importantly, it gave expression to the very means by which royal authority could be communicated and maintained – through the 'manifest' presence of the king as he achieved victory in war, made his *epidēmia* (or 'divine arrival') among his subjects, was laid open to view in state pageantry, was honoured in the rituals of ruler cult, and was viewed in the form of his image, whether sacred *agalma*, honorific *eikōn* or numismatic portrait.[56] The blurring of honorific and divine qualities in the title *Epiphanēs* accords precisely with the ambiguous status that Hellenistic kings held as the recipients of *isotheoi timai* – honours equal to those that were bestowed upon the gods.[57] While kings may not have held the same transcendent status as deities, the *timai* awarded to them and the powers they wielded over human affairs as saviours (*sōtēres*), benefactors and liberators invested them with a divine *agency*.[58] Like the gods,

---

[55] The title was also officially adopted by Nicomedes II of Bithynia (149–127) and Ariarathes VI of Cappadocia (120–111). It is first attested on the Rosetta Stone (dated 196 BCE) as a title of Ptolemy V: Pfister (1924: 308–9) and Nock (1972: vol. I, 152–6). On the use of the epithet by Antiochos IV, see Mittag (2006: 128–39), who emphasises the importance of his additional epithet *Theos* ('divine'); on Ptolemy V, see Nock (1972: vol. I, 147), who downplays the title's Egyptian associations, and Koenen (1993: 65), on its similarity to the Egyptian notion of the pharaoh as the god 'who comes forward'; on the application of *epiphanēs* and *epiphanestatos* to the Roman emperors, see Price (1984a: 86–8), who emphasises that the title 'is not a uniquely religious term', and La Rocca (1994).

[56] On Hellenistic ruler-cult and its function in the traditional Greek city, see L. Robert (1966), Habicht (1970), Nock (1972: vol. I, 134–59, 202–51), Price (1984b: 25–40), Walbank (1984: 87–98; 1987), Gauthier (1985: 42–7), Ma (1999: 219–26) and Chaniotis (2003, with further bibliography). On the importance of images for the visual projection of royal ideology and kingly presence, see R. R. R. Smith (1988, 1993), A. Stewart (1993), M. Bergmann (1998: 13–84) and Kroll (2007). On the distinction between *eikōn* and *agalma* (not always strictly maintained) in ruler cult, see Walbank (1984: 87–8). On *epidēmia* as a form of epiphany, see Petridou (2006: 230–3).

[57] See Nock (1972: 724–5), Price (1984a: 88; 1984b: 48–9) and Irskine (2003: 433).

[58] On Greek conceptions of divinity as 'an unstructured abstract signifying varying levels and nuances of power' (Delia, 1993: 197), see Price (1984b), Goedicke (1986: 57–8) and Gradel (2002: esp. 28–31). On the divine connotations of the title *Sōtēr*, adopted by Ptolemy I (305–283), Ptolemy IX (116–107), Antiochos I (281–261), Seleukos III (226/5–223), Demetrios I (162–150), Demetrios III (95–88), Attalos I (241–197) and Eumenes II (197–159/8), see Nock (1972: 720–35) and R. R. R. Smith (1988: 50). On *theoi sōtēres* as epiphanic deities, see Koch Piettre (1996: 430–61).

Hellenistic rulers were able to bypass the normal constraints within which their subjects were bound to operate; as Arthur Darby Nock points out, Ἐπιφανής as a divine epithet 'implies . . . the making of sudden ἐπιφανεῖαι, appearances in person or manifestations of power', conveying an immediacy and unpredictability that is characteristic of divine epiphany.[59] Yet, like the gods, kings were also drawn by their subjects into a reciprocal series of ritual honours and commitments that nevertheless sought to constrain and rationalise that power.[60] Significantly, divine honours were usually awarded by cities rather than the kings themselves.[61] The emphasis on visibility in the title *Epiphanēs* thus expresses the king's godlike agency in visual terms, yet is offset by an emphasis on visibility in the civic machinery by which relationships between kings and their subjects were played out: the strategic use of spectacle works both ways. In this sense the king's external manifestations of authority are balanced by civic rituals, festivals, inscriptions and images, in a relationship that echoes the more traditional bond between externally generated epiphany and internally generated ritual response that I traced in Chapter 1.[62]

This double significance of *epiphanēs*, as both a divine quality of kings and a tangible quality of civic government, offers a productive means of interpreting the epiphanic language of a text that has long troubled historians of religion. In the infamous Athenian *Hymn to Demetrius Poliorcetes*, dated to 291/0 and preserved by Athenaeus as an example of the ultimate degradation of 'the victors at Marathon', the general is welcomed as a divine liberator, in line with his reception in 307/6 BCE when, having rescued Athens from servitude to Cassander and driven out the 'tyrant' Demetrius of Phaleron, he was hailed as a 'benefactor' (*euergetēs*) and 'saviour' (*sōtēr*).[63]

---

[59] Nock (1972: 154). Here the association between *epiphanēs* and *phaō*, 'to give light, shine, beam, especially of heavenly bodies' (LSJ s.v. φάω) is important: see R. R. R. Smith (1988: 42, 50), Koenen (1993: 65), who notes similarity between Ptolemaic use of *Epiphanēs* and manifestations of the Egyptian sun-god Re, and Mittag (2006: 128–39), who stresses the astral symbolism employed by Antichos IV Epiphanēs, especially in his use of a radiate crown, on which see R. R. R. Smith (1991: 42) and M. Bergmann (1998: 61–6).

[60] This two-way relationship is subtly traced by Ma (1999: 179–242), on Antiochos III and the cities of Asia Minor, summarised in Ma (2003a). On the Hellenistic king as benefactor, see also Bringmann (1993).

[61] Chaniotis (2003: 439–40).

[62] On the king as a manifestation of power external to the Greek city, see Price (1984: 30).

[63] Athenaeus 6.253e = *FGrH* 76 F13, quoted by Duris of Samos and attributed to the otherwise unknown poet Hermocles or Hermippus. Demetrius is hailed with the titles *Euergetēs* and *Sōtēr* in Plutarch *Demetrius* 9.1. For relations between Demetrius and Athens, see Habicht (1970: 44–55) and Mikalson (1998: 75–104). On the Athenian cult of Demetrius and Antigonus Sōtēres and Demetrius' other cultic honours, see Scott (1928a, 1928b) and Mikalson (1998: 78–104). On hymns in Hellenistic ruler-cult, see Dunand (2002: 70).

The Athenians contrast the manifest presence of the king (σεμνόν τι φαίνεθ' – 'what a holy sight!', 9) with the absence of the 'other gods', who 'are far away, or do not have ears, or do not exist, or pay us no attention' (15–17). Demetrius' divine status is thus explicitly expressed in terms of his immediate visibility: 'We see your very presence (σὲ δὲ παρόνθ᾽ ὁρῶμεν), not in wood or stone, but in truth (ἀληθινόν)' (18–19). The *parousia* facilitated by his earthly corporeality is cast as a virtue in contrast to the elusiveness of divine form, which can be made present only through the metonymic strategies of statuary.[64]

The text has been interpreted as an example of religious crisis in the Hellenistic period (prompted by the great upheavals generated by conflict between the *Diadochoi*), as an expression of callow Athenian sophistry and even as an articulation of incipient atheism; as John Ma writes, it inevitably appears in accounts of Hellenistic ruler-cult as 'a compulsory tut-tutting quote'.[65] Yet read as a strategic employment of the language of manifestation, the hymn actually has more in common with contemporary religious modes of expression than might first appear. It begins with the statement that 'The greatest and most beloved of the gods are present (πάρεισιν) in the city' (1–2), including Demeter, who has made her *epidēmia* together with her protégé to perform the Eleusinian mysteries (5–6). The claim that 'the other gods are far away' does not then refer to *all* the gods, but only those who are not primarily concerned with Athens. Significantly, all the evidence suggests that Demetrius' cult at Athens supplemented traditional religious practice rather than supplanted it: he supposedly inhabited the Parthenon as a *sunnaos theos* with Athena rather than as her successor, for example.[66] In the context of the hymn, Demetrius is addressed as a present god precisely because of his ability to influence the city's fate, specifically to protect the polis against the Aetolian 'Sphinx' threatening Attica from its base in central Greece (20–9).[67] The opening χαῖρε section (1–19), which establishes Demetrius' claim to godlike status, is therefore immediately followed by a prayer, which

---

[64] On *parousia* as an epiphanic term, see Pfister (1924: 278) and Koch Piettre (1996: 384–7); on epiphanic language in the *Hymn to Demetrius*, see Weinreich (1926: 647) and Chaniotis (2003: 431–3); on the hymn's significance for Hellenistic interest in epiphany as spectacle, see Koch Piettre (in press).

[65] Ma (2003a: 179). See, e.g., Dodds (1951: 242) 'When the old gods withdraw, the empty thrones cry out for a successor, and with good management, or even without management, almost any perishable bag of bones may be hoisted into the vacant seat' (quoted by Price, 1984b: 37 n. 58). On the hymn's potential atheism, see Dunand (2002), who ultimately rejects this interpretation; on its possible relationship to Euhemerism, see Price (1984b: 38–9).

[66] Plutarch *Demetrius* 23.3: see Scott (1928a, 1928b) and Nock (1972: vol. I, 204).

[67] On Aetolian prominence in this period, see Grainger (1999) and my discussion below.

asks him to bring peace (21–34). In this way the epiphanic language of the opening lines works to bind the ruler into the reciprocal honours system of the city. The hymn itself functions as part of this *do ut des* exchange, for each performance of the text confirms the illustriousness of its addressee in a way that boosts the very claim made in its opening lines. Demetrius is *epiphanēs* not just because of his godlike agency, but also because the Athenians make him so.[68]

But what of the contrast between the 'real' Demetrius and gods 'of wood and stone'? Do we find here an implicit rejection of traditional image-worship, along the lines of Xenophanes? Arguably the hymn presents a wilfully reductive mode of viewing the material *sēmata* of divine presence that underlines the arbitrariness of the representational bond between a deity and his or her image, making an explicit play on the contrast between 'wooden' (λίθινον) and 'true' (ἀληθινόν, 19). Yet it does so in service of an alternative form of material manifestation that is concentrated in the 'merry, beautiful and laughing' body of the king (7–8), rather than an argument about the transcendent nature of the divine. Whereas traditional hymns employ the language of epiphany in order to make sense of the elusive, shifting nature of divine form (as we saw in the *Homeric Hymns*), the *Hymn to Demetrius* compares absent deities and present ruler in order to make sense of the religious and political challenges raised by ruler cult. In both cases self-consciousness about the accessibility of divine form is rooted in the hymn's politics of praise. The Athenian hymn's claim for the ontological inferiority of sacred images does not, therefore, constitute an outright rejection of image worship, but merely intensifies the dilemmas intrinsic to the relationship between divinity and materiality in order to stress the epiphanic force of Demetrius' corporeality. For what kings lacked in terms of immortality, they made up for by their manifest presence, as the most *epiphanestatoi* of *theoi*.

As we saw in Chapter 2, the relationship between gods and their images could be construed in a variety of ways in antiquity, many of which allowed for the fact that deities operated independently of their material *sēmata*, for an image's epiphanic aura is always in tension with the potential for direct encounter with the god it denotes. Hellenistic evidence suggests a particular self-consciousness about this distinction, which is demonstrated by the language of *technē* in Damophon's epigraphic corpus as well as the contrast between image and prototype drawn by the *Hymn to Demetrius*.[69]

---

[68] Athenaeus comments that the song was so popular the Athenians even sang it at home (6.253e).
[69] This concept is explored in more detail in Chapter 4.

While this need not reflect a decline in religiosity, the notion of presence that drives the *Hymn to Demetrius* does suggest that traditional image-worship continued alongside an intensified desire for *unmediated* encounter with the divine. The 'other gods', as well as their royal flesh-and-blood counterparts, were required to be present 'in truth' (ἀληθινόν) for Hellenistic viewers. Accordingly, epigraphic evidence from the third to the first centuries BCE demonstrates that the language of manifestation employed in civic decrees and ruler cult was matched by an emphasis on the manifestations of gods themselves, as *theoi epiphanes*.[70] The stress on kingly presence in the *Hymn to Demetrius* is thus balanced in the contemporary record by a stress on divine presence, for while kings might have generated epiphanies, they were also witnesses to them (as Attalos II's foundation of the cult of Zeus Sabazios suggests). And while kings could be invoked as *sōtēres* by Greek cities, so could the Olympians themselves.

To traditional poleis precariously balanced between self-government and submission to a series of more centralised royal power-bases, epiphany offered a powerful diplomatic tool by which the blessings of divine presence could be tightly bound to issues of civic security and autonomy. Significantly, one of our earliest extant inscriptions referring to the epiphany of gods in war relates to the deliverance of Argos from Macedonia by Demetrius Poliorcetes in 303 BCE. Situated in the Argive sanctuary of Apollo Pythaeus, it refers to the dedication of statues of Apollo and Artemis to Leto, and promises a monthly sacrifice to commemorate Apollo's nocturnal expulsion of the Macedonian general Pleistarchus, brother of Cassander.[71] Wilhelm Vollgraff suggested that, although Demetrius is not mentioned by name in the inscription, he may be implicitly assimilated to Apollo.[72] Yet the most striking aspect of the text is that, in contrast to the Athenians' hymn, any potential allusions to ruler cult are firmly subordinated to the traditional

---

[70] On *Epiphanēs* as a divine epithet, see Picard (1912, 1922: 362–84), Steinleitner (1913: 15–21), on epigraphic evidence, Pfister (1924: 301), Pax (1955: 832–909), Troiani (1988: 49–52) and Koch Piettre (1996: 395–6). The term is employed in literary contexts by, e.g., Herodotus 3.27 (the epiphany of Apis) and Diodorus 1.17.20 (Isis and Osiris), 5.79.4 (the heroes Idomeneus and Merion) and 6.6.2 (the Dioscuri).

[71] Published by Vollgraff (1908) and revised by Picard (1912: 75–7) and Moretti (1967–2002: vol. I, no. 39). While Vollgraff read [ἐπιφ]ανεῖ[ς] θεο[ὶ] at line 2, Picard corrects this to ἔνθεοι, although the reference to Apollo's nocturnal epiphany still stands (Πλείσταρχον νύκ[τ]ωρ | ἐξήλασε Ἀπόλλων, 5–6). Vollgraff (1908: 240–1) reminds us that only thirty years later Demeter would be hailed by the Argives for murdering the invading Pyrrhus by hurling a tile from a rooftop (Paus. 1.13.8, 2.21.6). On Demetrius' activities in the Argolid in 304–2, see Billows (1990: 170–3). For a parallel inscription from Olymos which honours Leto in thanks for epiphanies of Apollo and Artemis, see *I. Mylasa* 895, published by Blümel (1989: 7–9).

[72] Vollgraff (1908: 240).

gods of the Olympian pantheon, who are made the focus of the Argives' ritual response. Apollo's liberation of the city is ascribed an aetiological force that stands in a long line of crisis epiphanies in Greek culture, such as the appearance of the Dioscuri at the River Sagra (555–540) or of Pan at Marathon (480).[73] The epigraphic commemoration of the event, however, reflects trends that would be particularly influential in Hellenistic Greece. The prominent acknowledgement of visible demonstrations of divine power in inscriptions both sacralised the language of manifestation and invested epiphany with a physical alternative to the image, preserving its elusive memory in the form of a material text that could function as both a religious and civic monument. In this way the visible agency of Hellenistic gods in their unmediated form (ἀληθινόν) would prove inseparable from their visibility on stone (λίθινον). The second half of this chapter explores the ways in which these epigraphic *sēmata* of divine presence were deeply implicated in wider forms of cultural, political and military activity in the Hellenistic world.

The epiphanic habit: monumentalising the language of manifestation

Strabo attributes the fame of the sanctuary of Asclepius at Epidaurus to both the 'manifest presence' (τὴν ἐπιφάνειαν) of Asclepius and 'the votive tablets (τῶν ἀνακειμένων πινάκων) on which his cures have been inscribed' (8.6.15). Like many of the epiphanic inscriptions that followed them, these fourth-century *pinakes* forged a close relationship between divine presence, sacred location and material object, in which the third element – the creation of a physical *sēma* of divine manifestation – played a key role in recording visionary experience and communicating it to other viewer-worshippers. As H. S. Versnel comments, the tablets give us our earliest extant example of 'the structural advertising function of miracles' within a Greek sanctuary, for these were not individual dedications (like the inscription set up by Meneia on the Athenian Acropolis discussed in Chapter 1), but constituted a carefully compiled and officially published 'body of evidence' for

---

[73] Dioscuri: Diodorus 8.32, Strabo 6.1.10.261, Justin 20.2–3. Pan: Herodotus 6.105, Paus. 8.54.6. These and other battle epiphanies are collected by Pritchett (1979: 11–46) and discussed by Speyer (1980), Giangiulio (1983), on the Sagra, and Petridou (2006: 97–117). On the significance of battle epiphanies of the Dioscuri in Graeco-Roman tradition, see Platt (in press a).

Asclepius' *aretai*.[74] In this sense the tablets anticipated Hellenistic catalogues of epiphanies, in which systematic documentation and categorisation gave credence to the phenomenon by chronicling the repeated manifestations of specific deities. At Epidaurus the inscribed cures derived their legitimacy from narratives of sceptics won over by Asclepius' manifest power and the sheer number of incorporated tales, as votive inscriptions and oral traditions were collected into an authoritative master-text.[75] From the third century, however, we start to see epigraphic catalogues that are more overtly integrated into civic life beyond the sanctuary and therefore make broader claims for epiphany's significance. A third-century inscription from Chersonesus on the Crimean peninsula, for example, commemorates the public reading of a work by one Syriskos, the son of Herakleidas, who 'wrote about the *epiphaneiai* of the Parthenos and investigated truthfully and appropriately for the city the existing privileges for the cities and the kings' (16–20).[76] For this service Syriskos has been publicly praised by the *boulē* and *dēmos* and awarded a golden crown. The inscription testifies to a series of epiphanies by the city's patron goddess, Tauric Artemis, which demonstrate her concern for her people; the relationship between the blessings conferred by her manifestations and the city's political affiliations; the painstaking documentation of these epiphanies by a respectable scholar – Syriskos has worked 'diligently' (φιλοπόνως, 3–4), 'truthfully' (ἀλαθινῶς, 19) and 'appropriately' (ἐπιεικέως, 20); the public performance of this work at Chersonesus; an official decree celebrating the work's composition and publication; and, finally, the commemoration of all these elements in epigraphic form.[77] In this way Artemis' appearances are given full ratification, inextricably tied to the religious authority of her sanctuary and the political status of the city through literary documentation, public performance, civic bureaucracy and inscribed monument.

The Chersonesus inscription is important evidence for several developments in attitudes to epiphany in the Hellenistic period. First, it alludes to the scholarly documentation of divine appearances. Syriskos' enquiry into

---

[74] Versnel (1990: 191). See Chapter 1, n. 22, on the Meneia inscription.

[75] On this process of priestly editing, see LiDonnici (1995: 40–9) and Petridou (2006: 153, 280–1).

[76] *IOSPE* I² 344 = *FGrH* 807 TI. Text from Chaniotis (1988: E7), translation adapted from Higbie (2003: 275–6). Lines 16–20: ὅτι τὰ]ς ἐπιφανείας τᾶς Πα[ρ]||[θένου ἔγρα]ψε καὶ τὰ ποτὶ τὰς [πό]||[λεις καὶ τοὺς] βασιλεῖς ὑπάρξ[αν]||[τα φιλάνθρωπα] ἱστόρησεν ἀλαθιν[ῶς] | [καὶ ἐπιεικέως] τᾶι πόλει. See also Rostovtzeff (1920: 203–6) and Petridou (2006: 124–8). See also Bresson (2006: 534–5), who dates the inscription to the first half of the third century.

[77] On the Chersonese cult of Tauric Artemis, see Ustinova (1999: 54–8), Bilde (2003) and Braund (2007). On Syriskos' historiographical virtues and role within the polis, see K. Clarke (2008: 248, 344–5, 369).

epiphanies of the Parthenos parallels the contemporary work of the Alexandrian author Istros, who we know published works listing the epiphanies of Apollo and Heracles (Ἀπόλλωνος ἐπιφάνειαι and Ἡρακλέους ἐπιφάνειαι), and Phylarchos, who is listed in the *Suda* as the author of a work 'On the Epiphanies of Zeus' (Περὶ τῆς τοῦ Διὸς ἐπιφανείας).[78] Despite their diverse locations, all three authors respond to an impulse to collect and preserve examples of divine manifestation that resonates with the broader encyclopaedic and paradoxographical interests of Hellenistic scholars.[79] Yet while the works of Istros (who seems to have been a member of Callimachus' circle) may have been more antiquarian in approach, divorced from a specific sacred context and more closely related to the burgeoning intellectual culture of a sophisticated urban elite in Alexandria, Syriskos' work is clearly related to the cult of Tauric Artemis and the religious and political concerns of Chersonesus. The inscription's reference to a public reading, in particular, suggests that catalogues of *epiphaneiai* not only were a serious subject of scholarship, but also had a significant part to play within lived religion, enhancing the sanctity of temples and festivals by confirming the power and immanence of their patron deities. As we shall see, this is also the case with the so-called 'Lindian Chronicle'.

The second significant development that the Chersonesus inscription charts is the use of the substantive noun *epiphaneia* to refer to divine manifestation.[80] Like *epiphanēs*, the term is used in pre-Hellenistic texts in a literal sense to mean 'that which is visible', often to indicate a surface. It is used by Democritus to mean 'plane', and thereafter is frequently employed in technical literature to refer to the external appearance of a body or object.[81] Koch Piettre comments that Strabo, for example, only uses *epiphaneia* in a religious sense to refer to Asclepius' presence at Epidaurus (as discussed above), and otherwise uses the term to mean 'surface', 'renown' or a

---

[78] For Istros, see *FGrH* 334 F50–3; on Phylarchos, see *FGrH* 81 T1 and J. Kroymann, *RE* Suppl. 8, 1956: 475. The *Suda* also lists a work Περὶ θείων ἐναργειῶν ('On Divine Appearances') by the second-century CE author Aelian. Epiphanies of local deities are also recounted by the second-century BCE author Leon of Samos (*FGrH* 540 T1, on Hera): see Chaniotis (1988: 53–4, 145–6, 308–9) and Petridou (2006: 7). On epigraphic evidence for regional sacred histories, including catalogues of epiphanies, see Boffo (1988), Chaniotis (1988), Isager (1998), Lloyd-Jones (1999), Wiemer (2001: 27–32), Shaya (2002: 26–35), Higbie (2003: 273–88), Dillery (2005) and K. Clarke (2008).

[79] See, e.g., Giannini (1966), Gabba (1981), Schepens and Delcroix (1996) and W. Hansen (1996, 1998).

[80] See Introduction, n. 54.

[81] Democritus fr. B155, followed by, e.g., Euclid 1 Df. 5 and 11 Df. 2: see Vlastos (1995: 293 n. 39) and Koch Piettre (1996: 396–8), who also notes Arist. *HA* 1.16, 494b19 (τὴν ἔξω ἐπιφάνειαν) and Polybius 6.23.3 (τὴν ἐκτὸς ἐπιφάνειαν).

'sudden striking appearance'.[82] Why, then, do we find *epiphaneia* employed in Hellenistic inscriptions to refer specifically to manifestations of divine presence? In order to document and publicise divine appearances in material form, Hellenistic cities and sanctuaries needed a concise, formulaic term that would capture the force and import of the divine agency they hoped to direct for strategic ends.[83] The language of epiphany in traditional texts such as the *Homeric Hymns* is by its very nature reticent and ambivalent, expressing both the elusive nature of divine form and the limitations of human subjectivity, while a term such as *opsis*, 'vision', as used in the Meneia inscription, focuses upon the passive experience of a single human viewer rather than the deity's will to appear (as is fitting in a private dedication).[84] In contrast, *epiphaneia* emphasises *active presence*, a 'coming into appearance' 'upon', 'near' or 'by' a mortal beholder that, crucially, occurs at the god's initiative.[85] Beyond this the term is conveniently ambiguous: although it suggests a visual experience of deity, *epiphaneia* gives a minimum of detail. It leaves open the possibility of single or multiple viewers, and is applied to a broad range of supernatural incursions into the everyday, from fully anthropomorphic visitations to extreme meteorological conditions.[86] The epigraphic use of *epiphaneia* thus leaves anything beyond the manifest nature of the event to the imagination of the reader, allowing the text to concentrate on the epiphany's immediate significance for the community – whether the safety and status of a city or sanctuary, or the vowing of appropriate honours for the deity in question. Most importantly, the substantive noun allows the fact of epiphany to be engraved concisely in stone, reifying and perpetuating divine presence while providing an accessible language within which to imagine such events in the future.

Epiphaneia thus provided a means of transforming the elusive, ephemeral nature of epiphany into a verbal and physical *sēma* of divine favour.

---

[82] Koch Piettre (1996: 397 n. 9): see, e.g., Strabo 8.6.15 (on Epidaurus, as above), 6.2.9 (an underground river rising to the 'surface' near Metaurus in Sicily), 8.3.30 (the 'fame' of Olympia) and 15.2.13 (the striking 'appearance' of elephants).

[83] On the sacred authority of the inscribed word, see Beard (1991) and Elsner (1996c).

[84] *IG* 2².4326 (*Syll.*³ 1151): see Chapter 1, 38–9. The participle ἐπιφανέντα is used only once to describe Asclepius' oneiric appearance in the fourth-century Epidaurian *iamata* (at A23), but ὄψις is far more common, appearing twenty-one times, reflecting the personal nature of each experience collected into the master-text. On the use of *opsis* in narratives of dream epiphany, see Chapter 6.

[85] On the importance of divine initiative in such contexts, see Potter (2003: 415).

[86] See below, on the ambiguous nature of the *epiphaneia* that expelled the Gauls from Delphi. *I. Stratonikeia* 10 (discussed below) is rare in the degree of detail it provides about the epiphanies of Zeus Panamaros, which include thunderstorms and, in an aural twist, the sound of snarling dogs and phantom troops. On individual and collective epiphanies, see Graf (2004b).

Moreover, as the Chersonesus inscription demonstrates, its formulaic quality allowed the phenomenon to be officially ratified by the machinery of state. While Syriskos claims the authority of rigorous scholarship, the significance of his work – and therefore the goddess's epiphanies – is confirmed by an official decree issued by the city's *boulē* and *dēmos*. Like the decrees in honour of Damophon, the text confirms the *technē* and *theosebeia* of Syriskos' work, and therefore the religious authority (or cognitive reliability) of its content. But this work is explicitly two-pronged: it documents the *epiphaneiai* of Artemis in order to confirm and reinforce certain political relations, calling attention to privileges (φιλάνθρωπα) designed to forge strategic alliances between Chersonesus and the kings of other Tauric states such as Bosporus, and so fend off Scythian invasion from the north.[87] In this respect the inscription's diplomatic function stands firmly within Hellenistic political tradition and anticipates high-profile epigraphic texts such as the declaration from Magnesia-on-the-Maeander, which records an epiphany of Artemis Leucophryene ('Of the White Brow') in 221 BCE.[88] Here we see the full ritual, diplomatic and economic significance invested in epiphany by vulnerable Hellenistic poleis, for Artemis' appearance (ἐπιφανοῦς δὲ γενομένης [Ἀρτέμιδος], 10–11) prompted an oracular consultation at Delphi that led not only to the foundation of a festival and games known as the Leucophryena in her honour, but also encouraged the Magnesians to seek recognition across the Hellenised world of their city's status as sacred and 'inviolable' (ἄσυλον, 32). The inscription records how, after their initial attempts were 'fobbed off', the Magnesians successfully persuaded the Greek cities and kings some time after 208/7 to accept the Leucophryena – now of crowned (stephanitic) status, equal to the Pythian Games – and to recognise their city's *asylia*.[89]

---

[87] As suggested by Molev (2003). See also Rostovtzeff (1920: 204–5), who emphasises Chersonesus' close relationship to its parent city Heraclea on the south shore of the Black Sea, and thus the kings of Bithynia. For an inscription dated *c.* 107 BCE commemorating the presence of the Parthenos to aid Chersonesus and the general Diophantos during Mithridates Eupator's war against the Scythians, see *IOSPE* 1² 352 (*Syll.*³ 709), translated by Bagnall and Derow (2004: no. 56) and discussed by Pritchett (1979: 38), Chaniotis (2005: 210–11) and Petridou (2006: 124–5).

[88] *IvM* 16 (*Syll.*³ 557), revised by Ebert (1982), Rigsby (1996: no. 66, with commentary) and again most recently by Slater and Summa (2006). Translated by Bagnall and Derow (2004: no. 153). See Dunand (1978), Gehrke (2001), Parker (2004) and further bibliography below.

[89] On Magnesia's first and second attempts to establish a stephanitic contest, see Slater and Summa (2006) and Thonemann (2007); for the reading 'fobbed off' (παρηλκύσθησ[αν, 24), see Rigsby (1996: 185–6) and Slater and Summa (2006: 276). On the concept and significance of *asylia* (the declaration of a place as 'sacred and inviolable' and therefore free from attack and spoliation, particularly by pirates or through excessive legal redress) in the Hellenistic world,

Displayed in the agora, the inscription makes a very public claim for Magnesia's position among the cities of the Greek East, relating its sacred and inviolable status directly to the epiphanic presence of its patron goddess. The epiphany's validity is ratified by several authorities: first, the epiphany's significance is explained by the Delphic oracle, an alternative form of active communication with the divine that confirms the authenticity of the original epiphany;[90] second, the epiphany's implications for the religious, cultural and political standing of Magnesia are confirmed by positive replies – also publicly inscribed – from cities located from Sicily to the Persian Gulf and from powerful kings, including Antiochos III, Philip V, Ptolemy IV and Attalos I.[91] In this way the language of divine manifestation was woven into the political, intellectual and physical fabric of civic life, and provided a diplomatic tool by which Magnesia's status might be communicated abroad.[92] In particular, Magnesia's request for *asylia* to apply not only to the sanctuary of Artemis but to the entire city reveals the very real influence that epiphany wielded over issues of state security (even if the request was not entirely successful).[93]

The Magnesian dossier crops up in almost every handbook to the Hellenistic period as an example of the politics of inviolability and the promotion or augmentation of games, festivals and other religious phenomena for political ends.[94] Less emphasis is laid, however, on the monumentality of the inscriptions themselves and their contribution to the physical fabric of the

see Chaniotis (1996), Rigsby (1996: esp. 179–279), on Magnesia, and Flashar (1999). On the significance of panhellenic games for Hellenistic states, see Parker (2004), and on the augmentation of festivals, including the Leucophryena, see Dunand (1978, 2003), Ebert (1982), Dušanić (1983) and Chaniotis (1991).

[90] On oracles as a source of authority and an 'active' form of religious activity, see Potter (1994: 12–13; 2003: 426–9).

[91] The decrees of acceptance are published by Kern as *IvM* 18–87 (see also *Syll.*³ 558–62) and re-edited with commentary by Rigsby (1996: nos. 67–131), excluding the fictional *IvM* 20, on which see Chaniotis (1999). See also Welles (1934: nos. 31–4), Bagnall and Derow (2004: nos. 154–5) and Austin (2006: nos. 189–90).

[92] The noun *epiphaneia* is used to refer to Artemis' appearance in several of the replies as part of the phrase ἐπιφάνειαν τῆς θεοῦ / τᾶς θεοῦ / τῆς θεᾶς / τῆς Ἀρτέμιδος / τᾶς Ἀρτέμιτος / τᾶς Λευκοφρυηνᾶς, including *IvM* 25b.8–9, 31.26, 32.14, 34.8, 35.7, 36.7, 37.15, 38.11, 39.13, 43.14, 44.12, 45.19, 46.8, 47.13, 48.7, 50.14, 53.19, 54.11, 61.35–6, 63.11, 71.7, 72.14, 86.6.

[93] See Welles (1934: 146) and Austin (2006: 342 n. 9), who point out that while every published reply welcomes the institution of games in Artemis' honour, the only king to acknowledge Magnesia's inviolability is Ptolemy IV, who had little territorial interest in the area. On the ambiguous significance of *asylia*, claimed in 'hope' and to honour a patron deity rather than as an official guarantee of immunity from war, see Rigsby (1996: 16–25) and Chaniotis (2005: 156–7). On the dossier's potential connection to a political collaboration between the Magnesians and Philip V, see Dušanić (1983).

[94] See, e.g., Giovannini (1993: 276–81) and Mikalson (2006: 217).

city. Over 60 responses survive out of a possible 90, with further lists of up to 100 cities that 'voted in the same way'. Displayed on the interior walls of the grand stoa that defined the west side of the agora, the replies both provided a magnificent testimony to the presence and authority of Magnesia's patron goddess and constituted a 'cognitive map' by which the city's diplomatic relations across the Hellenised world could be apprehended by citizens and visitors alike.[95] In occupying such a prominent position in the city's built environment, they also defined an important conceptual and rhetorical space for their viewers and readers, constructing a *milieu de mémoire* in which epiphany provided the catalyst for spectacular ritual, local history and international relations to coalesce.[96] Positioned opposite the entrance to the sanctuary of Artemis Leucophryene, the dossier also functioned as a civic counterpart and aetiological guide to the monumental altar and Ionic temple that were built shortly afterwards, the latter designed by the architect Hermogenes and considered one of the most beautiful in Asia Minor.[97]

Together with the enhanced Leucophryena, this flurry of building activity speaks of a community keen to establish and secure its status in a world that was rapidly recentring itself during the third century.[98] The strategic use of religious phenomena such as epiphany by Hellenistic states bears strong similarities to the contemporary evocation of mythical genealogies in inter-polis kinship diplomacy (such as Pergamon's use of the Arcadian-born hero Telephos on the Great Altar): both are forms of 'constructed' history, which, though deeply rooted in the religious and cultural imagination, also have immediate political application.[99] Indeed, the Magnesian dossier refers to

[95] *IvM* 11–12 and pl. 2. I borrow the phrase 'cognitive map' from Ma (2003a: 21). Cf. Rogers (1991: esp. 19–24), on Ephesus.

[96] Cf. J. K. Davies (2003), on the progressive monumentalisation of Greek epigraphy, and Elsner (1996c), on the monumentality of Augustus' *Res Gestae*. On *milieux de mémoire*, see Nora (1996–8: vol. I, xv–xxiv, 1–20), with Nelson (2003: 74): 'A *milieu de mémoire* is communal, belongs to public life, functions through a network of associations with diverse places, spaces, and groups, relies upon metonymic constructions, and, like human memory, condenses, abridges, alters, displaces, and projects fragments of the past, making them alive in the present for particular groups.'

[97] Strabo 14.1.40, Vitruvius 3.2.6, 7.*praef*.12. Hoepfner (1990) and Kreeb (1990) date the temple to the late third or early second century (and thus to the epiphany of Artemis and augmentation of the Leucophryena), while some scholars (e.g., Akurgal, 1990) prefer a late second-century date on stylistic grounds. On the altar, see Linfert (1995: 132–4, with bibliography); on the temple's Amazonomachy frieze, see Yaylalı (1976) and Davesne (1982). On the doors of the temple's west pediment, which may have been designed to facilitate an epiphanic viewing of the goddess's statue within, see Bingöl (1999).

[98] See Parker (2004: 16).

[99] See Gehrke (2001) on 'intentional history' (298) in the Magnesian dossier. On kinship diplomacy, see Curty (1995) and C. P. Jones (1999). On the Telephos frieze on the Pergamene

the city's foundation by the Thessalian hero Magnes in order to claim kinship ties (*syngeneia*) with the Kephallenians, the Aeolians and (conveniently) the Macedonians.[100] Epiphanies, too, could be evoked as foundation narratives (like the Athenian myth of Athena and Poseidon); yet, significantly, the appearance of Artemis Leucophryene at Magnesia – which functions as the prime *aition* for the city's claims to sacred and inviolable status – is clearly located in the historical *present*. The Magnesians' rapid ritual and diplomatic response to the event demonstrates how epiphany offered an immediate source of divine ratification that could bypass conventional constraints and open the possibility of forging new traditions and relationships, as well as looking to the past.

The Magnesians' decision to consult the Delphic oracle, however, demonstrates a certain anxiety about the wider significance of Artemis Leucophryene's appearance, and a desire to boost the influence of their local goddess by recourse to a religious authority long established in the very *omphalos* of the Greek world. Indeed, by appropriating epiphany for strategic ends, cities such as Chersonesus and Magnesia were employing a model that is first attested at Delphi itself. Our first recorded example of the religious use of *epiphaneia* in an epigraphic context is a text dated to 278 BCE that was displayed in the sanctuary of Asclepius on the island of Cos.[101] This takes the form of a decree giving thanks for the recent expulsion of the Gauls from Delphi by Apollo in the winter of 279, and promises both to send a delegation of *theōroi* to the Delphic festival of the Soteria (an annual festival of 'salvation') and to make appropriate sacrifices on Cos.[102] The stele refers to the tradition – well attested in the epigraphic and historiographical record – that an epiphanic manifestation of divine power, combined with extreme weather conditions, was responsible for the repulsion of aggressive Galatian forces from this important religious centre, and, ultimately, from Greece. It therefore testifies to the frenzy of myth-making that took place in the wake of the Galatians' retreat, as various regional groups attempted to

---

altar, see Dreyfus and Schraudolph (1996) and Scheer (2003: 220–6). Epiphanic inscriptions in western Asia Minor are known from Ilion (Plutarch *Lucullus* 10.34), Pergamon (see above) and Knidos, Stratonikeia, Bargylia and Mylasa (discussed below).

[100] *IvM* 17 = *FGrH* 482 F3: see Prinz (1979 no. 92), Dušanič (1983), Scheer (1993), Chaniotis (1999) and Gehrke (2001: 291–3).

[101] *Syll.*[3] 398, edited by Herzog 1904: 164–73 and translated by Bagnall and Derow (2004: no. 17). See also Nachtergael (1977: no. 1, 401–3) and Austin (2006: no. 60). On epiphanies in the Gallic Wars, see Nachtergael (1977: 152–64), Pritchett (1979: 30–4) and Petridou (2006: 115–18).

[102] On the Soteria, see Roussel (1924), Pfister (1927), Nachtergael (1977: 209–382) and Grainger (1999: 144–6).

claim responsibility for the victory by evoking the divine support of Apollo. The prime movers in this situation were the Aetolians, who claimed to have borne the brunt of the Galatian attack, and now took control of the Delphic sanctuary, reorganising the Soteria in order to commemorate the victory as one of Greeks over barbarians, and thereby stress their own (somewhat precarious) role as guardians of Hellenic identity.[103] Their increasing influence at Delphi, and on the panhellenic stage, is demonstrated by a series of decrees recognising the reorganised festival from poleis including Athens, Chios, Tenos and Smyrna.[104]

Given the rival claims for divine support in the wake of the Galatians' defeat (and Delphi's prominence as a focus of interstate competition), it is not surprising that the precise nature of the sanctuary's epiphanic narrative is disputed. Typically the epigraphic evidence does not provide details of the manifestation that occurred: *epiphaneia* may refer to a 'miracle' (as a manifestation of divine power) or an 'appearance' (as a manifestation of divine form).[105] While the Coan decree (which does not mention the Aetolians) refers to a single *epiphaneia* of Apollo (16–18), the decree from Smyrna refers to an ἐπιφάνειαν τῶν θεῶν, implying several deities (6).[106] In later historiographical tradition, Diodorus and Justin refer to an epiphany of Apollo and two 'white maidens' identified as Athena and Artemis, while Pausanias claims that the Delphic heroes Hyperochus, Amadocus, Pyrrhus, Laodocus and Phylacus appeared during the battle, confirming that divine forces were behind the sudden storm, earthquake, snow and avalanche that hampered the barbarians' attack.[107] This reference to the repulsion of invaders at

---

[103] On Aetolian power at Delphi, see Flacelière (1937), Bousquet (1957), Nachtergael (1977: 209–33), Grainger (1999: 105–12) and Scholten (2000: 31–45, 100–2); on Aetolian propaganda in the wake of the Galatians' defeat, see Champion (1995).

[104] These latter decrees are associated with the reorganisation of the annual Amphictionic festival of the Soteria into an Aetolian penteteric festival in 246/5 BCE, and are published by Nachtergael (1977) as *Actes* nos. 21–7, 435–47: *EM* 7400 (*IG* 2/3².680, *Syll.³* 408) (Athens); *Delph.Inv.* 2275 (*IG* 9.1².194b, *FD* 3.3.215, *Syll.³* 402) (Chios); *Delph.Inv.* 688 (*IG* 12 suppl. 309, *FD* 3.1.482) (Tenos); *Delph.Inv.* 2158, 2159 (*FD* 3.1.481) (Cyclades); *Delph.Inv.* 697, 698, 699 (*FD* 3.1.483) (Smyrna); *Delph.Inv.* 6377, 2872 (Abdera); *Delph.Inv.* 6203 (origin unknown).

[105] On this distinction, see Versnel (1987: 42–3), Cancik (1990: 290) and Graf (2004b: 113).

[106] On the difference in wording between the Smyrna decree (which may be later in date) and others recognising the reorganisation of the Soteria, see Elwyn (1990, with bibliography). It is worth noting that the Smyrnean inscription also mentions the city's recently granted inviolability (*asylia*); as at Magnesia, civic inviolability is linked with divine protection through the motif of epiphany.

[107] Diodorus 22.9.5, Just. *Epit.* 24.8 (see also Cic. *Div.* 1.81); Paus. 1.4.4, 10.23.1–2. On these conflicting accounts, see also Graf (2004b: 120–1). On the epiphanic nature of such *Wundertopoi*, see Chaniotis (1998).

Delphi by an epiphany of local heroes strongly echoes Herodotus' account of the Persians' attempt to sack the sanctuary in 480 and their repulsion by the heroes Phylacus and Autonous, drawing a pointed parallel between the Galatians' defeat in 279 and the iconic events of the early fifth century, which had done so much to define Greek identity against foreign invaders.[108] The divergence between the two traditions has been attributed to competing accounts of the Galatians' defeat; the Phocians claim the presence of their local heroes, while the Aetolians look to their patron goddesses Athena and Artemis.[109] Yet it is noteworthy that documents issued in the immediate aftermath of the event – recorded in stone and publicly displayed – refer only to a non-specific *epiphaneia* of divine power. The emphasis is not on local tradition so much as the *panhellenic* significance of the manifestation: the Coan inscription explicitly states that a decree has been passed 'so that it may be manifest that the people / shares in the joy of the Greeks over the victory and is repaying thank-offerings for the epiphany that took place during the perils which confronted the sanctuary and for the safety of the Greeks'.[110] It emphasises how, in recognising the significance of Apollo's epiphany, the Coans subscribed to an authoritative narrative of Hellenicity; for the threat posed by the Galatians, like the Persians before them, was a threat not only to Delphi, but to the entire Greek *oikoumenē*. In this respect the Delphic Soteria was an influential model. Not only did it relate epiphanic salvation in battle to the autonomy and survival of Greek culture, but also the communicative measures taken to publicise the festival legitimised the role of epiphany in the formal discourse of 'peer polity interaction' by which structurally homologous Hellenistic poleis understood and engaged with each other.[111] It is most fitting, in this regard,

---

[108] Herodotus 8.38–9, also mentioned by Polybius (2.35.7) and Plutarch (*Cimon* 1.1): see Nachtergael (1977: 161–4), Alcock (1996: 256–8), on Pausanias, Champion (1995: 213), Fantuzzi and Hunter (2004: 356–7), on Callimachus' *Hymn to Delos* 165–76, and Graf (2004b: 116–17). The analogy seems to have been suggested by the Aetolians themselves, who, Pausanias tells us, dedicated shields upon the west and north metopes of the Temple of Apollo at Delphi to complement those set up in the east and south metopes by the Athenians after the battle of Marathon (10.19.3): see Amandry (1978) Hannestad (1993: 16–19) and Scholten (2000: 40).

[109] See Bearzot (1989: 80–2) and Champion (1995: 217). On the contested nature of the Delphic epiphanic tradition in relation to the Galatian invasion, see Segre (1927: 38–42) and Flacelière (1937: 93–111).

[110] Translation Austin (2006: no. 60), with modifications. *Syll.*³ 398, 14–21: ὅπως οὖν ὁ δᾶμος φανε|ρός ἦι συναδόμενος ἐπὶ τᾶι γεγενημέ|ναι νίκαι τοῖς Ἕλλασι καὶ τῶι θεῶι χαρισ|τήρια ἀποδιδοὺς τάς τε ἐπιφανείας | τὰς γεγενημένας ἕνεκεν ἐν τοῖς περὶ | τὸ ἱερὸν κινδύνοις καὶ τὰς τῶν Ἑλλά|νων σωτηρίας.

[111] On peer polity interaction, see Renfrew and Cherry (1986); the concept is applied to epigraphic records of communication between Hellenistic cities by Ma (2003b), including the Magnesian dossier (12–13).

that the Magnesians mention their own involvement in the repulsion of the Gauls from Delphi in the epigraphic corpus referring to the epiphany of Artemis Leucophryene.[112]

The Delphic sequence of epiphany–victory–festival–inscription is subsequently found in many locations in Asia Minor. At Knidos we see the influence of the Soteria in a decree from Cos acknowledging the 200 BCE augmentation of the Hyakinthotrophia, which commemorated Knidos' salvation due to *epiphaneiai* of Artemis Hyakinthotrophos that possibly took place during Philip V of Macedon's unsuccessful siege of the promontory in 201: as a result of her repeated manifestations, the goddess is even ascribed the new epithet *Epiphanēs* (8–9).[113] An early second-century BCE inscription from Chios refers to the establishment of a new festival in honour of Rome, related to a pre-existing *theophania* seemingly founded in honour of an *epiphaneia* of the Dioscuri.[114] In Caria a festival was instituted at Bargylia in the late second century in honour of Artemis Kindyas, to commemorate her *epiphaneia* at a time when 'many great dangers were besetting the city' ([πολλῶν καὶ μεγάλων]‖ περιστάντων κινδύνων τήν τε πόλιν, 2–3).[115] In the late first century BCE the festival of the Panamareia was founded at Panamara near Stratonikeia, where an inscription details the 'many manifest deeds' (μεγάλας ἐπιφανεῖς . . . ἐνεργείας, 2) wrought by Zeus Panamaros for the *sōtēria* of his city, describing the dramatic supernatural events that helped repel an attack on the god's sanctuary by the forces of Labienus Parthicus in 42.[116] At Mylasa, also in Caria a first-century BCE inscription commemorated the 'many great manifest deeds' (πολλὰς καὶ μεγάλας ἐπιφανεῖς | [ἐνεργείας, 4–5) of the god Zeus Osogo, and praised him as the city's 'saviour and benefactor' (σωτῆρος καὶ εὐεργέτου, 3).[117]

Epiphany was thus absorbed into the Hellenic cultural and linguistic *koinē*, testifying to divine protection for cities and their sanctuaries from both Greek kings and barbarian invaders such as the Persians, Galatians and, later, the Romans. The strong sense of civic unity such inscriptions

[112] See *IvM* 46.9–10, with 35.20–1, 36.7–8, 44.13–14, 45.21–3, discussed by Gehrke (2001: 293).

[113] *I. Knidos* 220 (with commentary and bibliography). See also Pritchett (1979: 36), Pugliese-Caratelli (1987: 114–15) and Habicht (1989).

[114] Published by Sarikakis (1975), discussed by Derow and Forrest (1982), with revised text, and Garbrah (1986).

[115] *I. Iasos* 613. See L. Robert (1937: 459–65), with Pritchett (1979: 37–8), Blümel (2000) and Zimmermann (2000).

[116] *I. Stratonikeia* 10. See Roussel (1931), Pritchett (1979: 6–7), Chaniotis (1998: 408–10; 2005: 159), Graf (2004b: 118–29), Petridou (2006: 89–90, 126–7, 131–5) and Belayche (in press). The text refers to several manifestations of Zeus Panamaros' aid during Labienus Parthicus' invasion, including a burning lance that appeared during the night, extreme weather conditions, and the sound of snarling dogs and reinforcement troops.

[117] *I. Mylasa* 306, with bibliography (LBW 400).

convey also underlines the phenomenon's importance for local forms of self-representation. Their prevalence in first-century BCE Caria and the for-mulaic language they share, for example, suggest a particularly 'epiphanic' landscape in which, while subject to the rivalries of more mighty political actors, small poleis followed each other in celebrating the manifestations of their own patron gods, attributing to them a powerful role in maintaining civic stability and independence; the Mylasa inscription even claims that Artemis Kindyas' *epiphaneia* 'saved our native autonomy'.[118] Their display in town sanctuaries and civic spaces suggests that, as well as acting as documentary records, epiphanic inscriptions projected a particular symbolic – even talismanic or apotropaic – force, evoking the protective and salvific power of each city's patron deity. References to multiple manifesta-tions at Knidos, Panamara, Bargylia and Mylasa reinforce this relationship between epiphany and state security by suggesting that divine salvation is a constant potential.[119] The inscriptions thus stand as a thank-offering to the god, ensuring future patronage; a warning to potential aggressors during a time of near-constant warfare; and, perhaps most importantly, a statement of unity, moral superiority and reassurance to anxious inhabitants of the polis: with divine support, it is implied, even the most powerful foreign invader or acquisitive king can be repelled.

The vocabulary of manifestation does not, however, apply solely to the gods. For in all these inscriptions, the visual force of divine epiphany is matched by an emphasis on visible honours and diplomatic exchange. The polysemous nature of *epiphanēs* – as conspicuous or illustrious, political or sacred – applies in these texts as in any other epigraphic texts of the period. In the so-called 'hortative clause' that explains a city's aims in pass-ing a decree, for example, the language of visibility (*phaneros*) is frequently employed to construct a relationship of manifest reciprocity between the *dēmos* and those it honours, whether gods, kings, fellow cities or private

---

[118] *I. Iasos* 613.3–4: διὰ τὴν τῆς Ἀρτέμιδος | ἐπιφάνειαν τὴν τε πάτριον αὐτονομίαν διέσωσε. I thank Mathieu Carbon for bringing this inscription to my attention. On the precarious or ambiguous nature of civic *autonomia* in the Hellenistic period, see Gauthier (1987–9), M. H. Hansen (1995) and Ma (1999: 160–7), who comments (at 160 n. 190) that Mylasa was granted freedom by Seleukos II, and was allowed to retain it under the Roman settlement of Asia Minor in 188 BCE (see Polybius 21.45.4).

[119] *I. Knidos* 220, 8–9 (see above). The Panamaran inscription refers to 'the many and great epiphanies for the salvation of the city from ancient times to the present' (*I. Stratonikeia* 10, 2–4; see also *I. Stratonikeia* 1101, 3–5); a Bargylian inscription (*EA* 32, 90) refers to 'the ongoing epiphanies of Artemis Kindyas'; *I. Mylasa* 306, 5–6, refers to the 'many great, manifest deeds' of Zeus Osogo both 'before in the time of our ancestors and [now] throughout the world'. These recurrent epiphanies are discussed in an unpublished paper by Jan-Mathieu Carbon.

citizens.[120] In epiphanic inscriptions this is applied both to the vertical relationship between manifest gods and their grateful worshippers, and to the horizontal relationship between cities. The Coans' response to the Knidians' invitation to celebrate the *epiphaneiai* of Artemis Hyakinthotrophos, for example, accepts the augmentation of her festival 'so that the *damos* might make manifest (φαίνηται) the policy it has appointed towards the goddess', while their recognition of the Delphic Soteria states that a decree has been passed 'so that it may be manifest (φανε | ρός) that the people / shares in the joy of the Greeks over the victory and is repaying thank-offerings for the epiphany that took place (τᾶς τε ἐπιφανείας | τᾶς γεγενημένας)'.[121] In this way both epiphanies are explicitly matched by the Coans' visible response, which also functions as a diplomatic demonstration of their commitment to good relations with their fellow Greeks.

Likewise, the reply from Antioch in Persis regarding the Magnesian Leucophryena records that the Magnesians 'wished to make manifest (φανερὸν θέλοντες ποιεῖν) that they are admitting all deserving men to a share in all libations, sacrifices and other religious honours' (22–3), and responds that 'The people in its reverence for the gods we share with the Magnesians, . . . believes it a matter of great importance not [to let] pass [any suitable] opportunity / for displaying (ἐ[να](π)οδείξεται) privately [to each individual and] publicly to all the zeal [which] it continually displays [for the] interests of the people of Magnesia' (40–7).[122] While the language of manifestation applies to the formal texts by which such diplomatic exchanges were enacted and recorded for posterity, it also applies to ritual celebrations. Angelos Chaniotis points out that the term *epiphanestatos* is applied in second-century BCE inscriptions to both a sacrifice at Magnesia (to celebrate the dedication of Artemis Leucophryene's cult statue in the newly built temple) and a 'most beautiful procession' in honour of Athena and Homonoia held by Antioch on the Pyramos.[123] The reciprocity of such language is explicitly highlighted when applied to festivals that commemorate divine appearance, where the visual force of epiphany is matched by a visible act of recognition. An inscribed regulation from Bargylia, for example, states that, because of multiple *epiphaneiai* of Artemis Kindyas, the gratitude of the *dēmos* has 'become more visible'

[120] For this point I am grateful to John Ma, who discusses the function of the hortative clause in Ma (1999: 183–5).
[121] *I. Knidos* 220, 13–14: *Syll.*³ 398, 16–21 (translation Austin, 2006: no. 60, with modifications).
[122] *IvM* 61 (*OGIS* 233), translation Austin (2006: no. 190).
[123] Chaniotis (1995: 159 n. 101): *LSAM* 33, 23–4, μετὰ θυσίας τῆς ἐπιφανεστάτης; *LSAM* 81 Z, 8–9, πομπὴν . . . ὡς καλλίστην καὶ ἐπιφανεστάτην.

(ἐκφανεστέραν γεγονέναι), and that processions and sacrifices in her honour are now 'more conspicuous' (ἐπισημότεραι).[124] Like the Magnesian dossier, it records the city's efforts to expand the cult, yoking the conspicuous piety of the Bargylians to the manifest presence of their patron goddess.

Should we read these promotional tactics as a form of interstate competition in which, as Chaniotis has commented, 'The representation of divine miracles turns out to be a self-asserting representation of human success'?[125] Certainly, the Magnesians' renewed attempts in 208/7 to upgrade the Leucophryena have recently been interpreted as a response to the acquisition of inviolate status and establishment of crowned games in honour of Apollo by their neighbouring city (and bitter rival) Miletus.[126] Yet the web of language, ritual and physical commemoration by which epiphany was incorporated into the religious and political life of the Hellenistic city suggests that the notion of the 'manifest' had far deeper relevance than such cynically short-term ends would suggest. For the impulse to 'make manifest' lay at the heart of Hellenistic modes of communication, and, while rooted in traditional political and religious systems, became an increasingly valuable tool in the self-consciously revelatory culture of the third and second centuries BCE. The marked presence of the divine in Hellenistic affairs is in this sense inseparable from the self-reflexivity of contemporary civic discourse and the emphasis on visual display in religious ritual, royal self-presentation and state pageantry. It is thus misguided for Chaniotis to suggest that 'the collective belief in miraculous divine interventions . . . almost acquired the dimensions of a massive delusion'.[127] Rather, the notion of manifestation – and its verbal expression – spoke naturally to people's awareness of divine agency, their desire for direct encounter and their need to mobilise such authority for their own ends; epiphany was culturally effective because all the tools of ritual, text and monument were in place for *dēmos* and *boulē*, king and priest, to record, magnify and perpetuate its significance.

---

[124] Blümel (2000), lines 7–8 (also *SEG* 50.1101).   [125] Chaniotis (2005: 160).

[126] See Slater and Summa (2006: 284) and Thonemann (2007), who dates the foundation of the Milesian Didymeia between 217/16 and 206/5. Rigsby (1996: 352 n. 172) suggests that a similar combination of crowned games and *asylia* at nearby Colophon was prompted by an *epiphaneia* of Apollo of Claros in the late third century BCE: see *SEG* 33.973 (I am grateful to Georgia Petridou for this reference). On the trend for panhellenic games in this period, see Parker (2004).

[127] Chaniotis (2005: 145).

Cataloguing presence: text and object in the Lindos stele

The concluding section of this chapter examines an inscription commonly known as the 'Lindian Chronicle', which is perhaps our most eloquent expression of the relationship between epiphany and epigraphy.[128] Dated to 99 BCE, this substantial text was originally displayed in the sanctuary of Athena Lindia on Rhodes, which had been progressively enhanced with a new temple and two grand stoas during the third century, following a destructive fire in 392/1 (Figure 3.8).[129] The decree inscribed across the top of the stele (section A) claims that, as 'the most archaic and the most venerable / in existence', Athena's sanctuary 'has been adorned with many beautiful offerings (καλοῖς ἀναθέμασι) from the earliest times on account of the visible presence of the goddess (διὰ τὰν τᾶς θεοῦ ἐπιφάνειαν, 2–3)'.[130] Because most of these *anathēmata* have been 'destroyed by time' (4), it stipulates that two local authors – Tharsagoras and Timakhidas – should 'inscribe from the / letters and from the public records and from the other evidence' whatever should prove a fitting source of evidence for Athena's epiphanies and the votives dedicated in her honour (6–8).[131] Displayed in the *temenos* on a stele 2.37 m tall, the inscription would have been visible to anyone visiting the temple and its venerable *agalma* of the goddess, serving as an important framing device for those viewing the sanctuary and its treasures.[132] Though forbiddingly long, the text is clearly marked into columns and subsections with visible headings: it both asks to be read and

---

[128] *Syll*[3].725 (*FGrH* 532; Chaniotis, 1988: T 13). First published by Blinkenberg (1912), in French, then again in revised form in 1915 (in German; published with an English introduction, 1980) and 1941 (no. 2, in French, with bibliography).

[129] On the sanctuary, see Dyggve (1960: vol. I) and Higbie (2001). On the cult statue, see below. On Hellenistic Rhodes, see Gabrielen *et al.* (1999) and Wiemer (2001, 2002).

[130] Text (based on Blinkenberg, 1941: no. 2, with some modifications) and translation from Higbie (2003).

[131] On the inscriptions' authorship, see Blinkenberg (1912: 32), Richards (1929) and Higbie (2003: 62–3). On the destruction of dedications, see Higbie (2003: 256–7) and Bresson (2006: 543–4), who comments that the first thirty-four votives listed (75 per cent) all predate the fire of 392/1. As section D 41–2 states explicitly, the items dedicated by Datis were burned in the fire, which implies that this was most likely the fate of those others that ever 'actually' existed. Those that postdate 392/1 (nos. 35–42) were theoretically still visible in the sanctuary, as suggested by a change in tense from ἐπεγέγραπτο ('had been inscribed') to ἐπιγέγραπται ('has been inscribed') and a smaller number of citations.

[132] The stele is 2.37 m high, 0.85 m wide and 0.32 m deep: see Shaya (2002: 65–7, 212–13) and Higbie (2003: 155–7), who each describe the text's structure and organisation in detail. The stele was discovered in the Byzantine church of Aghios Stephanos, where it has been used (face up, alas) as a paving-stone. Its original position within the sanctuary is unknown.

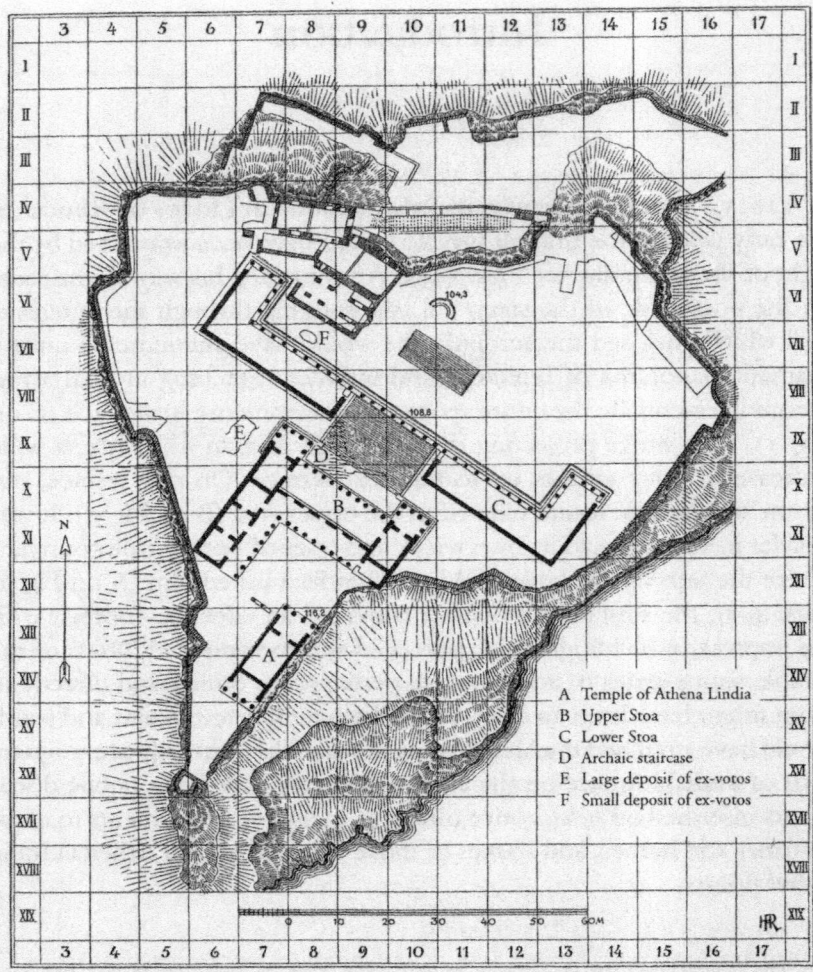

Figure 3.8 Plan of the Acropolis of Lindos

displays text as monument, functioning as a highly visible *anathēma* in its own right (Figure 3.9).

Juxtaposing a catalogue of votive offerings (B–C) with a series of epiphanic narratives (D), the inscription establishes in visual-verbal form the necessary and symbiotic relationship that bound manifestations of divine presence to the material record in Greek culture. Although it has received much attention, especially in recent years, scholars have tended to focus on the extensive evidence the text provides for local historiography and archival documentation in antiquity (at least 126 citations of 24 works),

Figure 3.9 The Lindos temple stele, 99 BCE

reading the inscription as a form of 'constructed history' that situates the sanctuary of Athena Lindia in space and time.[133] Josephine Shaya has related the catalogue of votives to the concept of the Greek temple as a community 'museum', in which the symbolic display of treasured objects helped to forge local identity, constructing and representing memory through the highly manipulated organisation of knowledge.[134] Both these modes of analysis illuminate the ideological concerns behind the inscription's rich blend of literary, historical and material evidence. Shaya's work, in particular, reminds us of the importance of context for understanding how the stele functioned as a written document. In such discussions, however, the sheer quantity of evidence the text provides for practices of composition, citation and dedication inevitably takes priority over the more slippery concept of epiphany.[135] The combination of votive list and what we might call 'epiphanography' has led to considerable confusion over the inscription's epigraphic category: should it be compared to temple inventories, such as those that survive from Delos and the Athenian Acropolis?[136] Or is it a work of historiography? If so, is it appropriate to follow the stele's excavator Christian Blinkenberg in calling it an *Anagraphē* ('Chronicle')?[137] For Felix Jacoby, the lack of annalistic data and juxtaposition of votives and epiphanies created a *mixtum compositum*, which juxtaposed works that could have been entitled 'On the Votives at Lindos' (Περὶ τῶν ἐν Λίνδῳ ἀναθημάτων) and 'On the Epiphanies of Athena Lindia' (Περὶ τῆς Ἀθηνᾶς Λινδίας ἐπιφανείας).[138]

---

[133] See Higbie (2003), with Bresson (2006), for an extensive discussion of the stele's historiographical significance, together with a translation and detailed commentary. The text's status as a valid literary and historical source was examined by Blinkenberg (1912), while its sociocultural significance as an example of local history inscribed on stone has been addressed in relation to broader Hellenistic trends by Boffo (1988: 27–8), Chaniotis (1988: 52–7), Wiemer (2001: 27–32) and K. Clarke (2008: 321–5). On the inscription's use of citation, see Higbie (2003: 188–203).

[134] Shaya (2005); see Shaya (2002) for a more extended discussion of the inscription's museological significance, together with a translation and commentary.

[135] A notable exception is Koch Piettre (2005).

[136] See, e.g., Richards (1929: 76), who entitles the inscription 'A Historical Inventory of the Temple Treasures'. Parallels with inventories from Delos, Didyma and the Athenian Asclepieion and sanctuary of Artemis Brauronia are discussed by Shaya (2002: 128–37); see also Higbie (2003: 260–2). On temple inventories in general, see Linders (1972, 1988, 1992), Aleshire (1989), D. Harris (1995), Hamilton (2000) and Dignas (2002).

[137] Blinkenberg (1912).

[138] See *FGrH* 532, vol. 3B, 445, followed by Chaniotis (1988: 53–4) and Wiemer (2001: 27–32), who stress the inscription's historiographical function. Shaya (2002) employs the term 'Lindos stele' (which I adopt here, in reference to the inscription's status as an inscribed object rather than a dematerialised text), while Higbie (2003: 159) employs the conventional term 'Chronicle'.

Considered in the light of the relationship I have traced between divine, ritual and epigraphic modes of manifestation in Hellenistic culture, however, the juxtaposition of inventory and epiphanography on an inscribed monument appears as a logical outcome of the epigraphic habits displayed at Chersonesus, Knidos or Magnesia. The demonstration of Athena's power in her visitations to temple priests (as recorded in the three epiphanic narratives that survive) is balanced and reinforced by votive dedications that testify to her efficacy throughout Lindian history, from the epochs of Lindos, Heracles, Helen and Menelaus to those of Alexander and Ptolemy I. In turn, these lost material *sēmata* of Athena's authority are substituted by the inscription itself, which functions as a textual and physical marker of both the dedications' former presence and the intangible presence of the goddess.[139] In this sense the avalanche of objects, texts, names and events listed on the Lindos stele is an understandable response to the problem of absence – whether divine elusiveness or material decay. Like Syriskos' work on the epiphanies of the Parthenos at Chersonesus, painstaking documentation is precisely what provides the cognitive reliability required for the goddess's elusive presence to be strategically employed by her worshippers. Furthermore, the textual evidence provided by scholarly citation is balanced by the reassuring solidity of the stele itself, a piece of local stone (from nearby Lartos) that, in a reflexive reference to its own materiality, is explicitly ordered in the opening decree (5–6).[140] Together, textual citation and physical inscription act to re-materialise both votives and epiphanies for the reader within Athena Lindia's sanctuary.

Within the text itself, this act of re-materialisation takes many forms, generating a plausible system of proofs and corroborations that are boosted by appeals to the reader's imagination. The list of *anathēmata* stretches in chronological order from the sanctuary's foundation prior to the Trojan War, through the 'mythical' period of Greek history to the age of the colonisers, and thence to the Persian Wars and, finally, the conflicts of the *Diadochoi*. Within this vast chronological and geographical span, repeated motifs suggest the plausible authenticity of the various offerings listed. Inscriptions are recorded, even when in foreign scripts, such as the 'Phoenician letters' on a bronze cauldron dedicated by Cadmus (B 15–16), or the 'sacred letters' (ἱερῶν γραμμάτων) on phiales dedicated by Amasis

---

[139] On this point, see also Koch Piettre (2005: 102), who suggests that the stele is 'une relique de reliques, une relique au carré'.

[140] See also Bresson (2006: 537), on the stele's possible use of the verb ἀναγράφω (6, 8) to refer to the specifically *epigraphic* (rather than literary) nature of the text.

(C 53).[141] The authority ascribed to these inscribed texts reinforces the authority of the stele itself, reminding the reader of the materiality of the written word and its active role in ritual. Likewise, we find objects that commemorate specific ritual acts, such as the phiales dedicated by Lindos, Tlapolemos, Telephos and Amasis (B 2–8, 37–41, 48–53, C 53), or the 20 cattle skulls that recall a sacrifice made by Ptolemy (C 110–13). Many votives are personal objects closely connected to the body of the dedicator – Minos' silver drinking vessel (B 18–22), Helen's bracelets (B 70–2), Amasis' linen corselet (C 36–9) – or weapons that testify to their engagement in major military campaigns, from Meriones' quiver, inscribed 'Spoils of those from Troy' (B 78–81), to Alexander's caltrops, dedicated after his defeat of Darius (C 103–8). Vessels, jewellery and clothing are of course traditional kinds of offering, attested in sanctuaries throughout the Greek world. As metonymic substitutes for the body, they facilitate the dedicator's continued presence in the sanctuary and encourage a sense of corporeal identification from future visitors.[142] The bodily traces of such charismatic individuals as Heracles and Helen, however, are particularly exciting; they, too, had visited Athena Lindia and performed the customary rituals. The traces they leave behind – preserved only in textual form on the stele – provoke a longing for contact that parallels the desire for divine encounter engendered by the catalogues of epiphanies. This bond between votives and the bodies of their dedicators finds a particularly provocative demonstration in Pliny the Elder's comment that Helen had dedicated at Lindos a goblet of electrum in the shape of her breast.[143]

The material plausibility of these objects is further boosted by close analogy between the list of *anathēmata* and the catalogue of epiphanies: C 65–74 lists 'a torque and a Persian cap and armlets and a Persian curved short sword and trousers', all dedicated by 'the general of the king of the Persians, Darius', while the first epiphany relates how, after Athena saved the Lindians with a sudden thunderstorm during their siege by the Persian admiral Datis, 'the enemy was astounded at the *epiphaneia* of the goddess and took off his own accoutrements covering his body', dedicating his mantle, torque, armlets, Persian cap and curved sword (D 33–8). The name of the general is damaged, and has been identified as Datis, Artaphernes or Artaxerxes, yet the correspondence between the two entries and the sources they cite (such

---

[141] On Amasis' dedications, see Francis and Vickers (1984). On the documentation of inscriptions on the stele, see Higbie (2003: 174–9).

[142] Compare the dedication of representations of *actual* body-parts in healings cults: see van Straten (1981: 99–151) and Petsalis-Diomidis (2005).

[143] Plin. *HN* 33.23.

as Eudemos' *Lindian Topics*, Polyzalos' *Investigations* book 4, Hieron's *About Rhodes* book 1) suggests to the careful reader that ritual responses to Athena's epiphany mirror precisely the practices of dedication in her sanctuary, reinforcing the aetiological relationship between the goddess's presence and her material treasures.[144] By implication, any of the votives listed on the stele can thus be read as a witness to her manifest efficacy. Indeed, this connection between epiphany and dedication may have been explicitly made on another famed treasure within Athena's temple – a painting of Heracles by Parrhasius inspired by his appearance to the artist in a dream. Athenaeus tells us that it was inscribed, 'As he appeared (φαντάζετο) in the watches of the night, oft visiting Parrhasius while he slept, even so he stands here to behold'.[145]

The stele's concern with appropriate dedicatory responses to epiphany is echoed in both catalogues by consideration of the ritual treatment of Athena's foremost material *sēma* – the *agalma* within the temple. Several of the *anathēmata* are designated as *kosmos*, adornment for Athena's statue, including a golden circlet, necklaces and clothing (C 2, 81–3).[146] As I mentioned in Chapter 2, the image of Athena Lindia was classed as one of the oldest in Greece; Callimachus compares it to the ancient statue of Hera on Samos, employing the term λιτὸν ... ἕδος ('unadorned seat'), and claims it was dedicated by the early Greek king Danaos during his flight from Egypt.[147] It seems to have survived the fourth-century fire that destroyed many of the temple's treasures; the early third-century temple includes the foundations of a statue base in the centre of the *cella*, while an inscription records that over 260 local citizens contributed to the cost of new ornaments for the image.[148] The conventional *kosmēsis* of the statue in the votive catalogue echoes the treatment of *xoanon*-type images such as the Athena Polias. This is supplemented, however, by a singular dramatic occasion in the epiphanography, which relates how Athena appeared to her priest to give

---

[144] On the identification of the Persian dedicator, see Higbie (2003: 121–6) and Bresson (2006: 529). Artaphernes was suggested by Blinkenberg (1912: 379; 1941: cols. 194–8), Datis by Richards (1929: 77, 82) and Heltzer (1989), Artaxerxes by Baslez (1985: 140–1).

[145] Athenaeus 12.543f: οἷος δ' ἐννύχιος φαντάζετο πολλάκι φοιτῶν | Παρρασίῳ δι' ὕπνου, τοῖος ὅδ' ἐστὶν ὁρᾶν. Translation by Gulick, Loeb Classical Library edition (1933). On images inspired by dream visions, see Chapter 6. On Parrhasius' claims to close relations with the divine, see Platt (2007b: 267), and on the worship of Heracles at Lindos, see Croon (1953).

[146] See Higbie (2003: 102–3, 128). Francis and Vickers (1984) suggest that the circlet was intended to crown one of the two gold statues given by Amasis (C 41), though there is no evidence for this connection.

[147] Callimachus fr. 100 Pfeiffer, preserved in Plutarch *De Daedalis Plataeensibus* = *Moralia* fr. 158 Sandbach 1969: see Chapter 2, 84, Blinkenberg (1917), Dyggve (1960: 108–13, fig. IV, 5–6), Romano (1980: 213–20), Shaya (2002: 23) and Higbie (2003: 277–8).

[148] Blinkenberg (1941: no. 51, dated *c.* 325 BCE). See Shaya (2002: 45, with further bibliography).

advice on the correct purification of her *agalma* after a man had hanged himself from the struts that secured the image within the temple: the roof is to be opened above the statue for three days, until it is 'cleansed by the washings of her father' (D 60–78). These references to Athena's statue shed interesting light on the relationship between image, ritual and epiphany in the Hellenistic sanctuary: while practices of dedication and *kosmēsis* are focused upon the *agalma* as a material marker of the goddess's presence, the epiphany emphasises Athena's existence independently of her image, if only to reinforce the importance of the image itself as an object for which she has particular concern.

This complex relationship echoes the modes of viewing established by the inscription as a whole, for while the epiphany narratives direct one's attention away from material objects towards the transcendent form of the goddess (as she manifests herself to prominent Lindians and her priests), the votive offerings listed in the catalogue and the first epiphany direct the reader back to the material *sēmata* of Athena's authority. Athena is never described in the epiphanies: we are told only that she appeared 'standing over' (ἐπιστᾶσα) each witness in his sleep in order to give advice (D 14, 68, 98).[149] Collective experience of Athena's power is experienced instead in the form of rainstorms sent by Zeus (D 27–32, 73–4). Although each narrative is longer than the brief references given in other epiphanic inscriptions, the focus, as at Magnesia, is on the immediate implications of Athena's appearance: she saves the Lindians from the Persians in the early fifth century (D 1–59), ensures the correct purification of her image and temple at some point in the fourth century (D 60–93) and suggests a strategic alliance with Ptolemy I to save the Lindians from the besieging Demetrius Poliorcetes in 304/3 (D 94–119).[150] So while the elusive quality of her self-manifestation in the dream world is under-signified (resting only on the authority of her privileged viewers), the practical benefits of her appearance for Lindos are emphatically supported by historical documentation.

The inscription, then, sets up a series of tensions between presence and absence, the material and transcendent. Both forms of catalogue negotiate the problem of the historical trace – whether that of the lost votive,

[149] On *epistasis* as an epiphanic term used specifically for dream visitations, see van Straten (1976: 17) and Petridou (2006: 157–8, 292–3, n. 1324).

[150] On Demetrius' infamous siege of Rhodes, see Berthold (1984: 59–80). Ptolemy's title *Sōtēr* was reportedly granted by the Rhodians in thanks for his help during the siege, though it is interesting that the surviving section of narrative on the Lindos stele locates divine agency specifically with Athena and does not apply epiphanic language to the king himself. See Hazzard (1992).

heroic visitor or elusive dream epiphany. In each case, acts of citation and inscription serve to create a literary and monumental *mnēma* to preserve and celebrate these now imperceptible demonstrations of Athena's efficacy. In offering two categories of 'proof', the stele also presents two forms of history. The first, expressed in terms of material *anathēmata*, looks to the distant (we would say 'mythical') past, in order to demonstrate the significance of the shrine from earliest antiquity to the Hellenistic kings and the enduring nature of its ritual practices.[151] The varied geographical origins of its many dedicators – from Sicily and mainland Greece to Egypt and Persia – act like the inscribed replies at Magnesia by situating Lindos at the centre of the known world; together with the catalogue's chronological span, they too generate a cognitive map that defines Athena Lindia's authority across space and time. The second form of history, as articulated in the epiphanic narratives, looks *only* to the recent past – historical crises of foreign invasion, sacred pollution and civic vulnerability. As at Magnesia, epiphany is shown to have immediate significance for the city's security, status and international relations. The dynamic repetition of Athena's epiphany, which takes the same form each time (even six nights in a row in the most recent epiphany, 109–10), sets the stage for her immanence; rather than stretching back to the murky realms of distant history, its formulaic insistence looks to the future.[152] Each of these modes reinforces the other, for while the treasures that define and adorn sacred space yoke elusive epiphanies to the material world, the enduring potential for divine encounter legitimises and secures the sanctity of the votives and their location. Together these forms of history construct the sanctuary of Lindos as an *epiphanestatos topos* in both its senses: it is both illustrious and full of divine presence. Most importantly, the manifest nature of both offerings and deity is materialised and communicated in the form of the manifest inscription itself.

[151] On the relationship between myth and history in the inscription, see Higbie (2003: 206–9, 247–50), and in Hellenistic culture in general, Gehrke (1994) and Scheer (2003).

[152] See Bresson (2006: 533–4), who comments that an epiphany of Isis was reported to have saved the city of Rhodes during its siege by Mithridates in 88 BCE (App. *Mith.* 27), eleven years after the Lindos stele was commissioned.

Facing the gods in the 'birdcage of the Muses'

While epigraphic evidence from the Hellenistic period suggests that epiphany played a vital role in political and religious life (as I explored in Chapter 3), the converse has often been held of contemporary literature, produced for a learned elite in self-consciously intellectual institutions such as the libraries of Alexandria and Pergamon or the philosophical schools of Athens.[1] The poster-girl for this approach to Hellenistic thought is a second-century BCE marble version of Phidias' Athena Parthenos, originally displayed in a large *oikos* accessed through the north stoa of the Pergamene sanctuary of Athena Nikephoros traditionally associated with the Attalids' library (Figure 4.1). One of our earliest identifiable 'copies' of a Greek cult statue, the Pergamene Athena has been interpreted as a de-sacralised *objet d'art*, harbinger of the replicatory practices so familiar to Roman art, and a symbol of Pergamon's cultural, rather than religious, self-presentation.[2] Created from a different medium from Phidias' Parthenos, she is no longer the gleaming focus of religious ritual, but stands instead as a personification of wisdom, an embodiment of the intellectual activity conducted in the building she adorns. Likewise, for the 'cloistered book worms, endlessly arguing in the birdcage of the Muses' (as Timon of Phlius satirised the library at Alexandria), literary texts – like sacred images – were no longer necessarily bound to their

---

[1] On Hellenistic library culture, see (from a vast bibliography) Fraser (1972: 305–35), Canfora (1990), El-Abbadi (1990), R. Blum (1991), Erskine (1995), MacLeod (2000), Staikos (2000), Casson (2001: 30–60) and Bagnall (2002), who debunks many of the myths associated with the Alexandrian library.

[2] See, e.g., Pollitt (1986: 167, 235), Robertson (1993: 73–5), who nevertheless acknowledges the significance of the sculpture's religious setting, and Kousser (2008: 140–2), who emphasises its political implications. Note that the identification of this chamber and its adjoining rooms as Pergamon's famous library has recently been challenged by Strocka (2000), who identifies the large *oikos* as a *hestiatorion* designed for ritual feasting. Whatever the room's function, however, it is clear that the image's primary role was that of a votive dedication to the city's patron goddess: see Mielsch (1995) and Platt (2010: 201–3). On replications of the Athena Parthenos, see Gaifman (2006), Tanner (2006: 229–30) and my discussion in Chapter 2, 87–9.

Figure 4.1 Athena Parthenos, from the sanctuary of Athena Nikephoros, Pergamon: Hellenistic copy after Phidias' Athena, *c.* 190 BCE

original ritual or performative context.[3] As collected objects they formed the focus of encyclopaedic catalogues and academic enquiry, or inspired the composition of self-consciously allusive poetry, performed under the aegis

---

[3] Timon fr. 12 Diels: see Canfora (1990: 37–44) and Barnes (2000: 62). On the separation of text from performative context in Hellenistic literature, see Fantuzzi and Hunter 2004: 17–26.

of court patronage or circulated in the form of the book.[4] The implication of this secularising model of cultural production is that any vestigial religiosity could be experienced only through the prism of human *technē*, resulting in a profound sense of distance from the divine.

As Hellenistic inscriptions show, however, elite literary production was often firmly integrated within civic or religious contexts; the practices of citation and historiography exhibited by a text such as the Lindos temple stele demonstrate that academic qualities conventionally associated with the library could be readily mobilised in celebration of the divine. Intellectualism did not necessarily entail a move away from traditional religious practice. Likewise, to emphasise the secularism of the Pergamene Parthenos is to ignore both the context of the Attalids' library, and the enduring sanctity of her form. Just as the Alexandrian library bore a close relationship to a scholarly institution called the *Mouseion* (a 'Shrine of the Muses') and was presided over by a priest, so the Pergamene library was directly connected to the sanctuary of Athena: neither foundation was entirely secular in spirit.[5] Indeed, Pergamon's cultural ambitions were inseparable from its relationship to its patron goddess. While the marble Parthenos may not have formed the focus of ritual activity, she nevertheless invoked the authority of her Athenian model as a *lebende Statue* – a 'living image' within the Greek cultural imagination.[6] As I discussed in Chapter 2, it was precisely the representational nature of Phidias' Parthenos (rather than its own debatable ritual function) that made this form of replication both possible and meaningful for Greek viewers.[7] In this sense the Pergamene Athena echoes the epiphanic quotation we saw on the Great Altar, in which a composition borrowed from the Athenian Parthenon did not simply demonstrate the city's *arriviste* cultural mentality, but employed a form of visual citation that was entirely appropriate for the structure's function and the relations it sought to establish between human and divine. The library context of the Parthenos does not, then, de-sacralise her form, but establishes a productive tension between her status as an artistic object presented for connoisseurial viewing and her status as a deity. Like the altar – and Damophon's statues

---

[4] On Hellenistic texts as artefacts, see Gutzwiller (2007: 43–9). On kingship and literary patronage, see Weber (1993).

[5] Strabo 17.18. See Fraser (1972: vol. III, 312–19) and El-Abbadi (1990: 84–90), who points out that Plato's *Academy* and Aristotle's *Lyceum* also included *mouseia*.

[6] See Chapter 2, 87–9, and Gaifman (2006).

[7] Note that when Athena visited Aelius Aristides in the form of the Parthenos years later, he was at the Pergamene Asclepieion at the time (*Hieroi Logoi* 2.41)! See Chapter 6, 262.

at Lykosoura – she demonstrates the close bond between epiphany and allusion in Hellenistic art, in which the immediacy of the divine is paradoxically accessed through the models of the past. In this sense she raises interesting questions about the parallel de-contextualisation of literary genres that took place during the Hellenistic period, and their corresponding treatment of the concept of epiphany. What happens when texts are divorced from the sacred environs of the sanctuary and performed in court settings or read as part of a literary collection? Does *technē* triumph over *theosebeia* (or 'reverence for the gods'), turning epiphany into a matter of pure poetics? Or can the text itself function as a medium through which to encounter the divine – a literary equivalent to the inscribed *epiphaneiai* that adorned contemporary cities and sanctuaries?

Rather than exploring the general theme of epiphany in Hellenistic poetry (which deserves a book in itself), this chapter focuses on the poetic treatment of sacred images and their role as epiphanic *sēmata*, examining Callimachus' *Hymn to Athena* before turning to some examples of ekphrastic epigram.[8] We shall see that the same qualities that made cult statues exciting yet problematic for their viewers also made them useful vehicles for poets to explore the tensions between religiosity and mortal *technē* that characterised their own literary production. On one hand, the ontological status of sacred images as mimetic products of human artistry provided a constructive parallel to the work of the poet, particularly in those genres such as the literary hymn or epigram that were now 'imitative' of earlier poetic practice. Yet, on the other hand, the phenomenological impact of those same images – as forms that generated a sense of encounter with the deities they embodied – held out the possibility of a less mediated form of aesthetic experience. In Hellenistic poetry the *enargeia* that characterised epiphanic encounter in the Homeric corpus, for example, is reformulated as the *enargeia* of ekphrasis – a descriptive rhetorical device 'that brings the thing shown clearly into vision (ἐναργῶς ὑπ' ὄψιν)'.[9] Like naturalistic representations of the gods, ekphraseis are bound to self-conscious acts

---

[8] For some recent approaches to epiphany in Hellenistic poetry, see Bing (1993), Hunter and Fuhrer (2002), Vestrheim (2002) and I. Petrovic (2007: 142–81).

[9] As defined by the second-century CE rhetorician Aelius Theon, *Progymnasmata* 118.6–120.11 (Patillon, 1997). See Dubel (1997), R. Webb (1999: 11–15), Elsner (2002: 1–3, with further bibliography) and Goldhill (2007). Although the ancient *progymnasmata* treat ekphrasis as a description of a broad range of visual phenomena, from battle scenes to festivals, I here focus on ekphrasis as the verbal evocation of a work of art, an identifiable ekphrastic subcategory with a long life of its own, from the Homeric shield of Achilles to the *Imagines* of Philostratus: see Friedländer (1912: 1–103).

of *technē*: both image and text (if produced with enough skill) have the potential to provoke a sense of direct encounter with the divine for their viewers and readers. Yet in displaying the technical ability of the artist or poet, both media have the potential to undermine their enargeic exercise by diverting attention to their own facture. Ekphrasis, like the sacred image, thus shuttles between the poles of cognitive reliability (correspondence between text and object, or image and god) and cognitive dissonance (a sense of distance and incommensurability). In this way ekphrasis and the epiphanic image are natural partners: both strive to make present that which is other, and in so doing to elide their status as strategic devices. And both inevitably reassert themselves through the dazzling nature of their own fashioning.[10]

The corollary of this emphasis on visual production and presentation is an emphasis on its reception, specifically the experience of viewing a god through his or her image, or an image through a text. Here as well, two modes of looking are juxtaposed: the connoisseurial eye – educated, urbane, critical – and the imaginative eye, which enters into the scopic fantasy presented by image or text. Think of Parmenion's epigram about Polyclitus' Hera, for example (with which I began Chapter 2): the witty play on divine law and the appropriateness of representation intersects with a serious desire to view the statue as an embodiment of the goddess. We might associate the first with the sense of detached voyeurism generated by naturalistic art (as I discussed in Chapter 2), and the second with the notion of *theōria*, the act of 'going to see' a divinity as an act of pilgrimage.[11] In Hellenistic poetry, not only are these two modes of viewing more clearly distinguished from each other than in earlier literature: they are then staged for the reader as an interpretative exercise which (in Simon Goldhill's words) 'dramatize[s] the viewing subject seeing himself seeing'.[12] Thus not only is epiphany problematised in such texts: the problematisation of epiphany is itself presented as a subject for examination (and even humour). In this way Hellenistic decontextualisation of traditional poetic genres, while distancing texts from ritual performance or display, nevertheless set the stage for a rigorous examination of religious modes of artistic representation. The practice of poetics, in this sense, was never too far from theology.

---

[10] Cf. Bartsch and Elsner (2007: vi).

[11] These modes of viewing are defined and discussed by Elsner (2007: 1–26), though applied to different categories of image (the 'naturalistic' and the 'sacred'); here I define them as conflicting modes that can influence the viewing of a single image.

[12] Goldhill (2007: 2); see also Goldhill (1994: 205).

Here comes the goddess! Hope, fear and representation in Callimachus' *Hymn to Athena*

The shift from a Homeric model of epiphanic *enargeia* to a self-consciously mimetic model is most cogently demonstrated by the *Hymns* of Callimachus, composed in the first half of the third century. In his *Hymn to Athena* the poet openly marks the text's distance from a ritual context and emphasises its status as a 'literary' composition by dramatising the circumstances of its own presentation.[13] He thus presents us with a mimetic evocation of an Argive ceremony in which the cult statue of Athena (an *agalma* identified as the Trojan Palladion) was washed in the waters of the River Inachus.[14] The speaker (a cult official) begins by summoning the goddess in the form of her image, thrice calling ἔξιθ', Ἀθαναία, 'Come forth, Athena!'[15] This animating device is reinforced by the proposed ritual performance, which centres upon an anthropomorphising *loutron* in which the Palladion is to be stripped 'naked' (γυμνάν, 53) and washed as if it were the body of the goddess herself, despite the fact that this manly maid is more interested in fighting than her toilette (5–26).[16] The poet playfully blurs his description of Athena's attitude to bathing and the ritual invocation of her image, straining the bond between goddess and statue. He alludes to the flight of Athena's priest Eumedes from Argos with the Palladion (35–42), claiming 'He placed you, goddess, upon precipitous rocks' (41–2), addressing image as deity while simultaneously reminding his audience of

---

[13] For ritual frames suggestive of epiphanic encounter, see also Callimachus' hymns to Apollo and Demeter. Fantuzzi and Hunter (2004: 364) comment that these texts 'actually script a context for performance, whereas such a context needed no such script when the poem was indeed part of a real performance'. See also Falivene (1990), Hunter (1992), Harder (1992), Depew (1992, 1993, 1994, 2000: 78–9), Hunter and Fuhrer (2002) and Vestrheim (2002), though Alan Cameron (1995: 63–7) has suggested that Callimachus' hymns could have been performed outside formal ritual frameworks (following Cahen, 1929: 281, Fraser 1972: vol. II, 916 n. 289, and Bulloch, 1985: 4–6). On the *Hymns* as a published collection designed for reading, rather than performance, see Haslam (1993) and Hunter and Fuhrer (2002). I. Petrovic (2007: 124–77), however, stresses correspondence between the *Hymns* and the staging of divine presence in contemporary Hellenistic festivals, noting Callimachus' very contemporary expression of religiosity.

[14] Callimachus' hymn is our only source for the ritual, which may in fact be fictional (Hunter, 1992: 14). Scholars have noted similarities to the Athenian Plynteria (at which the statue of the goddess may have been ritually bathed and dressed) and the Arrephoria (associated with the Cecropides myth, and so the perception of the goddess's sexual secrets and the ritual revelation of sacred objects): see Chapter 2, n. 53, with Bulloch (1985: 9–10). On bathing rituals in general, see Ginouvès (1962: 283–98).

[15] Lines 33 and 43: ἔξιθ', Ἀθαναία; line 55: πότνι Ἀθαναία, σὺ μὲν ἔξιθι. Text from Bulloch (1985), with my translation.

[16] See Depew (1994: 417–21) and Heyworth (2004: 139–40).

its status as a portable object, a *xoanon*-type statuette that must have been very ancient (if not aniconic) in form.[17] To what extent could such an object have been viewed as an embodiment of Athena herself, particularly when stripped of its adornments?[18] Was there, in fact, anything to see? Hymns, of course, had always dealt with the problematic nature of divine form as part of their encomiastic enterprise (as we saw in Chapter 1).[19] Where Callimachus differs is in recasting the Homeric theme of elusive divine *eidos* in terms of visual representation.[20] Like the *Hymn to Demetrius Poliorcetes*, the *Hymn to Athena* couches the question of divine accessibility in terms of the material object: will we see Athena 'in wood or stone' or 'in truth'? Yet as a highly self-conscious literary text (as opposed to a popular song), Callimachus' hymn presents a further meta-poetic twist, whereby the ambiguous status of Athena's image echoes that of the text itself – a mimetic composition that is also concerned with the tension between divine reality and its simulation.

The sense of epiphanic expectation generated by the hymn's ritual frame, however, proves problematic within the *pars epicum* that follows. The introductory passage provokes in the reader an ekphrastic desire to see an image treated as an embodiment of Athena, and therefore to encounter the goddess. Yet it addresses only the goddess's female worshippers – the 'fair-haired daughters of Pelasgus' (4). The mimetic frame thus allows its male readers virtual access to a ritual from which they are prohibited, enhancing the frisson generated by the statue's impending arrival with the cry 'Pelasgian, / beware lest you unintentionally see the queen!' (51–2).[21] The speaker then

---

[17] See Bulloch (1985: 145–7), who follows the scholiast in explaining Eumedes' escape from Argos with the Palladion as an attempt to take the talisman to the Heracleids, who had been wrongfully expelled from the Peloponnese by Eurystheus.

[18] Cf. Callimachus' *Iambi* 6 and 7, in which the grandeur of Phidias' Olympian Zeus is juxtaposed with the aniconic, humble form of Hermes Perpheraios. Ironically, while the former can be only be viewed in terms of its numerical qualities, it is the shapeless wood of the latter that speaks in the god's 'voice'. In this way the poet explicitly problematises the limits of both visual and verbal representation: epiphanic form cannot be conveyed in words, while aniconic form paradoxically allows for greater textual *enargeia*. On these texts, see Manakidou (1993: 238–42), Kerkhecker (1999: 147–96), Acosta-Hughes (2002: 265–300), I. Petrovic (2006, 2010) and Payne (in press).

[19] On Callimachus' relationship to the *Homeric Hymns* and treatment of the hymnic genre more generally, see Hunter and Fuhrer (2002). While the *Homeric Hymns* may have been performed as *prooimia* to epic recitation (see Chapter 1, 61), Callimachus conspicuously 'drops the epic sequel as inconsistent with his aesthetic goals and [makes] the hymn stand on its own' (Bing, 1993: 182).

[20] On the role played by cult images in Callimachus' other hymns, see Manakidou (1993: 212–38).

[21] The speaker addresses a single male viewer: Πελασγέ, / φράζεο μὴ οὐκ ἐθέλων τὰν βασίλειαν ἴδῃς.

proceeds to a narrative *muthos* that explores the dangers of epiphany for men who *do* encounter the goddess.[22] While the Argive festival focuses on bathing Athena in the form of her image, the *pars epicum* focuses on the myth of Teiresias, who suffered the consequences of crossing the mimetic barrier and beholding the actual goddess bathing.[23] As a male viewer who unwittingly entered the fantasy set in motion by the opening section of the hymn, Teiresias 'unwillingly saw what is forbidden by divine law' (οὐκ ἐθέλων δ᾽ εἶδε τὰ μὴ θεμιτά, 78), and is therefore blinded; fittingly, the angry goddess claims, 'Never again will you take back your eyes' (80).[24] In her *consolatio* to Teiresias' mother Chariclo, Athena draws upon the myth of Actaeon, presenting us with our earliest account of the young hunter's fatal epiphany of Artemis (107–18).[25] While the Callimachean versions of the Teiresias and Actaeon myths probably have textual antecedents, the poet is the first (as far as we know) to identify both transgressions as sight of a virginal goddess bathing, and to draw a parallel between the heroes' fates.[26] The theme of male visual transgression thus encourages a specifically

[22] Cf. Hunter and Fuhrer (2002: 160).

[23] In earlier versions of the myth, such as the pseudo-Hesiodic *Melampodia* (fr. 275), Teiresias' blindness is attributed to his bisexual experiences and claim, so offensive to Hera, that women enjoy greater pleasure than men: see Brisson (1976), Ugolini (1995) and Loraux (1995). We learn from Apollodorus 3.6.7, however, that the Teiresias and Athena myth was originally told by the fifth-century mythographer Pherecydes: see Bulloch (1984: 225–8; 1985: 17–19, 163, 189), Lacy (1990: 29 and n. 26), Haslam (1993: 122), Depew (1994: 411–13) and Ugolini (1995: 66–78). As Callimachus' speaker informs us, μῦθος δ᾽ οὐκ ἐμός, ἀλλ᾽ ἑτέρων ('The tale is others', not mine', 56). On parallels with other narratives of voyeurism such as Herodotus' tale of Gyges (1.8–12) and Euripides' *Bacchae*, see Hunter (1992: 18–28).

[24] τὸν ὀφθαλμὼς οὐκέτ᾽ ἀποισόμενον. On this passage, see Henrichs (1993a: 144 n. 42). The question of who may experience epiphany, of elite access to the deity, is something that Callimachus repeatedly explores in the hymns, from the *esthlos* – the 'good man' – who is privileged to see Apollo at 2.9, to the gender split in Hymn 5. Only those sanctioned by status and ritual experience may approach the divine with due piety, a factor that reflects the relationship between epiphany and initiation in actual cult practice, while reinforcing the exclusivity of Callimachus' own poetics. On the 'poetics of exclusion', see Bassi (1989), Bing (1993: 193) and Dickie (2002).

[25] In earlier versions of the myth, Actaeon was punished by Zeus because he lusted after Semele (Paus. 9.2.3, referring to a lost poem by Stesichorus: *PMG* no. 236) or, in a classic tale of hubris, because he boasted that he was a better hunter than Artemis (Euripides, *Bacchae* 337–40, and Diodorus 4.81.4–5). In Pausanias' own interpretation, Actaeon's hounds were simply rabid, 'and were sure to tear to pieces without distinction everybody they chanced to meet' (9.2.4). Following Callimachus, the motif of Artemis' nudity and the implied eroticism of the myth becomes standard, and is employed by Apollodorus 3.4.4, Ov. *Met.* 3.138–252 and *Tr.* 2.103–8, Seneca *Oedipus* 751–63, Statius *Thebais* 3.201–5, Apuleius *Golden Ass* 2.4 and Nonnus *Dionysiaca* 5.287–551. On the Actaeon myth in classical literature, see Lacy (1990), who discusses early sources for the myth in detail, Heath (1992: 25–52) and Depew (1994: 411–12). On visual representations of Actaeon's fatal epiphany, see Leach (1981) and Platt (2002).

[26] Cf. Haslam (1993: 124).

gendered reading of the hymn, highlighting the gap between the poet's (male) voice and the hymn's (female) speaker, and between male readers (presumably Callimachus' dominant audience) and the hymn's internal (female) worshippers.[27]

This serves, of course, to remind us of the role of the poet and the mimetic nature of the text itself, alerting us to the tension between ritual frame and internal narrative. While the former seeks to induce epiphany via the ekphrastic animation of a cult image, the latter demonstrates what can happen when mimesis becomes 'reality' and the limits of epiphanic representation are overstepped by the wrong viewer. The warning given in the context of performance becomes a reality within the myth itself, while the reader's desire for an encounter with the goddess (a desire that is always implicit in the voyeuristic myths of Teiresias and Actaeon) is revealed to be fraught with danger. The hymn creates a scopic trap, manipulating us as participants in its ritual structure into anticipation of an experience that is later revealed to be a χαλεπὰν ὁδόν – a 'painful path' (81). The text's authority thus lies in its ability to reveal just what is at stake in the mimetic enterprise, probing the unsettling boundary between *enargeia* as vivid literary production and *enargeia* as direct encounter with deity. When, in its closing lines, the speaker finally announces 'Athena is really coming now!' (ἔρχετ᾽ Ἀθαναία νῦν ἀτρεκές), do we actually want to see her?[28]

By flirting with the epiphanic potential of mimesis, Callimachus also problematises the tradition of anthropomorphism: how can humans create images of a goddess that are designed to be *viewed*, when the very viewing of Athena is prohibited, as she herself admits, by 'the laws of Kronos' (100)?[29] The virginal Athena, he notes – unlike the mirror-loving Aphrodite – will not even look at herself (21–2).[30] If to view is, in some form, to possess, then how can male worshippers ever view a divinity whose very identity is bound up in her resistance to the male gaze? The converse of this problem lies in the Palladion's status as an object. Are male viewers banned from the

[27] Cf. Vestrheim (2002).

[28] The use of ἀτρεκές ('certainly', 'indeed') surely has an ironic ring to it, although Bulloch (1985) observes that the word can also mean 'real', in which case it 'would stress that Athena's appearance is not illusory . . . and would emphasise the identity of the Palladion with the goddess herself' (244). On a similar use of the word in Apollonius Rhodius' ekphrasis of Aphrodite at 1.745, see below, 207–8. On the ambiguous epiphany of the hymn's close, see Hunter (1992: 12–13).

[29] Note Diodorus Siculus' suggestion that Actaeon was punished because he attempted to effect 'a marriage' (τὸν γάμον) with the goddess in her temple (4.81.4–5), perhaps a reference to an assault on the goddess's image, and thus a variation on the infamous blemish on the Knidian Aphrodite's thigh (discussed below).

[30] On Athena's problematic relationship to the mirror, see Loraux (1995: 216–19). On Aphrodite, see below.

loutron because of the anthropomorphic implication that this is Athena's *body*, or are they banned because the act of removing the statue's costume and adornments exposes its mundane materiality, its very lack of epiphanic authority? The same question applies to Teiresias' fatal epiphany of the goddess herself. As Nicole Loraux has asked, did Teiresias come face to face with the fascinatory power of the Gorgon, the goddess's aegis? Does Athena's apparel actually conceal the 'phallic body' of a virile virgin? Did Teiresias see nothing at all? Or is there in fact no surprise? Is Athena's body merely that of a woman, blinding in its familiarity?[31] Loraux questions whether a corporeal Athena is actually an *adunaton*, 'the body of a goddess who is never reduced to her body alone, because her being is in the multiple appearances that she assumes'.[32]

By keeping his audience within the realm of mimesis, then, there is a sense in which Callimachus presents the only form of epiphany that he can. For Teiresias and Actaeon, visionary experience results in an uncomfortable transfiguration of the self; as a result, Teiresias loses his sight, yet gains a form of inner vision (in the form of mantic powers) ordinarily inaccessible to mortals. Callimachus makes a claim for the authority of his own poetry by demonstrating how this intensely difficult and transformative experience can be communicated to others only by mimetic means, because, in its 'real' form, epiphany is beyond human capabilities. Mimesis makes epiphany possible within the world of lived experience. In this sense, the necessary insufficiency of representation is transformed into a religious and poetic virtue, making a forceful claim for the text's sacred efficacy. The gap that Callimachus' hymn marks between goddess and image, reader and text, is thereby essential for a proper understanding of the relationship between human and divine. This is where the hymn both echoes and elaborates upon its Homeric forebears; for while the themes of dangerous epiphany and evasive immortal form are intrinsic to texts such as the *Hymn to Aphrodite* or *Hymn to Dionysus*, Callimachus yokes the problematic nature of divine encounter more explicitly to the dilemmas of mortal production, reformulating the epiphanic *aporia* of the *Homeric Hymns* as a claim for the efficacy of his own poetry.[33] Here we see a significant contrast to the mimetic enterprise of the Delian maidens in the *Homeric Hymn to Apollo*, whose perfect fusion of sign and referent stands as a metaphor for the hymn's complete absorption of its audience (3.156–64).[34] For Callimachus, it is the

---

[31] Loraux (1995: 213).   [32] Loraux (1995: 220); see also Llewellyn-Jones (2001).

[33] Cf. Vestrheim (2002: 176), who comments that Callimachus' *Hymn to Apollo* 'puts forth epiphany as a metaphor for poetry'. I think it would also be possible to say the converse, which is that poetry is a metaphor for epiphany.

[34] See Chapter 1, 70–2.

gap between model and copy and the overtly constructed nature of the poem that paradoxically make epiphany possible. Both these are fundamentally bound to the written status of the text as a mimetic object divorced from the circumstances of ritual performance.

This paradox is exhibited most explicitly in Callimachus' own *Hymn to Apollo*, which also employs a mimetic frame (possibly the Carneia festival in Callimachus' home town of Cyrene).[35] While Apollo's immanence is indicated by the shaking of his laurel branch, the nodding of the Delian palm tree and the singing of swans, his corporeal presence is withheld from the poem's sacred space; he is merely imagined 'kicking the doors with his beautiful foot' (4).[36] Yet when Apollo is finally made present at the hymn's close, it is to make a statement about Callimachean poetics (105–12), contrasting the 'filthy' waters of the mighty Euphrates with water that 'flows forth pure and undefiled from a holy spring'.[37] Again, Callimachus draws upon his archaic model (the *Homeric Hymn to Apollo* famously includes a reflexive passage in which the poet refers to his own *kleos*, 3.165–78); yet again, he goes further, this time putting his poetic *cri de cœur* in the mouth of a god whose very name can be read as a pun on Callimachean aesthetics (ά-πολύς, 'not much').[38] True access to the divine is thus facilitated by consuming the poet's own literary output – the 'crown of waters'. Significantly, the 'foot' with which Apollo kicks Envy and finally makes his corporeal appearance within the hymn turns out to be the metrical 'foot' of poetry itself. In this sense, the god *is* the poem.[39]

Writing desire in stone: epiphanies of Aphrodite in ekphrastic epigram

Ἡ Παφίη Κυθέρεια δι᾽ οἴδματος ἐς Κνίδον ἦλθε,
βουλομένη κατιδεῖν εἰκόνα τὴν ἰδίην.

---

[35] On epiphany and ritual in the *Hymn to Apollo*, see Bing (1993) and Vestrheim (2002: 176–80).

[36] See Henrichs (1993a) and Hunter and Fuhrer (2002: 150), who associate these epiphanic *sēmata* with the gods' original epiphany – his birth on Delos. On epiphanic feet and footprints, see Dunbabin (1990) and Takács (2005).

[37] The famous Callimachean statement, 'Great is the stream of the Assyrian river, but much filth of earth and much refuse it carries on its waters' (108–9). On the poetics of this passage, see Köhnken (1981), Kahane (1994), Traill (1998) and Cheshire (2008). As Fantuzzi and Hunter (2004: 358) comment, when Apollo speaks, 'he sounds very like Callimachus'.

[38] This delightful pun is drawn attention to by Hunter and Fuhrer (2002: 152).

[39] Cf. Bing (1993: 186): 'the literary work is itself the sacrament, the hymn itself is an epiphany in the process of being accomplished'.

πάντη δ' ἀθρήσασα περισκέπτῳ ἐνὶ χώρῳ,
  φθέγξατο. Ποῦ γυμνὴν εἶδέ με Πραξιτέλης;

Paphian Cytherea came through the waves to Knidos,
  Wishing to see her own image.
Having viewed it from all sides in its open shrine,
  She cried, 'Where did Praxiteles see me naked?'[40]

Callimachus' *Hymns* demonstrate how the shift from performance to text that characterised much Hellenistic poetry did not necessarily entail distance from the divine, but opened up new realms of possibility, in which the difficult, elusive nature of epiphany offered a constructive and exciting parallel to the representational concerns of poetry. In the *Hymn to Athena* the goddess's *agalma* serves as a visual metaphor within the text for the problems faced by the poet in making Athena present for his audience. While the hymn does not offer an ekphrasis of the statue, as such, this focus on a material *sēma* of divinity anticipates a theme that would become hugely popular in Hellenistic epigram, in which sacred images frequently form the focus of succinct and enigmatic ekphraseis concerned with the relationship between gods and their artistic representations.[41] Like the literary hymn, epigrams were one of the most overtly decontextualised genres of the period, collected in the form of single-authored volumes such as the recently rediscovered works of Posidippus (dated to the third century), or gathered into anthologies, such as the early first-century BCE *Garland of Meleager* and the *Garland*

[40] *Anth. Plan.* 160, 1–4, attributed to 'Plato' (lines 5–6, discussed below, are usually interpreted as a later addition, following Jacobs, 1794–1814: vol. IV, 345–6). All translations from the *Greek Anthology* are from W. R. Paton's Loeb Classical Library edition (1918), with some modifications. 'Plato' is possibly the same 'Plato Junior' who is excluded from the *Garland of Philip* by GP 1968 (xxvi), but may, according to Page (1981: 82), be a comic playwright of the first century CE. Except where stated, all epigrams are cited according to the numeration of the Loeb edition of the *Greek Anthology*. Book 16 comprises the epigrams collected in the 1301 *Anthologia Planudea* which were not included in the tenth-century manuscript of the *Anthologia Palatina*, including most of *Anth. Plan.* book 4, which includes the ekphrastic poems; see Alan Cameron (1993: 16–17) and Manakidou (1993: 254–69). Those devoted to the Aphrodite of Knidos number *Anth. Plan.* 159–70.

[41] See Gutzwiller (2002a: 85 n. 1), who points out that although the term 'ekphrasis' is not specifically applied to epigrams on works of art in antiquity, they clearly 'formed an identifiable category within the broader genre of epigrammatic literature'. Ekphrastic epigrams playing with the deceptive lure of naturalism became particularly popular from the late Hellenistic period, as a subgenre of the rhetorical epigrams that dominate the *Garland of Philip* (in contrast to the more erotic subject-matter of the earlier *Garland of Meleager*). The literature is vast and ever-growing, but see most recently Manakidou (1993), Goldhill (1994 – fundamental – and 2007), Gutzwiller (2002a, 2004b, 2004c), Petrovic and Petrovic (2003), Männlein-Robert (2007), Platt (2007b), Prioux (2007), Squire (2010) and the literature on Posidippus in nn. 42 and 44 below.

of Philip, compiled around 40 CE.[42] As literary texts, Hellenistic epigrams continued to draw attention to their poetic origins as a genre designed for visual display on stone. Traditionally they were themselves the most material of poems, literally 'written upon' the physical environment, and often composed to accompany images such as votive dedications, funerary reliefs or honorific statues.[43] Once divorced from their original function, literary epigrams now bore a dematerialised relationship to their subjects, whether real images (such as famous sculptures or paintings) or works of fiction. Rather than being displayed in the sanctuary, cemetery or agora, they were now read separately from these viewing contexts, sometimes even arranged into virtual collections according to the category of object on which they focused, as we see in Posidippus' *lithika* ('On Stones') and *andriantopoiika* ('On Statues').[44] Too brief and elliptical to present a full rhetorical *descriptio*, as we find in more conventional ekphraseis, epigrams offered 'the poetic identification of a work of art and the poetic *mise en scène* of an important interpretative pronouncement upon it'.[45] They thus established a fictional scenario in which viewing and reading are juxtaposed. The text alludes to its lost materiality as an inscription as well as the materiality of its actual subject-matter, with the reader encouraged to bring both categories of physical object to his or her mind's eye.[46]

The tension between the ekphrastic epigram's original visual function and the absence of its partner object thus lies at the heart of its poetics. In this sense the presence/absence dilemma generated by the sacred image made it a natural epigrammatic theme, for while the image must make present a divinity that defies representation, the epigram must conjure up in verbal form an image that cannot be seen. The constraints of materiality, in this sense, are parallel to the constraints of language. Most importantly,

[42] For Posidippus' epigrams as a single-authored collection, see Austin and Bastianini (2002), together with Gutzwiller (2004a) and the papers collected in Gutzwiller (2005b, especially Bing, Gutzwiller and Krevans). On the collection of epigrams into multi-authored anthologies, see GP 1965 and 1968, Page (1981), Alan Cameron (1993), Gutzwiller (1998), Krevans (2007) and Argentieri (2007).

[43] See Day (1989, 2000, 2007), Svenbro (1993), Bing (2002) and A. Petrovic (2007); on the shift from inscribed to literary epigram in the Hellenistic period, see Bing (1998), Gutzwiller (1998: 47–114) and D. Meyer (2007).

[44] See Austin and Bastianini (2002: nos. 1–20, *lithika*, and 62–20, *andriantopoiika*), together with Falivene (2002), Gutzwiller (2002b), Kosmetatou (2003, 2004), G. Zanker (2003), Hunter (2004), Papalexandrou (2004), Petrain (2005), Prauscello (2006) and the papers collected in Gutzwiller (2005b), particularly Kuttner, Sens and Stewart.

[45] Männlein-Robert (2007: 252).

[46] For an example of an actual inscribed epigram juxtaposed with the image on which it comments, see Gutzwiller (2004b), on a replacement copy of Praxiteles' Eros at Thespiae.

the particularly self-reflexive nature of the Hellenistic epigram, as a literary device that presents the poet 'seeing himself seeing', meant that ekphrastic epigrams about sacred images did not just negotiate the relationship between epiphany and representation, but also drew attention to the poet's reflection upon this very process.[47]

Callimachus' *Hymn to Athena* gains much of its enargeic charge from the potential eroticism of the goddess's epiphany. The act of viewing the statue disrobed of its *kosmos* is presented as equivalent to viewing the naked form of Athena herself. The text's ability to draw in its audience and the frisson of danger it generates thus play upon our desire *to see*. The inevitable distancing effect of mimesis, however, establishes a triple parallel between a frustrated desire for encounter with the divine, the desire for sacred images to 'be' the deities they represent, and the desire to 'see' an image that is conjured up in words. Epiphany, representation and ekphrasis thus form a bewildering textual prism in which the eroticised divine body serves as both a bait for the viewer/reader and a metaphor for the poetics of frustrated vision. In this respect it is not surprising that one of the most popular themes in ekphrastic epigram was the representation of Athena's sensual antithesis Aphrodite, particularly Praxiteles' sculpture of the goddess at Knidos, created around 350 BCE and one of the most highly prized cult images in the Greco-Roman world.[48]

While Aphrodite personified both the force and caprice of desire itself, the Knidia stood as the ultimate example of naturalism's Pygmalionesque potential to make the absent present.[49] The quality of Praxiteles' workmanship (which gave the marble a highly polished surface, possibly tinted with wax) and the image's graceful nudity lent it a beguiling sexual and numinous power, creating a strong charge between (male) viewer and (female) goddess.[50] The Knidia therefore inspired not only an endless series of artistic reproductions (Figures 4.2–3), but also a proliferation of literary responses,

---

[47] Goldhill (1994: 205).

[48] Tragically, the original sculpture was destroyed in a fire in Constantinople in 476 CE (see Mango *et al.*, 1992). On the Knidia and its copies, see Havelock (1995), with Blinkenberg (1933), Kraus (1957), Pfrommer (1985), A. Stewart (1990: vol. I, 176–8, 277–80; 1997: 96–105), R. R. R. Smith (1991: 79–81), Todisco (1993: 71–2), Moreno (1994: vol. I, 108–10, 221–2), R. Osborne (1994), Ridgway (1997: 263–5; 2004: 713–25) and Corso (2007: 9–186). On the eroticism of statues in archaic and classical Greece, see Steiner (2001: 186–250), and, more generally, Freedberg (1989: 317–44).

[49] See K. Gross (1992: 69–75).

[50] On the sculpture's possibly painted surface, see Havelock (1995: 13–16, 51–2), A. Stewart (1997: 99) and Ridgway (2004: 719). On the painting of sculptures in antiquity, see Brinkmann (2003), and, on deities in particular, Brinkmann and Wünsche (2004).

Figure 4.2 Aphrodite of Knidos (Venus Colonna), Roman copy

which explore the intense passion, fear and curiosity the statue aroused in her viewers.[51] As an embodiment of desire itself, the sculpture's magnetism

---

[51] E.g., Plin *HN* 36.20–1, Athenaeus 13.591a and Pseudo-Lucian *Amores* 15–16, discussed below; for literary sources on the Knidia, see Overbeck (1868: 1227–45). On the Aphrodite epigrams, see also Havelock (1995: 22–3, 48–9, 117–26) and Gutzwiller (2004b: 396–9), on Praxiteles' Eros at Thespiae. Another welcome Posidippus discovery would be his work Περὶ Κνίδου,

Figure 4.3 Rear view of Figure 4.2

lay in its ability to inspire *erōs* in every man who beheld it. Yet this desirability was, to a certain extent, at odds with the statue's divine status: Aphrodite's nudity maintains a delicate balance between manifesting the erotic potency

known to us only from a brief reference by Clement of Alexandria (*Protrepticus* 4.53.5; see Austin and Bastianini, 2002: no. 147), in which he seems to have recounted the tale, also in Pliny and Pseudo-Lucian, of a youth who fell in love with the Knidia.

of the goddess, on one hand, and yet inviting transgressive possession by the male gaze, on the other. In this sense the Knidia encapsulates the ability of naturalistic illusionism to absorb and deceive the viewer – to generate an experience of epiphany. Yet the very popularity of the statue as a literary theme also reflects its status as an artistic object.[52] The epigram ascribed to 'Plato' above illustrates this duality with great elegance: Aphrodite is impressed by the verisimilitude of her image, and confirms its sanctity by suggesting that Praxiteles has seen her unawares, yet the scene the epigram conjures up is of the goddess evaluating her representation for its naturalistic skill, not unlike the women in Herodas' fourth *mimiambus*, who comment on the illusionism of the paintings and sculptures they encounter in the sanctuary of Asclepius on Cos.[53] The goddess thus performs *theōria* at her own sanctuary, in a move that both confirms the Knidia's sanctity and introduces a profound rupture between goddess and statue, emphasising the ontological distinction between image and prototype. A variation on this theme makes the Knidia's status as both subject and object even more emphatic, prefixing the goddess's cry 'Where did Praxiteles see me naked?' with the phrase 'Cypris, seeing Cypris in Knidos, said ... ' (ἁ Κύπρις τὰν Κύπριν ἐνὶ Κνίδῳ εἶπεν ἰδοῦσα).[54] Both epigrams demonstrate how the Knidia stands as both an embodiment of divinity and a symbol of artistic skill (of *theosebeia* and *technē*), generating a nexus of fraught encounters between viewer and image, artist and object, man and woman, lover and beloved, and, perhaps most importantly, mortal and divine.

That the Knidia's provocative nudity and aura of divine presence were problematic, even as they were thrilling, is demonstrated by Pliny's *aition* of the sculpture's presence on the otherwise insignificant promontory of Knidos (*HN* 36.20–1). We are told that the statue was turned down by its commissioners (the islanders of Cos) in favour of a draped image, also by Praxiteles, because the nude was considered too risqué. Consequently, 'the people of Knidos bought the rejected statue, the reputation of which became immeasurably greater.'[55] Pliny goes on to narrate the infamous tale (also recounted in Pseudo-Lucian's *Amores* 15–17) of a youth who, inflamed

---

[52] See Arscott and Scott (2000: 5): 'Since Venus is preeminent in beauty, as well as in sexual love, her presence in art triggers a meditation on the domain of the aesthetic. The special power of art can be presented and contemplated in terms of the libidinal sway of the goddess.' For the influence and re-presentation of Venus statues in Western art, see the catalogue of the Louvre's 2000 exhibition *D'après l'antique* (Cuzin *et al.*, 2000), particularly 'Dalí, la Vénus de Milo et la persistence de la mémoire antique' (462–7).

[53] Herodas 4.20–38, 56–78 (cf. Theocritus 15.78–86); see Gelzer (1985), Manakidou (1993: 18–39), Goldhill (1994: 216–23) and J. Burton (1995: 93–122).

[54] *Anth. Plan.* 162; cf. Gutzwiller (2004b: 396).   [55] *HN* 36.20.

with desire for the image, visited the shrine by night, and in an excess of 'enthusiasm' left his mark on the object of his passion.[56] It is no accident that the boy in question is said to have then committed suicide in mysterious circumstances with an Actaeon-esque flavour of divine punishment, which imbued the sculpture itself with a sinister power.[57] Pseudo-Lucian goes so far as to describe the unfortunate viewer as a 'New Anchises' (16), a reminder of the hero's fear in the *Homeric Hymn to Aphrodite* that 'No man who sleeps with immortal goddesses is full of vigour (βιοθάλμιος)' (189–90), since for a mortal man to love a goddess is to risk impotence and even death. He frames this tale with a discussion of the respective merits of homo- and heterosexual love, set in the context of the Knidian sanctuary itself. Viewing the cult image within its shrine (which seems to have been an open structure in which the statue could be viewed from various angles), the author's companions, one of each sexual orientation, respond in dramatically different ways to the statue's erotic sway.[58] Viewing the goddess from the front, the heterosexual visitor, Charicles, is overcome by her feminine beauty and tries to kiss her, while his friend Callicratidas is unmoved by her form until, walking round to view her from behind, he becomes aroused by her perfect buttocks and compares her to Ganymede (14). It is a mark of both Praxiteles' genius and the statue's divinity that the Knidia is not only the ultimate classical representation of the feminine body, but also the ideal boy. Observed from all sides in an open shrine, her naked body fully revealed, she is Greek

---

[56] See Corso (1988: vol. I, 24–5, 42–4, 91–3, 127–40). For a discussion of these texts, see Elsner (1991), K. Gross (1992: 81–2), R. Osborne (1994), Goldhill (1995: 102–5), A. Stewart (1997: 86–105) and Vout (2007: 27–9).

[57] Pseudo-Lucian *Amores* 16: 'The youth concerned is said . . . to have hurled himself over a cliff or down into the waves of the sea and to have vanished utterly' (translation by M. D. MacLeod, Loeb Classical Library, 1967). For an echo of this story in nineteenth-century France, see Prosper Mérimée's 1837 novella *La Vénus d'Ille*, in which a young man who jokingly places an engagement ring upon the finger of a bronze Venus discovered nearby is subsequently crushed to death by the statue on his wedding night: 'How I pity her lovers!' the narrator proclaims, 'She must have delighted in making them die of despair'. For this literary tradition, which dates back to the twelfth century, see Baum (1919), Ziolkowski (1977: 18–77) and Freedberg (1989: 333, 491 n. 25).

[58] The claim by Iris Love (1972) to have discovered a tholos temple that housed the statue at Knidos has now been proven invalid; epigraphic evidence suggests that the structure was in fact associated with Athena. See Bankel (1997). Although the Knidia's home has not yet been found, Pliny tells us that 'her shrine is completely open, so that the image of the goddess can be seen from all sides' (36.21), while Pseudo-Lucian claims that 'the temple had a door on both sides for the benefit of those also who wish to have a good view of the goddess from behind' (13). A copy of the Knidia discovered at Tivoli certainly suggests that, by the imperial period, three-dimensional displays of the statue were considered *de rigueur* (see MacDonald and Pinto, 1995: 58–9). Havelock (1995: 58–63) suggests that the Knidia was redisplayed in an open shrine during the second century BCE; see also Ridgway (2004: 721–2).

man's perfect sexual object.[59] Nevertheless, the apocryphal mark of sexual frustration on her thigh demonstrates that any attempt to consummate the erotic narrative she sets in motion is doomed to failure, for she is both a stone (impenetrable) image and divine (unpossessable) goddess. Praxiteles' skill may conjure up the goddess's presence for the Knidia's viewers, yet the very existence of the statue as a material object which 'represents' Aphrodite is a reminder of her absence.

The Knidia's ambiguous relationship to her viewers is also key to the literary conceits employed by ekphrastic epigrams, many of which respond to the aura of presence she generates by suggesting that image and prototype are one and the same. In this sense they stand within a broader ekphrastic tradition that celebrates the deceptive lure of naturalism, echoing popular themes such as Myron's Cow, which became a popular topos in the Hellenistic period and was imitated in 'variations on a theme' for several centuries, testifying to Graeco-Roman culture's ongoing flirtation with the alluring and problematic nature of mimesis.[60] These and other epigrams repeatedly exploit the ambiguities of naturalism in order to play with the idea that a statue or painting blurs the boundaries between an image and its prototype; for instance, on Myron's Cow, 'It is the base to which it is attached that keeps back the heifer, and if freed from this it will run off to the herd.'[61] In playing this game the epigrams present in verbal form the implicit achievements of naturalistic art: they imbue the image with life, realise the potential of its *veritas*. In several poems this ambiguity is dramatised still further by the motif of prosopopoeia (the verbal summoning of dead or divine persons before the eyes of the reader or listener) in which, as I shall discuss below, the image is actually given a voice and, animated by the verbal power of the text, comments upon its own status.

Revelation

Aphrodite's great mythic triumph is the Judgement of Paris, in which it is the goddess's influence over her male viewer that exalts and confirms her divine status and identity: in contrast to Athena, it is when Aphrodite is *seen* that she is victorious. A popular image of Aphrodite in ancient art is that of the goddess carrying out her toilette in preparation for her lovemaking with

---

[59] For a feminist response to the Knidia, see Salomon (1997).

[60] On the Myron's Cow series (*Anth. Pal.* 9.713–42), see Fua (1973), Speyer (1975), Gutzwiller (1998: 245–50), Corso (2006) and Squire (2010).

[61] *Anth. Pal.* 9.740 (attributed to Geminus) = GP 1968: Geminus no. 5.

Ares.[62] The fact that she looks at herself in a mirror is essential to this image, for her erotic power (as demonstrated by the subsequent seduction) lies in the beguiling effects of her physical manifestation. Crucial to this power is the goddess's own awareness of her effect upon the viewer; in the visual tradition, she is repeatedly shown looking at herself, and is often represented on the backs of mirrors.[63] We find the same motif in Hellenistic poetry: in Apollonius' *Argonautika*, Aphrodite is embroidered on the cloak that Hypsipyle gives to Jason, looking at her image reflected in the shield of Ares (1.742–5, discussed below); in Callimachus' *Hymn to Athena* she is explicitly contrasted to Athena and Hera, who, we are told, did *not* look at themselves prior to Paris' judgement, whereas 'Cypris took the shining bronze and often altered and again altered the same lock' (21–2). Likewise, in 'Plato's' epigram on the Knidia (quoted above), the poet describes how the goddess visited her sanctuary at Knidos, 'wishing to see her own image' (βουλομένη κατιδεῖν εἰκόνα τὴν ἰδίην). In making this claim the poet represents the encounter between goddess and statue as that between the goddess and her reflection. Significantly, the Knidia is referred to as an *eikōn*, a term that is more commonly used for portraits and suggests a mimetic 'likeness', rather than the ritual function suggested by the term *agalma*.[64] By applying the motif of Aphrodite looking at herself to the goddess's relationship with Praxiteles' image, the epigrammatist distinguishes between image and prototype, yet simultaneously makes a claim for the statue's authenticity. This is then

---

[62] E.g., *The Courtship of Mars and Venus* from the house of Marcus Lucretius Fronto, Pompeii. For images of Aphrodite looking at her reflection, see *LIMC* s.v. Aphrodite, nos. 494–6, 836, 1105, 1192; for depictions of her on mirrors themselves, see nos. 87–97, 111–22; for a recent discussion, see Taylor (2008: 39–47). A number of mosaics from the eastern provinces depict Venus Triumphans looking at herself in a mirror while resplendent on her conch-shell: see Balensiefen (1990: 244 and nos. K 50–2, pl. 13–14). Arscott and Scott (2000: 11) testify to the ongoing association of Venus with her reflection, informing us of the Venus de Milo that 'A much favoured "restoration" of the Melian goddess had her staring at her own reflection in the shiny glare of a polished shield, a variation on ancient narratives of Venus's pleasure in her own image'; on the Melian Aphrodite, and the related Aphrodite of Capua (who also held a shield), see Havelock (1995: 95–7) and Kousser (2008). The relationship between epiphany and reflection is further discussed in Chapter 5, 222–3.

[63] E.g., a late classical red-figure pelike in the Louvre (K 95), which represents Aphrodite looking at herself in a hand-mirror while she is carried by winged Erotes, and a Hellenistic mirror, also in the Louvre (27663), with an incised Aphrodite and Eros. The major work on case mirrors is Züchner (1942); on the use and representation of mirrors in Greek culture, see Frontisi-Ducroux and Vernant (1997); for Berger-influenced readings of the relationship between women and the images on fourth-century BCE case mirrors (i.e., contemporary with the Knidian Aphrodite), see A. Stewart (1996, 1997: 171–81) and Roussos (1999: 230–305). Statius refers to an image of Venus as being imprisoned in a case mirror: 'speculum reclusit imagine rapta' (*Silvae* 3.4.97).

[64] On this distinction, see Chapter 2, nn. 80 and 159.

confirmed by the second couplet of the poem, in which the goddess expresses her astonishment at its lifelike qualities.

It is as if the Narcissus myth, which also plays upon the reflexive nature of beauty, desire and reflection, is transposed to the goddess's relationship with her own image. What could be a more eloquent way in which to praise the *technē* of its creator than to claim his representation is on a par with the naturalistic powers of reflection itself? There is, however, a significant difference: whereas the mortal Narcissus was, as a negative paradigm of reflection, fatally transfixed by his mirror image, Aphrodite's delight in her sculpted image confirms and magnifies her divine beauty. While this contrast can be read as a demonstration of gendered attitudes to the relationship between self and body (in Berger's infamous – and problematic – maxim, 'Men look at women. Women watch themselves being looked at'), it can also be read as an expression of the difference between the mortal and divine.[65] Whereas images of Narcissus serve to warn the viewer of naturalism's mesmerising ability to ensnare the gaze, images of Aphrodite present a positive erotic narrative in which self-admiration is not caught in an endless solipsistic loop, but serves to reinforce the deity's sphere of authority.[66] Crucially, Aphrodite traditionally remains in control both of her own act of viewing, and of the way in which she is viewed. Her glance into the mirror is a demonstration of her ability, both as a woman and as a goddess, to manipulate her epiphanic self-presentation.

In dramatising the viewing of the Knidia as equivalent to viewing the goddess herself, several poems in the *Greek Anthology* accordingly construct their epigrammatic conceit around the Judgement of Paris, that mythic moment of triumphant epiphany in which Aphrodite, as goddess of the desirous gaze, makes her power fully manifest:

Πρόσθε μὲν Ἰδαίοισιν ἐν οὔρεσιν αὐτὸς ὁ βούτας
    δέρξατο τὰν κάλλευς πρῶτ᾿ ἀπενεγκαμέναν.
Πραξιτέλης Κνιδίοις δὲ πανωπήεσσαν ἔθηκεν,
    μάρτυρα τῆς τέχνης ψῆφον ἔχων Πάριδος.

---

[65] J. Berger (1972: 47). For a reading of a female image which, in contrast to Berger's formulation, 'takes over and dominates both viewer and lover' rather than presenting herself as static spectacle, see Bal (1995: 165); for evaluations of Berger's claim, see Fuller (1980), Doane (1982), Kaplan (1983), de Lauretis (1984) and Pointon (1990: 4, 15–17).

[66] On Narcissus, see most recently Bartsch (2000; 2006: 84–96), Elsner (2000b; 2007: 132–76), Frontisi-Ducroux (2000), Platt (2002), Bettini and Pellizer (2003), Iaculli (2003) and Taylor (2008: 56–77).

The shepherd himself beheld on the mountains of Ida
She who gained first prize on account of her beauty.
But Praxiteles has set her in full view of the Knidians,
Having the vote of Paris as witness to his skill.[67]

Here the poet Evenus implies that the mythic epiphany of the Judgement
has been recreated in the form of the Knidia in such a way that the goddess
has now become *panōpēessa*, from *panopsios* – 'wholly visible,' or 'visible to
all'. To view the sculpture, the epigram implies, is to enter into the *enargeia*
of the myth, to behold the goddess in all her naked glory and experience
her *kallos*. Every man to visit Knidos can now be a latter-day Paris. Just as
Aphrodite promised fulfilment of desire (in the form of Helen) to the Trojan
prince, so her image, as an embodiment of the goddess's beauty made 'all-
visible', promises fulfilment to its viewers. Indeed, an epigram also ascribed
to 'Plato' claims that the Knidia is so obviously a manifestation of the
goddess (even addressing the statue as if it were Aphrodite herself), that she
transcends the realm of 'art' altogether. Here the viewer does not enter into a
recreation of the Judgement of Paris, but actually sees the goddess as she then
appeared:

Οὔτε σε Πραξιτέλης τεχνάσατο, οὔθ' ὁ σίδαρος.
  ἀλλ' οὕτως ἔστης, ὥς ποτε κρινομένη.

Neither Praxiteles nor the chisel formed you,
But so you stand, just as when you came to judgement.[68]

In line with the Judgement theme, another major series of epigrams is
based upon Apelles' painting *Aphrodite Anadyomene*. Depicting the goddess
'Rising from the Waves', this focused on the other significant moment of
epiphanic revelation in the goddess's myth-cycle, which, as the moment of
her birth, was arguably the most important. Just as Praxiteles supposedly
'saw' Aphrodite at the moment of judgement, Apelles is claimed to have
seen the goddess emerging from the ocean:

Αὐτὰν ἐκ πόντοιο τιθηνητῆρος Ἀπελλῆς,
  τὰν Κύπριν γυμνὰν εἶδε λοχευομέναν.
καὶ τοίαν ἐτύπωσε, διάβροχον ὕδατος ἀμφῶ
  θλίβουσαν θαλεραῖς χερσὶν ἔτι πλόκαμον.

---

[67] *Anth. Plan.* 166 (Evenus) = GP 1968: Evenus no. 11.
[68] *Anth. Plan.* 161 ('Plato'; see above, n. 40).

Apelles saw Cypris herself brought forth naked
By the sea, her nurse;
And so he drew her, still wringing with her hands
Her locks soaked with the foam of the water.[69]

Here, the beauty and naturalism of Apelles' painting are attributed to the
artist's vision of Aphrodite's genesis. His own epiphanic encounter and our
viewing of the painting are presented as equivalent experiences; the goddess
is represented τοίαν, 'just as' she appeared at the moment of her birth. This
sense of transmitted epiphanic experience – from artist to poet to reader –
is reinforced by the verb ἐτύπωσε (3), from τυπόω, to 'impress' or 'mould'.
Often used in connection with *phantasia* and Stoic theories of vision, the
language of *tupōsis* ('impression') implies a chain of images emanating from
a prototype, a direct link between an object and its representation.[70] It is
thus closely linked to Hellenistic materialist epistemologies, and the notion
that knowledge can be acquired through sense perception. In this respect the
Anadyomene presents a theory of representation that counters the Platonic
notion of mimesis and makes a claim for the validity of both image and
epiphany. This is reinforced by the sensuous tactility of the poem's final
couplet: the poet's emphasis on the seawater in Aphrodite's hair, and her
iconic posture as she wrings out her locks, is such that the reader might
expect the painting to be wet too; the liquid nature of the paint itself
(especially at the painting's own moment of inception, as Apelles himself
'gives birth' to the goddess) echoes and once more engenders Aphrodite.
Indeed, the late antique epigrammatist Julianus (who demonstrates a keen
sense of continuity with his Greek predecessors) takes this conceit to its
logical conclusion when he warns the viewer:

ἀλλὰ τάχος γραφίδων ἀποχάζεο, μή σε διήνῃ
    ἀφρὸς ἀποστάζων θλιβομένων πλοκάμων.

---

[69] *Anth. Plan.* 179 (Archias) = GP 1968: Archias no. 34.

[70] E.g., Diogenes Laertius *Lives of the Philosophers* 7.45–6. On the relationship between *tupōsis*
and the visual arts, see Platt (2006). On *phantasia* and Stoic theories of vision, see Sandbach
(1971), Lindberg (1976: 9–11), Imbert (1980), G. Simon (1988), Watson (1988: 38–58),
Ioppolo (1990), Zagdoun (2000: 160–70) and Bartsch (2006: 65–7). On *phantasia* and
epiphany in Greek imperial literature, see my discussion in Chapter 7, 320–9. The vocabulary
of *tupōsis* is also found in *Anth. Pal.* 7.169, 7.730, 12.56, 12.57, 13.2 and 15.51, and *Anth. Plan.*
30, 136, 143 and 216 (see Manakidou, 1993: 160–2). Note that *Anth. Plan.* 216 (Parmenion's
epigram on Polyclitus' Hera) describes the statue as τυπωσάμενος, 'moulded' by the sculptor.
The relationship between Epicurean epistemology and epiphanic vision is discussed by Mackey
(in press).

But back quickly from the picture, in case you are made wet
By the foam that drips from her tresses as she wrings them![71]

In this example the painting's blurring of image and prototype is so strong that, just as Evenus' epigram purports to lead the viewer into the Judgement of Paris itself, so here the viewer stands on the seashore and, with Apelles, is witness to Aphrodite's birth. Furthermore, every time the epigram itself is read, the genesis occurs again, in an infinite recession of births and viewings directly related to the original epiphany of the goddess.

Creation

Despite their superficial simplicity, the Knidia epigrams present a sophisticated commentary on the relationship between reading, viewing, naturalistic art and desire. Relying upon their readers' acquaintance with the sculpture, they construct a mode of viewing within the text which, while not conventional ekphrastic 'description' as such, performs a similar role to ekphrasis in that it attempts to construct a visual medium through the power of the verbal. The epigrams thus employ a wide variety of mimetic scenarios: they address the statue and/or the goddess, give voice to the goddess through prosopopoeia, or comment upon the image as if directing a remark to another viewer. Our response to the image is dictated by the text, and in each case the mode of viewing offered is epiphanic: we apprehend the statue as Aphrodite herself. In this sense, the strategies of image and text coincide. However, this literary epiphany is created by a double process of mimesis – a verbal representation of the visual (i.e., the image within the text), and a visual representation of the divine (i.e., the goddess behind the image). So, while the epigram purports to break down the opposition between the visual and the verbal, the artificial and the real, this strategy is so self-consciously displayed that it calls attention to the epigram's own 'literary' status, and so, too, to the constructed nature of the image within the text. In this way the poems seem, paradoxically, to undermine their own epiphanic enterprise.

One of the key ways in which the image's object status is stressed is by a repeated emphasis on the artist's *technē*. This points to the conundrum that although each image appears to be Aphrodite herself, this epiphanic quality is a result of the mortal artist's craftsmanship of inert material. The equivalence between the genesis of Aphrodite qua goddess and her creation

---

[71] *Anth. Plan.* 181, 3–4 (Julianus).

as an image becomes a motif by which the epiphanic qualities of the image are revealed to be the product of mortal skill. This is particularly well demonstrated by an epigram attributed to the third-century poet Antipater of Sidon:

Τὰν ἀναδυομέναν ἀπὸ ματέρος ἄρτι θαλάσσας
    Κύπριν, Ἀπελλείου μόχθον ὅρα γραφίδος.
ὡς χερὶ συμμάρψασα διάβροχον ὕδατι χαίταν
    ἐκθλίβει νοτερῶν ἀφρὸν ἀπὸ πλοκάμων.
αὐταὶ νῦν ἐρέουσιν Ἀθηναίη τε καὶ Ἥρη.
    Οὐκέτι σοὶ μορφᾶς εἰς ἔριν ἐρχόμεθα.

Look at the labour of Apelles' pencil: Cypris, just
Rising from the sea, her mother;
How, grasping her dripping hair with her hand,
She wrings the foam from the wet locks.
Athena and Hera themselves will say,
'We compete with you in the beauty contest no longer.'[72]

The epigram overtly complicates the nature of Aphrodite's birth: while Antipater pointedly describes the sea as the goddess's 'mother', the imperative in the first couplet of the poem exhorts the reader to look at the Ἀπελλείου μόχθον . . . γραφίδος, the 'labour of Apelles' pencil', encouraging us to view the image, and Aphrodite herself, as the product of the artist's own endeavours (the word μόχθον implying the labour of childbirth). Hence Apelles is not, as in Archias' epigram, a witness to the goddess's epiphanic appearance from the sea, but is held responsible for her very existence as a visible entity. Julianus' epigram on the Anadyomene even claims that Aphrodite has been 'delivered by Apelles' midwife hand' (μαῖαν Ἀπελλείην εὑραμένη παλάμην).[73] The goddess's 'birth' as an artistic image designed to be viewed is thus presented as being inseparable from her birth in myth.

This emphasis on artistic creativity is, of course, entirely appropriate to images of Aphrodite, who is herself the ultimate *creatrix*; as Lucretius claims in the *De rerum natura*, 'without [her] nothing comes forth into the shining borders of light, nothing lovely or joyous is made'.[74] However, creative power is here wrested from the goddess herself, who is presented as a product created by the (male) artist. As any ancient reader would have known, although Aphrodite rose from the sea, this was because she was the

---

[72] *Anth. Plan.* 178 = GP 1965: Antipater no. 45.   [73] *Anth. Plan.* 181, 2.
[74] *De rerum natura* 1.22–23: 'nec sine te quicquam dias in luminis oras / exoritur neque fit laetum, neque amabile quicquam' (translation by W. H. D. Rouse, Loeb Classical Library edition, 1982).

product of the castrated phallus of Ouranos; that is, the goddess's *paternity* was most crucial to the story of her birth.[75] The fact that this element of the myth goes unmentioned raises the question of her paternity, only to imply that perhaps Apelles himself should be credited with this role, for it is he who has given birth to the goddess in the form of her image. The popularity of the Anadyomene in ekphrastic epigram is due, then, not only to the beauty of Apelles' painting itself, but also to the fact that it is a representation of creative genesis. While the Anadyomene series is ostensibly about visual creativity, the absorption of such a motif into the literary medium of the epigram invites the reader to reflect simultaneously on the *technē* of the poet himself, and thus the literary conception of the text. That the artist was the 'father' of his work is an oft-repeated motif in the Western tradition; in the context of epigram, Geminus describes the Eros of Praxiteles at Thespiae as the offspring of the poet and *Technē*.[76] This paternal relationship also applies to the relationship between an author and his work. Jesper Svenbro casts the relationship between writing and reading as one between parent and child. Claiming that, 'for the Greeks, the writer was normally seen as a father', he refers to a passage in Artemidorus' *Oneirocritica* in which any man who dreams he is a writer will subsequently conceive offspring.[77] The implication is that, while Apelles has produced the Anadyomene, the poet himself has produced the epigram and, by extension, the image within; it is ultimately literary *technē* that has reproductive power (a potency that is reinforced by the poem's status as an infinitely replicable text).

While Apelles is presented as an epigrammatic paradigm of the artist as parent, Praxiteles represents the artist as lover. Many epigrams play with the idea that the sculptor must have been sexually involved with Aphrodite, while a parallel literary tradition claims that he used his mistress Phryne as a model.[78] This notion of the creative process as a form of erotic appreciation is closely related to the myth of Pygmalion.[79] Here we find a similar tension

---

[75] Hesiod *Theogony* 154–206, Epimenides DK 3 B19; see Dalby (2005: 9–11).

[76] *Anth. Plan.* 205 = GP 1968: 9.   [77] Svenbro (1993: 85); *Oneirocritica* 1.53.

[78] The primary reference is Athenaeus 13.590f–591a. See also *Anth. Plan.* 203–6, which play with the notion that Praxiteles' sculpture of Eros was a gift to Phryne. For further Phryne references and discussion, see Raubitschek (1941), Pollitt (1990a: 86–7), Havelock (1995: 42–9), Corso (1997), McClure (2003: 126–36), Gutzwiller (2004b: 385–6) and Ridgway (2004: 715–18). On romantic ties between artists and their models, see Kris and Kurz (1979: 40–41, 116–20). In an echo of Parmenion's Hera, Athenaeus tells us that Phryne was 'more beautiful in the unseen parts (ἐν τοῖς μὴ βλεπομένοις)' (590f).

[79] On Ovid's Pygmalion (*Met.* 10.243–97), see Sharrock (1991b, 1991b) and Elsner (2007: 113–31). Cf. Zeuxis' painting of Helen at Croton, based on the most beautiful parts of five different naked models (Cicero *De inventione* 2.1.1–3, Plin. *HN* 35.64), on which see E. Mansfield (2007: 19–38).

between the idea of the animated image (desire has the transformative ability to make marble flesh) and the image as a created object. Again, the emphasis on artistic *technē* refers us to the skill of the poet himself in constructing such a conceit. As Alison Sharrock has persuasively argued for Ovid's *Metamorphoses*, the paradigm of the artist as lover is a metaphor for the role of the poet himself.[80]

By shaping a verbal viewing of the Knidia that emphasises her creation by man, these epigrams not only reflect the authority of the poet but also neutralise the sexual energy of the image, even as they praise it. The numinous sway the Knidia has over her viewers in the prose accounts of Pliny and Lucian is curtailed and transformed into a metaphor for the skill of the poet, when shaped by epigram and subordinated to his literary concerns. This neutralisation also results from the formulation of the image's naturalistic charisma in verbal terms. The aura of divinity projected by the actual statue – the phenomenological impact of the image *as* goddess – cannot be captured fully by language, for the naturalistic image relies on its powers of visual absorption to lure the viewer into a narrative of desire. Such absorption cannot be communicated by the epigram, which is, by nature, an exercise in the verbal facility to express an ironic distance from any subject matter discussed. Because of its rhetorical and agonistic concerns, the epigram is, ultimately, an exercise in self-promotion; it is all about the *poet*. In celebrating the Knidia's naturalism, the epigram appropriates the stylistic mode to express the authority of the word; it presents, in effect, a form of anti-naturalism that threatens the status of the very object it praises.

By celebrating the potency of artistic *technē* and calling attention to the artificial nature of representation, the Anadyomene and Knidia epigrams thus appropriate the achievements of the visual for their own, verbal medium. Yet they praise the achievements of artifice by, paradoxically, emphasising the epiphanic potency of the image, deliberately merging the mythical genesis of Aphrodite with the creation of the Anadyomene by Apelles, or the manifestation of the goddess at the Judgement of Paris with Praxiteles' creation of the Knidia. This exploration of the relationship between image and prototype is not simply a means of praising the artist; it is also a key element of each text's poetics, a tool by which the epigram can construct its 'conceit' – the verbal quip that gives each poem its rhetorical force, satisfying the reader's literary expectations and seeking his or her admiration. Although each poem may present us with a mode of 'viewing', this viewing is ultimately subject to a mode of 'reading'. As W. J. T. Mitchell

---

[80] Sharrock (1991b: 37).

points out, 'All ekphrasis is notional, and seeks to create a specific image that is to be found only in the text as its "resident alien".'[81]

This subtle line between the word's ability to animate and subordinate the image is demonstrated by an epigram from the *Garland of Philip* attributed to the first-century BCE Roman aristocrat Geminus, who employs the motif of prosopopoeia in order to give voice to a painting by Polygnotus of the Elean king Salmoneus. Said to have mimicked Zeus by using a bronze cauldron and torches to simulate thunder and lightning, the king was consequently killed by a thunderbolt sent by the god:

Χείρ με Πολυγνώτου Θασίου κάμεν. εἰμὶ δ' ἐκεῖνος
    Σαλμωνεύς, βρονταῖς ὃς Διὸς ἀντεμάνην,
ὅς με καὶ εἰν Ἀΐδῃ πορθεῖ πάλι, καί με κεραυνοῖς
    βάλλει, μισῶν μου κοὐ λαλέοντα τύπον.
ἴσχε, Ζεῦ, πρηστῆρα, μέθες χόλον. εἰμὶ γὰρ ἄπνους
    ὁ σκοπός. ἀψύχοις εἰκόσι μὴ πολέμει.

The hand of Thrasian Polygnotus made me. I am that
Salmoneus, mad rival of the thunders of Zeus,
Who destroys me again even in Hades and strikes me with his
Bolts, hating even my voiceless figure.
Zeus, restrain your fiery blast, put aside your anger. For I,
Your target, am without breath. War not with lifeless images.[82]

The epigram's conceit is constructed around the paradox that Salmoneus, as an image, is 'lifeless' (*apsuchos*, 6), yet manipulates this fact in order to persuade Zeus to cease punishing him, so demonstrating poetry's ability to exploit the motif of animation. The tension between Polygnotus' lifelike representation of the mythical king and Salmoneus' status as a mere painted image is echoed by that between the silent painting evoked for the viewer and the accompanying epigram which, when spoken aloud, brings the image to life. The contrast between the image's silence and the power of speech

---

[81] W. J. T. Mitchell (1994: 157 n. 19).

[82] *Anth. Plan.* 30 = GP 1968: Geminus no. 6. Gow and Page identify the writer as C. Terentius Tullius Geminus, *consul suffectus* in 46 CE. Ten epigrams are attributed to him altogether (seven in the *Palatine Anthology* and three in the Planudean manuscript). He is hurriedly dismissed by Gow and Page (1968: 295), who show little interest in ekphrastic literature, with the somewhat unfair claim that he 'is among the least gifted of Philip's authors. Most of the epigrams are descriptions of works of art. The sentiments are commonplace, sometimes foolish; the phrasing is generally undistinguished and occasionally incompetent.' On Salmoneus, see Hesiod fr. 30.22–3 M-W (from the *Catalogue of Women*), Diodorus Siculus 6.6.4–5, Virgil *Aeneid* 6.585–94, Apollodorus 1.9.7 and Hyginus *Fabulae* 61, 239; the myth also seems to have been the subject of a lost satyr play (*Salmoneus*) by Sophocles.

conferred by literature is repeatedly stressed. While Salmoneus speaks, he describes himself as 'unspeaking' (οὐ λαλέοντα, 4) and 'without breath' (ἄπνους, 5). It is a commonplace of the ekphrastic tradition to describe an image as 'breathing'; indeed, Geminus uses the word ἔμπνοος in an epigram praising the naturalistic qualities of Myron's Cow, just as Martial later writes of his painted portrait 'spirat . . . picta tabella'.[83] It is a measure not only of Salmoneus' sophistic character, but also of Geminus' poetic skill, that he contradicts this topos in order to make his epigrammatic point.

Indeed, Geminus' sophisticated approach to his literary enterprise is demonstrated by his rather obscure choice of subject.[84] For Salmoneus' story is about representation itself. In creating the son et lumière effects of thunder and lightning, the mythical king simulates Zeus, presenting himself as an embodiment of the god (or potential rival) upon earth. In the context of a genre concerned with the practice and limits of mimesis, this creative form of role-playing is almost an enactment of the artist's own enterprise. Assuming the identity of another is, like naturalistic representation, a form of imitation. When representation can so easily be viewed as 'reality' (as both Polygnotus' painting and the Knidia demonstrate), the artist's naturalistic endeavour seems to echo Salmoneus' fatal hubris. The ambiguous relationship between visual representation and the process of simulating, animating or 'becoming' a prototype is cleverly demonstrated by Salmoneus' description of himself as a σκοπός: he is both a 'mark' or 'target' of Zeus' wrath, and 'one that watches or looks out', even 'one who lies in wait'.[85] As an animated representation Salmoneus is simultaneously a passive image, subjected criminal, viewed object and an active prototype, holder of the gaze, master of mimesis, just as the Knidian Aphrodite maintains an ambiguous position as both subject and object, viewer and viewed, goddess and image.

Salmoneus' fate also offers a neat counterpart to that of the Knidia's frustrated lover: whereas the Elean king attempts to manifest himself as an immortal by appropriating the attributes of divinity (thunder and lightning), the youth of Knidos attempts to possess an immortal by raping a goddess in the form of her statue. While Salmoneus demonstrates a narcissistic desire to equate himself with a deity, the Knidian youth succumbs

---

[83] *Anth. Pal.* 9.740, 3 = GP 1968: Geminus no. 5: ἴδ᾽, ὡς ἔμπνουν ὁ τεχνίτας | θήκατο ('See how alive the artist has made it!'); Martial 7.83.2. Cf. Chapter 3, 130.

[84] *LIMC* 7.1.653–5 s.v. Salmoneus. The king may have featured in Polygnotus' *Nekyia* in the *Leschē* of the Knidians at Delphi, though is not mentioned in Pausanias' description (which does refer to Salmoneus' daughter Tyro at 10.29.7).

[85] LSJ s.v. σκοπός.

to the temptations of voyeuristic desire, pursuing the erotic narrative set in motion by Aphrodite's beguiling image. Both men attempt to transgress the limits of representation, exploiting the visual strategies by which the divine is manifested to man in art.[86] Yet their attempts at animation must necessarily fail, for they have tried to wrest epiphanic agency from the gods themselves.

Possession

Ekphrastic epigrams, then, do not simply praise beautiful images or play literary games: these elements are combined in such a way that they also comment upon the complex nature of the divinity beyond the image. In their probing of the relationship between presence and absence in art and text, they also touch upon another aspect of divinity and its representation by man – that of *themis*, or divine law. One of the most striking elements of 'Plato's' epigram is Aphrodite's expression of surprise and uncertainty: 'Where did Praxiteles see me naked?' This response is also suggested by the statue itself, which seems to have depicted the goddess instinctively moving to conceal her groin and grasping her drapery, as if she has either just disrobed, or is about to conceal her body (Figures 4.2–3).[87] The viewer is thus cast as a trespassing voyeur. Aphrodite's power lies in the revelation of body, yet here she has been caught unawares and is not necessarily in control of the gaze. Is the viewer then cast as an Actaeon, or a Teiresias? As Callimachus' *Hymn to Athena* makes clear, he who unwittingly beholds a naked goddess must suffer the consequences; he has transgressed *themis*.

The Knidia elicits a certain tension between erotic excitement and mortal fear, for to behold her naked is, by extension, to possess her, and yet, as Adonis and Anchises fatally discovered, for a mortal to possess the goddess of love results in impotence, crippling and even death. That to see is to possess sexually is playfully demonstrated by certain epigrams from the *Anthologia Latina* about dinner plates adorned with representations of the nymph Galatea, one of which warns the viewer that if he does not conceal her naked body with food, he will lose his appetite owing to sexual desire.[88] Food, sex and art are presented as consumables, with the implication that, in viewing an erotic image, one simply exchanges one kind of appetite

---

[86] On the simulation of epiphany by mortals, see, e.g., Polyaenus 1.41.1 and 6.1.3, with Krentz and Wheeler (1994: ix–xvi), Petridou (2006: 135–45) and Platt (in press a).

[87] On the suggestion (by Bernoulli, 1873) that the Knidia is caught as she is about to bathe, or has just emerged from her bath, see Havelock (1995: 16–37), who emphasises the prudish anachronism of this interpretation.

[88] *Codex Salmasianus* no. 143 SB; see also nos. 140–2, attributed to Florus.

for another. The epigrams are very much in the spirit of other sympotic literature such as Athenaeus' *Deipnosophistae*, where 'food and women perform analogous functions for the discussants of the dinner party', yet the Galatea poems, by combining the association of food and sex with the trope of ekphrasis, explicitly associate the 'Edible Woman' with the pornographic nature of representational art.[89] This nexus of associations is specifically applied to a statue of a goddess by Athenaeus in an unpleasant twist on the tale of the Knidia's blemished thigh:

> [Cleisophus the Selymbrian] fell in love with the *agalma* made of Parian marble at Samos and locked himself in the temple, so that he might have intercourse with it. When he was unable to, because of the cold and unyielding nature of the stone, he thenceforth desisted from his desire, and setting out a piece of meat, had intercourse with that.[90]

Here the sense of absence provoked by an image that proffers the consummation of desire and yet resists it is crudely reduced to its physical essentials: the statue cannot be possessed simply because it is made of stone. The viewing of the cult image is stripped of all epiphanic ambiguity, and the goddess's representation as a desirable female form is equated, in a hideous subversion of the Pygmalion myth, with a piece of meat that substitutes for the flesh she is not – neither as a divinity, nor as a representation.[91]

This desire to 'make the goddess flesh' so that the passion she arouses can actually be consummated is demonstrated by a series of epigrams from the *Anthologia Latina* in which flowers spring from statues of Venus. On one hand, the theme plays with the conceit that the generative powers of the goddess of fertility have, in a variation on the epiphanic motif, permeated her own image. On the other hand, the topos is made explicitly sexual by an epigram that claims she has 'roses in her loins' (*inguinibus rosas*), as if the locus of animation, the place in which epiphanic encounter is located, is her vagina.[92] For, by logical extension, if the image of the goddess is actually

---

[89] M. M. Henry (1992: 251–2). Galatea reflects the women in the *Deipnosophistae* who 'speak only to the extent that they participate in their own commodification and when they themselves reinforce their status as objects', and where 'the acts of beholding and eating food can become acts of seduction, rape, dismemberment, and murder' (M. M. Henry, 1992: 254, 257). On the association between food and sex in classical Athens, see Davidson (1997: 8–11).

[90] *Deipnosophistae* 13.605f4–10: see Freedberg (1989: 331, 491 n. 21) and M. M. Henry (1992: 257).

[91] For a discussion of the Knidia literature in the context of the Pygmalion myth, see Elsner (1991: n. 3).

[92] *Anthologia Latina* vol. 1, *Codex Salmasianus* no. 351 SB, line 6, attributed to Luxorius. See also *Cod. Sal.* nos. 34 and 56 SB. On ῥόδον and *rosa* as metaphors for female genitalia, see H. White (1980: 17–20), McIntosh Snyder (1989: 78–9) and Skinner (1991: 93 n. 29).

empnoos, if the viewer 'really' has an epiphanic encounter with her, then, made flesh, she *can* fulfil his desire. One of the most striking characteristics of the classical female nude is that, in contrast to her male counterparts, her genitals are never visually defined: she is, ultimately, impenetrable.[93] Yet naturalism's ability to deceive the viewer into thinking that an image is 'real' constantly threatens to transgress *themis* by making the body appear available. Indeed, several of the Knidia epigrams playfully suggest that Praxiteles must have somehow possessed Aphrodite, so neutralising the image through the artist-as-lover paradigm discussed above. In one example the goddess asks:

Γυμνὴν εἶδε Πάρις με, καὶ Ἀγχίσης, καὶ Ἄδωνις.
  τοὺς τρεῖς οἶδα μόνους. Πραξιτέλης δὲ πόθεν;

Paris, Anchises and Adonis saw me naked.
I know only those three. But how did Praxiteles contrive it?[94]

There is a humorous aspect to this particular twist of the epigrammatic conceit. Aphrodite is presented as if counting the notches on her bedpost, wondering if she might have imbibed rather too much nectar at an Olympian symposium. But there is also a deeper element to the joke, which lies in the role of *technē*. For the statue to be so successfully infused with eroticism, it must have been created by someone intimately acquainted with the goddess's charms: Praxiteles must have, in some way, 'known' Aphrodite. The relationship between erotic representation and sexual possession is also demonstrated by the tradition, recorded by Athenaeus, that the Knidia was actually modelled upon Praxiteles' mistress, the courtesan Phryne.[95] It is as if there is an imperative to deny a direct relationship between goddess and mortal, displacing it onto a mortal woman because of the sense of transgression elicited by the image's seeming availability.

---

[93] On the female nude and the 'containment and regulation of the female body', see Nead (1992: 6) and A. Stewart (1997: 100), in addition to R. R. R. Smith (1991: 83), who states, 'It was a basic principle of Greek art that it record all visible essentials of the human body. The smooth, unparted genital surface of the Aphrodites is a rare and presumably highly significant departure from this principle ... Accurate female genitals on statues, we can only surmise, might have been deemed too immodest, or have been felt unconsciously to be too sexually aggressive.' Ridgway (2004: 719) suggests that the original sculpture's hand adhered to the pubis and so made its rendering unnecessary, or that it might have been painted. For a feminist reaction to the way in which the vulva has been 'annulled, smoothed down and idealised', see Parker and Pollock (1981: 127–30). It is perhaps significant that the epigram which is most explicit in its 'opening' of a statue's genitals is attributed to Luxorius (above, n. 92), a sixth-century CE poet who, as a Christian, could perhaps view the image in a more straightforwardly pornographic sense – that is, as a woman open to his sexual possession, rather than a goddess.
[94] *Anth. Plan.* 168 (Anon.).   [95] See above, n. 78.

A later addition to 'Plato's' epigram (above) attempts to absolve the sculptor from such transgression by explicitly denying the idea of an epiphanic viewing of the goddess, claiming:

Πραξιτέλης οὐκ εἶδεν ἃ μὴ θέμις. ἀλλ᾽ ὁ σίδηρος
  ἔξεσεν οἷ ἂν Ἄρης ἤθελε τὴν Παφίην.

Praxiteles did not look on forbidden things,
But the chisel carved the Paphian as Ares would have her.[96]

The locus of divinity is here transferred from the image itself to the σίδηρος – the 'iron' which has created it. The epiphanic conceit is constructed around the association of metal weaponry with the god of war, as if the possessive erotic gaze did not emanate from Praxiteles himself, but from his divinely inspired 'tools'. Thus the notion that the artist must have beheld a deity in order to create his image – whether Praxiteles, Apelles or Phidias – exists side by side with the caveat that he must not have seen 'too much'. Furthermore, the epigram denigrates the goddess, and therefore reduces her erotic sway, by making a playful reference to her adultery: σίδηρος ('iron') suggests through allegorical means the ultimate divine craftsman, and Aphrodite's husband, Hephaestus. While Aphrodite has, in a playful transgression of *themis*, been carved as she appealed to her lover Ares, she has been 'created', it is implied, by her official divine consort. This is 'womanufacture' at its most overt: the goddess is thrice represented as a male construct, according to the fantasies and demands of her lover, her husband and the artist, who, the epigram implies, has been divinely inspired by Hephaestus himself.[97]

The epigrams flirt with the transgressive animation of the divine through their use of prosopopoeia; by giving voice to Aphrodite with the cry, 'Where did Praxiteles see me naked?', 'Plato' commits a similar crime to Salmoneus. The uneasy ambiguity of the Knidia's nudity, which seems to invite scopic possession and to reduce the goddess to the status of a sexual and artistic object, is made complete by her representation in literature, where, although she is made a speaking subject, her words are imposed by a mortal viewer.[98] The image is thus further neutralised by the poet's scripting of Aphrodite's reaction to her own representation. Derrida claims that, although works of art are ostensibly mute, they are in fact 'already talkative, full of virtual

---

[96] *Anth. Plan.* 160 ('Plato'; see n. 40).   [97] Sharrock (1991b).

[98] See Kappeler (1986: 90–1): 'The assumption of the female point of view and narrative voice – the assumption of linguistic and narrative female "subjectivity" ... goes one step further in the total objectification of woman. It is indeed one of the well-tried pornographic devices to fake the female's, the victim's, point of view.'

discourses', yet the attribution of words to an image within an ekphrastic text imposes a *single* discourse, denying the polysemousness that is an essential element of the Knidia's visual charisma.[99] As Peter Wagner argues, 'Ekphrasis . . . has a Janus face: as a form of mimesis, it stages a paradoxical performance, promising to give voice to the allegedly silent image even while attempting to overcome the power of the image by transforming and inscribing it.'[100] Salmoneus' plea, 'War not with lifeless images', captures the way in which the voice projected upon an image through the mastery of text simultaneously emphasises the limits of the visual, even when the words seemingly express the 'lifelike' nature of the image they purport to animate. In this sense 'Plato' and Geminus demonstrate the superiority of literature; they indulge in their own ability to transgress boundaries, to present the unrepresentable and thereby commit the very act of simulation for which Salmoneus was punished.

The Knidia epigrams exploit the issues of gender, desire and divine accessibility that are raised by the statue itself as part of their exploration of the relationship between art and text. While each poem appears to celebrate the authority of the visual, as demonstrated by the sculpture's erotic charms, it also seeks to enhance the status of the written word by simultaneously neutralising the Knidia's divinity, emphasising her status as a man-made object and usurping her own power as a generative force. Without an accompanying text, the Knidia can mean many things, can have multiple effects upon the viewer (as Pseudo-Lucian's *Amores* testify), yet the epigrams repeatedly view Aphrodite through her relationships with men – whether her mythical lovers and admirers, her mortal viewers or her divine and artistic progenitors. Moreover, by dictating Aphrodite's response to the Knidia, they control her relationship with her own image, and thus the gaze of the goddess herself. In imposing such control the epigrams purport to neutralise the curse of Anchises, implying that, through the power of the written word, one might possess the image (and, by extension, the goddess) with impunity.

Frustration

We are then, as readers, subject to the literary 'viewing' presented to us in the text; as Don Fowler has written of ekphrasis, 'a point of view is necessarily inscribed,' and we can focalise only through the poet himself.[101] While each epigram purports to generate a form of epiphanic encounter with Aphrodite through the medium of her image, the literary strategies employed to do so reveal the motif to be a rhetorical construct, and so actually distance the

---

[99] Derrida (1994: 12–13).   [100] Wagner (1996: 13).   [101] D. Fowler (1991: 29).

reader even further from both the statue and the goddess it represents. By emphasising the Knidia's status as a 'man-made' object, the figure of Prax-iteles becomes another distancing device, for epigrams that emphasise how the statue is based upon the artist's epiphany of Aphrodite herself introduce yet another focaliser.[102] This motif is also found in epigrams praising the ultimate *agalmatopoios*, Phidias; for example, an epigram ascribed to Philip, editor of the eponymous *Garland*, claims:

Ἡ θεὸς ἦλθ' ἐπὶ γῆν ἐξ οὐρανοῦ, εἰκόνα δείξων,
Φειδία, ἢ σύ γ' ἔβης τὸν θεὸν ὀψόμενος.

Either God came down from heaven to earth to show you
His image, Phidias, or you went to see God.[103]

This epigram suggests that Phidias had a pure epiphany of Zeus, upon which his cult image of the god at Olympia was based, yet there is a note of equivocation. The reader must still experience the image through the text, and is reliant upon the viewings experienced by both Phidias and the poet. Furthermore, although the epigram states that Phidias must have 'seen' Zeus, the claim that the god must have shown the artist his *eikōn* implies a degree of separation in the viewing process. While *eikōn* suggests a close relationship between image and prototype – in which Phidias' Zeus is an intimate 'portrait' of the god – it nevertheless involves an element of ambiguity, implying representation, shadow, seeming, rather than the 'thing itself'.[104] Whereas *tupōsis* presents a theory of representation that allows for direct transmission, the *eikōn* draws upon a Platonic model of mimesis in which the image is always ontologically inferior to its prototype.

The ambiguous status of the divine *eikōn* is a particularly rich subject for the paradoxical play beloved by epigram precisely because of the contradic-tions that characterise mimetic representations of the gods. We might call it the 'naturalistic paradox' that, as one of the finest examples of classical sculpture, the Knidia represents a goddess whose true status lay *beyond* the reaches of human vision. It is one thing to praise Myron's Cow for its nat-uralistic portrayal of an animal; in this case, image and prototype can be easily compared. But it is quite another to make such a claim for an image of a deity, hence the emphasis in the Anadyomene series on Apelles' role

---

[102] See D. Fowler (1991: 31): 'In literary ecphrasis the presence of the intermediary – usually fictional – visual artist introduces another potential focaliser.'

[103] *Anth. Plan.* 81 (Philip) = GP 1968: Philip no. 67. On Phidias, see Chapter 2, Chapter 5, 224–35, and Chapter 7, 321–3.

[104] See Chapter 2, nn. 80 and 159.

as progenitor of the image. The artist had indeed helped to 'give birth' to the goddess, for she could only be culturally known by her representation on earth. In this sense the goddess behind the representation is revealed to be as much a cultural construct as the painting itself, and the image and its prototype become, in essence, one and the same; to view the Anadyomene or the Knidia is to experience an epiphany of the divine, because such images are essential to the way in which we form our understanding of Aphrodite herself.[105]

The lure of the goddess within the text depends upon the viewer's desire to see. Ekphraseis of Aphrodite's image derive their potency from the fact that this desire is never actually satisfied: the epiphanic conceit offers wholly to reveal the goddess – to make her *panōpēessa* – but in fact this revelation is always withheld. In her discussion of the Knidia epigrams, Havelock claims that 'the only thing that mattered to these authors, whose readers were predominantly men, was that the nude goddess could be seen totally, either in reality or in the imagination. [They] stress more than anything the visibility and accessibility of the goddess.'[106] Yet in suggesting a visibility that is eternally suspended by ekphrasis, the poems actually play with *non*-accessibility; therein lies their epigrammatic conceit, and therein lies the secret of Aphrodite's power, both within the epigrammatic discourse and within her broader role as a personification of desire. For if the play between presence and absence, possession and non-possession, lies at the heart of ekphrasis, it also lies at the heart of desire itself. As a personification of desire, Aphrodite acts as an ever-shifting arouser and potential facilitator of *erōs*. Indeed, an epigram attributed to Posidippus suggests this most eloquently with the lover's complaint:

Δάκρυα καὶ κῶμοι, τί μ᾽ ἐγείρετε, πρὶν πόδας ἆραι
    ἐκ πυρός, εἰς ἑτέρην Κύπριδος ἀνθρακιήν;
λήγω δ᾽ οὔποτ᾽ ἔρωτος. ἀεὶ δέ μοι ἐξ Ἀφροδίτης
    ἄλγος ὁ μὴ κρίνων καινὸν ἄγει τι Πόθος.

---

[105] Which does, of course, raise the question of how women could respond to a goddess whose representation on earth was facilitated entirely by men. R. Osborne (1994) has to conclude that, in contrast to archaic representations of women, the sculpted girl of late classical and Hellenistic art does *not* speak to women too. Compare Freedberg (1989), who suggests that, for female viewers, 'male possession of the female body offers the possibility of female sexual arousal' (322), and Winkler (1990b: 162–87), who explores the idea of 'double consciousness'. For attempts to construct a female viewing experience from ancient sources (particularly in religious contexts), see Sourvinou-Inwood (1978), Stehle and Day (1996), Hackworth Petersen (1997) and, on the Knidia herself, Roussos (1999: 148–221) and Gutzwiller (2004b).

[106] Havelock (1995: 62–3).

Tears and revels, why do you spur me on, before my feet
Are out of the fire, into other coals lit by Cypris?
I never cease from love, but always indiscriminate Desire
Brings me some new pain from Aphrodite.[107]

This process of deferment, the continuous *algos* prompted by desire, can
also be applied to the literary motif of ekphrasis: for the image we desire to
see, which is so delectably presented in *words*, must always be held within the
text itself. The epigram exists as a substitution between the reader and the
artwork it describes, just as a statue of Aphrodite stands between the viewer
and the goddess herself.[108] An anonymous epigram on the Knidia expresses
the eternal frustration engendered by this triangulation with the question,
'Who wrought such desire (*himeron*) in stone?,' for the statue promises so
much, and yet must always refuse to yield.[109]

   This relationship between ekphrasis and desire is not only to be found in
epigram. It is typical of Ovid's use of art (for instance, the Pygmalion episode
in the *Metamorphoses*), and in later literature is a key element not only of
the ancient novel, but also of both Lucian's and Philostratus' *Imagines*.[110] Its
roots in Hellenistic poetry are demonstrated by Moschus' *Europa*, but the
relationship is most astutely captured with reference to Aphrodite herself
in the first book of Apollonius' *Argonautika*, where the poet describes an
image of the goddess embroidered upon the cloak Jason wears for his first
meeting with Hypsipyle.[111] Fittingly, for a poem that breaks new ground in
its depiction of *erōs* in an epic context, Aphrodite is the first deity to make
an appearance, yet the elusive nature of both the divine sphere and the
desire she embodies is demonstrated by the fact that she appears within an
ekphrasis:

Ἑξείης δ' ἤσκητο βαθυπλόκαμος Κυθέρεια
Ἄρεος ὀχμάζουσα θοὸν σάκος. ἐκ δέ οἱ ὤμου
πῆχυν ἔπι σκαιὸν ξυνοχὴ κεχάλαστο χιτῶνος

---

[107] Posidippus 129 (Austin and Bastianini) = *Anth. Pal.* 5.211 = GP 1965: Posidippus no. 3. See
also Loraux (1995: 205), on *erōs* and flight: 'The Greek structure of desire dictates that one
needs wings to approach what flies and is ever elusive. But the (Greek) structure of desire also
dictates that even as one beholds the winged object, one is painfully deprived of it.'

[108] Cf. Elsner (2004).   [109] *Anth. Plan.* 159, 2.

[110] See above, n. 79. On ekphrasis and desire in the *Imagines*, see Elsner (2004), on Philostratus,
and Vout (2007: 213–39), on Lucian, and in the ancient novel, Goldhill (2001b) and Morales
(2004: esp. 96–151).

[111] On the cloak of Hypsipyle, see Fränkel (1968: 100–3), Shapiro (1980), G. Zanker (1987: 68–70,
75–6), Hunter (1993: 52–9) and Manakidou (1993: 101–42). On Moschus, see Fantuzzi and
Hunter (2004: 215–24).

νέρθε ὑπὲκ μαζοῖο. τὸ δ᾽ ἀντίον ἀτρεκὲς αὔτως
χαλκείη δείκηλον ἐν ἀσπίδι φαίνετ᾽ ἰδέσθαι.

Next in order had been wrought long-haired Cytherea,
Wielding the swift shield of Ares; and from her shoulder
To her left arm the fastening of the tunic was loosed
Beneath her breast; and opposite in the shield of bronze
Her image appeared clear to view as she stood.[112]

The meeting between man and god (such a traditional element of epic poetry) is subjected to a complex distancing effect in which the goddess is presented on a different ontological plane to that of the heroes.[113] Not only is Aphrodite distanced by one medium (as an image within the text): she is also distanced by the contradictory claim that she is 'correctly to be seen' (ἀτρεκὲς ... ἰδέσθαι) in the form of a reflection in her lover's shield. The word δείκηλον is an ambiguous term meaning not just 'representation' or 'image' but also a 'phantom'; the Aphrodite we encounter in the text is but a ghostly presence distanced by mirrors, images and words, and, crucially, *presented* to us (from δείκνυμι – to 'show') through the author's own verbal and literary ingenuity. Apollonius reminds his readers that any epiphany here is stage-managed only by the poet. Any deity who exists beyond the string of signifiers that take us from linguistic to visual sign is but a pale ghost, apprehended through the mediating inventions of art(ifice); the only goddess beyond the poetry is a fictional woven construct (and it is no surprise that the cloak itself was originally a gift from Athena, goddess of weaving, with all its connotations of fiction and lies).[114]

Indeed, this distancing effect is confirmed by the final image of the ekphrasis, that of Phrixus and his ram, of whom Apollonius claims, 'Beholding them, you would be silent and would deceive your desire (ψεύδοιό τε θυμόν) with the hope of hearing some wise speech from them, and would gaze for a long time with that hope' (1.763–6). The comment captures the element of frustrated desire (the θυμός and the ἐλπίς) that is always an element of ekphrastic description – the desire *to see and hear* the image, to

---

[112] *Argonautika* 1.742–6 (translation by R. C. Sheaton, Loeb Classical Library edition, 1961, with modifications).

[113] On the poetic distancing of the divine in Apollonius' *Argonautika*, see Hunter (1986) and Feeney (1991: 70), who comments, 'Here we have, in an epic poem which has not yet embodied a god in action, the first representation of a god. And it is a representation in words of a representation in cloth of a representation in marble of a goddess – and her reflection.'

[114] On the poetics of weaving in ancient literature, see McIntosh Snyder (1981), Kennedy (1986), N. K. Miller (1986), Scheid and Svenbro (1996) and Salzman-Mitchell (2005: 117–49).

transgress the boundaries between nature and artifice.[115] How appropriate that the centrepiece of this description should be the goddess of desire herself, who offers the hope of satisfaction, who is always presented as an available object, yet who is ultimately beyond possession.

In contrast to the epic ekphraseis of the *Argonautika*, the Knidia epigrams are based upon an actual image, so allowing us to compare the visual or verbal strategies each medium adopts in order to elicit a particular audience response. This does not change the fact that each epigram's reader is dependent upon a kind of 'verbal viewing'. Yet a certain correspondence between image and text is demonstrated by the fact that the aporetic quality of the epigrams, with their systematic presentation and denial of epiphany, is not merely a paradox wrought by words, but is also a quality of the statue itself. Knidian Aphrodite's nudity suggests that she is utterly subject to the desirous gaze, that the voyeur who disturbs her bath can possess her merely by a glance; indeed the erotic (and often specifically phallic) aspect of the gaze is a well-documented phenomenon in the ancient world.[116] Yet she simultaneously resists such scopic possession due to the complexities of her pose, which, as far as can be deduced from 'copies' of the original statue, incorporates a certain ambiguity (Figures 4.2–3).[117] While from one side her hand conceals her pudenda, as if from an unexpected intruder, from a frontal view she seems to point towards her genitals in a deliberate gesture of revelation.[118] Nanette Salomon interprets this ambiguity as a form of degradation, claiming that 'Woman, thus fashioned, is reduced in a humiliating way to her sexuality.'[119] Yet this response ignores the Knidia's status not just as a woman, but also as a divine personification of desire itself. A viewing of the statue *as goddess* sheds a rather different light on her

---

[115] NB: the extended ekphrasis in Catullus 64, also of a woven tableau, purports to transgress the boundaries of visual description by providing the sound that Apollonius pointedly withholds from Phrixus and the ram; this transgression takes the form of a speech by Ariadne about unrequited desire: see Laird (1993). On ekphrastic hope, see W. J. T. Mitchell (1994: 152–4) and Bartsch and Elsner (2007: i–ii).

[116] See Keuls (1985), Frontisi-Ducroux (1996), Goldhill (2001b), Bartsch (2006: 67–83) and, for a theoretical formulation of the gaze as phallic activity in Western culture, Irigary (1991) and Jay (1993: 493–542).

[117] On the difficulty of determining the original stance of the Knidia from Roman variations of the type, see Ridgway (2004: 716–18).

[118] Cf. A. Stewart (1997: 103–4).

[119] Salomon (1997: 204): 'The hand that points also covers and that which covers also points. We are, in any case, directed to her pubis, which we are not permitted to see.' Contra Ridgway (1997: 263): 'I am completely convinced that the gesture of her right hand is meant to point to, not to hide, her womb, emphasizing her fertility.'

pose.[120] The texts' emphasis on the fact that the statue could be seen from all sides reinforces the way in which any viewing of the Knidia necessarily required that her admirers should move between an ever-shifting series of roles; whether the viewer plays the part of voyeuristic intruder or expected lover, there must always be someone else involved in the scenario. As Robin Osborne has written, 'Praxiteles' goddess does not feed the male appetite in at all a straightforward way ... placed in such a way as to be seen all round it is in fact up to the viewer which position he adopts, and as he adopts a particular position so he opens up or forecloses the possible narratives.'[121]

This triangulation of the viewing process, involving statue, viewer and a mysterious other (Ares? Adonis? Anchises?) means that the visitor to the shrine never 'possesses' the image in the manner that her apparent accessibility would initially suggest, just as the reader of an epigram never views the goddess or her image in the way that the ekphrasis purports to present. Both statue and epigram perform a narrative of desire itself, eternally unrequited; through both words and images they present us with, to quote the Symbolist painter Odilon Redon, 'the logic of the visible at the service of the invisible'.[122] If Aphrodite is an embodiment of desire itself, then the act of viewing ultimately celebrates the goddess's true divinity, and yet this act is by definition a reminder of absence, of the fact that the goddess, like the force she embodies, is elusive. In his *Amores*, Pseudo-Lucian describes how the Knidia 'arrogantly smiles a little as a grin parts her lips', as if, rather than responding with fear to an intruder, she is well aware, and in control, of the frustration she arouses.[123]

The image thus resists not only possession by the viewer but also complete neutralisation by the epigrams that purport to celebrate her. For in suggesting how her presence actually lies in absence, the texts paradoxically allow a certain space for the polysemy that they initially seem to deny. It is in their very use of ekphrasis that they allow the goddess herself to enter the reader's experience, for it is this literary trope that performs the ever-unrequited nature of desire. In this they take their lead from the image itself; the process of viewing produced by the actual sculpture is mirrored in the process of *reading* produced by the text. While the epigrams fulfil their own literary concerns by appearing to neutralise the Knidia's power, they

---

[120] See R. Osborne (1994: 83), Ridgway (2004: 723–4).   [121] R. Osborne (1994: 84).

[122] Odilon Redon, *A soi-même. Journal, 1867–1915*, quoted by Jay (1993: 157).

[123] *Amores* 13: ὑπερήφανον καὶ σεσηρότι γέλωτι μικρὸν ὑπομειδιῶσα. Cf R. Osborne (1998: 230–5). A. Stewart (1997: 107) relates the statue's open mouth to the Greek medical theory that a woman's mouth was directly connected to her womb, on which see King (1998: 27–8).

nevertheless demonstrate their debt to the sculpture beyond the text, and the deity it represents.

A later epigram attributed to Lucian captures this paradox with unrivalled economy and elegance. The couplet purports to be an inscription accompanying a votive offering to Aphrodite which is, entirely appropriately, an image of herself:

Σοὶ μορφῆς ἀνέθηκα τεῆς περικαλλὲς ἄγαλμα,
      Κύπρι, τεῆς μορφῆς φέρτερον οὐδὲν ἔχων.

To you, Cypris, I dedicate the beautiful image of your form,
Since I have nothing better than your form.[124]

What does Lucian mean here by *morphē*? While it is clear that the 'form' of the first line is associated with a votive statue, an *agalma*, the *morphē* of the second line purports to refer to the 'form' of Aphrodite herself. As in much of his prose work, Lucian here plays with the problematic nature of representation, particularly of the divine.[125] As goddess of beauty, fertility and desire, Aphrodite is an embodiment of body itself; our confrontations with the deity are to be located in our viewing and touching of desirable form. Yet the epigram's conceit lies in the fact that, as a deity, Aphrodite is beyond our comprehension, and, while being an embodiment of 'form', has no 'form' herself that can act as a prototype for the formal representations that, like the Knidia, act as a focus of worship. Thus while Lucian's devotee recognises that the most fitting form of worship is to view the goddess as an embodiment of *morphē* (for there is φέρτερον οὐδέν – 'nothing better'), he also realises that the only *morphē* he himself can apprehend is necessarily incomplete. Any attempt to press this poem for meaning necessarily destroys its subtle ambiguities. For what is the reader left with? Only the exquisitely crafted *morphē* of Lucian's epigram itself. Again, the act of viewing is located within the text, and we are reminded of the delicate facility of words to express the paradoxical nature of representation. Yet it is the

---

[124] *Anth. Plan.* 164 ('Lucian').

[125] See in particular the representation of 'Panthea' in the *Imagines* (Steiner, 2001: 295–306; J. A. Francis, 2003: 580–2; Vout, 2007: 213–39), an extended ekphrasis of the emperor's mistress, whose various features are compared to the body parts of famous works of art (she has the head of the Knidia, 6), and *Jupiter Tragoedus* 6–12 (Bracht Branham, 1989: 167–77), which satirises the conception of gods in the form of their material representations. For a parallel confusion of facture and divine nature in Philostratus' *Imagines*, compare the use of *schēma* ('type', 'figure' or 'form') at 2.1.1: 'The figure (σχῆμα) of the goddess is that of Aphrodite goddess of Modesty, naked and well-figured (εὐσχήμων).'

paradox wrought by the *visual* image which provides the model of presence and absence that inspires the poet.

As Parmenion's epigram on Polyclitus' Hera demonstrated, the goddess herself must always remain at a distance from her image, even as it expresses the force she personifies. The gaze's power to possess must, ultimately, belong only to the gods: just as the Knidia can only have been formed by Hephaestus' chisel, so the erotic parts of Hera's form can only be apprehended by Zeus. The manifestation of the divine in material form should express the elusiveness and impenetrability of the goddess (her *agnostoi morphai*), even as it communicates her desirability by co-opting the lure of naturalism to reveal the erotic body. These epigrams demonstrate how, while the battle between art and text must always be ostensibly won by literature (for images are necessarily mute until they are given voice by the text itself), the games ekphrastic texts play in order to assert the superiority of their own medium are often dependent upon modes of viewing established by images themselves. The Knidia epigrams present the reader with multiple forms of viewing. They purport to engender an 'epiphanic' viewing of the image, a kind of *theōria*, with its concomitant religious connotations, in which the statue can be perceived as a manifestation of the goddess herself. Yet they also present us with a self-consciously intellectual mode of viewing that praises *technē*, demonstrating a form of connoisseurship in their recognition of the artist's naturalistic skill. These diverse approaches to the image within the text are exploited, simultaneously, as a comment upon the relationship between art and literature. Religious and intellectual modes of viewing are often deliberately confused, so that the praise of visual *technē* is expressed through self-consciously clever verbal 'conceits' that ultimately point to the *technē* of the poet. Yet within this concern for the complexities of cultural expression is also an awareness of the nature of divinity. These epigrams are not simply verbal quips indulging in clever little games with the trope of ekphrasis (although they are that, too). In their exploration of the forces at play in sculpting and writing, viewing and reading, they explore how Aphrodite may be culturally known, and find her in the eternal play of desire and denial, or presence and absence, that characterises representation. As they perform this elusive phenomenon, they proclaim the status of statue and poem as cultural markers of this process, which, in evading epiphany, ultimately generate a space in which mortal and goddess can meet.

PART II

5 | Virtual visions: piety and *paideia* in Second Sophistic literature

τί δ᾽ ἄν τις τὰ παλαιὰ λέγοι;
ἔτι γὰρ καὶ νῦν ἐναργὴς ἡ κίνησις τοῦ θεοῦ.

But why should we speak of ancient history?
For the activity of the god is still now manifest.[1]

Aelius Aristides, Hymn to Heracles, 12

It is no accident that Part I of this book, which explores the relationship between epiphany and representation prior to the first century CE, is so often reliant upon the evidence provided by later Greek literature – from Pausanias' discussion of archaic *xoana* to (Pseudo?) Lucian's playful treatment of the Aphrodite of Knidos.[2] Despite scholars' best methodological efforts to tell the story of pre-imperial Greek art or religion from contemporary sources alone, the obsessive interest of second- and third-century CE writers in their cultural heritage (combined with the replicatory practices of Roman art) has provided a wealth of evidence that is difficult to ignore.[3] Part II therefore considers this evidence on its own terms, not simply as the product of a stale antiquarianism or nostalgia for former glories, but as a vibrant engagement with the cultural models through which Hellenic identity was constructed and negotiated under the Roman Empire. The now customary labelling of this period as the 'Second Sophistic' highlights the secular, intellectual aspects of its culture, particularly the rhetorical concerns of the sophists themselves.[4] Although a buzzword in contemporary classical studies, the term actually comes from Philostratus' *Lives of the Sophists*, where it refers to the antiquarian flourishing of a style of rhetorical

---

[1] Translation by Behr (1981).   [2] See Chapter 2, 92–100, and Chapter 4, 186–8.

[3] For a methodologically rigorous but ultimately aporetic examination of this problem, see Donohue (1988), who is left with very little evidence for attitudes to Greek religious art prior to the second century CE. Steiner (2001) and Tanner (2006) choose to proceed regardless, making generous use of Second Sophistic sources. On Roman art and practices of replication, see most recently Marvin (2008, with bibliography).

[4] See Brunt (1994), with Bowersock (1969, 1974), Bowie (1982) and Schmitz (1997). Recent scholarship has sought to redress the balance by emphasising the importance of religion within Second Sophistic culture: see in particular Alcock *et al.* (2001), Elsner (2001c; 2007: 29–48), Lightfoot (2003), Aitken and Maclean (2004), Galli (2004) and Bowie and Elsner (2009).

performance founded by Aeschines; its broader application to Greek literary culture of the imperial period is thus a modern construct, but nevertheless underlines this prolific author's contribution to the literature of the third century, as well as his debt to the Greek past.[5] The urge to construct an elite Greek identity in the imperial period (both in relation to Rome and, later, to the rise of Christianity) saw an increasing emphasis on the acquisition and demonstration of a self-consciously Hellenic *paideia* and *sophia*.[6] Yet such intellectualism also existed alongside a thriving culture of ritual activity and religious pilgrimage, accompanied by an intense awareness of and curiosity about the divine.[7] While it is often impossible to separate secular from sacred concerns in Second Sophistic texts, so it is difficult to draw distinctions between 'elite' and 'popular' attitudes towards religion, for intimate acquaintance with high Hellenic culture – the result of extensive literary and philosophical training – existed alongside a fascination with traditional cult practice and direct encounter with the divine. Together, these elements produced a climate of knowing religiosity in which rigorous intellectual enquiry and traditional piety often converged.[8]

As Aelius Aristides claims in his *Hymn to Heracles* (quoted above), the religious *sēmata* of the past are not simply ancient history (τὰ παλαιά) for his second-century CE audience, but part of a continuing engagement with the sacred that is very much alive in the present: Heracles' presence and authority are still 'manifest', *enargēs*. In this sense Second Sophistic approaches to epiphany demonstrate continuity with those we noted in the Hellenistic period: a desire for divine presence in the here and now is nevertheless expressed through visual and verbal strategies that are themselves based upon earlier models, so that epiphanic modes of representation are often also a form of citation. The *enargeia* of epiphany is thus increasingly inseparable from the *enargeia* generated by cultural forms of production.

---

[5] *Lives of the Sophists* 481. For a discussion of the term and its problems, see introduction to Goldhill (2001a: esp. 14–15) and Whitmarsh (2001b: 42–4). Philostratus' corpus finally forms the sole focus of an edited volume in Bowie and Elsner (2009); for monographs, see G. Anderson (1986) and Billaut (2000).

[6] On *paideia* in the Second Sophistic, see Marrou (1956), Jaeger (1961), Bowie (1970), T. Morgan (1998: 190–273), Whitmarsh (1998a; 2001a: 5–9, 90–130), G. Anderson (1993: 83–5), Swain (1996: 18–64), Schmitz (1997), Rousselle (2001) and Borg (2004b).

[7] On attitudes to epiphany in this period, see Lane Fox (1986: 104–67). On pilgrimage in the Second Sophistic, see Elsner (1992; 1995: 127–55; 2001b), Rutherford (2001, 2009), Elsner and Rutherford (2005: especially papers by Galli, Hutton, Petsalis-Diomidis and Williamson) Petsalis-Diomidis (2001) and my discussion in Chapter 7.

[8] On the problematic nature of the 'two-tier' theory of elite and popular religious sensibilities, see Brown (1971; 1981: 12–22, 27–30, 48–9), Momigliano (1972: 18) and Averil Cameron (1981: 7–8, 32, 36–9).

Yet while epiphany and learning were intimately connected in Hellenistic
Greece (as typified by a text such as the Lindos stele), the rise of a self-
consciously 'Hellenic' intellectualism under the Roman Empire seems to
have intensified this bond between visionary encounter and the cultivation
of *paideia*. The further Greek thinkers moved in time and status from the
building blocks of their cultural identity, the more intensely they desired to
reinhabit them, whether through the use of obsolete dialects (such as Attic
Greek), nostalgic political alliances (such as Hadrian's Panhellenion) or the
enargeic power of rhetorical devices such as ekphrasis and prosopopoeia.[9]
In these texts language triggers a dynamic process of imaginative viewing,
in which the verbally conjured image almost streams from the (papyrus)
page. Encounters with works of art – whether direct or via ekphrastic literature such as Philostratus' *Imagines* – are presented as a pedagogic process
in which sophisticated erudition alternates and merges with moments of
absorption, when the image itself is animated and experienced as a form of
virtual reality.[10] In such a climate epiphany offered the ultimate strategy by
which Second Sophistic viewers, readers and worshippers might reanimate
the past in the present. The ability to encounter the divine through the
mediatory power of rituals, images and texts was one of the gifts conferred
by *sophia*, and therefore a goal of *paideia*. Knowledge of the appropriate
cultural models and practices, combined with religious and philosophical
understanding, led to a pattern of initiation and revelation that was fundamentally intertwined with notions of Greek identity and education.[11]
Epiphany thus facilitated a form of 'time travel', providing cognitive reliability for earlier models of religious practice in service of a Greek cultural
autonomy that could soothe the sting of Roman imperium.[12] Crucially, it

---

[9] See Bowie (1970), Swain (1996: 65–100), Schmitz (1997, 1999), J. Connolly (2001), Whitmarsh
(2001b: 26–9, 41–89) and R. Webb (2006a). On the use of Attic Greek, see Bompaire (1994),
Swain (1996: 17–42), Horrocks (1997: 78–86), Schmitz (1997: 67–83), and the standard work,
Schmid (1887–97); on the use of the Ionic dialect in a religious literary context, see Elsner
(2001b: 125–8) and Lightfoot (2003: 91–7). On the Panhellenion, see Spawforth and Walker
(1985, 1986), Arafat (1996: 12–13), C. P. Jones (1996) and Whitmarsh (2001b: 24–5). On
visionary rhetorical texts, see Zeitlin (2001).

[10] On the pedagogic process of viewing in the *Imagines*, see Maffei (1991) and Elsner (1993; 1995:
21–39); on verbal animation of the text, see Bryson (1995), R. Webb (2006b) and Squire
(2009); on the Philostratean play of absorption and erudition, see Newby (2009), and my
discussion in the Introduction, 1–7.

[11] On Second Sophistic attitudes to Hellenism in the Roman Empire, see in particular Elsner
(1992, 1994), Alcock (1993, 1996), Woolf (1994), Arafat (1996: 43–79), Swain (1996: 330–56)
and Whitmarsh (2001b).

[12] On 'time travel' in relation to the Greek sublime in Pausanias and Longinus, see J. I. Porter
(2001).

underlined the continued value and efficacy of such models in the present, re-enchanting the sacred landscape by emphasising the vibrant numinosity of Greece itself.

Facing the gods through the mirror of Pausanias

No ancient author could be said to have charted the numinosity of the Greek landscape with greater commitment than Pausanias. The *Description of Greece* is threaded with epiphanic narratives, often presented as *aitia* for the foundation of temples and the dedication of cult images and votive objects. Like the epiphanic epigraphy of Hellenistic cities such as Magnesia on the Maeander, manifestations of divine agency within Pausanias' text serve to construct a 'cognitive map' that imbues physical topography with sacred presence.[13] Pausanias is certainly a reader of inscriptions, and takes his lead from the epiphanic *sēmata* he encounters within the landscape itself (supported by oral traditions related by local *exēgētai*).[14] Yet within the text of the *Periēgēsis Hellados*, these physical markers and local narratives are brought together in service of a more panhellenic discourse (Pausanias claims he will represent 'all things Greek' – πάντα... τὰ Ἑλληνικά, 1.26.4) that testifies to the *longue durée* of Greek religion.[15] Epiphanies serve to unite both the material and the sacred, and the past and present, proving the continuity of divine favour within a landscape that had been politically (if not culturally) transformed into the Roman province of Achaea.[16] Significantly, many of the epiphanic *aitia* that Pausanias chooses to include record moments when local autonomy was threatened by outside forces and saved by the aid of Hellenic gods or heroes.[17] At Argos, for example, Demeter's

---

[13] On Pausanias' relationship to the Greek landscape, see Alcock (1993: esp. 173–9; 1996; 2001; 2002) and Hutton (2005a). On epiphany at Magnesia, see Chapter 3, 151–4.

[14] See Habicht (1985: 64–94), Tzifopoulos (1991) and C. P. Jones (2001a).

[15] On this phrase, see J. I. Porter (2001: 68–9) and Hutton (2005a: 55–8).

[16] See Elsner (1992, 1994, 2007: 32–45). On Pausanias and Rome, see Habicht (1985: 117–40), Tzifopoulos (1993), Arafat (1996), Bowie (1996), Swain (1996: 330–56), Auffarth (1997), Lafond (2001) and Hutton (2008, with further bibliography). On the province of Achaea, formed during the Augustan period, see Alcock (1993: 8–24).

[17] Battle epiphanies in Pausanias can be found at 1.13.8 (Demeter at Argos); 1.15.3 (Theseus and Echetlaeus at Marathon); 1.32.4 (Echetlaeus at Marathon); 1.36.1 (Kychreus in snake form at Salamis); 3.18.3 (Zeus Ammon); 3.19.12–13 (Ajax); 4.16.5 (Dioscuri); 4.32.4 (Aristomenes); 6.20.3–4 (Sosipolis at Elis, discussed in Chapter 6); 8.10.8 (Poseidon); 1.28.4, 8.54.6 (Pan to Philippides after Marathon); 9.22.2 (Hermes Promachos at Tanagra); 10.13.10 (Taras and Phalanthos); 1.4.4, 10.23.3 (the heroes Hyperochus, Laodocus, Pyrrhus and Phylacus at Delphi). Pritchett (1979: 44) comments that Pausanias 'records more epiphanies than any other writer' in the context of battle.

rooftop epiphany as a woman who killed the Epirote leader Pyrrhus with a well-aimed tile is commemorated by a sanctuary 'built at the command of the oracle, on the spot where Pyrrhus died' (1.13.8). At Marathon, the appearance of the hero Echetlaeus ('He of the Plough-Tail') during battle against the Persians in 490 is commemorated by a white marble plough on the battlefield (1.32.5). Pausanias later claims at 8.10.8–9 that, after a battle between the Lacedaemonians and Greek allied forces, 'the Mantineans affirmed that Poseidon too manifested himself (φανῆναι) in their defence, and for this reason, they erected a trophy as an offering to Poseidon'. To prove the identifiably Hellenic nature of this phenomenon, he continues:

That gods were present at war and slaughter of men has been told by the poets who have treated of the sufferings of the heroes at Troy, and the Athenians relate in song how gods sided with them at Marathon and at the battle of Salamis. Very plainly (ἐκδηλότατα) the host of the Gauls was destroyed at Delphi by the god, and manifestly (ἐναργῶς) by spirits (δαιμόνων). So there is precedent for the story of the Mantineans that they won their victory by the aid of Poseidon.

While the epiphanies at Troy, Marathon and Salamis are located within the world of poetry and song, Pausanias goes out of his way to emphasise the authenticity of epiphanies that occurred during the Gallic invasion of Delphi in 279, stressing their clarity and vividness (ἐκδηλότατα... ἐναργῶς). Close to the beginning of the *Periēgēsis* at 1.4.4, he had referred to the 'terrible shapes (δείματα) dressed as hoplites' who haunted the enemy ranks at Delphi in the form of the Greek heroes Hyperochus, Amadocus and Pyrrhus; again, at 10.23.2, he refers to the φάσματα of Hyperochus, Laodocus, Pyrrhus and the local Delphic hero Phylacus, who appeared during the battle, which he describes as 'the greatest of the Greek exploits against the barbarians' (10.19.5).[18] These manifestations of divine power in response to an external threat to the *omphalos* of the Greek world itself (which, as we saw in Chapter 3, had been so influential on Hellenistic models of epiphany) thus frame Pausanias' entire narrative.[19] They demonstrate how the sacred landscape of Greece is not simply a catalogue of monuments, but a living religious system that (with Roman imperium conveniently ignored) is safeguarded by the very powers it celebrates.[20] The *enargeia* of epiphany is thus

---

[18] See Chapter 3, 154–7.

[19] On the Gallic invasion in Pausanias, see Bearzot (1992: 103–26), Alcock (1996: 256–9) and Akujärvi (2005: 255–61); on Delphi as a site of inspiration not just for the Pythia but also Pausanias himself, see J. I. Porter (2001: 80); on Pausanias' use of Hellenistic history, see Bearzot (1992) and Ameling (1996).

[20] On the exclusion of Roman monuments from the text, see Elsner (1992: 15–18).

a means whereby Pausanias can animate the world he has explored and described for his readers, generating a verbal form of *enargeia* that allows the text itself to function as a virtual experience of sacred *theōria*.[21]

Most importantly, the numinosity of the sacred is manifested for Pausanias and his fellow viewer-worshippers in material markers of divine presence and ritual activity encountered within the landscape itself. Pausanias does not simply describe the objects and structures that mark his route, but through telling vignette or anecdote conveys a sense of religiosity that animates these antiquarian details for the viewer/reader, and contributes to what Jaś Elsner has described as 'a deep sense of place' within the narrative.[22] Pausanias' repeated negotiation of the gap between the material and the sacred, the past and present, is particularly well illustrated by those occasions where his text can be directly compared with surviving archaeological evidence, revealing the ideological influences at work behind his processes of selection, omission or creative supplementation.[23] In Chapter 3 I explored the epiphanic qualities of the surviving cult images at the sanctuary of Despoina at Lykosoura, attributed to the local sculptor Damophon. Significantly, Pausanias provides our only surviving literary evidence for Damophon and, in line with his connoisseurial interests elsewhere, describes the statue group in great detail (8.37.3–6).[24] His ekphrasis concurs with surviving marble fragments from the site (Figures 3.2–5), with one notable exception. For at 8.37.3, he claims,

The actual *agalmata* of the goddesses, Mistress and Demeter, the throne on which they sit, along with the footstool under their feet, are all made out of one piece of stone (ἑνὸς ὁμοίως λίθου) . . . This stone was not brought in by them, but they say that in obedience to a dream (κατὰ ὄψιν ὀνείρατος) they dug up the earth within the enclosure and so found it.

Given Pausanias' familiarity with sculptural media and techniques, it is particularly surprising that he ignores the obviously acrolithic composition of the Despoina statue group in order to emphasise that the two central

---

[21] On the *Periēgēsis* as form of pilgrimage narrative, see Elsner (1992; 1994; 1995: 129–31, 143–6; 2007: 246–51), Rutherford (2001) and Hutton (2005a: 303–11; 2005b). On ekphrasis and *enargeia* in Pausanias' text, see Hutton (2005a: 49–51).

[22] Elsner (1992: 9).

[23] On the general reliability of Pausanias' accounts, see Habicht (1985: 28–63, esp. 47–57, on Damophon), and on his errors, Arafat (1996: 18–29, with bibliography). On the ideological (and especially religious) influences upon Pausanias' processes of selection and organisation, see Elsner (1992, 2001c) and, from a literary point of view, Hutton (2005a).

[24] See Jost (in Casevitz *et al.* 1998: 249–53) and Moggi and Osanna (2003: 468–74). On Pausanian 'connoisseurship', see Elsner (2007: 49–58).

figures were carved from a single block of marble.[25] Indeed, the 'piecing' of the sculptures must have been obvious to the careful viewer, given the contrast between the dark drapery of the two goddesses and their marble heads, hands and feet, not to mention the fact that the figures were hollowed out at the back.[26] Pausanias even mentions that Damophon was responsible for repairing Phidias' statue of Zeus at Olympia following an earthquake, a task that must have been dependent upon his familiarity with the acrolithic techniques employed for chryselephantine images (4.31.6).[27]

The reason for this erroneous emphasis upon the structural integrity of the group's main figures soon becomes clear, however. Rather than illustrating Damophon's *technē*, the rendering of Despoina and Demeter from a single block is related to the stone's discovery in the Lykosoura sanctuary itself, 'following a vision seen in a dream' (κατὰ ὄψιν ὀνείρατος). Pausanias' (perhaps willing) oversight thus allows the group to be related to a whole network of sacred images referred to in the *Periēgēsis* using this very formula that are based upon, or commissioned as the result of, an epiphany.[28] In this case, however, the tale ascribes an epiphanic origin not to the statues' form (which has been admirably shaped by Damophon) but to the raw material from which they have been wrought, so seeking to reconcile their status as the products of artifice with the numinous presence they project within the temple. In keeping with Pausanias' efforts to emphasise the actively sacred nature of the Greek religious landscape, the material source of this divine presence is appropriately located within the earth of the actual sanctuary.[29] Directed by an external manifestation of Despoina's authority (the *opsis oneiratos*), the statues' projection of divine presence is thus facilitated by the internal revelation of their very matter. In his *Rhodian Oration*, Dio Chrysostom emphasises the importance of sculpture for Greek identity with the comment that 'It is the *stones* which reveal the grandeur and the greatness of Hellas!' (31.159).[30] For Pausanias, this association between geology and Hellenicity is explicitly religious. Like the colossal bones of heroes that testify to their historical authenticity in Philostratus' *Heroicus*,

---

[25] On Pausanias' understanding of artistic techniques, materials and period styles, see Arafat (1996: 45–75). Note that Pausanias identifies a statue of Aphrodite at Megalopolis as acrolithic (8.31.6), but does not recognise the same technique at Lykosoura.

[26] See Themelis (1996: 178) and Chapter 3, 125–31.   [27] Lapatin (2001: 78, 86).

[28] E.g., 3.14.5, 4.1.5, 4.13.2, 4.26.3, 7.5.2, 9.23.3, 9.29.8 and 10.2.6; see Pirenne-Delforge and Pumelle (1997) s.v. ὄψις. This phrase is discussed in more detail in Chapter 6, 266–75.

[29] The statues are indeed made from a local variety of Arcadian marble, but this is unlikely to have been quarried from within the sanctuary itself; recall the importance of using local stone for the Lindos temple stele, as discussed in Chapter 3, 165.

[30] See Platt (2007b: 257–8). Translation J. W. Cahoon, Loeb Classical Library edition, 1940.

the epiphanic origin of Damophon's raw materials locates divinity within the rocky substrata of Greece itself.[31] Indeed, as Pausanias goes on to claim, 'Of all the *poleis* which the earth has sent forth on the mainland or the islands, Lykosoura is the oldest (πρεσβυτάτη), and the first one which the sun beheld' (8.38.1).

Pausanias' desire to view sacred *agalmata* through an epiphanic lens is reinforced by an observation he makes as he leads his readers out of the temple back into the Lykosoura sanctuary (8.37.7): 'On the right as you go out of the temple there is a mirror fitted into the wall. If anyone looks into this mirror, he will see himself very dimly indeed (ἀμυδρῶς) or not at all, but the actual *agalmata* of the gods and the throne can be seen quite clearly (ἐναργῶς θεάσασθαι).' The passage suggests that, rather than reflecting the viewer-worshipper, the temple mirror reflects the statues towering behind him or her in such a way that they dominate the visual field, generating an optical paradox: it is by perceiving the gods indirectly, via a reflection, that one can actually see them clearly (ἐναργῶς).[32] The *enargeia* generated by Damophon's illusionistic sculptural style is thus transformed into the *enargeia* of epiphany via a further form of representation that is tradition-ally associated with deception (the curse of Narcissus).[33] Within the sacred space of the sanctuary the Platonic view of reflection as 'something that appears real, but is not real itself' is recast, so that the analogy between art and the mirror rests not on the ontological status of image and reflec-tion, but on their phenomenological impact – the way in which they are *seen*.[34] At Lykosoura one looks *through* the mirror rather than beholding the object itself.[35] Within a ritual context the mimetic distance generated by several layers of representation can, paradoxically, lead to clearer perception of the divine forms that the cult statues embody, for reflection performs a dematerialisation of Damophon's *agalmata*, giving them a visible yet elu-sive form that is phenomenologically closer to the immaterial *eidea* of the goddesses themselves. Significantly, this encounter with the deities in their dematerialised form takes place as worshippers leave the temple, forming

---

[31] *Heroicus* 8.1–14; Herodotus mentions the bones of Orestes (1.67), while catalogues of huge bones are also found in Pausanias (1.33–5, 2.10.2, 8.29–35): see Boedeker (1993), Alcock (2004: 159), Rusten (2004), Whitmarsh (2009) and, on the *Heroicus*, my discussion below. On the prehistoric fossils that may have influenced these accounts of heroic relics, see Mayor (2000).

[32] Cf. Frontisi-Ducroux and Vernant (1997: 196–9) and Taylor (2008: 2–3).

[33] See Chapter 4, n. 66.   [34] See *Republic* 596e.

[35] Compare the practice of catoptromancy and lecanomancy, in which mirrors or bowls of liquid are used as mantic devices: see Halliday ([1913] 2003: 145–62), Delatte (1932), Balensiefen (1990: 174–209), Frontisi-Ducroux and Vernant (1997: 191–7), Cassimatis (1998) and Taylor (2008: 102–36).

the culmination of the ritual sequence that structures their visit to the sanctuary; it thus represents the knowledge that comes with initiation into Despoina's mysteries and the negation of self that occurs in the face of unmediated encounter with the divine.[36] As an epiphany that occurs as the viewer looks *back*, the catoptric effect at Lykosoura parallels epiphanic narratives in which it is the lingering trace or impression of divine presence that leads to *anagnōrisis*, from Poseidon's footprints in the *Iliad* to Virgil's Venus, who is only recognised by her son Aeneas in her departing step ('vera incessu patuit dea').[37]

Epiphany thus lies in the interstices between presence and absence, image and reflection. In this sense the mirror at Lykosoura typifies what James Porter has defined as the Pausanian 'sublime', '"a positive, material object elevated to the status of [an] impossible Thing" that, simultaneously fascinating and fearful, both invites and resists integration into symbolic frameworks of understanding'.[38] By virtue of their paradoxical or ineffable nature, these moments within Pausanias' text both excite the reader's own desire for *theōria*, and underline the insufficiency of the work itself as a means of experiencing 'all things Greek'. Like Despoina's mirror, the *Periēgēsis* offers a reflection of the Hellenic sacred landscape that purports to cross the ekphrastic barrier and facilitate the reader's own experience of *theōria*; yet like the mirror, the text offers a dematerialised vision of this world, a form of *phantasia* that can be clearly apprehended only through full initiation and active pilgrimage. Pausanias generally leaves it open as to whether this can be achieved through the acquisition of religious memory by means of literary *sophia*, or by literally retracing his steps and encountering the physical *Realien* and supernatural inhabitants of Greece itself (for in order to leave a sacred site with the knowledge gained through enargeic encounter, one has to visit it in the first place). Yet, tellingly, he repeatedly draws attention to *lacunae* in his text, 'signalled absences' that indicate where the ritualistic structure of the *Periēgēsis* must stop short of full revelation.[39] One of these follows naturally from the *agalmata* at Lykosoura; for while Pausanias alerts

---

[36] Cf. Elsner (2001b: 153; 2007: 289).

[37] *Il.* 13.71–2: see Chapter 1, 58–9; *Aeneid* 1.405: see Dunbabin (1990) and Platt (in press a). On 'trace-objects' in Pausanias' text, see J. I. Porter (2001: 70). See also *Heroicus* 13.2–3, on the footprints of Protesilaos.

[38] J. I. Porter (2001: 65), quoting Žižek (1989: 71).

[39] Elsner (2001c: 18): '[Pausanias'] text is a spur to do what he did and see what he saw (including the necessary rituals and initiations); it can never be a replacement'; see also Foccardi (1987), Elsner (1992: 22–7 – fundamental), J. I. Porter (2001: 74–5) and Henrichs (2003: 242–50), with Petsalis-Diomidis (2006b) on parallel rhetorical devices in Aelius Aristides' *Sacred Tales* (e.g., 47.3, 48.58).

us to a mirror that can *show* Despoina 'clearly' (ἐναργῶς), he pointedly refrains from *telling* her name, stating at 8.37.9:

This Mistress the Arcadians worship more than any other god, declaring that she is a daughter of Poseidon and Demeter. Mistress is her surname among the many, just as they surname Demeter's daughter by Zeus 'the Maid' (*Korē*). But whereas the real name of the Maid is Persephone, as Homer and Pamphos before him say in their poems, the real name of the Mistress I am afraid to write to the uninitiated (τῆς δὲ Δεσποίνης τὸ ὄνομα ἔδεισα ἐς τοὺς ἀτελέστους γράφειν).

In this way Pausanias draws attention to his privileged knowledge of Despoina's identity, yet places a clear obstruction between the goddess and his uninitiated readers. In order to gain such intimate access to the Mistress, one must not only experience autopsy at Lykosoura, but also perform liturgy, joining the ranks of Despoina's *telestai*. Pausanias' stated fear (ἔδεισα) of divulging sacred truths may distance the reader, yet it also animates the text with a sense of active piety by revealing the very real risks of 'writing' (γράφειν).[40] The knowledge imparted by the *Periēgēsis* may skirt the boundaries of sacred wisdom, yet those moments when the author passes where we cannot follow guarantee the authenticity of his *sophia* and his reliability as a guide.[41] By marking the limits of the reader's knowledge, they also have an apophatic function, for in defining the point where mystery begins they create a space for the ineffable, generating a frisson of anticipation that magnifies the power of the divine. This is the point at which we are invited to enter the world Pausanias describes, and to experience its numinosity for ourselves.

Phidias' Zeus and the sophistic imagination

Tension between revelation and concealment forms a leitmotif of the *Periēgēsis*, an inevitable corollary of Pausanias' desire to describe and preserve the facticity of the Greek sacred landscape, on one hand, and to safeguard its most precious mysteries on the other. Like the hymns discussed in Chapter 1, the text's act of withholding is a sign of its own religiosity;

---

[40] Loucas-Durie (1991) shows no such ritual reticence and identifies Despoina as Artemis (see Chapter 3, n. 3). Compare Pausanias' refusal to describe the Athenian Eleusinion or the sanctuary of Eleusis because of 'a vision in a dream' (see 1.14.3 and 1.38.7, where he states that 'the uninitiated are of course not permitted to learn [by reading] what they are prevented from seeing'); this passage is further discussed in Chapter 6, 287–8.

[41] Cf. B. Bergmann (2001: 166).

it is also, as we saw in Chapter 4, the inevitable effect of ekphrasis.[42] Such tensions frequently arise within Second Sophistic texts, which often invite the reader to enter their imaginative space, yet exhibit continual anxiety over the power of words or images to facilitate the very form of unmediated encounter they promote. This problem is addressed with particular acuity in relation to the commanding centrepiece of the *Periēgēsis* (and arguably of Greek religious art) – Phidias' chryselephantine statue of Zeus at Olympia (5.11.1–9).[43] After a detailed description of the statue, Pausanias claims, 'I know that the height and breadth of the Olympic Zeus have been measured and recorded; but I shall not praise those who have made the measurements, for even their records fall far short of the impression made by a sight of the image' (5.11.9). The inadequacy of language and number to convey the grandeur and numinosity of the Zeus echoes Callimachus' Sixth *Iambus*, which parodies numerical accounts of the statue and impresses upon the reader the need for direct encounter.[44] In the hallowed context of the *Periēgēsis*, however, this self-conscious ekphrastic failure also underlines the image's status as a paradigmatic example of the Hellenic 'sublime', for Pausanias' aporetic attempt to convey the Phidian statue's visual impact is immediately followed by a vignette that, like the epiphanic discovery of a single block of stone at Lykosoura, confirms the object's sanctity.[45] Stating that 'the god himself according to legend bore witness (μάρτυρα) to Phidias' *technē*', Pausanias recalls that when Phidias 'prayed to the god to show by a sign (ἐπισημῆναι) whether the work was to his liking', the floor of the temple was immediately struck by a thunderbolt, in a spot now covered by a bronze jar. Like the marks left by Poseidon's trident in the porch of the Erechtheion on the Athenian Acropolis, the mark functions as a *sēma* of epiphanic presence, so providing a powerful demonstration of the statue's cognitive reliability.[46]

By drawing attention to both the inadequacy of description and the artist's need for external validation, however, Pausanias demonstrates an anxiety about the authority of anthropomorphic representation, hinting at an element of cognitive dissonance that is expressed (with varying levels of browbeating) by a number of Second Sophistic thinkers. Zeus' thunderbolt

[42] Cf. Bryson (1995: 279), on Philostratus' *Imagines*, and J. I. Porter (2001: 278 n. 50), on Pausanias.

[43] Cf. Elsner (2001c: 17–18), with Trendelenburg (1914: 71–102) and Maddoli and Saladino (1995: 238–46). On the image itself, see Chapter 2.

[44] On *Iambus* 6, see Chapter 4, n. 18.   [45] See J. I. Porter (2001: 72).

[46] See Chapter 2, 107–8, and Maddoli and Saladino (1995: 245), who discuss the possibility of an opening in the temple roof and local evidence for the cults of Zeus Kataibates and Keraunios.

may enchant the object by performing an epiphanic consecration of his image, yet the very inclusion of this externally generated proof-mechanism emphasises the statue's status as a mortal construct. As at Lykosoura, Pausanias' connoisseurial interest in the image's facture is accompanied by a need for this process to be divinely directed or guaranteed. Epiphanic aetiology offered a means of incorporating the living oral traditions that must have accrued around objects themselves, but the special attention Pausanias gives to these tales is also illustrative of the ideological weight carried by such *sēmata* of active religiosity within his text. In this sense, the *Periēgēsis* typifies many literary works of the imperial period, in which a sophisticated awareness of the problematic nature of anthropomorphism lay in tension with a concerted attempt to justify and promote the status of sacred *agalmata* within Hellenic religious tradition. For authors such as Dio Chrysostom, Maximus of Tyre and Philostratus, the great cult statues of the fifth and fourth centuries BCE stood as both historic symbols of Hellenic *technē* and cultural achievement, and the focus of a living religious tradition they were determined to uphold. The significance of Greek *agalmata* thus rested upon both the artistry of their creators and the authenticity of their rendering – factors that were not always mutually reinforcing. For this reason the question of how and why the gods were viewed and represented as they were was repeatedly thematised. As the ultimate source of cognitive reliability, epiphany provided the deus ex machina by which anthropomorphic tradition might be verified, whether through the visionary inspiration of the artist, or the subsequent appearance of gods in the forms of their images. Yet in order to reconcile any potential tension between external divine manifestation and internal cultural production, epiphany was increasingly bound to the principle of *paideia*: true perception of the divine, whether directly or in the form of enargeic representations, was thus intimately connected to the acquisition of appropriate knowledge.

Phidias' Olympian Zeus was, of course, *the* sacred image of the Graeco-Roman world. Epictetus comments that it was considered a calamity (ἀτύχημα) to die without having seen it, for, as the definitive example of anthropomorphic representation, the Olympian god was also the ultimate object of *theōria*.[47] In viewing Phidias' creation, one beheld not simply a statue, but a visual embodiment of Hellenic religious tradition itself. The sense of epiphanic encounter generated by the image thus demonstrated the Greek world's privileged relationship with the divine, symbolising not

---

[47] *Dissertationes* 1.6.23. For Second Sophistic texts on the Phidian Zeus, see Overbeck (1868: nos. 692–743) and Clerc (1915: 194–229). On the later history of the statue, see Lapatin (2001: 88–90).

only the piety and virtue of worshippers at Olympia, but also the vibrancy and vitality of Hellenic culture. Jerome Pollitt traces this view back to the (now lost) nostalgic art histories of the Hellenistic period, which influenced the retrospective nature of subsequent studies of art with 'the view that the great artists of the Classical period had been inspired seers, visionaries of a sort, who had been able to grasp the nature of divinity and convey it to their fellow men through the medium of the visual arts'.[48] This attitude is echoed in the praise bestowed upon the *pulchritudo* of the Phidian Zeus by Roman orators: for Cicero, Phidias 'did not look at any person whom he was using as a model, but in his own mind there dwelt a surpassing vision of beauty (*species pulchritudinis eximia quaedam*); at this he gazed and all intent on this he guided his artist's hand to produce a likeness of the god'.[49] This emphasis upon the artist's imaginative vision may have drawn upon the language of replication (the statue is a *similitudo*), yet also challenged the idea that as an *eikōn*, the statue was automatically ontologically inferior to its prototype.[50] Indeed, in Quintilian's formulation of the relationship between god and image, the statue's *pulchritudo* is presented as a key element in the construction of the god's identity and power, for he claims that the artist 'is even thought to have *added* something to the accepted religion'.[51]

Phidias' perceived contribution not only to the worship but also the identity of his divine subject thus placed the Olympian Zeus at the centre of Graeco-Roman discourse about the formation of human concepts of the divine, and the role played in the development of such concepts by visual or literary cultural models. The so-called *Olympian Oration* of Dio Chrysostom, delivered *c.* 97 CE in front of the Phidian image itself, is the most extended example of this debate.[52] Espousing the Stoic view that men

---

[48] Pollitt (1974: 52).

[49] Cicero *Orator* 8–9: 'Nec vero ille artifex cum faceret Iovis formam aut Minervae, contemplabatur aliquem e quo similitudinem duceret, sed ipsius in mente insidebat species pulchritudinis eximia quaedam, quam intuens in eaque defixus ad illius similitudinem artem et manum dirigebat' (translation from H. M. Hubbell's Loeb Classical Library edition, 1971). On the *pulchritudo* of Phidias' statues, see also Cicero, *Brutus* 257; Plin. *HN* 34.54 and 36.18; and Quint. *Inst.*. 12.10.9, with Pollitt (1974: 423–6). See also Seneca *Controversiae* 10.5.8, discussed by Watson (1988: 71).

[50] Compare the use of the term *eikōn* in Anth. Plan. 81 (Philip) = *GP* 1968: Philip no. 67, discussed in Chapter 4, 204.

[51] *Quint. Inst.* 12.10.9: 'cuius pulchritudo adiecisse aliquid etiam receptae religioni videtur'. On the relationship between representation and declamation, see Gunderson (2003: 91–4).

[52] See Russell (1992: 14–19, 155–211), with discussions by Clerc (1915: 194–229), B. F. Harris (1962), Fazzo (1977: vol. I, 21–58), Watson (1988: 71–95), Sharrock (1996: 103–5), Klauck (2000), Zeitlin (2001: 220–4) and Betz (2004a). On the speech's date, see Russell (1992: 16). All Dio translations are from J. W. Cahoon's Loeb Classical Library edition, 1939.

have an innate concept of the gods (and particularly of the 'leader of the universe') owing to their kinship with the divine (27, 39), Dio examines how humans try to make sense of and communicate this 'acquired concept' of divinity (ὑπόληψις) through poetry, law, art and philosophy (40).[53] The orator does not, therefore, frame his debate around the problem of epiphanic vision (how can we see Zeus? What does he 'really' look like?), but instead concentrates upon the ways in which Zeus can be apprehended via the cultural *sēmata* that mediate between human and god. Speaking of drawing, painting and sculpture, Dio argues that artists

were not satisfied to display their cleverness and skill (δεινότητα καὶ σοφίαν) on commonplace subjects, but by exhibiting all sorts of likenesses and representations of gods (θεῶν εἰκόνας καὶ διαθέσεις) they secured for their patrons both private persons and the states, whose people they filled with an ample and varied conception of the divine (πολλῆς ἐνέπλησαν ὑπονοίας καὶ ποικίλης περὶ τοῦ δαιμονίου, 45).

Significantly, Dio speaks of such images not only as *eikones* but also as *diatheseis* ('representations', 'descriptions' or 'arrangements' of an artificially created nature), a form of cultural synthesis that is as much a demonstration of the artist's *technē* and *sophia* as a visionary presentation of divinity. In both personal and civic contexts, the viewer is thus cast as a recipient of the artist's own conception, or *huponoia*, of the gods.

In this sense Dio anticipates certain arguments about the practice of representing the divine in Maximus of Tyre's didactic speech (or *dialexis*) 'Should statues be made to the gods?', dated to the mid second century CE.[54] Assuming (in line with Middle Platonic tradition) that true deity is imperceptible and that humans cannot grasp its essence, Maximus nevertheless concedes that visual aids are useful in prompting their viewers to piety.[55] Although he argues that anthropomorphism is the most pious form of representation, because 'the human soul is something very close to god' (3), he also grudgingly accepts the validity of theriomorphism (the worship of gods in the form of animals) and aniconism: 'If it is the art of Phidias

---

[53] On Dio's Stoic theology, see Desideri (1978: 362–4 n. 12, with bibliography), Schofield (1991: 57–92) and Swain (1996: 195–206). On the Stoic argument for the existence of God from consensus, see Dragōna-Monachou (1976: 44, 186–7, 195–9) and Meijer (2007: 117–19).

[54] *Dial.* 2, εἰ θεοῖς ἀγάλματα ἱδρυτέον; Translation by Trapp (1997: 15–24), with some modifications. On Maximus of Tyre, see Clerc (1915: 230–2), Koniaris (1982, 1983), Szarmach (1985) and Trapp (1997, 1999). On Maximus and Dio, see Puiggali (1982).

[55] On Maximus' non-sectarian form of Platonism, see Dillon (1977: 399–400), Koniaris (1983) and Trapp (1997: xxii–xxx, 15–16; 1999: 1948–50). In an echo of Dio's *Olympian Oration*, Maximus also draws upon Stoic theorising about the sources of human notions of divinity, emphasising the naturalness of religious ideas in section 1 and relating them to the use of aniconic images.

that arouses recollections of God for the Greeks, while for the Egyptians it is the worship of animals, and a river or fire for others, I have no objection to such diversity' (10).[56] The very range of strategies by which different cultures denote divine presence, however, is for Maximus proof of the arbitrariness of such semiological practices. Indeed, he compares the relationship between images and deities to that between written and spoken language:

One can, I think, compare spoken utterances, which can easily be articulated without recourse to written characters, be they Phoenician, Ionian, Attic, Assyrian, or Egyptian... In just the same way, divinity in its own nature has no need of statues and dedications (οὐδὲν ἀγαλμάτων οὐδὲ ἰδρυμάτων); but humanity, an utterly feeble species that lies as far from the divine as heaven from earth, contrived them as symbols (σημεῖα) through which to preserve the gods' names and their reputations (2).

Fittingly for an orator, Maximus draws a parallel between speech and the divine, condemning both written text and artistic objects to an inferior position in an ontological hierarchy that owes much to Plato's discussion of writing in the *Phaedrus*.[57] Whereas spoken words, like gods, are fluid, immaterial entities, texts and images strive to reify their elusive signifieds as fixed, physical objects, and in doing so inevitably lose the very qualities that define them. The sacred image, then, functions as a mere aide-mémoire, by which unimaginative mortals can be prompted to a lesser form of religious understanding. In this way the oration presents an ardent denial of the image's epiphanic potential, for in Maximus' theology god is ineffable and invisible – 'tongues cannot speak of him, and eyes cannot see him' (ἄρρητος φωνῇ καὶ ἀόρατος ὀφθαλμοῖς, 10).[58] In a further echo of the *Phaedrus*, mortal worshippers are thus 'like lovers, for whom the sweetest thing of all is the sight of their loved ones' forms (εἰς θέαμα οἱ τῶν παιδικῶν τύποι), but who also find pleasure in the recollections stirred by a lyre or a javelin or a seat or a racetrack or in general by anything that arouses memory (μνήμην) of the beloved' (10).[59] By implication,

---

[56] On Greek attitudes to Egyptian theriomorphism, see Smelik and Hemelrijk (1984); on the Greek notion that the Persians worshipped fire, see Herodotus 1.131, Strabo 15.3.13–14 and Luc. *JTr.* 42; on aniconism, see my discussion in Chapter 2, 100–5.

[57] See esp. *Phaedrus* 274d–275b, with Derrida (1981) and Trapp (1990).

[58] Cf. *Dial.* 11, 'On Plato's Theology' (τίς ὁ θεὸς κατὰ Πλάτωνα), especially section 9, on defining god by means of negation. On negative attitudes towards the sacred image in Greek thought, see Barasch (1992: 49–62), who does not, unfortunately, discuss Maximus of Tyre.

[59] Cf. *Phaedrus* 251a, on vision of the beloved as akin to epiphany of the form of Beauty (discussed by Nightingale, 2004: 86–9); see also *Phaedo* 73d, on sight of the beloved's lyre prompting a mental image (*eidos*) of its owner.

the sacred image is merely a trace or vestigial sign of the former presence of the divine, and epiphany can occur only in the memory of such *theamata.*

Maximus may exhibit an incipient iconophobia in his oration (which prompted considerable interest among later Christian readers), yet by emphasising the importance of mental contemplation as a means of accessing the divine, he is in tune with Second Sophistic authors who, like Dio, sought to reconcile the concept of *huponoia* with that of artistic production itself.[60] While reducing all sacred images to mere *sēmeia,* or 'symbols', Maximus nevertheless emphasises the superiority of Hellenic anthropomorphic tradition, praising the Greeks for their practice of honouring the gods 'with the most beautiful things the earth affords: pure materials, the human form, and the precise craftsmanship (τέχνῃ δὲ ἀκριβεῖ) of the artist' (3). Likewise, the relationship he draws between vision and memory parallels expressions of the nostalgic nature of epiphany and its relationship to the trace or vestige that have been noted in numerous epiphanic contexts.[61] Significantly, while Maximus emphasises the necessary insufficiency of sacred images, he draws upon the same repertoire of philosophical terms and concepts as iconophiles such as Philostratus.[62] His use of the term *tupos* to refer to the 'form of the beloved', for example, derives not from a Platonic model of mimetic representation, but from the Stoic language of *phantasia* (or 'presentation'). As we saw in Chapter 4, the *tupos* could suggest a chain of images by which visionary encounter with the divine could be communicated to viewers in a serialised sequence of impressions, rather than a hierarchy of decreasing ontological values.[63]

Throughout this period the concepts of mimesis and *phantasia* offered competing theories of representation that were repeatedly confused or opposed, as Greek thinkers questioned the role of image worship in religious practice and its significance for Hellenic identity.[64] Like the term *enargeia,* which in post-classical Greek could refer to both direct epiphanic encounter and the ekphrastic potential of language, the vocabulary of *phantasia* acquired a convenient double meaning. While in Stoic thought it played a precise role in epistemology, for example in the term *phantasia kataleptikē* (the 'clear and distinct presentation' by which sense-perception could be transformed into knowledge), from the late first century CE it also acquired broader significance as a concept closer to our notion of 'imagination' or

---

[60] On the *Nachleben* of *Dial.* 2, see Trapp (1997: 16–17).   [61] See above, 223.

[62] See below and Chapter 7, 320–9.   [63] See 192.

[64] On the parallel problem of mimesis in relation to Second Sophistic literary production, see Whitmarsh (2001b: 46–87).

'mental visualisation'.[65] Both *enargeia* and *phantasia* carry the weight of technical precision (whether rhetorical or philosophical), yet simultaneously suggest an engagement with abstract, immaterial (and even divine) entities that, crucially, are experienced via the medium of sight. While experiences of *enargeia* or *phantasia* can be generated by literary or artistic representation, provoking secondary forms of vision such as that experienced in the 'mind's eye', they can also constitute the primary visual experiences that inspire such verbal or visual representations in the first place.[66] In this way both concepts facilitate a sleight of hand, whereby viewing an image or reading an ekphrastic text can be presented as a secondary mode of visualisation dependent upon culturally constructed *sēmata*, or as a form of direct encounter; consider, for example, Pausanias' use of ἐναργῶς in his description of the mirror at Lykosoura, in which the duplicative power of reflection actually leads to a more direct encounter with the image (and therefore deity) reflected.[67] This ambiguity provided a potent means of theorising the function and status of the sacred image. While Maximus emphasises the image's role as a secondary form of *phantasia*, allying it to the Platonic concept of mimesis, authors such as Philostratus explicitly contrasted these concepts in order to stress the image's transmission of a primary form of *phantasia* that was closer to epiphany (as we shall see in Chapter 7). Indeed, in Philostratus' *Life of Apollonius of Tyana*, the holy man addresses Phidias' statue of Zeus with the words 'Hail, kindly Zeus, since you are so kind as even to *make yourself available* (σαυτοῦ κοινωνῆσαι) to humans'; in such language, the statue does not function as a *sēmeion* of Zeus, but as an embodiment of his very godhead.[68]

The tensions between these models of apprehending the divine by means of images are tentatively addressed in Dio's *Olympian Oration*. While Dio does not emphasise the mimetic insufficiency of cult images (on the contrary, he is most vocal in his praise of Phidias' statue), he nevertheless anticipates Maximus' emphasis upon the arbitrary relationship between deity and its mortal representation. His main concern is not whether such images are justifiable (for he presents himself as a defender of traditional

---

[65] See Watson (1988: 38–95; 1994: 4766–84) and, on *phantasia* as imagination, Fattori and Bianchi (1988). On *phantasia kataleptikē*, see Sandbach (1971), Imbert (1980), Frede (1983) and Annas (1994: 71–88). On the relationship between *phantasia* and *enargeia* in ekphrastic texts, see Elsner (1995: 26–8), Graf (1995), Dubel (1997), R. Webb (1997a, 1997b) and Zeitlin (2001).

[66] Cf. Elsner (1995: 26).

[67] Cf. Whitmarsh (2001b: 56), on Plutarch's use of the mirror metaphor in *Aemilius Paulus* 1.2.

[68] Philostr. *VA* 4.28: Ἀγαθὲ Ζεῦ, σὺ γὰρ οὕτω τι ἀγαθός, ὡς καὶ σαυτοῦ κοινωνῆσαι τοῖς ἀνθρώποις. Translation from C. P. Jones's Loeb Classical Library edition, 2005–6. On attitudes to sacred images in the *Life of Apollonius*, see Chapter 7.

Hellenism), but how, in a world of competing representations of god, we can decide which concept of divinity to adopt.[69] With such a plethora of cultural models on which to base our understanding (for to poetry, law and art Dio adds the crucial input of the philosopher as *exēgētēs*, or 'interpreter', 47), how can we know which model 'adheres to the truth most closely' (ξυνέπεται τῷ ἀληθεῖ μάλιστα, 48)? Putting to one side the social and metaphysical influences of law and philosophy, Dio frames his question around the familiar topos of the contest between image and text, setting the visual impact of the Phidian image against the verbal picture of Zeus conjured up in Homer's *Iliad*.[70] As in ekphrastic epigrams, the very medium of the speech conspires to attribute a greater potential for divine revelation to text, rather than image (for after all, what does Dio's epithet 'Chrysostom' refer to but the power of words?).[71] Called upon through the use of *prosōpopoiia* to defend the 'shape and form' of his Zeus (σχήματός τε καὶ μορφῆς, 52), Phidias not only must use the unfamiliar medium of rhetoric (rather than sculpture) within the context of the *Oration*, but, by attributing his conception of Zeus to that presented by Homer, testifies to the influence of poetry, rather than images, over his particular vision of the divine (57, 62).

However, while it may suit Dio's personal verbal agenda to allow Homer such an advantage, the orator ultimately yields to the phenomenological impact of the statue before which he speaks, and allows Phidias' justification of visual *technē* to triumph. In an extensive series of arguments, the sculptor stresses the disadvantages of working with physical media, rather than words; for although the poet is able to represent Zeus 'vividly and with conviction' (ἐναργῶς καὶ πεποιθότως, 26), drawing forth 'an immense volume of verses, as if from a gushing spring of water, before the vision and conception (τὸ φάντασμα καὶ τὴν ἐπίνοιαν) he had grasped can leave him

---

[69] As he comments, it was Phidias himself who, 'by the power of [his] art first conquered and united Hellas and then all others by means of this marvelous presentment' (53). On Dio's sense of Greek identity, see Desideri (1978: 524–36), C. P. Jones (1978: 125–7), Bowie (1991: 194–202), Swain (1996: 191–5), J. I. Porter (2001: 85–90) and Platt (2007b).

[70] The idea that the Phidian image was based upon Homer's description of Zeus in *Il.* 1.528–30 is first extant in Polybius 30.10.6, followed by Strabo 354A (who relates how Phidias' brother, the painter Panainos, asked him which *paradeigma* he would use for his statue) and Plu. *Aem.* 28.2. On Dio's use of Homer, see Mestre (1990: 89–101), Sharrock (1996: 104) and Zeitlin (2001: 220–4). Watson (1988: 72) comments, 'The fact that he begins with Phidias, indeed that Phidias is the only one whose supposed views are given, adds to the impression that Dio is handling a familiar topos, because his speech is concerned not with what we should expect, the problem of forming a notion of the divinity at all, but rather with contrasting the contributions made by the plastic arts and literature to the picture we have.'

[71] See Watson (1988: 74, 83).

and flow away' (70), the sculptor is bound by matter, and 'must keep the same image in his mind continuously (ἀνάγκη παραμένειν τῷ δημιουργῷ τὴν εἰκόνα ἐν τῇ ψυχῇ τὴν αὐτὴν ἀεί) until he finishes his work, which often takes many years' (71). Despite this drawback, the sculptor is able to harness the image's visual and material immediacy for religious ends, for 'all men have a strong yearning to honour and worship the deity from close at hand', as children long for their parents, 'being eager in every possible way to be with them and to hold converse with them' (61–2). Significantly, Dio's Phidias does not define the image's mediation of divine form as an inferior mode of re-presentation, but as a direct channel of communication and a conjuring of presence. Phidias' description of holding an *eikōn* of the god in his mind echoes the *species pulchritudinis* referred to by Cicero, which 'resided in [Phidias'] own mind'. Moreover, this *eikōn* is perfected to communicate 'the whole of god's nature and power' (70), 'insofar as it is possible for a mortal man to frame in his mind and to represent (διανοηθέντι μιμήσασθαι) the divine and inimitable nature' (74). As Froma Zeitlin comments, 'The implication is that [Phidias] here has grasped the true nature of the godhead in Zeus' powerful pose, while Homer, for all his dazzling reproduction of sights and sounds, trails behind the sculptor's truer, more stable, vision.'[72]

In the *Olympian Oration* Dio is still bound by the Platonic language of mimesis: the statue that communicates Phidias' vision is termed an *eikōn*; the god is very much 'represented' (μιμήσασθαι); Dio's Phidias strikes a particularly Socratic pose, employing dialogic formulae and making continual allusions to Plato – particularly in his description of god as 'the first and most perfect *dēmiourgos*' (82), which recalls the *Timaeus*.[73] However, despite the limitations of the terminology with which he has been trained, Dio strives to transcend the notion of ontological hierarchies and to set the agenda for a new way of conceptualising and viewing the sacred image, rehabilitating its relationship to divine 'truth' (*alētheia*).[74] For example, he wonders (26) if 'there is some sort of influence which in some way actually moulds and forms an impression upon (ἀμηγέπη πλάττον καὶ ἀνατυποῦν) man's

---

[72] Zeitlin (2001: 222).

[73] See Trapp (2000: 228). Zeitlin (2001: 222) comments that from here, 'It is but a short step to the notion that the sculptor is the mortal counterpart of the "first and foremost artificer", Zeus himself, the *dēmiourgos* who fashioned the entire universe.'

[74] On mimetic illusionism in Plato's *Republic*, see Chapter 2, n. 163, and Halliwell (2002: 110–11), although the concept of a divine demiurge advanced in the late dialogue *Timaeus* perhaps hints at a more positive notion of 'cosmic' mimesis (see Pollitt, 1974: 47–8, and Halliwell, 2002: 71 n. 79, 125–6). Trapp (2000: 227) comments that in his treatment of Homeric mimesis at 12.68, Dio draws upon Plato's criticism of Homer at *Republic* 397ff. 'in order radically to revalue it'.

conception of the deity', drawing upon the language of *phantasia* by positing the idea of a chain of impressions that can transmit divine truth by means of cultural representations. While this notion can implicitly lend itself to both images and texts, Dio's *prosōpopoiia* of Phidias goes on to stress the greater reliability of visual media. Claiming that Homeric poetry makes greater use of *mimēmata*, Phidias argues that while the poet can 'excite and cheat' the ear through the 'spell of metre and sound', viewers of images 'require greater *enargeia* to be convinced', because 'the eye agrees exactly with what it sees' (71). He thus plays upon the double meaning *enargeia* had acquired by the late first century CE. As a property of ekphrasis, *enargeia* is applied to Homer's verbal representation of Zeus by Dio (26), and there expresses the power of words to conjure up an image of the entities they describe (a form of secondary vision). He refers (45) to the representation of the divine by both artists and poets as *eidōlopoiia* ('image-making'), a term that emphasises their 'created' nature, but is also, according to 'Longinus', used in the same sense as *phantasia* when, in a rhetorical context, 'you think you see what you describe, and you place it before the eyes of your hearers'.[75] Dio's Phidias, however, reclaims *enargeia* as a visual experience in its own right, emphasising the image's ability to communicate a more authentic vision of god that allows the statue to function in phenomenal (and, by implication, epiphanic) terms. Like Pausanias' mirror at Lykosoura, visual representation can thus facilitate a clearer apprehension of the divine.

As we shall see, the *Olympian Oration* is one of a series of Second Sophistic texts that seek to reconcile the tensions generated by the sacred image. Like his later biographer Philostratus, Dio's religious conservatism and philosophical interests align so as to incorporate anthropomorphism into his intellectual framework, affirming its status as a cultural practice through which the divine can be apprehended by the pious viewer.[76] Through Dio's subtle rhetoric, Phidias' statue is presented as a creation of informed sophistication, culturally and intellectually equal in its conception to any poetic or philosophical text. For Dio, Phidias' conception of Zeus is communicated by art, but has been formed through a process of *paideia*; knowledge of

---

[75] 'Longinus' 15.1 (translation, Watson, 1988): '*Phantasiai* conribute greatly to dignity, elevation and power as a pleader. This is the name I give them; some call them *eidōlopoiiai*'. Discussed by Watson (1988: 67; 1994: 4773–4).

[76] Philostratus classes Dio among those whose eloquence has earned them the title of sophist 'though they were not sophists in fact' (*Lives of Sophists* 487–8), and portrays him as a rather slippery character in the *Life of Apollonius*, where he appears in a discussion of the ideal constitution with Vespasian (5.27–40); see Swain (2000: 23–4) and Whitmarsh (2001b: 225–44).

Homer's text is complemented by a learned familiarity with 'all the titles by which Zeus is known' (75), which, through Phidias' *technē*, are visually embodied by the statue itself (78). In this way the craftsman too is raised to the status of a *hermēneus* or *exēgētēs*, trusted with the task of communicating divine *alētheia* to mortal viewers. Together, art and literature thus form an important cultural resource for acquiring religious knowledge and understanding. Indeed, Dio ends his speech by uniting word and image, animating the statue itself for his audience. Claiming 'the god seems to us to have such an expression, altogether benevolent and solicitous, that I at least can almost imagine that he is *speaking* to us' (85), he moves from his *prosōpopoiia* of Phidias to speak in the voice of Zeus. In this way he conjures up an epiphanic confrontation with the god in order to praise his audience for their piety, while pitying their subjection to Rome with an appropriate quotation from the *Odyssey*: 'with deep concern I observe that "Yourself untended seem, and wretched age / With mean attire and squalor is your lot"'.[77] Dio's sophistic skill thus reinforces the power of the image, while demonstrating the perennial influence of the Homeric texts and defiantly confirming the importance of Hellenic religious tradition in the face of Roman imperium; it concludes a speech which, in true Second Sophistic style, is a seamless blend of aesthetic theory, literary sophistication and religious sensibility.

Holy moly! Animating the past in Philostratus' *Heroicus*

While Maximus of Tyre may claim that deity is ineffable and invisible, he has quite a different opinion on 'a race of secondary immortal beings, the so-called *daimones*, who have their station in the space between earth and heaven'.[78] As entities who are 'more closely related than men to the gods, but more closely concerned than the gods with men', *daimones* do not only speak to mortals, but also 'appear to them' (φανταζόμενον, 8.8).[79] For Maximus, even the tradition of Homeric epiphany is plausible if understood in terms

---

[77] 12.85; *Od.* 24.249–50. Russell (1992: 211) comments that this is 'an oddly pessimistic note on which to end a speech of celebration', which probably refers to Greece's 'old age and poverty'; Swain (1996: 100–3) reads the passage as a reference to Greece's enslavement by Rome. On the disputed meaning of the quotation, see also Klauck (2000: 157–9 nn. 428–30) and Betz (2004a: 138).

[78] *Dial.* 8.8, 'What was Socrates' Divine Sign?' (τί τὸ δαιμόνιον Σωκράτους;): see Trapp (1997: 67–83).

[79] Cf. *Heroicus* 16.5: 'The gods know everything; but the heroes know less than the gods but more than humans.'

of daemonic communication: Athena's famous appearances to Achilles, Diomedes and Telemachus in the *Iliad* and *Odyssey* are thus reformulated as epic examples of a widespread phenomenon that also embraces oracles, ghosts and the personal *daimonion* of Socrates, which Maximus' oration on *daimones* seeks to normalise through the enumeration of epiphanic *comparanda*.[80] In this, he takes his lead from Diotima's speech in Plato's *Symposium*:

> Everything that is daemonic is intermediate between God and mortal... Interpreting and transporting human things to the gods and divine things to men, and ordinances and requitals from above: being midway between, it makes each to supplement the other, so that the whole is combined in one... God has no contact with men; but the daemonic is the means of all society and converse of gods with men and of men with gods, whether waking or asleep. Whosoever has skill in these affairs is a daemonic man.[81]

Maximus thus employs the daemonic as a means of reconciling his philosophical commitment to monotheism with the weight of Greek religious tradition, a move that allows him to approve modes of 'active' religious engagement with the divine and so uphold the sanctity of phenomena such as Apollo's possession of the Delphic Pythia (8.1) and the visual and sonic epiphanies experienced by worshippers at the shrine of Trophonius near Lebadeia (8.2).[82] Maximus echoes Euhemeristic doctrine by including among the *daimones* divinised mortals such as Asclepius, Heracles, Dionysus and the Dioscuri, plus great heroes such as Achilles (9.7).[83] All these,

---

[80] See *Dial.* 8.5, where he quotes *Il.* 1.197, *Il.* 5.127–8 and *Od.* 3.26–7, and 8.8, where he quotes *Od.* 17.485–6: 'For indeed the gods, in the guise of strangers from abroad, / taking all manner of forms, visit the cities of men.' On Homeric epiphany, see Chapter 1, and on its relationship to demonology, Brenk (1986: 2071–82). Socrates' *daimōn* was also discussed by Maximus' contemporaries Plutarch (*De genio Socratis*) and Apuleius (*De deo Socratis*): see Dillon (1977: 216–24; 2001), J. Z. Smith (1978: 433), Brenk (1986), Trapp (1997: 67–8) and Baltes *et al.* (2004).

[81] Plato *Symposium* 202e–203a (translation adapted from W. R. M. Lamb's Loeb Classical Library edition, 1961). On the notion of a personal *daimōn* and its relationship to the soul (to which Maximus pays less attention in *Dial.* 8 and 9), see also *Phaedo* 107d and *Timaeus* 90a, with Dillon (2001). Dodds (1965: 37–8) comments that the concept of the daemonic was 'something of a novelty in Plato's day, but in the second century after Christ it was the expression of a truism'. On the 'daemonic' in Greek religion and philosophy, see François (1957), Detienne (1963), J. Z. Smith (1978), Ferguson (2003: 236–8) and, in Second Sophistic thought, Brenk (1977: 49–52, 85–112, 145–83; 1986; 1998) and Casadesús Bordoy (2001).

[82] On the role of *daimones* in pagan monotheism, see Frede (1999: 57–60) and Ferguson (2003: 237). On the oracle of Trophonius, see also Pausanias (9.39), who describes the process of consulting the oracle in great detail and, in another claim of sacred autopsy, states 'I have myself inquired of Trophonius' (9.39.14).

[83] On Euhemerism, see Price (1984b: 38–9).

he claims, are still visible to their mortal worshippers; indeed, he concludes his *Ninth Oration* with an emphatic statement of epiphanic autopsy, claiming 'I myself have never seen either Hector or Achilles, but I have seen the Dioscuri, in the form of bright stars (ἀστέρας λαμπρούς), righting a ship in a storm. I have seen Asclepius, and that not in a dream (ἀλλ'οὐχὶ ὄναρ). I have seen Heracles, in waking reality (ἀλλ' ὕπαρ, 9.7)'. These statements draw heavily upon epiphanic convention, alluding to the astral manifestation of the Dioscuri in the form of St. Elmo's Fire and the appearance of Asclepius in rites of incubation (though Maximus strengthens his statement by claiming to have seen the god during what Diotima calls 'the waking state', rather than dreams).[84] For the Homeric heroes, he must rely on others' accounts: Achilles, he claims, can still be encountered on the island where he dwells in the Black Sea (the so-called 'White Isle') – passing sailors 'have often seen a young man with tawny hair, clad in golden armour, exercising there' – while Hector 'can be seen sweeping over the plain [of Troy], flashing with light (φαντάζεται πηδῶν ἀνὰ τὸ πεδίον καὶ ἀστράπτων, 9.7)'. This reference to heroic epiphany on an ancient battlefield recalls Pausanias' accounts of the appearance of heroic *daimones* at Delphi (8.10.9) and Marathon (1.32.4).[85] In the latter location, the epiphany of heroes in the battle of 490 has now been superseded (as at Troy) by the ghostly presence of the heroised dead themselves: 'every night you can hear (αἰσθέσθαι) horses neighing and men fighting. No one who has expressly set himself to behold this vision (ἐς ἐναργῆ θέαν) has ever got any good from it, but the *daimones* are not angry with those who in ignorance chance to be spectators'.[86]

For both Maximus and Pausanias, then, the sphere of the daemonic is closely associated with the heroic, and thus to glorious victories of the mythic and classical past and enduring *milieux de mémoire* such as Troy and Marathon that can facilitate access to these lost worlds.[87] Both authors conjure up an impression of passing glimpses or echoes of beings who have a deeply ambivalent relationship with their viewer-worshippers, sometimes aiding them directly (like the *daimones* at Delphi) but often going about their

---

[84] On the relationship between epiphanies during sleep or while awake, see Petridou (2006: 155–8) and my discussion in Chapter 6. On astral epiphanies of the Dioscuri, see Lorenz (1992) and Platt (in press a); cf. *H. Hom.* 33, which describes the divine twins as 'deliverers of men on earth and of swift-going ships when stormy gales rage over the ruthless sea' (6–7).

[85] On the reception of Marathon in later Greek history, see Bridges *et al.* (2007). On the significance of Troy in the imperial period, see Erskine (2001).

[86] Compare Philostratus *Heroicus* 2.11 and 18.2 on the ghosts of heroes at Troy: 'They appear, I said. They still appear great and divine to herdsmen and shepherds on the plain, and they are seen whenever there is evil upon the land.'

[87] On heroic epiphany in particular, see Bravo (2004). On *milieux de mémoire*, see Chapter 3, n. 96.

own business in parallel spheres that can only be momentarily apprehended by mortals; one might hope to catch such heroes *in situ*, but, like the gods, they retain epiphanic agency in their own (ghostly) hands. Significantly, the verb Maximus uses to describe their appearance is φαντάζομαι, which shares the same root as ἐπιφαίνω and ἐπιφάνεια but has a narrower semantic field, being closely related to φάντασμα and φάσμα, both suggesting an 'apparition' or 'phantom'.[88] Indeed, φάσμα is frequently employed in Greek literature to refer to heroic epiphany: Theon refers to Ajax's appearance as a *phasma* at the battle of the Sagra, while Pausanias describes Helen and the Dioscuri as *phasmata* when they appear to aid the Messenian hero Aristomenes against the Spartans (4.16.9), as well as the local heroes who drive the Gauls from Delphi (10.23.2).[89] In such contexts *phasma* suggests a degree of corporeality that is more accessible to human sense-perception than that of *theos* (the divine), but which is nevertheless elusive, shifting and spectral; in this sense, it is akin to the *eidōlon* or 'double', a liminal entity that exists simultaneously in the human and supernatural realms and is often used to refer to both dream images and ghosts.[90]

This ambiguous form of embodiment is directly related to the heroes' 'historical' existence: great achievers such as Achilles and Hector attained daemonic status in death, and thus are accessible in epiphanic terms in the present; but as former mortals, they have also left traces on earth. Unlike the gods, whose distance from the realm of man and timeless immortality is emphasised by the fact that they have no tombs, epic heroes inhabiting the daemonic sphere are closely tied to mortal experience through the marks they have left on the landscape itself, whether battlefields, heroa or, as we saw above, the relics of their actual bones.[91] As the focus of hero cult, these physical traces provide a form of cognitive reliability that, like the relationship between gods and their images, exists in a mutually reinforcing relationship with epiphanic encounter. In Second Sophistic texts, however, authors increasingly emphasise the role of an alternative medium by which the daemonic can be accessed – that is, through the visual and textual

---

[88] See LSJ s.v. φαντάζω and φάντασμα, with Petridou (2006: 58).

[89] Theon, *FGrH* 26 F1, 18 = Phot. *Bibl.* 186.133b. These and other examples are discussed by Petridou (2006: 55–61; in press b).

[90] See Koch Piettre (1996: 342–50), with Vernant (1990b: 34–41; 1991: 167–70) and Tanner (2006: 106). On dream images, see Chapter 6. Note that *eidōlon* is also used to refer to epiphanies of Homeric heroes at *Heroicus* 21.1 (Palamedes) and 22.2 (Achilles), while Protesilaos is called a *daimōn* at 43.3.

[91] Cf. Callimachus *Hymn to Zeus* 5–9, on the fraudulent tomb of Zeus on Crete ('But you did not die, for you are eternal', 9). On tombs and hero cult, see Antonaccio (1995) and Ekroth (2002); on the Black Sea cult of Achilles, see Hedreen (1991) and Rusyaeva (2003).

traditions that celebrate heroic achievement. Indeed, the very status of the daemonic as a mediatory sphere available to human sense-perception seems to have facilitated a parallel with the mediatory nature of representation, whereby encounter with heroes could be experienced through acquaintance with the texts and images that had played a major role in their creation, characterisation and commemoration.[92] One could visit Troy and summon up the *daimōn* of Achilles, as Philostratus relates in his biography of Apollonius of Tyana, or one could draw upon the great store of *sophia* provided by texts such as the *Iliad*.[93] Deep engagement with these literary resources through the practice and acquisition of *paideia* thus offered an opportunity for exploring the workings of *phantasia* in both its primary and secondary senses – as a form of epiphanic encounter, and as a process of imaginative visualisation.

The privileged status given to vision in the Second Sophistic, combined with an urge to re-experience (and even rewrite) the literary and mythological past, meant that authors increasingly asked questions such as, 'What did Achilles look like?' or 'Was Homer right?'[94] In his twenty-first discourse, entitled *On Beauty*, Dio again explores how Homer's poetry encourages his audience to visualise the invisible, yet here focuses upon the heroes of the epic world, rather than Zeus. As in the *Olympian Oration*, the practice of viewing works of art and the verbal communication of aesthetic experience in the form of ekphrasis are presented as identifiably Hellenic activities. Dio lays particular emphasis upon the Greek tradition of celebrating athletic male beauty in statuary (as opposed to Persian preference for effeminate form, 3), and wonders whether there is a particularly 'Greek' form of beauty (16).[95] Yet turning to the *Iliad* for evidence (as Phidias did in the *Olympian Oration*), Dio has to concede that there is little ekphrasis of the Greek male form in Homer: the poet may state that the Achaeans 'gazed upon the wonderful form and beauty of Hector', but he does not supply the details.[96]

---

[92] See Vernant (1991: 164–85), who emphasises the 'paradoxical status of the image as an intermediary between nonbeing and being' in Platonism (181), a description that could just as well apply to the concept of the *daimōn*.

[93] *VA* 4.11, 16: see Zeitlin (2001: 248–55), Mestre (2004: 131–2), Grossardt (2009) and my discussion below. On traditions of necromancy in antiquity, see Ogden (2001: esp. 121–3), on Apollonius of Tyana.

[94] On the rewriting of Homer in Second Sophistic texts, see Mestre (1990, 2004) and (fundamental) Zeitlin (2001). As G. Anderson (1986: 243) comments, 'Correction of Homer is the sophistic device *par excellence*; the writer has to know his set text and then "improve" on it.'

[95] See Hawley (1998a, 1998b, 2000: 137–8) and Newby (2005: 126–9).

[96] *Il.* 22.371–2: οἳ καὶ θηήσαντο φυὴν καὶ εἶδος ἀγητὸν | Ἕκτορος, quoted by Dio at 21.16. Compare Dio's revision of the relationship between Paris and Helen in his *Troikos* oration (11.61–4), discussed by Mestre (2004: 129–30).

Although Dio purports to glean what he can from various narrative passages, he exhibits a highly ambivalent relationship to the text of the *Iliad* itself. Commenting that Homer describes Hector 'in greater detail than he describes any other of the most handsome men,' he continues, 'For he says that his head was graceful (τήν... κεφαλὴν χαρίεσσαν), his hair quite black (τὴν κόμην πάνυ μέλαιναν), and his body not too hard' (τὸ σῶμα οὐ σκληρόν, 17). Rather than quoting directly from the text of the *Iliad*, however, Dio is ostentatious in his use of *different* descriptive terms: Homer's Hector had hair which was κυάνεαι ('dark blue', or 'glossy', 22.402), rather than 'black', and his body was μαλακώτερος ('soft', 22.373), rather than οὐ σκληρόν ('not hard').[97] This slight modification of the textual record makes it clear that Dio is not employing the epics as a cast-iron source, but as a mediating cultural model through which the world of myth can be accessed and subsequently re-experienced on the reader's own terms; indeed, he criticises 'those of the present day [who] strive to name the ancients on any pretext' (12). Dio's attempt to visualise the Iliadic heroes is influenced by his literary knowledge, and yet opens up the text only to reimagine its content. Although he does not cross what we might call the 'ekphrastic barrier' to animate and give voice to the Hector whom he describes, Dio's creative and even irreverent use of the Homeric text opens the numinous world of the heroes to more 'direct' interaction.

The practice of rewriting Homer was by no means new to antiquity: a creative engagement with the Homeric epics is evident in Greek tragedy and, of course, in later epic poetry such as Apollonius' *Argonautika* and Virgil's *Aeneid*.[98] But Dio's aporetic attempt to find passages of visual description to inform his own visual conception of the ancient heroes suggests not just a literary game but also a *desire to see*, to use the text as a vehicle for engaging more directly with its subject matter, and to yoke it to broader representational practices that include the visual rendering of ideal masculine beauty. This desire is in large part fulfilled by a later Second Sophistic text – the third-century *Heroicus* of Philostratus, a dialogue between a travelling Phoenician and a mysterious 'vine-dresser' (ἀμπελουργός) near the

---

[97] On Homer's use of κυάνεος (often a synonym for μέλας), see Irwin (1974: 84–110, esp. 89–90) on its application to divine brows (*Il.* 1.528, 15.102) and heroic hair (22.402). Significantly, Irwin points out that the meaning of *kuaneos* shifted in the sixth century BCE from 'dark' to 'blue'; in this sense, Dio's use of *melainos* serves as a contemporary updating of Homer's archaic terminology.

[98] The bibliography on the reception and reworking of Homer in antiquity is vast, but see in particular Kindstrand (1973), H. Clarke (1981), who also looks at later Homeric reception, Lamberton and Keaney (1992), Cairns (2001: 1–56), Zeitlin (2001), Graziosi (2002) and Graziosi and Haubold (2005).

tomb of Protesilaos in the Thracian Chersonese, during which the local describes his epiphanic encounters with the Greek hero and relates Protesilaos' accounts of the Trojan War and the subsequent activities of heroes such as Achilles.[99] While Homer is frequently alluded to, the dialogue acts as a form of extended animation in which the reader is drawn into the daemonic world of the heroes through the mediatory strategies of cult arcana, a powerful conjuring of place and a broad spectrum of literary intertexts.[100] Like Dio's *Olympian Oration*, the text combines aesthetic and literary sophistication with a profound engagement with lived religion. Yet it does so not to construct a rhetorical critique of mortal attempts to visualise the divine, but actually to cross the ekphrastic barrier and give voice and form to the inhabitants of the supernatural realm, so facilitating a more direct form of engagement between reader and *daimōn* that purports to bypass the very sources of information on which the dialogue is based.[101] As the vine-dresser comments on his daemonic source of information, 'Among those who critically examine Homer's poems, who will you say reads and has insight into the poems as Protesilaos does?' (7.5).[102] The irony lies, of course, in the fact that the vine-dresser's daemonic source was famously the first hero to die at Troy: most of his knowledge, too, is gained second-hand (7.2).[103]

This difference between Dio and Philostratus is demonstrative of a shift in attitude towards the cultural models of the past between the late first and early third centuries CE, by which *paideia* is construed not only as acquired knowledge of canonical art and literature, but also as a more intense form of engagement with their content, whereby readers can reopen the past, move through its numinous world and come face to face – as Maximus of Tyre claims to have done – with its inhabitants. The Protesilaos and Achilles of the *Heroicus* are not just the creations of Homer: they are also *daimones* existing above and beyond the Homeric texts with whom the wise and pious can communicate. As the recipients of ritual honours, with a

---

[99] For a translation and notes on the *Heroicus*, see Maclean and Aitken (2001); for recent scholarship on the work, see C. P. Jones (2001b), the papers gathered in Aitken and Maclean (2004), Rutherford (2009) and Whitmarsh (2009).

[100] On cult arcana, see Pache (2004) and Rutherford (2009); on landscape and location in the dialogue, see Alcock (2004) and Whitmarsh (2004).

[101] Cf. Elsner's comment (in the introduction to Bowie and Elsner, 2009: 14) that the *Heroicus* 'takes *Homerkritik* into areas of mystic revelation from which it could hardly recover'.

[102] On the *Heroicus* as a form of *Homerkritik*, see G. Anderson (1986: 241–57), Beschorner (1999: 219–31), Zeitlin (2001: 255–66), Maclean and Aitken (2001: lx–lxxvi), Mestre (2004) and Grossardt (2006: 55–120).

[103] Cf. Whitmarsh (2009: 225).

power that extends from beyond the grave, they can generate epiphanic encounters with mortals, confer benefits, make demands and, in extreme cases, do them violence.[104] The vine-dresser's meetings with Protesilaos in the *Heroicus* and Apollonius' conjuration of Achilles both depend for their literary and numinous power upon the narrator's desire for unmediated access to the characters who were construed as being so important for Greek self-identity. In this sense the idea of epiphanic confrontation is used as a narrative device to allow for a sophistic rewriting of literary history, but this is not simply an arch demonstration of Philostratus' mastery over his literary sources.[105]

Ritual practice and epiphanic encounter both played an essential role in the revivification of Hellenism that Second Sophistic thinkers considered so important to their cultural identity.[106] Indeed, that such a desire spilled over into 'real' epiphanic experiences is demonstrated by texts such Aelius Aristides' *Hieroi Logoi*, in which he records his oneiric encounters with not only Asclepius and Athena but also Plato; in this way not only the sources of Hellenic *paideia* but also their very creators were accessible to those desiring to re-enter the past.[107] The epiphanies so tantalisingly described in texts such as the *Heroicus* thus combine intellectual and literary antiquarianism with a particularly contemporary desire for animation and imaginative visualisation (or *phantasia*).[108] Protesilaos, Philostratus' vine-dresser claims, has

[104] E.g., Protesilaos appears to a greedy landowner 'in a vision, as a result of which his eyes were stricken and he lost his sight' (4.2), and takes vengeance on adulterers (16.3); Achilles dismembers the last descendant of Priam from his home on the White Isle (56.1–10), and slaughters some invading Amazons (56.11–57.17). Compare Pausanias' comments on the dangers of viewing the *daimones* at Marathon (1.32.4), and Maximus of Tyre's account of Achilles' unpredictable behaviour on the White Isle (9.7).

[105] Compare Lucian's *Charon*, where the ferryman of the underworld just happens to have shared Homer's last voyage, and thus has privileged information regarding certain details of mythical history.

[106] Cult revival was one of the primary aims of Apollonius of Tyana during his travels (see Chapter 7); in a more general sense, such interest is demonstrated by Pausanias' *Description of Greece* and other Second Sophistic texts concerned with cult activity such as Aelius Aristides' *Sacred Tales*, the pseudo-Lucianic *On the Syrian Goddess* and Plutarch's *Moralia*. On the revival of hero cult under Caracalla in 211–17, see Mantero (1966: 21–47), G. Anderson (1986: 241–57), Beschorner (1999: 235–40), Alcock (2004: 161–2) and, more generally in the second and third centuries, C. P. Jones (2001b: 146–8), Betz (2004b), Pache (2004) and Rutherford (2009: 237–8). Nagy (in the introduction to Maclean and Aitken, 2001: xxxii) comments that 'The *Heroicus* bridges the chasm between the mythical world of the epic heroes and the ritual world of cult heroes . . . A continuum is still felt to exist between these two diverging worlds.'

[107] Aristides *Hieroi Logoi* 4.57.

[108] Cf. Zeitlin (2001: 263): 'Whatever the style of viewing, real or imaginary, the eyes, as no other faculty, give life and credence to vivid recollections of the past and the preoccupations of a shared cultural inheritance.'

unmediated access to the divine, and knows the gods 'not by worshipping *agalmata* and conjectures (ὑπονοίας), but by gaining visible association with them' (ἀλλὰ ξυνουσίας φανερὰς πρὸς αὐτοὺς ποιούμεναι, 7.3), a statement that explicitly rejects the model of *huponoia* advanced in Dio's *Olympian Oration*. In this way the literary conjuring of such experiences enabled a more fluid interaction with Greek cultural heritage, re-empowering the *daimones* who populated it in order to reappropriate them for contemporary lives and letters. This notion finds a fertile metaphor in the agricultural activities of Philostratus' vine-dresser, who says of his meetings with Protesilaos, 'Since I spend time with him and devote myself to the land, I am becoming wiser (σοφώτερος) than I used to be, because he excels in wisdom (σοφίας)' (4.10).[109]

This creative engagement with the literary and religious past is illustrated by an early episode from the *Heroicus* in which the Phoenician accounts for his presence in the numinous *locus amoenus* of his vine-tending interlocutor, where even the nightingales sing in Attic Greek (5.4):[110]

– Ask whatever you wish, my guest, and you will not say that you came in vain. For when Odysseus, far from his ship, was perplexed, Hermes, or one of his wise followers, had an earnest conversation with him (for we must believe the moly was this). So Protesilaos by means of me will fill you with information (ἱστορίας τε δι' ἐμοῦ ἐμπλήσει) and make you more content and wise (σοφώτερον). For knowing many things is very valuable.

– But I am not perplexed, my good friend. By Athena! I have come under the auspices of a god, and I finally understand my dream.

– How do you interpret your dream? You hint at something divine (θεῖον γάρ τι ὑποδηλώσεις).

– This is already about the thirty-fifth day, I suppose, that I have been sailing from Egypt and Phoenicia. When the ship put in here at Elaious, I dreamed I read the verses of Homer in which he recites the catalogue of the Achaeans, and I invited the Achaeans to board the ship, as if it were large enough for all. When I awoke with a start, for a sort of shuddering (φρίκης τι) came over me, I attributed the dream to the slowness and length of the voyage, since visions of the dead (τῶν ἀποθανόντων ὄψεις) mean little to those who travel in haste. Because I wished to receive a sign about the dream's meaning (for the wind has not yet allowed our sailing), I have disembarked here. While walking, as you know, you were the first person I encountered, and we are now talking about

[109] All translations of the *Heroicus* are from Maclean and Aitken (2001), with some minor modifications.

[110] Καὶ οὕπω, ξένε, τῶν ἀηδόνων ἤκουσας, οἶον τῷ χωρίῳ ἐναττικίζουσιν: see Pache (2004: 20–3) and Whitmarsh (2004: 239; 2009: 214–15).

> Protesilaos. We shall also converse about the catalogue of the heroes, for you
> say that we shall do so, and 'cataloguing them onto the ship' would mean that
> those who have compiled the story about them would then embark.
> – My guest, you have truly arrived under the auspices of a god, and you have
> interpreted the vision soundly (ὑγιῶς ἐξηγῇ τὴν ὄψιν). (6.1–7.1)

The passage presents us with two classic kinds of epiphanic encounter in
quick succession. First, the reference to Odysseus' meeting with Hermes and
the gift of moly (τὸ μῶλυ, the divine herb that Hermes gave to Odysseus
on Circe's island) suggests the revelation of knowledge by a divinity in
a Homeric-style encounter; second, the Phoenician experiences a vision
(*opsis*) of Homeric heroes in the dream world.[111] Both epiphanies involve a
certain cognitive realignment: the first recasts a hero–deity meeting within
epic myth (Odysseus and Hermes) as a meeting between an ordinary mortal
and a literary hero, with the vine-dresser's reported speech playing the role
of the moly; in the second, the oneiric context allows the dreamer to 'embark
the ship' and enter the Homeric text itself. The Phoenician's dream therefore
begins as a narrative of reading, only to shift to a direct interaction with the
characters within the text; it performs in miniature what the vine-dresser,
and through him, the Phoenician and the reader, experience in the *Heroicus*
as a whole. In this way we are allowed to enter into the myth and play with
the cultural building-blocks that form the educated reader's imaginative
world. The recording of first-hand experience and the secondary practice of
collecting *muthoi* from others become the same thing: literary 'reality' and
the reader's 'reality' coincide.

    The fluid nature of this kind of interaction with the past is expressed by
the vine-dresser's ambiguous use of the word *historia*. Through his mortal
interlocutor, Protesilaos will fill the traveller (and thus the reader) with a
form of *sophia* that is apparently imparted through the hero's epiphany, yet
which alludes semantically to systematic and scholarly enquiry along the
lines of Herodotean historiography.[112] Philostratus' animation of the past

---

[111] On the Homeric use of moly at *Od.* 10.274–306, see Clay (1972).

[112] On Herodotus' concept of *historia*, see R. Thomas (2000: 161–7), Bakker (2002b, 2006) and R.
Fowler (2006); on Herodotean elements in the *Heroicus*, Whitmarsh (2009: 209–10, 215–16);
see also Elsner (2001b: 127–8), on Herodotean elements in Lucian's *On the Syrian Goddess*.
Note that Protesilaos also appears in Herodotus' *Histories* at 9.120, where he takes vengeance
on the Persian Artaÿctes for violating his shrine: see Boedeker (1988) and Dewald (1997).
Compare the *Life of Apollonius*, in which Philostratus often adopts a historiographical pose by
means of Herodotean allusions (particularly in the more exotic travel sections of the
biography), yet much of his narrative appropriates elements from genres with a more fluid
relationship to 'real' events, such as hagiographical literature, and even the novel. For
similarities between the *Heroicus* and the *VA* see Solmsen (1940: 560) and G. Anderson (1986:

through the narration of epiphanic encounter thus flirts with the *Realien* of religious practice while maintaining a certain detachment; the experiences are numinously 'real', even as they are self-consciously contrived.[113] Here the moly is particularly significant: on one hand, it symbolises divine wisdom acquired through epiphany, yet, on the other, the vine-dresser interprets it in allegorical terms as discourse itself – the *logos* that takes place between Odysseus and Hermes, and by implication the *historia* acquired through conversation with Protesilaos that the vine-dresser then passes on to the Phoenician. In 'embarking the ship' through analysis of his dream, the Phoenician is then praised for 'interpreting his vision' (ἐξηγῇ τὴν ὄψιν), having acquired the role of a learned *exēgētēs* through the mediatory *paideia* of the vine-dresser.[114] In this sense, processes of verbal transmission are valued as highly as unmediated encounter itself.

In the Odyssey moly is acquired through epiphany, yet it is the magical object that enables Odysseus to retain his human form (and powers of reason) when confronted with Circe's powers of enchantment; in allowing Odysseus to seduce the enchantress herself and access her *sophia*, it is also the means by which he learns how to access the underworld, leading to Odysseus' own 'visions of the dead' (ἀποθανόντων ὄψεις) in the epic's *Nekuia*. The moly thus provides a potent symbol by which Philostratus can align the rational discourse of *logos* and *historia* with *paideia* gained through encounter with Greek heroes of the Trojan War – for in the *Heroicus*, too, moly gives access to the world of the dead, in that the text as a whole functions as a form of necromantic exercise. It is most fitting that attainment of this knowledge is symbolised by a plant with such a literary pedigree, for the true moly at work here is the text itself, which through narrative devices such as dream visions presents its readers with forms of sacred wisdom acquired through the author's creative relationship with his own Homeric heritage. Epiphanic viewing of the divine and heroic spheres is thus gained through a process of *paideia* in which acquaintance with appropriate cultural models (through structures of enquiry, *historia*) leads to *sophia*, and thence to a form of epiphanic *phantasia*.

---

241), who comments that the *Heroicus* 'certainly reveals the same outlook and literary technique, and has the same elusive relationship to the real world of the second and third centuries'. On genre in the *VA*, see Chapter 7.

[113] Cf. the Thessalian *theōria* to Achilles' tomb at Troy (*Heroicus* 67–70), which Rutherford (2009) suggests may be an elaborate literary invention threaded with many plausible details.

[114] Cf. 43.1, where the Phoenician alludes to *Od.* 9.82–104, claiming 'If they who in Homer ate the lotus, vine-dresser, were so readily addicted to the meadow as to forget utterly their own affairs, do not doubt that I am also addicted to the story just as to the lotus'.

Epiphany, however, is a predominantly visual phenomenon, and images, as well as texts, play a significant role in the *Heroicus'* game with the cultural *sēmata* of the past, particularly when the vine-dresser attempts to provide ekphraseis of both Protesilaos himself and his sacred *agalma* at Elaious:

– The *agalma* stood upon a ship, since its base has the shape of a prow, and the ship's captain dedicated it. Time has worn it away (περιτρίψας δὲ αὐτὸ ὁ χρόνος) and, by Zeus, those who anoint it and seal their vows here have changed its shape. But this means nothing to me. For I spend time with him and see him, and no *agalma* could be more pleasant than that man (οὐδὲν ἄν μοι γένοιτο ἄγαλμα ἐκείνου ἥδιον).
– Why don't you describe him to me and share what he looks like? (Ἦ καὶ διαγράψεις μοι αὐτὸν καὶ κοινωνήσεις τοῦ εἴδους;)
– Gladly, my guest, by Athena. He is about twenty years old at most. Because he sailed to Troy at such a young age, a light down grows on his chin and he smells sweeter than autumn myrtles. Cheerful eyebrows frame his eyes, which gives him a pleasant, friendly manner. When he exerts himself he looks intense and determined. But if we meet him at ease, how lovely and friendly his eyes appear! He has blond hair of moderate length. It hangs a little over his forehead rather than covering it. The shape of his nose is angular, just like an *agalma* (οἷον ἀγάλματος). His voice is more sonorous than trumpets, though it comes from a small mouth. It is most enjoyable to meet him nude, since he is well-proportioned and graceful, just like the herms set up in race courses (ὥσπερ οἱ δρομικοὶ τῶν ἑρμῶν). His height is easily ten cubits, and it seems to me that he would have exceeded this had he not died so young.
– I see the young man (εἶδον τὸν νεανίαν), vine-dresser, and I admire you because of your companion. Is he armed as a soldier, or how is he attired?
– He is clad in a riding cloak, my guest, in Thessalian style, just like this *agalma* (ὥσπερ τὸ ἄγαλμα τοῦτο). The cloak is sea-purple, of a divine lustre (θείου ἄνθους), for the lustre of purple cannot be expressed (ἄρρητον γὰρ τὸ τῆς πορφύρας ἄνθος). (9.6–10.5)

The vine-dresser explicitly states that his experience of Protesilaos as an *agalma* is entirely different from the 'real' Protesilaos with whom he converses. While the hero's cult image has been affected by cult practice, worn down (περιτρίψας) by the hands of those who pray to him as a *daimōn*, his epiphanic appearance is completely independent of any artistic representation: 'no *agalma* could be more pleasant'. Yet when the vine-dresser proceeds to describe this seemingly unmediated manifestation, he can only do so in terms of statues: his nose is angular, 'just like an *agalma*' (οἷον ἀγάλματος); he is well-proportioned and graceful, 'like the herms set up in race courses' (ὥσπερ οἱ δρομικοὶ τῶν ἑρμῶν); he wears a short Thessalian *chlamis*, 'just like the *agalma*' within the sanctuary itself (ὥσπερ τὸ ἄγαλμα τοῦτο).

The reanimation of Protesilaos is thus revealed to be a literary construct based upon the prior representation of such characters in Greek sculptural tradition. In a reversal of the Thessalian's dream, which began with reading and proceeded to epiphany, what begins as an ekphrasis of an epiphany (purporting to bypass the image altogether) ends as a traditional ekphrasis of a work of art. As well as conventional athletic statuary, the vine-dresser's *comparanda* even include herms, which, as we saw in Chapter 1, explicitly display their own object status through their semi-iconic form and lack of limbs.[115] Despite the fact that *daimones* are characterised by their non-corporeality (the vine-dresser reminds the Phoenician that 'to be cleansed of the body is the beginning of life for divine and thus blessed souls', 7.3), Protesilaos can ultimately be apprehended only as a body – specifically the culturally created body of the statue.[116]

Apollonius of Tyana is similarly tied to his cultural knowledge when he goes to raise the ghost of Achilles from his tomb at Troy: Philostratus tells us that the sage felt prepared to spend a night on the grave-mound of the Achaean heroes only once 'his mind was glutted with all the traditions of their past' (πάσης τῆς περὶ αὐτῶν ἀρχαιολογίας ἐμφορηθείς). Warned by his companions of Achilles' fearsome reputation, Apollonius reassures them, saying 'I know Achilles well (τὸν Ἀχιλλέα σφόδρα οἶδα) and he thoroughly delights in company' (4.11). Yet despite this statement of superior knowledge and acquaintance with the hero, the examples given of Achilles' *bonhomie* (his relationship with Phoenix, his kindness to Priam) all come directly from Homer! In their introduction to the *Heroicus*, Aitken and Maclean comment that:

Immediate engagement with the hero contrasts with other sources of similarly authoritative knowledge, such as dreams, visions, oracular utterances, ancient histories, and the interpretation of sacred texts. The word of the hero who has returned to life and speaks to his worshippers thus has ultimate truth value in the dialogue. This revealed knowledge functions as the final authority in the *Heroicus*.[117]

Yet we are continually reminded that this knowledge is actually gained from the very cultural models that the device of epiphany seeks to render irrelevant.

---

[115] See Chapter 1, 33–6.

[116] This corporeal ambiguity is echoed in Protesilaos' physical engagement with the vine-dresser; although he allows himself to be kissed, and the mortal to 'cling to his neck' (11.2), he never eats or drinks in front of him; the vine-dresser leaves offerings and discreetly departs, and 'the things are eaten and drunk faster than the blink of an eye' (11.9). On the erotic element of the encounter, see Whitmarsh (2009: 219–25).

[117] Maclean and Aitken (2001: lxii). It is not clear how 'immediate engagement with the hero' differs from 'visions' here.

The Second Sophistic reader is thus caught in a self-consciously recursive pattern, whereby any attempt to re-engage with the past in a dynamic manner is thoroughly dependent upon the static monoliths – the *archaiologiai* – of earlier cultural achievement. In such a context the mutually reinforcing relationship between Protesilaos and his *agalma* serves a meta-textual function, giving form to the very tension between nostalgia and innovation that characterises Philostratus' literary enterprise. Yet, critically, this relationship works both ways: while the vine-dresser's description of Protesilaos moves from epiphany to ekphrasis, for example, his later account of Hector's statue at Ilion moves from ekphrasis to epiphany (19.3–7). The *agalma* 'reveals (ἐπιφαίνει) many delineations of his character to one inspecting it with the right perspective (ξὺν ὀρθῷ λόγῳ)', and is 'so alive (ἔμπνουν) that the viewer is drawn to touch it', features that draw upon conventional ekphrastic topoi such as those found in Hellenistic epigram, as well as the pedagogical principles of the *Imagines*.[118] Yet those who dismiss Hector's *agalma* as a mere representation come to a sticky end, notably a young visitor who, having disparaged the hero's achievements, is subsequently drowned by a sudden flood directed by 'an immense, heavily armed soldier'. In particular, Hector's wrath seems to be aroused by the youth's critique of his statue's iconography, which he claims 'must be Achilles on the basis of the hair, which Achilles had shorn for Patroclus'. Here, reliance on Homer's text (through the allusion to *Iliad* 23.141–2) is revealed as not only misguided, but also highly dangerous, and traditional practices of connoisseurship are explicitly rejected in favour of more pious modes of viewing. In this way the cognitive bond between epiphanies and cult images is reaffirmed, even as it is problematised.

The potential *aporia* of the *Heroicus* is written into the programmatic dream of the Phoenician, expressed by his fear that such visions are ἀργοί ('fruitless' or 'idle') to those in a hurry. Although his dream facilitates a meeting, at his precise moment of entry into the world of the heroes he awakes; the 'shudder' (φρίκης τι) he experiences is both a response to his brushing encounter with the supernatural and a reminder of the impossibility of such a meeting.[119] Through the extended process of enquiry,

---

[118] On the use of *empnous* in Hellenistic epigram, see Chapter 4, 198. On the *Imagines*, see above, n. 10.

[119] For examples of *phrikē*, 'shuddering' with religious awe, see Herodotus 6.134, S. *OT* 1306 and Euripides *Phoenissae* 1284. Philostratus uses it elsewhere to describe the Athenians' reaction to the birth of Athena at *Imagines* 2.27.1 (φρίττουσι δὲ τὴν Ἀθηνᾶν), while Aelius Aristides suggests in the *Sacred Tales* that to narrate his dream visions without extraneous detail would be 'more awe-inspiring [lit. 'shudder-making'] and vivid' (φρικωδέστερον καὶ ἐναργέστερον), 48.29 Keil: see Introduction, n. 51.

description and reported narrative that structures the dialogue of the *Hero-icus*, the Phoenician feels as if he has gained knowledge of θείους λόγους, 'divine tales' (58); the text ends with his statement, 'I am persuaded by you (πείθομαί σοι), vine-dresser, and so shall it be', as he vows to listen the next day to further *logoi*. Yet this statement of belief is preceded by recognition of the limits of such knowledge, when the Phoenician concedes that he cannot ask about 'how [Protesilaos] himself returned to life', since this is 'inviolable and secret' (ἀβεβήλῳ τε καὶ ἀπορρήτῳ). The text thus ends with an acceptance of mortality – the pivotal factor that separates the reader from the divine and daemonic spheres.[120] Only Apollonius, who is presented by Philostratus as the kind of 'daemonic man' of whom Dio-tima speaks in the *Symposium*, can engage with a hero such as Achilles on his own terms, employing his extraordinary *sophia* in order to call up the hero through a theurgic rite learned from the Indian Brahmans.[121] Whereas the vine-dresser is presented as a passive figure who says little on his own authority and is dependent upon the whims of Protesilaos for his epiphanic encounters, Apollonius persuades Achilles to appear by informing the hero, 'you would be much obliged to my eyes, if you used them to attest to your existence' (καὶ γὰρ ἂν ὄναιο ἄγαν τῶν ἐμῶν ὀφθαλμῶν, εἰ μάρτυσιν αὐτοῖς τοῦ εἶναι χρήσαιο 4.16). The philosopher thus offers himself as a witness (*martus)* to Achilles' very authority, presenting himself as a heroic equal, capable of challenging and bargaining with this most powerful of *daimones*.[122]

Despite its final withholding of knowledge, the *Heroicus* is nevertheless structured as a revelatory narrative, wherein reference to cultural models and the process of ekphrasis act as the moly that enables us, as read-ers, to enter the daemonic realm for ourselves. If only we can accept the authority of the text, then, like the Phoenician, we too can claim 'I believe you' – πείθομαί σοι. But can we? The encounters with heroic figures that take place in the *Heroicus* and the *Life of Apollonius* are described by internal narrators – by the vine-dresser to the sailor, and by Apollonius to

---

[120] For death and resurrection in literature of the imperial period, see Bowersock (1994: 99–119), J. Davies (1999) and Hershbell (2004).

[121] 4.16: 'Show us your form' (δεῖξον ἡμῖν τὸ σεαυτοῦ εἶδος). On Apollonius as a 'daemonic man', see Chapter 7. Compare Homer's epiphanic encounter with Odysseus at *Heroicus* 43.12–16, in which the poet gains divine knowledge, yet is emotionally blackmailed into reporting events to favour Odysseus rather than Palamedes.

[122] See Grossardt (2009), who points to the fascinating tradition – attested in the *Vita Romana* (6 Allen) and the scholion to Plato's *Phaedrus* 243a – that Homer's blindness was a result of an epiphanic encounter with Achilles at the hero's tomb. Apollonius' ability to act as Achilles' all-seeing witness is thus another example of his ability to surpass all previous models, as discussed in Chapter 7.

his men. They are presented as ekphraseis of visual experiences that may occur within locations charged with cultural and religious significance, but are nevertheless highly intertextual. In this way they confirm the influence of the literary canon while simultaneously challenging its authority.[123] Both Philostratean texts therefore raise questions about the relationship between vision and knowledge, and literature's potential both to mediate and generate such experiences. Like pilgrimage narratives and ekphraseis of sculptures or paintings, reports of epiphanic encounter reconstruct an experience for the reader, making vicarious or 'virtual' vision possible. Yet, like the tension between 'absorption and erudition' in ekphrastic texts, or the 'signalled absences' of Pausanias' *Periēgēsis*, they also vacillate between the conjuring of presence and aporetic reminders of distance.[124] On one hand, Protesilaos' statement that he can 'see through' (διορᾷ) the Homeric poems in order to present his own definitive version of events is an example of the same kind of creative reading that allowed Dio's Phidias to conceive his own vision of Zeus from the *Iliad*. In this way awe at the artistic genius of the past is combined with a supreme creative confidence. Dio and his successors do not simply celebrate their models, but continually reactivate them; the reader is not simply presented with an ekphrasis of the statue, for example, but is actually encouraged to think himself into the creative mind of Phidias. On the other hand, the fact that Homer's text is repeatedly rewritten means that the authority of *any* literary source is questioned, including the texts of Dio and Philostratus themselves.

How might the active revisionism so enthusiastically undertaken by these texts inform our understanding of the Second Sophistic? In that Philostratus and his contemporaries conduct a sustained engagement with the Greek past (whether linguistic, cultural, religious or political), their intellectual movement is certainly 'secondary'. As much recent scholarship has argued, however, this need not mean 'lesser'.[125] On the contrary, works such as the *Heroicus* demonstrate a desire not only to reopen and animate the founding texts of the past, but also to improve upon them. A reading of the *Heroicus* manages to cap a reading of the *Iliad* because it introduces the experience of epiphanic *phantasia*, drawing upon readers' own *paideia* in order to dramatise and illuminate their confrontation with the cultural models that

---

[123] This is most strikingly demonstrated in the rebranding given to the hero Palamedes, who in both texts is presented as the ultimate Greek hero, left out of Homer's narrative because of some careful bargaining with the bard engineered by the jealous ghost of Odysseus (*Heroicus* 21.1–8, 33.1–34.7; *VA* 3.22.2, 4.16.6).

[124] See Newby (2009), on ekphrasis, and Elsner (2001c: 18), on 'signalled absences', together with my discussion above.

[125] See, e.g., Whitmarsh (2001b: 41–89), on 'the crisis of posterity'.

underpin their Hellenic identity. In this way the *Heroicus* explores how artistic and literary material can be appropriated as building blocks from which one can construct an individual yet culturally informed mode of vision. Yet, crucially, the close association between vision and place in the dialogue (combined with the wealth of cultic detail it provides) holds out a third means of accessing the daemonic. The purple of Protesilaos' cloak, for example, may be 'like' the cloak of his *agalma*, yet it is also 'beyond speech' (ἄρρητον). How is the reader to experience such a colour for himself, if its lustre, as the vine-dresser claims, it is in fact 'divine' (θείου ἄνθους)? The only way is to follow in the Phoenician's footsteps and *go to see*, engaging with the 'sublime' relics of the living sacred past through the act of *theōria*, just as the vine-dresser claims Hadrian 'embraced and kissed' the bones of heroes at Troy (8.1), and Pausanias claims in the *Periēgēsis* to have consulted the oracle of Trophonius at Lebadeia, undergone initiation at Eleusis and learned the unspeakable name of the mysterious Despoina at Lykosoura.[126] As the vine-dresser charges the Phoenician at the beginning of the *Heroicus*, 'Why are you going so proudly and ignoring everything at your feet?' (βαδίζεις δὲ ποῖ μετέωρός τε καὶ ὑπὲρ πάντα τὰ ἐν ποσί; 1,2).[127] In this sense the limits of the *paideia* that the *Heroicus* can transmit are also the points at which the reader is encouraged not only to continue his voyage through Greek literary history, but also to embark upon a more literal journey and experience epiphanic autopsy.

In both the *Heroicus* and the *Periēgēsis*, piety and *paideia* converge, requiring readers to conduct their own imaginative journey through the sacred *sēmata* of Greece and the Troad. Each functions as a kind of 'hyperpilgrimage', in which ekphraseis of epiphanies and sacred monuments act as a form of verbal moly that activates a 'phantastic' mode of reading.[128] This link between epiphany and pilgrimage was not, however, a purely imaginative activity, for the desire to see also characterises what may be called the 'pagan universalism' of the second and third centuries CE in a more literal sense.[129] From Aelius Aristides' sojourn at the sanctuary of Asclepius at Pergamon to Hadrian's tours of Greece and Egypt and recreation of key religious

---

[126] See above, on the sublime qualities of the *Periēgēsis*, with J. I. Porter (2001). This association between the *Heroicus* and Porter's Pausanian sublime is also drawn by Whitmarsh (2009: 214). On Hadrian's travels, see below.

[127] Cf. Alcock (2004: 159).

[128] On the text as a 'hyperpilgrimage', see Rutherford (2001: 42). On the act of writing about pilgrimage as a surrogate form or repetition of the ritual, see Harbsmeier (1987: 337) and Elsner (1997a: 28). On *phantasia* in the *Heroicus*, see Zeitlin (2001: 255–62).

[129] On third-century 'universalism', see Fowden (1993: 37–60). On the flourishing of religion in the Second Sophistic, 'a vibrant paganism serving the community as a whole', see Swain (1996: 108–9; 1999: 168) and, more generally, MacMullen (1981) and Lane Fox (1986: 27–261).

sites in his villa complex at Tivoli, pilgrimage (which cannot be clearly separated from tourism) and the visual experience of *theōria* are repeatedly presented as an identifying feature of Hellenic cultural experience.[130] Like Dio's *Olympian Oration*, Pausanias' *Description of Greece*, Aelius Aristides' *Sacred Tales* and, as we shall see, Philostratus' *Life of Apollonius*, the *Heroicus* is firmly located within a specific set of locales, transporting its readers to both Thrace and the site of Troy with an *enargeia* that draws its vivid power from the sacred dimensions of the landscape itself. It is fundamental to the text that this *enargeia* is understood in both its primary and secondary meanings – as a visual experience in its own right (to be accessed through autopsy), and as an imaginative experience (generated by visual or verbal representation); in both senses, it is left to the reader to find his own way, interpreting his own experiences so that he, too, can aspire to the role of an *exēgētēs*. In this way the tension between unmediated encounter and human artifice (or cognitive reliability and cognitive dissonance) that we have observed in earlier explorations of the relationship between epiphany and representation is self-consciously reformulated, generating a mode of cultural practice in which visionary experience and religious, literary and artistic knowledge are inextricably intertwined. As the Phoenician acknowledges in the *Heroicus*, 'I am not surprised that I continue to marvel (θαυμάζειν), because what is divine is full of wisdom (σοφὸν γὰρ τὸ θεῖον, 9.4).'

[130] On Hadrian's travels, see Millar (1977: 28–40), Bowersock (1984), Halfmann (1986: 143–56), Clinton (1989), Holum (1990), Birley (1997: esp. 151–88), Rutherford (2001: 49–50) and my discussion in Chapter 7, 301. On the Villa Adriana at Tivoli – which included, among others, reconstructions of the Egyptian Canopus, the shrine of Aphrodite at Knidos and even, according to the *Historia Augusta* (*Hadrian* 26.5–6), an underworld – see MacDonald and Pinto (1995), Elsner (1998: 171–9), Packer (1998) and B. Bergmann (2001: 164–6), who comments that 'Hadrian's villa typifies the middle empire's recollective, eclectic nature. It was a place of "remembrance" reinforcing Rome's link to Greece' (165). On pilgrimage in Pausanias, see above, n. 21; on the problem of distinguishing pilgrimage from tourism, see Rutherford (2001).

The visionary dialogue of Philostratus' *Heroicus* is precipitated by a dream which, in prompting the Phoenician to leave his ship in search of an interpretation, leads him to the sanctuary of Protesilaos and thus the acquisition of epiphanic *paideia*. Encouraged by the vine-dresser to describe his dream's 'divine' content, the Phoenician explains that, while dreaming that he was reading Homer's *Catalogue of the Achaeans*, he suddenly found himself inviting the heroes to board his ship (6.3–6). As we saw in Chapter 5, this shift from literary to epiphanic encounter is typical of a Second Sophistic interest in the relationship between vision, knowledge and 'phantastic' modes of reading. But the episode also makes an important point about the relationship between dreams, epiphanies and textual narrative. In the *Heroicus* the Phoenician's shift from Homeric poem to heroic epiphany is made possible within a liminal realm of experience in which ontological distinctions are frequently collapsed: in the dream world it is possible to move between 'reading' and 'seeing' without being frustrated by the hierarchies of representation that inhibit such manoeuvres in waking reality. Dreams thus provide the ultimate playground for *phantasia*, wherein mental images acquired through conventional sense-perception can merge and interact with the wildest fancies of the imagination. Indeed, Aristotle asserts that dreams are produced by 'the imaginative part of the soul (τὸ φανταστικὸν τῆς ψυχῆς), while Plutarch explicitly likens *poiētikai phantasiai* to dreams in his *Amatorius*, because both forms of visionary experience 'impose themselves with such *enargeia*' (16).[1] As the Phoenician realises in the *Heroicus*, this *enargeia* can be simultaneously experienced in both its primary and secondary senses – as a direct form of encounter with the dream's inhabitants, and as a mode of viewing that is highly mediated by the cultural *sēmata* that structure his imaginative inner world.

The dream realm is one of images. From the figurative *oneiroi* that wend their way from Homer's gates of horn and ivory to the Isle of Dreams in

---

[1] Aristotle *On Dreams* 458b29 (cf. Plato *Timaeus* 45b–46a); Plutarch *Ethika* 759c: see Rist (2001) and Bartsch (2006: 70–1). On the dream as a *phantasia*, see also Hanson (1980: 1408, with Diodorus Siculus 1.65.5), Weber (2000: 32) and Holowchak (2002: 41–4); on the enargeic quality of the dream, see van Lieshout (1980: 18–19).

Lucian's *Verae Historiae,* oneiric experience is presented in ancient literature as predominantly visual.[2] Even the briefest glance at Artemidorus of Daldis' *Oneirocritica,* a second-century CE guide to dream interpretation, demonstrates that the narrative complexities of Freudian dream analysis and its relationship to the subconscious are out of place here: Greek interpretation rests instead upon the decoding of a series of *phantasiai* which function as signs relating to future events.[3] Rather than 'having' a dream, Greek authors write of 'seeing' a dream (*onar idein, enhypnion idein*).[4] As E. R. Dodds argues, 'the language used by the Greeks at all periods in describing dreams of all sorts appears to be suggested by a type of dream in which the dreamer is the passive recipient of an objective vision'.[5] This vision, often presented as a specific *figure* rather than a general *experience,* can take the form of the ghost of a dead friend or relative, a divine messenger, an authority figure such as a priest or king, or, in many cases, an actual deity.[6]

---

[2] *Od.* 19.562–7; Lucian *Verae historiae* 2.32–4. On the dream in Homer, see Messer (1918), Amory (1966), Kessels (1978) and Koch Piettre (1997), with subsequent imitations in classical literature listed by Hanson (1980: 1398–9 n. 25). For general accounts of ancient dream vision and its analysis, see Del Corno (1962, 1978), Meier (1966), Kessels (1969), Hanson (1980), van Lieshout (1980), Guidorizzi (1988a), Cox Miller (1994), Walde (1999, 2001, 2004), Weber (2000) and W. V. Harris (2009). Modern oneirology, influenced by psychoanalysis and critical theory, prefers to see dreams as episodic narratives: see Kilroe (2000a), though for a more visual focus, see Hartmann (1996).

[3] For a comparison of Freudian and Artemidoran approaches to dream analysis, see Oberhelman (1977), Price (1986), L. Martin (1991: 102–3) and Walde (1999), with a bibliographical review by Weber (2000: 531–6).

[4] Dodds (1951: 105). On Greek terminology for the perception of dreams, see Björck (1946), Kessels (1978: 156–7), Hanson (1980: 1407–8) and Oberhelman (1987: 48–9). On the parallel phenomenon of audio dreams (which also employ the terminology of dream *vision,* e.g., Plutarch *Agesilaus* 6.5, *Acts* 18.9), see Hanson (1980: 1411–12) and van Lieshout (1980: 20–4), who claims not to know of a single auditive dream-experience unaccompanied by visual images. As Oberhelman (1981, 1987) points out, much ancient dream interpretation rested upon the recognition of puns, that is, the exploitation of polysemy and homonymy, often dependent upon tensions between visible objects and their verbal definitions. For a modern interpretation of the ways in which dream puns represent abstract thought in concrete form, see Kilroe (2000b).

[5] Dodds (1951: 105). van Lieshout (1980: 12–13) terms this kind of dream the 'passive' or 'enstatic' type, as opposed to the 'active' or 'ecstatic' dream, in which the dreamer visits a person or place elsewhere, or the 'subjective' dream, in which meaning is conveyed in symbolic or allegorical terms.

[6] Examples are too numerous for a comprehensive list, but, for a friend or relative, see, e.g., Paus. 4.13.2–4, Plutarch *Gracchus* 1.6, Xenophon of Ephesus 2.8.2; for a priest, see Paus. 4.26.6, Aristid. *Or.* 47.15 (= *Hieroi Logoi* 1.15). Many dream visions of the dead take their inspiration from Achilles' vision of Patroclus in *Il.* 23.65–107. Dream visions of authority figures are found in Aelius Aristides' *Sacred Tales* and prose hymns, in which he recounts oneiric meetings with not only the emperor and the Parthian king, but also Socrates, Lysias and Sophocles (50.60), Demosthenes and Alexander the Great. For a list of the gods who appear in dreams (predominantly Asclepius, Isis and Serapis), see Newhall (1911: 92–113). On the dream as a form of 'figuration', see Cox Miller (1994: 14–38).

The dream realm, unbound by the ontological or practical constraints of the waking world, thus acts as a primary medium through which mortals can view and communicate with the gods themselves.[7] Indeed, literary references to epiphany often pair 'dreams and waking visions' (*onar* and *hypar*) as distinct but commensurate categories of encounter. In his critique of excessive personal piety in Plato's *Laws*, the Athenian describes how impressionable members of society (notably women and the sick) make dedications, vow sacrifices, and found altars and shrines in response to 'fears caused by waking visions or dreams' (ἔν τε φάσμασιν ἐγρηγορότας διὰ φόβους καὶ ἐν ὀνείροις, 910a), juxtaposing *phasmata* with *oneiroi*; likewise, in describing the sphere of the daemonic in the *Symposium*, Diotima explains that *daimones* have contact with humans 'in the waking state or during sleep' (καὶ ἐγρηγορόσι καὶ καθεύδουσι, 203a).[8]

Plato's use of *oneiros* in the *Laws* anticipates Artemidorus' later use of the same term in the *Oneirocritica*, where he contrasts the *oneiros*, which 'calls to the dreamer's attention a prediction of future events', with the *enhypnion*, which is prompted by the internal content of the dreamer's mind and simply acts as 'a reminder of a present state' (1.1).[9] These distinctions do not always hold, yet they do point to a culturally constructed hierarchy of oneiric experience in which the mantic dream functions in very similar ways to the epiphany.[10] While dream visions can be invoked by means of ritual

---

[7] On epiphanic dreams, see Koch Piettre (1996: 323–42) and most recently W. V. Harris (2009: 23–90, with bibliography).

[8] On dreams in Plato, see Gallop (1971), van Lieshout (1980: 105–64) and Rotondaro (1998). On the difficulty of distinguishing between dreams and waking visions (often both referred to simply as *opseis*), see Hanson (1980: 1408–9).

[9] At 1.1, Artemidorus gives an etymological explanation for the significance of the *oneiros*, suggesting that it either 'arouses the soul' (ὀρείνειν τὴν ψυχήν) or 'speaks the truth' (τὸ ὂν εἴρειν). See Hanson (1980: 1399, 1407–8) and, on oneiric terminology more generally, Kessels (1969), Oberhelman (1977), Casevitz (1982), Guidorizzi (1988b), Vinagre (1996) and Weber (2000: 31–4). On Oneiros himself as *le dieu-songe*, see Koch Piettre (1997). On the distinction between *oneiros* and *enhypnion* in Artemidorus, see also Price (1986: 371–2), Winkler (1990b: 24–5), Bowersock (1994: 80) and Cox Miller (1994: 80–4). Aristotle, of course, was circumspect about the idea that dreams had any mantic significance at all, preferring to see correspondence with future events as mere coincidence (*De divinatione per somnia* 463b1–464b6); dreams are not god-sent but 'daemonic' (δαιμόνια), 'for nature is daemonic, but not divine' (463b13–15): see Chroust (1974), Hanson (1980: 1399–400), Gallop (1990) and Holowchak (1996: 418–22; 2002: 49–50).

[10] Kessels (1969) warns against the assumption that Plato had any systematic form of dream classification, while van Straten (1976: 12) points out that there is a significant diachronic shift in the epigraphic terminology of dream visions, which are more often referred to as *enhypnia* prior to the first century CE, and *oneiroi* thereafter. On the equivalence of dream vision and epiphany, cf. Weber (2000), on dreams and visions ascribed to Roman emperors. On contradictions even within synchronic Greek attitudes to the dream, see Brelich (1966: 293–4).

acts (most importantly the practice of incubation), their authority lies in the acknowledgement that oneiric agency rests with the gods themselves; like predictive dreams, the epiphanic dream is *theopemptos*, 'god-sent'.[11] Indeed, epiphanies and dream visions function in such similar ways that the two categories are frequently blurred.[12] On the Lindos temple stele, for example, Athena's nocturnal visits to her priest are simply categorised as *epiphaneiai*, while many inscriptions from healing sanctuaries employ the general term *opsis* ('vision') to refer to epiphanies that must have been experienced during incubation, in addition to more explicit formulae such as *kat' oneiron* or *kat' onar* ('according to a dream').[13]

The dream vision proves to be a particularly slippery medium in which to communicate with the divine, however. As we saw in Chapter 5, Maximus of Tyre claims that both dreams and waking visions provide access to the daemonic realm, yet he feels the need to qualify his statements of epiphanic autopsy with the claim that he saw Asclepius, 'but not in a dream' (ἀλλ' οὐχὶ ὄναρ), and beheld Heracles 'in waking reality' (ἀλλ' ὕπαρ, 9.7).[14] The subjectivity of oneiric experience and the inevitable lack of witnesses mean that the dream's cognitive reliability is particularly open to challenge.[15] Accordingly, dream visions are often supported by external 'proof' mechanisms, such as daylight epiphanies that corroborate the dreamer's experience; identical dreams experienced by another individual; the leaving of symbolic tokens by the visitor ('apport' dreams); or, like Athena at Lindos, repeated visitations by which the deity stresses that this is an externally generated *oneiros* rather than an internal *enhypnion*, and must be taken seriously.[16]

---

[11] Artemidorus 1.6, 4.3: *oneiroi* are god-sent 'in the same way that we customarily call all unforeseen things god-sent'. On the *theopemptos oneiros*, see Oberhelman (1977: 685–6; 1981: 418–19; 1987: 50) and L. Martin (1991: 100). The term is also used by the fourth-century BCE physician Herophilus, quoted in Aëtius *Maxims* 5.2.3.

[12] See Kessels (1978: 194–7).

[13] *Syll.*[3] 725, D1: see Chapter 3, 168. On epigraphic records of dream visions, see van Straten (1976), Veyne (1987), Renberg (2003), who advises against reading all *kat' onar* or *ex iussu* inscriptions as explicitly epiphanic, and Petridou (2006: 11), who claims that the terms most commonly employed for dream visions are *opsis*, *oneiros* and *epistasis*, as used on the Lindos stele, D 14, 68, 98. For *kat' onar* dedications from the Asclepieion at Pergamon, see Habicht (1969): nos. 75, 65, 77, 91, 116 (κατ' ὄνειρον); 117, 127 (κατ' ὄναρ); and 132 (κατὰ ἐνυπνίου ὄψιν), a votive altar on which ὄψιν, 'vision', is centrally positioned in strikingly prominent letters. On those from Epidaurus, see Chapter 3, 147–8.

[14] Cf. Weber (2000: 33–4).

[15] See W. V. Harris (2003) on scepticism about the predictive value of dreams, which were 'a by-word for the insubstantial and deceptive' throughout antiquity (21).

[16] For a dream vision corroborated by a waking epiphany, see *POxy.* 11.1381.91–145, discussed below; for double dreams, see, e.g., Dionysius of Halicarnassus 1.57.304, with Wikenhauser (1948) and Hanson (1980: 1415–16); on 'apport' dreams (e.g., Pi. *O.* 13.61–80, Paus. 10.38.13,

The dream's liminal status, combined with the elusive quality of oneiric images, places it in a similar category to the *phasma* or *eidōlon* (while in the *Odyssey*, the *dēmos oneirōn*, or 'Village of Dreams', is situated just outside the realm of the dead).[17] As a fugitive phenomenon that is only tangentially related to the dreamer's waking life, the *oneiros* can be a vehicle for both truth and deception. This innate ambiguity is reified in Homer's gates of horn and ivory: while dreams issuing from the former 'have power in reality, whenever any mortal sees them' (οἵ ῥ' ἔτυμα κραίνουσι, βροτῶν ὅτε κέν τις ἴδηται), those sent through the latter 'are dangerous to believe, for they bring messages which will not issue in deeds' (οἵ ῥ' ἐλεφαίρονται, ἔπε' ἀκράαντα φέροντες, *Od.* 19.563–7).[18] One line of interpretation (recorded by the Homeric scholiast Eustathius) relates Homer's ivory gates to the teeth, and thus the unreliability of speech, while horn, he claims, symbolises the hard covering of the eye, and thus the more dependable faculty of vision (for what is seen is more reliable than what is reported).[19] Eustathius also suggests an etymological connection whereby horn (κέρας) echoes the verb 'accomplish', or 'bring to pass' (κραίνω), while ivory (ἐλέφας) resembles 'deceive' (ἐλεφαίρομαι). As with the false relationship drawn between *theōria* and *theos* in antiquity, such etymologies often reveal more about patterns of cultural association than about linguistic origins.[20] It is telling that Eustathius constructs a web of meaning around the concepts of dreaming, sight and duplicity that echoes the language of deceptive naturalism associated with ivory images: like Pygmalion's ivory statue, dream visions, too, have the potential to beguile and mislead.[21]

If the dream's truth value is problematised in texts from the earliest archaic poetry to the medieval scholia, then what is the status of the oneiric epiphany for Greek viewer-worshippers? How are deities to be recognised during sleep when, as Homer makes clear, they often employ strategies of obfuscation and disguise? Do dreams really facilitate direct encounter with the deities who appear within them, or do they introduce a mediating element in the form of an *eidōlon* or *mimēma* of the divine? Indeed, we shall

IG 10.2.1, no. 255), see Dodds (1951: 102–6) and van Lieshout (1980: 21–3); on the Lindos visitation, D 60–79, see Chapter 3, 167–9, and for further examples of repeated dream visions, Hanson (1980: 1411 n. 69).

[17] *Od.* 24.10–14. See Rotondaro (1998: 274–89), with Brillante (1988: 22–3). As Petridou (2006: 57–8), points out, *phasma* is often used to refer to dream visions themselves (e.g., E. *IT* 42 and 1263 and Plutarch *Caesar* 69.9). On the status of the *eidōlon* as a form of double, see Vernant (1991: 166–8, 186–92).

[18] See Amory (1966), Kessels (1978: 100–10), Cox Miller (1994: 14–17) and Koch Piettre (1997).

[19] Eustathius, *Commentaria ad Iliadem et Odysseam* 1877.26–39, translation from Amory (1966: 4–6). Eustathius also suggests that horn is transparent, whereas ivory is opaque.

[20] See Introduction, 11.   [21] See Introduction, 2.

see that the dream's slipperiness – the fact that it is *amēchanos*, 'difficult to handle' (*Od.* 19.560) – is fundamentally related to its visual character, and thus its kinship with the problems raised by representation. As Aristotle comments in his treatise *On Prophecy during Sleep*, dreams function as 'likenesses' (τὰς ὁμοιότητας), mental pictures 'like reflections in water' (τοῖς ἐν τοῖς ὕδασιν εἰδώλοις) in which the relationship between image and prototype continually shifts and distorts.[22] His argument stems from a naturalistic theory of dreaming that denies or downplays any potential theological significance, yet it illustrates the very aspect of dream visions that allows them to attain epiphanic status. For insofar as they are like reflections or *eidōla*, dreams function as dematerialised images; like Pausanias' mirror at Lykosoura, they generate fleeting visual experiences that may echo representations of deities familiar from the dreamer's waking life, yet retain an elusive quality that seems closer to the immaterial forms of the gods themselves.[23]

This chapter examines how the cognitive and hermeneutic dilemmas raised by epiphanic dream vision are parallel to those raised by the sacred image, as addressed in a series of Second Sophistic texts concerned with access to the divine. Dreams play an important role in the mutually reinforcing relationship that exists between epiphanies and artistic representations. Gods frequently appear in the form of their cult images in dream narrative, not only because traditional iconography informed divine appearances within the cultural imagination, but also because, as a realm of images liberated from material constraints, the dream world facilitated the coalescence of deity and image that was always implicit in the form of cult statues themselves, allowing the *lebende Statue* to be fully animate.[24] To the religious outsider the influence of artistic convention over subjective experiences of the divine in dreams might seem glaringly obvious: gods appear as their images because images are themselves responsible for 'constructing' gods in the cultural (and thus oneiric) imagination.[25] We might recall Bell's theory

---

[22] *De divinatione per somnia* 54.464b5: see Meier (1966: 306) and, on Aristotle's 'psychobiological' interpretation of dreams, Gallop (1990), Cox Miller (1994: 42–4) and Holowchak (2002: 39–52).

[23] Paus. 8.37.7: see Chapter 5, 222–3.   [24] Schefold (1937: 33): see Chapter 2, 88.

[25] On the coalescence of god and cult statue in the context of the dream, see MacMullen (1981: 61), Brillante (1988), Lane Fox (1986: 153–63), Barasch (1992: 31–33) and Cox Miller (1994: 28–35). Surprisingly, Freedberg (1989) only refers to the relationship between images and dreams in passing, commenting that 'Visions and dreams involving images which move, speak, suffer, or act beneficently provide strong illustrations – all the better because they are unconscious – of the ways in which people think of the potentiality of images, and therefore of the ways in which they respond to them' (304).

of 'misrecognition' (discussed in Chapter 1), according to which religious practice 'does not see the production process that constitutes the "object"', and Dodds's claim that dreams follow culture patterns.[26] Yet in texts written by those invested in a living Greek religion, such as Pausanias' *Periēgēsis*, we shall see that this pattern of influence is also reversed, for dream visions repeatedly inspire the artistic creation of statues and paintings themselves, acting as a form of epiphanic *aition*. As Gell commented on the sacred image, the object's sanctity lies in the attribution of divine agency – the belief that 'the causal arrow is orientated in the other way'.[27] Artistic representations may provide a guide to identifying divine *oneiroi* (the god is the god because he looks like his statue), but dream visions themselves are presented as a primary source of cognitive reliability for traditional religious practice. In this way a firm relationship is established between oneiric modes of epiphanic encounter and the material, waking world of the dreamer-worshipper, mapping the divine realm onto both the physical landscape and the subjective imagination.

The equivalence between god and image in dreams was so prevalent in Greek culture that Artemidorus famously claimed that 'Statues of the gods have the same meaning as the gods themselves' for the interpreter (κοινὸν δὲ λόγον ἔχουσιν οἱ θεοὶ καὶ τὰ ἀγάλματα αὐτῶν, 2.39).[28] Just as the dream world's location outside real time and space allows Philostratus' Phoenician to move from 'reading' to 'seeing' and thus enter the text, so it collapses the ontological distinction between image and prototype, ascribing deity and statue the same semiotic value.[29] Yet while Artemidorus' statement has often been cited as an example of the epiphanic qualities of the cult image, we shall see that this relationship was not always so straightforward, even within the *Oneirocritica*.[30] Rather, the fluidity of dreams, combined with the inherent ambiguities of epiphanic narrative, generated a hall of mirrors wherein the status of the image was continually questioned and re-evaluated. In the visually sophisticated milieu of the Second Sophistic, this combined with a very real belief in the epiphanic or mantic significance of the *oneiros*

[26] Bell (1992: 87); Dodds (1965: 112): '[Dream experiences] reflect a pattern of belief which is accepted not only by the dreamer but usually by everyone in his environment; their form is determined by the belief, and in turn confirms it; hence they become increasingly stylized'. Dodds quotes (1951: 112) the anthropologist E. B. Tylor's comment that 'it is a vicious circle: what the dreamer believes he therefore sees, and what he sees he therefore believes' (1871: vol. II, 49).
[27] Gell (1998: 25); see Chapter 1, 76.
[28] All translations of Artemidorus are from R. J. White (1990), with minor modifications.
[29] Cf. Brelich (1966: 300).
[30] E.g., Brillante (1988: 18), Barasch (1992: 32–3), Elsner (2007: 30) and Squire (2009: 115–16).

to generate a self-conscious combination of hermeneutic gymnastics and committed piety that reflected the broader religious and literary concerns of the culture at large.

Dream, statue and body in Aelius Aristides' *Sacred Tales*

Our most eloquent first-person account of dream epiphany in antiquity is a collection of *Hieroi Logoi* (or 'Sacred Tales') composed by the second-century orator and invalid Aelius Aristides, which relate his experiences of incubation and medical treatment at a series of healing sanctuaries in north-west Asia Minor, particularly the Asclepieion at Pergamon.[31] As a narrative of epiphanic autopsy composed by a highly educated member of the Hellenised elite, the *Hieroi Logoi* have much in common with Second Sophistic texts such as the *Heroicus* and Pausanias' *Periēgēsis*, particularly a deep commitment to traditional Greek cult, combined with self-conscious demonstrations of the author's *paideia*.[32] In Aristides' case, however, the relationship he draws between piety, *paideia* and epiphany is not demonstrated through antiquarian description or fictional dialogue, but takes the form of a serious statement of personal religious experience in which narrative subjectivity is fundamentally related to his bodily suffering.[33] Dreams, for Aristides, are not just a means of collapsing ontological categories in

---

[31] *Orations* 47–52: numbers correspond to the position of the *Hieroi Logoi* in Keil's edition of Aelius Aristides. See Behr (1968, 1981) and Festugière and Saffrey (1986). On the *Hieroi Logoi* in their Second Sophistic context, see Bompaire (1993: 199–202), S. Harrison (2000–1), Petsalis-Diomidis (2001, 2006b, 2010), Dorandi (2005), Korenjak (2005), Downie (2008a, 2008b, 2009) and Holmes (2008). On the notion of *hieroi logoi*, see Henrichs (2003). On incubation, see Chapter 1, 44–8. For attempts to psychoanalyse Aristides' conception of himself and relationship to his body and society, see, e.g., Dodds (1965: 39–45), on Aristides' mental fragility and need for a strong father-figure; Brown (1978: 41–5), on Aristides' illness as a means of displacing an overweening sense of superiority; and Cox Miller (1994: 184–204), on a 'crisis of the subject' caused by a conflict between Aristides' inner self and the expectations imposed by public models of masculine achievement.

[32] The professional, as opposed to apologetic, autobiographical or psychological, aspects of the *Hieroi Logoi* are addressed in their Second Sophistic context by Horstmanshoff (2004) and Downie (2008a), who argues that Aristides has 'a discernible rhetorical project, by which he seeks to reinforce his position of preeminence in professional oratory and to enhance his status as a public figure' (7). On the relationship between Aristides' religious, rhetorical and political lives, see Boulanger (1923), Quet (1993), Moreschini (1994), Cortés Copete (1995, 1999), Swain (1996: 254–97), Flinterman (2002) and the essays gathered in Harris and Holmes (2008).

[33] On Aristides' relationship to his body, see Cox Miller (1994: 185–8), Perkins (1995: 173–92) and Holmes (2008). On 'personal' dream reports (a problematic notion discussed below), see Nock (1933: 138–55), Festugière (1955: 85–104), W. V. Harris (2005) and, on Aristides, Nicosia (1988), Quet (1993), S. Harrison (2000–1) and Petsalis-Diomidis (2006b).

order to generate a literary effect (like the Homeric dream of Philostratus' Phoenician), but a means of accessing the sacred knowledge that just might restore his bodily health.[34] One of the most striking aspects of the various dream narratives woven through the text is Aristides' highly developed sense of location, whether within the sanctuary of Asclepius at Pergamon (where he spent his *kathedra*, or 'sitting period' of 145–7 CE), or at the other temples, altars, *agorai*, gymnasia, baths and even tombs that he visits in his dreams, both in Pergamon and further afield in Smyrna, Athens and his ancestral estate in Mysia.[35] These structures form the backdrop to Aristides' dream-scape, demonstrating how his oneiric experiences are located within the architectural and topographical spaces of his waking world. Through their relationship to the public life of the Roman Mediterranean, such locations also emblematise the religious, political and intellectual ideologies that inform Aristides' rhetorical enterprise.[36] It is in the midst of this monu-mentalising culture that his visual apprehensions of divinity are located, for while his oneiric epiphanies of Asclepius (and a panoply of other deities) are directly influenced by the environs of the sanctuary at Pergamon, they also reflect the broader sacred topography through which he constructs his identity as both orator and pilgrim.[37]

Amid the shifting landscape that shapes Aristides' visions, statues of the gods, particularly Asclepius, repeatedly appear either as a focus of worship, the identifying feature of a specific sanctuary within which Aristides meets a divinity, or, most dramatically, as animated forms of the deities they represent. During incubation he converses with 'the god' (Asclepius), who

---

[34] On the diagnostic value of dreams within Greek medicine, see Hanson (1980: 1397), Oberhelman (1981, 1987, 1993), Holowchak (2001; 2002: 125–64) and Walde (2001: 106–26). On dreams in the *Hieroi Logoi*, see Michenaud and Dierkins (1972), Nicosia (1988), Pearcy (1988), Cox Miller (1994: 184–204), Walde (2001: 52–105), Downie (2008b) and Holmes (2008).

[35] On Aristides' relationship to the Pergamene Asclepieion, see Remus (1996) and C. P. Jones (1998); on his patterns of pilgrimage, see Rutherford (1999); and on his attempts to situate himself within a landscape, see Petsalis-Diomidis (2008). While the term *kathedra* implies a period of 'inactivity' or even 'retreat', Cox Miller (1994: 189) points out that 'it also denotes the chair of a teacher, the seat from which one professes. The choice of name suggests that Aristides found his profession – his professing voice – not in spite of the illness that had brought him to Asclepius, but *in* it'.

[36] On the Second Sophistic orator's relationship to public space, see Gleason (1995) and Platt (2007b).

[37] See Petsalis-Diomidis (2005) on the physical space of the Pergamene Asclepieion, and the ways in which it 'provided the physical and conceptual frameworks in which pilgrims experienced the process of sickness and healing' (185). On Aristides' dedications within the sanctuary itself (and his literary representation of them), see Downie (2009); on statues in the *Sacred Tales*, see also L. Martin (1987: 68–70).

appears 'in the posture in which he is represented in his statues' (ἔχων ἤδη τὸ ἑαυτοῦ σχῆμα ἐν ᾧπερ ἔστηκεν, 50.50), and even receives surgical treatment from Serapis (who was often identified with Asclepius in healing cult) 'in the form of his seated statues' (ὥσπερ κάθηται τῷ σχήματι, 49.47).[38] Aristides relates (48.41–3) how, when on the brink of death during the Antonine plague of 165 CE, 'Athena appeared with her aegis and the beauty and the magnitude and the whole form of the Athena of Phidias in Athens' (ἡ Ἀθηνᾶ φαίνεται τήν τε αἰγίδα ἔχουσα καὶ τὸ κάλλος καὶ τὸ μέγεθος καὶ σύμπαν δὴ σχῆμα οἷα περ ἡ Ἀθήνησιν ἡ Φειδίου), her aegis emanating a scent of wax and also 'wondrous in beauty and magnitude' (θαυμαστὴ καὶ αὕτη τὸ κάλλος καὶ τὸ μέγεθος).[39] Here, Aristides explicitly draws upon the formulae of Homeric epiphany, the *kallos kai megethos* so familiar from the *Homeric Hymns*.[40] A sophist to the end, he recalls his experience as if it were an animated parallel to the pairing of Homer and Phidias in Dio's *Olympian Oration*: Athena appears as the Phidian Parthenos (complete with attributes), and when she speaks to him it is, he claims, 'to remind me of *The Odyssey* . . . I myself was indeed both Odysseus and Telemachus, and she must help me'.[41] Attempting to interpret the vision's import according to the cultural associations of the Phidian statue, Aristides realises that his clue lies in its location, and that the appropriate cure for his fever is 'an enema of Attic honey'. Just as the nightingales in Philostratus' sanctuary of Protesilaos sing in Attic Greek, even Aristides' digestive remedies must testify to his Athenocentric notion of sophistic *paideia*![42]

Indeed, the unapologetic connection Aristides draws between the Athena Parthenos and the emphatically physical processes of his body is one of the most fascinating aspects of what we might call his 'agalmatophany'. While the dream's epiphanic quality collapses the distinction between image

---

[38] All translations of Aelius Aristides are from Behr (1981), with some modifications. On the relationship between Asclepius and Serapis in Aristides' works (including 45, his *Hymn to Serapis*, which advances a form of monotheism), see Pearcy (1988: 378). On the syncretism of the two healing deities more generally, see Stambaugh (1972: 75–8) and Meier (2003: 43–8). Aristides explains (49.46) that 'Serapis appeared on the same night, both he himself and Asclepius. They were both marvellous in their beauty and magnitude, and in some way like one another (καί τινα τρόπον ἀλλήλοις ἐμφερεῖς)'.

[39] On this passage, and the theatrical metaphor of the preceding dream, in which Aristides 'seemed even to be at the conclusion of the play and to put aside my buskins' (48.40), see Holmes (2008: 87–9). On Aristides' inspiration by Athena (as discussed in 28, 'Concerning a Remark in Passing'), see Quet (2001).

[40] See Chapter 1, 63–4.

[41] Cf. the opening to the first *hieros logos* (47.1), in which Aristides claims, 'It seems to me that I shall speak like Homer's Helen'. On Aristides' adoption of an Odyssean persona in the *Sacred Tales*, see Kindstrand (1973: 73–97), Schröder (1987) and Holmes (2008).

[42] *Heroicus* 5.4: see Chapter 5, 243.

and divine prototype, giving voice to Athena herself, Aristides' familiarity with the image *as statue* encourages him to think topographically, and so leads him to his 'cure'. Just as epiphanies exist in a mutually reinforcing relationship with material images and commemorative *mnēmata*, so the ultimate significance of Aristides' dream vision lies in its tangible impact upon his corporeal self. Yet the difficulty of bridging the gap between the waking realm of the physical body and the visionary realm inhabited by the god is one of the most salient features of Aristides' attempts to express his epiphanic experiences in language. In an oft-quoted episode in the second *Sacred Tale*, he describes an encounter with Asclepius as if he were caught between these very states:

> For there was a seeming as it were to touch him and to perceive that he himself had come, and to be between sleep and waking, and to wish to look up and to be in anguish that he might depart too soon, and to strain the ears and to hear some things as in a dream, some as in a waking state.[43]

This struggle to meet the god with all the senses, to translate a dematerialised form of oneiric *theōria* into conscious embodied experience (and thence into language), is arguably a driving force within the text. It is telling, in this regard, that when Aristides is oneirically operated upon by Serapis – when his body experiences the direct touch of a divine figure, who 'made an incision around my face, going somehow under the gum itself in the root of the lips' – the god takes the form of his statue.[44] The implicit materiality of the image-as-god makes contact between the mortal and immortal body plausible and comprehensible within the logic of the dream. The mutual dependency of transcendent deity and material image thus resonates in the *Sacred Tales* with the continually reiterated bond between dream vision and suffering body. As Brooke Holmes has observed, the interior of the body, with its unpredictable pathologies, is mysterious, uncharted territory to Aristides, parallel to divine mysteries in that it is unseen by all but the god.[45]

---

[43] 48.32: καὶ γὰρ οἷον ἅπτεσθαι δοκεῖν ἦν καὶ διαισθάνεσθαι ὅτι αὐτὸς ἥκοι, καὶ μέσως ἔχειν ὕπνου καὶ ἐγρηγόρσεως καὶ βούλεσθαι ἐκβλέπειν καὶ ἀγωνιᾶν μὴ προαπαλλαγείη, καὶ ὦτα παραβεβληκέναι καὶ ἀκούειν, τὰ μὲν ὡς ὄναρ, τὰ δὲ ὡς ὕπαρ. On this passage, see Petsalis-Diomidis (2006b: 200–1) and Downie (2008a: 30–1, 157–8), who concentrate on Aristides' use of the language of initiation, for he goes on to say, 'What man could describe these things in words? If any man has been initiated (εἰ δέ τις τῶν τετελεσμένων ἐστίν), he knows and understands'.

[44] 50.50. For a parallel example of a dream vision involving direct treatment at the god's hands, see the Archinos relief from the Amphiareion at Oropos discussed in Chapter 1, 44–7.

[45] Holmes (2008): 'Grasping the hidden experiences or condition of the body requires opening up channels of knowledge as mysterious as the passages through which the disease first entered' (94). Note 47.8, in which Aristides has a dream vision (ὄψις δὲ ὀνείρατος) of his own innards.

The unintelligibility of Aristides' body and its resistance to conventional medical interpretation is what drives him to Asclepius, for dream visions give access to a divine knowledge that also penetrates the unknown parts (or *agnostoi morphai*) of the human form itself.[46]

It is in the light of this equivalence between dream epiphany and oneiric access to the internal mysteries of the embodied self that we might read one of the more striking (and difficult) passages of the *Hieroi Logoi*, in which, during a dream-time visit to the sanctuary of Asclepius at Smyrna, Aristides encounters a statue of himself in a space which, in a characteristic example of oneiric condensation, he experiences as both the temple and its vestibule, or *pronaos*:[47]

περιεσκόπουν δὲ ὡς ἐν τῷ προνάῳ δὴ τούτῳ ἀνδριάντα ἐμαυτοῦ. καὶ τότε μέν γε ὡς ἐμαυτοῦ ὄντα ἑώρων, πάλιν δὲ ἐδόκει μοι εἶναι αὐτοῦ τοῦ Ἀσκληπιοῦ μέγας τις καὶ καλός.

I examined, as it were, in this vestibule, a statue of me. At one time I saw it as if it were of me, and again it seemed to be a great and fair statue of Asclepius (47.17).

Significantly, the image Aristides encounters here is not an *agalma* of the god, but an *andrias*, a sculptural term that, derived from *anēr* ('man'), is applied to portraits rather than divine figures.[48] The merging of Aristides' own image – displayed in the temple *pronaos* as if an honorific portrait or votive offering – with the image of the god is facilitated by Asclepius' anthropomorphic iconography and the typical *Mischbildung* (identified by Freud) by which people and places can appear in dreams with more than one identity.[49] This slippage between vestibule and temple, Aristides and Asclepius, facilitates a longed-for union between worshipper and deity that enhances Aristides' sense of corporeal and intellectual well-being through a transformative process that simultaneously subsumes the dreamer into the realm of the god and confers a special status and identity.[50] Indeed, in the fourth *Sacred Tale* Aristides claims to have been hailed in a dream as 'Theodorus', a title he readily accepts, 'since everything of mine was a gift of

[46] *Anth. Plan.* 216.4 = GP 1968: Parmenion 14.4, on the 'unknown forms' of Polyclitus' chryselephantine statue of the Argive Hera, discussed in Chapter 2, 77–81.

[47] On the condensation of multiple entities into 'collective figures' in dreams through the device of the *Mischbildung*, see Freud (1953: 292–3), with Didi-Huberman (2005: 144–56), on Freud's analysis of dream figuration and its relationship to the visual arts.

[48] See Chapter 2, n. 80.   [49] See above, n. 47.

[50] Cf. 50.50, with Quet (1993: 243), Cox Miller (1994: 34–5) and Downie (2008a: 174–8).

the god' (ὡς ἄρα πᾶν τοὐμὸν εἴη τοῦ θεοῦ δωρεά, 50.53).[51] It is telling that, in the second part of his dream (at 47.17), he views the same hybrid statue 'as if it were in the long portico of the Gymnasium', precisely the location in which honorific portraits of philosophers and orators would have been encountered.[52] In this way the blessings conferred by union with the god within sacred space are extended to the paideutic spaces in which Aristides seeks public recognition, uniting his identities as pilgrim and sophist. Again, it is the statue's paradoxically fluid physicality that provides an intermediate state between human and god in which union with the divine can occur, while the topographical associations it carries allow Aristides to reconcile his experiences during incubation with the social and intellectual demands of his waking world.

The repeated convergence of deity and image in the *Sacred Tales* thus serves several functions. First, Aristides' ability as a *pepaidoumenos* to recognise and interpret each deity's iconography leads him to *anagnōrisis*, confirming the cognitive reliability and interpretative value of his visions. Second, the correspondence between immaterial divine bodies and their material images acts in parallel with that between Aristides' dematerialised dream visions and the corporeal challenges presented by his ailing body, thereby authenticating the practical therapeutic benefits of incubation and the 'exertions of the Saviour' (τὰ τοῦ Σωτῆρος ἀγωνίσματα, 47.1) on his behalf. For Aristides, the deities whose help he seeks are not simply incorporeal products of the imagination existing above and beyond the world of lived experience, but real entities operating within and around the public and sacred landscapes that the dreamer-worshipper inhabits. Their visible presence *within* this world in the recognisable forms of iconographic tradition is proof of the efficacy of the rituals and sacred institutions upon which Aristides' health – and therefore his life – depends. Finally, each deity's manifestation in image form facilitates the verbal transmission of Aristides' epiphanic experience to the reader, so that the unmediated *enargeia* of his vision can be transformed into the literary *enargeia* of the *Sacred Tales* by means of a familiar ekphrastic shorthand. In order to visualise Aristides' oneiric encounter for ourselves, we need only draw upon a familiar repertoire of sacred schemata. In this way the fleeting, intangible nature of the

---

[51] See also 50.70, with Cagnat *et al.* (1911: 369–70, no. 1070), Puech (2002: 140–5, no. 44) and Petsalis-Diomidis (2006b: 208 n. 47), on an inscription (possibly from Smyrna) honouring Aristides as Publius Aelius Aristides Theodoros.

[52] See Delorme (1960) and Newby (2005: 229–71), who notes that gymnasia such as that at Ephesus also displayed statues of Asclepius (243).

narrator's dream world is not only anchored to the *Realien* of the sacred spaces in which he persists in his quest for health, but also preserved in the verbal testimony of the text itself.

Landscape and dreamscape in Pausanias' *Description of Greece*

While the coalescence of god and statue in Aristides' dreams draws upon public representations in order to authenticate and reify his private experiences, we can trace an inverse relationship in Pausanias' *Description of Greece*, which repeatedly draws upon the epiphanic quality of personal dream-visions in order to confirm the sanctity of objects and locations within the public realm. In particular, Pausanias accounts for the creation and appearance of cult images through tales of oneiric inspiration, whereby artists claim legitimacy for their depictions of deities through narratives of epiphanic autopsy.[53] In this sense his use of the mutually reinforcing relationship between dream vision and sacred object reflects the aetiological function of mantic dreams throughout the text (and, indeed, in Greek culture more generally), where they are repeatedly employed to explain the location and foundation of sanctuaries and cities.[54] Oneiric epiphanies thus play an intrinsic role in the network of reported tales, *aitia* and assertions of divine presence that suggest continuity between the most ancient origins of Greece and the Second Sophistic present, bringing the sacred landscape alive for Pausanias' readers.

As we saw in Chapter 5, Pausanias claims that the marble employed by Damophon for the statues of Demeter and Despoina at Lykosoura was discovered buried within the goddess's sanctuary κατὰ ὄψιν ὀνείρατος, 'according to a vision seen in a dream'.[55] Similarly, a *xoanon* of Artemis is stolen from Sparta by Preugenes of Patrae κατὰ ὄψιν ὀνείρατος, an event which then forms an *aition* for a local festival of Artemis.[56] The phrase

---

[53] See, e.g., 6.25.4 (Sosipolis at Olympia) and 8.42.7 (Demeter Melaina at Phigalia), discussed below.

[54] See, e.g., Paus. 2.33.1 (the foundation of a sanctuary of Athena Apaturia on Sphaeria following a dream vision of Athena, κατὰ δή τι ἐξ Ἀθηνᾶς ὄνειρον); 3.23.6 (the foundation of Epidauros Limera in Laconia by Epidaurians following warnings in dreams, ἐξ ἐνυπνίων γενομένων σφίσι καταμείναντες); 4.26.6 (the refoundation of Messene according to Epaminondas' vision of a priest of Demeter 'standing over him during the night', νύκτωρ ἐπιστάντα); and 7.5.2 (Alexander's foundation of Smyrna after a dream vision of the Nemeses, κατ' ὄψιν ὀνείρατος). On the role of epiphany within the *Periēgēsis*, see Chapter 5, 218–25.

[55] 8.37.3: see Chapter 5, 220–2.

[56] 7.20.8: see Frazer (1898: vol. IV, 149) and Lafond (in Casevitz and Lafond, 2000: 187–8).

is used so often that, like epigraphic records of dream vision, it acquires a formulaic quality, impressing upon the reader the close and recurring relationship between oneiric epiphany and sacred object: dream visions inspire the theft of images, the discovery of images and, most significantly, the *creation* of images.[57] While the Despoina example echoes the tradition of *acheiropoiēta*, whereby ancient cult objects (often aniconic in form) fall from heaven, are fished up from the sea or are discovered in mysterious locations characterised by much numinous activity, we also find examples where identifiable artists working within the tradition of classical naturalism are inspired by dreams.[58] Such tales are not unique to Pausanias. As I noted in Chapter 3, Athenaeus tells us that the Lindos Temple of Athena displayed a painting of Heracles attributed to Parrhasius accompanied by the inscription, 'As he appeared in the watches of the night, oft visiting Parrhasius while he slept, even so he stands here to behold'.[59] Tales of Parrhasius' hubris were legendary in antiquity, and in the context of the *Deipnosophistae* his claims to an oneiric hotline to Olympus are presented as characteristic of the painter's self-mythologising (likened to his habit of dressing, like Zeus, in purple and gold).[60] Yet the association the tale draws between oneiric access to the divine and artistic creativity echoes the visionary language that surrounds famed *agalmatopoioi* such as Phidias, and finds many serious analogies in Pausanias.[61] As we shall see, however, the relationship between dream epiphany and sacred image in the *Periēgēsis* is by no means straightforward. In keeping with the religious hermeneutics of the text (in which Pausanias repeatedly draws attention to the limits of the *theōria* he can generate for the reader), the role of oneiric inspiration is closely related to the play of concealment and revelation that characterises the author's presentation of sacred knowledge.[62]

---

[57] For further narratives of dream visions that employ the phrase, see Paus. 3.14.5 (discovery of the *xoanon* of Thetis brought to Sparta from Messenia); 4.13.2 (the suicide of Aristodemus following a dream vision of his dead daughter); 4.26.3 (a vision of Heracles Manticlus by his priest); 6.1.5 (a vision of the athlete Deinolochus with a victor's crown by his mother, commemorated by his statue at Olympia); 7.5.2 (recovery of the *agalma* of the Heracles of Erythrae from the sea, on which see Chapter 2, 97); 9.23.3 (Pindar's dream of Persephone and ensuing death), 9.29.8 (a dream commanding Philip to take the bones of Linus to Macedonia) and 10.2.6 (Phaylus' dream vision of a bronze corpse, followed by his death from wasting disease).

[58] On *acheiropoiēta*, see Chapter 2, 96–8.   [59] Athenaeus 12.543f: see Chapter 3, n. 145.

[60] On Parrhasius' reputation as an artist concerned with flouting the technical and ethical limits of mortal creativity, see Morales (1996) and Platt (2007b: 268–9).

[61] E.g., Quint. *Inst.* 12.10.9 and Him. *Ecl.* 32.10; on Phidias, see Chapter 5, 224–35.

[62] On these 'signalled absences' within the text, see Elsner (1992: 22–7) and my discussion in Chapter 5, 223–4.

Let us take, for example, two passages from the description of Olympia that refer to Sosipolis, the patron child god of Elis.[63]

In the front part of the temple [of Eileithyia], for it is built in two parts, is an altar of Eileithyia and an entrance for the public; in the inner part Sosipolis is worshipped, and no one may enter it except the woman who tends the god, and she must wrap her head and face in a white veil . . .

It is said that when the Arcadians had invaded the land of Elis, and the Eleans were set in array against them, a woman came to the Elean generals, holding a baby to her breast, who said that she was the mother of the child but that she gave him, because of dreams (ἐξ ὀνειράτων), to fight for the Eleans. The Elean officers believed that the woman was to be trusted, and placed the child before the army naked. When the Arcadians charged, the child turned at once into a snake. Thrown into disorder at the sight (ἐπὶ τῷ θεάματι), the Arcadians turned and fled, and were attacked by the Eleans, who won a very famous victory, and so call the god Sosipolis ['Saviour of the City']. On the spot where after the battle the snake seemed to them to go into the ground they made the sanctuary. With him the Eleans resolved to worship Eileithyia also, because this goddess to help them brought her son forth unto men. (6.20.3–5)

Sosipolis too is worshipped in a small shrine on the left of the sanctuary of Fortune. The god is painted according to a vision seen in a dream (κατὰ δὲ ὄψιν ὀνείρατος γραφῇ μεμιμημένος ἐστὶν ὁ θεός): in age a boy, wrapped in a star-spangled robe, and in one hand holding the horn of Amaltheia. (6.25.4)

Dream vision here manifests itself in two ways: it is responsible for both the actions that save the city in battle (the setting of the mysterious child in front of the troops) and the subsequent creation of a painting (or painted statue), which recalls the god's appearance in Elis and, through its close topographical relationship to the sanctuary of Tyche, ensures the city's safety in the future. The passage thus forms part of a network of episodes in the *Periēgēsis* which, following the model of the Trojan Palladion, link communal security with cult images and sacred objects, such as the 'secret thing' ([ἦν] τι ἐν ἀπορρήτῳ) of the Messenians, which, Pausanias tells us, would lead to the destruction and annihilation of the state if lost or damaged; buried by Aristomenes when the polis is under threat, the mysterious object is later retrieved by the Messenians on their return from exile, also upon the

---

[63] On this myth, see C. Robert (1893), Kearns (1990: 323–6), Elsner (1995: 132–4), who points out the relationship between *theos* (the god) and *thea(ma)* in this episode, and Jacquemin (in Casevitz *et al.*, 2002: 249–52, 301–2).

promptings of a dream.[64] Sosipolis functions, in Emily Kearns's formulation, as an 'improbable' agent of salvation, a marginal and vulnerable being (here, a tiny child) who, in the counterintuitive manner so typical of religious paradox, has the strength to save an entire community from destruction.[65] The infant god appears from outside the polis, in contrast to salvation epiphanies by civic deities, such as Athena at Lindos or Artemis Soteria at Pellene.[66] In this case, however, the role played by Eileithyia, the goddess of childbirth, and the boy's subsequent transformation into a snake suggest a chthonic origin that associates Sosipolis with the landscape of Elis itself as a local hero, or *epichōrios daimōn*.[67] A salvific epiphany-from-without thus turns out to be an epiphany-from-within, commemorated in a shrine that preserves the deity's mysterious identity and enhances his epiphanic potential by restricting access to all but the cult's elderly attendant, whose ritual function recalls the maternal *kourotrophos* who accompanied the god's original manifestation, but who must herself remain veiled within his presence.[68]

The first Sosipolis dream narrative ensures the efficacy of the god's epiphany by confirming the divine origin of Eileithyia's injunction to set the child in front of the Arcadian troops, ensuring that the strange woman is 'trusted' (πιστά): reported *oneiros* thus paves the way for a salvific spectacle (*theama*), which is then commemorated in rites that once more hide the god from his worshippers. Yet while entry to the shrine of Sosipolis within the Temple of Eileithyia at the foot of Mount Cronius is forbidden, Pausanias

---

[64] Paus. 4.20.4; see also 4.26.7–8 for the object's recovery, where it is revealed to be a copy of the mysteries of the Great Goddess engraved on a sheet of tin. On talismans designed for civic protection, see Frazer (1898: vol. IV, 433–4), Torelli and Musti (1991: 232–3) and Faraone (1992: 18–35), with my discussion of *palladia* in Chapter 2, 93–8. On the legends associated with Aristomenes, see Ogden (2004: esp. 89–103), with Alcock (2001: 149–51) and Henrichs (2003: 245–50) on the significance of the sacred texts at 4.26.7–8.

[65] Kearns (1990: 323–6). On battle epiphanies, see Pritchett (1979: 11–46, esp. 19–20, on Sosipolis) and my discussion in Chapter 3, 154–8. On the influence of 'counter-intuitive ontologies' on religious modes of cognition, see Boyer (1994: 91–125; 2001: 52–105) and Pyysiäinen (2002).

[66] On the epiphany of Artemis Soteria at Pellene (Plutarch *Aratus* 32.1–2), see the Introduction, 13–17.

[67] See Jacquemin (in Casevitz *et al.*, 2002: 249), with Pirenne-Delforge (1998: 132–5). On the relationship between autochthony and state security, see Loraux (1993: 37–71).

[68] On restricted access to the Temple of Eileithyia at Elis and the role of the cult's female attendants, see Steiner (2001: 87–8), Petridou (2006: 86, 270) and Connelly (2007: 91, 104, 202–3). On temple access more generally, see Hewitt (1909), Corbett (1970) and, on Pausanias in particular, Pritchett (1998: 178 n. 72). On the possible location of the Temple of Eileithyia and Sosipolis (now lost), see Kastenholz (1996).

suggests that his shrine next to the sanctuary of Tyche near the Elean agora is accessible. It is here, several paragraphs later, that we hear about a second *oneiros*, which, in bypassing the forbidden mysteries of the god's primary cult, facilitates the creation of a physical testimony of divine presence that gives form to Sosipolis' continued patronage of Elis, and ensures the availability of such a *theama* for subsequent viewer-worshippers. The painting thus not only continually re-enacts the dream epiphany which led to its own creation, but also recalls the child god's original manifestation. In doing so, it provides further iconographic details that reveal the boy-snake's true identity. For while the horn of Amaltheia – the fabled cornucopia, or horn of plenty – is associated with numerous deities, including Sosipolis' Elean neighbour Tyche, its possession by a divine boy wearing a cloak embroidered with stars (presumably the constellation Capricorn) alludes directly to the infancy of Zeus, when he was suckled by the kindly goat Amaltheia on Crete.[69] In this way, the mysterious saviour of Elis is revealed to be the king of the gods and patron deity of Olympia himself.

Like the dream that leads to the 'secret thing' of the Messenians, the Sosipolis episodes demonstrate the dream's potential to override problems of access, revealing what is hidden or unknown. Whereas Aelius Aristides' dreams provide a mediating sphere in which his divine protector might reveal and heal the suffering human body, dreams in the *Periēgēsis* repeatedly reveal the gods' capacity to act upon and assert their presence within the physical paraphernalia of religious practice. Yet, tellingly, Pausanias invokes this mutually reinforcing bond between dream vision and the materiality of cult at moments when the form or accessibility of sacred images is most in doubt. Such is the case at Phigalia in Arcadia, which he visits in order to see the statue of 'Black Demeter', named for her costume of mourning and worshipped in the cave where she was said to have grieved for Persephone.[70] As the mother of the Arcadian goddess Despoina, born after a union with Poseidon Hippios, Demeter Melaina was famed for her highly unusual

[69] On Pausanias' interest in the iconography of the Horn of Amaltheia and its association with Tyche in her sanctuaries at Smyrna (4.30.4) and Aegeira (7.26.8), see Hutton (2005a: 313–17). On the constellation of the goat, see, e.g., Aratus *Phaenomena* 162ff., Ovid *Fasti* 5.111–26, Ant. Lib. *Met.* 36 and Paus. 2.13.6. On the possible existence of an 'Idaean Cave' at Olympia, see Hampe (1951).

[70] 8.42.1–13. On this passage, see Jost (1973: 249–50; Casevitz *et al.*, 1998: 262–5), who suggests that Demeter's black garments and snaky locks suggest an underworld, chthonic association, Heer (1979: 160–7), Bruit (1986), Elsner (1992: 8) and J. I. Porter (2001: 74–5). On the cult of Demeter at Phigalia, see also Jost (1985: 312–17; 1992: 219–21, 233–4; 2003: 143–4; 2005: 97–8), and on the goddess's 'mixanthropic' aspects in their Arcadian context, Aston (2007: 142–5, 169–76).

iconography, for she 'was seated on a rock, like to a woman in all respects save the head. She had the head and hair of a horse, and there grew out of her head images of serpents and other beasts. Her tunic reached right to her feet; on one of her hands was a dolphin, on the other a dove' (8.42.4).[71] Although Pausanias famously claims that 'It was mainly to see this Demeter that I came to Phigalia', he finds that the statue no longer exists, and that 'most of the Phigalians were ignorant that it had ever existed at all', save for an ancient inhabitant who points out the holes in the cave roof from which stones had fallen and destroyed the statue, 'three generations before his time'.[72] Pausanias, however, is familiar with the tale of the image's creation, telling us that when the original *xoanon* was destroyed by fire and not replaced, the Phigalians suffered terrible famine until they were ordered by the Delphic oracle to adorn Demeter's cave with honours:

When the Phigalians heard the oracle that was brought back, they held Demeter in greater honour than before, and particularly they persuaded Onatas of Aegina, son of Micon, to make them an *agalma* of Demeter at a price. The Pergamenes have a bronze Apollo made by this Onatas, a most wonderful marvel both for its size and workmanship (θαῦμα ἐν τοῖς μάλιστα μεγέθους τε ἕνεκα καὶ ἐπὶ τῇ τέχνῃ). This man then, about two generations after the Persian invasion of Greece, made the Phigalians an *agalma* of bronze, guided partly by a picture or copy of the ancient wooden image (γραφὴν ἢ μίμημα τοῦ ἀρχαίου ξοάνου) which he discovered, but mostly (so goes the story) by a vision that he saw in dreams (κατὰ ὀνειράτων ὄψιν). (8.42.7)

As at Elis and Messene, the well-being of Phigalia is intimately connected to its citizens' relationship with their protector deity, enacted and symbolised through their treatment of a cultic object. The relationship between the goddess and her image is reinforced by the communication of divine power through both verbal oracle and visual dream, and again we find a variant of the formula, κατὰ ὀνειράτων ὄψιν. Although the Black Demeter is no longer visible in the Pausanian present (save for the signs of her destruction), the statue's history is itself presented as one of recurrent loss and recovery, in which mortal skill is able to reveal the goddess to her worshippers when aided by an oneiric epiphany. In the Sosipolis episode, the sacred image's relationship to the dream is spoken of in the language

---

[71] 8.42.4. On the relationship between Demeter Melaina and Demeter Erinys ('Fury') at Thelpousa, where she was raped by Poseidon Hippios, see Paus. 8.25.4–7, with Jost (in Casevitz *et al.*, 1998: 211–13, 262–3).

[72] 8.42.11–13. See Habicht (1985: 13–40), who cites Wilamowitz's denial that Pausanias ever visited Phigalia at all (1931: vol. I, 402–3), and J. I. Porter (2001: 75).

of mimesis: the god is 'imitated in painting' (γραφῇ μεμιμημένος ἐστίν) according to the artist's dream vision. At Phigalia, however, the dream's power to present an unmediated vision of the divine is contrasted with the less helpful evidence provided by a 'picture or copy' of the ancient *xoanon* – a *graphē* or *mimēma*. Onatas, then, is no mere imitator, but an artist whose work elsewhere demonstrates his ability to create wondrous images, *thaumata* famed for their great size and skill.[73] Like Damophon's *agalmata* of Demeter and Despoina at Lykosoura nearby, Onatas' work combines *technē* and *theosebeia*, using his skills in bronze, rather than wood, to create an image that bypasses the lost original, transmitting the *phantasia* of an unmediated vision to its viewer-worshippers, rather than a mere image of an image.[74]

The Phigalian episode of the *Periēgēsis* is particularly striking in its juxtaposition of the language of cult with that of connoisseurship and antiquarianism. Pausanias not only refers to Onatas' *opsis oneiratos* and quotes the Delphic verse-oracle given to the 'acorn-eating' Phigalians, demonstrating his familiarity with Arcadian religious arcana (8.42.6), but also alludes in great detail to several of the sculptor's works. He first proves Onatas' skill as an *agalmatopoios* through the example of his bronze Apollo at Pergamon, and then verifies his dates by reference to specific statues dedicated at Olympia (complete with their inscriptions) in order to conclude that his floruit was contemporary with the early fifth-century sculptors Hegias of Athens and Agelados of Argos.[75] In this way, Onatas' dream vision confirms the authenticity of his statue, yet is in turn anchored by visible demonstrations of his craftsmanship that survive in other locations in Greece and Asia Minor. As elsewhere in the *Periēgēsis*, piety and *paideia* converge in order to

---

[73] Frazer (1898: vol. IV, 408) tells us that a pedestal bearing the inscription Ὁνάτας] Σμίκωνος Αἰγινήτης [ἐποίησεν ('Onatas an Aeginetan, son of Micon, made this statue') was found at Pergamon (*Inschr. Perg.* 48), where Pausanias tells us Onatas' Apollo could be seen, presumably among the numerous 'Old Masters' brought to the city by the Attalids. On Pergamene practices of collecting, see Chapter 4, 170–3. On *thauma* as a term of popular criticism referring to 'the feeling that works of art have the capacity to take on a magical life of their own', see Pollitt (1974: 190–1), and, on the role of *thauma* in the language of epiphany, my discussion in Chapter 1, 56–7.

[74] On the language of skill and piety in relation to the *agalmatopoios*, see Chapter 3, 131–4. On Pausanias' celebration of Damophon at 8.37.3–6, see Chapter 5, 220–3.

[75] See also Paus. 5.25.8 and 5.25.12 (on statues by Onatas at Olympia), with further textual evidence for Onatas' sculptural activities in Pollitt (1990a: 36–9) and A. Stewart (1990: 252–3). On Pausanias as a reader of inscriptions, see Habicht (1985: 64–94). M. Robertson (1975: 184 n. 48) dates Onatas' period of artistic activity from the 480s to the 440s, and associates him with the Peloponnesian school of early classical sculptors. See also Ridgway (1970: 62–5, 72), who associates Onatas with an early classical school and considers him the possible creator of the Omphalos Apollo, a monumental bronze work (possibly even that at Pergamon?) known through Roman copies in marble.

provide the reader with the tools required to reanimate the lost sacred past for him- or herself.

Yet in spite of (or indeed because of) this valiant attempt to recover the lost Demeter's appearance, the most memorable feature of the episode at Phigalia is that Pausanias sees nothing at all, save the gaps in the cave's roof left by the stones that destroyed the statue in their fall. Porter sees these markers of absence as one of the most concentrated examples of the Pausanian sublime, a sign of '*the very loss of loss*', for 'nowhere are the sites of memory more compelling than where they are least visibly supported'.[76] In this sense Onatas' dream vision stands as proof of the authentic religiosity of a visual experience that is no longer available to Pausanias or his readers, providing a model of dematerialised encounter with the 'Black Demeter' that echoes (or anticipates) the *enargeia* that can now only be experienced in the statue's absence. Indeed, Onatas' ability, because of his oneiric epiphany, to ignore the *mimēma* of the original *xoanon* points to a means of experiencing the goddess that bypasses the need for her image altogether and, in offering an alternative mode of viewing, rescues the text from an utter sense of bereavement. The prominence of the dream in Pausanias' narrative suggests that, despite the close bond he stresses between statue and deity, the goddess exists independently of her image; although her presence can no longer be experienced in material form, she is nevertheless to be encountered in the ritual practices that persist within her sanctuary, the fireless offering of 'grapes and other cultivated fruits, with honeycombs and raw wool still full of its grease' (8.42.11) that Pausanias witnesses during his visit.[77]

This anxiety about the relationship between deity and statue (and implicit acknowledgement of the image's insufficiency) is also demonstrated by a passage in Pausanias' guide to Laconia, where he describes the shrine and *agalmata* of the Leucippides at Sparta:[78]

τὸ μὲν δὴ ἕτερον τῶν ἀγαλμάτων ἱερασαμένη τις ταῖς θεαῖς Λευκιππὶς ἐπεκόσμησε, πρόσωπον ἀντὶ τοῦ ἀρχαίου ποιησαμένη τῆς ἐφ᾽ ἡμῶν τέχνης. τὸ δὲ ἕτερον μὴ καὶ τοῦτο ἐπικοσμεῖν αὐτὴν ἀπεῖπεν ὄνειρον.

One of the images was adorned by a Leucippis who had served the goddesses as a priestess. She gave it a face of modern workmanship instead of the old one: she was forbidden by a dream vision to adorn the other one as well. (3.16.1)

---

[76] J. I. Porter (2001: 75 his emphasis). On the Pausanian sublime, see my discussion in Chapter 5, 223–4.

[77] On these 'bloodless sacrifices', see Bruit (1986).

[78] On the Spartan cult of the Leucippides, see Larson (1995: 64–9) and S. B. Pomeroy (2002: 118–19).

As at Elis and Phigalia, the episode asserts a close relationship between divine manifestations in dreams and the appearance of sacred images. The Leucippis' concern for her statue echoes, for example, the second epiphany of Athena inscribed upon the Lindos stele, when the goddess gave instructions for the purification of her *agalma* following a suicide in the temple.[79] Yet in contrast to Sosipolis and Demeter Melaina, the Leucippis does not reveal her form for the artist to imitate; on the contrary, she forbids an attempt to update her image in a style that would presumably have been more naturalistic than that of the original *agalma*. At Phigalia, Pausanias' celebration of Onatas' *technē* and detailed attempt to date his work suggest that, through his skilled use of bronze, the artist was able to form a compellingly lifelike image of Demeter (despite her theriomorphism) by employing the more naturalistic technique of the severe style, rather than the archaic forms of the original *xoanon*. As we saw in Chapter 2, this kind of updating would not have been unusual in a fifth-century context.[80] In Sparta, however, a pious priestess's attempt to replace the *archaikon prosōpon* of one of the Leucippides with a face 'in the style of our time' (τῆς ἐφ' ἡμῶν τέχνης) is explicitly rejected in the dream, in which the goddess forbids any changes to be made to the second statue.[81] In each case the dream offers a means of engaging with the material cultic realities that Pausanias encounters. In the absence of a cult statue at Phigalia, Onatas' dream vision points to a means of bypassing the image and beholding the deity directly. In the presence of hybrid archaic and classicising *agalmata* at Sparta, the priestess's dream vision facilitates a form of heritage management, asserting and preserving the superior sanctity of antique image-types that Pausanias elsewhere describes as the 'holiest' (ἁγιώτατον) of their kind.[82]

By reminding the reader of the enduring relationship between gods and their sanctuaries, the dream vision thus allows Pausanias to draw attention to those markers of sanctity he considers most 'worthy of seeing' (θέας δὲ ἄξιον), whether in terms of visiting sites themselves, or by means of the virtual *theōria* offered by the text of the *Periēgēsis*.[83] The visual quality of the dream facilitates a continuity between the visible sites of Greece's

---

[79] D 60–78; see Chapter 3, 167–8.

[80] On the commissioning of more naturalistic cult statues during the classical period, see Chapter 2, 83–4.

[81] Compare the supposed updating of the Athena Polias on the Athenian Acropolis by Endoios (Chapter 2, n. 52), which Kroll (1982) suggests involved the addition of figurative details to the semi-iconic form of the older *xoanon*.

[82] 1.26.6, on the Athena Polias: see Chapter 2, 106. On Pausanias' attitude to the styles of different periods, see Donohue (1988: 195–200).

[83] 1.1.3, on the sanctuary of Athena and Zeus in the Piraeus. See also 2.10.4, 2.13.3, 2.20.7, 2.23.7, 2.25.4, 2.29.1, 2.30.10, 3.19.6, 8.54.7 and 10.32.1, with Elsner (1992: 10).

sacred past and the 'phantastic' imagination required to reanimate such religiosity in the present, providing a model by which the image can travel between the material relics of cult and the *enargeia* of the text. At the same time, however, dreams alert the reader to moments of *aporia*, when mortal means of apprehending divine nature are most in doubt.[84] Sosipolis, for example, remains a hidden deity after his initial manifestation – even his attendant is compelled to veil herself in his presence – while Demeter Melaina possesses a strikingly unusual iconography that Pausanias pointedly refuses to explain and the Spartan Leucippides offer a confusing doubleness of form.[85] Dreams may provide cognitive reliability for sacred images, then, but they also point to the limitations of human knowledge of the divine and the very precariousness of the religious traditions Pausanias is endeavouring to preserve.

Artemidorus and the ontology of the dream image

If the gods' appearance is as elusive and problematic as such Pausanian episodes suggest, then what is the status of divine forms revealed to mortal eyes in dreams? Does an *opsis oneiratos* provide an unmediated vision of godhead, which can then be preserved and transmitted in material form through human skill? Or are dream visions replicable in painted or sculpted form precisely because they already have the status of representations? Do *oneiroi* of the gods have the status of true epiphanies, or – like the disguises adopted by the gods in Homeric dream visions – are they *eidōla* (or 'doubles') crafted for human consumption?[86] The dream image's very resistance to such questions is what makes it an ideal medium in which to facilitate

[84] Compare MacAlister (1996: 34), who comments that dreams are employed at pivotal moments of uncertainty in the Greek novel, for as 'chance events cannot be predicted or controlled by human or rational initiatives such as forethought, experience or analysis, an alternative means of revelation – such as the dream – is brought into play'. Note that when the Nymphs appear to Daphnis in a dream in Longus' *Daphnis and Chloe*, it is in the form of their images (2.23).

[85] See 8.42.4, on Demeter Melaina: 'Now why they had the image made after this fashion is plain to any intelligent man who is learned in traditions'. Pausanias is rarely reluctant to share such *paideia*, save when he is forbidden to pass on cultic knowledge by sacred law. Is this, then, a 'signalled absence' akin to his ritual silence at Eleusis (1.38.7)? On the characteristic dualism of epiphanies associated with the Dioscuri and Leucippides, see Platt (in press a).

[86] E.g., *Il.* 2.20–1, 56–8, *Od.* 4.795–8, 6.22–4; cf. Aelius Aristides 48.9, in which Asclepius appears to his foster-father in the form of the consul ordinarius L. Salvius Julianus, and necromantic dreams such as Herodotus 5.92, in which Periander's deceased wife appears as an *eidōlon*. See Dodds (1951: 104–5, 111), Kessels (1978) and, on the 'double', Vernant (1991: 166–8, 186–92), for whom the category encompasses phenomena such as shades (*skiai*) and apparitions (*phasmata*), as well as the *oneiros*, which function simultaneously in both the physical and spiritual worlds, as both a marker or signifier, and the thing which it signifies.

communication between the mortal and divine, for, as Vernant comments, 'The double plays on two contrasting levels at the same time; at the moment that it shows itself to be present, it also reveals itself as not being of this world but rather as belonging to an inaccessible elsewhere.'[87] As a liminal space between, in which the supernatural reveals itself in visible yet ambiguous terms, the dream image is thus a primary vehicle of prophecy.

The question of the dream image's ontological status is approached from a divinatory angle in Artemidorus' *Oneirocritica*, or 'Taxonomy of Dreams'.[88] Whereas Pausanias looks to dream visions to explain the form and significance of sacred images, Artemidorus uses the visual data provided by images in order to explain the mantic significance of dreams, proclaiming that, on an oneiric level, 'Statues of the gods have the same meaning as the gods themselves' (2.39). In both cases the dream's ability to collapse ontological registers facilitates correspondences between an inaccessible divine realm and the *Realien* of the waking world. Yet rather than drawing upon private oneiric experience as a source of authority for public religious life like Pausanias, Artemidorus draws upon the semiological systems of the public world in order to shed light upon the personal fate of each individual dreamer.[89] Here it is important to note that the mantic *oneiroi* subjected to interpretation in the *Oneirocritica* are not, for Artemidorus, equivalent to the epiphanic dream visions reported by Aristides or Pausanias, even when they feature visitations by the gods.[90] In his introduction Artemidorus breaks down the category of the *oneiros* into *theōrēmatikoi*, in which future events correspond precisely to what is seen in the dream vision, and *allēgorikoi*, which 'signify one thing by means of another' (δι' ἄλλων ἄλλα σημαίνοντες, 1.2).[91] It is this latter subcategory that forms the object of his oneirology, which proceeds as a rigorous form of demystified divination (or, as Christine Walde argues, a highly secularised branch of

---

[87] Vernant (1991: 187).

[88] This translation (based on the significance of *krinein*, 'to distinguish' or 'separate') rather than the 'Interpretation of Dreams' (*oneirohermeneia*), is suggested by L. Martin (1991: 107–8): '*Oneirocritica* signifies an ordering or systematic classification whereby those dreams that are true, that is, that are predictive, may be distinguished from those that are not.'

[89] On the relationship between Artemidorus' interpretative method and the social context of his subjects, see Pack (1955), Del Corno (1978: 1607–13), L. Martin (1987: 65–6; 1991), A. J. Pomeroy (1991), I. Hahn (1992) and Weber (1999), who possibly overstates the size of Artemidorus' readership: see W. V. Harris (2003: 32 n. 92) and Bowersock (2004: 61).

[90] See L. Martin (1987).

[91] Artemidorus' first example of a theorematic dream is that 'a man who was at sea dreamt that he suffered a shipwreck, and it actually came true in the way that it had been presented in sleep' (1.2).

'applied science').[92] Despite an ambivalent attitude towards the creative interpretation by cult personnel of dreams experienced during incubation, Artemidorus does not actually deny the possibility of epiphanic dreams: he introduces (1.2) two further categories of *oneiros* parallel to the *theōrēmatikos* – the *horama* ('vision') and the *chrēmatismos* ('oracular' or 'revelatory' dream), the latter of which corresponds to the dream visions experienced by Aelius Aristides during incubation, and includes *therapeiai* sent by Serapis (2.44).[93] Yet Artemidorus goes on to state that 'I have deliberately omitted a detailed explanation of these phenomena, since I suspect that any man to whom these things are not immediately evident will be unable to follow closely another man's detailed explanation of them' (1.2). Whereas gods that appear in *chrēmatismoi* might be viewed as epiphanic visitations, then, gods that appear in *allēgorikoi* are semiological vehicles that require a further process of decoding. Although he considers both categories of *oneiros* to be *theopemptos*, 'god-sent', Artemidorus makes a point of stating, 'I do not, like Aristotle, inquire as to whether the cause of dreaming is outside us (ἔξωθεν) and comes from the gods (ὑπὸ θεοῦ) or whether it is motivated by something within (ἔνδον), which disposes the soul in a certain way and causes a natural event to happen to it' (1.6). Rather, he is concerned with the classification of oneiric knowledge once it has been acquired. It is in such a spirit that he tackles the relationship between deity and statue in dream visions: statues have the same meaning as gods themselves because, in effect, all oneiric images that interest him exist on the same ontological level. As Patricia Cox Miller has suggested, dreams function as an 'imagistic resource' for mantic exegesis.[94] Yet as part of this visual databank, both gods and their statues also operate within a broader symbolic economy in which the phenomenological impact of dream vision (a sense of epiphanic encounter with the divine) is subordinated to a play of signs, for deities that appear in allegorical dreams necessarily mean something other than themselves.

The parallel Artemidorus draws between god and statue within the hermeneutic space of the *oneiros allēgorikos* means, therefore, that each

---

[92] Walde (1999: 127–8) – contra, Holowchak (2002: 93–105); see also Walde (2001: 144–99; 2003). L. Martin (1987: 102) describes Artemidorus' oneiromantic theory as 'a systemic play of resemblances that might be envisioned during sleep through strategies of moral purification', so contributing to 'the circle of late antique epistemological possibility'.

[93] On Artemidorus' attitude towards incubation and the medical interpretation of dreams, see Walde (1999: 123–4). On categories of *oneiroi* and their correspondence to other systems of dream classification in antiquity (such as those of Cicero and Macrobius), see Kessels (1969).

[94] Cox Miller (1994: 76). See also Pack (1955: 280–90). On the tension between epiphany and sign in ancient systems of divination, see Burkert (2005).

dream's interpretation requires a form of iconographic and cultural decoding, which draws upon the very traditions of visual *paideia* celebrated by Second Sophistic authors such as Pausanias and Philostratus. As a product of Antonine culture, the *Oneirocritica* is at no pains to conceal its author's status as a *pepaidoumenos*; indeed its first three books are dedicated to none other than Maximus of Tyre, 'the greatest Greek orator ever to come before the public'.[95] Artemidorus does not present himself as a sophist, however, despite occasional displays of literary and philosophical learning; as Glen Bowersock comments, he 'belonged to the age of the Second Sophistic but was not a part of the movement'.[96] Rather, he declares himself a rigorously trained professional (more akin to medical specialists such as Galen) who has paid his dues in both the library and the agora, and whose technical expertise rests predominantly upon careful autopsy.[97] In the *Oneirocritica* a familiarity with artistic conventions of dress, pose, attribute and style (indeed, knowledge of art history) thus has a highly practical application. For example:

Ἑρμῆς ἀγαθὸς τοῖς ἐπὶ λόγους ὁρμωμένοις καὶ ἀθληταῖς καὶ παιδοτρίβαις καὶ πᾶσι τοῖς ἐμπορικὸν <τὸν> βίον ἔχουσι καὶ ζυγοστάταις διὰ τὸ πάντας τοὺς τοιούτους ἐπίκουρον τὸν θεὸν νομίζειν. καὶ τοῖς ἀποδημεῖν βουλομένοις. πτηνὸν γὰρ ὑπειλή-φαμεν εἶναι τὸν θεόν. τοῖς δὲ λοιποῖς ἀκαταστασίας καὶ θορύβους προαγορεύει. νοσοῦντας δὲ ἀναιρεῖ διὰ τὸ ψυχοπομπὸς νενομίσθαι. Ἑρμῆς ὁ τετράγωνος <καὶ> σφηνοπώγων φιλολόγοις μόνοις συμφέρει, ὁ δὲ τετράγωνος καὶ ἀγένειος οὐδὲ τού-τοις συμφέρει. τὸ γὰρ περικεκομμένον αὐτοῦ τῶν περὶ τὸν ἰδόντα πάντων ὄλεθρον μαντεύεται.

Hermes is good for those who are studying oratory, for athletes, for gymnastic instructors, for all those whose life is devoted to trade and commerce, and for

---

[95] 1.*praef.* On the identification of Artemidorus' 'Cassius Maximus' as Maximus of Tyre (the name 'Cassius' possibly acquired together with Roman citizenship from Avidius Cassius, governor of Asia 166–75 ᴄᴇ), see Pack (1955: 7, 9), Price (1986: 10) and Bowersock (2004: 56). Artemidorus seems to mention Aristides (4.2), Fronto (4.22) and Plutarch (4.72) by name, but does not suggest personal acquaintance. On the Second Sophistic context of the *Oneirocritica*, see Bowersock (1994: 80–7; 2004), who suggests that Artemidorus' Aristides was an Ephesian magistrate called Q. Aemilius Aristides rather than the author of the *Hieroi Logoi* (2004: 55–6).

[96] Bowersock (2004: 59). Artemidorus claims (2.70) to be quite capable of 'inventing ingenious arguments' (εὑρησιλογεῖν) if need be, but to have no time for 'word merchants' (λογέμποροι).

[97] See 1.*praef.*: 'I . . . have not only taken special pains to procure every book on the interpretation of dreams, but have consorted for many years with the much-despised diviners of the marketplace'; see also 2.70 and 4.*praef.* On parallels between Artemidorus and Galen, see C. Blum (1936: 81–91) and Oberhelman (1987: 51–2), as well as Price (1986: 23–9), who claims that Artemidorus was inspired by the principles of the empiricist school: tradition (*historia*), analogy (*metabasis tou homoiou*) and experience (*peira*). Artemidorus is even cited by Galen as an empirical authority on bird divination (*Corpus medicorum Graecorum*, v.9.1, pp. 128–30).

inspectors of weights and measures, since all these men regard him as their tutelary deity. He is also good for those who wish to travel abroad. For we interpret him as being winged. But for other men, he foretells unrest and disturbances. He portends death for the sick because he is believed to be the conductor of souls. A quadrangular Hermes, if he has a wedge-shaped beard, signifies benefits only for literary men. But a quadrangular Hermes that is beardless does not signify benefits even for them. For the fact that he has been mutilated foretells the death of the dreamers' relatives [*lit.* the destruction of everything around the viewer]. (2.37)

Although Artemidorus is here ostensibly discussing the significance of seeing Hermes qua god, rather than statue, his interpretative strategy is nevertheless dependent upon material signs of Hermes' presence in contemporary Greek culture. His roll-call of professions under Hermes' protection evokes a typology of places in which the god's statues would have been displayed, such as *gymnasia* and *agorai*. In a neat reversal of Pausanias' oneiric *aitia*, the cultural conventions by which Hermes is already represented are then used to decode his mantic significance: he bodes well for travellers, Artemidorus claims, because we 'interpret' or 'understand' him to be winged (ὑπειλήφα-μεν). This act of imaginative visualisation both makes the god representable in human terms and inspires his appearance in the oneiric realm, generating a circular relationship between dream image and cultural representation. The god's iconography provides information about his divine nature, yet it is his divine nature that has inspired his iconography.[98] We might compare Aelius Aristides' comment in his *Hymn to Heracles* that 'Heracles especially appears to have the flower of youth. Indeed, there are now *agalmata* shared between Hermes and Heracles', where the existence of syncretistic images of the two gods is employed to gloss Heracles' divine identity, rather than the deity's characteristics inspiring his image.[99]

That the god's mantic significance depends upon his sculptural schema becomes even more apparent in the second half of the paragraph, in which Artemidorus refers to Hermes *tetragōnos* – the quadrangular herm. Here, without acknowledging any distinction between the god and his statues, he moves from anthropomorphic iconography (Hermes Psychopompos, the 'conductor of souls') to a semi-iconic form that, as we saw in Chapter 1, explicitly draws attention to the image's object status.[100] His theory of the

---

[98] On the oneiric *cercle herméneutique*, see also Veyne (1987: 386).

[99] Aelius Aristides *Hymn to Heracles* 40.19. On Aristides' prose hymns, see Russell (1990b) and Saïd (2008).

[100] See Chapter 1, 34–7, with Frontisi-Ducroux (1991: 213–20).

herm's mantic significance therefore no longer refers to the god's imagined, animate form (as the winged Hermes did), but decodes the dream according to his history as a material sign, alluding specifically to the famous mutilation of Athenian herms recorded by Thucydides, who reports in his *Histories* that, on the eve of the Athenians' fated Sicilian expedition,

ὅσοι Ἑρμαῖ ἦσαν λίθινοι ἐν τῇ πόλει τῇ Ἀθηναίων (εἰσὶ δὲ κατὰ τὸ ἐπιχώριον ἡ τετράγωνος ἐργασία, πολλοὶ καὶ ἐν ἰδίοις προθύροις καὶ ἐν ἱεροῖς), μιᾷ νυκτὶ οἱ πλεῖστοι περιεκόπησαν τὰ πρόσωπα. . . . καὶ τὸ πρᾶγμα μειζόνως ἐλάμβανον. τοῦ τε γὰρ ἔκπλου οἰωνὸς ἐδόκει εἶναι, καὶ ἐπὶ ξυνωμοσίᾳ ἅμα νεωτέρων πραγμάτων καὶ δήμου καταλύσεως γεγενῆσθαι.

The stone statues of Hermes in the city of Athens – they are the pillars of square construction which according to local custom stand in great numbers both in the doorways of private houses and in sacred places – nearly all had their faces mutilated on the same night . . . The matter was taken very seriously; for it seemed to be ominous for the expedition and to have been done withal in furtherance of a conspiracy with a view to a revolution and the overthrow of the democracy.[101]

This act of iconoclasm (and the Athenian defeat it supposedly foreshadowed) was so intimately related to the herm's later reception that by the second century CE it had passed into dream-lore. For Artemidorus, a beardless herm (ἀγένειος) is thus directly associated with mutilation.[102] A comparison of the passages reveals that the *oneirokritikos* even uses similar language to Thucydides, not only in the use of τετράγωνος to convey the herm's quadrangular form, but also the term περικεκομμένον to describe the images' desecration, which echoes the historian's περιεκόπησαν.[103] Given the learned nature of Artemidorus' interpretation, it is not surprising that a dream vision of a herm has specific import for *philologoi*, a significance derived as much from the popular use of herms in post-classical portraits of

---

[101] 6.27 (translation from Charles Forster Smith, Loeb Classical Library edition, 1966).

[102] See also Plutarch *Alkibiades* 19–23, for a second-century CE account of the event. On the mutilation of the herms, see R. Osborne (1985), Winkler (1990a), Furley (1996), Parker (1996: 199–200), Wohl (2002: 154–9, 205–14), Todd (2004) and Quinn (2007).

[103] R. Osborne (1985: n. 94) argues that περικοπή/περικόπτω is first used in extant texts in relation to the mutilation of the herms, and conveys the act of shaving or trimming the edges of an object. For a more positive interpretation of an oneiric visit to the barber, free of the associations raised by the herm, see *Oneirocritica* 1.22, where 'to have one's hair cut' (καρῆναι) is related to 'rejoice' (χαρῆναι), for 'a neat appearance is the concern of those who are free from pain and are not in difficulty'. Note that the term *tetragonos* was specifically employed by Simonides as a sculptural metaphor for moral integrity – *PMG* fr. 542 'It is difficult for a man to become truly noble (*agathos*), foursquare (*tetragonon*) in hands, feet, and mind, crafted without flaw'; see Pollitt (1974: 263–9), Svenbro (1976: 153–54), Rouveret (1989: 146 n. 44) and Neer (2010: 36–40).

philosophers and intellectuals as it is from the god Hermes (whose wily eloquence often associated him with orators and sophists).[104] For the dreaming
philologos, the coalescence of deity and statue in the form of the herm thus
also embraces the public representation of the dreamer himself – an image
whose authority and identifiability rested to a great deal on the presence of a
beard.[105] In his analysis of the Thucydidean episode, Robin Osborne claims
that the shock of the herms' mutilation, particularly that of the face, lay in
the fact that 'the face of the herm was the face of every Athenian'.[106] This
sense of a violated civic identity – and threat to the entire political system –
is transformed by Artemidorus into a harbinger of personal fate, interpreted
according to the visible *habitus* of the Second Sophistic intellectual.[107] For
a *philologos* to dream of a mutilated herm thus signifies 'the destruction of
everything around the viewer', an emphasis on sight (ἰδόντα) reinforcing
the dream's imagistic quality and the text's corresponding investment in
contemporary modes of visuality.

This analogy between iconographic detail and the personal affairs of the
dreamer is drawn repeatedly in the *Oneirocritica*: the import of a dream
vision of Aphrodite, for example, shifts according to whether she appears
as the 'vulgar' Pandemos (good for innkeepers and courtesans), 'heavenly'
Ourania (good for marriages and farmers), Pelagia (good for sailors) or
Anadyomene (2.37).[108] As Pausanias demonstrates in his description of the
Temple of Aphrodite in Elis, each of these epithets was closely related to
a sculptural type characterised by a particular pose, costume or attribute:
as Ourania the goddess is represented by Phidias 'standing with one foot
on a tortoise' (its muteness and privacy symbolic of her modesty), and
as Pandemos she is represented by Scopas in rather more ribald form,
'riding a bronze he-goat'.[109] Pausanias keeps his own foot tortoise-bound

---

[104] On Hermes as the god of speech and communication, see L. Kahn (1978), Conte (1999) and
Jaillard (2007: 167–236). On the display of bearded herm portraits in gymnasia during the
second and third centuries CE, see Krumeich (2004).

[105] Note that Artemidorus, like Thucydides, ignores the question of the herms' castration in order
to concentrate on the mutilation of the face. On the importance of beards for Second
Sophistic intellectual identity, see P. Zanker (1995b: 198–266), R. R. R. Smith (1998), Borg
(2004a), Vout (2006) and Sidebottom (2009: 81–5). The long hair and beards of
second-century charismatics were often remarked upon (e.g., Philostr. *VS* 529, 536, *VA* 1.32,
7.34), while Epictetus declared that he would sooner let his head be cut off than his beard, so
essential was it to his very sense of self (*Diss.* 1.2.28, discussed by P. Zanker, 1995b: 260).

[106] R. Osborne (1985: 65).

[107] For an analysis of the *habitus* of second-century sophists, see Gleason (1995), with Bourdieu
(1977), and Sidebottom (2009).

[108] On the distinction between Aphrodite Ourania and Pandemos, see Plato *Symposium* 181a–d.

[109] 6.25.1: 'The goddess in the temple they call Heavenly (*Ourania*); she is of ivory and gold, the
work of Phidias, and she stands with one foot upon a tortoise. The precinct of the other

in responding to these contrasting manifestations of the goddess, merely commenting, 'the meaning of the tortoise and of the he-goat I leave to those who care to compare them (εἰκάζειν)'. Such niceties are unnecessary, however, within the encyclopaedic exegesis of the *Oneirocritica*, according to which the significance of the Aphrodite Anadyomene (and, one imagines, the dreamer's state of arousal) depends explicitly upon the extent of her nudity:

> If the upper part of Aphrodite's body, as far down as her waist, is unclad, it is always considered a good sign, since the breasts, which are the most nourishing part of the body, are uncovered and exposed to view. But if Aphrodite is completely naked, it is auspicious for courtesans alone and signifies profit. But in regard to other things, it foretells shame. (2.37)

Artemidorus here places the reader/dreamer in the same viewing position as Pausanias' virtual visitor to Elis, providing descriptions of pose and attribute in an abbreviated form of ekphrasis. Both authors depend upon their readers' familiarity with the typology of divine statuary, just as Aelius Aristides depends upon his readers' ability to visualise Phidias' Athena Parthenos. The Anadyomene, for example, might take the form of the Aphrodite of Capua type (if semi-clad), or Praxiteles' Knidia (if fully nude).[110] For Artemidorus, then, in order to 'read' a dream, one must be able to 'read' a statue, relating subtle distinctions of visual detail to specific epithets and divine identities, before examining them in relation to one's profession and sexual ethics.[111] Visual *paideia* thus enables the reader to interpret fleeting, immaterial *oneiroi* according to tangible images seen in waking life that are already fully integrated into a coherent semiological system. The image's ability to travel between hard material object and elusive dream as a *lebende Statue* thereby provides a means of locating each dreamer within the coherent network of relationships that divination presupposes between individual, society and the cosmos.[112]

Aphrodite is surrounded by a wall, and within the precinct has been made a base, upon which sits a bronze image of Aphrodite upon a bronze he-goat. It is a work of Scopas, and the Aphrodite is named Common (*Pandēmos*).' Plutarch claims that Aphrodite's tortoise 'typifies for womankind staying at home and keeping silent' (*Moralia* 142d): see Llewellyn-Jones (2003: 189–91).

[110] On the dissemination of Aphrodite types in post-classical sculpture, see Havelock (1995) and Kousser (2005, 2008).

[111] On the sexual ethics of the *Oneirocritica*, see Foucault (1986: 4–16), Winkler (1990b: 23–44) and C. Stewart (2002: 282–6).

[112] On the Stoic concepts underlying Artemidorus' theory of oneiromancy (particularly that of the soul's relationship to a divine principle or cosmic *sympatheia*), see C. Blum (1936: 52–71), on the influence of Posidonius, and L. Martin (1991: 103–8), who argues that divination by

While the coalescence of deity and image within the *oneiros* facilitates Artemidorus' practice of allegoresis, allowing for a system of resemblances to be established between dreams and waking life, we should not rush to take his statement that 'Statues have the same meaning as the gods themselves' at face value. Cox Miller is correct in her statement that 'the oneiric imagination confounds the conventional distinction between (real) thing and (false) copy', yet, despite the fact that image and prototype have the same general import for the dreamer in Artemidorus' interpretative model, any details that draw attention to the god's status qua image necessarily generate a further layer of signification that, as he fully recognises, must then be subjected to further analysis.[113] For example, towards the beginning of book 1, Artemidorus offers as an example of dreams that are good in both their appearance and mantic import: 'Seeing the Olympians themselves (αὐτούς), or statues of them that have been made out of an incorruptible material (<τὰ> ἀγάλματα αὐτῶν ἐξ ὕλης <τῆς> ἀσήπτου πεποιημένα), cheerful, smiling, giving or saying something good' (1.5). At first reading this might seem a straightforward anticipation of his comment in book 2 that gods and their statues have the same meaning, yet his reference to *agalmata* immediately leads to a qualification referring to the statue's materiality (or *hulē*), which, he suggests, must be as enduring as the gods themselves in order to have positive significance for the dreamer. Indeed, immediately following his statement that 'Statues of the gods have the same meaning as the gods themselves' (2.39), he comments that:

agalmata that are fashioned from a substance that is hard and incorruptible as, for example, those that are made from gold, silver, bronze, ivory, stone, amber or ebony are auspicious. *Agalmata* fashioned from any other material as, for example, those that are made from terra cotta, clay, plaster or wax, those that are painted and the like, are less auspicious and often even inauspicious.

The dream's import here depends on both value and perishability – friable, malleable and cheap materials suggest a degree of impermanence that neutralises the positive significance of the god's appearance and, by introducing

---

dreams was 'a literate reading of the objective signs of the world as ordered by the syntax of fate' (108). On Stoic theories of oneiromancy (as advanced by Quintus Cicero in book 1, 39–65 of Cicero's *De divinatione*), see Pease (1920: 20–4), Schofield (1986: 51–2), Cox Miller (1994: 52–5), Wardle (2006: esp. 206–70) and Engels (2007: 135–40, 146–50).

[113] Cox Miller (1994: 30). As she goes on to suggest, 'When these *simulacra* appeared in dreams, they were not derided as mere copies of copies; on the contrary, their emotional and epistemological charge was heightened by virtue of their double imaginal character' (33).

a disjunction between divine inviolability and the instability of base matter, even foreshadows negative events in the dreamer's waking life.

Whereas an *oneiros* featuring a god's statue provides Artemidorus with further information to decode, suggesting that, in mantic terms, an 'agalmatophany' has more hermeneutic value than an 'epiphany', he makes a distinction (2.35) between god and image that draws more explicitly upon a notion of ontological hierarchy. For those who dream of Artemis, he suggests that:

οὐδὲν <δὲ> διαφέρει τὴν θεὸν ἰδεῖν ὁποίαν ὑπειλήφαμεν ἢ ἄγαλμα αὐτῆς. ἐάν τε γὰρ σάρκινοι οἱ θεοὶ φαίνωνται ἐάν τε ὡς ἀγάλματα ἐξ ὕλης πεποιημένα, τὸν αὐτὸν ἔχουσι λόγον. θᾶττον δὲ καὶ τὰ ἀγαθὰ καὶ τὰ κακὰ σημαίνουσιν αὐτοὶ οἱ ὁρώμενοι ἤπερ τὰ ἀγάλματα αὐτῶν.

It makes no difference whether we see the goddess herself as we have imagined her to be, or a statue of her. For whether gods appear in the flesh or as statues fashioned out of some material, they have the same meaning. But when the gods have been seen in person, it signifies that the good and bad fulfilments will take place more quickly than they would have done if statues of them had been seen.

While god and statue have the same eventual significance (or *logos*) for the dreamer, the rate at which the dream's import is felt within the dreamer's waking life depends upon the representational status of the *oneiros*. Whereas the appearance of a god qua statue generates an intensification of signification, then, the appearance of a god qua god generates an intensification of mantic efficacy. This rests upon a clear discrepancy between the way in which we see Artemis 'as we have *imagined* her to be' (ὑπειλήφαμεν), which Artemidorus conflates with how she is 'in the flesh' (σάρκινοι), and the way in which she is represented as an *image*, despite the coalescence of 'imagined' and 'imaged' deity in passages such as that on Hermes, discussed above. He thus introduces a Platonic notion of mimetic hierarchy (the statue is only an imitation of the deity, after all, and thus less efficacious in prophetic terms), which contradicts the model of phenomenological unity suggested by his statement that 'Statues of the gods have the same meaning as the gods themselves.'

Putting aside the deeply problematic notion of how a deity (particularly Artemis) might appear 'in the flesh', how, then, is the dreamer then meant to distinguish between god and statue? Artemidorus provides little advice, save for explicit signs of materiality. Indeed, when he describes *oneiroi* of the gods, he does so by reference to the iconographic schemata by which they were represented in art, as we saw in the cases of Hermes and Aphrodite. We return, inevitably, to the hermeneutic circle with which this chapter began, and the question of whether it was at all possible to imagine a deity independently of artistic tradition, given that the mutually reinforcing relationship between gods and their images was so firmly entrenched in the Greek cultural consciousness. Artemidorus demonstrates some awareness of this problem in his comment that 'the gods appear in the image and likeness of men, since we have conceived of them as resembling us in their form' (φαίνονται δὲ οἱ θεοὶ ἐν ἀνθρώπων ἰδέᾳ τε καὶ μορφῇ, ἐπειδὴ νενομίκαμεν αὐτοὺς τὰ εἴδη ἡμῖν ἐοικέναι, 2.44), a statement that harks back to Xenophanes' critique of anthropomorphism.[114] We might recall the fact that the first three books of the *Oneirocritica* are dedicated to Maximus of Tyre, who argued in his *Second Oration* that images of the gods are *sēmeia* akin to spoken utterances, with an arbitrary and culturally constructed relationship to their divine prototypes.[115] Artemidorus implies a similar conception of the sacred image in his use of the verb ὑπολαμβάνω (*lit.* 'to take up by getting under', and thus 'to interpret' or 'understand') in relation to the iconography of specific deities: Hermes is winged because 'we have understood' him to be so (ὑπειλήφαμεν); Artemis appears in dreams 'as we have understood her' (ὑπειλήφαμεν).[116] The term echoes the Stoic notion of an 'acquired concept' (ὑπόληψις) of divinity that is interrogated by Dio in the *Olympian Oration*, and underlines the role played by human imagination in the visualisation of anthropomorphic divine beings.[117]

This attitude to mental imag(in)ings of the gods echoes Artemidorus' more general theory of oneiric content, according to which even dreams that are 'god-sent' (*theopemptos*) are formed by the human soul in response to an external stimulus, and are thus dependent upon the experience and critical faculties of the dreamer in question. The dreams of learned men, for example, are more semiologically complex than those of ignorant ones, while Artemidorus takes it as an interpretative axiom that 'a man will not dream about things to which he has never given a thought (πεφρόντικεν)' (1.2).[118] In this sense his emphasis upon the role of human creativity in the formation of dreams echoes the oneirological approach illustrated by a fragment attributed to the second-century novelist Iamblichus (author of

---

[114] Xenophanes DK B14–16: see Chapter 1, 51–2.

[115] *Dial.* 2.2, 'Should Statues be made to the Gods?', discussed in Chapter 5, 228–30.

[116] See LSJ s.v. ὑπολαμβάνω.   [117] Dio 12.40: see Chapter 5, 228.

[118] 4.*praef.*: 'Whatever the masses desire or dread, they also see in precisely that form in their sleep, whereas those who are qualified experts in this field see their wishes expressed in symbols'; 4.59: literary dreams 'are seen only by those who are cultured and have some degree of education. From this anyone can clearly perceive that dreams are products of the mind and are not caused by any outside influence'. Cf. Walde (1999: 134–5).

the *Babyloniaka*), which states that 'Dreams are sent by the divine, but the soul of each individual dreamer shapes them. God is the principal patron of their nature, but we ourselves are the fashioners of their form' (τὰ ἐνύπνια ὑπὸ μὲν τοῦ δαιμονίου πέμπεται, ὑπὸ δὲ τῆς ἑκάστου ψυχῆς τῶν ὁρώντων πλάττεται. καὶ τῆς μὲν φύσεως αὐτῶν ὁ θεός ἐστι χορηγός, τῆς δὲ ἰδέας ἡμεῖς αὐτοὶ δημιουργοί).[119] Iamblichus' Platonic language here suggests that, as entities akin to the eternal 'forms' (*ideai*), dreams can transmit divine truths, but that each dreamer determines their visual appearance, playing the role of craftsman (*dēmiourgos*). The dream vision, then, may have mantic significance because of its divine origin, but in terms of its content and appearance it functions as a man-made *mimēma*. If humans have the ability to 'shape' or 'mould' their dreams (πλάττεται), then it is no wonder that oneiric epiphanies take the form of statues, whose appearance is equally dependent upon the creative facility of the human imagination. Whereas in sacred contexts dream visions of the gods inspire artists, in the rationalising tradition inspired by Greek philosophy humans are themselves the artists of their dreams.

Although the mutually reinforcing relationship between *agalma* and *theos* influences the function and interpretation of dreams in a great range of Second Sophistic texts, the relationship between *oneiros* and epiphany is, therefore, construed very differently by authors invested in the dream vision's power to provide cognitive reliability for traditional religious practice. For Aelius Aristides and Pausanias, the dream's assumed origin *outside* the circle of human representation is precisely what lends it authority within the text, offering a channel of communication between the human and divine through which images can travel between the physical and incorporeal. The dream's ability to collapse ontological registers so that god and statue inhabit the same sphere of experience blurs the distinction between sign and referent, allowing cultural *sēmata* of the divine to be apprehended as 'gods themselves'. Artemidorus, however, explicitly states his lack of interest in the external origin of dreams, beyond a general principle of cosmic *sympatheia* that stimulates the human soul into producing oneiric images that anticipate natural events. In an effort to impose an interpretative system upon the slippery, subjective realm of the oneiric imagination, he subordinates the dream's phenomenological effect to its semiological import, interpreting dream visions as the encoded product of culture patterns familiar to

---

[119] Iamblichus fr. 34 Habrich = *codd. Laur.* 57, 12, and *Vat.* 1354; Stephens and Winkler (1995: 210). The fragment relates to a trial brought by a husband against his wife because she dreamt she had sex with a slave. On Iamblichus, see Stephens and Winkler (1995: 179–245). On dreams in the Greek novel, see MacAlister (1996).

each individual dreamer. In his professional mission to outline a theory of oneiromancy that rests upon principles of natural philosophy rather than superstition, Artemidorus effectively detaches the visual form of epiphany from its sacred content. By excluding an external origin (ἔξωθεν) for divine appearances in dreams, he thereby exposes the visual paradox that structures the relationship between gods and their representations.

Oneiric inspiration and the dream as text

Artemidorus was not, however, immune to the epiphanic potential of *oneiroi* as far as his own literary claims were concerned. In his address to Cassius Maximus at the end of book 2, he defends the structural and intellectual integrity of the *Oneirocritica* with the claim that 'Apollo has encouraged me in the past and now especially, when I have made your acquaintance, he clearly presides over me (ἐναργῶς ἐπιστάντι μοι) and has all but commanded me to compose this work. It is no wonder, then, that Apollo of Daldis, who is called *Mystes* according to our local tradition, urged me to this undertaking' (2.70). It is here, in a *Dichterweihe* related to the patron deity of his home town, that Artemidorus explicitly draws upon the enargeic language of epiphany, placing himself in a long line of authors inspired to literary achievement through divine encounters that take place within the very medium that forms the subject of his work.[120] In this way he claims a cognitive reliability for the form and content of his text that is parallel to the authority attributed to oneiric inspiration by Pausanias and Aelius Aristides, both of whom acknowledge the direct influence of dreams upon their narrative structures.

In each case the role played by the *oneiros* provides a meta-textual commentary upon the author's literary enterprise. While describing the monuments on the Athenian Acropolis, Pausanias writes, 'After I had intended to go further into this story, and to describe the contents of the sanctuary at Athens, called the Eleusinion, I was stayed by a vision in a dream (ἐπέσχεν ὄψις ὀνείρατος)'.[121] Just as the other *opseis oneiratōn* scattered through the *Periēgēsis* expose the difficulties of accessing sacred knowledge, so Pausanias' own dream draws attention to the necessary limitations of his descriptive project, and introduces an apophatic element that, in

---

[120] E.g., Hesiod *Theogony* 9–34 (discussed in Chapter 1, 50–4). On the use of ἐφίστημι in accounts of dream epiphany, see above, n. 13.

[121] 1.14.3: see Chapter 5, 223–4.

preserving sacred mysteries, also enhances the religiosity of the text itself.[122] In the *Sacred Tales* direct responsibility for the text's loose, episodic configuration is attributed to Asclepius: Aristides claims that 'straight from the beginning, the god ordered me to write down my dreams', which resulted in a dream diary, or *apographē*, of over 300,000 lines (48.1–3).[123] This immense work has only a tangential relationship to the present text, however, partly because it is no longer accessible, and partly because of the impossibility of transcribing events as they were experienced; as Aristides comments, 'each of our days as well as our nights has a story' (47.3). He has been urged to overcome the impossibility of putting such experiences into words, however, by *opseis oneiratōn* that 'compel [him] to bring these things somehow to light' (48.2). Despite the fact that the *Hieroi Logoi* will offer the reader a compressed and apparently random narrative, 'compiled as I remember different things from different sources', Aristides claims that 'the god will lead and stimulate me' (48.4), and indeed is diverted 'in the midst of composing' by a dream (50.68).[124] These explicit acknowledgements of Asclepius' intervention within the text provide a means of understanding its seemingly chaotic, even transgressive composition (described by Behr as an 'unbelievable confusion'), generating a reading experience that, in echoing the shifting, unpredictable nature of dreaming itself, ratifies the text's claims to epiphanic intimacy with the god.[125]

In foregrounding the relationship between god-sent dreams and textual authenticity, all three authors emphasise the role played by language in shaping and understanding divine encounter. Not only are dreams inaccessible to all but the dreamer until transformed into verbal discourse,

---

[122] Cf. 4.33.5: 'I may not reveal (ἀπόρρητα ἔστω μοι) the rite of the Great Goddesses, for it is their mysteries which they celebrate in the Carnasian Grove, and I regard them as second to the Eleusinian in sanctity. But my dream did not prevent me (οὐκ ἀπεῖργε τὸ ὄνειρον) from making known to all that the brazen urn, discovered by the Argive general, and the bones of Eurytus the son of Melaneus were kept here.' Elsewhere, Pausanias is quick to acknowledge the influence of dream visions not only upon Greece's physical monuments, but also upon the literary achievements that contribute to its cultural distinction: see 1.21.1–2 (on Sophocles and Aeschylus) and 9.23.2–4, where he presents an extraordinary triple narrative of oneiric inspiration associated with Pindar.

[123] On this (possibly fictional) text, see Pearcy (1988: 383–4), Quet (1993: 218–20), Petsalis-Diomidis (2006b: 196–8) and Downie (2008a: 25–7).

[124] Cf. Petsalis-Diomidis (2006b: 198–9).

[125] Behr (1968: 118). On the *Hieroi Logoi* as a form of *lalia* (or 'talk'), an informal and comparatively flexible structure associated with rhetorical improvisation, see Downie (2008a: 26–7). As Pearcy (1988: 379) comments, 'The *Sacred Tales* proceed from an awareness that the human desire to perceive reality in the shape of a story must give way when the subject is divine, and that sequence, causality, and the other determiners of Aristotelian narrative (*Poetics* 1450 B24) cannot take their accustomed place if the narrative is to represent the condensations and displacements common to dreams and miracles'.

but also it is in their retelling that they are invested with structure and mean-ing. These, however, depend entirely upon the hermeneutic lens employed by the dreamer/interpreter. In this sense, dreams are both parallel to and rep-resentative of epiphany in general: both are fleeting, intangible encounters resistant to conventional hermeneutic strategies, which only gain cultural significance through their commemoration by human acts of representa-tion. At the same time, dreams are comparable to literary texts, in that both generate imaginative spaces in which (as I suggested of ekphrasis in Chap-ter 4) ontological distinctions can be collapsed, and mortal and immortal can meet. Just as Aristides revels in the fluid relationship between gods and statues in his dreams, for example, so he delights in collapsing the bound-aries between texts. The introduction to his *Hymn to the Sons of Asclepius* opens with the statement,

Κλῦτε φίλοι, θεῖός μοι ἐνύπνιον ἦλθεν ὄνειρος, ἔφη αὐτὸ τὸ ὄναρ. ταύτην γὰρ δὴ ἐδόκουν ἀρχὴν ποιεῖσθαι τοῦ λόγου, ὡς ὕπαρ τὸ ὄναρ σκοπῶν ἐπ᾽ ἐμαυτοῦ.

'Hearken, friends, a divine dream came to me in sleep,' said the dream itself. For I dreamed that I made this the opening of my speech while I beheld the dream before me as if it were a reality. (38.1–3)

Here, the dream's ability to fold different layers of experience within itself is presented as parallel to the framing of texts within texts, exhibiting a self-consciousness of form that echoes (or foreshadows) the self-reflexivity of Aristides' hymn, in which the orator is both speaker and audience, viewer and viewed, dreamer and interpreter. The speech already exists within the imagined 'reality' of the *theios oneiros* before it is summoned into the wak-ing world through Aristides' performance, while the fluidity of experience between dream and reality within the dream itself facilitates a corresponding fluidity between the dream and Aristides' actual speech. A similar manoeu-vre is employed in the *Sacred Tales*, where the dream that intervenes in Aristides' narrative (50.68–9) features an oneiric address to Asclepius which the orator then discovers written down: 'Behold, what I dreamed that I said, I find written in the book!' Again, a text encountered in the dream world is echoed in the *hieros logos* of the work itself: the process of 'secondary elaboration' necessary for oneiric interpretation has already been enacted within the sacred space of the dream, and can thus be transmitted to the reader without further intervention.[126] In this way, the text makes a claim

---

[126] On the phenomenon of 'secondary elaboration', in which the dreamer recognises the dream's oneiric status while still asleep, so that 'the dream loses the appearance of absurdity and incoherence, and approaches the pattern of an intelligible experience', see Freud (1953: 390–2, at 391).

for the reliability of its own discursive practices at the very same moment that it demonstrates the ineluctable subjectivity of visionary experience.

It is because they bring questions of cognition, representation and interpretation centre stage, then, that dreams prove such a fertile medium in which to explore the relationship between images and epiphanies. They therefore offer a means of understanding how divinity can be apprehended within the boundaries of human experience, and how sacred knowledge (including that of divine form) might pass between the mortal and immortal realms. Perhaps most compellingly, dreams offer a model of god–human relations that simultaneously acknowledges divine authority (the dream is *theopemptos*), while functioning as a creative medium that allows for a degree of mortal agency. In this sense they concentrate the mutually reinforcing relationship between divine form and human creativity that characterised Greek culture at large into a singular phenomenon that is accessible to every individual who remembers his or her oneiric adventures. Each model of dream vision explored in this chapter negotiates the relationship between external divine influence and human subjectivity in different ways, whether Artemidorus' model of interaction between cosmic structures and the social conditions that shape his clients' daily lives; the influence of Aristides' healing god upon the internal struggle between his suffering body and intellectual exertions; or the symbiotic relationship Pausanias traces between deities that safeguard Greek religious tradition and the material traces left by their worshippers upon the sacred landscape. Most importantly, the discursive practices that give dream visions meaning in each case are shaped by the textual requirements of different literary genres, whether the pseudo-technical treatise, religious autobiography or encyclopaedic topographical description.

The dream's ability to draw attention to the hermeneutics of the text is powerfully demonstrated in the very final paragraph of Pausanias' *Periēgēsis*, for while dreams often provide an original *aition* for literary creativity (as in the *Dichterweihe* topos), they can also stand at the work's end, functioning as a framing mechanism that establishes (or problematises) the text's relationship to the world of the reader:

The sanctuary of Asclepius I found in ruins, but it was originally built by a private person called Phalysius. For he had a complaint of the eyes, and when he was almost blind the god at Epidaurus sent to him the poetess Anyte, who brought with her a sealed tablet. The woman thought that the god's appearance was a dream (ὄψις ὀνείρατος), but it proved at once to be a waking vision (ὕπαρ). For she found in her own hands a sealed tablet; so sailing to Naupactus she bade Phalysius take away the seal and read what was written. He did not think it possible to read the writing with his eyes in such a condition, but hoping to get some benefit from Asclepius he took away the seal. When he had looked at the wax he recovered his sight, and gave to Anyte what was written on the tablet, two thousand staters of gold. (10.38.13)

Here, as he reaches the port of Naupactus in Locris on the Corinthian Gulf and – whether by accident or design – bids goodnight to his readers, Pausanias presents us with an 'apport' dream that fearlessly asserts the relationship between an invisible divine realm and the physical world described and preserved within his text.[127] The parallel visions of patient and poet – one experienced during incubation, the other as a form of daydream – establish an equivalence between the oneiric and waking worlds that is realised in the form of the sealed tablet received by the Hellenistic poetess Anyte of Tegea, and prompts a voyage in search of the blind man she is destined to help.[128] While many have doubted that this passage is indeed the official end of the *Periēgēsis*, expecting more formal closure, the episode's concentration of themes related to Pausanias' literary and religious enterprise builds to a powerful statement of the text's ambition that presents a

---

[127] We may have been robbed of Pausanias' formal ending by a lacuna in the manuscript tradition: see Habicht (1985: 6–7, with earlier bibliography), for the suggestion that 'Pausanias either became tired or died before he could put the finishing touches to his work'. Habicht nevertheless rejects the idea of an eleventh book, and asserts that 'only a very few pages can be missing'. If 10.38.13 was not Pausanias' closing paragraph, it was almost certainly one of the final episodes of the *Periēgēsis* as a whole. For positive readings of the episode as a form of closure, see Alcock (1996: 267–8), J. I. Porter (2001: 91) and Sidebottom (2002: 498–9), who points out that the text also lacks a formal preface. Nörenberg (1973: 250–2) compares the ending to that of Herodotus. On 'apport' dreams, see above, 256.

[128] In its double narrative of visionary experience combined with miraculous healing and the production of a text, this Pausanian episode bears a strong parallel to *POxy*. 11.1381, a second-century CE papyrus on the 'marvellous epiphanies' (τερατώδεις . . . ἐπ[ι]φανείας, 219–20) of Imouthes, an Egyptian deity identified with Asclepius. This opens with an account of how the author – struck down with a fever due to that all-too-human sin of procrastination ('for to gods, not to mortals, is it permitted to describe the mighty deeds of the gods', 40–2) – is finally forced to begin work following a healing visitation from Imouthes, 'clothed in shining raiment and carrying in his left hand a book' (117–21), both to himself and his concerned mother within the god's temple at Memphis. This leads to an aretalogy of the divine dedicatee that anticipates the healing epiphanies which were probably narrated in the (now lost) work that followed. See Grenfell and Hunt (1928: 221–34), whose translation I have borrowed, Nock (1933: 86–9) and Hanson (1980: 1416–17). For a comparison of the Pausanian passage and evidence for epiphanic healing in Asclepian cult, see Nörenberg (1973: 244–50), who emphasises how, in the Pausanian passage, the epiphany of the god reaches its climax through the figure of the *poet*. On Anyte of Tegea, see S. Barnard (1978: 208–10; 1991), Geoghegan (1979), Gutzwiller (1993; 1998: 54–74), Greene (2000) and Skinner (2001: 209–11, 217–18), who suggests that the association between Anyte and Naupactus may have arisen from a hymn to Asclepius that she composed for the dedication of Phalysius' shrine (217).

compelling case for an authentic ending.[129] For despite the ruinous decay
of the final sanctuary Pausanias describes, and the sense of nostalgia for lost
tradition this evokes, the episode demonstrates how divine presence lives
on in the memory of an *opsis oneiratos* that literally places a divine text in
the hands of an author. At the very point that marks the limits of his own
literary enterprise, then, Pausanias offers the reader an example of a text
with the potential to reach beyond itself, to transmit its god-sent message
in such a way that, when its mysteries are unsealed, the blind are literally
compelled *to see*. In recovering his sight, Phalysius is finally able to read the
sacred text that is offered to him, and, in so doing, to realise its value – a
final twist that is surely a tongue-in-cheek hint at the importance of recognising the worth of Pausanias' work itself.[130] In the Phalysius episode the
author thus reifies his own literary project, uniting the theme of divinely
inspired travel with the word's power to perform its own kind of *thera-
peia*, preserving the fragile memory of epiphanic encounter and living cult
through its own verbal strategies of *enargeia*.[131] Crucially, amid the loss,
longing and hope that imbue Pausanias' ekphrastic project, it is the paradoxical logic of the dream that asserts the porous nature of the text and
facilitates the miracle of vision.

[129] See above, n. 127.
[130] Sidebottom (2002: 499 n. 40) points out the delightful pun by which the verb ἀνύτω can
       mean 'to complete', 'to finish a journey' and 'to gain'.
[131] Note that θεραπεία ('service', 'care' or 'cure') is also used in Hellenistic inscriptions to refer to
       the maintenance or repair of temples: see LSJ s.v. θεραπεία, with *Syll.*³ 1102.8 and 1106.49.

In a striking passage of Philostratus' *Life of Apollonius of Tyana*, we follow the heroic first-century CE philosopher to the Athenian port at Piraeus, where he seeks passage to that ultimate Graeco-Roman pilgrimage destination, Egypt (5.20).[1] Denied space on a ship bound for Ionia, Apollonius discovers that its precious cargo comprises *agalmata* of the gods made of gold, ivory and marble, intended not for direct dedication in the temples of Asia Minor, but 'for sale to those who wish to dedicate them (ἀποδωσό-μενος . . . τοῖς βουλομένοις ἱδρύεσθαι)'.[2] Claiming that he does not fear the statues' theft, but that they will be 'infected by bad company and the way of life on ships', the captain reveals a contradictory attitude to the sacred image that reverberates throughout the *Life*, and which Apollonius will feel compelled to resolve. On one hand, the captain treats his statues as manifestations of the deities they represent, fearing for their sanctity; yet on the other, he treats them as mere tradable objects, available for purchase in the markets of the Greek East. The sage's response is emblematic of his approach to practices of religious representation elsewhere, in that he emphatically endorses the object's sanctity over its materiality, while asserting the importance of philosophical enquiry as a means of accessing the divine: 'Are you foolishly banning philosophers from your ship,' he asks, 'men whom the gods approve more than all others, and yet you are trafficking in the gods?' The market in deities, he suggests, is in violation of earlier practices of image worship, when *agalmatopoiia*, the 'making of sacred statues', was practised by itinerant craftsmen who did not circulate the products of their artistry

---

[1] The text of the *Life* suggests that Apollonius was active in the first century CE, from the reign of Tiberius (14–37 CE, Philostr. *VA* 1.12.2) to that of Nerva (96–98 CE, *VA* 8.27). On the work's Greek title, Τὰ ἐς τὸν Τυανέα Ἀπολλώνιον ('In Honour of Apollonius of Tyana'), and its relationship to the thorny problem of genre, see G. Anderson (1986: 121, 235–6). On historical evidence for the 'real' Apollonius, see Grosso (1954), with caution, B. F. Harris (1969), G. Anderson (1986: 175–97), Dzielska (1986), Swain (1996: 395–6), J. A. Francis (1998) and C. P. Jones (2005–6: vol. III). On the *Life* as a work of fiction, see Bowie (1978), Schirren (2005, 2009) and Gyselinck and Demoen (2009).

[2] All translations of the *Life of Apollonius* are taken from C. P. Jones's Loeb Classical Library edition (2005–6), with some minor alterations. This passage is also discussed by Lapatin (2001: 122).

like any old commodity, but 'brought merely their own hands with them' and, 'taking raw material, plied their crafts in the sanctuaries themselves'. The traditional *agalmatopoios*, by implication, lived the life of a philosopher, touring the holy sites of Greece (like Apollonius) with little to peddle save his wisdom and skill. This is in stark contrast to the art dealer: 'to live off the gods themselves, and never to be satisfied – what a horrible trade!' The superiority of philosophy to image-making is confirmed when the sage and his companions finally reach the island of Rhodes; asked by his faithful disciple Damis whether he thinks there is anything greater than the famous colossus, Apollonius claims, 'A true man who pursues wisdom honestly and sincerely' (ἄνδρα φιλοσοφοῦντα ὑγιῶς τε καὶ ἀδόλως, 21.1). In this sense Apollonius emphasises his own superiority as a conduit through which his followers (and, by implication, Philostratus' readers) might gain access to the sacred. Yet, crucially, he does not deny the religious efficacy of traditional *agalmata*; indeed, Apollonius' rejection of the statue's status as a tradable art object anticipates a passionate defence of its epiphanic potential in book 6, in which he emphasises the relationship between image-making and *phantasia*.[3] Throughout the *Life*, sacred images play an important role within Apollonius' theological and philosophical promotion of paganism. As a form of third-century apologetic, the *Life of Apollonius of Tyana* thus serves to justify and reassert the significance of *agalmatopoiia* in Greek religious tradition.[4]

Commissioned by the empress Julia Domna and dedicated some time after her death in 217 CE, Philostratus' highly fictionalised biography performs many impressive feats in its representation of the Greek sage as a paradigmatic 'divine man', or *theios anēr*.[5] In its encyclopaedic range the text

---

[3] *VA* 6.19, discussed below.

[4] On the *Life of Apollonius* as a defence of Apollonius' reputation, a response to Roman *imperium* or a rival to Christian promotions of Jesus, see M. Smith (1978: 84–93), Talbert (1978: 1621–2), Flinterman (1995: 60–2), J. A. Francis (1995: 83–129), Swain (1997a: 28–9; 1999), Gasparro (2007: 281–2), König (2007: 136), Whitmarsh (2007: 50–1) and Elsner (2009b), contra, Bowie (1978: 1666). A more explicit promotion of Apollonius as a rival to Christ is attributed to the fourth-century pagan apologist Sossianus Hierocles, ridiculed by Eusebius in his *Contra Hieroclem*: see Forrat and des Places (1986), Junod (1988) and Schirren (2009: 177–86), with Cox (1983: 73–4), Swain (1996: 382–3) and Elsner (2009b).

[5] Bowie (1978: 1652–99) suggests a date between 222 and 235; see also J. A. Francis (1998: 419–20). In using the phrase *theios anēr*, I allude to Ludwig Bieler's 1935–6 study of holy men in late antiquity; see also Betz (1982). On Apollonius as the archetypal holy man, see also Talbert (1978), Belloni (1980), Gallagher (1982: 1–26), G. Anderson (1986: 227–240; 1994: *passim* – on Apollonius as a 'virtuoso religious activist', 3), Corrington (1986: 1–43), Phillips (1986), Koskenniemi (1994: 169–89), Flinterman (1995: 60–6), J. A. Francis (1995: 122–6) and Gasparro (2007). For a critique of the scholarly tradition, see Koskenniemi (1994), who emphasises the influence of Philostratus' portrait of Apollonius rather than the historical figure

manages to penetrate the geographical limits of the known world, to cover radically different approaches to religious practice, philosophical enquiry and systems of government, and even to traverse time and rewrite Greek literary history. In this way the *Life* appropriates and reformulates virtually every aspect of the intellectual culture of its time, all to further Philostratus' promotion of Apollonius as the Hellene extraordinaire, demonstrating his all-encompassing wisdom, his ability to embrace and master the familiar and the foreign, the practical and the intellectual, the human and the divine.[6] Working towards this end, the narrative repeatedly plays with the topoi of Greek literary tradition, allowing Apollonius to subvert and surpass his models in terms of *paideia, sophia* and piety, while demonstrating Philostratus' own skills in outstripping the literary achievements of his predecessors. Indeed, the author clearly states his agenda at the beginning of book 7, when, relating the feats 'performed by truly wise men against tyrants' (7.1), he claims that he is obliged to downplay the accomplishments of even Zeno, Plato and Diogenes: 'Not that they are not honourable or generally famous, but they fall short of Apollonius' deeds, even if they surpass those of everyone else' (7.2.3).[7]

Key to this pattern of appropriation and transcendence is the text's use of material images, and their relationship to epiphanic encounter with the divine.[8] As the ultimate representative and safeguard of Greek religion (and yet a Pythagorean who rejects the practice of animal sacrifice, 5.25), it is essential that Apollonius should justify and promote the worship and artistic representation of anthropomorphised gods, particularly temple statues such as the Zeus of Phidias regarded as central to Hellenic cultural and religious identity.[9] As paradigmatic holy man, and yet archetypal philosopher, Philostratus' Apollonius has to find a way of reconciling popular religious practice with sophisticated intellectual enquiry in a manner that will both validate

---

himself, Flinterman (1996), who defends the category of miracle workers in the first and second centuries, and Du Toit (1997: esp. 275–320), who argues that *theios* and its cognates refer in such contexts to philosophical and moral excellence rather than ontological status.

[6] Zeitlin (2001: 248) comments that 'Philostratus' portrait of the sage . . . is also a prime illustration of Greek self-identity at work in the promotion of a Philhellenism in its many aspects, among which are *paideia*, philosophical wisdom, devotion to learning, love of freedom and defense of ethical values'. On the *Life* as a symbolic form based upon archetypal lives of the Greek philosophers, see Schirren (2005).

[7] On Apollonius' spirited stand against Roman emperors, see Flinterman (1995: 128–230) and Whitmarsh (2001b: 225–44).

[8] On the 'appropriation and transcendence' of literary models in Second Sophistic texts, see Whitmarsh (2001a: 273), with Bowie (2009) on citation and allusion in the *VA*.

[9] On Apollonius' abstention from sacrifice, see J. A. Francis (1995: 105–6) and C. P. Jones (2009: 250–1).

Hellenic tradition and demonstrate his own status as an all-embracing symbol of Greek religious and philosophical achievement.[10] Throughout the *Life*, Philostratus thus stages examples of the viewing of sacred images in which Apollonius is cast as a pedagogic guide, or *exēgētēs*, leading a series of Socratic-style discussions that, as the narrative progresses, move towards a specific elucidation of the means by which traditional anthropomorphic representations (and, through them, the gods) might be apprehended by pious and thoughtful viewers.[11]

As the Piraeus scene in book 5 demonstrates, this gradual delineation of Apollonius' theory of representation is mapped onto the *Life*'s narrative framework of travel, particularly the performance of pilgrimage. The visiting of key sacred sites and the viewing of sacred images are essential to Philostratus' hagiographical agenda, while they contribute to the novelistic and paradoxographical qualities of the text.[12] The various images that the sage and his followers view and discuss during their adventures are thus presented as the conventional subjects of exotic travel narratives, while they simultaneously reflect and advance the Hellenic philosophical and religious concerns that are threaded through the work as a whole.[13] As Apollonius points out to his follower Damis in Babylon, 'To a wise man, Greece is everywhere' (σοφῷ ἀνδρὶ Ἑλλὰς πάντα, 1.35.2). In line with many Greek literary encounters with the 'other', the exotic details of such foreign climes are thus ultimately subordinated to the text's exploration and promotion of its own cultural framework.[14] Travel, pilgrimage, the viewing of sacred images and the attainment of *sophia* all come together in the Greek notion of *theōria*, which, as we saw in Chapter 5, can apply to the individual pilgrim who visits foreign lands in search of knowledge and wisdom (often of

---

[10] See J. A. Francis (1995: 126), who comments that 'Apollonius does not look forward to Byzantine saints as much as he recapitulates classical philosophers and heroes, a point reinforced by his consistent action on behalf of established norms and values.'

[11] On Apollonius as an interpreter, see Miles (2009). On the influence of Socrates as a biographical paradigm, see Cox (1983: 7), who points out that hagiographical biography owes a certain debt to Plato's *Apology* and Xenophon's *Life of Socrates*, both of which 'present an intermingling of fantasy and historical reality with the intent of capturing the ideals suggested by the actual life'. On the biography as a major vehicle for the communication of religious and philosophical ideas in this period, see Cox (1983), Momigliano (1987), Swain (1996: 385–6; 1997a) and Hägg and Rousseau (2000).

[12] See E. Meyer (1917), Elsner (1997a: 24), who argues that Philostratus' travel narrative can be read as an allegory for 'the spiritual journey of Apollonius as paradigmatic holy man', and Montiglio (2005: 213–20). In line with this emphasis on travel, another model that Philostratus frequently employs for his protagonist is Homer's Odysseus: see van Dijk (2009).

[13] For Philostratus' attitudes to Hellenism in the *VA* and elsewhere, see Follet (1991: 205–15), Flinterman (1995: 89–127) and Swain (1999).

[14] Cf. Elsner (2001b), on Lucian's *De Syria dea*.

a religious nature), as well as state pilgrimages to religious festivals.[15] The concept of *theōria* is also, crucially, where religion and philosophy meet, and desire for knowledge of the divine is aided by processes of intellectual enquiry. As Andrea Nightingale has commented on Plato's use of the term, 'the philosopher . . . is a new kind of *theoros*: a man who travels to the metaphysical realm to see the sacred sights in that region. The goal of philosophy, as Socrates claims, is to engage in the "*theoria* of all being."'[16] In this sense Socrates provides Philostratus with an ideal model for Apollonius, whose habit of 'wandering and wondering' entwines the practices of journeying, seeing, thinking and revering.[17] Throughout the biography the practice of *theōria* is intertwined with Apollonius' intellectual journey – his acquisition and demonstration of *sophia*. As part of this process Philostratus repeatedly brings together the quest for wisdom and the epiphanic perception of divinity through the mediatory functions of sacred and allegorical representations.

Following the work of Ella Birmelin in the 1930s, three key passages have been regarded as significant for our understanding of Philostratus' use of art in the *Life*.[18] The first takes place in book 2, where Apollonius explains the imagery on the metalwork reliefs in Taxila to his follower Damis, their depiction of Alexander's defeat of the Indian king Porus leading to a discussion about the nature of mimesis (2.22). The second is a discussion of the relative merits of the Zeus of Homer and the Zeus of Phidias (4.7), in which Apollonius promotes the literary representation of the god – which 'could be sensed in every corner of the universe (τὸν δὲ ἐς πάντα ἐν τῷ οὐρανῷ ὑπονοεῖσθαι)' – over the chryselephantine statue at Olympia, which is only 'visible on earth' (τὸν μὲν γὰρ ἐν γῇ φαίνεσθαι). The final, most overtly polemical passage forms part of Apollonius' extensive debate with Thespesion, the spokesman of the naked philosophers (or 'gymnosophists') of Ethiopia in book 6. Here the sage promotes Greek systems of anthropomorphic representation over the Egyptian practice of theriomorphism, and presents his theory of *phantasia* as a solution to the epistemological problems raised by the concept of art as mimesis (6.19). Each episode tackles the cognitive issues at stake in the creation and the viewing of images, setting

---

[15] On *theōria*, see Koller (1957), Rausch (1982), Rutherford (1995, 2000, 2001) and my discussion in Chapter 1, 59–60.

[16] Nightingale (2001: 36, on *Republic* 486d); see also Rutherford (2001: 47) and Nightingale (2004, 2005).

[17] I borrow the phrase 'wandering and wondering' from Nightingale (2001). See also Montiglio (2005: esp. 213–20), on Philostratus' Apollonius.

[18] See Birmelin (1933), Schweitzer (1934), Manieri (1998: 60–6), Schirren (2005: 272–85) and Miles (2009: 147–56). On images in the *VA*, see also Rousselle (2001: 393–9).

Hellenic modes of naturalistic representation against the ekphrastic powers of literature, on one hand, and the visual schemata of foreign cultures, on the other.

Apollonius' Socratic pose and defence of anthropomorphism demonstrate Philostratus' debt to the *Olympian Oration* of Dio (whose influence can be detected throughout the *Life*, and who even makes a dramatic appearance to discuss kingship in book 5).[19] Yet, as with the *Heroicus* and the *Imagines*, the text's scenes of viewing are structured according to Philostratus' choice of genre. The sage's presentation as a philosophical pedagogue means that (as in the *Heroicus*) *paideia* acquired through acts of viewing is reached through dialogue between Apollonius and his interlocutors. Yet the biographical structure of the *Life* means that we also find narrative episodes in which images are referred to in passing (as the Piraeus scene above), or described by Apollonius' companion, Damis (as I shall discuss below).[20] For this reason, not only the passages of overt *Kunsttheorie* identified by Birmelin are relevant to our subject, but also the more general narratives of viewing scattered through the text. In this sense the *Life* can be compared to the ancient novel, where the viewing of works of art is often associated with the acquisition of crucial knowledge and the characters' journey from ignorance to knowledge, such as the related statues of Diana, Actaeon and Isis in Apuleius' *Golden Ass*, or the painting of Andromeda that plays such an important role in the plot of Heliodorus' *Aethiopica*.[21] Nor should we forget the pedagogic structure of Philostratus' *Imagines*, which demonstrates a keen awareness of the role played by viewing in the progression from ignorance to knowledge.[22] In the *Life* the roles of teacher and pupil are recast for their sacred context, so that Apollonius, as *exēgētēs*, employs images to communicate his religious and philosophical teachings to his companions. The reader's experience is carefully controlled as he or she, like Damis, is put into the role of an uneducated viewer. To view through the prism of Philostratus' narrative is thus a process of education and initiation by which we can gain access to higher truths through a combination of description

---

[19] See Chapter 5, n. 76; note that Dio also appears (in a rather negative light) in Philostratus' *Lives of the Sophists* (487–8).

[20] On the novelistic elements of the *Life*, see Bowie (1978, 1994) and G. Anderson (1986: 227–39; 1996). Flinterman (2009: n. 1) favours parallels with imaginative histories such as Xenophon's *Cyropaedia* and the *Alexander Romance* (as suggested by G. Anderson, 1986: 231–2).

[21] Apuleius *Metamorphoses* 2.4, 11.1; Heliodorus 4.8: see Peden (1985), Too (1996), M. J. Anderson (1997b), Laird (1997), N. Slater (1998) and Platt (2002: 103–4). On ekphrasis in the novel, see Harlan (1965), Bartsch (1989: 26–31, 42–4), Zeitlin (1990), Morales (1995, 2004), Stoneman (1995) and Whitmarsh (2002).

[22] See Chapter 5, n. 10.

and allegory comparable to the religious and philosophical ideals explored in ekphrastic texts such as the *Tabula* of Cebes.[23]

In order to explore these aspects of the *Life* in more detail, this chapter focuses on the third section of *Kunsttheorie* outlined by Birmelin – the Ethiopian debate in book 6, which forms part of a sequence of episodes in which Apollonius and his companions view or discuss works of art with a specifically sacred function.[24] Here, we are repeatedly presented with images (or references to images) that, in keeping with the religious focus of the *Life*, raise important questions about the vision and representation of the divine, and the attainment of wisdom through theological enquiry. In doing so, they appropriate popular philosophical ideas in an attempt to reconcile the tensions generated by the sacred image, thereby offering a guide to viewing that confirms Apollonius' status as spokesman and champion of Greek religious tradition.

The mis-viewing of Memnon

I met a traveller from an antique land
Who said: Two vast and trunkless legs of stone
Stand in the desert. Near them on the sand,
Half sunk, a shatter'd visage lies.

(P. B. Shelley, *Ozymandias*)

The first image with which Apollonius and his retinue are confronted as they enter Ethiopia is the colossus of Memnon at Thebes (6.4). Famed for the eerie 'twang' it emitted at dawn, the statue and its partner were a popular attraction on the Egyptian pilgrimage circuit, survivors of the great temple of Amenhotep III, fifteenth-century BCE ruler of the Eighteenth Dynasty (Figure 7.1).[25] Memnon's colossus was a *thauma*, a marvel combining the sacred, ancient, mysterious and pseudoscientific – perfect subject-matter for paradoxography. Indeed, Pausanias tells us that the colossus 'made me marvel (θαυμάσαι) more than anything else' (1.42.3). He goes on to explain,

---

[23] On the pepaideutic qualities of the *Tabula* of Cebes and its relationship to the reader, see Elsner (1995: 39–48).

[24] *VA* 6.19; Birmelin (1933: 392–414).

[25] On the popularity of Memnon in Second Sophistic sources, see Bravi (2007). Note also the significance of the Memnonion at Abydos as a Greco-Roman pilgrimage destination, on which see Rutherford (2003). On pilgrimage to Egypt in the Roman period, see also Bernand and Bernand (1960), Nock (1972: 53–104) and Frankfurter (1998).

Figure 7.1 Colossus of Memnon (Amenhotep III) and its twin, fifteenth century BCE

This statue was broken in two by Cambyses, and at the present day from head to middle it is thrown down (ἀπερριμμένον); but the rest is seated, and every day at the rising of the sun it makes a noise, and the sound one could best liken to that of a harp or lyre when a string has been broken (καὶ τὸν ἦχον μάλιστα εἰκάσει τις κιθάρας ἢ λύρας ῥαγείσης χορδῆς).[26]

The sonic phenomenon recorded by Pausanias was the paradoxically fortuitous result of the statue's desecration: once its upper body had been destroyed, the thermal strength of the rising sun, warming and expanding the stone of the statue's base, came into contact with the cool channels of air running through the crevices of the statue's interior, so producing a mysterious sound-effect, which many chose to interpret as an epiphanic animation of the image.[27] Once the statue was repaired (possibly under the orders of Septimius Severus after his visit to Egypt in 199), this collision of

---

[26] Other literary references to the colossus of Memnon are made by Strabo 17.1.46 (our earliest Greek reference to the statue), Tacitus *Annals* 2.61 (the visit of Germanicus), Plin. *HN* 36.58 ('Memnonis statuae dicatus, quem cotidiano solis ortu contactum radiis crepare tradunt') and Lucian *Toxaris* (or, *On Friendship*) 27.12 and *Philopseudes* 33.8.

[27] Note that Strabo attributes the damage to Memnon's upper body to an earthquake rather than Cambyses' troops (17.46).

hot and cold could not take place, and Memnon was silenced.[28] Neverthe-less, the colossus became a focus of *theōria* for generations of Greek and Roman pilgrims, who recorded their experiences on its legs and base, often with the simple formula ἤκουσα Μέμνονος, or *audi Memnonem*.[29] It was even the focus of at least three imperial visits, including one by Hadrian and Sabina that was detained for three days because, intriguingly, Memnon chose to remain silent.[30]

Memnon is thus a highly appropriate focus for Philostratus' Apollonius, whose paradigmatic status means that he must surpass every theoric model in his journeys to distant and exotic sacred destinations.[31] Fittingly, the colossus stands both at the beginning of book 6, and close to the border between Egypt and Ethiopia, so acting as a textual marker of transition into the mysterious world that would later be appropriated as a paradoxograph-ical backdrop by Heliodorus.[32] Within the structure of the *Life*, Ethiopia forms a southern counterpart to the eastern limit of the known world marked by the Indian episode. Memnon was the paradigmatic Ethiopian, a symbol of otherness, and yet, through his presence in the *Iliad*, he forms a Homeric link to the world of Achilles and the Greek heroic past explored by Apollonius in book 4.[33] The statue's role as an indication of transition hints that Memnon also has a programmatic function, showing the way in which religious images will be central to the subsequent narrative:[34]

---

[28] See Bowersock (1984: 31–2), who suggests the colossus was repaired by Zenobia in the late third century CE.

[29] On the Memnon inscriptions, 107 texts in Latin and Greek, dating from the first to the third centuries CE, see Bernand and Bernand (1960: nos. 30, G 24, and 93–6); see also Kaibel (1878: nos. 987–1014).

[30] On the visits of Hadrian and Septimius Severus, see Bowersock (1984) and Bravi (2007: 82–89); on Germanicus, who, appropriately for a Philhellenic pilgrim on the Egyptian *thaumata* trail, dressed as a Greek, see Tacitus *Annals* 2.61; on imperial travel more generally, see Millar (1977: 28–40) and Halfmann (1986: 143–56). That not all visitors to the sacred sites of Egypt were entirely serious in their viewing is suggested by a graffito from one temple site which is signed: 'Ammun, son of Nile, Crocodile' ([Ἀ]μμώνιου Νειλέως Κροκοδείλου: *Sammelbuch* 151, quoted by Smelik and Hemelrijk, 1984: 1939). On Greek attitudes to Egypt, see Vasunia (2001), and on the relationship between Greek and Egyptian models of epiphany, Rutherford (in press).

[31] On Apollonius' 'orgy of temple-visiting' elsewhere in the *Life*, see Elsner (1997a: 22–8).

[32] On similarities between the *VA* and the *Aethiopica*, see Rohde (1974: 466–73), Maillon's introduction to the 1943 Budé Heliodorus (vol. 1, 86), G. Anderson (1986: 230–1) and J. R. Morgan (2009). On paradoxography and the negotiation of Hellenism in the *Aethiopica*, see Whitmarsh (1998b: 93–124), and in the ancient novel in general, Morales (1995: 39–50). On attitudes to Ethiopia in the Greco-Roman world, see Romm (1992: 45–81).

[33] On Apollonius' epiphanic encounter with Achilles at 4.11, see Chapter 5, 247.

[34] Compare the use of herms as textual markers at the end of book 2 and beginning of book 3 in Pausanias's *Periēgēsis*, where they also mark the boundary between Argos, Arcadia and Laconia: see Elsner (1995: 136–7) and Cole (2004: 178–80).

Περὶ δὲ τοῦ Μέμνονος τάδε ἀναγράφει Δάμις . . .

Τὸ δὲ ἄγαλμα τετράφθαι πρὸς ἀκτῖνα μήπω γενειάσκον, λίθου δὲ εἶναι μέλανος, ξυμβεβηκέναι δὲ τὼ πόδε ἄμφω κατὰ τὴν ἀγαλματοποιίαν τὴν ἐπὶ Δαιδάλου, καὶ τὰς χεῖρας ἀπερείδειν ὀρθὰς ἐς τὸν θᾶκον, καθῆσθαι γὰρ ἐν ὁρμῇ τοῦ ὑπανίστασθαι. τὸ δὲ σχῆμα τοῦτο καὶ τὸν τῶν ὀφθαλμῶν νοῦν καὶ ὁπόσα τοῦ στόματος ὡς φθεγξομένου ᾄδουσι, τὸν μὲν ἄλλον χρόνον ἧττον θαυμάσαι φασίν, οὔπω γὰρ ἐνεργὰ φαίνεσθαι, προσβαλούσης δὲ τὸ ἄγαλμα τῆς ἀκτῖνος, τουτὶ δὲ γίγνεσθαι περὶ ἡλίου ἐπιτολάς, μὴ κατασχεῖν τὸ θαῦμα.

Φθέγξασθαι μὲν γὰρ παραχρῆμα τῆς ἀκτῖνος ἐλθούσης αὐτῷ ἐπὶ στόμα, φαιδροὺς δὲ ἱστάναι τοὺς ὀφθαλμοὺς δόξαι πρὸς τὸ φῶς, οἷα τῶν ἀνθρώπων οἱ εὐήλιοι. τότε ξυνεῖναι λέγουσιν, ὅτι τῷ Ἡλίῳ δοκεῖ ὑπανίστασθαι, καθάπερ οἱ τὸ κρεῖττον ὀρθοὶ θεραπεύοντες. θύσαντες οὖν Ἡλίῳ τε Αἰθίοπι καὶ Ἠῴῳ Μέμνονι, τουτὶ γὰρ ἔφραζον οἱ ἱερεῖς, τὸν μὲν ἀπὸ τοῦ αἴθειν τε καὶ θάλπειν, τὸν δὲ ἀπὸ τῆς μητρὸς ἐπονομάζοντες, ἐπορεύοντο ἐπὶ καμήλων ἐς τὰ τῶν Γυμνῶν ἤθη.

About Memnon Damis gives this account . . .

The *agalma* itself faces the sun, and is still beardless. It is of black stone, with both its feet together, according to the style of *agalmata* in Daedalus' time, and presses its arms straight down on its throne, in the position of a sitter just getting up. This position, the expression of its eyes, and the celebrated look of its lips, as if it was about to speak, did not seem particularly wonderful to them at first, they say, because the statue did not appear clearly. But when the sun's ray struck the statue, as it did at sunrise, they could not withhold their amazement.

It immediately spoke as the ray touched its lips, and fixed its eyes cheerfully upon the light, as men do who are fond of basking in the sun. It was then, they say, that they realised that it seemed to be rising in honour of the Sun, like those who stand to worship powers above. So they sacrificed to the Ethiopian Sun and Memnon of the Dawn, as the priests instructed them (they give these titles to the sun because he 'heats' and 'glows', to Memnon because of his mother). The party then travelled on camels to the region of the Naked Ones.

We have a situation here that is most unusual in classical studies – a literary account of the viewing of an image that survives in tandem with the image itself, as well as epigraphic records of the statue's viewing by Graeco-Roman contemporaries. Significantly, Philostratus presents us with a narrative of religious revelation that echoes the non-fictional epiphanic experiences we find inscribed upon the colossus.[35] For example, one Petronius Secundus, prefect of Egypt, wrote in 92 CE, 'You spoke' (φθέγξαο), which is followed by

---

[35] On the literary qualities of the Memnon epigrams ascribed to the empress Sabina's companion Julia Balbilla and others, see Bowie (1990: 61–6) and Bravi (2007: 87–8), with a brief note by West (1977).

a quotation from the *Odyssey* describing the statue as ἀκτεῖσιν βαλλόμενος πυρίναις, 'struck by the fiery rays of the sun', just as Damis' account here speaks of the statue's utterance (φθέγξασθαι) 'when the sun's ray struck the statue' (προσβαλούσης . . . τῆς ἀκτῖνος).[36]

The Philostratean passage also bears strong similarities to an epiphanic inscription famously discussed by Nock from the south portico of the Temple of Mandulis at Talmis, dated to the third century CE.[37] Here, too, the pilgrim writes of the manifestation of a divine being in the form of light, and refers to the image of a deity within a shrine, recounting a dream vision of the god Helios which anticipates (or mirrors) the effect produced by the rays of the rising sun streaming into the dark temple and illuminating the god's *xoanon*.[38] Nock compares the Mandulis vision to the statue of Serapis in his temple at Alexandria, where the first rays of the sun supposedly touched the cult image on the lips, so that, according to the Christian writer Rufinus, 'Serapis seemed to be greeted by the Sun with a kiss'.[39] In both the inscription and Philostratus' biography, the pilgrims begin in ignorance, unclear as to how they should view the sacred image and, by means of an epiphany generated by the statue's 'animation' by the light of the rising sun, experience a revelation about the identity of the image and the deity it represents. The pilgrims subsequently perform ritual actions, guided by the priests of the cult. This movement from ignorance to wisdom is also implied by an inscription located behind Memnon's left foot, which reads:

[Α]ὐδήεντά σε, Μέμνον, ἐγὼ Παιὼ|ν ὁ Σιδήτης
τὸ πρὶν ἐπυνθα|νόμην, νῦν δὲ παρὼν ἔμαθον.

[36] Bernand and Bernard (1960: no. 13.7–8), a Greek couplet inserted into a longer Latin inscription. The literary pretensions of many of these testimonies are exemplified by one inscription, which proclaims, 'I will make mention of you in my books' (Bernand and Bernard, 1960: no. 22, dated to 122/3 CE). Compare the inscriptional evidence from the Temple of Seti I at Abydos, known as the Memnonion, where a group of visitors recorded that each of them 'viewed' (ἐθήσατο): see Rutherford (2000: 140; 2003: 178), on Perdrizet and Lefebvre (1919: no. 424).

[37] *Sammelbuch* no. 4127; revised version by Nock (1972: vol. I, 357–400).

[38] The inscription continues: 'I had a vision (ἐνθεασάμενος) and found rest for my soul. For thou didst grant my prayer and show me thyself (κατ]εδειξάς μοι σεαυτόν) going through the heavenly vault; then washing thyself in the holy water of immortality thou appeardst (φαί[νη) again. Thou didst come at due season to thy shrine, making thy rising, and giving to thy *xoanon* and to thy shrine divine breath (ἔμπνοιαν) and great power. Then I knew thee (ἔνθα σε ἔγνων), Mandulis, to be the Sun, the allseeing Master, king of all, allpowerful Eternity (Αἰῶνα)' (9–20, translation A. D. Nock).

[39] Nock (1972: 376); Rufinus *Historia Ecclesiastica* 11.23: 'ita ut inspectante populo osculo salutatus Serapis videretur a Sole'.

I, Paion of Side, who previously enquired about your speaking,
Memnon, have now experienced it right here.[40]

Paion's movement from enquiry to experience (from ἐπυνθανόμην to
ἔμαθον) figures precisely the process of *theōria* – curiosity about the sacred
and a desire for proximity to the divine, followed by the acquisition of
knowledge through the act of going to see (or in this case, to hear). It is
not, perhaps, surprising that in the fourth century Jerome was moved to
claim (following Eusebius) that the colossus of Memnon had been silenced
at the birth of Christ, for the image's eerily numinous power gave it a
fame that spread throughout the Graeco-Roman world, constructing it as a
paradigmatic focus of the theoric urge to experience sacred mysteries.[41]

Despite these correlations between Damis' description of Memnon and
epigraphic evidence for the statue's epiphanic effect, however, certain details
in Philostratus' text do not add up. Pausanias writes that the colossus
was 'broken in two', and that the upper part was 'thrown down' on the
ground, rather in the manner of Shelley's *Ozymandias*. Yet in Damis' account
Memnon's dawn cry is described not as a twang emerging from the bowels
of the colossus, but an utterance that comes from his very lips, while the light
of the sun is caught and reflected by the statue's eyes. As we can see from
Figure 7.1, if the colossus' upper half was lying in ruins on the ground, the
lips and eyes cannot have been visible. Even if its torso and head had been
restored by the time that Philostratus was writing in the early third century,
they cannot have been during Apollonius' lifetime in the first century (i.e.,
earlier than Hadrian or Pausanias). Moreover, there was never a time at
which the statue both uttered a cry at dawn *and* had a visible torso and
head, for we are told by later sources that once the image was repaired,
it ceased to make a sound. There are further errors in Damis' account:
he only mentions one figure, whereas the singing statue was (and still is)
accompanied by an identical, silent figure; he tells us that the statue is black
(μέλας), whereas it is actually made of yellow-grey quartzite sandstone; and
he claims the statue 'presses its arms straight down on its throne, in the
position of a sitter just getting up'. In fact, as can still be seen today, both
figures' arms rest upon their knees rather than their thrones, and rather than

---

[40] Bernand and Bernand (1960: no. 12, dated 89–91 CE). On Paion's career as a professional poet,
see Bowie (1990: 66).

[41] Bowersock (1984: 24), from Jerome (Eusebius) *Chron.* ed. Helm, 17. Bowersock comments that
a ninth-century manuscript in Merton College, Oxford, adds 'cuius statui usque ad adventum
Christi sole oriente vocem dare dicebatur'.

appearing to be in the process of rising, they are firmly rooted to their seats (Figure 7.1).

How are we to interpret these anomalies? Glen Bowersock has claimed that, since Damis' account is so erroneous, 'Philostratus can never have seen the colossus of Memnon or spoken to anyone who did, nor have read an account from someone who had seen it. So much for Damis'.[42] Yet, as Jaap-Jan Flinterman has commented, 'Rivers of ink have flowed over the poor Syrian and his scrapbook', and it is now generally accepted that the 'scraps from the manger' (ἐκφατνίσματα, 1.19.3) that Philostratus attributes to his source function as a fictional *Beglaubigungsapparat*, or 'plausibility-enhancing device', rather than as an authentic citation.[43] At key points within the text, Philostratus seems to problematise his source's unreliability overtly, so drawing attention to the biography's fictional aspects; he even introduces a conversation reported by Damis during the Indian episode with the non-committal comment, 'I should not leave it out, since one might do well neither to believe nor to disbelieve all the details' (καὶ γὰρ κέρδος εἴη μήτε πιστεύειν, μήτε ἀπιστεῖν πᾶσιν, 3.45.1). It must, therefore, be significant that the awkward Memnon passage is introduced with the phrase 'About Memnon Damis gives this account' (Περὶ δὲ τοῦ Μέμνονος τάδε ἀναγράφει Δάμις), and is written entirely in reported speech.

Why should Philostratus wish to highlight the fictional nature of his text in relation to the colossus of Memnon? As I suggested above, most viewing episodes within the *Life* are led by Apollonius in the role of *exēgētēs*. At Olympia, for example, he acts as an *Imagines*-style pedagogue, explaining the iconography of an archaic kouros statue of the athlete Milo to viewers within the sanctuary (4.28).[44] Why, rather than giving us a scenario in which Apollonius explains the *thauma* that is Memnon to his confused followers, emphasising his knowledge of religious arcana and pious attitude towards ancient cults and Homeric heroes, does Philostratus' narrative parade a

---

[42] Bowersock (1984: 28).

[43] Flinterman (1995: 79); Whitmarsh (2001b: 229). For summaries of the Damis debate, see Bowie (1978), G. Anderson (1986: 169 n. 1), Koskenniemi (1994: 9–15) and Flinterman (1995: 79–88). On Damis as a fictional device, see E. Meyer (1917), Bowie (1978), Raynor (1984), Dzielska (1986: 19–49), J. A. Francis (1995: 83–9), Swain (1996: 383–4), Whitmarsh (2001b: 227–9) and, on the fictionality of the text in general, Schirren (2005: 38–50). On Philostratus' possible use of a pseudepigraphic text from the second century CE, see Speyer (1974: 48–53) and Goulet (1981: 176–8). For attempts to defend Damis as a historical figure, see Phillimore (1912) and Grosso (1954).

[44] See Rousselle (2001: 395–6), who points out that Apollonius' analysis of the Milo statue is also erroneous; although Milo competed at Olympia from 532 to 516 BCE, Apollonius' description conforms to the Daedalic style, dated to the seventh century BCE. On the statue's latent Pythagorean associations (left to the reader to surmise), see Miles (2009: 135–9).

mis-viewing of the colossus, ostentatiously attributed to an unreliable source?[45] It is suggestive that in the *Heroicus*, where Memnon's colossus is described in less detail, the vine-dresser merely claims that 'whenever the sun sends out its first ray (ἀκτῖνα πρώτην) the statue breaks out with a voice by which it greets the cult attendants', and makes none of the ostentatious 'errors' we find in Damis' account (26.16). In the *Life of Apollonius*, by contrast, we are dependent upon a less reliable narrator, and Apollonius is not mentioned at all, but fades into the background while the narrator's attempt to describe the image and its effect is focalised through Damis. This shift in the text's presentation of images, combined with Damis' apparently erroneous method of viewing, presents the reader with a conundrum: what is the correct way to look at works of art? In the case of statues such as the colossus of Memnon, where issues of vision, cult practice and religious knowledge are foregrounded, what is the correct way to view *sacred* images? Without Apollonius to guide him or her, the reader is put into the same position as the confused and ignorant Damis (or, indeed, the merchant-sailor in the Piraeus). In Ethiopia, the carefully staged errors within the text suggest that there may be clues hidden within Damis' account, and that his mis-viewing may actually have certain import for the reader's experience of the Memnon phenomenon.

That Memnon featured prominently in Second Sophistic literature is suggested by Lucian's satirical dialogue *Philopseudes* ('The Lover of Lies'), where he appears in the liar's report of his experiences with a certain 'holy man' in Egypt.[46] He tells his interlocutor:

When I was living in Egypt during my youth (my father had sent me travelling for the purpose of completing my education), I took it into my head to sail up to Koptos and go from there to the statue of Memnon in order to hear it sound that marvellous salutation to the rising sun. Well, what I heard from it was not a meaningless voice (ἄσημόν τινα φωνήν), as is the general experience of common people; Memnon himself actually opened his mouth and delivered me an oracle in seven verses. (33)[47]

Here we find a humorous adaptation of the Memnon phenomenon, in which listening to the singing statue is presented as a classic case of religious gullibility. Part of the joke must lie in the fact that Lucian's readers realised

---

[45] On the ironic qualities of the *VA*, see Schirren (2005: 286–318; 2009); on the function of Damis' erroneous interpretations in relation to Apollonius' authority elsewhere in the text, see Miles (2009).

[46] On this text, see Ogden (2007).

[47] Translation from A. M. Harmon's Loeb Classical Library edition, 1921.

that Memnon actually had no mouth. The liar had visited in Egypt ἐπὶ παιδείας ('for his education'), yet the pattern of epiphany and revelation – the experience of *theōria* underlying the actual testimonies of Memnon's visitors – is subverted by the comically exaggerated nature of his claim. Why, then, in an apparently serious account of the viewing of Memnon by Apollonius and his followers, do we find a similar exaggeration – that sound actually issues from Memnon's lips – attributed to Damis? Bowersock argues that, 'Unlike Philostratus, Lucian was a humorist of the first rank . . . The sober Philostratus may have been seriously misled into composing his novel about Apollonius by a piece of witty but deliberate misrepresentation.'[48] Yet one of the most ostentatious aspects of the *Life* is Philostratus' repeated demonstration of his superior, playful command of his source material. If he does echo Lucian's references to Memnon, then it is more likely that our author has appropriated the satiric sketch for his own ends, emphasising the relationship between viewing and imagination that a dramatic moment of mis-viewing can spotlight. If Damis is also a 'lover of lies', then he is so for a reason.

In answer to this conundrum, we might look to Nock's comparison of the Mandulis vision to the statue of Serapis in his temple at Alexandria, where the first rays of the sun supposedly touched the cult image on the lips.[49] Read in the light of such pilgrimage practices in Roman Egypt, Philostratus' narrative appears to conflate Memnon's sonic phenomenon with the visual effect produced by Serapis, as if to present his readers with a synthesised, archetypal experience of an 'Egyptian statue greeting the dawn'. This is no heavy-handed amalgam of traditions, but a sophisticated blend of Egyptian *exempla* that blends seamlessly into the religious *Realien* that form the backdrop for Apollonius' travels. Like the Thessalian pilgrimage to Achilles described in the *Heroicus*, the Memnon passage is ostensibly a plausible (yet probably fictional) account of religious practice designed to serve a particular purpose within the text as a whole.[50] This creative relationship to social context characterises the *Life of Apollonius* in general, which is on one hand a historiographical work deeply embedded in Greek religious and cultural tradition, and on the other hand a highly contrived piece of imaginative biography in which fictional elements are frequently employed in order to access deeper truths.[51] Significantly, in contrast to the ubiquitous statement of the inscriptional evidence ('I heard'), Philostratus' passage shifts the emphasis from the experience of hearing Memnon to the

---

[48] Bowersock (1984: 29).   [49] Nock (1933: 77).
[50] *Heroicus* 67–70: see Chapter 5, n. 113.   [51] Cf. J. A. Francis (1998) and Schirren (2005).

way the statue is *seen*; the statue is not a *thauma* until it 'appears clearly' (ἐνεργά φαίνεσθαι) in the light of the rising sun. Damis describes Memnon's posture in detail, constructing an elaborate ekphrasis that draws the reader into the transformative experience narrated by the text. Ultimately, the dominant impression with which we are left is not one of sound but of light. Yet this epiphanic – and potentially programmatic – experience is of an image that *does not exist* in the form in which it is described.

The shift from an aural to visual experience is reinforced by Damis' erroneous description of the statue's posture, which continues the theme of animation by claiming that Memnon presses his arms down upon his throne, thus seeming to rise 'in honour of the Sun, like those who stand to worship powers above'. This dynamic shift imbues the image with an incipient movement, enhancing its epiphanic qualities. Damis' comment is also, perhaps, an allusion to Phidias' Zeus, which, as Strabo commented, would 'unroof the temple' if the statue's epiphanic potential were fulfilled and the god 'arose and stood erect'.[52] The description of Memnon as not only a god, but also a celebrant, however, simultaneously links the statue's function to that of its viewers, as worshippers of the sun. Momentarily infused with the spirit and power of the divinised hero, the statue does not only speak; he also *sees*. The process of revelation is thus transmitted from the light of the sun, via the eyes of the image, which are 'fixed cheerfully upon the light', to the eyes of those who view it: *theōria* is successfully achieved through the visual (rather than aural) interaction of god, statue and pilgrim.

The pilgrims' passage from ignorance to knowledge is completed in the final passage of the Memnon episode, in which an exegetical conversation with local priests leads to aetiological explanations that reinforce the revelation facilitated by the statue's animation. Despite the fact that Memnon stands at the entrance to Ethiopia, the colossal *sēma* of a foreign, ancient culture, the mythological *aition* that provides final proof of the statue's religious significance is constructed according to Greek etymologies and epic poetry.[53] Revelation experienced in visionary terms is thus explained by recourse to language and Hellenic literary tradition. In this sense the episode is paradigmatic of the scenes of viewing and *Kunsttheorie* that take place throughout the *Life* (and, as we saw in Chapter 5, the *Heroicus*):

---

[52] Strabo 8.3.30: see Chapter 2, 89–90.

[53] On the role of Memnon in the epic poem *Aithiopis* and its relationship to the *Iliad*, see Willcock (1997: 179–84) and West (2003). On the relationship between Hellenes and non-Greeks in the *Life*, see Swain (1996: 386–8).

although the acquisition of philosophical knowledge and religious understanding is repeatedly presented as a visual experience, *sophia* is ultimately
communicated in verbal form, expressed in both the intellectual heritage
through which Apollonius constructs himself as the Hellene extraordinaire
or the self-conscious intertextuality of the biography as a whole.

It is telling that Philostratus' emphasis upon the importance of verbal
transmission in the Memnon episode of the *Life of Apollonius* also characterises his ekphrasis of the hero in the *Imagines*, where the description of
a painting of the dead Memnon at Troy suddenly segues into an epiphanic
viewing of the deified warrior's colossal image in Ethiopia (1.7.15–25):

Look! Memnon has been stolen away and is at the edge of the painting. Where is
he? In what part of the earth? No tomb of Memnon is anywhere to be seen but in
Ethiopia he himself has been transformed into a statue of black stone (μεταβεβληκὼς
εἰς λίθον μέλανα). The attitude is that of a seated person, but the figure is that of
Memnon yonder, if I mistake not, and the ray of the sun falls on the statue (καὶ
προσβάλλει τῷ ἀγάλματι ἡ ἀκτὶς τοῦ Ἡλίου). For the sun, striking the lips of
Memnon as a plectrum strikes a lyre, seems to summon a voice from them, and by
this speech-producing artifice (λαλοῦντι σοφίσματι) consoles the Goddess of the
Day.[54]

Philostratus appropriates the epiphanic effects of the colossus in order to
introduce the notion of sound to his ekphrasis, literally 'summon[ing] a
voice' from Memnon. Yet it is ironic that in order to animate the subject of
the painting, he must resort to a statue within it, performing an ontological
shift that is signalled by a sudden leap in location and medium, and the
speaker's injunction, 'Look!' (ἰδού).[55] As in the *Life of Apollonius*, Philostratus claims the colossus is made of 'black stone' (εἰς λίθον μέλανα), yet
here the reasoning behind this apparent error is more overt, for the material
of the statue directly echoes the skin of the real Memnon's corpse at Troy,
where 'the pure black shows a trace of ruddiness' (ἀκράτως ἐν αὐτῷ μέλαν
ὑποφαίνει τι ἄνθους); despite the contradictory visual evidence in Ethiopia,

[54] Translation from A. Fairbanks's Loeb Classical Library edition, 1931.
[55] Cf. Bryson (1995: 186–7): 'This strange, hallucinatory power of ekphrasis calls on the capacities
of words and pictures to describe the world, but goes beyond their several powers into a
visionary moment when "Look!" becomes the only appropriate response'. Note that the
relationship between Memnon the Homeric hero and Memnon the colossus is also
problematised in the *Heroicus*, where the vine-dresser claims that there were in fact two
Memnons – an Ethiopian king who ruled during the time of the Trojan War, and a Trojan
youth who came of age during the war and performed the deeds celebrated in the epic cycle
(26.16–19). Here the 'rewriting' of Homer is thus employed to explain inconsistencies between
literary and archaeological evidence for past events.

Memnon's image can be viewed in a Greek context only through the prism of his epic identity as a dark-skinned hero.[56] Again, we find a reference to the mouth (στόμα) of the statue, which ignores the damaged upper body of the Theban image. Significantly, the Ethiopian statue's ability to emit sound is called a 'speaking *sophisma*', a neat reminder of the persuasive authority of verbal representation, and the author's ability to direct the ways in which his protagonists respond to the images within his text.

The verbal pyrotechnics of Memnon's treatment in the *Imagines*, then, suggest that rather than resting on faulty research, Philostratus' description of the statue in the *Life of Apollonius* is rather more subtle. Damis' viewing of Memnon actually offers a highly creative response to the statue, imaginatively supplementing the incomplete figure with visual details that enhance the epiphanic qualities of the viewing process. This manoeuvre does not necessarily annul Damis' value as a narrative voice, but demonstrates the degree to which he has absorbed the teachings of Apollonius himself. When discussing the Porus reliefs in book 2, Apollonius had stressed the importance of regarding mimesis as a creative process required not just of the artist creating a naturalistic image, but also of the viewer, for 'those who view the works of painters need the imitative faculty (μιμητικῆς)'; in order to view and respond appropriately, they must first conceive in their minds an εἴδωλον of the thing represented (2.22). This is, in effect, what Damis presents us with in his ekphrasis of the colossus of Memnon. It is as if he has fully internalised the lesson given to him in Taxila, to the extent that he no longer sees what the image presents in physical terms, but (perhaps a little too enthusiastically) presents his *mental* picture of the statue, which is informed by both Memnon's Homeric identity and a general familiarity with sacred Egyptian statuary. In this way his viewing runs counter to the very materiality of the object, replacing it with a *huponoia* (or 'intellectual conception') of its perceived prototype. Damis even incorporates an example given by Apollonius in book 2, where he refers to the use of mimesis in the representation of racial characteristics:

If we draw one of these Indians with a white line, he will surely seem black (μέλας δήπου δόξει); the snub nose, fuzzy hair, prominent jaw, and a look of surprise, as it were, in the eyes, lend blackness to the picture (μελαίνει τὰ ὁρώμενα), and convey an Indian at least to an educated observer (τοῖς γε μὴ ἀνοήτως ὁρῶσιν).

To Apollonius, the viewer's ability to generate a *mimēma* of Indian ethnicity in his mind allows him to perceive dark skin in a painting by identifying

---

[56] Cf. Newby (2009) on the tension between the literary and the visual in the *Imagines*.

other racial characteristics, even when the image he beholds is painted in white.[57] We have already noted how Damis explicitly mentions that Memnon's colossus was made 'of black stone' (λίθου δὲ εἶναι μέλανος), despite the lighter colour of the colossus itself, and that when the sun's rays struck at dawn, the statue 'fixed its eyes cheerfully upon the light, as men do who are fond of basking in the sun (οἷα τῶν ἀνθρώπων οἱ εὐήλιοι)'. Is Damis here applying Apollonius' ekphrasis of the Indian 'Other' to his own ekphrasis of the Ethiopian 'Other', trying a little too hard to please his teacher – to be an 'educated observer' of representations of ethnic difference, and thereby behold the heroic Memnon himself by means of his statue?[58]

The Memnon passage expresses the pilgrim's desire to encounter the divine through the mediatory powers of sacred images. Yet Philostratus' text overtly destabilises its own narrative, thereby highlighting the complex combination of influences upon practices of viewing. The epiphanic qualities of the Memnon experience are not simply generated by beholding the colossus itself, but are also driven by internalised mental concepts formed through knowledge of language and myth, while the act of viewing becomes yet more complex when it is subsequently narrated in verbal form (as Philostratus repeatedly reminds us in the *Imagines*).[59] The most important element for both viewers and readers is the engagement of the intellect: the *theōria* achieved by Apollonius' followers, while prompted by a visual image, can only be truly experienced as a mental phenomenon in which the visual is supplemented by religious and philosophical *sophia*. It is not surprising that the Memnon passage finishes with a Greek etymology, for this seemingly sophistic twisting of Ethiopian cult back to Hellenic linguistic concerns demonstrates precisely the cognitive processes required – in Apollonius' philosophy – for the attainment of true wisdom. As he comments in book 4, in similar language to Dio, whereas the Zeus of Phidias is only 'to be seen' (φαίνεσθαι), the Zeus of Homer 'is imagined' (ὑπονοεῖσθαι): the superior mode of visualisation is that which involves the faculty of mind.[60] In this sense both the Phidias-Homer debate and Damis' mis-viewing of Memnon highlight the problematic issues involved in looking at religious images according to notions of mimesis. While Apollonius' mimetic theory may be appropriate for looking at the historical narrative reliefs at Taxila,

[57] On this passage, see also Birmelin (1933: 163–5).

[58] On the representation of dark-skinned peoples in Greco-Roman art, see Snowden (1991).

[59] See Elsner (1995: 28), who comments that 'These descriptions were not seen as dependent on prior images (as a modern art historian's description would be); they were independent and self-sufficient works of rhetorical art in their own right.'

[60] Cf. Watson (1988: 63–4, 71–2).

the concept of 'imitation', which relies on the viewer's acquaintance with a visible prototype, is unhelpful when it comes to representing and viewing gods and *daimones*. That Damis is required to mis-view Memnon in order to gain his epiphanic experience implies that pious viewers need *something else* in order to engage correctly with the anthropomorphic images of traditional Greek religion. This is the question that Apollonius subsequently addresses in his conversation with the gymnosophists.

Through philosophy to vision: the allegory of Prodicus

Leaving behind the colossus of Memnon, Apollonius and his followers travel to a hill beyond the Nile where the community of 'naked philosophers' is centred. They immediately encounter problems owing to a slanderous envoy sent by Apollonius' rival Euphrates, who accuses him of intellectual arrogance, the promotion of Indian philosophy over other doctrines, and the practice of false magic (6.7). Apollonius' subsequent debate with the gymnosophists' leader, Thespesion, is accordingly presented as a form of *apologia*, in which the sage justifies the importance of Brahman precepts while setting them within a Hellenic context, thereby demonstrating his superior wisdom. The apologetic character of the *Life* has been discussed by Simon Swain in relation to Apollonius' troubled confrontations with imperial power.[61] We might also read Apollonius' refutation of the charges of magic and absorption of Eastern wisdom into a Greek world-view as part of a strategy of conspicuous philhellenism espoused by intellectuals such as Philostratus in response to the rapid spread of Christianity.[62] Certainly, the Ethiopian episode allows him to present a triumphant form of philosophical and religious self-legitimation that complements and anticipates the more political apologetic of the biography's climax. While Thespesion may seek to cast Apollonius in the role of plaintiff, the sage subverts his attempts in order to present himself once more as a pedagogue and *exēgētēs*, no longer learning (as he did from the Brahmans), but taking the role of supreme teacher. 'I have not come here to take your advice about a way of life,' he

---

[61] E.g., the Nero episode (4.35–47), his persecution by Domitian (7.1–34) and his defence speech (8.1–10); see Swain (1996: 381–95; 1999: 158, where he comments that Apollonius' self-defence at 6.11 forms a 'lengthy technical *apologia* for philosophy as a spiritual system of personal living').

[62] See above, n. 4. On the ambivalence surrounding the concept of γοητεία (sorcery) in the imperial period and Philostratus' defence of Apollonius from this charge, see Gasparro (2007), together with Versnel (1991) and Frankfurter (1997).

proclaims to the gymnosophists, for 'I am better qualified to advise *you* about choosing a philosophy . . . I will teach you how right I was to choose my path, since no better has ever come to my attention' (6.11).

Thespesion calls upon Apollonius to justify his adoption of Indian thinking by contrasting the gymnosophists' avowedly simple doctrine with the elaborate complexities of the Brahmans' approach. Yet throughout his extended debate with the sage, Thespesion continually appeals to the traditions of Greek religion and philosophy in order to support his arguments in favour of Ethiopian wisdom; again, the attractions of foreign lore are explored through the prism of Hellenism. Apollonius' sophistic skill as the ultimate Hellene, however, naturally allows him to appropriate the Greek *exempla* that Thespesion employs in order to justify and promote his own teachings. Ultimately, Apollonius' influence as not only a representative of traditional religious values but also a guide to how to think and worship (so improving upon those traditions) is demonstrated by his justification of Greek anthropomorphism through the doctrine of *phantasia* (6.19). By formulating a means of viewing the gods that unites the intellectual and the sacred, Apollonius presents a model of *theōria* that seemingly reconciles the tensions intrinsic to Greek forms of image worship, thus completing his self-presentation not as a sorcerer (*magos*, 1.2), but as the ultimate arbiter of relations between the human and divine.[63]

While Damis' description of the colossus of Memnon anticipates the religious themes of the *phantasia* debate, Thespesion presents us with an image that anticipates its philosophical aspect. In contrasting the philosophical systems of Ethiopia and India (6.10), the gymnosophist employs the allegory of Heracles' choice between Virtue and Vice attributed to the fifth-century BCE sophist Prodicus, charging Apollonius to 'think of yourself standing between the Wisdom of India, and that of our land'. Following Xenophon's association of the 'Choice of Heracles' with Socrates in his *Memorabilia* (2.1.21–34), Greek authors had frequently exploited the allegory's juxtaposition of competing abstract ideas in the form of personifications.[64] Unsurprisingly, Philostratus modifies the tradition in ways that complement his presentation of Apollonius elsewhere in the *Life*. The most notable of these is Thespesion's introductory comment that, 'In the *logoi* of painting you

[63] On Apollonius' self-defence against the charge of sorcery (as suggested by, e.g., Lucian *Alexander* 5 and Cassius Dio 77.18.4) at 8.7, see Swain (1999) and Flinterman (2009).

[64] See Alpers (1912), Panofsky (1930), Nestle (1936) and Sansone (2004). Alpers compares the allegory to the Persians' choice of democracy, oligarchy or monarchy at Herodotus 3.80–4 and the struggle between the personified *Dikaios* and *Adikos Logos* in Aristophanes' *Clouds*.

have seen the *Heracles* of Prodicus' (εἶδες ἐν ζωγραφίας λόγοις καὶ τὸν τοῦ Προδίκου Ἡρακλέα). This immediately raises a problem, for just as Damis' description of Memnon was ultimately of an image that does not exist, so Thespesion's account of the allegory of Prodicus erroneously presents the scene not as a philosophical parable, but as a painting (*zōgraphia*). Yet despite the allegory's popularity in literary sources, there exist no extant references to an actual visual representation of the Choice of Heracles in antiquity, nor any suggestion that Prodicus' allegory was presented as an ekphrasis.[65] Panofsky's study of 'Hercules am Scheidewege' in later Western art, for example, can offer as an antique model only a relief of Heracles with two of the Hesperides.[66] If there was a famous painting of the scene in antiquity, then every trace of it has been lost.

That Philostratus was familiar with the allegory in its literary form is demonstrated by two references to Prodicus in the *Lives of the Sophists*, in both of which it is presented as a textually transmitted *logos*.[67] Yet it suits Philostratus' creative employment of images in the *Life of Apollonius* as a whole that such a painting never existed at all. Significantly, Thespesion emphasises the visual quality of the allegory by opening with the statement 'You have seen' (εἶδες), yet the oxymoron that follows in the phrase ἐν ζωγραφίας λόγοις (literally 'in the words of painting') perfectly captures the problematic relationship between image and text (6.10). Is he referring to literary ekphraseis of a painting, or to a form of narrative painting that communicates Prodicus' *logos* in visual terms?[68] Such ambiguity anticipates the imaginary ekphrasis that follows, in which Thespesion adapts the

---

[65] Xenophon introduces the allegory with the words, 'In the essay *On Heracles*' (ἐν τῷ συγγράμματι τῷ περὶ Ἡρακλέους), with no reference to an image. Maximus of Tyre refers to Prodicus' allegory in *Dial.* 14 and adapts the choice of Virtue and Vice to 'Friend and Flatterer', but although he describes the women's clothing, he does not refer to a painting, only to Prodicus' text. For imitations and adaptations of the motif, see Philo *Sacr.* 20–44, *De merc. mer.* 2–4; Ovid *Amores* 3.1, *Tabula* of Cebes 5–7, 9–10, 15–22, Dio *Or.* 1.64–84, Sil. *Pun.* 15.18–128, Luc. *Somn.* 6–16, Gal. *Protr.* 2–5 and Them. *Or.* 22. See also Joly (1956) and Snell (1967).

[66] Panofsky (1930: pl. 45, fig. 66, a relief now in the collection of the Villa Albani, Rome). See also Picard (1951, 1953), who likewise struggles to find any convincing evidence.

[67] *VS* 1.482–3: 'Prodicus of Ceos had composed a certain pleasant fable, in which Virtue and Vice came to Heracles in the shape of women . . . For this story Prodicus wrote a rather long epilogue, and then he toured the cities and gave recitations of the story in public, for hire.' At *VS* 496 we find again, 'Even Xenophon did not disdain to relate the fable of Prodicus (τὸν τοῦ Προδίκου λόγον) called *The Choice of Heracles*'; the verbal nature of the tale is emphasised still further by Philostratus' comment: 'As for the language of Prodicus, why should I describe its characteristics, when Xenophon has given so complete a sketch of it?' Translations from W. C. Wright's Loeb Classical Library edition, 1922.

[68] Note that while Jones's Loeb edition (2005–6) translates the phrase as 'descriptions of pictures', F. C. Conybeare's Loeb translation (1912) opts for the visual emphasis 'in painted narratives'.

Prodican image into an elaborate orgy of description distinctly different from Xenophon's more restrained text, complete with a deliciously sophistic hint at nudity that is entirely fitting for a 'naked philosopher': Virtue 'would show herself naked (γυμνὴ δ' ἂν ἐφαίνετο) except that she knows womanly proprieties'. It is surely provocative that this most Hellenic of philosophical allegories, composed by an Attic sophist, placed in the mouth of Socrates and then extensively employed by Cynic thinkers, is employed by an Ethiopian sage in order to contrast two distinctly un-Greek philosophical systems.

By turning Prodicus' fable into a painting, Philostratus echoes allegorical ekphraseis such as the *Tabula* of Cebes and Lucian's *Calumny*, while emphasising the importance of vision for the biography's presentation of the practice of wisdom.[69] Apollonius responds to Thespesion's visual challenge by reapplying Prodicus' allegorical forms to his own adoption of Pythagorean doctrine, which is presented not as an ekphrasis, but as an epiphanic encounter with Philosophia herself.[70] In this way he appropriates and recasts the exemplum so that it once more refers firmly to Greek models of wisdom, while presenting his own philosophy as an all-embracing union of vision and knowledge.[71] In Xenophon's account of the Choice of Heracles in the *Memorabilia*, Virtue advises the hero, 'If you want the favour of the gods, you must worship the gods: . . . if you covet honour from a city, you must aid that city: if you are fain to win the admiration of all Hellas for virtue, you must strive to do good to Hellas' (2.1.28).[72] Such responsibilities, of course, are easily fulfilled by our Philostratean hero, who, through his repeated demonstrations of *sophia*, surpasses every model incorporated into Thespesion's model of the allegory, including that of Socrates himself (a factor that will be significant in his subsequent critique of mimesis). Yet, as Anton-Hermann Chroust points out, Xenophon's portrayal of Socrates owes much to theories laid down by the Cynic philosopher Antisthenes,

[69] On the *Calumnia non temere credendum* and its reception, see Massing (1990, 2007).

[70] On the tradition that Apollonius himself composed a *Life of Pythagoras* (mentioned in the *Suda*, A 3420) see Flinterman (1995: 77–9), who notes that the work is not mentioned by Philostratus, but that Apollonius does emerge from the Oracle of Trophonius at 8.19.2 with a book containing the doctrines of Pythagoras (δόξαι Πυθαγόρου), an association between epiphanic encounter and Pythagorean doctrine that echoes the allegory of book 6.

[71] Compare 8.7.17, where Apollonius defends his long hair by alluding to the Dorian traditions of Sparta, and 2.40, where he refuses valuable gifts but accepts linen from the Indian king Phraotes because 'it resembles a philosopher's cloak of the old-fashioned, genuine Attic kind'. On Pythagoreanism in the *Life of Apollonius*, see Flinterman (1995: 167–89; 2009) and J. A. Francis (1995: 105–8, 126–7).

[72] Translation from O. J. Todd's Loeb Classical Library edition, 1979.

who developed Heracles' role as a model for philosophical *ponos*.[73] The allegory therefore implies that Apollonius' true model is in fact Heracles, paradigmatic benefactor of Greece and, ultimately, a deified mortal. Such philosophical syncretism allows Apollonius not only to absorb his Socratic heritage, but also to appropriate and surpass the *sophia* of the Cynic school, with its negative attitude to oracles, cult practices and religious metaphysics. The sage thus presents himself as a new Heracles – the embodiment of Cynic heroism – while simultaneously embodying the traditional religious values to which the Cynics were opposed.[74] That he finds a superior philosophical model in the personification of Pythagoreanism reminds us that the Prodican allegory actually had its roots in Pythagorean doctrine, specifically Pythagoras' comparison of life's progress to the letter Y, where the adolescent has to choose between the paths of virtue and vice (or, the philosophical or non-philosophical life).[75] Just as his protagonist incorporates and re-presents the ideas of his philosophical predecessors, so Philostratus demonstrates his superior mastery of his sources, placing an Athenian *exemplum* in the mouth of an Ethiopian, problematically turning a text into a painting, extensively elaborating its visual detail and, ultimately, restoring the image to its rightful founder through the agency of Hellas' new benefactor – Apollonius himself.

In line with the visionary language of the Memnon episode, Apollonius repeatedly associates his espousal of Pythagorean intellectual enquiry with the act of viewing, claiming, 'I saw (κατιδών) a sign of greatness in Pythagoras', then, 'Philosophy set the whole range of her doctrines before me, adorning each with its own special charms, and then told me to look at them (ἐκέλευσεν ἐς αὐτὰς βλέπειν) and choose wisely'. Finally, he tells us, 'I saw an ineffable form of wisdom (εἶδον σοφίας εἶδος ἄρρητον), which once won the devotion of Pythagoras'. The doctrine's status as ἄρρητον – *beyond the capabilities of language* – justifies the role of allegory in this passage, and thus the importance of visual experience for the communication of wisdom. Indeed, Apollonius' initiation into Pythagoreanism included a five-year vow of silence, following a practice that Philostratus, in his introduction to the *Life*, relates directly to the acquisition of sacred knowledge.[76] In this way,

---

[73] See Chroust (1957: esp. 101–34), with Böttiger (1829) and Alpers (1912: 8).

[74] On Apollonius' assimilation to Heracles in his 'ascension' from the Temple of Athena at Lindos, reported by Philostratus at 8.30, see Flinterman (2009: 237–40).

[75] Ruyt (1931). See also Guthrie (1987: 158, fig. 12, a picture from Geoffrey Tory's *Champfleury*, 1529, in which an ornamented Y figure is accompanied by a verse ascribed to one 'Maximinus' with a verse inspired by Xenophon's original allegory).

[76] 1.1.3: 'All Pythagoras's revelations his disciples considered law, and they honored him as an envoy from Zeus. Hence they practiced silence on celestial subjects, having heard many sacred

the ineffability of epiphanic encounter and the inadequacy of language in religious matters form a recurring theme that echoes the text's repeated interrogation of the limits of artistic representation. In both cases Apollonius offers a means of passing beyond the forms of *aporia* that can so easily inhibit the reader's own religious and intellectual journey.

Apollonius' choice of Pythagoreanism and espousal of its doctrines throughout the *Life* help to define the philosophy as the 'core element of Hellenism', reflecting its popularity and significance in the early third century CE, by which point certain Pythagorean precepts had been enthusiastically adopted by mainstream Platonism.[77] Apollonius' 'ekphrasis' of his initiation into philosophy in book 6 thus describes an experience of revelatory *theōria* that offers a crucial link between his intellectual quest for wisdom and the cognitive reliability that epiphany provided for traditional religious practice. This union of vision and knowledge is expressed by the personification of Pythagoreanism herself, who promises Apollonius:

καθαρῷ δὲ ὄντι σοι καὶ προγιγνώσκειν δώσω καὶ τοὺς ὀφθαλμοὺς οὕτω τι ἐμπλήσω ἀκτῖνος, ὡς διαγιγνώσκειν μὲν θεόν, γιγνώσκειν δὲ ἥρωα, σκιοειδῆ δ' ἐλέγχειν φαντάσματα, ὅτε ψεύδοιντο εἴδη ἀνθρώπων.

When you are pure, I will grant you the gift of foreknowledge, and I will so fill your eyes with light that you will recognise gods, know heroes, and unmask insubstantial *phantasmata* when they disguise themselves in human form. (6.19)

Here recognition (προγιγνώσκειν) is explicitly associated with the eyes (τοὺς ὀφθαλμούς), while Pythagoreanism's promise to fill Apollonius' eyes with light ([οὕτω] τι ἐμπλήσω ἀκτῖνος) echoes Damis' description of the eyes of Memnon, which gleamed in the light of the rising sun, thus recalling the text's earlier presentation of a narrative of revelation gained through the viewing of a sacred image. The epiphanic insight acquired through philosophy raises Apollonius to a higher plane of existence, as it were: he becomes a Memnon-like figure himself through the transformative power of true *sophia*. Like Protesilaos in the *Heroicus*, our sage can clearly distinguish between different supernatural categories and perceive the gods 'not by worshipping *agalmata* and conjectures, but by gaining visible association with

secrets which it would have been difficult to keep, except that they had learned first that even silence is a form of discourse'; see also 1.14–15 and 6.11.5. On silence in Pythagoreanism, see Flinterman (2009).

[77] Swain (1999: 159). On the growing popularity of Neopythagoreanism in this period, see Dillon (1977: 341–83), Flinterman (1995), Swain (1999: 165–78, 185–9) and Kahn (2001: 94–138), with sources in Guthrie (1987).

them'.[78] This is a crucial stage in Apollonius' progression to godlike status, which is also demonstrated by his faculty of precognition, and culminates in his own transformation into an object of *theōria* within the sanctuary of Olympia (8.15), where Philostratus tells us that 'the Greeks assembled in such excitement for his sake as they had never for any Olympics', to the extent that 'Hellas could barely keep from worshipping him (οὐ πόρρω τοῦ προσκυνεῖν αὐτόν)'.[79]

Apollonius' superior powers of vision, which enable him to distinguish between the divine, the heroic and the evil, are demonstrated by a number of episodes in the *Life*. He rids the city of Ephesus of a plague (4.10) by encouraging its inhabitants to stone an old beggar in the theatre who is simulating blindness by 'artfully blinking his eyes' (ἐπιμύων τοὺς ὀφθαλμοὺς τέχνῃ):

The Ephesians were puzzled by his meaning and shocked at the thought of killing someone who was a visitor and so destitute . . . But Apollonius was relentless, urging the Ephesians to crush him without pity. Some of them had begun to lob stones at him when, after seeming to blink, he suddenly glared and showed his eyes full of fire (ἀνέβλεψεν ἀθρόον, πυρός τε μεστοὺς τοὺς ὀφθαλμοὺς ἔδειξε). The Ephesians realised he was a demon and stoned him so thoroughly as to raise a pile of stones on him.

On removing the stones, the citizens discover that in his crushed state the demon has assumed its natural form as a rabid beast with the body of a Molossian hound, and a statue of Heracles Apotropaios (the 'Averter') is set up over the spot 'where the *phasma* was stoned'. Philostratus' use of the term *phasma* here anticipates Pythagoreanism's claim that by adopting her philosophical system, Apollonius will be able to 'unmask insubstantial *phantasmata* when they disguise themselves in human form'.[80] Significantly, the sage's extraordinary powers of perception, and the beast's fiendish

---

[78] *Heroicus* 7.3: see Chapter 5, 242–3.

[79] On Apollonius' godlike status, see Flinterman (2009), though contra, see Du Toit (1997: 307–10), who argues that Apollonius lives under the guidance of a personal *daimōn*, like Socrates, rather than attaining to daemonic status himself. Philostratus seems to leave the question of Apollonius' status deliberately open (see below): while he declines divine honours at 4.31 and claims he is not a *daimōn* at 7.32, we are told that he was worshipped at Tyana and called a son of Zeus (1.6), and that Damis regards him as 'godlike and superhuman' (θεία τε εἴη καὶ κρείττων) when he shakes off his fetters when imprisoned by Domitian at 7.38.2. Apollonius' prophetic powers are referred to throughout the life: see, e.g., 1.2.2, 3.42, 6.11.6 and 8.7.30, with Gasparro (2007).

[80] On the relationship between *phasmata* and *daimones*, see Chapter 5, 238. On this miracle, see G. Anderson (1986: 140–1), who rationalises the event as a misunderstanding of a conflict between Apollonius and a Cynic (κύων, i.e., 'a dog').

nature, are both expressed in terms of vision: it is the old man's *ophthalmoi* that give him away, emitting a demonic fire that contrasts with the divine rays of sunlight that animate the eyes of Memnon and mark his divinity, or Pythagoreanism's promise that she will 'fill [Apollonius'] eyes with light'.[81] Later (6.27) Apollonius once more proves his superior powers of vision by locating the *phasma* of an invisible satyr who had been assaulting the women of an Ethiopian village. In a particularly vivid scene, the sage lulls the demon to sleep with wine, the liquid disappearing as if by magic from the village trough as it is greedily drunk by the predictably alcoholic creature, who is subsequently revealed sleeping off his hangover in a local cave of the nymphs.[82]

In both these exempla Apollonius demonstrates his ability to perceive the true form of *daimones* who are invisible to humans without his superior powers of cognition, even those such as the Ephesian beggar who employ all the supernatural *technē* at their command.[83] In each case Apollonius' method of dealing with the *phasma* culminates in his revelation of its true form to a crowd of spectators. While presented in novelistic, even humorous, terms, such episodes demonstrate the sage's superior *sophia* in practice, giving vivid expression to the powers granted him by Pythagorean philosophy; we might recall his claim to Achilles that 'you would be much obliged to my eyes, if you used them to attest (μάρτυσιν) to your existence' (4.16).[84] In this sense he emulates the visionary faculties of Pythagoras himself, whom Philostratus had referred to programmatically (1.1.2): whereas others 'merely guessed about the divine', he claims, Pythagoras received actual visitations from deities including Apollo, Athena, the Muses and 'other gods, whose shapes and names were quite unknown to humanity' (ὧν τὰ εἴδη καὶ τὰ ὀνόματα οὔπω τοὺς ἀνθρώπους γιγνώσκειν). Likewise, Iamblichus tells us in *On the Pythagorean Life* that the philosopher 'was also the cause of his disciples holding converse with the gods in the form best suited to us,

---

[81] Note the contrast here between the concept of the hero as benign *daimōn* and the *daimōn* as an evil spirit closer to the Christian concept of the devil. On this distinction, see Dillon (1977: 217–19) and J. Z. Smith (1978).

[82] 'Without the creature becoming visible, the wine began to go down as if being drunk' (ὁ δὲ οὔπω μὲν ἑωρᾶτο, ὑπεδίδου δὲ ὁ οἶνος, ὥσπερ πινόμενος, 6.27.3). On this passage and its relationship to Midas' capture of a satyr in Xenophon's *Anabasis* 1.2.13, see Gyselinck and Demoen (2009: 118–19) and Schirren (2009: 168–70), who sees the episode as an allusion to the sculptural type of the Barberini Faun.

[83] Note that the beggar 'artfully' blinks his eyes (ἐπιμύων τοὺς ὀφθαλμοὺς τέχνη). Such visionary power is confirmed at 8.15–16, where Apollonius (in Ephesus) witnesses the murder of Domitian at midday, precisely when the event is taking place in Rome.

[84] See Chapter 5, 249.

waking visions and dreams' (70).[85] Apollonius, of course, demonstrates his
acquaintance with the supernatural through his meetings with Achilles and
Trophonius, as well as his many oracular dreams.[86] His ability to initiate
and control such confrontations is repeatedly presented as a result of his
extraordinary *sophia*, often demonstrated through his knowledge of obscure
details of Hellenic culture, and acquaintance with the arcana of religious
cult. In line with the novelistic tone of the *Life*, these biographical topoi
are not layered with the philosophical complexities of the later Neoplatonic
lives of Pythagoras, but instead employ the language of vision in order to
manifest Apollonius' superior *sophia* by means of narrated adventure.[87]
The strikingly visual nature of their performance constructs a discourse
of miracle-working in which Apollonius' extraordinary deeds are founded
directly upon his ability to view with knowledge, and to transmit such
knowledge to others.[88] In this way Philostratus presents a model of charismatic sanctity that appeals specifically to the values of piety, *paideia* and
visionary perception that characterised the culture of the Second Sophistic.

Sight, insight and *phantasia*

If the Prodican allegory presented in book 6 associates the power of philosophy to give true sight with Apollonius' power to perceive divinity itself,
this relationship between epiphanic vision and sacred knowledge is also
suggested by the name of the gymnosophist Thespesion, which recalls that
of Thespesios, the hero of Plutarch's myth of the soul in the *De sera numi-
nis vindicta* (itself modelled upon Plato's Myth of Er in the *Republic*).[89]

---

[85] Translations of Iamblichus are from Clark (1989). On the tradition of Pythagoras' epiphanic
powers of vision, see Flinterman (2009). On Iamblichus' treatment of Pythagoreanism and its
relationship to earlier formulations of the doctrine, see O'Meara (1989: 30–105), von Albrecht
et al. (2002) and Staab (2002).

[86] 4.11, 4.16, 8.19.1–2, 1.23, 4.34: see Chapter 5, 247, 249. Apollonius' privileged access to the
Homeric heroes through his knowledge of religious ritual learned from the Brahmans (itself a
form of *sophia* which surpasses that of Pythagoras) forms a parallel to Pythagoras' own
privileged access to the Homeric world through knowledge of his former life as Euphorbus; see
1.1.1 and 3.19.1–2, and Diogenes Laertius *Life of Pythagoras* 4 (in Guthrie, 1987).

[87] On Neoplatonic biography as a guide to the philosophic life, see Cox (1983) and Clark (2000).

[88] On the 'rational' nature of Apollonius' miracles, see G. Anderson (1986: 139–40), Dzielska
(1986: 91–4), Koskenniemi (1991: 60), J. A. Francis (1995: 118–26) and Schirren (2005:
213–318), who argues that such passages overtly signal their own fictionality.

[89] On Plutarch's Thespesios, see Alesse (2001) and Pérez Jiménez (2001). On the use of such
terms in texts of the imperial period, see Du Toit (1997: 309–12 and *passim*). On Plutarch's
influence on the *VA*, see Van der Stockt (2009), who concentrates on the biographical model
offered by Plutarch's *Lives*.

These multiple allusions to philosophical allegory, combined with Philostratus' presentation of the Choice of Heracles as an ekphrasis, encourage
the reader to associate the viewing of images within the text with the visionary quest that directs the process of philosophical enquiry; indeed, Plato had
called the philosopher's vision of the Forms in the *Republic* a 'divine *theōria*'
(517d).[90] The theoric experiences prompted by the colossus of Memnon
and the Choice of Heracles anticipate the model of viewing that is finally
put forward in Apollonius' discussion of the nature of anthropomorphism
with Thespesion (6.19), where, having criticised the 'strange and ridiculous
(ἄτοπα καὶ γελοῖα)' practice of Egyptian theriomorphism, Apollonius is
forced to defend Hellenic traditions of representation:[91]

δυσχεράνας δὲ ὁ Θεσπεσίων "τὰ δὲ παρ' ὑμῖν" εἶπεν "ἀγάλματα πῶς ἱδρῦσθαι
φήσεις;" "ὥς γε" ἔφη "κάλλιστόν τε καὶ θεοφιλέστατον δημιουργεῖν θεούς." "τὸν
Δία που λέγεις" εἶπε "τὸν ἐν τῇ Ὀλυμπίᾳ, καὶ τὸ τῆς Ἀθηνᾶς ἕδος, καὶ τὸ τῆς
Κνιδίας τε καὶ τὸ τῆς Ἀργείας, καὶ ὁπόσα ὧδε καλὰ καὶ μεστὰ ὥρας."

"Οὐ μόνον" ἔφη "ταῦτα, ἀλλὰ καὶ καθάπαξ τὴν μὲν παρὰ τοῖς ἄλλοις ἀγαλματοποιίαν ἅπτεσθαί φημι τοῦ προσήκοντος, ὑμᾶς δὲ καταγελᾶν τοῦ θείου μᾶλλον
ἢ νομίζειν αὐτό." "οἱ Φειδίαι δὲ" εἶπε "καὶ οἱ Πραξιτέλεις μῶν ἀνελθόντες ἐς οὐρανὸν,
καὶ ἀπομαξάμενοι τὰ τῶν θεῶν εἴδη, τέχνην αὐτὰ ἐποιοῦντο, ἢ ἕτερόν τι ἦν,
ὃ ἐφίστη αὐτοὺς τῷ πλάττειν;" "ἕτερον" ἔφη "καὶ μεστόν γε σοφίας πρᾶγμα."
"ποῖον;" εἶπεν "οὐ γὰρ ἄν τι παρὰ τὴν μίμησιν εἴποις." "φαντασία" ἔφη "ταῦτα
εἰργάσατο σοφωτέρα μιμήσεως δημιουργός. μίμησις μὲν γὰρ δημιουργήσει, ὃ
εἶδεν, φαντασία δὲ καὶ ὃ μὴ εἶδεν, ὑποθήσεται γὰρ αὐτὸ πρὸς τὴν ἀναφορὰν τοῦ
ὄντος, καὶ μίμησιν μὲν πολλάκις ἐκκρούει ἔκπληξις, φαντασίαν δὲ οὐδέν, χωρεῖ γὰρ
ἀνέκπληκτος πρὸς ὃ αὐτὴ ὑπέθετο.

"Δεῖ δέ που Διὸς μὲν ἐνθυμηθέντα εἶδος ὁρᾶν αὐτὸν ξὺν οὐρανῷ καὶ ὥραις
καὶ ἄστροις, ὥσπερ ὁ Φειδίας τότε ὥρμησεν, Ἀθηνᾶν δὲ δημιουργήσειν μέλλοντα
στρατόπεδα ἐννοεῖν καὶ μῆτιν καὶ τέχνας καὶ ὡς Διὸς αὐτοῦ ἀνέθορεν. εἰ δὲ ἱέρακα
ἢ γλαῦκα ἢ λύκον ἢ κύνα ἐργασάμενος ἐς τὰ ἱερὰ φέροις ἀντὶ Ἑρμοῦ τε καὶ Ἀθηνᾶς
καὶ Ἀπόλλωνος, τὰ μὲν θηρία καὶ τὰ ὄρνεα ζηλωτὰ δόξει τῶν εἰκόνων, οἱ δὲ θεοὶ
παραπολὺ τῆς αὐτῶν δόξης ἐστήξουσιν."

Annoyed, Thespesion said, 'How will you describe the way your *agalmata* are
represented?' 'In the most beautiful and pious way for representing gods', said
Apollonius. 'You must mean the Zeus at Olympia, said the other, 'the image of
Athena, of the Knidian goddess, and the Argive one, all the images that are as
beautiful as those and full of charm.'

---

[90] See Nightingale (2005: 82).
[91] On Greek attitudes to Egyptian theriomorphism, see Smelik and Hemelrijk (1984). On
phantasia in this passage, see Birmelin (1993: 393–414) and Watson (1988: 60–4, 76–93).

'Not those merely,' said Apollonius, 'but in general I hold that the sculpture of other peoples aims at propriety, but you mock divinity rather than honouring it.' 'Your Phidias,' said Thespesion, 'your Praxiteles, they did not go up to heaven and make an impression of the gods' forms before turning them into art, did they? Was it not something else that set them to work as sculptors?' 'It was,' said Apollonius, 'and something of supreme wisdom.' 'What is that?' asked Thespesion; 'for you cannot mean anything but Mimesis.' 'Phantasia created these objects,' replied Apollonius, 'a wiser artist than Mimesis. Mimesis will create what it knows, but Phantasia will also create what it does not know, conceiving it with reference to the real. Terror often frustrates Mimesis, but nothing will frustrate Phantasia, as it goes imperturbably towards its own appointed purpose.

'Doubtless if you envisage the form of Zeus, you must see him together with heaven, the seasons and the planets, as Phidias ventured to do in his day. If you are planning to portray Athena, you must think of armies, intelligence, technical skills and how she sprang from Zeus himself. But if you create a hawk, an owl, a wolf or a dog, and bring it into your holy places instead of Hermes, Athena or Apollo, people will think animals and birds worth envying for their images, but the gods will fall far short of their own glory.'

The debate between Apollonius and Thespesion directly tackles the issues of epiphanic promise and mimetic *aporia* raised by the anthropomorphic cult images of classical Greece. By taking the great chryselephantine statues of Phidias – the Athena Parthenos and Olympian Zeus – as well as the Argive Hera and Knidian Aphrodite of Praxiteles as his exempla, Thespesion challenges Hellenic culture at its very core. As with the Choice of Heracles, the Ethiopian sage appropriates Greek visual exempla in order to further his own argument, and as in the Taxila and Memnon episodes, it is in the meeting of Greek and non-Greek that Philostratus' readers are encouraged to think about the nature of Hellenic modes of artistic representation. In order to defend the symbolic schemata of Egyptian theriomorphism against the mimetic tendencies of classicism, Thespesion asserts the necessary gap such images mark between object and deity, suggesting that the relationship between image and prototype in anthropomorphic art is just as arbitrary as in other traditions of *agalmatopoiia*, despite the special claims of the Greeks.[92]

In effect, the gymnosophist here exploits the problem of cognitive dissonance I set out in Chapter 2: although the naturalistic forms of Greek tradition assert an identity with their prototype, this claim is always potentially undermined by their status as products of human artistry, thereby requiring

[92] Indeed, Thespesion claims in answer to Apollonius' critique that Egyptian artists deliberately use forms that are 'more symbolic and suggestive, since in that way they seem more venerable' (ξυμβολικὰ δὲ αὐτὰ ποιεῖσθαι καὶ ὑπονοούμενα, καὶ γὰρ ἂν καὶ σεμνότερα οὕτω φαίνοιτο).

the authority of epiphany in order to confirm their authenticity (as in Aphrodite's cry, 'Where did Praxiteles see me naked?').[93] In order to expose the false promise of such claims, Thespesion subverts the traditional topos of the artist as a visionary creator; we might recall the Hellenistic epigram that proclaimed, 'Either God came down from heaven to earth to show you / His image, Phidias, or you went to see God.'[94] Yet rather than undermining the cognitive reliability provided by vision alone, the gymnosophist sarcastically suggests that Phidias, Praxiteles *et al.* actually made physical impressions, or casts, of the gods (ἀπομαξάμενοι τὰ τῶν θεῶν εἴδη) which they then used to create their sculptures, in a direct chain of transmission from divine body to material image. While this reductio ad absurdum begs the question of the physicality of divine *eidos*, it also recalls Lucian's *Jupiter Tragoedus* (6–12), in which the corporeality of cult statues is rigidly projected onto the gods themselves, who are than categorised according to the material of their most famous artistic avatars.[95] Most importantly, by employing the language of impression (*tupōsis*), Thespesion draws upon Stoic theories of sense-perception, parodying the notion of an unmediated relationship between god, artist and object that had been suggested in a broad spectrum of post-Hellenistic epiphanic texts, from ekphrastic epigrams to Philostratus' *Heroicus*. He thus demonstrates how traditional notions of *phantasia* derived from Stoic epistemology are incompatible with Greek practices of *agalmatopoiia* dependent upon the notion of a mimetic relationship between god and statue, and, in doing so, undermines the delicate balance maintained by classical cult images between epiphanic appearance and mortal construct.

As the ultimate representative of Hellenic cult practice, Apollonius must defend anthropomorphic representation in a manner that marries rigorous philosophical enquiry with religious tradition. The coup de théâtre in his response to Thespesion therefore rests upon a theory of image-making that moves not only beyond Platonic notions of representation as imitation, but also beyond a concept of *phantasia* derived from reductive forms of Stoic materialism. Instead, the model of representation he puts forward relies upon a concept of internal vision more akin to our notion of 'imagination' (or, in Pollitt's translation, 'intuitive insight').[96] The relationship between deity and image thus implied does not rely upon the kind of

[93] *Anth. Plan.* 160, 4: see Chapter 2 and Chapter 4, 180–1.

[94] *Anth. Plan.* 81 (Philip) = GP 1968: Philip no. 67. See Chapter 4, 202.

[95] See Bracht Branham (1989: 167–77).

[96] Pollitt (1974: 53), 'since the word implies not simply fabricating something in the mind but actually "seeing" something that is not perceptible to the senses'. On this shift, see also Watson (1988: 59–95).

'mimetic faculty' (τὸ μιμητικόν) that Apollonius proposed at Taxila, but a philosophical faculty that builds upon the model of viewing with *sophia* that he outlined in response to the allegory of Prodicus. At Olympia, Apollonius had addressed Phidias' statue with the words, 'Hail, kindly Zeus, since you are so kind as even to make yourself available (σαυτοῦ κοινωνῆσαι) to humans' (4.28), thereby suggesting an equivalence between deity and image that bypasses the notion of mimetic imitation.[97] In Ethiopia he explains how such a mode of viewing might be possible, pointing to a holistic strategy of visualisation that incorporates the god's cosmic as well as anthropomorphic identity, for 'you must see him together with heaven, the seasons and the planets', just as one must view Athena with understanding of her military, intellectual and technical skills and knowledge of her descent from Zeus. In this way Apollonius incorporates the lessons taught by Damis' mis-viewing of Memnon and Prodicus' allegory, demonstrating how the practice of viewing with knowledge can lead to informed epiphanic encounter.

The model of imaginative viewing Philostratus puts forward in book 6 owes much to Dio's formulation of an 'acquired concept' (ὑπόληψις) or 'conception' (ὑπόνοια) of divinity in the *Olympian Oration*.[98] In book 4, Apollonius had echoed Dio's juxtaposition of the Zeus of Phidias with that of Homer in order to stress that whereas the Olympian statue could only 'be seen' (φαίνεσθαι), the Iliadic Zeus could 'be imagined (ὑπονοεῖσθαι) everywhere in heaven' (4.7.2). Yet in book 6 he expands upon Dio's theory of *huponoia* in order to apply it to Phidias' creative enterprise too, describing his Zeus as 'imaged in the mind' (ἐννοεῖν, 6.19.3). In this way he liberates the image from dependence upon a visible prototype, claiming that *phantasia* can 'create what it does not know', conceiving it (ὑποθήσεται) according to a model of reality (τοῦ ὄντος) generated by the application of knowledge rather than mere sense-perception.[99] The theory of *phantasia* advanced in

---

[97] See Chapter 5, 231.   [98] 12.40, 45; see Chapter 5, 228.

[99] See Halliwell (2002: 310), who comments that the Philostratean formulation of *phantasia*, 'an insistence that the possibilities of representation extend beyond the boundaries of the observable world', is not incompatible with older formulations of mimesis, such as Aristotle's theory of artistic idealism in the *Poetics* (25.1460b8–11); this interpretation is also suggested by Birmelin (1933: 399–401), who sees a parallel between Apollonius' model of unshaken *phantasia* and Aristotle's contrast between *phantasia* and belief at *De anima* 3.3, 427b21, but also stresses the influence of Plato's *Timaeus* (esp. 28a, on the distinction between 'thought (*noēsis*) with the aid of *logos*' and 'opinion (*doxa*) with the aid of *aisthēsis*') on the concept of forming an image in the mind, particularly its reception by Middle Platonists such as Antiochus; see also Miles (2009: 152–4). Schweitzer (1925, 1934) stresses the influence of Stoic doctrine, while Watson (1988: 80–93) also acknowledges Philostratus' debt to the *Timaeus*, but emphasises the additional influence of Stoic theological concepts of Nature as divine creator and the doctrine of *phantasia aisthētikē*, positing a Stoic commentary on the *Timaeus* as a source for Philostratus.

book 6 thus raises the Phidian image to equal status with the Homeric text, suggesting that through the faculty of imagination the sculptor's *huponoia* of Zeus can – like the poet's – be seen and imagined everywhere. Apollonius shows that text and image can ultimately work together in a reformulation of Dio's oration whereby media are no longer in competition but can mutually inform each other, enabling the reader/viewer to formulate his or her own vision of the divine.[100] This approach surmounts not only the problem of model and copy intrinsic to the concept of mimesis, but also that of materiality, neutralising Thespesion's satirical treatment of divine *eidos* as material object and allowing the created image to float free of the physical limitations that had troubled Dio's Phidias.

While Philostratus may appropriate Dio's concept of imaginative viewing, he nevertheless improves upon his model by providing a more precise language with which to give it expression. Whereas Dio had still employed the language of mimesis, referring to Phidias' vision as an *eikōn* and describing Zeus as 'represented' (μιμήσασθαι), Apollonius explicitly rejects such Platonisms, while retaining a Platonic emphasis upon the superiority of abstract reasoning.[101] Understood according to the Apollonian formulation of *phantasia*, visual images need no longer be unreliable, incomplete *mimēmata* that appeal to the lower part of the soul – to imagination rather than reason, in Plato's formulation – but imagination is raised to the level of reason itself; the two work together in order to construct a mode of visualisation that is no longer dependent upon shadows in the cave, but facilitates unmediated encounter with divine truth. Apollonius' most striking move, however, is to give his theory of *phantasia* a label derived from the very philosophical language that Thespesion had implicitly criticised in his reference to 'casting' the gods. Rather than drawing upon the Stoic notion of *phantasia* as a form of presentation by which external objects are impressed upon the *psuchē* (which suggests a passive model of sense perception), Apollonius makes *phantasia* refer to the active role played by human agency in generating an internal mental concept of divinity. Whereas Thespesion relies on a model of external, inaccessible deity (which renders the idea of artists visiting heaven ridiculous), Apollonius thus presents a model of internal visualisation in which deity is made accessible through the divine qualities of mind itself. In this way he provides a corrective to the gymnosophist's

---

[100] Indeed, Philostratus the Younger uses the concept of *phantasia* to emphasise the similarity between art and text in the proem to his *Imagines*, where, in a discussion on the nature of *symmetria* in art, he states that 'One finds that the art of painting has a certain kinship with poetry and that an element of *phantasia* is common to both' (*Proem* 6).

[101] On the Platonic elements of Apollonius' model, especially their relationship to the *Timaeus*, see above, n. 99.

model of *phantasia* by stressing the role of logical thought and the communication of mental concepts by means of language (and, by implication, visual representations). In a remarkable feat of philosophical syncretism, Apollonius thus unites the notion of *phantasia* as an unmediated encounter with the divine not only with Platonic concepts of abstract reasoning, but also with Stoic formulations of rational perception as *phantasia katalēptikē* (in which *phantasiai* are subjected to a rigorous process of examination before being granted assent), and *phantasia logikē* (in which this process is explicitly related to structures of language).[102] According to this model, the cognitive reliability required by sacred images is attained through active mental processes rather than the passive reception of epiphanies sent by the gods. In this way Apollonius not only demonstrates the value of philosophy for theology, but also ascribes a specifically religious agenda to aesthetic and epistemological discourse.

Such bold syncretism emphasises Apollonius' power to embrace both the philosophical and the sacred in his advocacy of Greek cultural values, while offering a means of accessing the divine that is an active component of not only viewing but also reading. As a cognitive tool concerned with perception through language as well as sense perception, *phantasia* embraces both the visual and the linguistic, so allowing the text, too, to overcome the limits of ekphrasis and implicate the reader in its pursuit of religious knowledge. Philostratus' formulation of *phantasia* as a creative theological enterprise also solves the dilemma raised by the problematic ekphraseis of Damis and Thespesion. In both cases the idea of 'viewing with imagination' explains the complex synthesis of elements that led the narrator to elaborate upon the image he described and to create an 'impossible' visual experience. Just as a worshipper of Athena Parthenos must view her image with an awareness of the skills and aetiologies that construct her anthropomorphic persona, so Damis viewed the colossus of Memnon according to his knowledge of Egyptian cult statues and the hero's ethnic and genealogical origin. In such cases the image's ability to facilitate an experience of epiphany is dependent upon both its visual form and the application of the viewer's mental processes.[103] If Damis is somewhat unreliable in his record of this experience, it is because he has not attained the same levels of *sophia*

---

[102] See Sandbach (1971), Imbert (1980), Frede (1983), Watson (1988: 38–60, 84) and Ioppolo (1990). On the use of this terminology in non-philosophical Second Sophistic contexts such as the ancient novel, see Goldhill (2001b).

[103] See Zeitlin (2001: 219): *phantasia* 'shifted attention from the mimetic faculty and technical excellence in the production of images to the valorization of a kind of interior vision'. See also Watson (1988: 59–95).

as his perceptive companion, who embodies the kind of *exēgētēs* that Dio celebrates in the *Olympian Oration* – 'the philosopher, the one who by means of reason interprets and proclaims the divine nature most truly, perhaps, and most perfectly' (47).[104]

Apollonius thus offers a solution to the question of how to look at sacred images, reconciling the familiar problems of mortal artistry and the transmission of authentic vision by uniting the visual and the intellectual. In this way he justifies the tradition of Hellenic anthropomorphism while opening the door to more complex philosophical explorations of the means by which divinity can be apprehended.[105] His formulation of *phantasia* is not a particularly sophisticated presentation of the highly complex epistemological issues raised by the term, but then the *Life of Apollonius* is not a purely philosophical text, despite the Socratic and Pythagorean personae adopted by its protagonist. Rather, it selectively employs a range of philosophical doctrines in order to construct an all-encompassing image of its hero, just as it also employs historiographical and novelistic elements. Before the action shifts to Rome in book 7, Apollonius' promotion of *phantasia* concludes the biography's series of viewing episodes and *Kunsttheorie*, allowing Apollonius to transform a concept appropriated from Stoicism in order to defend Hellenic practices of anthropomorphism from the Platonic critique of mimesis. In doing so, he unites intellectual and religious concerns in a model of theoric viewing that draws inspiration from cult statues regarded as central to Hellenic cultural and religious identity, while providing a range of pedagogic tools for viewing such images according to principles of *sophia*. In this way, just as Apollonius confronts Achilles in book 4 in order to 'rewrite' Homer, so in book 6 he reformulates Greek attitudes to representation. Like Plutarch in the *Delphic Orations*, Philostratus is here in the position of defender and proselytiser of a pagan universalism deeply concerned with the traditions of the past, but which also stresses the reality of religious experience in the present.[106] The concept of *phantasia*, which marries philosophy with the potential for epiphanic (in)sight, thus enables him to put the language of philosophy at the service of traditional *agalmatopoiia*. Indeed, later traditions held that a statue of Apollonius was worshipped at Tyana long after the time of Philostratus, and that he created talismans for the cities of

---

[104] λέγω δὴ τὸν φιλόσοφον ἄνδρα, ἢ λόγῳ ἐξηγητὴν καὶ προφήτην τῆς ἀθανάτου φύσεως ἀληθέστατον ἴσως καὶ τελειότατον.

[105] As Cox (1983: xiv) writes of biography in late antiquity, 'philosophy itself, which had once resisted the incursions of religious speculation, came increasingly to denote the search for God'.

[106] On Plutarch's theology, see the Introduction, n. 57.

Antioch and Constantinople; as Philostratus' text suggests, his *Nachleben* was closely intertwined with investment in the power of images to wield sacred authority.[107]

Despite Apollonius' defence of Greek practices of *agalmatopoiia*, however, his theory of *phantasia* has implications that compromise his position in provocative ways. In his second *Oration*, Maximus of Tyre had justified the use of cult statues by claiming they were useful aids for 'feeble' humans to apprehend the divine, yet commented that 'People whose memories are strong and who can reach straight out for the heavens with their souls and encounter the divine may perhaps have no need of images' (2.2). By suggesting that the ultimate form of *theōria* is located in the power of the mind to visualise and communicate with the divine, Apollonius implies that he embodies this type of ideal viewer, outlining a theory of internal visualisation that actually bypasses the need for images altogether, as well as mortal artists, for in the sage's formulation *phantasia* is itself the δημιουργός by which the gods are visualised.[108] By dissolving the problems of materiality and human artistry, he implicitly nullifies any need for physical *sēmata* of divine form, and by emphasising the importance of viewer-supplementation, plays down the phenomenological impact of images themselves.

Indeed, when responding to Thespesion's subsequent defence of theriomorphism as a symbolic and venerable mode of representation, Apollonius argues that Egyptians and Ethiopians would do better to worship no images at all, claiming that 'rather than introducing an *agalma*, you could leave the forms of the gods to those visiting your holy places, for the mind portrays and imagines an object better than creation does (ἀναγράφει γάρ τι ἡ γνώμη καὶ ἀνατυποῦνται δημιουργίας κρεῖττον, 6.19.4)'. Despite his continued adherence to a hierarchy of divine forms, in effect, Apollonius here outlines a theory of programmatic empty-space aniconism in which the language of impression (note the use of ἀνατυποῦνται) refers only to a process of mental visualisation, and material images become surplus to religious requirements.[109] In this sense he ends up defending a Platonic theory

[107] [Justinos], *Quaestiones et responsiones orthodoxorum*, PG 6.1269 and 1272. I am grateful to Jaap-Jan Flinterman for this reference. On fourth-century talismans and amulets of Apollonius, see the Antiochene chronographer John Malalas, *Chron.* 10.51 (Thurn), with Speyer (1974), Dzielska (1986: 68, 99–101), Potter (1994: 34) and Elsner (1997b: 178), who relates a passage from the *Historia Augusta* in which Apollonius reveals himself in a vision to Aurelian, 'in the form in which he was usually portrayed', i.e., his statue (*HA Divus Aurelianus* 24.2–9). On the mutually reinforcing relationship between holy men and their portraits in late antiquity, see J. A. Francis (2003: esp. 582–3, 592, on Apollonius).

[108] On this point, see also Miles (2009: 154–5).

[109] On programmatic (as opposed to *de facto*) aniconism, see Mettinger (1995: 18) and my discussion in Chapter 2, 100–4.

of the image, despite his original rejection of Platonic language and the role of mimesis in image-making. Furthermore, despite his appeal to Hellenic tradition, the near-iconoclastic implications of Apollonius' *apologia* go beyond his specific critique of Egyptian *agalmatopoiia*, demonstrating contradictory impulses that are illustrative of broader cultural shifts in the early third century, particularly transformations in artistic practices that anticipate the so-called *Stilwandel* of late antiquity. The move away from naturalism in art of the third and fourth centuries CE was driven by a complex network of religious, cultural and social factors, not least of which was a preference for symbolic forms and a heightened emphasis upon the role of sacred knowledge in practices of viewing (ultimately demonstrated by the guiding role of scripture in early Christian art). It is ironic, then, that in his very attempt to provide an *apologia* for earlier forms of Greek image-worship, Philostratus' Apollonius appeals to the very impulses that would eventually lead to its demise.

Apollonius: 'daemonic man'?

As Patricia Cox has written of late antique biography, 'The myth of the holy man is here considered to be an imaginal "place between" where the history of a man's life and his biographer's vision of human divinity meet and mingle. Biographies of holy men are the literary expressions of this play between fact and fantasy; they are the "place between" come to life as an embodied ideal, imaginal history.'[110] In *The Life of Apollonius* the liminal qualities of the *bios* itself also apply to the text's protagonist, a daemonic figure who stands between the realms of human and divine, fiction and reality. Crucial to this liminality is his ability *to see*, as he states in his reformulation of the Choice of Heracles. Vision – whether epiphanic, ekphrastic or imagined – is crucial to the crossing of boundaries facilitated by Apollonius and expressed in his theory of *phantasia*. Presented within the narrative's framework of travel, the power of vision to penetrate beyond conventional limitations is demonstrated in scenes of epiphanic image-viewing (such as the colossus of Memnon), by encounters with the supernatural (such as Achilles, Trophonius, the Ephesian demon and the Ethiopian satyr), by allegorical epiphany (the Prodican choice of Pythagoreanism) and by Philostratus' reanimation

---

[110] Cox (1983: xii) evokes Plutarch's notion of biography as 'revelatory discourse', in which 'the biographer's task was to capture the gesture which laid bare the soul', claiming that 'Biographies of holy men did not "translate" or "represent" their heroes' lives; like Plutarch, they were engaged in revelation.'

of the literary and cultural past (particularly the first century CE). In this sense Apollonius' visionary experiences anticipate his eventual presentation as an epiphanic being in his own right, in which the text performs the act of *theōria* that structures its own narrative, presenting an ekphrastic epiphany of Apollonius to the reader/viewer.[111]

The Life of Apollonius may anticipate certain late antique attitudes to religious art, from Christian models of typological viewing to Neoplatonism's emphasis upon the visionary potential of the image (particularly the practice of theurgy).[112] Traditionally, however, Philostratus' text has been read as evidence for the popularity of the *theios anēr* in the later empire, and the promotion (intentional or not) of a pagan equivalent to Jesus.[113] After all, in a famous example of third-century CE syncretism, Alexander Severus was said to have included images of Apollonius and Christ in his *lararium* together with his penates, Orpheus and Abraham.[114] While the validity of the 'divine man' category has recently been questioned and Apollonius' own status within the *Life* called into doubt, it is surely significant that Philostratus seems to leave the question of Apollonius' divinity open for the reader to decide.[115] Tellingly, the first epiphany he associates with the sage is that of Proteus to Apollonius' mother, his announcement that she will 'give birth to himself' giving potent expression to the elusive nature of both the protagonist and the text itself (1.4).[116] Certainly, characters within the text repeatedly demonstrate their willingness to regard Apollonius as

---

[111] On the meta-poetic function of both mimesis and *phantasia* in the *VA*, see also Schirren (2005: 272–85).

[112] On theurgy and its relationship to Neoplatonism, see Shaw (1985, 1995, 1999). While E. R. Dodds's influential piece on theurgy (1947, reprinted in 1951) followed later Christian criticism in presenting it as a mere magical technique, a 'manifesto of irrationalism' (1951: 287), other scholars have emphasised the more complex relationship between theurgical ritual and philosophical contemplation of the divine in Neoplatonism, whether we should view them as 'practical' and 'mystic' alternatives, or 'lower' and 'higher' forms of approaching 'the One'. For an overview, see Lloyd (1967: 269–325), Sheppard (1982) and Athanassiadi (1993); on theurgy's place within the broader ritual traditions of late antiquity, see Janowitz (2002).

[113] See n. 4 above.

[114] Lampridius *Alexander* 29: see B. F. Harris (1969: 189), Settis (1972) and Swain (1996: 382).

[115] See above, n. 79. Such reticence was certainly not maintained in later texts: the fourth-century pagan historian Eunapius, for example, claimed that Apollonius was 'not merely a philosopher but a demigod, half man, half god' (οὐκέτι φιλόσοφος, ἀλλ᾽ ἦν τι θεῶν τε καὶ ἀνθρώπου μέσον), and even that the life of Philostratus himself should have been called the ἐπιδημίαν ἐς ἀνθρώπους θεοῦ (*Vit. Phil.* 454). On Apollonius as the object of pilgrimage, see Elsner (1997a: 27–8) and Miles (2009: 146–7), and, on his divinity, Talbert (1978: 1635, 1638–9).

[116] 'Why should I describe to the readers of the poets how great Proteus was in wisdom, how versatile, changeable in form, masterful in escape, and how he was reputed to know and foreknow everything?' Cf. J. A. Francis (1995: 120–1), Elsner (2009a) and Flinterman (2009: 232–6).

divine: I mentioned above that, at Olympia, Apollonius himself became a focus of *proskynesis* (8.15); likewise, we are told that he was worshipped at Tyana and hailed as a son of Zeus (1.6), while the people of Alexandria 'look on him as a god' (5.24), and Damis explicitly regards him as 'godlike and superhuman' (θεία τε εἴη καὶ κρείττων) when he miraculously shakes off his fetters in Domitian's jail as proof that he has been imprisoned by the emperor merely by choice (7.38.2).[117]

Yet all these celebrations of Apollonius' divine status are focalised through internal viewers. Significantly, at 4.31.1, enthusiasm for the sage among the Spartans leads some cynical Corinthians to ask 'whether they were also going to celebrate a *theophania* for him', as if he were one of the Dioscuri, an act of ritual invocation that Apollonius discourages. Yet at 6.35, Philostratus explicitly compares the transmission of Apollonius' knowledge to 'visits from the sons of Asclepius' (ταῖς τῶν Ἀσκληπιαδῶν ἐπιδημίαις).[118] In this sense he marks Apollonius' status as a spokesman of religious truth yet refrains from directly identifying him as *theios*, while making a more overt claim for the quality of the text itself, which thus performs the epiphanic function of an *epidēmia* for the reader. This ambiguity is echoed at 7.32.2, when Apollonius criticises Domitian for mistaking him for a *daimōn*, expressing surprise that he does not have the cognitive insight of Diomedes at Troy, when Athena 'took away . . . the mist (τὴν . . . ἀχλύν) that prevents men seeing fully, and gave him the power to distinguish gods and men'.[119] Yet we know from Apollonius' *apologia* in book 6 that he possesses this faculty himself (as, indeed, he goes on to point out to Domitian). In this sense he *is* a *daimōn*, if understood according to Diotima's formulation in Plato's *Symposium*, when she claims that 'the daemonic is the means of all society and converse of gods with men and of men with gods, whether waking or asleep. Whosoever has skill in these affairs is a daemonic man'.[120]

Apollonius' attainment to daemonic status in death is certainly not in doubt at 8.31, when, after disappearing from earth in a veritable ascension, the sage appears in a dream to a doubtful follower to prove that his soul

[117] On προσκύνησις as a traditional response to epiphany, see Dickie (2004: 169–72).

[118] Cf. Montiglio (2005: 213–20), who notes that Apollonius' travels are not presented as *planē* by Philostratus (the seemingly aimless wandering of philosophers), but more like 'the sweeping movements of the gods. If his travels are wandering, they are divine wandering' (217).

[119] *Il.* 5.127–8: ἀχλὺν δ' αὖ τοι ἀπ' ὀφθαλμῶν ἕλον ἣ πρὶν ἐπῆεν, / ὄφρ' εὖ γιγνώσκῃς ἠμὲν θεὸν ἠδὲ καὶ ἄνδρα.

[120] Plato, *Symposium* 202e–203a: see Chapter 5, 236. Cf. J. A. Francis (1995: 124): 'The overall impression Philostratus conveys of Apollonius is not one of superhuman power . . . but of supernatural *insight*' (my italics).

is immortal.[121] Waking up, the youth cries, just like the Phoenician sailor in the *Heroicus*, 'I believe you!' (πείθομαί σοι) and berates his companions, 'Don't you see (οὐχ ὁρᾶτε) the wise Apollonius? He is with us listening to our conversation, and rhapsodising marvellously about the soul.'[122] The closing section of the *Life* thus dramatises the very challenge of *phantasia* that Apollonius had outlined in Ethiopia, focusing the reader's desire-to-see upon the sage himself. In this way the *Life* offers itself as a means of acquiring the *sophia* necessary for true vision in a manner that both parallels the Christian tale of 'Doubting Thomas' and relates the issue of Apollonian faith directly to the principles of Hellenic *paideia* espoused throughout the narrative.[123] That Apollonius' young follower experiences his dream vision among fellow students 'concentrated on their books' suggests that it is crucial to Philostratus' text that epiphanic encounter with the sage should not result from passive reception, but from an active process of visualisation dependent upon the pursuit of wisdom. Whereas Phidias' *phantasia* of Zeus (6.19) is a composite of details derived from cosmology, literature, art and allegory, so our *phantasia* of Apollonius must depend upon acquisition of all the knowledge available. Where is this conveniently to be found? Surely in the encyclopaedic eight-book tome presented to us by Philostratus, a thorough synthesis of all available source material, conceived in comparison with a series of earlier paradigms from Odysseus to Socrates and animated by the enargeic powers of his own imagination. Through his necromantic confrontation with Achilles, Apollonius had proved that the literary and religious past was permeable, suggesting it could be animated, reread and re-experienced in ever-shifting ways. So, by extension, Philostratus' text, too, is open. Readers distanced from Apollonius by time and mortality must remember that *phantasia*, as he proclaims to Thespesion, 'goes imperturbably towards its own appointed purpose'; all we need do is to state 'I believe you' – πείθομαί σοι – to the author himself.

---

[121] On this passage, and the multiple narratives of Apollonius' 'ascension' at 8.30, see Schirren (2005: 309–12) and Flinterman (2009).

[122] See J. A. Francis (1995: 100).

[123] On the epistemological crisis presented by Thomas, see most recently Most (2005).

PART III

But in the self-same fixed trance he kept,
Like one who on the earth had never stept.
Aye, even as dead-still as a marble man.

> Keats, *Endymion* (1818), 1.403–5

Safe in the arms of Sleep, a beautiful young shepherd reclines on the bucolic slopes of Mount Latmos, while before him Selene, goddess of the moon, alights from her chariot (Figure 8.1).[1] A cupid leads the way, his flaming torch illuminating her beloved, while Hypnos gently raises his cloak to reveal the youth's naked torso. Centrally positioned, the goddess is framed by whorling drapery, which billows around her body and presses against her breasts and thighs as she moves towards him. On tenterhooks, we wait for him to awake to Selene's glorious epiphany. Yet suspended in slumber, as 'dead-still' as Keats's marble man, Endymion can see her only in his dreams. Like Gerontia, the little girl once laid to rest in this marble sarcophagus, his sleep – and by implication his beauty and desirability – is eternal.[2]

Dreams may generate a liminal space in which mortal and immortal can meet, yet the ultimate *limen* whose crossing is marked by epiphanic encounter is that of Hades. Death, after all, demands its own form of *theōria*, which constitutes both the survivors' visits to the tomb in order to remember the departed and the mythic *katabasis* performed by the deceased, whose journey to the *au-delà* is punctuated by divine figures such as Hermes Psychopompos (the 'conductor of souls'), Charon the ferryman and

---

[1] Museo Capitolino, Rome, inv. 325 discovered near the Porta Ostiense, and one of the earliest examples of an Endymion sarcophagus. See Sichtermann and Koch (1975: 27–8), Sichtermann (1992: 103–5, *ASR* 12.2, no. 27), Koortbojian (1995: 65–8) and Zanker and Ewald (2004: 317–19).

[2] The inscription (*CIL* 6.19037) reads, 'D[is] M[anibus] | Gerontiae | filiae KRM [*karissimae*]', and was added in late antiquity once the central motif (possibly a mask of Oceanus) was removed: see Zanker and Ewald (2004: 319). At 1.32 m long, the sarcophagus was clearly intended for a child, although the identity of its original mid-second-century occupant is unknown. On the relationship between mythological sarcophagus reliefs and the gender of the deceased, see below. On children's sarcophagi, see Huskinson (1996: esp. 25–7, on this example).

Figure 8.1 Selene and Endymion child's sarcophagus, c. 130–40 CE

the gods of the Underworld.[3] Moreover, in antiquity death itself is often figured as a moment of epiphany, whether abduction (such as Hades' rape of Persephone) or joyous union (such as Dionysus' discovery of Ariadne on Naxos, or Selene's nocturnal visits to Endymion). It should not be surprising, then, that our largest and best preserved corpus of visual evidence exploring the phenomenon of epiphany in the second and third centuries CE comes from the funerary sphere, where the relationship between death and divine manifestation was thematised in the stucco, mosaic and painted interior decorative schemes of tombs and, most strikingly, upon marble sarcophagi. This chapter explores how the representational concerns raised by discussions of epiphany in the literary-philosophical tradition explored in Part II are played out in the contemporary material context of death and remembrance. The cultural and economic resources invested in Roman commemoration of the dead mean that not only do sarcophagus reliefs compose the Graeco-Roman world's largest corpus of objects abundant in visual narrative, but also that the dynamics of epiphany they so adeptly explore are invested with a particularly rich and sophisticated set of resonances. Indeed, one might argue that all the ambivalences of epiphany this book has traced thus far are sublimated in – or conversely become a form of sublimation for – the ambivalences of death itself.

Classicism, culture and *res religiosae*

The majority of epiphanic sarcophagus reliefs come neither from mainland Greece nor Asia Minor but, like Figure 8.1, from metropolitan Rome, where Second Sophistic values of *paideia* were espoused within the funerary sphere with great vigour and erudition.[4] Epiphanic scenes are symptomatic of a proliferation of myth in imperial funerary art, as Roman patrons shifted from the *mos Romanus* of cremation to Greek traditions of inhumation, and the increasing use of sarcophagi (rather than ash chests) provided a larger visual field for sculptural narrative.[5] These changes in funerary tradition

---

[3] On Greek eschatology, see Albinus (2000) and Bremmer (2002), with, e.g., Sourvinou-Inwood (1995: 321–53) and Oakley (2004: 113–44), on encounters with Hermes, Charon *et al.* on Attic lekythoi. On personifications of death in Western culture, see Guthke (1999) and D. Burton (2005).

[4] See Müller (1994: 139–70), Koortbojian (1995: 15–18), Elsner (1998: 146–52), Ewald (1999), Zanker and Ewald (2004: 36–8) and Caliò (2007), with Newby (2002), on parallel trends in non-funerary relief sculptures such as the Spada reliefs.

[5] Tacitus (*Annals* 16.6) calls cremation the 'mos Romanus'. On the shift from cremation to inhumation in the second century CE and the influence of Greek burial traditions, see Nock (1932) and I. Morris (1992: 31–69). Müller (1994: 158–63) also emphasises the influence of

formed part of a broader philhellenic movement during the Hadrianic and Antonine periods, during which contemporary Greek interest in the arts, rituals and myths of the Hellenic past was co-opted by Roman elites, while Rome itself acted as a flourishing locus of rhetorical, paideutic and artistic activities typical of the Second Sophistic.[6] Despite their ambivalent relationship with Roman power, Greek intellectuals flocked to the imperial centre as performing sophists, as resident philosophers in private homes or to hold positions *ab epistulis graecis* in the imperial court, while Latin literature of the period demonstrates a deep familiarity with Greek traditions of rhetoric, including epideictic forms such as funeral orations that were performed in honour of deceased individuals and characterised by their use of mythological exempla.[7]

The use of Greek myths together with classicising styles and iconographic formulae on Roman sarcophagi is in this sense reflective of cultural preoccupations across the Hellenised Mediterranean. Indeed, Greek forms provided a visual lingua franca that was employed in the construction of cultural identity throughout the empire. At the same time, metropolitan traditions of sarcophagus decoration are closely bound to their Roman context, drawing upon customs of funerary ritual and tomb decoration that date back to the Republican period, as well as conventions of artistic production characteristic of domestic décor and ideal sculpture.[8] Attic sarcophagi, for example, do not employ portrait heads within mythological scenes, preferring to confine portrait elements to reclining figures on the lid, whereas a Roman predilection for inserting portrait heads within narrative reliefs relates, as we shall see, to a strong tradition of funerary portraiture in Rome itself.[9]

older Roman traditions of inhumation practised by aristocratic clans such as the gens Cornelia, and relates its revival to a need for new status symbols and a representative manner of burial among a reactionary Roman elite following the restoration of the senate under Trajan.

[6] On Rome as a prime centre of the Second Sophistic, see Bowersock (1969: 43–58), Fantham (1996: 222–46) and, in the visual sphere, Elsner (1998: 169–85).

[7] On the office *ab epistulis graecis* see Bowersock (1969: 50–7), and on sophists in Rome, Hahn (1989: 46–53, 148–55), Pernot (1997), Galli (2002), on Herodes Atticus, and Whitmarsh (2002: 181–246). On Greek traditions of funerary eulogy, see Hani (1972), on the pseudo-Plutarchan *Consolatio ad Apollonium*; Russell and Wilson (1981), on Menander Rhetor 2.9 (the *paramuthetikos*), 2.11 (the *epitaphios*) and 2.16 (the monody); and, for its influence on Roman traditions of *consolatio*, Kierdorf (1980) and Müller (1994: 143–7). On sarcophagi as forms of *consolatio*, see Turcan (1999), Gessert (2004) and Zanker and Ewald (2004: esp. 62–115).

[8] On Roman funerary tradition, see Toynbee (1971), Hopkins (1983), Prieur (1986), Bodel (1999) and Hope (2007: 85–127).

[9] See Ewald (2004: 233, 250) and, on Attic mythological sarcophagi, Koch and Sichtermann (1982: 366–475), Giuliani (1989) and Rogge (1995). On the Roman tradition of using wax *imagines* in funerary ritual, see Plin. *HN* 35.2, with Lahusen (1982, 1985), Dupont (1987), Bianchi (1994), Flower (1996) and Bodel (1999: 260–1, 271–3). On the use of portrait heads on sarcophagi, see my discussion below.

Likewise, the Roman enthusiasm for erotic epiphanies such as Hades and Persephone, Selene and Endymion or Dionysus and Ariadne is not echoed on sarcophagi produced in Attica or Asia Minor, where heroic myths such as the Achilles and Meleager cycle and battle scenes such as Amazonomachies and centauromachies prevail over scenes of erotic abduction or union with the divine.[10] The greater permeability between the divine and human spheres on Roman sarcophagi parallels local traditions of assimilating the deceased to divine figures (as, for example, in funerary statuary depicting married couples as Mars and Venus), and perhaps reflects the broader influence of imperial iconography, which from the mid first century CE frequently depicted the emperor and his relatives as deities.[11] We might also read a Roman desire for the individual to insert him- or herself within the mythic realm in the light of the monumental mythological statuary so popular during the high empire, when colossal figures such as the Farnese Hercules transformed the monumental spaces of grand public baths, gardens and palaces into a veritable Olympus.[12] Yet these trends date as far back as the late Republic, and played a fundamental role in Rome's appropriation, replication and transformation of Hellenic visual culture.[13] By the second century CE the play between 'absorption and erudition' generated by Greek naturalistic styles had long been appreciated with great sophistication by Roman viewers.[14] The adoption of such practices in the funerary sphere thus drew upon a deep familiarity with classical and Hellenistic modes of representation, and spoke to viewers who had

[10] Ewald (2004) provides a statistical comparison of mythological scenes on Roman and Attic sarcophagi. Dionysus and Ariadne, Selene and Endymion, and Mars and Venus are very rare on Attic examples, in which myths relating to Achilles, Hippolytus and Meleager (all of which also appear on Roman sarcophagi) are the most popular. Aside from generic mythological topoi such as Dionysiac scenes, marine *thiasoi* and cupids, the most popular subjects on Roman sarcophagi are Endymion and Persephone. For a rare example of a scene of human–divine union on an Attic sarcophagus, see Perry (2001), who discusses an example associated with the daughter of Herodes Atticus depicting Leda and the Swan juxtaposed with Helen and the Dioscuri, which she relates to family connections to Sparta.

[11] On the commemoration of deceased individuals as divine figures, see Wrede (1971, 1981), Kleiner (1981), D'Ambra (1993b, 1996, 2000), Hallett (2005c: 199–270) and Kousser (2007). On the use of divine iconography in imperial portraiture, see Mikocki (1995) and M. Bergmann (1998), and, on the cosmic and eschatological implications of imperial funerary monuments in relation to notions of apotheosis, P. Davies (2004).

[12] On monumental statue groups such as the Farnese Hercules and Dirce and the Bull in their Second Sophistic context, see Elsner (1998: 169–85), C. Kunze (1998) and von den Hoff (2004), with Manderscheid (1981) and Marvin (1983), on statue groups in the imperial *thermae*, and Cima and La Rocca (1998) and Graepler (2002), on Roman *horti*.

[13] The bibliography on Roman practices of emulation and replication is vast, but see most recently B. Bergmann (1995), Gazda (2002), Hallett (2005a, 2005c), Perry (2005), Varner (2006), Wyler (2006b), Kousser (2008), Marvin (2008) and Trimble (2009).

[14] See Newby (2009).

already claimed the visual heritage and complex mythological language of the Greek past as their own.[15]

It is against this background that we might understand the philhellenic *paideia* behind the choice of epiphanic myths in Roman funerary art, but what about Second Sophistic interests in the sacred? It is here that scholarship runs aground on the notorious difficulties of relating iconographic choices within the tomb to the religious beliefs and practices of those who viewed and commissioned them. Epiphanic scenes such as those of Selene and Endymion or Dionysus and Ariadne have proven to be rallying points in the fierce debates that have raged over the symbolic significance of Roman funerary art, precisely because they figure death as an encounter between a mortal and an immortal in which the human partner is implicitly elevated to the divine sphere. Such myths cry out for eschatological interpretation, yet simultaneously resist any definitive reading. Those who have succumbed, most famously Franz Valéry Marie Cumont, have risked downplaying the material's polyvalence in an effort to shoehorn it into theological frameworks (such as Neopythagoreanism) that are derived from mystery cult and anachronistically influenced by Christianity.[16] Conversely, since the 1950s the trend has been to emphasise the importance of social display and cultural identity in the selection and presentation of funerary iconography, a move strongly influenced by Arthur Darby Nock, who in his review of Cumont's 1942 study *Recherches sur le symbolisme funéraire des romains* claimed that the forces behind sarcophagus reliefs were 'classicism and culture' rather than eschatological doctrines of salvation and rebirth (as if 'religion' and 'culture' were two separable entities easily compartmentalised by cynical Roman viewers).[17] Despite Nock's sophisticated grasp of the religious complexities of the Roman world, his verdict on sarcophagi was to prove most convenient for the secularising agenda of classical archaeology in the later twentieth century.

---

[15] See Koortbojian (1995: 15–18), who emphasises how sarcophagus reliefs chart a transformation of Greek imagery from *mythos hellenikos* to *mythologia romana*.

[16] See Cumont (1942), with parallel approaches in Lehmann-Hartleben and Olsen (1942) and Turcan (1966), on Dionysiac iconography, and Hanfmann (1951), on personifications of the Seasons.

[17] Nock (1946: 166); see also North (1983: 169), who argues that 'survival of death remains a marginal idea rather than central to any religious structure' in Roman society. Turcan (1999) offers a noble attempt to find a compromise between the Nock and Cumont positions. On sarcophagi as expressions of cultural identity, see, e.g., D'Ambra (1988, 2006). For a rigorous analysis of sarcophagi in relation to Roman senatorial history, see Wrede (2001). On the limitations of such socio-historical readings, see Ewald (2003).

Indeed, 'classicism and culture' has proven to be an all-too-flexible category, and demonstrates further how the significance attributed to sarcophagus reliefs depends entirely upon the interpretative lens through which such objects are studied. Read as an embodiment of Roman moral virtues influenced by contemporary rhetorical literature (as in Michael Koortbojian's *Myth, Meaning, and Memory on Roman Sarcophagi*), Endymion and Selene function as rhetorical analogies, designed to elevate the status of the deceased and embed him or her within a broader system of values by means of visual strategies of abstraction and typology.[18] As a Greek myth in a Roman setting, the scene functions as an expression of learned cultural display, so that for Frank Müller '[t]he frame of reference of the mythological sarcophagi is the complex of purely profane, at most paraphilosophical or popular philosophical topoi which were associated with dying and death in the aristocratic circles of the Greek East and the hellenised West'.[19] Viewed through the experience of the mourner (as in Paul Zanker and Björn Ewald's more recent volume *Mit Mythen leben*), the image offers a soothing and consoling metaphor, preserving and enhancing the *memoria* of the deceased by functioning as a form of visual therapy, or *Trauerhilfe*.[20] While each of these interpretative models sheds important light upon the forces of cultural knowledge, social ambition, ritual tradition and personal anguish that Roman viewers brought to the tomb, the *tradition héllenique* that influenced their choice of funerary receptacle is in each case presented as an entirely secular phenomenon.

Given the multifarious and often ambiguous nature of Roman attitudes to death and the afterlife, this concern to downplay the influence of eschatological allegory or specific cultic affiliations upon sarcophagus iconography is surely legitimate. Rare examples give us insight into the religious identities of specific individuals, such as the Alcestis sarcophagus now in the Vatican Museums commissioned for a priestess of the Magna Mater, which juxtaposes a vision of Alcestis' triumphant return to her husband on the frontal relief with cymbals, drums and flutes related to the goddess's cult and an inscription that makes specific reference to its occupant's status as a *sacerdos*

---

[18] Koortbojian (1995: 63–99). As Elsner (1996d) points out, however, it is dangerous to employ a secular notion of typology without acknowledging Christian typological practices (often contemporary with 'pagan' sarcophagus production), wherein the notion of symbolic interpretation is fundamentally related to the religious identity of patrons and viewers.

[19] Müller (1994: 156–7).

[20] Zanker and Ewald (2004: 102–9, 316–25); see also Hallett (2005b). As Ewald has stated elsewhere (2004: 239), 'myth adds meaning to an otherwise meaningless or inexplicable fate, and it provides consolation by placing death in the perspective of a symbolic world order'.

Figure 8.2 Alcestis sarcophagus, *c.* 160 CE

on the lid (Figure 8.2).[21] Yet it is notoriously difficult to relate iconographic choices within the tomb to either cult practice in the world of the living or specific notions of the soul's fate after death. Where funerary epigraphy gives us any insight into such beliefs, the array of positions it reveals is so bewildering as to counter any dominant model of interpretation; as Nock claimed, paganism had 'unity in cultural inheritance and to some extent of feeling rather than a unity of belief'.[22]

Even so, a secularising drive to neutralise the presence of sacred iconography in funerary contexts by proclaiming it mere metaphor or self-conscious erudition risks draining such objects of their full cultural resonance and misrepresenting the conditions under which they were viewed. Amid the spectrum of interpretative possibilities offered by sarcophagus scholarship, there is seldom recognition of the alterity of death; yet within the categories of space recognised by Roman law, the realm of the tomb, like that of the sanctuary, was identifiably different from the *loci profani* that constituted the domestic, political and commercial spaces of the living.[23]

---

[21] Wood (1978), on the sarcophagus of C. Junius Euhodus and his wife Metilia Acte, Museo Chiaramonti, inv. 1195, discovered in Ostia and dated *c.* 161–70 CE (inscription, *CIL* 14.371): note that Wood revises her interpretation along more secular lines in a postscript to the paper's 1993 republication. See also C. Robert (1897–1919: vol. I, 31–3, *ASR* 3.1, no. 26), Sichtermann and Koch (1975: 20–1, no. 8), Blome (1978: 435–45), Koch and Sichtermann (1982: 136–8), Grassinger (1994, arguing against an eschatological interpretation in favour of Alcestis' status as an *exemplum pietatis*; 1999: 110–28, *ASR* 12.1, no. 76) and Zanker and Ewald (2004: 202–4, 298–301).

[22] Nock (1946: 169). See, e.g., the epitaphs collected in Lattimore (1962), with Knight (1970), Toynbee (1971: 33–42), J. Davies (1999), Bremmer (2002), on Greek, Jewish and early Christian evidence, and Hope (2007: 211–47). On attitudes to death and dying in Latin literature, see most recently C. Edwards (2007) and Erasmo (2008).

[23] See Y. Thomas (2004).

Of course, tombs were co-opted as vehicles for social display, related to very real issues of status and identity within the physical present, and iconography frequently crossed over from the public and domestic spheres to the sepulchral.[24] Nevertheless, a focus on the concerns of the living risks neglecting the unique status of space reserved for the dead; sarcophagi could never be 'purely profane' because they were designed for and viewed within a spatial category that was explicitly defined as *religiosus,* as opposed to *profanus.* First, tombs were located along roadsides in a liminal zone beyond the city boundaries that was, by its very nature, characterised by transition. Second, like sanctuaries (*loci sacri,* consecrated to the gods above), tombs (*loci religiosi,* sacred to the manes or 'shades') were inviolable, inalienable and immune from seizure, with perimeters that strictly demarcated those spaces allotted to the departed, whose corporeal presence was essential for defining the tomb's status as a *sepulcrum.*[25] Such dictates may tell us little about the social practices or mental representations that characterised attitudes to death in Roman culture, but, as Yan Thomas has suggested, they do underline the importance of demarcating a space for the manes, in which the presence of bodily remains generates the bonds of scrupulous ritual observance, the 'obligation' or 'conscientiousness' towards the dead that defines the concept of *religio.*[26]

As Zanker and Ewald have so elegantly demonstrated, funerary ritual provides a productive paradigm for interpreting many of the most popular motifs on mythological sarcophagus reliefs, where the display of torches, garlands and sympotic imagery provides visual bridges (*Brücken*) between the activities of the living and the honours paid to the dead.[27] In this sense they focus upon traditions of mourning and remembrance that characterise habits of viewing within the tomb, during funerary rituals and the annual festivals such as the *Parentalia* and *Rosalia* when the relatives of the deceased came to visit the departed.[28] Within the confines of this particular study, I want to question how the presence of *divine* figures affects the tomb's status as a space within which the living and the dead come together. By

---

[24] On the tomb as a form of 'house', see Wallace-Hadrill (2008); on tombs and public self-representation, see von Hesberg and Zanker (1987).

[25] See Visscher (1963), Toynbee (1971: 75–8) and Y. Thomas 2004. On inalienability, see, e.g., Ulpian *D.* 11.7.6.1. In Roman law temples, tombs and city perimeters fall respectively under the categories of the sacred (*sacer*), the religious (*religiosus*) and the holy (*sanctus*).

[26] Y. Thomas (2004: 66–8). On *religio* (and its Roman derivation from either *religare,* 'to bind', or *relegere,* 'to go back over'), see Beard *et al.* (1998: vol. 1, 215–19) and Scheid (2003: 22–3).

[27] Zanker and Ewald (2004: esp. 28–36).

[28] On ritual visits to the tomb and the cult of the dead, see Toynbee (1971: 43–64) and Hopkins (1983: 217–35).

focusing on the representation of epiphany, this chapter does not aim to provide an all-embracing interpretative model for the richly diverse range of funerary iconography employed during the second and third centuries CE; nor do I dare to ascribe specific beliefs or cultic affiliations to those who commissioned and viewed such objects. Rather, I wish to explore how the visual dynamics of epiphanic encounter I traced in earlier chapters might function when displayed upon objects designed as receptacles for the human body, and how they might have shaped attitudes to both the status of the deceased and the nature of death itself. For how does the Graeco-Roman tradition of naturalistic divine forms, with its sophisticated play of presence and absence, resonate within a context where every strategy of commemoration is designed to offset the bitter fact of human loss? After examining the status of sarcophagi as both a threshold between the living and the dead and a container for the corpse, I focus upon two major categories of epiphanic iconography employed upon their frontal reliefs – scenes of divine abduction, and myths in which a deity approaches a sleeping mortal. Concentrating on examples from the second century (which do not employ portrait features), I explore the implications of displaying eroticised divine bodies within the context of burial, asking how they engage and contrast with mortal characters who function as proxies for the dead. In a subsequent section I address the use of portrait features on examples of the same myths dating to the third century and the realignment of traditional epiphanic schemata within the tomb, whereby it is ultimately the dead themselves who form the focus of the epiphanic gaze.

Viewing the gods on the 'Threshold of Proserpina'

As *loci religiosi*, tombs act as both receptacles for the deceased and thresholds to the world beyond (however it might be conceived). Indeed, the tomb's status as a *limen* between life and death is frequently made literal in Roman funerary art by the motif of architectonic doorways, which appear on ash urns, sarcophagi and even the painted walls of tombs (such as that of Vestorius Priscus in Pompeii).[29] That these are to be understood as features of an imagined thanatological landscape is suggested by a late second-century

---

[29] On this motif, see Haarløv (1977) and G. Davies (1978), with Roosevelt (2006) on parallel motifs in Anatolia; on the tomb of Vestorius Priscus, dated *c.* 71 CE, see Dentzer (1962) and J. R. Clarke (2003: 187–203), who plays down the symbolic associations of the doorframe in order to concentrate on the tomb's simulation of an elite domestic interior.

Figure 8.3 Strigillated sarcophagus with Hercules and Cerberus emerging from the doors of Hades, *c.* 180 CE

sarcophagus in which Hercules peers around the doors to the underworld with Cerberus – an allusion, like Alcestis, to myths of return (Figure 8.3).[30] Here the sarcophagus is construed as the very threshold of Hades, its canine guardian offering a monstrous foretaste of epiphanic encounters to come, while Hercules is presented as one of those privileged few who were permitted, because of their extraordinary deeds, to recross the boundary that separates the viewer from the realm of the dead and, in practical terms, from the deceased within the sarcophagus. In other examples it is Hermes/Mercury in his role as Psychopompos who slips through the doorway into the sarcophagus's frontal relief, a deity who by his very nature defines the boundaries between different categories of space and experience (Figure 8.4).[31] Does his presence here allude to the possibility of return from the manes, or act as a reminder that only divine figures can traverse such boundaries at will? Is he about to conduct the couple depicted upon the sarcophagus to their final resting place? Alternatively, if he is returning from this particular assignment, who will accompany him next? It is significant that sarcophagi seldom permit their mortal viewers to pass through the doors of Hades and see what lies beyond, but compel us to remain (for now) within the world of the living. To cross that threshold – and, by implication, to enter the

---

[30] Rome, Museo Capitolino 1394: see Haarløv (1977: 139, no. D1), Koch and Sichtermann (1982: 149, 243–4, fig. 290) and Jongste (1992: 61–2).

[31] Museo dell'Opera del Duomo, Florence. See also a strigillated example in the Villa Rina, Genzano, dated 250–300, in which a figure (possibly holding a *kerykeion*) can be glimpsed through a narrow opening between the doors: see Morey (1924: 56–9), Haarløv (1977: cat. VI, C5 and D22) and G. Davies (1978: nos. 82 and 84), with G. Smith (2000) and Paolitti (2006) on Roman sarcophagi in Medici Florence. On Hermes as a marker of boundaries, see my discussion in Chapter 1, 35–6.

Figure 8.4 Sarcophagus with Hermes Psychopompos emerging from a central doorway, *c.* 200–50 CE

sarcophagus itself – is to enter the domain of the dead, a realm that (perhaps surprisingly, given the epic tradition of *katabasis*), is rarely depicted in Roman funerary art.[32] When we do see Pluto and Proserpina enthroned within the underworld, as on the far right of the Alcestis sarcophagus, they are clearly separated from the realm of the living by internal framing elements, while the viewer is diverted to the ghostly figure of Alcestis as she makes her extraordinary return to the court of Admetus (Figure 8.2). While doorway sarcophagi establish a channel of communication between these two spheres, then, they simultaneously reassert the necessary border that the tomb enforces between them – a notion that is often visually underlined by the presence of apotropaic *gorgoneia* and lion *protomai* on the doors' recessed panels, which emphasise the inviolability of the tomb at the same

[32] Toynbee (1977), followed by Grassinger (1994: 101), points out that on the rare occasions when the underworld is depicted on sarcophagi, it is to be found in lower relief on the shorter sides of the object, such as the punishments of Sisyphus, Ixion and Tantalus depicted on the right-hand side of the Protesilaos and Laodamia sarcophagus in the Vatican: *ASR* 3.3, no. 423; Zanker and Ewald (2004: 374–7). A striking exception is a mid-second-century CE sarcophagus in the Museo Civico at Velletri, with an upper register depicting Hades and Persephone enthroned within his palace, framed by doorways through which Alcestis returns to Admetus, and Protesilaos to Laodamia, and Heracles emerges with Cerberus. In the lower register, Hades abducts Persephone. See Lawrence (1965), Haarløv (1977: 26–30), Koch and Sichtermann (1982: 142), Jongste (1992: 39–43), Strong (1992: 190), Zanker and Ewald (2004: 29–30) and Platt (in press b). Note that, even here, the emphasis is still on passage *in and out* of Hades, rather than a *nekyia* in the tradition of the Greek monumental painting of Polygnotus, for example.

time as defining a clear boundary between the upper and lower worlds (Figure 8.4).

Threshold sarcophagi thus maintain a precarious balance between invitation and exclusion, which echoes the broader polyvalence of much Roman funerary iconography while giving visual expression to both the liminal status of the tomb itself and the viewer's conflicted desire for proximity to the deceased from a secure position within the realm of the living. On over thirty such sarcophagi, the object's status as a veil between the spheres of the living and the dead is reinforced by strigillated panels flanking its central architectural feature (for example, Figure 8.3). These shimmer over the surface like waves or rippling fabric, concealing what lies within while simultaneously dissolving and reinforcing the stone's materiality – a simple and affordable decorative motif, perhaps, but one that powerfully enhances the visual and eschatological ambivalence of the central doorway, while underlining the special conditions that characterise any act of viewing within the tomb.[33] A similar ambiguity is maintained by a number of Roman columnar sarcophagi on which a central doorway is flanked by personifications, or *genii*, of the Seasons (Figure 8.5).[34] These allude to cyclical patterns of life and death (and thus the possibility of return), yet keep the viewer firmly within a world where time is experienced as both the natural rhythm of the revolving year and a linear progression from youth to old age. In Figure 8.5, showing an Antonine example from Rome now in the Museo Capitolino, the inevitable linearity of temporal experience in the mortal realm is reinforced by the order in which the Seasons are depicted, according to which it is Winter and Autumn, clutching respectively a brace of fowl and a bunch of grapes, who flank the threshold of death.[35] Different experiences of time

[33] Here, I am indebted to Janet Huskinson's observations on strigillated sarcophagi, which she explores in detail in a forthcoming book. On strigillated doorway sarcophagi, see Haarløv (1977: 39–41, 139–49, cat. VI, D1–33).

[34] Museo Capitolino 1185: see Hanfmann (1951: vol. I, 24, 33–4, vol. II, no. 336), Haarløv (1977: cat. VI, C3) and Kranz (1984: no. 16, 187–8, with further bibliography). For parallel examples, see a sarcophagus in the Roman church of San Lorenzo in Panisperna dated *c.* 250–70 (discussed by Lawrence, 1958, and Kranz, 1984: no. 19, 189) and a child's sarcophagus in the Metropolitan Museum of Art, New York, dated to the late third century, in which the Seasons flanking the central doorway are displayed as statues upon bases (inv. 18.145.51, discussed by McCann, 1978: 133–7, no. 23, and Kranz, 1984: no. 9, 186).

[35] H. S. Jones (1926: 49); Lawrence (1958: 275); Kranz (1984: 188). On the Seasons as the four ages of man, see, e.g., Ov. *Met.* 15.199–212 and Horace *Odes* 4.7.7–16, with Putnam (1986: 133–44) and Feeney (2007: 213–15). On their significance in philosophical and religious texts of the second and third centuries CE, see Hanfmann (1951: vol. I, 150–209, a reading heavily influenced by the Cumont tradition, with 16–72 and 230–45), on the iconography of the Seasons in imperial funerary art. On the iconography pertaining to the *genius* of each season, see Kranz (1984: 119–27).

Figure 8.5 Seasons sarcophagus, *c.* 240 CE

may distinguish the living from the dead, but ultimately it is Time itself that will unite the sarcophagus's external viewers with those who lie within – a notion that is reinforced by the doubling of the Seasons in the form of miniature cupids on the very door panels that both invite and prohibit the viewer's entrance.

While the ash urn or sarcophagus can present itself as a portal, its primary function is nevertheless that of a container for the corpse (a concept taken to its logical extreme in the carved interior of the second-century Simpelveld sarcophagus, which depicts the deceased reclining upon a *klinē* surrounded by her household belongings).[36] While scholars have struggled to find a convincing explanation for the reasons behind the large-scale shift from cremation to inhumation that took place in the second century CE, one of the major implications of this change is the more enduring emphasis laid upon the body, as the focus of funerary ritual shifted from the public spectacle of the pyre to the privacy of the tomb's interior.[37] As Pliny the Elder pointed out, the etymology of the term sarcophagus (from the Greek *sarx,* 'flesh', and *phagein,* 'to eat') lay, after all, in the capacity of *sarkophagos* limestone

---

[36] Rijksmuseum van Oudheden, Leiden, l 1930/12.1: see Toynbee (1971: 281) and Zanker and Ewald (2004: 29).

[37] See above, n. 5.

from Assos to embrace and dissolve the corpses deposited within it.[38] In contrast to smaller ash-urns, sarcophagi draw attention to the dimensions of the human form(s) they contain, and their decorative reliefs, particularly on the long frontal panel, provide a screen or interface between the space of the living viewer and that occupied by the *corpus* within.[39] In this sense they operate as intermediary devices between moving and static bodies, invitations to meditation, interpretation and communication, rather than neat repositories of meaning. Given the proximity of viewer and (unseen) body in such contexts, it is telling that the figurative details employed on the frontal panels that stand between them often project an emphatic corporeality, which is enhanced on sarcophagi of the Antonine period by classicising, often eroticised, bodies carved in high relief.

The presence of immortal bodies in such narratives therefore offers a provocative contrast with the mortality of the form within the sarcophagus, signalling the deficiency of the human body while hinting at the potential for transcending its limitations – whether through piety, heroic achievement or acts of *memoria* performed by those left behind. Insofar as death marks a transition from one world to the next, deities appear as facilitators of this process, whether as guides (Mercury), abductors (Pluto and Proserpina; the Dioscuri and the Leucippidae), lovers (Selene and Endymion; Venus and Adonis) or agents of apotheosis (Dionysus and Ariadne).[40] Within the broad range of iconographic choices available to Roman patrons, scenes of an eroticised relationship between a god and a sleeping mortal form one of the most popular compositions, with over one hundred sarcophagi depicting

---

[38] On the 'flesh-eating' properties of *sarcophagus lapis* from Assos in the Troad, see Plin. *HN* 2.98 and 36.131, with Healy (1999: 239–40) and Denzey (2007: 6–7), who notes that although such material was not used for decorated Roman sarcophagi (which were predominantly made of marble), the high lime-content of marbles imported from the empire's eastern provinces may have hastened the corpse's decomposition.

[39] Y. Thomas (2004: 51–6) notes that, in the language of Roman burial, the body of the deceased is always referred to as a *corpus* rather than a *cadaver*: 'Bodies, not corpses, were buried in religious places, whether or not those bodies had been reduced to ashes. In relation to the tomb, a body figured as a *cadaver* only when its presence was forbidden' (53).

[40] For examples of the abduction of Persephone, see Sichtermann and Koch (1975: 56–9), Koch and Sichtermann (1982: 175–9) and Zanker and Ewald (2004: 91–5, 367–72); for the abduction of the Leucippidae, see Sichtermann and Koch (1975: 39), Koch and Sichtermann (1982: 157–8) and Zanker and Ewald (2004: 95–6, 331–6); for Aphrodite and Adonis, see Sichtermann and Koch (1975: 19–20), Koch and Sichtermann (1982: 131–3), Koortbojian (1995: esp. 19–62), Grassinger (1999: 70–90, *ASR* 12.1, nos. 43–67) and Zanker and Ewald (2004: 208–13, 288–94); for Dionysus and Ariadne, see Lehmann-Hartleben and Olsen (1942: 37–42), Matz (1969: *ASR* 4.3, nos. 207–29), Koch and Sichtermann (1982: 193–4), Turcan (1999: 101–10) and Zanker and Ewald (2004: 162–6, 306–12).

Figure 8.6 Dionysus and Ariadne sarcophagus, *c.* 180–90 CE

the Endymion myth.[41] We also find variations which, in a reversal of gender, depict Dionysus discovering the sleeping Ariadne on Naxos (Figure 8.6) and, more rarely, Mars descending to impregnate the Vestal virgin Rhea Silvia, mother of Romulus and Remus.[42] Indeed, by the third century, the three myths had acquired such an iconographic and thematic unity that the fates of Endymion and Rhea Silvia were depicted side by side in a reverse-gendered pair on a famous example now in the Vatican's Museo Gregoriano Profano (Figure 8.7), while a pair of sarcophagi now in the Louvre juxtaposes Endymion with Ariadne.[43] All three scenes of mortal–immortal union stage epiphanic confrontations in an explicit, and yet highly problematic, manner. For although the deity is in each case depicted by means of revelatory visual formulae, the sleeping figure is suspended in slumber and never perceives him or her directly (a feature to which I shall return below).

A simple narrative with a faint footprint in ancient literature, yet a powerful metaphor for death, the Endymion tale found its most eloquent expression in visual form, and became increasingly elaborate following its entry

---

[41] Zanker and Ewald (2004: 103).

[42] Figure 8.6: a sarcophagus still *in situ* within Tomb Z ('The Tomb of the Egyptians') in the necropolis beneath St Peter's Basilica, dated *c.* 180–90 CE: see Toynbee and Ward-Perkins (1956: 51–7), Mielsch and von Hesberg (1986: vol. II, 225–33) and Feraudi-Gruénais (2001: 172–3). On Mars and Rhea Silvia, see Sichtermann and Koch (1975: 66), Wrede (1981: 271–2), Koch and Sichtermann (1982: 104), Koortbojian (1995: 102–6), Turcan (1999: 97–8) and Zanker and Ewald (2004: 214–15).

[43] Figure 8.7: Museo Gregoriano Profano, Vatican, inv. 9558: see C. Robert (1897–1919: vol. I, 108–10, *ASR* 3.1, no. 88), Wrede (1981: 271, no. 200), Sichtermann (1992: 150–1, *ASR* 12.2, no. 99) and Zanker and Ewald (2004: 215–16). On the Louvre pair, see below.

Figure 8.7 Sarcophagus depicting Mars and Rhea Silvia and Selene and Endymion, c. 210–15 CE

Figure 8.8 Selene and Endymion *lēnos* sarcophagus, *c.* 190–200 CE

into the sarcophagus repertoire in the mid second century.[44] Figure 8.8, a *lēnos* sarcophagus from Ostia now in the Metropolitan Museum, New York, incorporates many elements that had become standard by the 190s.[45] To the left, a shepherd and his flock indicate the myth's bucolic setting, while Aura (a winged and booted personification of the breeze) brings Selene's rearing horses to a halt as they come into land above a personification of Tellus, the earth. In contrast to earlier, more experimental compositions (such as Figure 8.1), Selene now approaches Endymion from the left, her upper body framed by the *velificatio* motif formed by her billowing drapery.[46] She is accompanied by a cloud of winged cupids bearing torches, who urge the goddess towards her lover's now fully naked form, while above him a poppy-bearing personification of Night pours an opiate to ensure that he remains blissfully unaware of the dramatic motion and anticipation that surround him. To the right, Selene's billowing drapery is just visible as she departs from her nocturnal tryst, while the left side of the *lēnos* gives the scene a truly cosmic frame by depicting an ascending Sol with his radiate crown, to complement Selene's status as Luna. Endymion himself reclines in peaceful oblivion, his arm thrown back above his head in a pose familiar from depictions of the sleeping Ariadne (Figure 8.6); looking down with his eyes firmly closed, he remains a paralysed, static image amid a flurry of signification.[47]

Interpretations of such scenes have focused primarily upon the analogous relationship the composition establishes between the slumbering mortal on

[44] See *LIMC* s.v. Endymion (vol. III.1: 726–42, esp. 727–8) and Koortbojian (1995: 63–4), on literary sources for the myth. On Endymion sarcophagi, see C. Robert (1897–1919: vol. I, 53–111, *ASR* 3.1, nos. 39–92), Sichtermann (1992: 32–58, *ASR* 12.2, nos. 27–137), Koortbojian (1995: esp. 63–99), Turcan (1999: 92–6), Zanker and Ewald (2004: 102–9, 204–8) and, on Endymion in late antiquity, Sichtermann (1966) and Balch (2008).

[45] Metropolitan Museum of Art, New York, inv. 47.100.4. See C. Robert (1897–1919: vol. I, 103–6, *ASR* 3.1, no. 83), Matz (1956–7), McCann (1978: 39–45, no. 4), Koch and Sichtermann (1982: 145–6), Sichtermann (1992: 134–8, *ASR* 12.2 no. 80, with further bibliography), Koortbojian (1995: 75–82) and Zanker and Ewald (2004: 322–5). The lion *protomai* that appear on each side of the frontal panel are typical of *lēnoi* ('wine vats'), while the Cupid and Psyche depicted to the left represent another mortal–immortal coupling rich in allegorical associations (on which see Schlam, 1976, and Platt, 2007a). Most unusually for a Roman rather than Attic sarcophagus, the bucolic imagery is continued on the rear, though in more shallow relief; on the significance of such motifs as a *Glücksvision* of happiness close to nature, see Zanker and Ewald (2004: 167–77).

[46] On this shift in composition, see Koortbojian (1995: 68), who observes that few examples depicting the action from right to left date later than 180.

[47] On Hellenising depictions of the sleeping Ariadne in Roman art, see McNally (1985), Gallo (1988), Parise Badoni (1990) and Fredrick (1995).

the relief and the deceased individual within the sarcophagus.[48] While sleep is understood as a metaphor for death, the love of the god offers a means of emphasising (or enhancing) the youthful beauty and privileged status of the dead, while suggesting that death itself might be blessed by divinely influenced dreams (in the case of Endymion) or (in the case of Ariadne) the possibility of waking from a deathlike sleep to a joyful afterlife. In an extension of this analogical model, we might draw parallels between Selene's nocturnal visits to the sleeping Endymion and the mourner's cyclical, torch-lit visits to the tomb in order to honour the deceased – a compelling correspondence between the action depicted on the relief and the activities of the sarcophagus's viewers. Yet this reading suppresses the fact that, unlike the mortal viewer, the being who visits the sleeping beloved is in each of these cases a god. The internal dynamics of the scene itself thus revolve around an asymmetrical relationship between a passive mortal and a vital deity. Displayed in a locus where the very limits of mortality are repeatedly negotiated, they raise important questions about the nature of viewing in the context of death. To what extent is the tomb a sacred space that gives access to a different mode of vision from that which pertains in the profane spaces of the living? What, in fact, do the dead see? Is their experience at all accessible to, or representable by, those left behind?

In this sense the relationship between death and representation is parallel to the cognitive dilemmas raised by epiphany. Both are forms of dramatic and disturbing incursions into human experience, which by their very nature define the limits of mortality. They are thus resistant to human efforts to capture, preserve or communicate their qualities in visual or verbal form. To 'know' death in an unmediated sense is to cross the threshold of Pluto – and few can speak from beyond the tomb. For mere mortals, as Elisabeth Bronfen has suggested, death itself is beyond representation: any attempt to translate it into human terms must necessarily resort to strategies that transform it into something familiar, formulaic, aestheticised and therefore unlike itself.[49] At the same time one might argue that for those who remain within the realm of the living, death is *only* apprehensible as a cultural construct. Roman funerary art thus presents us with a complex system of metaphors and symbols that repeatedly signify death, but draw back from

---

[48] See above, 341.

[49] Bronfen (1992: x): 'The aesthetic representation of death lets us repress our knowledge of the reality of death precisely because it occurs *at* someone else's body and *as* an image'. See also Goodwin and Bronfen (1993), with an earlier exploration of the same themes by Burke (1952), who comments that 'The imaging of death necessarily involves images not directly belonging to it . . . [It lies] beyond the realm of such images as the living body knows' (369).

presenting the thing itself.[50] Instead, we encounter a *horror vacui* – the urge to fill the surface planes of the sarcophagus (and indeed the entire interior of the tomb) with a feverish number of signs that seek to suppress the threat death poses and allay potential grief through visual strategies that, as Karl Guthke has shown, 'give shape to the shapeless by approximating it to the familiar'.[51]

One of the most prevalent of these strategies in Graeco-Roman culture was the figuring of death as abduction by a divine lover. Here epiphany provides a striking metaphor for exploring the desirability of the dead, their sudden loss and violent transition to an altered state by means of a dramatic (and markedly gendered) asymmetry of power and agency between god and mortal.[52] As an act which is, in ancient terms, simultaneously destructive and creative, rape is deeply ambiguous, emphasising the seductive charm and tragic vulnerability of the female body – its potential for both fertility and corruption.[53] In the mid-fourth-century BCE 'Tomb of Persephone'

---

[50] While Hades/Pluto/Dis frequently appears as king of the underworld, Thanatos, the Greek personification of death, is seldom depicted in Roman funerary art, and his occasional presence is often disputed. See, e.g., Wood (1978: 501 n. 16) on the identity of the bearded figure with a dog in Figure 8.2, identified by C. Robert (1897–1919: vol. III, 32) as Thanatos, but by Grassinger (1994: 227) as the heroised Admetus, and Sichtermann (1992: 50–1), on failed efforts to identify the figure of Sleep on many Endymion sarcophagi as Thanatos. Death's female Latin equivalents Mors (the daughter of Erebus and Nox) and Libitina (the goddess of funerals) are literary figures but have no iconographic presence. Likewise, Jan Bazant points out in *LIMC* 7.1 (s.v. Thanatos) that the solemn putti with reversed torches often observed in Roman funerary art should be understood as funerary Erotes (or cupids) rather than personifications of death. For Mors as a personification in Latin epitaphs, see Lattimore (1962: 153 (*Carm. Epigr.* 441.3–4, 'mors tacita obrepsit subito facitque ruinam | quae tibi crescenti rapuit iuvenile figuram'), with, e.g., the female 'pallida mors' of Horace (*Odes* 1.4.13–14) and Seneca (*Hercules Furens* 555). On the complex gendering of death in antiquity, see D. Burton (2005: esp. 57–8), on Mors. On Orcus, a Roman name for the underworld, and, by extension, an equivalent deity to Hades–Pluto, see Wagenvoort (1956: 102–31). On Libitina and the metonymic use of her name in references to death and burial, see Bodel (2000: 132–7; 2004).

[51] Guthke (1999: 8), on personifications of death in Western culture.

[52] On the gendering of rape in Greek myths and its relationship to contemporary negotiations of power, gender and initiation into adult sexuality, see Zeitlin (1986), who points out that, in fifth-century BCE vase-painting, 'sexual aggression in its most unambiguous form as pursuit is mainly attributed to those who are not human actors – gods and satyrs' (131). On the inversion of gender roles in scenes of sexual pursuit, see A. Stewart (1995) and R. Osborne (1996); on their negotiation of human–divine relations, see Kaempf-Dimitriadou (1979) and Lefkowitz (2007: 70–81).

[53] See, e.g., Arieti (2002: 219–23), on rape in Livy. Rape, of course, is a notoriously slippery and difficult phenomenon that is subject not only to different cultural and legal definitions, but also multiple, often divergent narratives: see Brownmiller (1975), Tomaselli and Porter (1986) and Higgins and Silver (1991). On the law and politics of rape in classical Athens, see Omitowoju (2002). On the Roman concept of *raptus* ('carrying off by force') as a form of property offence against male guardians, see Burgess-Jackson (1999: 16), Wolfthal (1999: 9) and Dixon (2001: 45–55); on rape as *per vim stuprum* ('intercourse by force'), see Gardner (1986: 117–21) and Fantham (1991).

Figure 8.9 Hades abducting Persephone, mid fourth century BCE

at Vergina, for example, intense coloration and the naturalistic effects of *skiagraphia* and dramatic foreshortening are exploited to transform the painted wall into a dynamic epiphanic tableau in which the god of the underworld gallops towards the viewer in his chariot, the body of Persephone flung diagonally across the picture plane with a force that expresses death's sovereignty over those it desires (Figure 8.9).[54] The contrast between abductor god and helpless mourner is indicated by the seated figure of Persephone's mother, Demeter, on the adjacent wall (Figure 8.10): the numbness of grief is embodied by the static forms of those left behind, while death itself is figured as vigorous motion and violation, a terrifying confrontation with forces beyond mortal (and even immortal) control. It is questionable whether the Vergina image is intended for the living at all: concealed

[54] See Andronikos (1994: 49–134), who attributes the painting to Nicomachus (who Pliny tells us painted a *Rape of Persephone*, *HN* 35.108) or his pupil Philoxenus of Eretria. On the painting's use of colour, see Brecoulaki (2006: vol. I, 77–100), and on *skiagraphia*, see Bruno (1977: 31–40), Rouveret (1989: 16–63) and Summers (2007: 36–8). On the rape of Persephone in classical and Hellenistic art, see Schefold (1981: 259–65), Lindner (1984) and Cohen (1996), with G. Davies (1986) on Roman grave altars and ash chests and Koch (1978) on sarcophagi. For a feminist reading of the myth in the context of Roman funerary art, see Wood (2000).

Figure 8.10 Mourning Demeter, mid fourth century BCE

Figure 8.11 Pluto abducting Proserpina, *c.* 160–70 CE

within a tomb buried beneath a vast tumulus, the painting proffers its fatal epiphany to those who have already passed beyond the boundaries of mortality. As an iconographic schema, however, the image lived on, echoed for mourning viewers on the walls and floors of Roman tombs (Figure 8.11) as well as sarcophagus reliefs.[55] From the *korē* of Phrasikleia in sixth-century BCE Attica to the Roman catacombs of late antiquity, funerary inscriptions repeatedly drew upon this most archetypal of myths: a fourth-century BCE Athenian epitaph states of the deceased that 'Hades cast his dark wings about her', while a later Roman example claims in the voice of the dead

---

[55] Mosaic in the necropolis beneath St Peter's, Rome, Tomb I (the 'Tomb of the Chariot'): see Ferrua (1947: 226–8), Toynbee and Ward-Perkins (1956: 74–5), Lindner (1984: 59, no. 52), Mielsch and von Hesberg (1986: 219) and Feraudi-Gruénais (2001: 53–6).

Figure 8.12 Pluto and Proserpina sarcophagus, *c.* 160–70 CE

woman, 'Pluto rapuit me ad infera templa' ('Pluto snatched me away to his realms below').[56]

The ubiquity of such iconography, however, and its prominence within decorative schemes designed for entire tombs (as in Figure 8.11) as well as receptacles for female bodies, suggests that its dynamic contrast between wilful divine strength and mortal passivity provided a model for exploring asymmetrical relationships not only between men and women, but also between gods and mortals.[57] On a Pluto and Proserpina sarcophagus in Florence dated *c.* 160–70 CE, the deity and his victim form an arresting chiasmus that dominates a tug-of-war between Pluto, Mercury and Venus, on one hand, and Ceres and Minerva, on the other (Figure 8.12).[58] In contrast to the urgent motion of the deities attempting to advance their respective interests, Proserpina lies horizontally across the visual field, prostrate beneath the *velificatio* effect that indicates Pluto's sudden appearance and rapid,

---

[56] On Phrasikleia's epitaph (*CEG* 24, *IG* I³.1261: σῆμα Φρασικλείας· | κόρε κεκλέσομαι | αἰεί, / ἀντὶ γάμο | παρὰ θεõν τοῦτο | λαχõσ' ὄνομα, 'I am the marker of Phrasikleia. I shall always be *korē*, the gods having allotted me this name in place of marriage'), see Svenbro (1993: 8–25), Sourvinou-Inwood (1995: 242–51) and Derderian (2001: 79–80). A *korē* statue in Berlin, also once used as a funerary marker, offers an iconographic parallel between Persephone and the deceased by carrying a pomegranate (Antikensammlung no. 1800). For the Hellenistic example (*EG* 89.4: Ἅιδης [ο]ἱ σκοτίας ἀμφέβαλεν πτέρυγας), see Lattimore (1962: 88), with further examples. The Roman epitaph comes from the grave of a young woman called Bassa, and is preserved as *Carm. Epigr.* 1058, line 6 (*Carm. Sep.* 390; *CIL* 6.7898).

[57] Cf. Cohen (1996: 121), on the 'Tomb of Persephone', in which the remains of a man, woman and baby were discovered.

[58] Galleria Uffizi, Florence, inv. 86. To the left of the scene, Ceres begins the search for her daughter in a chariot pulled by serpents, and Minerva attempts to halt the abduction while Venus pulls her back by the rim of her shield; to the right, Mercury hastens Pluto's chariot on to its infernal destination. See Lindner (1984: 77, no. 94), Wood (2000: 83–4) and Zanker and Ewald (2004: 91–4). For a parallel example, see a sarcophagus dated 170–80 in the Palazzo Rospigliosi, Rome, discussed by Koch and Sichtermann (1982: 176, no. 203, pl. 25.1) and Lindner (1984: 79, no. 102, pl. 25).

Figure 8.13(a) Dioscuri and Leucippidae sarcophagus, *c*. 160 CE

Figure 8.13 (*cont.*) (b) and (c) Side panels of Figure 8.13(a)

inevitable departure. In examples depicting the abduction of the daughters of Leucippus by the Dioscuri, the sexual energy of the scene radiates from the central axis in a dramatic doubling, as elongated human bodies are thrown diagonally across the upright forms of their divine abductors, soft breasts and slim torsos juxtaposed with strong arms and jutting pectorals (Figure 8.13a).[59] The defenceless, outstretched bodies of Proserpina and the Leucippidae invite a double comparison, contrasting with the virility of their divine aggressors while evoking the supine bodies of the dead within

---

[59] Walters Art Museum, Baltimore (no. 23.32). This example formed part of the collection of sarcophagi associated with the 'Licinian tomb' in Rome and now in Baltimore: see Lehmann-Hartleben and Olsen (1942: 16–17, 42–5), Koch and Sichtermann (1982: 157–8, no. 176) and Zanker and Ewald (2004: 95–6, 333–6). On the problematic excavation of the tomb and provenance of its antiquities, see Bentz (1997–8), who is too trustful of the nineteenth-century sources, and Kragelund *et al.* (2003: 55–79), who rule out any direct relationship between the Baltimore sarcophagi and the tomb of the Licinii, and hesitate to assume that the Leucippidae sarcophagus (from 'Chamber Two') actually comes from the same tomb as the well-known Dionysiac sarcophagi (from 'Chamber Three'), thereby compromising attempts (such as Lehmann-Hartleben and Olsen, 1942) to interpret the objects as a group with a coherent set of eschatological themes related to the religious affiliations of their occupants. For parallel examples of the same composition, see C. Robert (1897–1919: vol. II, 223–4, *ASR* 3.2, no. 181, now in the Vatican Museums, Rome) and Zanker and Ewald (2004: fig. 222, now in the Uffizi, Florence, dated *c.* 150).

the sarcophagus. With their high relief, dramatic play of light and shadow, and richly modelled figures, such reliefs emphasise the body's tangible materiality at the very site where their occupants pass into an immaterial realm; indeed, if we take the etymology of the term *sarkophagos* literally, the object itself could be said to facilitate this transition.[60] As adornment and screen between the living and the dead, the container's frontal relief provides an interstitial space in which the boundaries between the material and immaterial are dissolved, and the body-as-image exists in a state of suspended animation. In this paradoxical zone, human *corpus* and elusive divine form can meet, and the erotics of epiphany are made possible.

How is the external viewer to engage with this ambiguous space? What is the ontological status of the immortal bodies that cavort within it, or indeed, of the mortals whom they force to submit to their will? The limits of representation are here put to effective use, for while the naturalistic style and dramatic composition of such scenes intensify the drama of loss through violent motion and heightened eroticism, the screen of discourse between viewer and narrative event is seldom punctured. Depictions of Proserpina's abduction on Roman sarcophagi tend to depict the wheels of Pluto's chariot, and thus the direction of the action, in profile: the living viewer observes the scene as if it were a theatrical performance, and is not invited to participate in its internal play of gazes (Figure 8.12).[61] Conversely, the diagonal thrust and strikingly foreshortened wheels of the chariot at Vergina suggest that Hades is galloping out of the picture plane into the space of the beholder, an effect that is enhanced by the large scale of the painting and its paucity of formal framing devices, as well as by the god's intense frontal gaze (Figure 8.9). This difference is partly due to the demands of the artistic medium: painting in the tradition of late classical *skiagraphia* favours a sense of illusionistic depth, whereas narrative sarcophagus reliefs concentrate their action within a narrow linear space that runs perpendicular to the viewer. In each locale, however, medium, style and composition are put to work in service of a specific set of ritual traditions.

In a Macedonian context where living viewers were denied access to the tomb after the funerary rites and any visual ornament was thereafter reserved for the dead, illusionistic absorption is entirely fitting; in encountering a Hades depicted in a manner that suppresses the image's act of mediation

---

[60] See above, n. 38.

[61] See, e.g., Lindner (1984: plates 14–26). On divine chariots in Roman art, see Schollmeyer (2001: 125–36). On the theatricality of sarcophagus reliefs, see Koortbojian (1995: 118–20), Gessert (2004) and Huskinson (2008), on the influence of pantomime.

and asserts a form of epiphanic presence, the tomb's occupant encounters a figure equated with 'death himself'.[62] Roman tombs, however, were visited by the relatives of the deceased on several occasions throughout the year, generating a ritual context that constructed the living viewer as primary bearer of the gaze. It is surely significant that the ontological status of the abductor god qua image is here more clearly signposted, whether by profile composition, concentric framing devices that stress the image's status as ornament, or symbolic motifs and subsidiary 'staffage' figures that divert the viewer from a sense of direct encounter by encouraging an allegorical mode of interpretation concerned with apotheosis and triumph over mortality. In this way the experiences of the dead (and their representational proxies) are repeatedly distanced from the living visitor to the tomb. The visual tradition of epiphany, which is fundamentally concerned with unmediated access to the gods, is here overtly co-opted by funerary art as a device for mediating or displacing the unpalatable phenomenon of death. For as parallel transgressions of the boundaries of human experience that are equally resistant to representation, epiphany and death provide compelling metaphors for each other: both phenomena lurk within Carson's 'darkness at the back of the painting'.[63]

Unlike abduction sarcophagi, scenes of a god approaching a sleeping mortal do not depict eroticised violence (although they may anticipate it). Yet despite the more gentle overtures made by divine lovers such as Selene, Dionysus and Mars, each myth depends upon the same notion of a stark disparity of agency between mortal and immortal. Like Pluto, Selene arrives (and departs) in a chariot from another realm, while her male equivalent, Mars, derives from a familiar corpus of rape myths in which a violent god descends from the sky to assault a vulnerable virgin. Like the rape of Proserpina, Selene's advances to Endymion take place within a bucolic landscape, indicated in examples of the latter myth by trees, personifications of Mount Latmos, shepherds and their flocks (Figures 8.1 and 8.14).[64] As a familiar element of epiphanic narrative that dates back as far as the *Homeric Hymns* and Hesiod's *Theogony*, the pastoral zone is no straightforward allusion to a blissful afterlife, but also evokes a space far from civic boundaries over which man has little dominion, where mortals

---

[62] On Macedonian tomb architecture, see Andronikos (1994: 29–48; 1997: 25–37) and Winter (2006: 87–90). For a parallel tradition of prioritising dead (rather than living) viewers in the decorative schemes of sealed Chinese tombs, see Wu Hung (2009).

[63] Carson (1999: 61); see my Introduction, 23.

[64] Figure 8.14: Museo Capitolino, inv. 725: see C. Robert (1897–1919: vol. I, 76–8, *ASR* 3.1, no. 61) and Sichtermann (1992: 114–16, *ASR* 12.2, no. 51).

Figure 8.14 Selene and Endymion sarcophagus, *c.* 200–20 CE

encounter forces far greater than themselves, and strange things happen to those who linger.[65] Like the tomb, it constitutes a space of alterity in which mortal and divine bodies can come together.

Within this zone the contrast between active deity and passive human is again expressed in terms of motion. While Endymion and Rhea Silvia recline in heavy slumber (enhanced on sarcophagi such as Figure 8.8 by an opium-bearing figure of Sleep or Night), the gods' arrival is marked by a rush of flying drapery, rearing horses, spinning chariot wheels and winged cupids; while mortals are depicted as frozen within the image realm, their divine lovers can come and go as they please.[66] Accordingly, a number of Endymion sarcophagi depict not only Selene's arrival, but also her departure (Figures 8.8 and 8.14).[67] If the tomb acts as a form of threshold to the *au-delà*, then it is one with very different sets of rules over each character's entrance and exit, as the doorway sarcophagi discussed above make clear. While Selene's comings and goings may be analogous to the mourner's repeated visits and carefully timed acts of ritual within the tomb, they also express the gods' power to cross the boundary between life and death at will. It is significant in this respect that Selene's chariot – that symbol of her transcendent powers of motion – is seldom depicted in domestic wall-painting, examples of which focus on the couple's impending erotic union rather than the goddess's passage in and out of the frame (Figures 8.17–18 below).[68] A striking compositional device with a similar effect is employed

---

[65] See Chapter 1, 55–6, with Petridou (in press a).

[66] For further examples of Hypnos or Nyx drugging Endymion with poppy juice, see Sichtermann (1992: 118–19, *ASR* 12.2, no. 57, dated *c.* 200 CE and now in the Louvre, Ma 607, and 125–7, *ASR* 12.2, no. 72, dated *c.* 220–40, also in the Louvre, Ma 1335), discussed below.

[67] For parallel examples to Figure 8.14, see Sichtermann (1992: 115–19, *ASR* 12.2, nos. 52–6, 'Group 3').

[68] On Selene and Endymion in Roman wall-painting, see below. The only Endymion painting I can find depicting Selene in her chariot is a now lost example from Pompeii 1.2.17 mentioned

Figure 8.15 Venus and Adonis sarcophagus, *c.* 190 CE

on a sarcophagus now in the Palazzo Ducale, Mantua, depicting Venus and Adonis (Figure 8.15).[69] In her urgency to hasten to the scene of her lover's fatal boar hunt on the right side of the relief, the goddess flings her arm in a *pathosformula* across the pilaster that separates the scene from that on the left, in which the couple are reunited in a final embrace while cupids tend to Adonis' wounds.[70] Venus' ability to breach the formal framing elements of the sarcophagus (adorned, we might note, with putti representing the Seasons) acts as an expression of both her passion and concern for Adonis, and her ability, if not to change the course of Fate, at least to transgress the spatial and temporal boundaries that shape normative mortal experience. It is only with the force of such divine agency behind them that the deceased might hope to surpass those limits themselves – a possibility that later Adonis sarcophagi render visible by including a scene of healing and enthronement that runs counter to the myth's traditionally tragic end.[71]

by Schefold (1956: 215–16) and Koortbojian (1995: 71, fig. 33, *LIMC* s.v. Endymion, no. 42). The illustration that survives, however, is of such poor quality that it is impossible to see Selene at all.

[69] Palazzo Ducale, Mantua, dated *c.* 190 CE: see C. Robert (1897–1919: vol. 1, 22–2, *ASR* 3.1, no. 20), Sichtermann and Koch (1975: 19, no. 6) and Grassinger (1999: 215, *ASR* 12.1, no. 55); note that this object has been heavily restored. For a parallel example in the cathedral sacristy, Blera, dated *c.* 200, see Grassinger (1999: 217, *ASR* 12.1, no. 61), although the left panel here depicts Adonis' departure for the hunt rather than the couple's farewell embrace, which is depicted in a third scene on the right. On Venus' gesture as a *pathosformula*, see Koortbojian (1995: 33–4).

[70] See Koortbojian (1995: 37–8, 42–4).

[71] E.g., a sarcophagus in the Vatican's Museo Gregoriano Profano dated *c.* 220 CE, inv. 10409: see C. Robert (1897–1919: vol. I, 22–4, *ASR* 3.1, no. 21) and Grassinger (1999: 74, *ASR* 12.1, no. 65). Koortbojian (1995: 49–62, 112–13) points out that, although Adonis sarcophagi include no explicit allusions to the Adonaia festival, which celebrated Adonis' botanical metamorphosis and symbolic rebirth, scenes of his recovery offer a 'prospective vision that augments the traditional analogy and evokes . . . a new fate for its protagonist' (49).

Divine lovers do not necessarily stand as analogies to the deceased's relatives, then, mourning the loss of those they have loved. Indeed, one might argue that the proleptic quality of their arrival before the sleeping bodies of Endymion, Rhea Silvia or Ariadne underlines the helplessness of the external viewer by suggesting an explicit contrast between the impotence of the grieving mortal outside the sarcophagus and the potential sexual agency of the immortal within the frame. Nor do such deities simply function as subordinate figures designed to enhance the beauty, desirability and heroism of the deceased, for their presence is too dynamic and insistent. Like Pluto and the Dioscuri, their resolute desire also serves to express death's ultimate power over the human body. As Anchises claims in the *Homeric Hymn to Aphrodite*, 'No man who sleeps with immortal goddesses is full of vigour (βιοθάλμιος)', since for a mortal to love a goddess is to risk impotence and even death, a 'terrible sorrow (αἰνόν . . . ἄχος)' that is echoed centuries later in Artemidorus' morbid interpretation of erotic dreams about the gods.[72] If sexual union with a deity is to be interpreted as an allegory of a blissful afterlife, then Selene, Mars and Dionysus represent the structural opposite of mortality: they are *im-mortales* (or, in the Greek, *a-thanatoi*), the 'undying ones'. And yet, in that each deity is responsible for the transformation of status – whether eternal sleep, pregnancy or mystic marriage – that renders Endymion, Rhea Silvia and Ariadne extraordinary, he or she also serves as a sublimation of death itself.

Although such reliefs employ every possible stylistic strategy to convey a glorious vision of divine epiphany, however, the dynamics of the scene portrayed condemn each deity to remain unacknowledged by his or her sleeping beloved. On the Endymion *lēnos* in New York, for example, the goddess's chariot, the *velificatio* effect of her drapery, the dramatic sense of swift motion and sudden arrival, and the myriad cupids all enhance the epiphanic effect of her divine *adventus*, while her exposed right breast and the crescent moon upon her brow emphasise her ambiguous status as both an embodied figure – a sensual corporeal presence – and a transcendent deity (Figure 8.8). In Graeco-Roman tradition, epiphanies demand an appropriate response from those who witness them.[73] Yet any awareness Endymion has of the heavenly spectacle being performed on his behalf lies within

---

[72] *H. Hom.* 5.189–90, 198–9; Artemidorus *Oneirocritica* 1.80: 'To have sexual intercourse with a god or a goddess . . . signifies death for a sick man. For the soul predicts meetings and intercourse with the gods when it is about to abandon the body in which it dwells' (see also 5.87). On the dangers of epiphany in the *Homeric Hymns*, see my discussion in Chapter 1, 63–8, with Chapter 6, 275–87, on Artemidorus.

[73] See Chapter 1, 54–6.

an oneiric realm that is inaccessible to both goddess and external viewer. Even subsidiary 'staffage' figures within the relief function as members of Selene's entourage or indicators of the location rather than internal mortal viewers, and therefore amplify the goddess's performance of self-revelation for Endymion rather than react to it (unlike the female companions who respond with alarm to the arrival of Pluto or the Dioscuri in Figures 8.9, 8.12 and 8.13a, for example).[74] Whereas abduction epiphanies underline the beholder's powerlessness over fate through the depiction of eroticised violence, scenes of sleep express loss and frustration by prohibiting not only an active response to the deity's arrival, but also any direct meeting of gazes – whether between divine lover and sleeping mortal, or between internal protagonists and external viewer.

For Koortbojian, Endymion's sleep acts as a rhetorical invitation to *phantasia*, a means of inducing imaginative involvement in the narrative, and the scene gains visual potency from the fact that Selene and Endymion 'are depicted in the recognizable and affective form of imminent sexual congress'.[75] Yet to accept the invitation of such erotic *prolepsis* is by no means a straightforward enterprise where goddesses are concerned (as I explored in Chapter 4).[76] An iconographic focus on the moment prior to congress may allow the viewer to imagine the scene for him- or herself (and indeed, Selene's exposure of a single breast in examples such as Figure 8.8 invites such an ocular undressing). At the same time, however, the narrative suspension signals the dangers and limitations of such voyeurism, while avoiding the awkward problem of *how* such a union might take place if Endymion is suspended in eternal slumber! In this sense Endymion sarcophagi enact a form of visual withholding: to pursue the narrative action beyond that which is shown is to enter a realm of experience that is prohibited to those who remain within the realm of the living. Furthermore, the delicate balance that the scene maintains between revelation and inhibition is not merely proleptic, for by isolating the sleeping mortal's visionary encounter within the dream world it actually situates each protagonist's experience within a

---

[74] On 'staffage' figures in depictions of the Endymion narrative, which function as 'stage dressing and decorative work that accompany the essential visualization of the myth', see Koortbojian (1995: 68–70, 73–5).

[75] Koortbojian (1995: 67–8).

[76] Consider, e.g., mortals who were blinded as a result of viewing gods engaged in sexual activity, from Apollo's son Erymanthus, who spied Aphrodite bathing after her union with Adonis (Ptolemy Hephaestion *ad* Photius, *Bibliotheca* Cod. 190, 146–7), to the tradition that Philip of Macedon lost the sight in one eye after witnessing Olympias with Jupiter Ammon in the form of a snake (Plutarch *Alexander* 3.1–4). See Buxton (1980: 30–2), Loraux (1990: 211–26) and Petridou (in press a).

discrete ontological category. Viewer, deity and dreamer thus occupy concentric realms of existence that lead deeper and deeper into obscurity, for, like any dream, the sleeper's *phantasia* is inaccessible to all but himself. In this sense, scenes of desirous gods approaching sleeping mortals constitute a self-consciously aporetic epiphanic mode that is peculiarly appropriate to the iconography of death.

The frustrating conjunction of revelatory performance, comatose sleep and withheld union on sarcophagi depicting Endymion, Rhea Silvia and Ariadne finds a thematic parallel in the iconography of abduction, which is also characterised by visual displacement. In the heroic tradition, sexual assault is rarely depicted explicitly; rather, we are presented with a sanitised moment of initial contact, when the realms of aggressor and victim first collide, while the subsequent act of possession and the locale where it will take place are left to our imagination.[77] So, too, is the event's potential allegorical significance. Just as epiphanies of Selene and Dionysus invite eschatological interpretations concerned with cosmological symbols of eternity or visions of a joyous afterlife gained through initiation into Bacchic cult, so Proserpina's abduction alludes to the Eleusinian mysteries, while sarcophagi depicting the abduction of the Leucippidae by the Dioscuri prompt consideration of the young women's divinisation and the brothers' eternal shuttling between the realms of Hades and Olympus (Figure 8.13a).[78] Yet in order to see the ensuing acts of sexual union, marriage or apotheosis that each myth foreshadows, the viewer must undergo a form of initiation,

---

[77] On the euphemistic suppression of explicit sexual acts in the rape iconography of the Western heroic tradition, see Cohen (1996), who suggests that, in the classical period, 'no artist ventured to visualize what happened after the chariot disappeared from view' (118), and Wolfthal (1999). On the gods' removal of their abductees to an alternative (often hidden) locale for the performance of the sexual act itself in narratives of erotic epiphany, see Petridou (2006: 199–200; in press a).

[78] On Selene's cosmological significance, see Cumont (1942: 177–252), with a review of symbolic interpretations in Sichtermann (1992: 40–44); on the eschatological significance of Dionysiac iconography in funerary contexts, see Lehmann-Hartleben and Olsen (1942) and Turcan (1966). On Roman familiarity with (and initiation into) the Eleusinian mysteries, see Clinton (1989); on allusions to the Eleusinian cult in funerary art, see Wood (2000: 79–81), with Clinton (1992: 137–8, no. 6; 2003: 59–60) on a sarcophagus now in the Palazzo Borghese depicting Hercules' initiation at Eleusis. On the eschatological significance of the Dioscuri, see Cumont (1942: 35–103), for whom the Dioscuri offer a rich symbol of Neopythagorean cosmological principles, and Lehmann-Hartleben and Olsen (1942: 42–5), who stress associations with the Bacchic mysteries. On the brothers' alternation between the lower and upper realms because of Castor's mortality and Pollux's divinity, see *Il.* 3.236–44 and Pindar *Nemean* 10.87–8 (though these roles are reversed in Rome, where Castor was worshipped as a deity). On the duality of the Dioscuri and their identity as epiphanic gods par excellence, see Platt (in press a).

whether that be conceived as cultic commitment to the mysteries themselves, or passage to the realm of the manes. The potential polyvalence of such iconography necessitates that this script is deliberately withheld, which generates the very combination of visual reticence and hermeneutic provocation that has mired scholars of Roman funerary art in Stygian swamps as they attempt to attribute 'meaning' to the narratives employed.

Rather than falling into such exegetical temptation, one could argue that the way in which such funerary objects prevaricate between knowledge and ignorance, the seen and unseen, actually offers a metaphor for the position occupied by the living viewer in relation to the deceased. Each relief's paradoxical combination of provocation and narrative inhibition – its 'signalled absences' – induces a viewing experience that reifies and dignifies the fear, longing, curiosity and frustration experienced by those left behind.[79] Like the protagonist Lucius upon his initiation into the cult of Isis in Apuleius' novel *The Golden Ass*, the external viewer stands 'on the threshold of Proserpina', eager 'to learn what was said and done'; unlike those who have crossed to the other side, he or she has not yet 'come face to face with the gods below and the gods above and paid reverence to them from close at hand' (11.23).[80] Likewise, the external viewer has not yet joined the ranks of *epoptai* (the fully initiated 'viewers' of Demeter's cult at Eleusis), but remains a *mystēs* ('one who closes the eyes'), who approaches the hallowed space but has yet to learn its secrets.[81] In this sense, scenes of erotic epiphany perform in narrative terms an equivalent to the formal device of the half-open door, offering a glimpse of the knowledge and experience to be acquired within, but positioning the sarcophagus's viewers carefully without. Indeed, the parallel is made explicit on the sides of the Baltimore Leucippidae sarcophagus, where each chariot-borne brother hurries his struggling bride away through a monumental archway (Figure 8.13b and c). Like Apuleius' Lucius, both iconographic schemata acknowledge the desire of the viewer/reader to penetrate further, and both resist such desire as an expression of the limitations not only of mortal knowledge, but also of representation itself.

---

[79] On 'signalled absences' in Pausanias' *Periēgēsis*, see Elsner (1992: 22–7), with my discussion in Chapter 5, 223–4.

[80] 'Accessi confinium mortis et, calcato Proserpinae limine, per omnia vectus elementa remeavi; . . . deos inferos et deos superos accessi coram et adoravi de proximo.' Translation from J. A. Hanson's Loeb Classical Library edition, 1989. On the representation of epiphany in *The Golden Ass* and the text's self-conscious shifting between reticence and revelation, see Laird (1997), van Mal-Maeder (1997), S. Harrison (2000: 238–52) and Elsner (2007: 290–302).

[81] On the ranks of *mystēs* and *epoptēs* at Eleusis and the etymology of each term, see Clinton (2003).

The hermeneutic complexities of mythological sarcophagus reliefs are imbued with a subtle playfulness, then, that is entirely in tune with the self-conscious sophistication of Roman visual culture beyond the funerary sphere. While they allude to religious patterns of thought and behaviour, their invitation to eschatological interpretation does not obviate self-reflexive games of revelation and concealment influenced by the function of the object and its display within the tomb. In their ambiguous relationship to the sacred, these reliefs echo the representational, theological and psychological complexities of images such as the Dionysiac paintings in the Villa of the Mysteries and texts such as Apuleius' *Golden Ass* – sophisticated artefacts that appropriate the hermeneutics of mystery cult (and potentially speak to the initiate) while maintaining a degree of ironic detachment and providing aesthetic pleasure for a broader community of viewers or readers.[82] Indeed, it is telling that the debate over the sacred or secular significance of sarcophagus iconography has run in parallel with scholarly conflict over the ancient novel, particularly *The Golden Ass*, which is contemporary in date to many of the sarcophagi discussed here (170–80 CE).[83] Just as Cumont's approach was rejected by Nock and his successors, so the mysticising interpretations of Reinhold Merkelbach have been side-lined by the secular readings of later twentieth-century scholars, who have prioritised the novel's narratological intricacies and ironic sense of *aporia* over its narrative of trial and conversion.[84] Surely, however, the point should be that such impulses do not have to be mutually exclusive.[85] As I hope this book has demonstrated, the hermeneutics of the sacred were a fundamental aspect of the very 'classicism and culture' that Nock saw as a unifying aspect of Graeco-Roman society; the modes of representation and engagement they

[82] On hermeneutic play in the Villa of the Mysteries, see in particular Henderson (1996), with Wyler (2006a, 2006b), on the visual sophistication of Roman allusions to Dionysiac iconography. On Apuleius, see below.

[83] For a helpful review of the scholarly literature, see S. Harrison (1999: xxxii–xxxviii; 2000: 235–38).

[84] See Cumont (1942) and Nock (1946), discussed above; on mystery religions and the novel, see Merkelbach (1962: 1–90; 1995: 266–303, 335–484), with critiques by Stark (1989) and Beck (1996). On the sacred aspects of *The Golden Ass*, especially its final book, see Griffiths (1975), Penwill (1975) and Shumate (1996), who interprets the novel according to models of religious conversion. Schlam (1992: 113–22) acknowledges the comic aspects of book 11 but does not rule out a more serious religious message. On narratological play and hermeneutic aporia, the primary text is Winkler (1985: esp. 204–47, on the novel's final sequence of epiphanies and initiations), who maintains a careful balance of emphasis between the novel's satirical humour and potential religious seriousness; S. Harrison (2000: 238–52), on the other hand, interprets book 11 as a more straightforwardly sophistic and satirical display of religious *paideia*.

[85] Here I echo the comments of Lightfoot (2003: 184–9, 196–221), on Lucian's *On the Syrian Goddess*, and Elsner (2007: 291 n. 4), on Apuleius.

engendered within the tomb could have serious cultural and theological resonances without demanding intense cultic or doctrinal commitments, nor precluding a sophisticated aesthetic response.

Corpus et imago: redistributing the epiphanic gaze

Within the charged space of the Roman tomb, it is important to remember that the promise and failure of representation does not play out solely in relation to the gods. Because she is denied the very response from Endymion that makes epiphany meaningful – that is, the look itself – Selene's multiple strategies of visual revelation on sarcophagus reliefs serve to realign epiphanic expectations. In keeping with the ritual focus of viewing within the tomb, the direction of desire, and thus the pattern of gazes within the picture plane, is focused instead upon her mortal beloved. On the New York *lēnos*, for example, Selene's powerful movement towards the right, the insistent tugging of the cupids and the glances of the other figures within the relief ultimately direct the external viewer's attention to the naked body of Endymion (Figure 8.8). Framed by his artfully draped chlamys, the youth is depicted on a larger scale and faces the frontal plane of the relief, inviting a lingering gaze upon his large expanse of smoothly modelled, fully exposed marble flesh. Indeed, on several Endymion sarcophagi, this invitation is made even more explicit by the unveiling of his form by Hypnos (Figure 8.1) or cupids (Figure 8.14), who peel back his cloak to reveal his naked body in a gesture that is echoed on reliefs depicting the sleeping Ariadne (Figure 8.6), and even doubled on the Vatican Endymion and Rhea Silvia sarcophagus in an act of simultaneous revelation (Figure 8.7). We might contrast this compositional balance with scenes of the same myth on engraved gems, in which the enhanced *velificatio* effect of Selene's descent stresses the overpowering physical force of her *adventus*, and Endymion is compressed into little more than a ground line (Figure 8.16).[86] This emphasis aligns with the function of the gem itself, which prioritises divine presence as a

---

[86] Chalcedony, Kestner Museum, Hanover (K 490), dated to the first century BCE: *AGD* 4, no. 252; *LIMC* s.v. Endymion, no. 38 (see also nos. 37, 39–40). For a fascinating appropriation of Selene and Endymion iconography to commemorate Sulla's dream epiphany of the Cappodocian goddess Ma (associated with the Roman Luna), see a coin now in the British Museum minted by Sulla's descendant L. Aemilius Bucca in 44 BCE (*RRC* no. 480/1), with Plutarch *Sulla* 9.4, *RRC* vol. I, 493, and Hallett (2005b: 154–5, pl. 88). Vollenweider (1958–9) argues that first-century BCE gems depicting Selene and Endymion are, in fact, a reference to Sulla's vision, although the absence of Victory in Figure 8.18 makes this identification rather tenuous.

Figure 8.16 Selene and Endymion chalcedony intaglio, first century BCE

means of stressing the sanctity of its iconographic device, and therefore the authority of its wax impression.[87] On sarcophagi, however, the unveiling of mortal bodies counters the traditional *velificatio* motif that signifies the gods' epiphanic arrival in order to stress the youthful beauty and vulnerability of the human form, transforming each episode into an epiphanic diptych in which deity and mortal are repeatedly made manifest before each other.

This doubling of revelatory gestures on sarcophagi echoes and re-contextualises the visual dynamics that are already at play within depictions of Selene and Endymion in Campanian wall-paintings dating to the mid first century CE. Within the Pompeian *domus* the eroticised epiphanies of Selene and Dionysus form part of a broader corpus of myths that explore the pleasures and dangers of the desirous gaze, from the fatal voyeurism of

---

[87] On the authority of divine figures on gems employed as seal stones, see Henig (1990) and Platt (2006: 234–5).

Actaeon to the scopophilic inertia of Narcissus.[88] Selene and Endymion are frequently placed within the context of other mortal–immortal unions: a fourth-style cubiculum in the Pompeian House of the Centenary, for example, juxtaposes the youth's fate with panels depicting a mournful Cassandra holding a branch of laurel (an allusion to her rejection of Apollo and his subsequent revenge) and Venus Piscatrix accompanied by two cupids.[89] The divine fisherwoman offers an allegory of the arbitrariness of desire, which in baiting even the gods can lead to ambivalent outcomes for their mortal partners, whether the fraught gift of prophecy or the dubious honour of eternal sleep – a reversal of traditional gender roles that, like paintings of Narcissus, transforms the virile hunter into a passive sexual object.

In the House of the Ara Maxima, this instability is thematised in a pair of Endymion paintings located in an adjacent tablinum and triclinium, where they are each juxtaposed with panels depicting the sleeping Ariadne (Figures 8.17 and 8.18).[90] In both rooms the fascinatory power of erotic revelation and the lure of the naturalistically rendered female body are stressed in the figure of Selene, whose drapery forms a nimbus that frames and reveals her naked form – a degree of eroticism that is never matched on sarcophagi. Yet while the goddess's epiphany is in each panel acknowledged in a humorous gesture by Endymion's hound, his master's response is rather more ambivalent.[91] In the tablinum (room F), the goddess appears from the left before an effeminate, pale-skinned youth whose slumber renders him oblivious to the explicit act of revelation performed on his behalf (Figure 8.17). In the triclinium (room G), Selene appears from the right and Endymion, now with the traditionally darker skin tone and defined musculature of the male hunter-warrior, sits upright and awake, looking away from Selene towards the viewer (Figure 8.18).[92] As if to reinforce this unexpected balance of agencies in room G, the scene also includes internal

[88] See Fredrick (1995) and, on the dynamics of epiphany in Pompeian depictions of Diana's epiphany to Actaeon, Platt (2002). On Narcissus, see the bibliography listed in Chapter 4, n. 66. On Endymion in Roman *domus*, see also Balch (2008).

[89] Pompeii IX.8, 3.7, cubiculum 42: see *LIMC* s.v. Endymion, no. 24, and *PPM* vol. IX, 1052–63. For a parallel example of Venus Piscatrix juxtaposed with epiphanic scenes of mortal–immortal union and transgression (here Diana and Actaeon, and Leda and the Swan), see cubiculum R in the House of the Gilded Cupids (Pompeii VI.16, 7.38): *PPM* vol. V, 833–45, and Seiler (1992: 56–8, figs. 382, 388–9).

[90] Pompeii VI.16, 15.17: see *LIMC* s.v. Endymion, nos. 16 and 22, *PPM* vol. V: 868–77, and Stemmer (1992: 24–5, 28–9), with Fredrick (1995: 283–4).

[91] In an example from the House of Ganymede, Endymion's hound even jumps forward to bark at Selene as she approaches (Pompeii VII.13.4, *LIMC* s.v. Endymion, no. 25).

[92] Cf. *LIMC* s.v. Endymion, nos. 15–18, for contemporary panels from Pompeii in which Endymion is awake.

Figure 8.17 Selene and Endymion: wall-painting from room F of the House of the Ara Maxima, Pompeii (VI.16, 15.17), mid first century CE

viewers in the form of an embracing couple who look in opposite directions – the man to Selene, and his female partner to Endymion. The doubling of scenes in the House of the Ara Maxima thus serves to cast the myth in divergent ways, offering a complementary scene of Endymion's sexual passivity to the Ariadne in room F, and a contrasting image of his heroised virility to the Ariadne in room G, which is echoed in adjacent panels depicting Hercules and an embracing Mars and Venus.[93] As David Fredrick has shown, the asymmetry of the Endymion myth's mortal–immortal pairing in first-century CE wall-painting offers a means of exploring the instability of gender boundaries in relation to the power structures that shape domestic space.[94] The naturalistic bodies displayed to the viewer's gaze in these

[93] See *PPM* vol. v, 871–5, and Stemmer (1992: 28–9, figs. 178, 181).
[94] Fredrick (1995).

Figure 8.18 Selene and Endymion: wall-painting from room G of the House of the Dioscuri, Pompeii (VI. 9, 6.7), mid first century CE

examples exploit the image's power to beguile and absorb, inviting an imaginative engagement with each painting that pursues (but can never fully access) the erotic promise of the scene portrayed. Indeed, in the House of the Ara Maxima, these themes are made explicit in a painting of Narcissus that forms the focus of the *fauces*–tablinum axis – the ultimate example of the image's power to provoke an impossible desire that transforms the active viewer into a passive object.[95]

As the Vatican Endymion and Rhea Silvia sarcophagus makes clear, Roman funerary art could play similar games with juxtaposition and inversion (Figure 8.7).[96] In funerary contexts, however, the self-conscious exploration of gender roles and illusionistic absorption so characteristic of

---

[95] Pseudotablinum D. See *PPM* vol. v, 880–1, and Stemmer (1992: 32–3, fig. 200).
[96] See Koortbojian (1995: 102–6).

Endymion scenes in Roman domestic wall-painting has a further resonance: death, after all, is the ultimate challenge to the inviolability of the Roman male. As a result of the tension Endymion embodies between heroic form and passive objectification, the stability of gender is called into question at the very place where boundaries between agency and passivity are most critically negotiated. In this sense it is fitting that the myth's inversion of sexual stereotypes does not map directly onto the gender of each sarcophagus's occupant. Those shown in Figures 8.1 and 8.8, for example, were both employed for females during antiquity: the Capitoline sarcophagus was reused for the young Gerontia, while an inscription in the centre of the lid of the New York *lēnos* states that one Aninia Hilara dedicated it for her 'peerless mother, Claudia Arria', who died aged fifty years and ten months, and is accompanied by a small panel to the right adorned with the portrait bust of a woman with the late second-century hairstyle of Julia Domna.[97] In such cases the eroticised relationship between deity and human on the relief can only have been compared to the bond between dedicator and deceased in a very loose manner, expressing a general sense of love and longing, while the objectification of Endymion's youthful strength serves to emphasise the terrible passivity that death demands of the human body, irrespective of gender.[98]

At the same time, death puts to work the push-me-pull-you paradox of naturalism. While eroticised bodies in domestic wall-painting might flirt with the image's power to excite and to tease, the emphatic corporeality of classicising forms within the tomb asserts a presence-in-absence that gains added poignancy from its display within a space associated with grief and remembrance. Such provocation of desire and frustration is intensified on sarcophagi, in particular, by the proximity of the visual field to the physical remains of the dead themselves, so that each relief's tangible corporeality purports to give form to the deceased, while acting as a reminder of their

---

[97] *CIL* 14.92, no. 565: 'Aninia Hilara | CL Arriae matri | inconparabili | fecit vixit | ann L men | X.' See McCann (1978: 43–4) and Sichtermann (1992: no. 80, 135). Zanker (in Zanker and Ewald 2004: 106) does not rule out the idea that the inscription is related to a later period of usage, and that Arria's bust has been re-cut from an earlier male portrait; see also Sichtermann (1992: 135). But even if this is the case, the sarcophagus was clearly deemed appropriate for a female occupant at some point within the late second / early third century CE. For a parallel example of an analogy between a romantic and parent-child relationship, see the Phaedra and Hippolytus sarcophagus in the Museo Nazionale Romano (inv. 112444) dedicated by a mother to her dead son, discussed by Sichtermann and Koch (1975: 36, no. 30), Koch and Sichtermann (1982: 152), Zanker (1999), Zanker and Ewald (2004: 328–9) and Newby (in press).

[98] For Koortbojian (1995: 109), the burial of women in Endymion sarcophagi suggests that the deceased is to be identified with Selene, a possible interpretation discussed below.

passage to a state that is both immaterial and inaccessible. Indeed, the popularity and enduring potency of the decorative sarcophagus as a funerary receptacle must lie partly in the nature of relief sculpture as a medium, which can create three-dimensional forms that assert corporeal presence while simultaneously confining them within a series of shallow planes that must ultimately be experienced as a two-dimensional image. A similar tension between two-dimensional outline and fully plastic form is found on Attic grave reliefs, which exploit the illusionistic potential and representational failure of naturalistic relief sculpture as part of their rhetoric of loss and remembrance.[99] The striking feature of the Roman sarcophagi I have discussed here, however, is that this cycle of manifestation and abnegation is explicitly explored through the iconography of mythological epiphany. The bittersweet presence-in-absence of the dead is thus allied to the aporetics of divine presence in a compelling panorama of mortal and immortal bodies in which everything is possible and nothing is guaranteed. On Selene and Endymion sarcophagi, the revelatory diptych of divine self-manifestation and mortal unveiling serves to thematise the image's power to make present, while the continual deferment of the couple's mutual acknowledgement or union gives form to the complex cocktail of grief, desire and hope that the mourning viewer must have brought to the tomb. In this way manipulation of the visual language of epiphany within the ambiguous space of the relief provides both a screen for the projection of fantasy and desire, and a platform for the contemplation of mortality, loss and life after death.

Given these parallels between funerary and epiphanic modes of viewing, it should be no surprise to find that, with the introduction of portrait features into mythological scenes during the first half of the third century CE, the dead are assimilated not only to sleeping mortals, but also to their divine lovers.[100] Just as Endymion provides a model for the contemplation of death as blissful sleep, so Selene offers a means of figuring the deceased as an elusive, desirable being who can be apprehended only in an imagined afterlife or in fleeting visions grasped in dreams – a notion that is perhaps conveyed on a sarcophagus now at Cliveden where Selene has been given portrait features, but retains the soft centre-parting and long ringlets of a goddess

---

[99] See Turner (2007, 2009) and Neer (2010: 182–214), with Summers (2003: 448–50), on planarity in classical relief sculpture.

[100] On the use of portrait heads on mythological sarcophagi, see Fittschen (1970: 188; 1984), Engemann (1973: 28–35), Schauenburg (1980), Koch and Sichtermann (1982: 607–14), Huskinson (1996: 98), on parallel developments on children's sarcophagi, Zanker and Ewald (2004: 45–50, 193–24) and (most helpfully) Newby (in press), with Blome (1992: 1062–5) and Zanker (1999) on individual myths.

Figure 8.19 Selene and Endymion sarcophagus with portrait heads, c. 240 CE

rather than the hairstyle of a contemporary Roman matron (Figure 8.19).[101] Significantly, abductor gods such as Pluto and the Dioscuri never receive portrait features, one suspects because the metaphor of death as violent abduction was less open to romantic reinterpretation than the more gentle epiphanic model offered by scenes of sleep.[102] Likewise, Dionysus is rarely identified directly with the deceased, despite the fact that Ariadne is one of the most popular figures for the reception of portrait features: indeed, on a well-known pair of Endymion and Ariadne sarcophagi in the Louvre (probably commissioned for a couple), Selene and Endymion retain blank features ready to receive portraits, while their companion piece retains them only for Ariadne, and diverts the male portrait from Dionysus to a togate bust on the sarcophagus's lid.[103] Traditionally scholars have assumed this is because the drunken deity is a dubious role model for the upstanding Roman citizen, but considering the frequency of seemingly inappropriate analogies on sarcophagus reliefs elsewhere (such as Achilles and Penthesilea, or Phaedra and Hippolytus), this explanation fails to convince.[104] Could it be, rather, because the cultic and eschatological significance of Dionysus was too strong for his relationship with Ariadne to be reappropriated as an expression of mortal love beyond the grave? Certainly, as Zahra Newby has pointed out, Ariadne's discovery on Naxos is often visually subordinated on Dionysiac sarcophagi to the god's arrival amid the bacchanalian revels of his *thiasos*; his status qua deity is in this sense of greater interpretative

---

[101] Astor Collection, Cliveden, Bucks. (formerly in the Villa Borghese, Rome), dated *c.* 240 CE: see Wrede (1981: 264, no. 21) and Sichtermann (1992: 145–6, *ASR* 12.2, no. 95), with compositional parallels in the Palazzo Doria Pamphilj (*ASR* 12.2, no. 93), on which Selene also has ringlets, and Woburn Abbey (*ASR* 12.2, no. 94). On Selene as a vision of the deceased glimpsed in dreams, see Koortbojian (1995: 106–11), citing Propertius' dream vision of the dead Cynthia in 4.7 and an inscription (*CIL* 6.18817) in which a bereaved wife expresses a hope to see her husband in dreams, Zanker and Ewald (2004: 102–6) and Newby (in press).

[102] See Newby (in press), with a helpful tabulation and analysis of the range of mythological reliefs incorporating portrait features. Sarcophagi depicting the abduction of the Leucippidae do not appear after 200 CE, although the rape of Proserpina continued in popularity (see below).

[103] Musée du Louvre, Ma 1335 and 1346, discovered in a tomb in St Médard d'Eyran, Bordeaux, dated *c.* 220–40 CE: see Matz (1969: 394–7, *ASR* 4.3, no. 222) and Sichtermann (1992: 125–7, *ASR* 12.2 no. 72), with Zanker and Ewald (2004: 108–9, figs. 91–2). On the practice of leaving faces uncarved, perhaps for the projection of fantasies relating to the fate of dead, see Andreae (1984) and Huskinson (1998). For sarcophagi depicting Ariadne with portrait features, see Wrede (1981: 209–12, nos. 44–57), who considers identification with Ariadne a form of apotheosis, but not Endymion, who, despite the inclusion of sarcophagi featuring Selene/Luna portraits, is absent from his catalogue of ordinary Romans commemorated *in formam deorum*. Among images of Dionysus with portrait features, only two are on sarcophagi rather than free-standing statues – a strigillated example in the Catacomb of Praetextatus, dated *c.* 250, and a scene of Dionysus and Ariadne enthroned with unfinished faces in the Museo Nazionale Romano, dated *c.* 210–20 (124682): see Wrede (1981: 210, no. 48, and 263, no. 81), Zanker and Ewald (2004: 160, fig. 145) and Newby (in press).

[104] See, e.g., Zanker and Ewald (2004: 109).

value than any potential identification with a deceased male relative.[105] By contrast, the majority of Selene and Endymion sarcophagi employing portrait heads, and all examples of the Mars and Rhea Silvia myth (such as Figure 8.7), project the features of the deceased onto both partners and privilege the relationship within the composition.[106] In this way the dead enter the mythological space of the relief itself to form a double focus of the epiphanic gaze, offering a fantasy of eternal union and a testament to conjugal constancy.

Despite the positive associations of such double identifications, the composition of each scene still generates the cycle of revelation and withholding that I traced above, in which the lovers are eternally suspended on the brink of wakeful congress and never inhabit the same sphere of consciousness.[107] For when the promise of heroising or divinising analogy is made literal through the use of portraiture, the faces of the dead are incorporated into the narrative and representational dynamics of the scene portrayed, and are thus invested with the same ontological ambiguity as the otherworldly beings to whom they are assimilated. In death, ordinary mortals finally enter an epiphanic space that is only accessible to the living viewer in image form. In passing beyond the screen of discourse, they themselves are transformed into images for the contemplation of those left behind, thereby accruing all the tensions of presence and absence that such a metamorphosis entails. In this sense it is fitting that the Latin *imago* – a term synonymous with traditional Roman ancestor portraits – can refer not only to an image or likeness, but also (like the Greek *eidōlon*) to a ghost or phantom.[108] The

---

[105] Newby (in press). Consider, in this light, the group of Dionysiac sarcophagi discovered in the third chamber of the so-called 'Licinian tomb' (above, n. 59), in which an Ariadne sarcophagus was juxtaposed with examples depicting Dionysus' childhood and his Indian triumph.

[106] For Selene and Endymion with double-portrait features (or blank faces ready to receive them), see Wrede (1981: 265–7, nos. 185–91, s.v. Luna, *ASR* 12.2, nos. 56, 72, 73, 76, 77, 92, 93, 95). Several fragmentary reliefs employ portrait features on the figure of Endymion, but as Newby (in press) points out, the figure of Selene is missing (*ASR* 12.2, nos. 49, 85 and 90). Note that the double-narrative sarcophagus in the Vatican (Figure 8.7, *ASR* 12.2, no. 99) includes portrait features in the scene featuring Mars and Rhea Silvia, but that it is impossible to tell whether the same couple (or indeed, another pair) were identified with Selene and Endymion, as their heads have been restored. For further Mars and Rhea Silvia examples with double-portrait features, see Wrede (1981: 271–2, nos. 201–3, *ASR* 3.2, nos. 188, 190).

[107] On the importance of conjugal love for the interpretation of mythological sarcophagus reliefs during the high empire, see Ewald (2004: 251–2) and Zanker and Ewald (2004: 201–16, 242–5).

[108] On the use of *imago* as a social and moral, rather than aestheticising, term for Roman portraits, see Daut (1975) and Lahusen (1982); on its broader lexical range, including the concepts of 'ghost', 'reflection' and 'visible form', see Flower (1996: 33–5). On the concept of the *eidōlon*, see Chapter 6, 257–8.

portrait head thus embodies the very ambivalences that characterise the charged representational space of the tomb, which are at their most intense within the suspended animation of the mythological relief.

The convergence of portraiture and epiphanic iconography on third-century sarcophagi derives from two major traditions in Roman art. First, the perpetuation of individual presence by means of a veristic portrait echoes the Republican tradition of wax *imagines* (which preserved the form of the deceased and provided the potential for his reanimation in funerary ritual), and reiterates in relief form the three-dimensional portraits that crowded tombs in the form of statues, portrait busts and figures on sarcophagus lids.[109] Indeed, on sarcophagi, where portraits are also incorporated into *vita humana* reliefs and isolated within framed tondi, the image of the deceased also serves as a reminder of the body's presence within.[110] Significantly, Roman law did not recognise the sepulchral status of a cenotaph: to be guaranteed status as a *locus religiosus*, a tomb had to contain a body (whether cremated or inhumed), which had by rights to include the head.[111] The head of the deceased was therefore the primary component by which the tomb could be declared inviolable and inalienable.[112] Yet so close was the relationship between the body and its image in Roman funerary culture that, by law, an image could be allowed to stand for the body itself, so that 'imaginal' burial (*imaginaria*) formed a subcategory of legal burial (*legitima*): it was the physical presence of a *corpus* – whether real or represented – that was paramount.[113] The inclusion of an *imago* of the deceased upon the sarcophagus thus serves to assert a form of material continuity, so that the form within, while swiftly 'eaten' by its marble container, is perpetuated by

---

[109] On the Roman tradition of *imagines*, see the bibliography in n. 9, above. On the display of portraits in Roman tombs, see Kleiner (1987), Anderson and Nista (1988: 61–8), P. Stewart (2003: 83–7), Caliò (2007) and Fejfer (2008: 105–37).

[110] On *vita humana* sarcophagi, see Kampen (1981), Amedick (1991), Wrede (2001), Zanker and Ewald (2004: 185–93) and Newby (2007a: 237–40).

[111] See Y. Thomas (2004: 46–7), citing the jurist Florentinus 7 *Institutionum*, D. 11.7.42: 'Monument in its generic sense means something revealed and transmitted to posterity in memory: it becomes a tomb when it encloses a body or the remains of a body (*in qua si corpus vel reliquiae inferuntur, fiet sepulchrum*); but if it contains no such thing, it is built only to preserve a memory, and is what the Greeks calls a cenotaph (*erit monumentum memoriae causa factum, quod Graeci kinotaphion appellant*).' The same point is made by Ulpian 25 *ed.*, D. 11.7.2.6.

[112] Y. Thomas (2004: 50), citing the jurist Paul 3 *quaestionum*, D. 11.7.44: 'the true *locus religiosus* is the place where the principal part [of the body] is buried, that is to say the head, from which an image is taken'.

[113] Y. Thomas (2004: 48–9), citing Servius *ad Aen.* 6.325, 366, with Dupont (1987) on the metonymic relationship between the *imago* and the body of the deceased.

the form without.[114] Indeed, in his explanation of the properties of flesh-eating *sarcophagus lapis*, Pliny cites Mucianus' claim that grave goods placed within the casket, such as 'mirrors, body-scrapers, garments and shoes that have been buried with the dead, become transformed into stone': while the image consumes the body, then, its attributes are themselves transformed into images, and the substitution of *corpus* by *imago* is complete.[115]

Second, in identifying the dead with divinities through the use of portrait features, third-century sarcophagi apply to mythological relief a practice that had been established in three-dimensional funerary sculpture since at least the Flavian period, whereby veristic portrait heads were affixed to bodies derived from classical statues of deities such as Venus, Mars, Ceres, Hercules and Diana.[116] Consider, for example, the well-known (and often misunderstood) funerary portraits of Roman matrons in the guise of Venus, which employ sculptural types derived from Praxiteles' Aphrodite of Knidos (Figure 8.20).[117] Such objects may invest the deceased with the beauty and feminine qualities of Venus by borrowing the costume or *habitus* of the goddess's most familiar iconographic type; they may also make a claim for status and education by drawing upon the visual language of classicism.[118] Yet, in doing so, they simultaneously evoke the sanctity of the Greek original – not necessarily to make grand eschatological claims about apotheosis and immortality, but to mobilise the image's epiphanic authority in order to generate a sense of encounter for those engaged in the act of commemoration. In

---

[114] On this point, see also Ewald (2004: 230), who suggests that portraits on sarcophagi present an ideal social persona that is 'constructed in a crucial moment of transition: the moment in which a decomposing real body has to be replaced by an artificial body or image of the deceased'.

[115] *HN* 36.131: 'Mucianus specula quoque et strigiles et vestes et calciamenta inlata mortuis lapidea fieri auctor est'.

[116] The classic work on these images (and most accessible collection of examples) is still Wrede (1981), with Hallett (2005c: 237–70), on nude examples, and Fejfer (2008: 124–8). On the commemoration of Roman women as Ceres, see also Wood (2000), and, in this volume, the Roman copy of Polyclitus' Argive Demeter discussed in Chapter 2 (Figure 2.1), which originally supported a portrait head.

[117] Vatican Magazzini, inv. 2952, from the Tomb of the Manilii, Vigna Moroni on the Via Appia, Rome, dated to the Hadrianic period. The statue has the body of the Capitoline Venus type, and was juxtaposed with a man in the guise of Mercury, as well as several portrait busts: see Wrede (1971: 157, A.I.2; 1981: 274–5, no. 206, and 308, no. 293), D'Ambra (1996: 227–9), Hallett (2005c: B244 and B328) and Fejfer (2008: 119–21). On the depiction of Roman women as Venus, see Wrede (1971: 157–9, catalogue A; 1981: 306–15, nos. 292–308), D'Ambra (1993, 1996, 2000), Hallett (2005c: 199–201, 209–12, appendix B, nos. 327–42) and Kousser (2007). On the reception of the Aphrodite of Knidos as a cult statue, see Chapter 4.

[118] On the appropriation of Venus' body as a form of costume, see Bonfante (1989) and D'Ambra (1996); on the visual and ideological significance of classicism for funerary portrait groups of couples in the guise of Mars and Venus, see Kousser (2007).

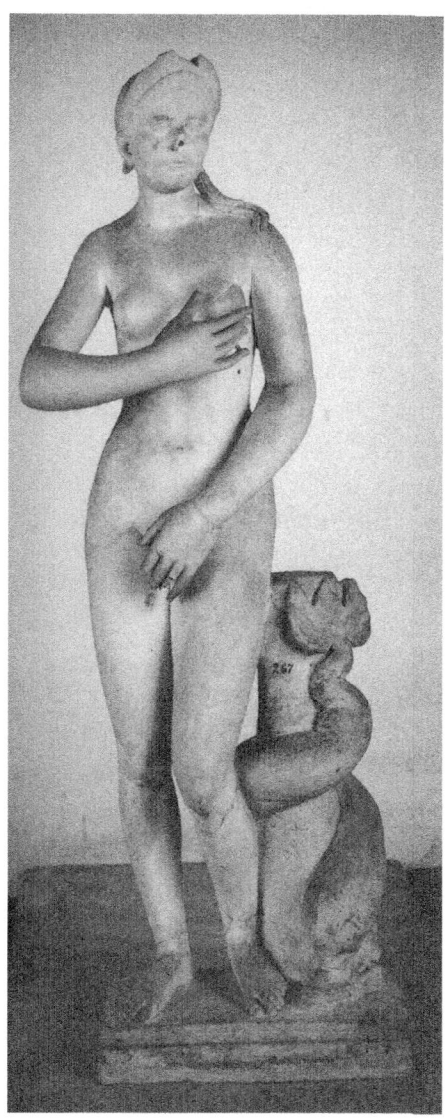

Figure 8.20 Portrait of a Roman woman with a body based on the Capitoline Venus type, early second century CE

such cases the identifiably 'Roman' practice of replication also functions as a form of epiphanic citation, standing in the same tradition as the Pergamene copy of the Athena Parthenos I discussed in Chapter 4 (Figure 4.1).[119] In

---

[119] See Chapter 4, 170–2.

the context of the tomb, however, citations of classical divine bodies have a further purpose: by drawing upon the ontological ambiguity of their divine models, they establish a dynamic shuttling between presence and absence that has its origins in sacred modes of viewing, yet perfectly embodies the distressing combination of remembered presence and present loss that characterises the act of mourning. While to our eyes the juxtaposition of veristic idiosyncrasy and *Idealskulptur* may be jarring, its visual distinction between divine body and mortal face allows the object to demand the epiphanic gaze while retaining the visual specificity of the deceased. This does not constitute an act of deification, but rather generates a 'multi-stable image' that draws upon the ambivalent corporeality of a divine model while asserting a form of physical continuity with the remains of the dead: like the bodies within the ambiguous space of the sarcophagus relief, the divinising portrait partakes of both the physical world of the viewer and the elusive realm of the shades.[120] In this way the ontological complexities of the Greek sacred image are allied to the ritual, legal and representational force of the Roman *imago*.

Conclusion: Selene takes flight

The reconfiguration of epiphanic schemata, the transformation of *corpus* into *imago* and the entry of the deceased within the sarcophagus' field of representation all articulate, as Keats wrote, 'the grandeur of the dooms / We have imagined for the mighty dead'.[121] Together they engage the power of *phantasia*, make vivid extraordinary experiences that figure death and yet defer it, and offer consolation through the assertion of presence while reminding their viewers, gently, of the grim fact of loss. The manifestation of divine figures within this process is crucial: they enhance the status of the deceased and dignify the ritual acts of mourners, while encouraging a meditation upon the boundaries between the material and transcendent, the human and divine. They mark the sarcophagus's status as a *limen* – a place where the external viewer comes into contact with a world beyond the *loci profani* of the living – while also asserting its status as a screen for the projection of fantasy and desire. In this way the visual language of epiphany is reconfigured so that Roman *religio* and Greek *paideia* can converge within

---

[120] On 'multi-stable images', see W. J. T. Mitchell (1994: 45–57, 74–6), with my discussion in Chapter 1, 37.

[121] *Endymion* (1818), 1.20–1.

the space of the tomb in myriad formulations, offering a spectrum of interpretative possibilities to those navigating the ritual demands and complex
cultural landscape of death.

In offering an interstitial space for the exploration of these themes, Roman
sarcophagus reliefs have more in common with Second Sophistic literature
than might initially appear to be the case. In particular, heroising or divinising mythological scenes take place within a mediatory sphere that is parallel
to the realm of the daemonic explored in contemporary texts such as Philostratus' *Heroicus*. As I showed in Chapter 5, the *daimōn* is a form of double
that is 'intermediate between god and mortal', inhabiting a liminal category equivalent to that of the *eidōlon, imago* or *oneiros*, and possessing an
ambiguous corporeality.[122] Indeed, given his prominence within the Second
Sophistic imagination as a *daimōn* capable of moving between the realms
of the living and the dead, the poetic and the real, it is not surprising that,
as well as forming the elusive protagonist of the *Heroicus*, Protesilaos also
features on sarcophagus reliefs as a heroising analogy for the deceased.[123]
In both cases, encounters with the departed take place at the site of the
tomb: the physical remains of the heroised dead constitute a material presence that is essential for anchoring the more fleeting acts of animation that
each cultural artefact purports to make possible.[124] The primary agent of
encounter, however, is the literary text or sculpted relief itself – an ekphrastic or representational space in which conventional categories of status
and ontology can be wilfully (and playfully) challenged. Like the visionary
accounts relayed by the vine-dresser to his Phoenician visitor, sarcophagus
reliefs – particularly those employing portrait features – facilitate 'visions
of the dead' (τῶν ἀποθανόντων ὄψεις), performing a kind of necromantic
exercise equivalent to the verbal moly offered by Philostratus' text.[125]

In generating a sense of intense encounter through self-conscious acts
of mediation, both visionary texts and mythologising sarcophagus reliefs
rely upon a deep store of cultural *paideia*. Through imaginative acts of
visualisation (or *phantasia*) the literary and visual schemata of the past
are appropriated and reformulated in order to answer the longings of the

---

[122] Plato *Symposium* 202e–203a, with Chapter 5, 235–9.

[123] On Protesilaos sarcophagi (including those mentioned above, n. 32), see Zanker and Ewald
(2004: 100–2, 374–7), with Newby (in press) and Platt (in press b), on the example in the
Vatican Galleria degli Candelabri (inv. 2465), dated *c.* 170 CE, with unfinished portrait heads
on the figures of Protesilaos and Laodamia (*ASR* 3.3, no. 423).

[124] See Chapter 5, 295, 319, with Rusten (2004), on the *Heroicus*' references to the bones of heroes.

[125] 'Visions of the dead': *Heroicus* 6.4. For moly, see *Od.* 10.274–306 and *Heroicus* 6.1, with my
discussion in Chapter 5, 244–5.

present, whether nostalgia for Greek cultural and political autonomy (in the case of Second Sophistic literature), or a desire to reanimate and enhance the memory of lost loved ones (in the case of funerary art). In neither case are earlier texts or images treated as cast-iron sources, but rather as mediating cultural models through which the mythologised past can be accessed and re-experienced on the viewer's or reader's own terms. For Philostratus, this offers an opportunity to 'rewrite' the epic cycle; on sarcophagi, it allows sculptors and their patrons to appropriate and reconfigure mythic narratives in sometimes surprising ways in order to dignify human qualities and relationships in the act of commemoration. Yet, like the vine-dresser's descriptions of Protesilaos, these sculpted visions of the glorious departed project a beauty and nigh-tangible corporeality that inspires a yearning for contact. Their sensuality of style prompts a desire that, as we saw in the ekphrastic language of the *Heroicus*, inevitably falls prey to the hermeneutic circle of the image, for the idealised *imagines* of the Roman dead prompt a cognitive dissonance equivalent to that generated by the sacred *agalmata* of the heroes, whereby unmediated vision is inevitably dependent upon cultural representation.[126] Significantly, the question of how Protesilaos 'returned to life' is passed over in the *Heroicus* in a self-conscious act of withholding that reasserts the very boundaries that the text purports to break down: knowledge that truly challenges the limitations of human experience is presented as 'inviolable and secret' (ἀβεβήλῳ τε καὶ ἀπορρήτῳ).[127] As in the *Heroicus*, so in the Roman tomb, mortality establishes the limits of *paideia*, as the viewer is repeatedly denied the opportunity to cross the 'threshold of Proserpina' and enter the epiphanic space of the relief (or, by extension, the domain of daemonic *manes*). In this sense the *aporia* of representation that the viewer/reader encounters in both the *Heroicus* and the paradoxical relief space of the sarcophagus is precisely the *aporia* of the human condition.

If mythological sarcophagi echo the cognitive and hermeneutic complexities that accompany epiphany elsewhere, then they also illustrate some of the critical reformulations of the relationship between vision and representation that would take place in late antiquity. With the introduction of portrait features into mythological scenes in the first half of the third century, we begin to see an increasing focus upon the *imago* of the deceased, while the narrative content of the relief is gradually de-emphasised. Take, for example, the well-known Pluto and Proserpina sarcophagus in the Museo

---

[126] On the heroes' beauty in the *Heroicus* and the eroticising language in which they are described, see Whitmarsh (2009).

[127] *Heroicus* 58.2: see Chapter 5, 249.

Figure 8.21 Pluto and Proserpina sarcophagus with portrait features, *c.* 230–40 CE

Capitolino, dated *c.* 230–40, which rejects the previous compositional motif whereby Proserpina was flung horizontally across the body of her divine abductor (as in Figure 8.12) in order to place her – now with the rather severe portrait features of the deceased – in an upright position in the centre of the relief (Figure 8.21).[128] The young woman shows no distress and does not engage with the deities around her, but as a still figure amid the narrative maelstrom she allows herself to be carried imperturbably towards her fate. Is this an indication of a shift in attitudes to death, influenced by the salvationist theologies of monotheistic cults such as Christianity?[129] The relief provides little clue. It does, however, chart the process of abstraction by which the mythological narrative that provided the initial subject of the relief is effectively relegated to the status of a frame that is visually differentiated (here by the use of the drill) from the iconic portrait at its centre. This shift in focus has important implications for the divine figures incorporated into the narrative composition, whose corporeally charged presence becomes less important than their interpretative value. Whereas sarcophagi of the second and early third centuries had maintained a careful balance between the representational complexities of embodied form (so fundamental to classical naturalism) and each scene's allegorical potential, later

---

[128] Museo Capitolino, Rome, inv. 249: see C. Robert (1897–1919: vol. III, 477–8, *ASR* 3.3, no. 392), Sichtermann and Koch (1975: 57–8, no. 61), Wrede (1981: 297–8, no. 269), Lindner (1984: 70–1, no. 81) and Zanker and Ewald (2004: 370–2).

[129] As suggested by Newby (2007a: 246–7).

Figure 8.22 Endymion sarcophagus, first half of the third century CE

examples tend to subordinate sensuous detail to symbolic function, which leads to a form of narrative abbreviation that has been identified with the process of 'demythologisation' that characterises third-century sarcophagi more broadly.[130]

Whatever the complex historical and cultural factors behind this shift, its implications for the corpus of epiphanic myths employed upon sarcophagi is dramatic, for it ultimately leads to the departure of divine figures from the visual field altogether. On a third-century Endymion sarcophagus now in the Palazzo Braschi, for example, the young man now reclines alone, accompanied on either side by visual quotations of well-known statue types – Dionysus, a satyr and a panther to the left, and Venus and Mars to the right (Figure 8.22).[131] While classicising divine forms are relegated to the status of symbolic pendants – visual cues rather than embodied presences – the figure of Endymion is accompanied by a large expanse of blank space, just where one would expect Selene to alight from her chariot and stride towards him. Likewise, on a comparable piece in the British Museum (mysteriously altered in antiquity from an Ariadne to an Endymion), the composition retains the gesture of unveiling, whereby a cupid draws back a cloak as if to reveal the sleeping mortal's torso to his divine lover, yet includes no deity within the frame to perform a corresponding act of self-revelation.[132] Indeed, Selene's absence on the Palazzo Braschi sarcophagus renders unnecessary the subtle aporetics of vision and revelation so characteristic of earlier Endymion sarcophagi; here, the youth actually gazes out at the viewer, the device of sleep being less important for the scene's allegorical interpretation than the abbreviated compositional schema that allows it to be identified. In order to complete each scene, therefore, and uncover the relief's potential significance, the viewer must supply the missing divine figure by him- or herself. In effect, each sarcophagus asks us to perform the very act of *phantasia* that Apollonius of Tyana had outlined in his conversation with the gymnosophists in Philostratus' *Life*: we are required to view with *sophia*, supplying the form, attributes and narrative occasion necessary for an informed epiphanic encounter, to the extent that any physical *sēma*

---

[130] On the *Entmythologisierung* of third-century funerary art, see Koortbojian (1995: 138–40) and Zanker and Ewald (2004: 255–61).

[131] Palazzo Braschi, Rome, dated to the first half of the third century CE: see Sichtermann (1966): 66; 1992: 155, *ASR* 12.2, no. 102), Koortbojian (1995: 135–41, with a review of the scholarly literature), Zanker and Ewald (2004: 106–7) and Newby (in press). On the miniature replication of well-known statue types in funerary art, see Boschung (1989).

[132] British Museum, London, mid to late third century: see C. Robert (1897–1919: vol. I, 110–11, *ASR* 3.1, no. 92), Sichtermann (1966: 66; 1992: 54–5), Koortbojian (1995: 135–7) and Elsner (1998: 152–6).

of divinity is ultimately rendered unnecessary.[133] In this way the model of initiate viewing that characterised the play of revelation and concealment in earlier mythological reliefs is allied to a more symbolic mode of viewing characteristic of late antiquity, and the play of presence-in-absence that had typified earlier epiphanic compositions is rejected in favour of a process of internal visualisation.

In charting the dramatic shifts that took place in the visual culture of the third century, these examples also mark the point at which a Second Sophistic model of *paideia* – or viewing with knowledge – began its transformation into the model of typological viewing so important for early Christian art. In asking the viewer to supply all the epiphanic detail necessary to identify and interpret the funerary significance of Endymion, the Palazzo Braschi sarcophagus parallels and anticipates the composition's appropriation by Christian iconography, in which the moon's reclining lover metamorphoses into Jonah, prostrate under the gourd vine after his expulsion from the belly of the whale. In its Christian form the composition requires no visual conjuring of divine presence, because its epiphanic potential is dependent upon a typological reading of scripture, whereby Jonah's three-day ordeal and eventual salvation in the Old Testament anticipate the death and resurrection of Christ in the New. In this sense Selene's disappearance from Endymion's side and transformation into a *dea abscondita* anticipate the profoundly different formulations of the relationship between deity, body and image that Christianity would entail. In the figure of Jonah we are encouraged to contemplate a mortal body which, in its typological foreshadowing of Christ, alludes to a salvationist model of incarnation that would fundamentally realign the relationship between death and epiphany, vision and representation.

In that they explore the final frontiers of mortal vision, knowledge and experience, mythological sarcophagi are (*pace* Nock) inescapably eschatological, for in representational terms they probe the *eschata*, the 'last things'. To admit this does not, however, necessitate a commitment to 'decoding' their meanings according to a narrow set of philosophical precepts or cultic identities, for, in general, funerary iconography spoke in a lingua franca that was polysemous, culturally inclusive and readily adapted to individual needs. Instead, we must acknowledge the unique status of the tomb in both Roman law and ritual practice, and the broader culture with which Roman funerary art was in dialogue. By the second and third centuries CE, any philhellenic notion of classicism or *paideia* entailed investment in a cultural

---

[133] *VA* 6.19.2–3: see my discussion in Chapter 7, 328–9.

inheritance characterised by a deep and sophisticated engagement with the aesthetics of the sacred. While this is overtly demonstrated in Greek prose literature of the period (as I explored in Part II), it is also intrinsic to the visual vocabulary inherited by contemporary artists, particularly the naturalistic modes of representation developed since the fifth century BCE in order to render anthropomorphic gods present for their viewers in image form. While the employment of such styles and motifs may not always have had an identifiably religious function, they nevertheless carried with them a set of concepts and problems that could be appropriated and put to work in diverse contexts: just as Roman funerary art reconfigures epiphanic *aporia* as a way of addressing (or deferring) the challenges of death and remembrance, so the *Hymn to Demetrius Poliorcetes*, for example, exploits the insufficiency of sacred modes of representation as a response to the difficulties raised by ruler cult, while Artemidorus demonstrates how the mutually reinforcing relationship between gods and their images could be of semiological value within his allegorical system of dream interpretation.

From the *Homeric Hymns* to Philostratus' *Heroicus*, one of the most striking aspects of the various textual and visual artefacts explored in this book is the irrepressible creativity and vigorous experimentation with which Graeco-Roman artists and writers strove to bring their gods to life, against the background of a living religious culture in which 'real' epiphanies were continually attested, and individuals from Syriskos of Chersonesus to Pausanias and Aelius Aristides worked 'diligently', 'truthfully' and 'appropriately' to record and preserve them.[134] Fundamental to all these projects was the symbiotic relationship between epiphany and material culture, through which divine presence both inspired and gained meaning from human acts of recognition and commemoration. The relationship between divine *eidos* and mortal representation was by no means constant, however, but was continually reformulated in the light of shifting historical, cultural and material conditions. Even within the same period and location, differences in medium, genre and function meant that the image's ability to bring the gods before mortal eyes was continually renegotiated, so that votive reliefs formulated a different relationship between deity, artefact and viewer from temple statues, for example, and temple statues themselves employed multiple and divergent means of engendering a sense of epiphanic encounter for their viewer-worshippers (as I demonstrated in Chapter 2). In this sense, complex aesthetic choices were inseparable from theological concerns about

---

[134] For the Chersonesus inscription, see *IOSPE* I² 344 = *FGrH* 807 TI; text from Chaniotis (1988: E7), translation adapted from Higbie (2003: 275–6): see Chapter 3, 148.

the nature of the gods and the means by which they could be made materially present, which generated a sophisticated vocabulary of aesthetic terms (such as *enargeia*) that may have become increasingly technical, but never entirely lost their function within a semantic framework concerned with the apprehension of divine presence.

From an early period in Greek history, visual and literary formulations of the divine were also characterised by a strong sense of historical self-consciousness – an awareness of their place in religious and cultural tradition. This was particularly marked from the Hellenistic period onwards, during which epiphanic artefacts not only mediated divine presence, but were also dense with allusions to the Greek past, from Damophon's epiphanic 'citations' of Phidian classicism to the use of scholarly citation to unite temple inventory and epiphanography on the Lindos stele. Thus while epiphany thrived as an active component of lived religion in this period (as Hellenistic inscriptions attest), it was also accompanied by an increasing intellectualism, which reached its zenith in the Second Sophistic valorisation of the relationship between epiphany and *paideia*. Graeco-Roman formulations of epiphany are thus characterised by the uneasy paradox that the immediacy of divine encounter in the present must be accessed through the models of the past – whether Callimachus' reworking of the *Homeric Hymns*, the Pergamene altar's allusion to the Parthenon pediments, or Dio's prosopopoeia of Homer and Phidias in his *Olympian Oration*. In each case a model of epiphany as aesthetically mediated religious experience (i.e., a phenomenological encounter with the divine by means of an image or text) rubs alongside a model of epiphany as literary or visual tradition (which tends to be more concerned with the ontology of representation). Such self-referentiality can operate as a sign of piety (as in the Kythnians' celebration of Damophon's *technē* and *theosebeia*), yet it can also prompt the kinds of intellectual play that typify ekphrastic epigram, as I traced in relation to the Aphrodite of Knidos in Chapter 4.[135]

Even here, however, epiphanic 'games' exploit the tension between self-conscious aesthetic detachment and the excitement (or fear) of divine encounter in such a way that to deny their potential seriousness is to drain them of their richness as cultural artefacts. Indeed, the same qualities that made cult statues exciting yet problematic for their viewers also made them useful vehicles for poets to explore tensions between religiosity and mortal skill in their own work: the problematic boundary between art object

---

[135] Decree from Kythnos: *SEG* 49.423, discussed in Chapter 3, 131–2.

and cult object, human invention and divine agency, is a fundamental feature of Hellenistic ekphrastic literature that resounds through the Second Sophistic, to be echoed in the 'libation of *logos*' from Philostratus' *Imagines* with which I opened my Introduction. Yet the self-conscious signposting of representational failure that characterises meta-poetic play in a text such as Parmenion's epigram on the *agnostoi morphai* of Polyclitus' Argive Hera, for example, has serious theological implications that are paralleled in hymnic negotiations of divine presence, aniconic cultic objects or the 'signalled absences' of pilgrimage literature such as Pausanias' *Guide to Greece*.[136] In this sense the representational dilemmas that mythological encounters with the divine raise upon Roman sarcophagi draw upon a broader cultural inheritance not merely to proclaim membership within a cult of learnedness, but as part of an active engagement with problems of vision and representation that endured throughout antiquity. A sophisticated attention to both the sacred and the aesthetic is thus a fundamental aspect of the very 'classicism and culture' that not only drove the creative appropriation and reconfiguration of epiphanic iconography within the Roman tomb, but also characterised the Graeco-Roman imagination at large.

[136] *Anth. Plan.* 216 = GP 1968: Parmenion 14, line 4. 'Signalled absences': Paus. 8.37.9, with Elsner (1992: 22–7).

Bibliography

Abbondanza, L. (2001) 'Imaggini della *phantasia*. I quadri di Filostrato tra pittura e scultura', *RM* 109: 111–34.

Acosta-Hughes, B. (2002) *Polyeidea. The* Iambi *of Callimachus and the Archaic Iambic Tradition*. Berkeley and Los Angeles.

Acosta-Hughes, B., E. Kosmetatou and M. Baumbach (eds.) (2004) *Labored in Papyrus Leaves. Perspectives on an Epigram Collection Attributed to Posidippus (P.Mil.Vogl. VIII 309)*. Washington, DC.

Aitken, E. B. and J. K. B. Maclean (eds.) (2004) *Philostratus's* Heroikos. *Religion and Cultural Identity in the Third Century C.E.* Atlanta.

Akujärvi, J. (2005) 'Researcher, Traveller, Narrator. Studies in Pausanias' *Periegesis.*' PhD diss., Lund University.

Akurgal, E. (1990) '*Grundzüge der hermogeneischen Architektur*', in Hoepfner and Schwander (eds.): 123–7.

Albinus, L. (2000) *The House of Hades. Studies in Ancient Greek Eschatology*. Aarhus.

Albrecht, M. von *et al.* (2002) *Pythagoras. Legende, Lehre, Lebensgestaltung*. Darmstadt.

Alcock, S. E. (1993) *Graecia Capta. The Landscapes of Roman Greece*. Cambridge.

(1996) 'Landscapes of Memory and the Authority of Pausanias', in Bingen (ed.): 241–67.

(2001) 'The Peculiar Book IV and the Problem of the Messenian Past', in Alcock *et al.* (eds.): 142–53.

(2002) *Archaeologies of the Greek Past. Landscapes, Monuments, and Memories*. Cambridge.

(2004) 'Material Witnesses. An Archaeological Context for the Heroikos', in Aitken and Maclean (eds.): 159–68.

Alcock, S. E., J. F. Cherry and J. Elsner (eds.) (2001) *Pausanias. Travel and Memory in Roman Greece*. Oxford.

Alcock, S. E. and R. Osborne (eds.) (1994) *Placing the Gods. Sanctuaries and Sacred Space in Ancient Greece*. Oxford.

Aleshire, S. B. (1989) *The Athenian Asklepieion. The People, Their Dedications, and the Inventories*. Amsterdam.

(1991) *Asklepios at Athens. Epigraphic and Prosopographic Essays on the Athenian Healing Cults*. Amsterdam.

Alesse, F. (2001) 'La tripartizione dell'uomo nel mito de Tespesio. La sua origine "socratica" e alcuni suoi effetti sulla filosofia del II sec. d.C', in Pérez Jiménez and Casadesús Bordoy (eds.): 45–56.

Allen, T. W., W. R. Halliday and E. E. Sikes (1936) *Homeric Hymns. A Commentary.* Oxford.

Aloni, A. (1980) '*Prooimia, Hymnoi*, Elio Aristide e i cugini bastardi', *QUCC* 4–6: 23–40.

Alpers, J. (1912) *Hercules in Bivio.* Hanover.

Alroth, B. (1989) *Greek Gods and Figurines. Aspects of the Anthropomorphic Dedications.* Uppsala.

(1992) 'Changing Modes in the Representation of Cult Images', in Hägg (ed.): 9–46.

Althusser, L. and É. Balibar (1979) *Reading Capital.* Trans. B. Brewster. London.

Amandry, P. (1978) 'Consécration d'armes galates à Delphes', *BCH* 102: 571–86.

Amedick, R. (1991) *Die Sarkophage mit Darstellungen aus dem Menschenleben. Vita privata.* Die antiken Sarkophagreliefs 1.4. Berlin.

Ameling, W. (1996) 'Pausanias und die Hellenistischen Geschichte', in Bingen (ed.): 117–66.

Amory, A. (1966) 'The Gates of Horn and Ivory', in G. S. Kirk and A. Parry (eds.), *Homeric Studies.* Yale Classical Studies 20. New Haven and London, 1–57.

Anderson, G. (1986) *Philostratus. Biography and Belles-lettres in the Third Century A.D.* London and Dover, NH.

(1993) *The Second Sophistic. A Cultural Phenomenon in the Roman Empire.* London.

(1994) *Sage, Saint and Sophist. Holy Men and Their Associates in the Early Roman Empire.* London and New York.

(1996) 'Philostratus on Apollonius of Tyana. The Unpredictable on the Unfathomable', in G. Schmeling (ed.), *The Novel in the Ancient World.* Leiden: 613–18.

Anderson, M. J. (1997a) *The Fall of Troy in Early Greek Poetry and Art.* Oxford.

(1997b) 'The σωφροσύνη of Persinna and the Romantic Strategy of Heliodorus' *Aethiopica*', *CPh* 92: 303–22.

Anderson, M. L. and L. Nista (1988) *Roman Portraits in Context. Imperial and Private Likenesses from the Museo Nazionale Romano.* Rome.

Ando, C. (2008) *The Matter of the Gods. Religion and the Roman Empire.* Berkeley and Los Angeles.

Andreae, B. (1984) 'Bossierte Porträts auf römischen Sarkophagen. Ein ungelöstes Problem', in Andreae (ed.), *Symposium über die antiken Sarkophage*, Pisa 5.–12. September 1982. Marburger Winckelmann-Programm 1984. Marburg: 109–28.

Andronikos, M. (1994) *Vergina, ɪɪ. The 'Tomb of Persephone'.* Athens.

(1997) *Vergina. The Royal Tombs and the Ancient City.* Athens.

Androutsopoulos, G. D. (1972) *The Amphiareion of Oropos.* Athens.

Annas, J. (1994) *Hellenistic Philosophy of Mind.* Berkeley and Los Angeles.

Antonaccio, C. M. (1995) *An Archaeology of Ancestors. Tomb Cult and Hero Cult in Early Greece.* Lanham, MD.

Arafat, K. W. (1996) *Pausanias' Greece. Ancient Artists and Roman Rulers.* Cambridge.

Argentieri, L. (2007) 'Meleager and Philip as Epigram Collectors', in Bing and Bruss (eds.): 147–64.

Arieti, J. A. (2002) 'Rape and Livy's View of Roman History', in Deacy and Pierce (eds.): 209–29.

Armstrong, A. H. (1979) 'The Escape of the One. An Interpretation of Some Possibilities of Apophatic Theology Imperfectly Realised in the West', *Plotinian and Christian Studies.* London: no. 23.

Arscott, C. and K. Scott (eds.) (2000) *Manifestations of Venus. Art and Sexuality.* Manchester and New York.

Arthur, M. B. (1983) 'The Dream of a World Without Women. Poetics and the Circles of Order in the *Theogony* Prooemium', *Arethusa* 16: 97–116.

Aston, E. (2007) 'Animal-Human Composite Deities in Greek Religion.' PhD diss., University of Exeter.

Athanassiadi, P. (1993) 'Dreams, Theurgy and Freelance Divination', *JRS* 83: 115–30.

Auffarth, C. (1997) '"Verräter-Übersetzer"? Pausanias, das römische Patrai und die Identität der Griechen in der Achaea', in H. Cancik and J. Rüpke (eds.), *Römische Reichsreligion und Provinzialreligion.* Tübingen: 219–38.

Austin, C. and G. Bastianini (eds.) (2002) *Posidippi Pellaei quae supersunt omnia.* Milan.

Austin, M. (2006) *The Hellenistic World from Alexander to the Roman Conquest. A Selection of Ancient Sources in Translation.* 2nd edn. Cambridge.

Back, F. (1883) *De Graecorum caeremoniis in quibus homines deorum vice fungebantur.* Berlin.

Bagnall, R. S. (2002) 'Alexandria. Library of Dreams', *PCPS* 146: 348–62.

Bagnall, R. S. and P. Derow (2004) *The Hellenistic Period. Historical Sources in Translation.* Rev. edn. Malden, MA, and Oxford.

Bain, D. (1975) 'Audience Address in Greek Tragedy', *CQ* 25. 13–25.

(1987) 'Some Reflections on the Illusion in Greek Tragedy', *BICS* 34: 1–14.

Bakker, E. J. (2002a) 'Remembering the God's Arrival', *Arethusa* 35: 63–81.

(2002b) 'The Making of History. Herodotus' *Historiēs Apodexis*', in E. J. Bakker, I. J. F. de Jong and H. van Wees (eds.). *Brill's Companion to Herodotus.* Leiden: 3–32.

(2006) 'The Syntax of *Historiē*. How Herodotus Writes', in Dewald and Marincola: 92–102.

Bal, M. (1995) 'Reading the Gaze. The Construction of Gender in "Rembrandt"', in B. Readings and S. W. Melville (eds.), *Vision and Textuality.* Basingstoke: 147–73.

Balch, D. (2008) 'From Endymion in Roman *Domus* to Jonah in Christian Catacombs: From Houses of the Living to Houses for the Dead. Iconography and
Religion in Transition', in Saller *et al.* (eds.): 273–302.

Balensiefen, L. (1990) *Die Bedeutung des Spiegelbildes als ikonographisches Motiv in
der antiken Kunst.* Tübingen.

Baltes, M., M.-L. Lakmann, J. M. Dillon, P.-L. Donini, R. Häfner and L. Karfikova
(eds.) (2004) *Apuleius. Über den Gott des Sokrates.* Darmstadt.

Bankel, H. (1997) 'Knidos. Der hellenistische Rundtempel', *AA*: 51–71.

Barasch, M. (1992) *Icon. Studies in the History of an Idea.* New York.

Barber, C. (2002) *Figure and Likeness. On the Limits of Representation in Byzantine
Iconoclasm.* Princeton, NJ.

Barber, E. J. W. (1992) 'The Peplos of Athena', in Neils (ed.): 103–17.

Barchiesi, A. (2005) 'The Search for the Perfect Book. A PS to the New Posidippus',
in Gutzwiller (ed.): 320–42.

Barnard, L. W. (1974) *The Graeco-Roman and Oriental Background of the Iconoclastic
Controversy.* Leiden.

Barnard, S. (1978) 'Hellenistic Women Poets', *CJ* 73: 204–13.
  (1991) 'Anyte. Poet of Children and Animals', in F. de Martino (ed.), *Rose di
  Pieria.* Bari: 163–76.

Barnes, R. (2000) 'Cloistered Bookworms in the Chicken-Coop of the Muses. The
Ancient Library of Alexandria', in MacLeod (ed.): 61–77.

Barton, S. C. (2007) *Idolatry. False Worship in the Bible, Early Judaism and Christianity.* London and New York.

Bartsch, S. (1989) *Decoding the Ancient Novel. The Reader and the Role of Description
in Heliodorus and Achilles Tatius.* Princeton.
  (2000) 'The Philosopher as Narcissus. Vision, Sexuality, and Self-Knowledge in
  Classical Antiquity', in Nelson (ed.): 70–99.
  (2006) *The Mirror of the Self. Sexuality, Self-Knowledge, and the Gaze in the Early
  Roman Empire.* Chicago.

Bartsch, S. and J. Elsner (2007) 'Introduction.: Eight Ways of Looking at an Ekphrasis', *CPh* 102: i–vi.

Baslez, M.-F. (1985) 'Présence et traditions iraniennes dans les cités de l'Egée', *REA*
87: 137–55.

Baslez, M.-F., P. Hoffmann and L. Pernot (eds.) (1993) *L'Invention de
l'autobiographie d'Hésiode à Saint Augustine. Actes du deuxième colloque
de l'Équipe de recherche sur l'hellénisme post-classique (Paris, École normale
supérieure, 14–16 juin 1990).* Paris.

Bassi, K. (1989) 'The Poetics of Exclusion in Callimachus' *Hymn to Apollo*', *TAPA*
119: 219–31.

Bastianini, G. and A. Casanova (eds.) (2002) *Il Papiro di Posidippo un anno dopo.*
Studi e Testi di Papirologia 4. Florence.

Baum, P. F. (1919) 'The Young Man Betrothed to a Statue', *Publications of the Modern
Language Association* 34 (n.s. 27): 523–79.

Beall, S. (1993) 'Word-Painting in the "Imagines" of the Elder Philostratus', *Hermes* 121: 350–63.

Beard, M. (1991) 'Writing and Religion. Ancient Literacy and the Function of the Written Word in Roman Religion', in J. H. Humphrey (ed.), *Literacy in the Roman World*. Ann Arbor: 35–58.

  (2003) 'The Triumph of the Absurd. Roman Street Theatre', in C. Edwards and G. Woolf (eds.), *Rome the Cosmopolis*. Cambridge: 21–43.

Beard, M., J. North and S. Price (1998) *Religions of Rome*. 2 vols. Cambridge.

Bearzot, C. (1989) 'Fenomeni naturali e prodigi nell'attacco celtico a Delfi', in M. Sordi (ed.), *Fenomeni naturali e avvenimenti storici nell'antichità*. Milan: 71–86.

  (1992) *Storia e storiografia ellenistica in Pausania il Periegeta*. Venice.

Becatti, G. (1940) 'Attikà. Saggio sulla scultura attica dell'ellenismo', *RIA* 7: 7–116.

Bechard, D. P. (2000) *Paul outside the Walls. A Study of Luke's Socio-Geographical Universalism in Acts 14: 8–20*. Rome.

Beck, R. (1996) 'Mystery Religions, Aretalogy and the Ancient Novel', in G. Schmeling (ed.), *The Novel in the Ancient World*. Mnemosyne Suppl. 159. Leiden: 131–50.

Beckwith, J. (1993) *Early Christian and Byzantine Art*. New Haven.

Behr, C. A. (1968) *Aelius Aristides and the Sacred Tales*. Amsterdam.

  (1981) *P. Aelius Aristides. The Complete Works*. 2 vols. Leiden.

Beja, M. (1971) *Epiphany in the Modern Novel*. London.

Belayche, N. (in press) '*A God is Born . . . in Carian Stratonicea (I Stratonikeia 10)*', in Petridou and Platt (eds.).

Bell, C. (1992) *Ritual Theory, Ritual Practice*. New York and Oxford.

Belloni, G. (1980) 'Aspetti dell'antica σοφία in Apollonio di Tiana', *Aevum* 54: 140–9.

Belting, H. (1996) *Likeness and Presence. A History of the Image before the Era of Art*. Trans. E. Jephcott. Chicago.

Benndorf, O. and C. Schenkel (1893) *Philostrati Maioris Imagines*. Leipzig.

Bennett, F. M. (1917a) 'A Study of the Word Ξόανον', *AJA* 21: 8–21.

  (1917b) 'Primitive Wooden Statues Which Pausanias Saw in Greece', *CW* 10: 82–6.

Bentz, K. M. (1997–8) 'Rediscovering the Licinian Tomb', *Journal of the Walters Art Gallery* 55–6: 63–88.

Berger, E. (1974) *Die Geburt der Athena im Ostgiebel des Parthenon*. Basel.

  (ed.) (1984) *Parthenon-Kongress Basel. Referate und Berichte. 4. bis 8. April 1982*. Mainz.

Berger, J. (1972) *Ways of Seeing*. London.

Bergmann, B. (1995) 'Greek Masterpieces and Roman Recreative Fictions', *HSCP* 97: 79–120.

  (2001) 'Meanwhile, Back in Italy . . . Creating Landscapes of Allusion', in Alcock *et al.* (eds.): 154–66.

Bergmann, M. (1998) *Die Strahlen der Herrscher. Theomorphes Herrscherbild und politische Symbolik im Hellenismus und in der römischen Kaiserzeit.* Mainz am Rhein.

Bergren, A. (1982) 'Sacred Apostrophe. Re-Presentation and Imitation in the *Homeric Hymns*', *Arethusa* 15: 83–108.

Bernand, A. and E. Bernand (1960) *Les Inscriptions grecques et latines du Colosse de Memnon.* Paris.

Bernoulli, J. J. (1873) *Aphrodite. Ein Baustein zur griechischen Kunstmythologie.* Leipzig.

Berthold, R. M. (1984) *Rhodes in the Hellenistic Age.* Ithaca, NY, and London.

Besançon, A. (2000) *The Forbidden Image. An Intellectual History of Iconoclasm.* Trans. J. M. Todd. Chicago.

Beschorner, A. (1999) *Helden und Heroen, Homer und Caracalla. Übersetzung, Kommentar und Interpretationen zum* Heroikos *des Flavius Philostratos.* Pinakes 5. Bari.

Bettinetti, S. (2001) *La statua di culto nella pratica rituale greca.* Bari.

Bettini, M. and E. Pellizer (2003) *Il mito di Narciso. Immagini e racconti dalla Grecia a oggi.* Turin.

Betz, H. D. (1982) 'Gottmensch II (Griechisch-römische Antike und Urchristentum)', *RAC* 12: 234–312.

 (2004a) 'God Concept and Cultic Image. The Argument in Dio Chrysostom's *Oratio 12 (Olympikos)*', *ICS* 29: 131–42.

 (2004b) 'Hero Worship and Christian Beliefs. Observations from the History of Religion on Philostratus's *Heroikos*', in Aitken and Maclean (eds.): 25–47.

Bianchi, L. (1994) 'Ὑπὸ τὴν ὄψιν. Polibio e le "vere immagini" del funerale romano', *AA* 7: 137–53.

Bickerman, E. J. (1976) 'Love Story in the *Homeric Hymn to Aphrodite*', *Athenaeum* 54: 229–54.

Bidney, M. (1997) *Patterns of Epiphany. From Wordsworth to Tolstoy, Pater and Barrett Browning.* Carbondale and Edwardsville.

Bielefeld, E. (1954–5) 'Götterstatuen auf attischen Vasenbildern. Eine religionsgeschichtlich-archäologische Studie', *Wiss. Zeitschrift der E. Moritz Arndt-Universität Greifswald* 4: 379–403.

Bieler, L. (1935–6) *Theios aner. Das Bild des 'göttlichen Menschen' in Spätantik und Frühchristentum.* 2 vols. Vienna.

Bierl, A. (2001) *Der Chor in der Alten Komödie. Ritual und Performativität (unter besonderer Berücksichtigung von Aristophanes'* Thesmophoriazusen *und der Phalloslieder fr. 851 PMG).* Munich.

 (2004) '"Turn on the Light!" Epiphany, the God-Like Hero Odysseus, and the Golden Lamp of Athena in Homer's *Odyssey* (especially 19.1–43)', *ICS* 29: 43–61.

Bilde, P. G (2003) 'Wandering Images. From Taurian (and Chersonesean) Parthenos to (Artemis) Tauropolos and (Artemis) Persike', in Bilde *et al.* (eds.): 165–83.

Bilde, P. G., J. M. Højte and V. F. Stolba (eds.) (2003) *The Cauldron of Ariantas. Studies Presented to A. N. Sceglov on the Occasion of his 70th Birthday.* Aarhus.

Billaut, A. (2000) *L'Univers de Philostrate.* Brussels.

Billows, R. (1990) *Antigonus the One-Eyed and the Creation of the Hellenistic State.* Berkeley and Los Angeles.

    (2003) 'Cities', in Erskine (ed.): 196–215.

Bing, P. (1993) 'Impersonation of Voice in Callimachus' *Hymn to Apollo', TAPA* 123: 181–98.

    (1998) 'Between Literature and the Monuments', in Harder *et al.* (eds.): 21–43.

    (2002) 'The Un-read Muse? Inscribed Epigram and Its Readers in Antiquity', in Harder *et al.* (eds.): 39–66.

    (2005) 'The Politics and Poetics of Geography in the Milan Posidippus, Section One. On Stones (AB 1–20)', in Gutzwiller (ed.): 119–40.

Bing, P. and J. S. Bruss (eds.) (2007) *Brill's Companion to Hellenistic Epigram.* Leiden.

Bingen, J. (ed.) (1996) *Pausanias historien.* Entretiens sur l'antiquité classique 41. Geneva.

Bingöl (1999) 'Epiphanie an der Artemistempeln von Ephesos und Magnesia am Mäander', in H. Friesinger and F. Krinzinger (eds.), *100 Jahre österreichische Forschungen in Ephesos. Akten des Symposions Wien 1995.* Österreichische Akademie der Wissenschaft, Phil.-Hist. Kl. Denkschriften 260. Vienna: 233–40.

Birge, D. (1994) 'Trees in the Landscape of Pausanias' *Periegesis'*, in Alcock and Osborne (eds.): 231–45.

Birley, A. R. (1997) *Hadrian. The Restless Emperor.* New York.

Birmelin, E. (1933) 'Die kunsttheoretischen Gedanken in Philostrats Apollonios', *Philologus* 88: 149–80, 392–414.

Björck, G. (1946) '"Οναρ ἰδεῖν. De la perception de rêve chez les anciens', *Eranos* 44: 306–14.

Blinkenberg, C. (1912) *La Chronique du temple lindien.* Copenhagen.

    (1915) *Die lindische Tempelchronik.* Bonn.

    (1917) *L'Image d'Athana Lindia.* Copenhagen.

    (1933) *Knidia.* Copenhagen.

    (1941) *Lindos. Fouilles de l'Acropole 1902–1914.* Vol. ii: *Inscriptions.* Berlin.

Blinkenberg, C., R. Clairmont and G. C. Richards (1980) *Timachidas of Lindus. The Chronicle of the Temple of Athena at Lindus in Rhodes.* Chicago.

Blok, J. (2000) 'Phye's Procession. Culture, Politics and Peisistratid Rule', in H. Sancisi-Weerdenburg (ed.), *Peisistratus and the Tyranny. A Reappraisal of Evidence.* Amsterdam: 17–28.

Blome, P. (1978) 'Zur Umgestaltung griechischer Mythen in der römischen Sepulkralkunst. Alkestis-, Protesilaos-, und Proserpinasarkophage', *RM* 85: 435–57.

    (1992) 'Funerärsymbolische Collagen auf mythologischen Sarkophagreliefs', *Studi Italiani di Filologia Classica* 10: 1061–73.

Blum, C. (1936) *Studies in the Dream-Book of Artemidorus.* Uppsala.

Blum, R. (1991) *Kallimachos. The Alexandrian Library and the Origins of Bibliography.* Trans. H. H. Wellisch. Madison, WI.

Blümel, W. (1989) 'Neue Inschriften aus der Region von Mylasa (1988)', *EA* 13: 1–15.

(2000) 'Ein dritter Teil des Kultgesetzes aus Bargylia', *EA* 32: 89–93.

Boardman, J. (1972) 'Herakles, Peisistratos and Sons', *RA* 1: 57–72.

(2002) *The Archaeology of Nostalgia. How the Greeks Re-created their Mythical Past.* London.

Bodel, J. (1999) 'Death on Display. Looking at Roman Funerals', in B. Bergmann and C. Kondoleon (eds.), *The Art of Ancient Spectacle.* London: 258–81.

(2000) 'Dealing with the Dead. Undertakers, Executioners and Potters' Fields in Ancient Rome', in V. M. Hope and E. Marshall. (eds.), *Death and Disease in the Ancient City.* London: 128–51.

'The Organization of the Funerary Trade at Puteoli and Cumae', in S. Panciera (ed.), *Libitina e dintorni.* Libitina 3. Rome: 149–70.

Boedeker, D. (1974) *Aphrodite's Entry into Greek Epic.* Leiden.

(1988) 'Protesilaos and the End of Herodotus' *Histories*', *ClAnt* 7: 30–48.

(1993) 'Hero Cult and Politics in Herodotus. The Bones of Orestes', in Dougherty and Kurke (eds.): 164–77.

Boeder, M. (1996) *Visa est Vox. Sprache und Bild in der spätantiken Literatur.* Frankfurt am Main.

Boehringer (2001) *Heroenkulte in Griechenland von der geometrischen bis zur klassischen Zeit. Attika, Argolis, Messenien.* Berlin.

Boffo, L. (1988) 'Epigrafi di città greche. Un'espressione di storiografia locale', in *Studi di storia e storiografia antiche per Emilio Gabba.* Pavia: 9–48.

Bompaire, J. (1993) 'Le Sacré dans les discours d'Aelius Aristide (xlvii–lii Keil)', *Revue des Études Grecques* 102: 28–39.

(1994) 'L'Atticisme de Lucien', in A. Billault (ed.), *Lucien de Samosate.* Lyon: 65–75.

Bonfante, L. (1989) 'Nudity as a Costume in Classical Art', *AJA* 93: 543–70.

Borg, B. (2004a) 'Glamorous Intellectuals. Portraits of Pepaidoumenoi in the Second and Third Centuries ad', in Borg (ed.): 157–78.

(ed.) (2004b) *Paideia. The World of the Second Sophistic.* Berlin and New York.

Borgeaud, P. (1988) *The Cult of Pan in Ancient Greece.* Trans. K. Atlass and J. Redfield. Chicago.

Boschung, D. (1989) '*Nobilia opera.* Zur Wirkungsgeschichte griechischer Meisterwerke im kaiserzeitlichen Rom', *AntK* 32: 8–16.

Botte, B. (1932) *Les Origines de la Noël et de l'Épiphanie. Étude historique.* Louvain.

Böttiger, C. A. (1829) *Hercules in bivio, e Prodici fabula et monumentis priscae artis illustratus.* Leipzig.

Boulanger, A. (1923) *Aelius Aristide et la sophistique dans la province d'Asie au IIe siècle de notre ère.* BEFAR 126. Paris.

Bourdieu, P. (1977) *Outline of a Theory of Practice.* Trans. R. Nice. Cambridge.

Bousquet, J. (1957) 'Les Aitoliens à Delphes au ive siècle', *BCH* 38: 21–37.

Bowden, H. (2005) *Classical Athens and the Delphic Oracle. Divination and Democracy.* Cambridge.

Bowen, Z. R. (1979) 'Epiphanies, Stephen's Diary, and the Narrative Perspective of *A Portrait of the Artist as a Young Man*', *James Joyce Quarterly* 16.4: 485–8.

Bowersock, G. W. (1969) *Greek Sophists in the Roman Empire.* Oxford.

(1974) *Approaches to the Second Sophistic.* University Park, PA.

(1984) 'The Miracle of Memnon', *Bulletin of the American Society of Papyrologists* 21: 21–32.

(1994) *Fiction as History. Nero to Julian.* Berkeley.

(2004) 'Artemidorus and the Second Sophistic', in Borg (ed.): 53–63.

Bowie, E. L. (1970) 'The Greeks and Their Past in the Second Sophistic', *Past & Present* 46: 3–41. Reprinted with some changes in M. Finley (ed.) (1974), *Studies in Ancient Society.* London: 166–209.

(1978) 'Apollonios of Tyana. Fiction and Reality', *ANRW* 2.16.2: 1652–99.

(1982) 'The Importance of Sophists', in J. J. Winkler and G. Williams (eds.), *Later Greek Literature.* Yale Classical Studies 27. Cambridge: 29–59.

(1990) 'Greek Poetry in the Antonine Age', in D. Russell (ed.), *Antonine Literature.* Oxford: 61–6.

(1991) 'Hellenism in Writers of the Early Second Sophistic', in S. Saïd (ed.): 183–204.

(1993) 'Lies, Fiction and Slander in Early Greek Poetry', in C. Gill and T. P. Wiseman (eds.), *Lies and Fiction in the Ancient World.* Exeter: 1–37.

(1994) 'Philostratus: Writer of Fiction', in J. R. Morgan and R. Stoneman (eds.), *Greek Fiction. The Greek Novel in Context.* London: 181–99.

(1996) 'Past and Present in Pausanias', in Bingen (ed.): 207–30.

(2009) 'Quotation of Earlier Texts in Τὰ ἐς τὸν Τυανέα Ἀπολλώνιον', in Demoen and Praet (eds.): 56–73.

Bowie, E. and J. Elsner (eds.) (2009) *Philostratus.* Cambridge.

Bowra, C. M. (1961) *Greek Lyric Poetry from Alcman to Simonides.* Oxford.

Boyer, P. (1994) *The Naturalness of Religious Ideas. A Cognitive Theory of Religion.* Cambridge.

(2001) *Religion Explained. The Human Instincts That Fashion Gods, Spirits and Ancestors.* London.

Bracht Branham, R. (1989) *Unruly Eloquence. Lucian and the Comedy of Traditions.* Cambridge, MA, and London.

Bradshaw, P. (1992) *The Search for the Origins of Christian Worship. Sources and Methods for the Study of Early Liturgy.* London.

Braginskaya, N. and D. Leonov (2006) '*La Composition des images de Philostrate l'ancien*', in Costantini *et al.* (eds.): 9–29.

Brahms, T. (1994) *Archaismus. Untersuchungen zu Funktion und Bedeutung archaistischer Kunst im Hellenismus.* Frankfurt.

Braund, D. (2007) 'Parthenos and the Nymphs at Crimean Chersonesus. Colonial Appropriation and Native Integration', in A. Bresson, A. Ivantchik and J.-L. Ferrary (eds.), *Une koinè pontique. Cités grecques, sociétés indigènes et empires mondiaux sur le littoral nord de la mer Noire (VIIe s. a.C.–IIIe s. p.C.).* Bordeaux: 191–200.

Bravi, F. (2007) 'Vocem Memnonis audivi. Il colosso di Memnon e i luoghi della memoria greco-romana in Egitto', in O. D. Cordovana and M. Galli (eds.): 79–91.

Bravo, J. (2004) 'Heroic Epiphanies. Narrative, Visual, and Cultic Contexts', *ICS* 29: 63–84.

Brecoulaki, H. (2006) *La Peinture funéraire de Macedoine. Emplois et fonctions de la couleur, IVe–IIe s. av. J.-C.* 2 vols. Meletemata 48. Athens and Paris.

Brelich, A. (1966) 'The Place of Dreams in the Religious World Concept of the Greeks', in von Grunebaum and Caillois (eds.): 293–301.

Bremer, D. (1975) 'Die Epiphanie des Gottes in den homerischen Hymnen und Platons Gottesbegriff', *Zeitschrift für Religions- und Geistesgeschichte* 27: 1–21.

Bremer, J. M. (1981) 'Greek Hymns' in Versnel (ed.): 193–215.

(1998) 'The Reciprocity of Giving and Thanksgiving in Greek Worship', in Gill *et al.* (eds.): 127–37.

Bremer, J. M. and W. D. Furley (2001) *Greek Hymns. Selected Cult Songs from the Archaic to the Hellenistic Period.* 2 vols. Tübingen.

Bremmer, J. N. (2002) *The Rise and Fall of the Afterlife.* London and New York.

Bremmer, J. N. and A. Erskine (eds.) (2010) *The Gods of Ancient Greece. Identities and Transformations.* Edinburgh.

Brenk, F. E. (1977) *In Mist Apparelled. Religious Themes in Plutarch's Moralia and Lives.* Leiden.

(1986) 'In the Light of the Moon. Demonology in the Early Imperial Period', *ANRW* 2.16.3: 2068–145.

(1987) 'An Imperial Heritage. The Religious Spirit of Plutarch of Chaironea', *ANRW* 2.36.2: 1300–22.

(1994) 'Greek Epiphanies and Paul on the Road to Damaskos', in U. Bianchi (ed.), *The Notion of 'Religion' in Comparative Research. Selected Proceedings of the XVIth International Association for the History of Religions, Rome 3rd – 8th September, 1990.* Rome: 415–24.

(1998) 'Genuine Greek Demons. "In Mist Apparelled"? Hesiod and Plutarch', *Relighting the Souls. Studies in Plutarch, in Greek Literature, Religion, and Philosophy, and in the New Testament Background.* Stuttgart: 170–81.

Bresson, A. (2006) 'Relire la *Chronique du temple lindien.* Carolyn Higbie, *The Lindian Chronicle and the Greek Creation of their Past*, Oxford (2003)', *Topoi* 14: 527–51.

Breytenbach, C. (1993) 'Zeus und der lebendige Gott. Anmerkungen zu Apostelgeschichte 14:11–17', *NTS* 39: 396–413.

Bridges, E., E. Hall and P. Rhodes (eds.) (2007) *Cultural Responses to the Persian Wars. Antiquity to the Third Millennium.* Oxford.

Brillante, C. (1988) 'Metamorfosi di un' immagine. Le statue animate e il sogno', in G. Guidorizzi (ed.), *Il sogno in Grecia.* Rome: 17–33.

Bringmann, K. (1993) 'The King as Benefactor. Some Remarks on Ideal Kingship in the Age of Hellenism', in Bulloch *et al.* (eds.): 7–24.

Brinkmann, V. (2003) *Die Polychromie der archaischen und frühklassischen Skulptur.* Munich.

Brinkmann, V. and R. Wünsche (eds.) (2004) *Bunte Götter. Die Farbigkeit Antiker Skulptur.* Munich.

Brisson, L. (1976) *Le Mythe de Tirésias. Essai d'analyse structurale.* Leiden.

Brommer, F. (1979) *Die Parthenon-Skulpturen. Metopen, Fries, Giebel, Kultbild.* Mainz am Rhein.

Bronfen, E. (1992) *Over Her Dead Body. Death, Femininity and the Aesthetic.* Manchester.

Brown, P. R. L. (1971) 'The Rise and Function of the Holy Man in Late Antiquity', *JRS* 61: 80–101. Reprinted in (1992) *Power and Persuasion in Late Antiquity. Towards a Christian Empire.* Wisconsin: 103–52.

(1978) *The Making of Late Antiquity.* Cambridge, MA.

(1981) *The Cult of Saints. Its Rise and Function in Latin Christianity.* Chicago.

Brownmiller, S. (1975) *Against Our Will. Men, Women and Rape.* New York.

Bruit, L. (1986) 'Pausanias à Phigalie. Sacrifices non-sanglants et discours idéologique', *Métis* 1: 71–96.

(1989) 'Les Dieux aux festins des mortels. Théoxènies et *xeniai*', in A.-F. Laurens (ed.), *Entre hommes et dieux. Le convive, le héros, le prophète.* Paris: 12–25.

Brunel, J. (1953) 'A propos des transferts de culte. Un sens méconnu du mot *aphydruma*', *Revue de Philologie* 27: 21–33.

Bruno, V. J. (1977) *Form and Color in Greek Painting.* New York.

Brunt, P. (1994) 'The Bubble of the Second Sophistic', *BICS* 39: 25–52.

Bryson, N. (1995) 'Philostratus and the Imaginary Museum', in Melville and Readings (eds.): 174–94.

Bulloch, A. W. (1984) 'The Future of a Hellenistic Illusion. Some Observations on Callimachus and Religion', *MH* 4: 209–30.

(1985) *Callimachus. The Fifth Hymn.* Cambridge.

Bulloch, A. W., E. S. Gruen, A. A. Long and A. Stewart (1993) *Images and Ideologies. Self-Definition in the Hellenistic World.* Berkeley and Los Angeles.

Bultmann, R. (1963) *History of the Synoptic Tradition.* Trans. J. Marsh. Rev. edn. New York.

Burgess-Jackson, K. (1999) 'A History of Rape Law', in K. Burgess-Jackson (ed.), *A Most Detestable Crime. New Philosophical Essays on Rape.* Oxford and New York: 1–31.

Burke, K. (1952) 'Thanatopsis for Critics. A Brief Thesaurus of Deaths and Dyings', *Essays in Criticism* 2: 369–75.

Burkert, W. (1985a) *Greek Religion. Archaic and Classical.* Trans. J. Raffan. Oxford.

(1985b) 'Herodot über die Namen der Götter. Polytheismus als historisches Problem', *MH* 42: 371–4.

(1990) 'Buzyge und Palladion. Gewalt und Gericht in altgriechischem Ritual', in *Wilder Ursprung. Opferritual und Mythos bei den Griechen.* Berlin: 77–85.

(1997) 'From Epiphany to Cult Statue. Early Greek *Theos*', in A. B Lloyd and W. Burkert (eds.), *What Is a God? Studies in the Nature of Greek Divinity.* London: 15–34.

(2004) 'Epiphanies and Signs of Power. Minoan Suggestions and Comparative Evidence', *ICS* 29: 1–23.

(2005) 'Signs, Commands, and Knowledge. Ancient Divination between Enigma and Epiphany', in S. Iles Johnston and P. T. Struck (eds.), *Mantikê. Studies in Ancient Divination.* Leiden: 29–49.

Burnyeat, M. (1982) 'Idealism and Greek Philosophy. What Descartes Saw and Berkeley Missed', *Philosophical Review* 91: 3–40.

Burton, D. (2005) 'The Gender of Death', in E. Stafford and J. Herrin (eds.), *Personification in the Greek World. From Antiquity to Byzantium.* Aldershot: 45–68.

Burton, J. (1995) *Theocritus's Urban Mimes. Mobility, Gender, and Patronage.* Berkeley and Los Angeles.

Buxton, R. (1980) 'Blindness and Limits. Sophokles and the Logic of Myth', *JHS* 100: 22–37.

(ed.) (1999) *From Myth to Reason? Studies in the Development of Greek Thought.* Oxford.

(2004) 'Similes and Other Likenesses', in R. Fowler (ed.), *The Cambridge Companion to Homer.* Cambridge: 139–55.

Cagnat, R., J. Toutain and P. Boudreaux (eds.) (1911) *Inscriptiones graecae ad res romanas pertinentes.* Vol. I. Paris.

Cahen, É. (1929) *Callimaque et son oeuvre poétique.* Paris.

Cain, C. D. (2001) 'Dancing in the Dark. Deconstructing a Narrative of Epiphany on the Isopata Ring', *AJA* 105: 27–49.

Cain, H.-U. (1995) 'Hellenistische Kultbilder. Religiöse Präsenz und museale Präsentation der Götter im Heiligtum und beim Fest', in Wörrle and Zanker (eds.): 115–30.

Cairns, D. L. (ed.) (2001) *Oxford Readings in Homer's Iliad.* Oxford.

Calame, C. (1991) 'Quand dire c'est faire voir. L'évidence dans la rhétorique antique', *EL* Oct.–Dec.: 3–22.

(1995) 'Variations énonciatives, relations avec les dieux et fonctions poétiques dans les *Hymnes homériques*', *MH* 52: 2–19.

(2001) *Choruses of Young Women in Ancient Greece. Their Morphology, Religious Role, and Social Functions.* Trans. D. Collins and J. Orion. Rev. edn. Lanham, MD.

Caliò, L. M. (2007) 'La morte del sapiente. La tomba di Valerius Herma nella necropoli vaticana', in Cordovana and Galli (eds.): 289–318.

Callaghan, P. J. (1981) 'On the Date of the Great Altar of Zeus at Pergamon', *BICS* 28: 115–21.

Cameron, A. (1939) 'Sappho's Prayer to Aphrodite', *Harvard Theological Review* 32: 1–17.

Cameron, Alan (1993) *The Greek Anthology. From Meleager to Planudes.* Oxford.

  (1995) *Callimachus and His Critics.* Princeton.

Cameron, Averil (1981) *Christianity and the Rhetoric of Empire.* Berkeley.

Cancik, H. (1990) 'Epiphanie/Advent', in Cancik *et al.* (eds): vol. II, 290–6.

Cancik, H., B. Gladigow and M. Laubscher (eds.) (1988–2001) *Handbuch religionswissenschaftlicher Grundbegriffe.* 5 vols. Stuttgart.

Canfora, L. (1990) *The Vanished Library.* Trans. M. Ryle. Berkeley.

Carson, A. (1996) 'The Justice of Aphrodite in Sappho 1', in Greene (ed.): 226–32.

  (1999) *The Economy of the Unlost. Reading Simonides of Ceos with Paul Celan.* Princeton.

Casadesús Bordoy, Y. (2001) 'La concepción plutarquea de los daímones', in Pérez Jiménez and Casadesús Bordoy (eds.): 23–34.

Casevitz, M. (1982) 'Les Mots du rêve en grec ancien', *Ktema* 7: 67–74.

Casevitz, M., M. Jost and J. Marcadé (eds.) (1998) *Pausanias. Description de la Grèce. Tome VIII, livre VIII. L'Arcadie.* Paris.

Casevitz, M. and Y. Lafond (eds.) (2000) *Pausanias. Description de la Grèce. Tome VII, livre VII. L'Achaïe.* Paris.

Casevitz, M, J. Pouilloux and A. Jacquemin (eds.) (2002) *Pausanias. Description de la Grèce. Tome VI, livre VI. L'Élide (II).* Paris.

Cassimatis, H. (1991) 'Les Autels dans la céramique italiote', in M.-T. Le Dinahet and R. Étienne (eds.), *L'Espace sacrificiel dans les civilisations méditerranéennes de l'antiquité. Actes du colloque tenu á la Maison de l'Orient, Lyon, 4–7 juin 1988.* Paris: 33–43.

  (1998) 'Le Miroir dans les représentations funéraires apuliennes', *MÉFRA* 110: 297–350.

Cassin, B. (1995) *L'Effet sophistique.* Paris.

Casson, L. (2001) *Libraries in the Ancient World.* New Haven.

Champion, C. (1995) 'The Soteria at Delphi. Aetolian Propaganda in the Epigraphical Record', *AJPh* 116: 213–20.

Chaniotis, A. (1988) *Historie und Historiker in den griechischen Inschriften.* Stuttgart.

  (1991) 'Gedenktage der Griechen. Ihre Bedeutung für das Geschichtsbewußtsein griechischer Poleis', in J. Assmann and T. Sundermeier (eds.), *Das Fest und das Heilige. Religiöse Kontrapunkte zur Alltagswelt.* Gütersloh: 123–44.

  (1995) 'Sich selbst feiern? Die städtischen Feste des Hellenismus im Spannungsfeld zwischen Religion und Politik', in Wörrle and Zanker (eds.): 147–72.

  (1996) 'Conflicting Authorities. Greek Asylia between Secular and Divine Law in the Classical and Hellenistic Poleis', *Kernos* 9: 65–86.

(1997) 'Theatricality beyond the Theater. Staging Public Life in the Hellenistic World', *Pallas* 47: 219–59.

(1998) 'Willkommene Erdbeben', in E. Olshausen and H. Sonnabend, *Stuttgarter Kolloquium zur Historischen Geographie des Altertums 6, 1996. Naturkatastrophen in der antiken Welt.* Stuttgart: 404–17.

(1999) 'Empfängerformular und Urkundenfälschung. Bemerkungen zum Urkundendossier von Magnesia am Mäander', in R. G. Khoury (ed.), *Urkunden und Urkundenformulare im klassischen Altertum und in den orientalischen Kulturen.* Heidelberg: 51–69.

(2003) 'The Divinity of Hellenistic Rulers', in Erskine (ed.): 431–45.

(2005) *War in the Hellenistic World. A Social and Cultural History.* Oxford.

Cheshire, K. (2008) 'Kicking Φθόνος. Apollo and His Chorus in Callimachus' *Hymn 2*', *CPh* 103: 354–73.

Chisholm, R. (1995) '"To Whom Shall You Compare Me?" Yahweh's Polemic against Baal and the Babylonian Idol-Gods in Prophetic Literature', in E. Rommen and H. Netland (eds.), *Christianity and the Religions. A Biblical Theology of World Religions.* Pasadena, CA: 56–71.

Chroust, A.-H. (1957) *Socrates, Man and Myth. The Two Socratic Apologies of Xenophon.* London.

(1974) 'Aristotle's *Protrepticus* versus Aristotle's *On Philosophy*. A Controversy over the Nature of Dreams', *Theta-Pi* 3: 168–78.

Cima, M. and E. La Rocca (eds.) (1998) *Horti romani.* Bulletino della Commissione archeologica communate di Roma Suppl. 6. Rome.

Clay, J. S. (1972) 'The Planktai and Moly. Divine Naming and Knowing in Homer', *Hermes* 100: 127–31.

(1989) *The Politics of Olympus. Form and Meaning in the Major Homeric Hymns.* Princeton.

Clark, G. (1989) *Iamblichus. On the Pythagorean Life.* Liverpool.

(2000) 'Philosophic Lives and the Philosophic Life. Porphyry and Iamblichus', in Hägg and Rousseau (eds.): 29–51.

Clarke, H. (1981) *Homer's Readers. A Historical Introduction to the Iliad and the Odyssey.* Newark, London and Toronto.

Clarke, J. R. (2003) *Art in the Lives of Ordinary Romans. Visual Representation and Non-Elite Viewers in Italy, 100 B.C.–A.D. 315.* Berkeley and Los Angeles.

Clarke, K. (2008) *Making Time for the Past. Local History and the Polis.* Oxford.

Clerc, C. (1915) *Les Théories relatives au culte des images chez les auteurs grecs du IIme siècle après J.C.* Paris.

Clinton, K. (1989) 'The Eleusinian Mysteries. Roman Initiates and Benefactors, Second Century B.C. to A.D. 267', *ANRW* 2.18.2: 1498–1539.

(1992) *Myth and Cult. The Iconography of the Eleusinian Mysteries. The Martin P. Nilsson Lectures on Greek Religion, Delivered 19–21 November 1990 at the Swedish Institute at Athens.* Stockholm.

(1994) 'The Epidauria and the Arrival of Asclepius in Athens', in Hägg (ed.): 17–34.

(2003) 'Stages of Initiation in the Eleusinian and Samothracian Mysteries', in M. B. Cosmopoulos (ed.), *Greek Mysteries. The Archaeology and Ritual of Ancient Greek Secret Cults.* London and New York: 50–78.

Cohen, A. (1996) 'Portrayals of Abduction in Greek Art. Rape or Metaphor?', in Kampen (ed.): 117–35.

Cole, S. G. (2004) *Landscapes, Gender, and Ritual Space. The Ancient Greek Experience.* Berkeley and Los Angeles.

Coleman, K. (1996) 'Ptolemy Philadelphus and the Roman Amphitheater', in W. J. Slater (ed.), *Roman Theater and Society.* E. Togo Salmon Papers 1. Michigan: 49–68.

Collins, D. (1999) 'Hesiod and the Divine Voice of the Muses', *Arethusa* 32: 241–62.

Comstock, M. B. and C. C. Vermeule (1976) *Sculpture in Stone. The Greek, Roman and Etruscan Collections of the Museum of Fine Arts Boston.* Boston.

Conan, M. (1987) 'The *Imagines* of Philostratus', *Word and Image* 3: 162–71.

Connelly, J. B. (1993) 'Narrative and Image in Attic Vase Painting. Ajax and Kassandra at the Trojan Palladion', in P. J. Holliday (ed.), *Narrative and Event in Ancient Art.* Cambridge: 88–129.

(1996) 'Parthenon and *Parthenoi.* A Mythological Interpretation of the Parthenon Frieze', *AJA* 100: 53–80.

(2007) *Portrait of a Priestess. Women and Ritual in Ancient Greece.* Princeton.

Connolly, A. (1998) 'Was Sophocles Heroised as Dexion?', *JHS* 118: 1–21.

Connolly, J. (2001) 'Problems of the Past in Imperial Greek Education', in Too (ed.): 339–72.

Connor, W. R. (1987) 'Tribes, Festivals and Processions. Civic Ceremonial and Political Manipulation in Archaic Greece', *JHS* 107: 40–50.

(1988) 'Seized by the Nymphs. Nympholepsy and Symbolic Expression in Classical Greece', *ClAnt* 7: 155–89.

Conte, G. (1999) *Il passaggio di Ermes. Riflessioni sul mito.* Florence.

Conticello, B. *et al.* (1987) *Alla ricerca di Fidia.* Padua.

Cook, A. B. (1914–40) *Zeus.* 3 vols. Cambridge.

Cooper, F. A. (ed.) (1992–6) *The Temple of Apollo Bassitas.* 4 vols. Princeton.

Corbeille, M. (2006) *Donner à voir, donner à lire. Mémoire et communication dans la Rome ancienne.* Paris.

Corbett, P. E. (1970) 'Greek Temples and Greek Worshippers. The Literary and Archaeological Evidence', *BICS* 17: 149–58.

Cordero, N. L. (1990) 'La Déesse de la raison en Grèce', in J-F. Mattéi (ed.) *La Naissance de la raison en Grèce.* Paris: 207–14.

Cordovana, O. D. and M. Galli (eds.) (2007) *Arte e memoria culturale nell'età della Seconda Sofistica.* Catania.

Cormack, R. (1985) *Writing in Gold. Byzantine Society and Its Icons.* Oxford.

(1997) *Painting the Soul. Icons, Death Masks and Shrouds.* London.

Corrington, G. P. (1986) *The 'Divine Man'. His Origin and Functions in Hellenistic Popular Religion.* New York.

Corso, A. (1988) *Prassitele. Fonti epigraphie e letterarie. Vite e opere.* 2 vols. Rome.

(1997) 'The Monument of Phryne at Delphi', *Numismatica e Antichità Classiche* 26: 123–50.

(2006) 'Mirone ovvero dell'arte animata', *Numismatica e Antichità Classiche* 35: 475–504.

(2007) *The Art of Praxiteles, II. The Mature Years.* Rome.

Cortés Copete, J. M. (1995) *Elio Arístides, un sofista griego en el Imperio Romano.* Madrid.

(1999) *Elio Arístides. Discursos XXXVI–LII. Introducciones, traducción y notas.* Madrid.

Costantini, M., E. Graziani and S. Rolet (eds.) (2006) *Le Défi de l'art. Philostrate, Callistrate et l'image sophistique.* Paris.

Cox, P. (1983) *Biography in Late Antiquity. A Quest for the Holy Man.* Berkeley.

Cox Miller, P. (1994) *Dreams in Late Antiquity.* Princeton.

Croon, J. H. (1953) 'Heracles at Lindus', *Mnemosyne* 6: 283–99.

Cumont, F. (1942) *Recherches sur le symbolisme funéraires des Romains.* Paris.

Curty, O. (1995) *Les Parentés légendaires entre cités grecques.* Geneva.

Cuzin, J.-P., J.-R. Gaborit and W. Pasquier (2000) *D'après l'antique. Paris, Musée du Louvre, 16 octobre 2000 – 15 janvier 2001.* Paris.

Dalby, A. (2005) *Venus. A Biography.* London.

Damaskos, D. (1999) *Untersuchungen zu hellenistischen Kultbildern.* Stuttgart.

D'Ambra, E. (1988) 'A Myth for a Smith. A Meleager Sarcophagus from a Tomb in Ostia', *AJA* 92: 85–100.

(ed.) (1993a) *Roman Art in Context. An Anthology.* Englewood Cliffs, NJ.

(1993b) 'The Cult of Virtues and the Funerary Relief of Ulpia Epigone', in D'Ambra (ed.): 104–14.

(1996) 'The Calculus of Venus. Nude Portraits of Roman Matrons', in Kampen (ed.): 219–32.

(2000) 'Nudity and Adornment in Female Portrait Sculpture of the Second Century AD', in Kleiner and Matheson (eds.): 101–14.

(2006) 'Imitations of Life. Style, Theme and a Sculptural Collection in the Isola Sacra necropolis, Ostia', in E. D'Ambra and G. Métraux. (eds.), *The Art of Citizens, Soldiers and Freedmen in the Roman World.* Oxford: 73–90.

Daut, R. (1975) *Imago. Untersuchungen zum Bildbegriff der Römer.* Heidelberg.

Davesne, A. (1982) *La Frise du temple d'Artémis à Magnésie du Méandre. Catalogue des fragments du Musée du Louvre.* Paris.

Davidson, J. M. (1997) *Courtesans and Fishcakes. The Consuming Passions of Classical Athens.* London.

Davies, G. (1978) 'The Door Motif in Roman Funerary Sculpture', in D. Whitehouse (ed.), *Papers in Italian Archaeology, I.* Oxford: 203–26.

(1986) 'The Rape of Proserpina on Roman Grave Altars and Ash Chests', *Shadow. The Newsletter of the Traditional Cosmology Society* 3: 51–60.

Davies, J. (1999) *Death, Burial, and Rebirth in the Religions of Antiquity.* New York.

Davies, J. K. (2003) 'Greek Archives. From Record to Monument', in M. Brosius (ed.), *Ancient Archives and Archival Traditions. Concepts of Record-Keeping in the Ancient World.* Oxford: 323–43.

Davies, P. (2004) *Death and the Emperor. Roman Imperial Funerary Monuments, from Augustus to Marcus Aurelius.* Austin.

Davreux, J. (1942) *La Légende de la prophétesse Cassandre.* Liège.

Day, J. W. (1989) 'Rituals in Stone. Early Greek Grave Epigrams and Monuments', *JHS* 109: 16–28.

(1994) 'Interactive Offerings. Early Greek Dedicatory Epigrams and Ritual', *HSCP* 96: 37–74.

(2000) 'Epigram and Reader. Generic Force as (Re-)Activation of Ritual', in Depew and Obbink (eds.): 37–57.

(2007) 'Poems on Stone. The Inscribed Antecedents of Hellenistic Epigram', in Bing and Bruss (eds.): 29–48.

de Jong, I. J. F. (1987) *Narrators and Focalizers. The Presentation of the Story in the Iliad.* Amsterdam.

de Lauretis, T. (1984) *Alice Doesn't. Feminism, Semiotics, Cinema.* London.

Deacy, S. and K. F. Pierce (eds.) (2002) *Rape in Antiquity. Sexual Violence in the Greek and Roman Worlds.* Paperback edn. London.

Deacy, S. and Villing, A. (eds.) (2001) *Athena in the Classical World.* Leiden.

Del Corno, D. (1962) 'Ricerche sull'onirocritica greca', *Rendiconti dell'Istituto lombardo, Classe di lettere, scienze morali e storiche* 96: 334–66.

(1978) 'I sogni e la loro interpretazione nell'età dell'impero', *ANRW* 2.16.2: 1605–18.

Delatte, A. (1932) *La Catoptromancie grecque et ses dérivés.* Liège.

Delia, D. (1993) 'Response to A. E. Samuel', in Green (ed.): 192–204.

Delorme, J. (1960) *Gymnasion. Étude sur les monuments consacrés à l'éducation en Grèce.* Paris.

Demoen, K. and D. Praet (eds.) (2009) *Theios Sophistes. Essays on Flavius Philostratus' Vita Apollonii.* Leiden.

Dentzer, J. M. (1962) 'La Tombe de C. Vestorius dans la tradition de la peinture italique', *MÉFRA* 74: 533–94.

Denzey, N. F. (2007) *The Bone Gatherers. The Lost Worlds of Early Christian Women.* Boston.

Depew, M. (1992) 'Ἰαμβεῖον καλεῖται νῦν. Genre, Occasion and Imitation in Callimachus, frr. 191 and 203Pf.', *TAPA* 122: 313–30.

(1993) 'Mimesis and Aetiology in Callimachus' Hymns', in Harder *et al.* (eds): 57–77.

(1994) 'POxy 2509 and Callimachus' *Lavacrum Palladis*: αἰγιόχοιο Διὸς κούρη μεγάλοιο', *CQ* 44: 410–26.

(2000) 'Enacted and Represented Dedications. Genre and Greek Hymn', in Depew and Obbink (eds.): 59–79.

Depew, M. and D. Obbink (eds.) (2000) *Matrices of Genre. Authors, Canons, and Society.* Cambridge, MA, and London.

Derderian, K. (2001) *Leaving Words to Remember. Greek Mourning and the Advent of Literacy.* Mnemosyne Suppl. 209. Leiden.

Derow, P. S. and W. G. Forrest (1982) 'An Inscription from Chios', *Annual of the British School at Athens* 77: 79–92.

Derrida, J. (1981) 'Plato's Pharmacy', in *Dissemination.* Trans. B. Johnson. Chicago: 61–84.

(1994) 'The Spatial Arts. An Interview', in P. Brunette and D. Wills (eds.), *Deconstruction and the Visual Arts.* Cambridge: 9–32.

Desideri, P. (1978) *Dione di Prusa. Un intellettuale greco nell'impero romano.* Messina and Florence.

Detienne, M. (1963) *De la pensée religieuse à la pensée philosophique.* La Notion de daïmon dans la pythagorisme ancien. Paris.

(1986) 'Dionysos en ses parousies. Un dieu épidémique', in *L'Association dionysiaque dans les sociétés anciennes. Actes de la table ronde organisée par l'École française de Rome, 24–25 mai 1984.* Rome: 53–83.

(1989) *Dionysos at Large.* Trans. A. Goldhammer. Cambridge, MA, and London.

(1994) *The Gardens of Adonis. Spices in Greek Mythology.* Trans. J. Lloyd. Princeton.

(1996) *The Masters of Truth in Archaic Greece.* Trans. J. Lloyd. New York.

Deubner, L. (1899) *De incubatione.* Leipzig.

(1932) *Attische Feste.* Berlin.

Dewald, C. (1997) 'Wanton Kings, Pickled Heroes, and Gnomic Founding Fathers. Strategies of Meaning at the End of Herodotus' Histories', in D. H. Roberts, F. M. Dunn and D. Fowler (eds.), *Classical Closure. Reading the End in Greek and Latin literature.* Princeton: 62–82.

Dewald, C. and J. Marincola (eds.) (2006) *The Cambridge Companion to Herodotus.* Cambridge.

Dibelius, M. (1935) *From Tradition to Gospel.* Trans. B. L. Woolf. Philadelphia.

Dickie, M. W. (2002) 'Who Were Privileged to See the Gods?' *Eranos* 100: 109–27.

(2004) 'Divine Epiphany in Lucian's Account of the Oracle of Alexander of Abonuteichos', *ICS* 29: 159–82.

Dickins, G. (1905–6) 'Damophon of Messene', *BSA* 12: 112–36.

(1910–11) 'Damophon of Messene, iii', *BSA* 17: 80–7.

Dickins, G. and K. Kourouniotis (1906–7) 'Damophon of Messene, ii,' *BSA* 13: 357–404.

Didi-Huberman, G. (2005) *Confronting Images. Questioning the Ends of a Certain History of Art.* Trans. J. Goodman. University Park, PA.

Dietrich, B. C. (1983) 'Divine Epiphanies in Homer', *Numen* 30: 53–79.

(1985–6) 'Divine Concept and Iconography in Greek Religion', *Grazer Beiträge* 12–13: 171–92.

(1994) 'Theology and Theophany in Homer and Minoan Crete', *Kernos* 7: 59–74.

Dignas, B. (2002) '"Inventories" or "Offering Lists"? Assessing the Wealth of Apollo Didymaeus', *ZPE* 18: 235–44.

Dikaios, P. (1961) *A Guide to the Cyprus Museum*. Nicosia.

Dillery, J. (2005) 'Greek Sacred History', *AJPh* 126: 505–26.

Dillon, J. (1977) *The Middle Platonists. A Study of Platonism*. London.

(2001) 'Iamblichus on the Personal Daemon', *Ancient World* 32: 3–9.

Dinsmoor, W. B. (1941) 'An Archaeological Earthquake at Olympia', *AJA* 45: 399–427.

(1956) 'The Sculpted Frieze from Bassae (a Revised Sequence)', *AJA* 60: 401–52.

Dixon, S. (2001) *Reading Roman Women. Sources, Genres, and Real Life*. London.

Doane, M. A. (1982) 'Film and the Masquerade. Theorising the Female Spectator', *Screen* 23: 74–87.

Dodds, E. R. (1947) 'Theurgy and Its Relationship to Neoplatonism', *JRS* 37: 55–69.

(1951) *The Greeks and the Irrational*. Berkeley.

(1965) *Pagan and Christian in an Age of Anxiety*. Cambridge.

Donnay, G. (1967) 'Les Comptes de l'Athéna chryséléphantine du Parthénon', *BCH* 91: 50–86.

(1968) 'La Date du procès de Phidias', *AntC* 37: 19–36.

Donohue, A. A. (1988) Xoana *and the Origins of Greek Sculpture*. Atlanta.

(1997) 'The Greek Images of the Gods. Considerations on Terminology and Methodology', *Hephaistos* 14: 31–45.

Dorandi, T. (2005) 'Il diario dei sogni di Elio Aristide. Per una interpretazione del primo Discorso Sacro (47 Keil)', *Segno e Testo* 3: 51–69.

Dougherty, C. and L. Kurke (eds.) (1993) *Cultural Poetics in Archaic Greece. Cult, Performance, Politics*. Cambridge.

Downie, J. (2008a) 'Professing Illness. Healing Narrative and Rhetorical Self-Presentation in Aelius Aristides' *Hieroi Logoi*'. PhD diss., University of Chicago.

(2008b) 'Proper Pleasures. Bathing and Oratory in Aelius Aristides' *Hieros Logos* I and *Oration* 33', in Harris and Holmes (eds.): 115–30.

(2009) 'A Pindaric Charioteer. Aelius Aristides and His Divine Literary Editor (*Oration* 50.45)', *CQ* 59: 263–9.

Dragōna-Monachou, M. (1976) *The Stoic Arguments for the Existence and the Providence of the Gods*. Athens.

Drexler, W. (1893) 'Die Epiphanie des Pan', *Philologus* 52: 731–2.

Dreyfus, R. and E. Schraudolph (eds.) (1996) *Pergamon. The Telephos Frieze from the Great Altar*. 2 vols. San Francisco and Berlin.

Du Toit, D. S. (1997) *Theios anthropos. Zur Verwendung von theios anthropos und sinnverwandten Ausdrücken in der Literatur der Kaiserzeit*. Tübingen.

Dubel, S. (1997) 'Ekphrasis et enargeia. La description antique comme parcours', in Lévy and Pernot 1997: 249–64.

(2009) 'Colour in the *Imagines* of Philostratus', in Bowie and Elsner (eds.): 309–21.

Dunand, F. (1978) 'Sens et fonction de la fête dans la Grèce hellénistique. Les cérémonies en l'honneur d'Artémis Leucophryéné', *Dialogues d'Histoire Ancienne* 4: 201–18.

(2002) 'L'Athéisme est-il vivable? Autour de l'hymne athénien à Démétrios Poliorcète', in G. Dorival and D. Pralon (eds.), *Nier les dieux, nier Dieu*. Aix-en-Provence: 69–80.

(2003) 'Fêtes et réveil religieux dans les cités grecques à l'époque hellénistique', in A. Motte and C. M. Ternes (eds.), *Dieux, fêtes, sacré dans la Grèce et la Rome antiques*. Turnhout: 101–12.

Dunbabin K. (1990) '*Ipsa deae vestigia . . .* Footprints Divine and Human on Graeco-Roman Monuments', *JRA* 3: 85–109.

Dupont, F. (1987) 'Les Morts et la mémoire. Le masque funèbre', in F. Hinard (ed.), *La Mort, les morts et l'au-delà dans le monde romain. Actes du colloque de Caen, 20–22 novembre 1985*. Caen: 167–72.

Dušaniç, S. (1983) 'The Κτίσις Μαγνησίας, Philip V and the Panhellenic Leucophryena', *Epigraphica* 45: 11–48.

Dyggve, E. (1960) *Fouilles de l'Acropole 1902–1914 et 1952*. Vol. iii: *Le Sanctuaire d'Athana Lindia et l'architecture lindienne*. Berlin.

Dzielska, M. (1986) *Apollonius of Tyana in Legend and History*. Trans. P. Pieńkowski. Rome.

Easterling, P. E. (1993) 'Gods on Stage in Greek Tragedy,' in J. Dalfen, G. Petersmann and F. Schwarz (eds.), *Religio graeco-romana. Festschrift für Walter Pötscher*. Grazer Beiträge Suppl. 5. Graz: 77–86.

Easterling, P. E. and J. V. Muir (eds.) (1985) *Greek Religion and Society*. Cambridge.

Ebert, J. (1982) 'Zur Stiftungsurkunde der Λευκοφρυηνά in Magnesia am Mäander (Inschr. v. Magn. 16)', *Philologus* 126: 198–216.

Eddy, S. (1977) 'The Gold in the Athena Parthenos', *AJA* 81: 107–11.

Edelstein, E. J. and L. Edelstein (1945) *Asclepius. A Collection and Interpretation of the Testimonies*. 2 vols. New York.

Edwards, C. (2007) *Death in Ancient Rome*. New Haven and London.

Edwards, C. M. (1985) 'Greek Votive Reliefs to Pan and the Nymphs.' PhD diss., New York University.

Ekroth, G. (2002) *The Sacrificial Rituals of Greek Hero-Cults in the Archaic to the Early Hellenistic Periods*. Kernos, Suppl. 12. Liège.

El-Abbadi, M. (1990) *The Life and Fate of the Ancient Library of Alexandria*. Paris.

Elderkin, G. W. (1937) 'The Marriage of Zeus and Hera and Its Symbol', *AJA* 41: 424–35.

Elkins, J. (1996) *The Object Stares Back. On the Nature of Seeing*. New York.

Else, G. F. (1958) '"Imitation" in the Fifth Century', *CPh* 53: 73–90.

Elsner, J. (1991) 'Visual Mimesis and the Myth of the Real. Ovid's Pygmalion as Viewer', *Ramus* 20.2: 154–68.

(1992) 'Pausanias. A Greek Pilgrim in the Roman World', *Past & Present* 135: 3–29.

(1993) 'Seductions of Art. Encolpius and Eumolpus in a Neronian Picture Gallery', *PCPS* 39: 30–47.

(1994) 'From the Pyramids to Pausanias and Piglet. Monuments, Travel and Writing', in Goldhill and Osborne (eds.): 224–54.

(1995) *Art and the Roman Viewer*. Cambridge.

(ed.) (1996a) *Art and Text in Roman Culture*. Cambridge.

(1996b) 'Image and Ritual: Reflections on the Graeco-Roman Appreciation of Art', *CQ* 46: 515–31.

(1996c) 'Inventing Imperium. Texts and the Propaganda of Monuments in Augustan Rome', in Elsner (ed.): 32–53.

(1996d) Review of Koortbojian 1995, *AJA* 100: 434.

(1997a) 'Hagiographic Geography. Travel and Allegory in the *Life of Apollonius of Tyana*', *JHS* 117: 22–37.

(1997b) 'The Origins of the Icon. Pilgrimage, Religion and Visual Culture in the Roman East as "Resistance" to the Centre', in S. Alcock (ed.), *The Early Roman Empire in the East*. Oxford: 178–99.

(1998) *Imperial Rome and Christian Triumph*. Oxford.

(2000a) 'Between Mimesis and Divine Power. Visuality in the Greco-Roman World', in R. Nelson (ed.) *Visuality before and beyond the Renaissance*. Chicago: 45–69.

(2000b) 'Caught in the Ocular. Visualising Narcissus in the Roman World', in L. Spaas (ed.), *Reflections of Narcissus*. Oxford: 89–110.

(2000c) 'Making Myth Visual. The *Horae* of Philostratus and the Dance of the Text', *RM* 107: 253–76.

(2001a) 'Cultural Resistance and the Visual Image. The Case of Dura Europos', *CPh* 96: 269–304.

(2001b) 'Describing Self in the Language of the Other. Pseudo (?) Lucian at the Temple of Hierapolis', in Goldhill (ed.): 123–53.

(2001c) 'Structuring "Greece". Pausanias's *Periegesis* as a Literary Construct', in Alcock *et al.* (eds.): 3–20.

(2002) 'Introduction. The Genres of Ekphrasis', *Ramus* 31: 1–18.

(2004) 'Seeing and Saying. A Psychoanalytic Account of Ekphrasis', *Helios* 31: 157–86.

(2005) Review of G. Zanker (2004), *AJPh* 126.3: 461–3.

(2006) 'Reflections on the "Greek Revolution" in Art. From Changes in Viewing to the Transformation of Subjectivity', in Goldhill and Osborne (eds.): 68–95.

(2007) *Roman Eyes. Visuality and Subjectivity in Art and Text*. Princeton.

(2009a) 'A Protean Corpus', in Bowie and Elsner (eds.): 3–18.

(2009b) 'Beyond Compare. Pagan Saint and Christian God in Late Antiquity', *Critical Inquiry* 35: 655–83.

Elsner, J. and I. Rutherford (eds.) (2005) *Pilgrimage in Graeco-Roman and Early Christian Antiquity. Seeing the Gods.* Oxford.

Elwyn, S. (1990) 'The Recognition Decrees for the Delphian Soteria and the Date of Smyrna's Inviolability', *JHS* 110: 177–80.

Engels, D. (2007) *Das römische Vorzeichenwesen (753–27 v.Chr.). Quellen, Terminologie, Kommentar, historische Entwicklung.* Stuttgart.

Engemann, J. (1973) *Untersuchungen zur Sepulkralsymbolik der späteren römischen Kaiserzeit.* Jahrbuch für Antike und Christentum Ergänzungsband 2. Münster.

Erasmo, M. (2008) *Reading Death in Ancient Rome.* Columbus, OH.

Erbse, H. (1969–88) *Scholia Graeca in Homeri Iliadem (Scholia Vetera).* Berlin.

Erskine, A. (1995) 'Culture and Power in Ptolemaic Egypt. The Museum and Library of Alexandria', *Greece & Rome* 42: 38–48.

(2001) *Troy between Greece and Rome. Local Tradition and Imperial Power.* New York and Oxford.

(ed.) (2003) *A Companion to the Hellenistic World.* Oxford.

Ewald, B. C. (1999) *Der Philosoph als Leitbild. Ikonographische Untersuchungen an römischen Sarkophagreliefs.* Mainz.

(2003) 'Sarcophagi and Senators. The Social History of Roman Funerary Art and Its Limits', *JRA* 16: 561–71.

(2004) 'Men, Muscle, and Myth: Attic Sarcophagi in the Cultural Context of the Second Sophistic', in Borg (ed.): 229–75.

Falivene, M. R. (1990) 'La mimesis in Callimaco: *Inni* ii, iv, v e vi', *QUCC* 65: 103–28.

(2002) 'Esercizi di Ekphrasis. Delle opposte fortune di Posidippo e Callimaco', in Bastianini and Casanova (eds.): 33–40.

Fantham, E. (1991) 'Stuprum. Public Attitudes and Penalties for Sexual Offences in Republican Rome', *Echos du Monde Classique / Classical Views* 35: 267–91.

(1996) *Roman Literary Culture. From Cicero to Apuleius.* Baltimore.

Fantuzzi, M. and R. Hunter (2004) *Tradition and Innovation in Hellenistic Poetry.* Cambridge.

Faraone, C. A. (1992) *Talismans and Trojan Horses. Guardian Statues in Ancient Greek Myth and Ritual.* New York and Oxford.

Farnell, L. R. (1896) *The Cults of the Greek States.* 2 vols. Oxford.

Fattori, M. and M. Bianchi (eds.) (1988) *Phantasia–imaginatio. V° Colloquio internazionale.* Rome.

Faulkner, A. (2008) 'The Legacy of Aphrodite. Anchises' Offspring in the *Homeric Hymn to Aphrodite*', *AJPh* 129: 1–18.

Faulstich, E. I. (1997) *Hellenistische Kultstatuen und ihre Vorbilder.* Frankfurt am Main.

Fazzo, V. (1977) *La giustificazione delle immagini religiose dalla tarda antichità al christianesimo.* Vol. I. Naples.

Feeney, D. (1991) *The Gods in Epic. Poets and Critics of the Classical Tradition.* Oxford.

(1998) *Literature and Religion at Rome. Cultures, Contexts and Beliefs.* Cambridge.

(2007) *Caesar's Calendar. Ancient Time and the Beginnings of History.* Berkeley and Los Angeles.

Fejfer, J. (2008) *Roman Portraits in Context.* Berlin and New York.

Feraudi-Gruénais, F. (2001) *Ubi diutius nobis habitandum est. Die Innendekoration der kaiserzeitlichen Gräber Roms.* Wiesbaden.

Ferguson, E. (2003) *Backgrounds of Early Christianity.* Rev. edn. Grand Rapids, MI.

Fernández Contreras, M. A. (1999) 'Las epifanías en la épica homérica', *Habis* 30: 7–17.

Ferrari, Giovanni (1988) 'Hesiod's Mimetic Muses and the Strategies of Deconstruction', in A. Benjamin (ed.), *Post-structuralist Classics.* London and New York: 45–78.

Ferrari, Gloria (1994–95), 'Heracles, Pisistratus and the Panathenaea.' *Métis* 9/10: 219–26.

(2000) 'The Iliupersis in Athens', *HSCP* 100: 119–50.

Ferrua, A. (1947) 'Un mausoleo della necropolis scoperta sotto S. Pietro', *RendPontAc* 23–4: 217–29.

Festugière, A. J. (1954) *Personal Religion among the Greeks.* Berkeley.

(1955) *Epicurus and His Gods.* Trans. C. W. Chilton. New York.

Festugière, A. J. and H. D. Saffrey (1986) *Discours sacrés. Rêve, religion, médicine au IIe siècle après J.-C.* Paris.

Feubel, R. (1935) *Die attischen Nymphenreliefs und ihre Vorbilder.* Heidelberg.

Finney, P. C. (1994) *The Invisible God. The Earliest Christians on Art.* New York and Oxford.

Fittschen, K. (1970) 'Zum Kleobis- und Biton-Relief in Venedig', *JDAI* 85: 171–93.

(1984) 'Über Sarkophage mit Porträts verschiedener Personen', in B. Andreae (ed.), *Symposium über die antiken Sarkophage, Pisa 5.–12. September 1982.* Marburger Winckelmann-Programm 1984. Marburg: 129–61.

Flacelière, R. (1937) *Les Aitoliens à Delphes.* Paris.

Flashar, M. (1999) 'Panhellenische Feste und Asyl', *Klio* 81: 412–36.

Flinterman, J.-J. (1995) *Power, Paideia and Pythagoreanism. Greek Identity, Conceptions of the Relationship between Philosophers and Monarchs and Political Ideas in Philostratus' Life of Apollonius.* Amsterdam.

(1996) 'The Ubiquitous Divine Man', *Numen* 43: 82–98.

(2002) 'The Self-Portrait of an Antonine Orator. Aristides, *Or.* 2.429ff.', in E. N. Ostenfeld (ed.), *Greek Romans and Roman Greeks.* Aarhus Studies in Mediterranean Antiquity 3. Aarhus: 198–211.

(2009) '"The Ancestor of My Wisdom". Pythagoras and Pythagoreanism in the *Life of Apollonius*', in Bowie and Elsner (eds.): 155–75.

Flower, H. I. (1996) *Ancestor Masks and Aristocratic Power in Roman Culture.* Oxford.

Flynn, T. (1997) 'Amending the Myth of Phidias. Quatremère de Quincy and the Nineteenth-Century Revival of Chryselephantine Statuary', *Apollo* no. 419: 6–10.

Foccardi, D. (1987) 'Religious Silence and Reticence in Pausanias', in M. G. Ciani (ed.), *The Regions of Silence. Studies on the Difficulty of Communicating.* Amsterdam: 67–113.

Follet, S. (1991) 'Divers aspects de l'hellénisme chez Philostrate', in Saïd (ed.): 205–15.

Ford, A. (1992) *Homer. The Poetry of the Past.* Ithaca.

Forrat, M. and E. des Places (1986) *Eusèbe de Césarée. Contre Hiéroclès.* Sources Chrétiennes 333. Paris.

Foster, H. (ed.) (1988) *Vision and Visuality.* Seattle.

Foucault, M. (1986) *The History of Sexuality.* Vol. iii: *The Care of the Self.* Trans. R. Hurley. New York.

Fournier, M. (1997) *The Episode at Lystra. A Rhetorical and Semiotic Analysis of Acts 14:7–20a.* American University Studies, Series 8, Theology and Religion 197. New York.

Fowden, G. (1993) *Empire to Commonwealth. Consequences of Monotheism in Late Antiquity.* Cambridge.

Fowler, D. (1991) 'Narrate and Describe. The Problem of Ekphrasis', *JRS* 81: 25–35.

Fowler, R. (2006) 'Herodotus and His Prose Predecessors', in Dewald and Marincola (eds.): 29–45.

Francis, E. F. and M. Vickers (1984) 'Amasis and Lindos', *BICS* 21: 119–30.

Francis, J. A. (1995) *Subversive Virtue. Asceticism and Authority in the Second-Century Pagan World.* University Park, PA.

(1998) 'Truthful Fiction. New Questions to Old Answers on Philostratus' "Life of Apollonius"', *AJPh* 119: 419–41.

(2003) 'Living Icons. Tracing a Motif in Verbal and Visual Representation from the Second to Fourth Centuries CE', *AJPh* 124: 575–600.

François, G. (1957) *Le Polythéisme et l'emploi au singulier des mots 'theos' et 'daimon' dans la littérature grecque d'Homère à Platon.* Paris.

Frangeskou, V. (1995) 'The *Homeric Hymn to Aphrodite.* A New Interpretation', *Scripta Classica Israelica* 14: 1–16.

Fränkel, H. F. (1968) *Noten zu den Argonautika des Apollonios.* Munich.

Frankfurter, D. (1997) 'Ritual Expertise in Roman Egypt and the Problem of the Category "Magician"', in P. Schäfer and H. G. Kippenberg (eds.), *Envisioning Magic. A Princeton Seminar and Symposium.* Leiden, New York and Cologne: 115–35.

(ed.) (1998) *Pilgrimage and Holy Space in Late Antique Egypt.* Leiden.

Fraser, P. M. (1972) *Ptolemaic Alexandria.* 3 vols. Oxford.

Frazer, J. G. (1898) *Pausanias's Description of Greece.* 6 vols. London.

Frede, D. and A. Laks (eds.) (2002) *Traditions of Theology. Studies in Hellenistic Theology, Its Background and Aftermath*. Leiden.

Frede, M. (1983) 'Stoics and Skeptics on Clear and Distinct Impressions', in M. Burnyeat (ed.), *The Skeptical Tradition*. Berkeley and Los Angeles: 65–93.

(1999) 'Monotheism and Pagan Philosophy in Later Antiquity', in P. Athanassiadi and M. Frede (eds.), *Pagan Monotheism in Late Antiquity*. Oxford: 41–68.

Fredrick, D. (1995) 'Beyond the Atrium to Ariadne. Erotic Paintings and Visual Pleasure in the Roman House', *ClAnt* 14: 266–303.

Freedberg, D. (1989) *The Power of Images. Studies in the History and Theory of Response*. Chicago.

Frenschkowski, M. (1995) *Offenbarung und Epiphanie*. Band I: *Grundlagen des spätantiken und frühchristlichen Offenbarungsglaubens*. Wissenschaftliche Untersuchungen zum Neuen Testament 2.79. Tübingen.

(1997) *Offenbarung und Epiphanie*. Band II: *Die verborgene Epiphanie in Spätantike und frühem Christentum*. Wissenschaftliche Untersuchungen zum Neuen Testament 2.80. Tübingen.

Freud, S. (1953) *The Standard Edition of the Complete Psychological Works of Sigmund Freud*. Trans. J. Strachey. Vol. IV: *The Interpretation of Dreams*. London: ix–627.

Frickenhaus, A. (1908) 'Das Athenabild des alten Tempels in Athen', *AthMitt* 33: 17–32.

Fried, M. (1980) *Absorption and Theatricality. Painting and Beholder in the Age of Diderot*. Berkeley.

Friedländer, P. (1912) *Johannes von Gaza und Paulus Silentarius. Kunstbeschreibungen justinianischer Zeit*. Berlin.

Fröhlich (2007) 'Les Tombeaux de la ville de Messène et les grandes familles de la cité à l'époque hellénistique', in C. Grandjean (ed.), *Le Péloponnèse d'Épaminondas à Hadrien. Unité et diversité*. Bordeaux: 203–27.

Frontisi-Ducroux, F. (1975) *Dédale. Mythologie de l'artisan en Grèce ancienne*. Paris.

(1986) 'Les Limites de l'anthropomorphisme. Hermès et Dionysos', in Malamoud and Vernant (eds.): 193–211.

(1988) 'Figures de l'invisible. Stratégies textuelles et stratégies iconiques', *AION* 10: 27–40.

(1991) *Le Dieu-masqué*. Paris.

(1996) 'Eros, Desire and the Gaze', in Kampen (ed.): 81–100.

(2000) 'Narcisse, à travers le miroir', in G. Sennequier, P. Ickowicz, N. Zapata-Aubé and F. Frontisi-Ducroux (eds.), *Miroirs. Jeux et reflets depuis l'antiquité*. Paris: 27–43.

Frontisi-Ducroux, F. and J.-P. Vernant (1997) *Dans l'œil du miroir*. Paris.

Fua, O. (1973) 'L'idea dell'opera d'arte "vivente" e la *bucola* di Mirone nell'epigramma Greco e Latino', *RCCM* 15: 49–55.

Fuchs, W. (1962) 'Attische Nymphenreliefs', *AthMitt* 77: 242–9.

Fuller, P. (1980) *Seeing Berger. A Revaluation.* London.

Fullerton, M. (1986) 'The Location and Archaism of the Hekate Epipyrgidia', *AA*: 669–75.

(2003) '"Der Stil der Nachahmer". A Brief Historiography of Stylistic Retrospection', in M. Fullerton and A. Donohue (eds.), *Ancient Art and Its Historiography.* Cambridge: 92–117.

Furley, W. D. (1995) 'Praise and Persuasion in Greek Hymns', *JHS* 115: 29–46.

(1996) *Andocides and the Herms. A Study of Crisis in Fifth-Century Athenian Religion.* Bulletin of the Institute of Classical Studies Suppl. 65. London.

Furtwängler, A. (1884–90) 'Athena in der Kunst', *Ausführliches Lexikon griechischen und römischen Mythologie.* Leipzig: 687–9.

Gabba, E. (1981) 'True History and False History in Classical Antiquity', *JRS* 71: 50–62.

Gabrielen, V., P. Bilde, T. Engberg-Pedersen, L. Hannestad and J. Zahle (eds.) (1999) *Hellenistic Rhodes. Politics, Culture, and Society.* Aarhus.

Gaifman, M. (2005) 'Beyond Mimesis in Greek Religious Art. Aniconism in the Archaic and Classical Periods.' PhD diss., Princeton University.

(2006) 'Statue, Cult and Reproduction', *Art History* 29.2: 258–79.

(2008a) 'The Aniconic Image of the Roman Near East', in T. Kaizer (ed.), *The Variety of Local Religious Life in the Near East in the Hellenistic and Roman Periods.* Leiden: 37–72.

(2008b) 'Visualized Offerings and Dedicatory Inscriptions on Votive Offerings to the Nymphs', *Opuscula* 1: 85–103.

(in press) *'The Absent Figure of the Present God. Aniconic Monuments on Greek Vases'*, in Petridou and Platt (eds.).

Gallagher, E. V. (1982) *Divine Man or Magician? Celsus and Origen on Jesus.* Chicago.

Galli, M. (2002) *Die Lebenswelt eines Sophisten. Untersuchungen zu den Bauten und Stiftungen des Herodes Atticus.* Mainz.

(2004) '"*Creating Religious Identities*". Paideia e religione nella Seconda Sofistica', in Borg (ed.): 315–56.

(2005) 'Pilgrimage as Elite Habitus. Educated Pilgrims in Sacred Landscape during the Second Sophistic', in Elsner and Rutherford (eds.): 253–90.

Gallo, A. (1988) 'Le pitture rappresentanti Arianna abbandonata in ambiente pompeiano', *RSP* 2: 57–80.

Gallo, I. (ed.) (1996) *Plutarco e la religione. Atti del VI convegno plutarcheo, Ravello, 29–31 maggio 1995.* Naples.

Gallop, D. (1971) 'Dreaming and Waking in Plato', in J. P. Anton and G. L. Kustas (eds.), *Essays in Ancient Greek Philosophy.* Albany: 187–94.

(1990) *Aristotle on Sleep and Dreams. A Text and Translation with Introduction, Notes and Glossary.* Peterborough, Ont.

Garbrah, K. (1986) 'On the Θεοφάνεια in Chios and the Epiphany of Gods in War', *ZPE* 65: 207–10.

García Valdés, M. (ed.) (1994) *Estudios sobre Plutarco. Ideas religiosas. Actas del III Simposio Internacional sobre Plutarco, Oviedo, 30 de abril a 2 de mayo de 1992.* Madrid.

Gardner, J. (1986) *Women in Roman Law and Society.* Bloomington.

Garland, R. (1992) *Introducing New Gods. The Politics of Athenian Religion.* London.

Gasparro, G. S. (2007) 'Il sofista e l'"uomo divino". Filostrato e la construzione della "vera storia" di Apollonio di Tiana', in Cordovana and Galli (eds.): 271–88.

Gauthier, P. (1985) *Les Cités grecques et leurs bienfaiteurs (IVe–Ier siècle avant J.-C.). Contribution à l'histoire des institutions.* Paris.

        (1987–9) 'Grandes et petites cités. Hégémonie et autarcie', *Opus* 6–8: 187–202.

Gazda, E. (2002) *The Ancient Art of Emulation.* Ann Arbor.

Geertz, C. (1973) *The Interpretation of Cultures.* New York.

Gehrke, H. J. (1990) *Geschichte des Hellenismus.* Munich.

        (1994) 'Mythos, Geschichte, Politik – antik und modern', *Saeculum* 45: 239–64.

        (2001) 'Myth, History and Collective Identity. Uses of the Past in Ancient Greece and Beyond', in N. Luraghi (ed.), *The Historian's Craft in the Age of Herodotus.* Oxford: 286–313.

Gell, A. (1998) *Art and Agency.* Oxford.

Gelzer, T. (1985) 'Mimus und Kunsttheorie bei Herondas. Mimiambus 4', in C. Schaeublin (ed.), *Catalepton. Festschrift für Bernhard Wyss zum 80. Geburtstag.* Basel: 96–115.

        (1993) 'Transformations', in Bulloch *et al.* (eds.): 130–51.

Gempf, C. (1995) 'Mission and Misunderstanding. Paul and Barnabas in Lystra (Acts 14:8–20)', in A. Billington *et al.* (eds.), *Mission and Meaning. Essays Presented to Peter Cotterell.* Carlisle: 56–69.

Geoghegan, D. (1979) *Anyte. The Epigrams.* Rome.

Gernet, L. (1981) *The Anthropology of Ancient Greece.* Trans. J. Hamilton and B. Nagy. Baltimore and London.

Gerson, L. P. (1990) *God and Greek Philosophy. Studies in the Early History of Natural Theology.* London.

Gessert, G. (2004) 'Myth as *Consolatio.* Medea on Roman Sarcophagi', *Greece & Rome* 51: 217–49.

Giakilis, A. (2005) *Images of the Divine. The Theology of Icons at the Seventh Ecumenical Council.* Leiden.

Giangiulio, M. (1983) 'Locri, Sparta, Crotone e le tradizioni leggendarie intorno alla battaglia di Sagra', *MÉFRA* 95: 473–521.

Giannini, A. (1966) *Paradoxographorum Graecorum reliquiae.* Milan.

Gill, C., N. Postlethwaite and R. Seaford (eds.) (1998) *Reciprocity in Ancient Greece.* Oxford.

Gill, W. J. and B. W. Winter (1994) 'Acts and Roman Religion', in W. J. Gill and C. Gempf (eds.), *The Book of Acts in Its Graeco-Roman Setting.* Carlisle: 79–104.

Ginouvès, R. (1962) *Balaneutikè.* Paris.

Giovannini, A. (1993) 'Greek Cities and Greek Commonwealth', in Bulloch *et al.* (eds.): 265–86.

Giuliani, L. (1989) 'Achill-Sarkophage in Ost und West. Genese einer Ikonographie', *Jahrbuch der Berliner Museen* 31: 25–39.

Giuman, M. (1999) *La dea, la vergine, il sangue. Archeologia di un culto femminile.* Milan.

Gladigow, B. (1985–6) 'Präsenz der Bilder, Präsenz der Götter. Kultbilder und Bilder der Götter in der griechischen Religion', *Visible Religion* 4–5: 114–33.

(1988) 'Anikonische Kulte', in Cancik *et al.* (eds.): vol. ı, 472–3.

(1990) 'Epiphanie, Statuette, Kultbild. Griechische Gottesvorstellungen im Wechsel von Kontext und Medium', *Visible Religion* 7: 98–121.

Gleason, M. (1995) *Making Men. Sophists and Self-Presentation in Ancient Rome.* Princeton.

Goedicke, H. (1986) 'God', *Journal of the Society for the Study of Egyptian Antiquities* 16: 57–62.

Goldhill, S. (1994) 'The Naïve and Knowing Eye. Ecphrasis and the Culture of Viewing in the Hellenistic World' in Goldhill and Osborne (eds.): 197–223.

(1995) *Foucault's Virginity. Ancient Erotic Fiction and the History of Sexuality.* Cambridge.

(1996) 'Refracting Classical Vision. Changing Cultures of Viewing', in T. Brennan and M. Jay (eds.), *Vision in Context. Historical and Contemporary Perspectives on Sight.* New York and London: 15–28.

(1999) 'Programme Notes', in Goldhill and Osborne (eds.): 1–29.

(ed.) (2001a) *Being Greek under Rome. Cultural Identity, the Second Sophistic and the Development of Empire.* Cambridge.

(2001b) 'The Erotic Eye. Visual Stimulation and Cultural Conflict', in Goldhill (ed.): 154–94.

(2006) 'Artemis and Cultural Identity in Empire Culture. How to Think about Polytheism, Now?', in Konstan (ed.): 112–61.

(2007) 'What is Ekphrasis For?', *CPh* 102: 1–19.

Goldhill, S. and R. Osborne (eds.) (1994) *Art and Text in Ancient Greek Culture.* Cambridge.

(eds.) (1999) *Performance Culture and Athenian Democracy.* Cambridge.

(eds.) (2006) *Rethinking Revolutions through Ancient Greece.* Cambridge.

Goodwin, E. W. and E. Bronfen (eds.) (1993) *Death and Representation.* Baltimore.

Goody, J. (1977) 'Against "Ritual". Loosely Structured Thoughts on a Loosely Defined Topic', in S. F. Moore and B. G. Myerhoff (eds.), *Secular Ritual.* Assen: 25–35.

Gordon, R. (1979) 'The Real and the Imaginary. Production and Religion in the Greco-Roman World', *Art History* 2: 5–34. Reprinted in R. Gordon (1996), *Image and Value in the Graeco-Roman World.* Aldershot.

Gosling, J. C. B. (1973) *Plato.* London.

Gould, J. (1985) 'Making Sense of Greek Religion' in Easterling and Muir (eds.), *Greek Religion and Society*: 1–33. Reprinted in J. Gould (2001), *Myth, Ritual, Memory, and Exchange. Essays in Greek Literature and Culture.* Oxford: 203–34.

Goulet, R. (1981) 'Les Vies de philosophes dans l'antiquité tardive et leur portée mystérique', in F. Bovon *et al.* (eds.), *Les Actes apocryphes des apôtres. Christianisme et monde païen.* Geneva: 161–208.

Gow, A. S. F. and D. L. Page (eds.) (1965) *The Greek Anthology. Hellenistic Epigrams.* 2 vols. Cambridge.

(eds.) (1968) *The Greek Anthology. The Garland of Philip and Some Contemporary Epigrams.* 2 vols. Cambridge.

Grabar, A. (1984) *L'Iconoclasme byzantin. Dossier archéologique.* 2nd edn. Paris.

Gradel, I. (2002) *Emperor Worship and Roman Religion.* Oxford.

Graepler, D. (ed.) (2002) *Barbarentod und Venuskult. Griechische Skulpturen aus den Gärten Roms.* Göttingen.

Graf, F. (1992) 'Heiligtum und Ritual. Das Beispiel der griechisch-römischen Asklepieia', in Schachter and Bingen (eds.): 159–99.

(1995) 'Ekphrasis. Die Entstellung der Gattung in der Antike', in G. Boehm and H. Pfotenhauer (eds.), *Beschreibungskunst-Kunstbeschreibung.* Munich: 143–55.

(2004a) 'Epiphany', in H. Cancik and H. Schneider (eds.), *Brill's New Pauly. Encyclopaedia of the Ancient World.* Vol. iv. Leiden: 1122–3.

(2004b) 'Trick or Treat? Collective Epiphanies in Antiquity', *ICS* 29: 111–30.

Grainger, J. D. (1999) *The League of the Aitolians.* Leiden.

Grandjean, Y. (1975) *Une nouvelle arétalogie d'Isis à Maronée.* Leiden.

Grassinger, D. (1994) 'The Meaning of Myth on Roman Sarcophagi', in *Fenway Court 1994. Myth and Allusion: Meanings and Uses of Myth in Ancient Greek and Roman Society.* Boston: 91–107.

(1999) *Die mythologischen Sarkophage. Achill, Adonis, Aeneas, Aktaion, Alkestis, Amazonen.* Die antiken Sarkophagreliefs 12.1. Berlin.

Graziosi, B. (2002) *Inventing Homer. The Early Reception of Epic.* Cambridge.

Graziosi, B. and J. Haubold (2005) *Homer. The Resonance of Epic.* London.

Green, P. (ed.) (1993) *Hellenistic History and Culture.* Berkeley.

Greene, E. (1996a) 'Apostrophe and Women's Erotics in the Poetry of Sappho', in Greene (ed.): 233–47.

(ed.) (1996b) *Reading Sappho. Contemporary Approaches.* Berkeley and Los Angeles.

(2000) 'Playing with Tradition. Gender and Innovation in the Epigrams of Anyte', *Helios* 27: 15–32.

Grenfell, B. and A. Hunt (1928) *The Oxyrhyncus Papyri.* Vol. xi London.

Griffiths, J. (1975) *Apuleius of Madauros. The Isis Book* (Metamorphoses *Book XI*). Leiden.

Grimes, R. L. (2006) *Rite out of Place. Ritual, Media and the Arts.* Oxford.

Gross, K. (1992) *The Dream of the Moving Statue.* Ithaca, NY, and London.

Gross, W. H. (1967) 'Xoanon', *RE* 9: 2140–9.

Grossardt, P. (2006) *Einführung, Übersetzung und Kommentar zum Heroikos von Flavius Philostrat.* Basel.

(2009) 'How to Become a Poet? Homer and Apollonius Visit the Mound of Achilles', in Demoen and Praet (eds.): 75–94.

Grosso, F. (1954) 'La vita d'Apollonios di Tiana comme fonte storica', *Acme* 7: 333–532.

Grottanelli, C. (1989–90) 'Do ut des?', *Scienze dell'Antichità* 3–4: 45–54.

Gruen, E. S. (2000) 'Culture as Policy. The Attalids of Pergamon', in Grummond and Ridgway (eds.): 17–31.

Grummond, G. N. T. de and B. S. Ridgway (eds.) (2000) *From Pergamon to Sperlonga. Sculpture and Context.* Berkeley, Los Angeles and London.

Guidorizzi, G. (ed.) (1988a) *Il sogno in Grecia.* Bari.

(1988b) 'Sogno e funzioni culturali', in Guidorizzi (ed.): vii–xxxviii.

Gunderson, E. (2003) *Declamation, Paternity and Roman Identity. Authority and the Rhetorical Self.* Cambridge.

Guthke, K. S. (1999) *The Gender of Death. A Cultural History in Art and Literature.* Cambridge.

Guthrie, K. S. (1987) *The Pythagorean Sourcebook and Library. An Anthology of Ancient Writings Which Relate to Pythagoras and Pythagorean Philosophy.* Michigan.

Gutzwiller, K. J. (1993) 'Anyte's Epigram Book', *SyllClass* 4: 71–89.

(1998) *Poetic Garlands. Hellenistic Epigrams in Context.* Berkeley.

(2002a) 'Art's Echo: the Tradition of Hellenistic Ecphrastic Epigram', in Harder *et al.* (eds.): 85–112.

(2002b) 'Posidippus on Statuary', in G. Bastianini and A. Casanova (eds.): 41–60.

(2004a) 'A New Hellenistic Poetry Book. P. Mil.Vogl. VIII 309', in Acosta-Hughes *et al.* (eds.): 84–93.

(2004b) 'Gender and Inscribed Epigram. Herennia Procula and the Thespian Eros', *TAPA* 134: 383–418.

(2004c) 'Seeing Thought. Timomachus' Medea and Ecphrastic Epigram', *AJPh* 125: 339–86.

(2005a) 'The Literariness of the Milan Papyrus, or, What Difference a Book?', in Gutzwiller (ed.): 287–319.

(ed.) (2005b) *The New Posidippus. A Hellenistic Poetry Book.* Oxford.

(2007) *A Guide to Hellenistic Literature.* Oxford.

Gyselinck, W. and K. Demoen (2009) 'Author and Narrator. Fiction and Metafiction in Philostratus' *Vita Apollonii*', in Demoen and Praet (eds.): 95–127.

Haarløv, B. (1977) *The Half-Open Door. A Common Symbolic Motif within Roman Sepulchre Sculpture.* Odense.

Habicht, C. (1969) *Die Inschriften des Asklepieions.* Berlin.

(1970) *Gottmenschentum und griechische Städte.* 2nd edn. Munich.

(1985) *Pausanias' Guide to Ancient Greece.* Berkeley and Los Angeles.

(1989) 'Gesandte der Knidier im hellenistischen Kos', *ZPE* 77: 92–4.

Habrich, E. (ed.) (1960) *Iamblichi Babyloniacorum Reliquiae.* Leipzig.

Hackworth Petersen, L. (1997) 'Divided Consciousness and Female Companionship. Reconstructing Female Subjectivity on Greek Vases', *Arethusa* 30: 35–74.

Hägg, R. (1986) 'Die göttliche Epiphanie im minoischen Ritual', *Mitteilungen des Deutschen Archäologischen Instituts, Athenische Abteilung* 101: 41–62.

  (ed.) (1992) *The Iconography of Greek Cult in the Archaic and Classical Periods.* Kernos Suppl. 1. Liège.

  (ed.) (1994) *Ancient Greek Cult Practice from the Epigraphical Evidence. Proceedings of the Second International Seminar on Ancient Greek Cult, Organized by the Swedish Institute at Athens, 22–24 November 1991.* Stockholm.

Hägg, T. (2002) 'Epiphany in the Greek Novels. The Employment of a Metaphor', *Eranos* 100: 51–61.

Hägg, T. and P. Rousseau (eds.) (2000) *Greek Biography and Panegyric in Late Antiquity.* Berkeley and Los Angeles.

Hahn, I. (1992) *Traumdeutung und gesellschaftliche Wirklichkeit, Artemidorus Daldianus als sozialgeschichtliche Quelle.* Xenia 27. Konstanz.

Hahn, J. (1989) *Der Philosoph und die Gesellschaft. Selbstverständnis, öffentliches Auftreten und populäre Erwartungen in der hohen Kaiserzeit.* Heidelberger althistorische Beiträge und epigraphische Studien 7. Stuttgart.

Halbertal, M. and A. Margalit (1992) *Idolatry.* Cambridge, MA, and London.

Haldane, J. A. (1968) 'Pindar and Pan, frs. 95–100 Snell', *Phoenix* 22: 18–31.

Halfmann, H. (1986) *Itinera Principum. Geschichte und Typologie der Kaiserreisen im Römischen Reich.* Wiesbaden.

Hallett, C. (2005a) 'Emulation versus Replication. Redefining Roman Copying', *JRA* 18: 419–35.

  (2005b) Review of Zanker and Ewald 2004, *Art Bulletin* 87: 157–61.

  (2005c) *The Roman Nude. Heroic Portrait Statuary, 200 BC – AD 300.* Oxford.

Halliday, W. R. (2003) *Greek Divination. A Study of Its Methods and Principles.* Whitefish, MT. Originally published London, 1913.

Halliwell, S. (2002) *The Aesthetics of Mimesis. Ancient Texts and Modern Problems.* Princeton.

Hamilton, R. (1985) 'Euripidean Priests', *HSCP* 89: 53–73.

  (2000) *Treasure Map. A Guide to the Delian Inventories.* Michigan.

Hampe, W. (1951) '"Idäische Grotte" in Olympia?', in G. E. Mylonas (ed.), *Studies Presented to David Moore Robinson on His Seventieth Birthday.* Vol. i. St Louis: 336–50.

Hanfmann, G. M. A. (1951) *The Season Sarcophagus in Dumbarton Oaks.* 2 vols. Cambridge, MA.

Hani, J. (1972) *Consolation à Apollonios.* Paris.

Hannestad, L. (1993) 'Greeks and Celts. The Creation of a Myth', in P. Bilde, T. Engberg-Pedersen *et al.* (eds.), *Centre and Periphery in the Hellenistic World.* Aarhus: 15–38.

Hansen, M. H. (1995) 'The "Autonomous City State". Ancient Fact or Modern Fiction?', in M. H. Hansen and K. Raaflaub (eds.), *Studies in the Ancient Greek Polis*. Historia Einzelschrift 95. Copenhagen.

Hansen, W. (1996) *Phlegon of Tralles' Book of Marvels*. Exeter.

(1998) *Anthology of Ancient Greek Popular Literature*. Bloomington.

Hanson, J. S. (1980) 'Dreams and Visions in the Graeco-Roman World and Early Christianity', *ANRW* 2.23.2: 1395–1427.

Harbsmeier, M. (1987) 'Elementary Structures of Otherness', in J. Céard and J.-C. Margolin (eds.), *Voyager à la Renaissance*. Paris: 337–55.

Harder, M. A. (1992) 'Insubstantial Voices. Some Observations on the Hymns of Callimachus', *CQ* 42: 384–94.

Harder, M. A., R. F. Regtuit and G. C. Wakker (eds.) (1993) *Callimachus*. Hellenistica Groningana 1. Groningen.

(1998) *Genre in Hellenistic Poetry*. Hellenistica Groningana 3. Groningen.

(2002) *Hellenistic Epigrams*. Hellenistica Groningana 6. Groningen.

Hardie, P. (2002) *Ovid's Poetics of Illusion*. Cambridge.

Harlan, E. C. (1965) 'The Description of Paintings as a Literary Device and Its Implications in Achilles Tatius'. PhD diss., Columbia University.

Harris, B. F. (1962) 'The *Olympian Oration* of Dio Chrysostom', *JRH* 2: 85–97.

(1969) 'Apollonius of Tyana. Fact and Fiction', *JRH* 5: 189–99.

Harris, D. (1995) *The Treasures of the Parthenon and Erechtheion*. Oxford.

Harris, W. V. (2003) 'Roman Opinions about the Truthfulness of Dreams', *JRS* 93: 18–34.

(2005) '*Insomnia*. The Content of Roman Dreams', in W. V. Harris and E. Lo Cascio (eds.), *Noctes Campanae. Studi di storia antica ed archeologia dell'Italia preromana e romana in memoria di Martin W. Frederiksen*. Naples: 245–60.

(2009) *Dreams and Experience in Classical Antiquity*. Cambridge, MA.

Harris, W. V. and B. Holmes (eds.) (2008) *Aelius Aristides between Greece, Rome and the Gods*. Leiden.

Harrison, E. B. (1965) *Archaic and Archaistic Sculpture*. Agora 11. Princeton.

(1977) 'Alkamenes' Sculptures for the Hephaisteion. Part II, the Base', *AJA* 81: 265–87.

(1981) 'Motifs of the City-Siege on the Shield of Athena Parthenos', *AJA* 85: 281–317.

(1996a) 'Pheidias', in Palagia and Pollitt (eds.): 16–65.

(1996b) 'The Web of History. A Conservative Reading of the Parthenon Frieze', in Neils (ed.): 198–214.

Harrison, S. (ed.) (1999) *Oxford Readings in the Roman Novel*. Oxford.

(2000) *Apuleius. A Latin Sophist*. Oxford.

(2000–1) 'Apuleius, Aelius Aristides, and Religious Autobiography', *Ancient Narrative* 1: 245–59.

Harrison, T. (2000) *Divinity and History. The Religion of Herodotus*. Oxford.

(2006) 'Religion and the Rationality of the Greek City', in Goldhill and Osborne (eds.): 124–40.

Hartmann, E. (1996) 'Outline for a Theory on the Nature and Functions of Dreaming', *Dreaming* 6: 147–70.

Hartog, F. (1999) 'Myth into *Logos*. The Case of Croesus, or the Historian at Work', in Buxton (ed.): 183–95.

Hartswick, K. J. and M. C. Sturgeon (eds.) (1998) *Stephanos. Studies in Honor of Brunilde Sismondo Ridgway*. Philadelphia.

Haslam, M. W. (1993) 'Callimachus' *Hymns*', in Harder *et al.* (eds): 111–25.

Haubold, J. (2007) 'Athens and Aegina (5.82–9)', in E. Irwin and E. Greenwood (eds.), *Reading Herodotus. A Study of the Logoi in Book 5 of Herodotus' Histories*. Cambridge: 226–44.

Hausmann, U. (1948) *Kunst und Heiltum. Untersuchungen zu den griechischen Asklepiosreliefs*. Potsdam.

(1960) *Griechische Weihreliefs*. Berlin.

Havelock, C. M. (1965) 'The Archaic as Survival versus the Archaistic as a New Style', *AJA* 69: 331–40.

(1995) *The Aphrodite of Knidos and Her Successors. A Historical Review of the Female Nude in Greek Art*. Ann Arbor.

Hawley, R. (1998a) 'The Dynamics of Beauty in Classical Greece', in D. Montserrat (ed.), *Changing Bodies, Changing Meaning. Studies on the Human Body in Antiquity*. London: 37–54.

(1998b) 'The Male Body as Spectacle in Attic Drama', in L. Foxhall and J. Salmon (eds.), *Thinking Men. Masculinity and Self-Representation in the Classical Tradition*. London: 83–99.

(2000) 'Marriage, Gender and the Family in Dio', in Swain (ed.): 125–39.

Hazzard, R. A. (1992) 'Did Ptolemy I Get His Surname from the Rhodians in 304?' *ZPE* 93: 52–6.

Healy, J. F. (1999) *Pliny the Elder on Science and Technology*. Oxford.

Heath, J. (1992) *Actaeon the Unmannerly Intruder. The Myth and Its Meaning in Classical Literature*. New York.

Hedreen, G. (1991) 'The Cult of Achilles in the Euxine', *Hesperia* 60: 313–30.

(2004) 'The Return of Hephaistos, Dionysiac Processional Ritual and the Creation of a Visual Narrative', *JHS* 124: 38–64.

Heer, J. (1979) *La Personnalité de Pausanias*. Paris.

Heidegger, M. (1997) *Plato's Sophist*. Trans. R. Rojcewicz and A. Schuwer. Bloomington and Indianapolis.

Heltzer, M. (1989) 'The Persepolis Documents, the Lindos Chronicle, and the Book of Judith', *La Parola del Passato* 44: 81–101.

Henderson, J. (1996) 'Footnote. Representation in the Villa of the Mysteries', in Elsner (ed.): 234–76.

Hendry, I. (1963) 'Joyce's Epiphanies', in S. Givens (ed.), *James Joyce. Two Decades of Criticism*. New York: 27–46.

Henig, M. (1990) 'A House for Minerva. Temples, Aedicula Shrines and Signet-Rings', in M. Henig (ed.), *Architecture and Architectural Sculpture in the Roman Empire*. Oxford: 152–62.

Henrichs, A. (1993a) 'Gods in Action. The Poetics of Divine Performance in the *Hymns* of Callimachus', in Harder *et al.* (eds.): 127–47.

(1993b) '"He Has a God in Him". Human and Divine in the Modern Perception of Dionysus', in T. H. Carpenter and C. A. Faraone (eds.) *Masks of Dionysus*. Ithaca, NY: 13–43.

(1999) 'Demythologizing the Past, Mythicizing the Present. Myth, History and the Supernatural at the Dawn of the Hellenistic Age', in Buxton (ed.): 223–48.

(2003) '"Hieroi Logoi" and "Hierai Bibloi". The (Un)Written Margins of the Sacred in Ancient Greece', *HSCP* 101: 207–66.

Henry, M. M. (1992) 'The Edible Woman. Athenaeus' Concept of the Pornographic,' in A. Richlin (ed.), *Pornography and Representation in Greece and Rome*. Oxford: 250–68.

Henry, P. (1977) 'What Was the Iconoclastic Controversy About?', *Church History* 46: 16–31.

Herington, C. J. (1955) *Athena Parthenos and Athena Polias*. Manchester.

(1985) *Poetry into Drama. Early Tragedy and the Greek Poetic Tradition*. Berkeley.

Herman, G. (1987) *Ritualised Friendship and the Greek City*. Cambridge.

Hershbell, J. P. (2004) 'Philostratus's *Heroikos* and Early Christianity. Heroes, Saints, and Martyrs', in Aitken and Maclean (eds.): 169–79.

Herter, H. (1981) 'L'inno omerico a Hermes alla luce della problematica della poesia orale', in C. Brillante, M. Cantilena and C. O. Pavese (eds.), *I poemi epici rapsodici non omerici e la tradizione orale*. Padua: 183–202.

Herzog, R. R. (1931) *Die Wunderheilungen von Epidauros. Ein Beitrag zur Geschichte der Medizin und der Religion*. Philologus Suppl. 22. Leipzig.

Hesberg, H. von and P. Zanker (eds.) (1987) *Römische Gräberstrassen. Selbstdarstellung – Status – Standard. Kolloquium in München vom 28. bis 30. Oktober 1985*. Munich.

Heubeck, A., S. West and J. B. Hainsworth (1988) *A Commentary on Homer's Odyssey*. Vol. I. Oxford.

Hewitt, J. W. (1909) 'Major Restrictions to Access to Greek Temples', *TAPA* 40: 83–92.

Heyworth, S. (2004) 'Looking into the River. Literary History and Interpretation in Callimachus, *Hymns* 5 and 6', in M. A. Harder, R. F. Regtuit and G. C. Wakker (eds.), *Callimachus II*. Hellenistic Groningana 7. Leuven: 139–60.

Higbie, C. (2001) 'Homeric Athena in the Chronicle of Lindos', in Deacy and Villing (eds.): 105–26.

(2003) *The Lindian Chronicle and the Greek Creation of Their Past*. Oxford.

Higgins, L. A. and B. R. Silver (eds.) (1991) *Rape and Representation*. New York.

Hill, G. F. (1899) 'Olba, Cennatis, Lalassis', *Numismatic Chronicle*, 3rd ser., 19: 181–207.

(1900) *Catalogue of the Greek Coins of Lycaonia, Isauria, and Cilicia in the British Museum.* London.

Himmelmann, N. (1998) 'Some Characteristics of the Representation of Gods in Classical Art', in W. Childs (ed.), *Reading Greek Art. Essays.* Trans. N. Himmelmann. Princeton: 103–38. A shortened and revised version of *Zur Eigenart des klassischen Götterbildes*, Munich, 1959.

Himmelmann-Wildschütz, N. (1957) *Theoleptos.* Marburg-Lahn.

Hoepfner, W. (1990) 'Bauten und Bedeutung des Hermogenes', in Hoepfner and Schwander (eds.): 1–34.

(1996) 'Zum Typus der Basileia und der königlichen Androne s', in W. Hoepfner and G. Brands (eds.), *Basileia. Die Paläste der hellenistischen Könige.* Mainz: 1–43.

Hoepfner, W. and E. L. Schwander (eds.) (1990) *Hermogenes und die hochhellenistische Architektur.* Mainz.

Hofkes-Brukker, C. and A. Mallwitz (1975) *Der Bassai-Fries in der ursprünglich geplanten Anordnung.* Munich.

Höghammar, K. (1993) *Sculpture and Society. A Study of the Connection between the Free-Standing Sculpture and Society on Kos in the Hellenistic and Augustan Periods.* Uppsala.

Holmes, B. (2008) 'Aelius Aristides' Illegible Body', in Harris and Holmes (eds.): 81–114.

Holowchak, M. A. (1996) 'Aristotle on Dreaming. What Goes on in Sleep When the "Big Fire" Goes Out', *Ancient Philosophy* 16: 405–23.

(2001) 'Interpreting Dreams for Corrective Regimen. Diagnostic Dreams in Greco-Roman Medicine', *Journal of the History of Medicine and Allied Sciences* 56: 382–99.

(2002) *Ancient Science and Dreams. Oneirology in Greco-Roman Antiquity.* Lanham, MD.

Holum, K. G. (1990) 'Hadrian and St Helena. Imperial Travel and the Origin of Christian Holy-Land Pilgrimage', in R. Ousterhout (ed.), *The Blessings of Pilgrimage.* Illinois Byzantine Studies 1. Urbana: 66–81.

Hope, V. M. (2007) *Death in Ancient Rome. A Source Book.* London and New York.

Hopkins, K. (1983) *Death and Renewal.* Social Studies in Roman History 2. Cambridge.

Hornblower, S. (2007) 'Epic and Epiphanies. Herodotus and the "New Simonides"', in D. Boedeker and D. Sider (eds.), *The New Simonides. Contexts of Praise and Desire.* Oxford: 135–47.

Horrocks, G. (1997) *Greek. A History of the Language and Its Speakers.* London.

Horstmanshoff, M. (2004) 'Aelius Aristides. A Suitable Case for Treatment', in Borg (ed.): 277–90.

Humphrey, C. and J. Laidlaw (1994) *The Archetypal Actions of Ritual.* Oxford.

Humphreys, S. C. (2004) *The Strangeness of Gods. Historical Perspectives on the Interpretation of Athenian Religion.* Oxford.

Hunter, R. (1986) 'Apollo and the Argonauts. Two Notes on Ap. Rhod. 2, 669–719', *MH* 43: 50–60.

    (1992) 'Writing the God. Form and Meaning in Callimachus, *Hymn to Athena*', *Materiali e Discussioni per l'Anali di Testi Classici* 29: 9–34.

    (1993) *The 'Argonautika' of Apollonius. Literary Studies.* Cambridge.

    (2004) 'Notes on the Lithika of Posidippus', in Acosta-Hughes *et al.* (eds.): 94–104.

Hunter, R. and T. Fuhrer (2002) 'Imaginary Gods? Poetic Theology in the *Hymns* of Callimachus', in F. Montanari and L. Lehnus (eds.), *Callimaque*. Entretiens sur l'antiquité classique 48. Geneva: 137–87.

Hurwit, J. M. (1995) 'Beautiful Evil. Pandora and the Athena Parthenos', *AJA* 99: 171–86.

    (1997) 'The Death of the Sculptor?' *AJA* 101: 587–91.

    (1999) *The Athenian Acropolis. History, Mythology, and Archaeology from the Neolithic Era to the Present.* Cambridge.

    (2004) *The Acropolis in the Age of Perikles.* Cambridge.

    (2005) 'Space and Theme. The Setting of the Parthenon', in Neils (ed.): 8–33.

Huskinson, J. (1996) *Roman Children's Sarcophagi. Their Decoration and Its Social Significance.* Oxford.

    (1998) '"Unfinished Portrait Heads" on Later Roman Sarcophagi. Some New Perspectives', *PBRS* 66: 129–68.

    (2008) 'Pantomime Performance and Figured Scenes on Roman Sarcophagi', in E. Hall and R. Wyles (eds.), *New Directions in Ancient Pantomime.* Oxford: 87–109.

Hutchinson, G. O. (2001) *Greek Lyric Poetry.* Oxford.

Hutton, W. (2005a) *Describing Greece. Landscape and Literature in the Periegesis of Pausanias.* Cambridge.

    (2005b) 'The Construction of Religious Space in Pausanias', in Elsner and Rutherford (eds.): 291–318.

    (2008) 'The Disaster of Roman Rule. Pausanias 8.27.1', *CQ* 58: 622–37.

Iaculli, G. (2003) 'L'iconografia di Narciso nell'arte classica', in A. Campanelli and M. P. Pennetta (eds.), *Attraverso lo specchio. Storia, inganni, e verità di uno strumento di conoscenza.* Pescara.

Imbert, C. (1980) 'Stoic Logic and Alexandrian Poetics', in M. Schofield, M. Burnyeat and J. Barnes (eds.), *Doubt and Dogmatism. Studies in Hellenistic Epistemology.* Oxford: 183–216.

Ioppolo, A.-M. (1990) 'Presentation and Assent. A Physical and Cognitive Problem in Early Stoicism', *CQ* 40: 433–49.

Irigary, L. (1991) 'This Sex Which Is Not One', in R. Warhol and D. Herndl (eds.), *Feminisms.* New Brunswick, NJ: 350–6.

Irskine, A. (ed.) (2003) *A Companion to the Hellenistic World.* Oxford.

Irwin, E. (1974) *Colour Terms in Greek Poetry.* Toronto.

Isager, S. (1998) 'The Pride of Halikarnassos. *Editio Princeps* of an Inscription from Salmakis', *ZPE* 123: 1–23.

Jacobs, F. (1794–1814) *Anthologia Graeca, sive, Poetarum Graecorum lusus.* Leipzig.

Jaeger, W. (1947) *The Theology of the Early Greek Philosophers.* Trans. E. S. Robinson. Oxford.

(1961) *Paideia. The Ideals of Greek Culture.* Trans. G. Highet. 3 vols. Oxford.

Jahn, O. (1866) *De Antiquissimis Minervae Simulacris Atticis.* Bonn.

Jahn, O. and Michaelis, A. (1901) *Arx Athenarum.* 3rd edn. Bonn.

Jaillard, D. (2007) *Configurations d'Hermès. Une 'théogonie hermaïque'.* Kernos Suppl. 17. Liège.

Jameson, M. H. (1999) 'The Spectacular and the Obscure in Athenian Religion', in Goldhill and Osborne (eds.): 321–40.

Janaway, C. (1995) *Images of Excellence. Plato's Critique of the Arts.* Oxford.

Janko, R. (1981) 'The Structure of the *Homeric Hymns.* A Study in Genre', *Hermes* 109: 9–24.

(1982) *Homer, Hesiod and the Hymns. Diachronic Development in Epic Diction.* Cambridge.

(1992) *The Iliad. A Commentary.* Vol. IV: Books 13–16. Cambridge.

Janowitz, N. (2002) *Icons of Power. Ritual Practices in Late Antiquity.* University Park, PA.

Jay, M. (1993) *Downcast Eyes. The Denigration of Vision in Twentieth-Century French Thought.* Berkeley, Los Angeles and London.

Jenkins, I. and D. Williams (1993) 'The Arrangement of the Sculptured Frieze from the Temple of Apollo Epikourios at Bassae', in Palagia and Coulson (eds.): 57–77.

Joly, R. (1956) *Le Thème philosophique des genres de vie dans l'antiquité classique.* Brussels.

Jonas, H. (1982) *The Phenomenon of Life. Toward a Philosophical Biology.* Chicago.

Jones, C. P. (1978) *The Roman World of Dio Chrysostom.* Cambridge, MA.

(1996) 'The Panhellenion', *Chiron* 26: 29–56.

(1998) 'Aelius Aristides and the Asklepieion', in H. Köster (ed.), *Pergamon, Citadel of the Gods. Archaeological Record, Literary Description, and Religious Development.* Harrisburg, PA: 63–76.

(1999) *Kinship Diplomacy in the Ancient World.* Cambridge, MA.

(2001a) 'Pausanias and his Guides', in Alcock *et al.* (eds.): 33–9.

(2001b) 'Time and Place in Philostratus' *Heroikos*', *JHS* 121: 141–8.

(2005–6) *Philostratus. Apollonius of Tyana.* 3 vols. Cambridge, MA.

(2009) 'Some Letters of Apollonius of Tyana', in Demoen and Praet (eds.): 249–61.

Jones, H. S. (1926) *The Sculptures of the Palazzo dei Conservatori.* Oxford.

Jong, I. J. F. de (1987) *Narrators and Focalizers. The Presentation of the Story in the Iliad.* Amsterdam.

Jongste, P. F. B. (1992) *The Twelve Labours of Hercules on Roman Sarcophagi*. Rome.

Jost, M. (1973) 'Pausanias en Megalopolitide', *Revue des Études Anciennes* 75: 245–67.

(1985) *Sanctuaires et cultes d'Arcadie*. Paris.

(1992) 'Sanctuaires ruraux et sanctuaires urbains en Arcadie', in Schachter and Bingen (eds.): 204–45.

(2003) 'Mystery Cults in Arcadia', in M. B. Cosmopoulos (ed.), *Greek Mysteries. The Archaeology and Ritual of Ancient Greek Secret Cults*. London and New York: 143–68.

(2005) 'Bêtes, hommes et dieux dans la religion arcadienne', in Østby (ed.): 93–104.

Joyce, J. (1963) *Stephen Hero*. New York.

Jung, H. (1982) *Thronende und Sitzende Götter. Zum griechischen Götterbild und Menschenideal in geometrischer und früharchaischer Zeit*. Bonn.

Junod, E. (1988) 'Polémique chrétienne contre Apollonius de Tyane', *Revue de Théologie et de Philosophie* 120: 475–82.

Kaempf-Dimitriadou, S. (1979) *Die Liebe der Götter in der attischen Kunst des 5. Jahrhunderts v. Chr*. Bern.

Kahane, A. (1994) 'Callimachus, Apollonius and the Poetics of Mud', *TAPA* 124: 121–33.

Kahil, L. (1983) 'Mythological Repertoire of Brauron', in W. G. Moon (ed.), *Ancient Greek Art and Iconography*. Madison: 231–44.

Kahn, C. H. (2001) *Pythagoras and the Pythagoreans. A Brief History*. Indianapolis.

Kahn, L. (1978) *Hermès passe, ou, Les ambiguïtés de la communication*. Paris.

Kaibel, G. (1878) *Epigrammata Graeca ex lapidibus conlecta*. Berlin.

Kallet, L.(2005) 'Wealth, Power, and Prestige. Athens at Home and Abroad', in Neils (ed.): 34–65.

(Kallet-Marx, L.) (1989) 'Did Tribute Fund the Parthenon?' *ClAnt* 8: 252–66.

Kaltsas, N. (2002) *Sculpture in the National Archaeological Museum, Athens*. Trans. D. Hardy. Los Angeles.

Kambylis, A. (1963) 'Zur Dichterweihe des Archilochos', *Hermes* 91: 129–50.

(1965) *Die Dichterweihe und ihre Symbolik. Untersuchungen zu Hesiodos, Kallimachos, Properz und Ennius*. Heidelberg.

Kampen, N. B. (1981) 'Biographical Narration and Roman Funerary Art', *AJA* 85: 47–58.

(ed.) (1996) *Sexuality in Ancient Art*. Cambridge.

Kaplan, A. E. (1983) 'Is the Gaze Male?', in A. Snitow, C. Stansell and S. Thompson (eds.), *Powers of Desire. The Politics of Sexuality*. New York: 309–27.

Kappeler, S. (1986) *The Pornography of Representation*. Minneapolis.

Karidas, P. (1968) *Das Amphiareion von Oropos in medizingeschichtlicher Sicht*. Nürnberg.

Karouzou, S. (1979) 'Bemalte attische Weihreliefs', in *Studies in Classical Art and Archaeology. A Tribute to P. H. von Blanckenhagen*. Locust Valley, NY: 111–16.

Kastenholz, R. (1996) 'Die Lokalisierung der Heiligtümer der Eileithyia, des Sosipo-lis und der Aphrodite Urania. Ein Beitrag zur Frühgeschichte Olympias', *Boreas* 19: 147–54.

Katz, J. T. and Volk, K. (2000) '"Mere Bellies?" A New Look at *Theogony* 26–8', *JHS* 120: 122–31.

Kauppi, L. A. (2006) *Foreign but Familiar Gods. Greco-Romans Read Religion in Acts.* London and New York.

Kavoulaki, A. (1999) 'Processional Performance and the Democratic Polis', in Gold-hill and Osborne (eds.): 293–320.

Kearns, E. (1990) 'Saving the City', in O. Murray and S. Price (eds.), *The Greek City from Homer to Alexander.* Oxford: 323–44.

Keesling, C. (2003) *The Votive Statues of the Athenian Acropolis.* Cambridge.

Kennedy, G. A. (1986) 'Helen's Web Unraveled', *Arethusa* 19: 5–14.

Kenney, J. P. (1993) 'The Critical Value of Negative Theology', *Harvard Theological Review* 86: 439–53.

Kerkhecker, A. (1999) *Callimachus' Book of Iambi.* Oxford.

Kessels, A. H. M. (1969) 'Ancient Systems of Dream Classification', *Mnemosyne* 22: 389–424.

(1978) *Studies on the Dream in Greek Literature.* Utrecht.

Kessler, H. L. (2000) *Spiritual Seeing. Picturing God's Invisibility in Medieval Art.* Philadelphia.

Keuls, E. (1985) *The Reign of the Phallus.* Berkeley.

Kiefer, A. (1929) *Aretalogische Studien.* Leipzig.

Kierdorf, W. (1980) *Laudatio funebris. Interpretationen und Untersuchungen zur Entwicklung der römischen Leichenrede.* Meisenheim am Glan.

Kilroe, P. A. (2000a) 'The Dream as Text, the Dream as Narrative', *Dreaming* 10: 125–37.

(2000b) 'The Dream Pun. What is a Play on Words without Words?', *Dreaming* 10: 193–209.

Kindstrand, J. F. (1973) *Homer in der Zweiten Sophistik. Studien zu der Homerlektüre und dem Homerbild bei Dion von Prusa, Maximos von Tyros und Ailios Aristeides.* Uppsala.

Kindt, J. (2006) 'Delphic Oracle Stories and the Beginning of Historiography. Herodotus' *Croesus Logos*', *CPh* 101: 34–51.

King, H. (1998) *Hippocrates' Woman. Reading the Female Body in Ancient Greece.* New York and London.

Kirk, G. S., J. E. Raven and M. Schofield (1983) *The Presocratic Philosophers. A Critical History with a Selection of Texts.* 2nd edn. Cambridge.

Kitzinger, E. (1954) 'The Cult of Images in the Age Before Iconoclasm', *Dumbarton Oaks Papers* 8: 83–150.

Klapaki, N. (2005) 'Versions of the Modern Literary Epiphany in Twentieth-Century Greek Poetry. Cavafy, Sikelianos, Seferis, Embirikos.' PhD diss., University College, London.

(in press) 'Accommodating the Divine in the Modern World. The Revival of Divine Epiphany in the Early Work of Angelos Sikelianos', in Petridou and Platt (eds.).

Klauck, H.-J. (2000) *Dion von Prusa. Olympische Rede, oder, Über die erste Erkenntis Gottes*. With B. Bäbler Darmstadt.

Kleiner, D. E. E. (1981) 'Second-Century Mythological Portraiture. Mars and Venus', *Latomus* 40: 512–44.

(1987) *Roman Imperial Funerary Altars with Portraits*. Rome.

Kleiner, D. E. E. and S. B. Matheson (eds.) (1996) *I, Claudia. Women in Ancient Rome*. New Haven, CT, and Austin, TX.

(eds.) (2000) *I, Claudia, ii. Women in Roman Art and Society*. Austin, TX.

Klöckner, A. (2006) 'Votive als Gegenstände des Rituals – Votive als Bilder von Ritualen. Das Beispiel der griechischen Weihreliefs', in J. Mylonopoulos and H. Roeder (eds.), *Archäologie und Ritual. Auf der Suche nach der rituellen Handlung in den antiken Kulturen Ägyptens und Griechenlands*. Vienna.

(2010) 'Getting in Contact. Concepts of Human/Divine Encounter in Classical Greek Art', in Bremmer and Erskine (eds): 106–25.

Knight, J. F. (1970) *Elysion. On Ancient Greek and Roman Beliefs Concerning Life after Death*. New York and London.

Knoepfler, D. and M. Piérart (eds.) (2001) *Éditer, traduire, commenter Pausanias en l'an 2000. Actes du colloque de Neuchâtel et de Fribourg (18–22 septembre 1998)*. Geneva.

Koch, G. (1978) 'The Walters Persephone Sarcophagus', *Journal of the Walters Art Gallery* 37: 74–83.

Koch, G. and H. Sichtermann (1982) *Römische Sarkophage*. Munich.

Koch Piettre, R. (1996) 'Le Corps des dieux dans les epiphanies divines en Grèce ancienne'. PhD diss., École pratique des hautes études, Paris.

(1997) 'Oneiros, le dieu-songe', *Uranie* 7: 115–40.

(1999) 'Les Dieux crèvent les yeux. L'enargeia dans la représentation du divin,' in D. Mulliez (ed.), *Ateliers 21. La transmission de l'image dans l'antiquité*. Lille: 11–21.

(2001) 'Images et perception de la présence divine en Grèce Ancienne', *MÉFRA* 113: 211–24.

(2005) 'La Chronique de Lindos, ou, Comment accommoder les restes pour écrire l'histoire', in P. Borgeaud and Y. Volokhine (eds.), *Les Objets de la mémoire*. Bern and Berlin: 95–121.

(in press) 'Anthropomorphism, Theatre, Epiphany. From Herodotus to the Hellenistic Historians', in Petridou and Platt (eds.).

Koenen, L. (1993) 'The Ptolemaic King as a Religious Figure', in Bulloch *et al.* (eds.): 25–115.

Koerner, J. L. (2004) *The Reformation of the Image*. London.

Köhnken, A. (1981) 'Apollo's Retort to Envy's Criticism (Two Questions of Relevance in Callimachus, Hymn 2, 105ff.)', *AJPh* 102: 411–22.

Kolde, A. (2003) *Politique et religion chez Isyllos d'Épidaure*. Schweizerische Beiträge zur Altertumswissenschaft 28. Basel.

Koller, H. (1957) 'Theoros and Theoria', *Glotta* 36: 273–87.

Koniaris, G. L. (1982) 'On Maximus of Tyre. Zetemata (ɪ)', *ClAnt* 1: 87–121.

(1983) 'On Maximus of Tyre. Zetemata (ɪɪ)', *ClAnt* 2: 212–50.

König, J. (2007) 'Greek Athletics in the Severan Period. Literary Views', in Swain *et al.* (eds.): 135–45.

Konstan, D. (ed.) (2006) *Greeks on Greekness. Proceedings of the Cambridge Philological Society.* Supplementary volume. Cambridge.

Koonce, K. (1988) 'Ἄγαλμα and εἰκών', *AJPh* 109: 108–10.

Koortbojian, M. (1995) *Myth, Meaning and Memory on Roman Sarcophagi.* Berkeley, Los Angeles and London.

Korenjak, M. (2005) '"Unbelievable Confusion". Weshalb sind die "Hieroi Logoi" des Aelius Aristides so wirr?', *Hermes* 133: 215–34.

Koskenniemi, E. (1991) *Der philostrateische Apollonios.* Helsinki.

(1994) *Apollonios von Tyana in der neutestamentlichen Exegese.* Tübingen.

Kosmetatou, E. (2003) 'Poseidippos Epigr. 8 and Early Ptolemaic Cameos', *ZPE* 142: 35–42.

(2004) 'Vision and Visibility. Art Historical Theory Paints a Portrait of New Leadership in Posidippus' *Andriantopoiika*', in Acosta-Hughes *et al.* (eds.): 187–211.

Kouroniotis, K. (1912) 'Τὸ ἐν Λυκοσούρα Μέγαρον τῆς Δεσποίνης', *ArchEph*: 142–61.

Kousser, R. M. (2005) 'Creating the Past. The Vénus de Milo and the Hellenistic Reception of Classical Greece', *AJA* 109: 227–50.

(2007) 'Mythological Group Portraits in Antonine Rome. The Performance of Myth', *AJA* 111: 673–91.

(2008) *Hellenistic and Roman Ideal Sculpture. The Allure of the Classical.* Cambridge and New York.

Kowalzig, B. (2007) *Singing for the Gods. Performances of Myth and Ritual in Archaic and Classical Greece.* Oxford.

Kragelund, P., M. Moltesen and J. S. Ostergaard (2003) *The Licinian Tomb. Fact or Fiction?* Meddelelser fra Ny Carlsberg Glyptothek 5. Copenhagen.

Kranz, P. (1984) *Jahreszeiten-Sarkophage. Entwicklung und Ikonographie des Motivs der vier Jahreszeiten auf kaiserzeitlichen Sarkophagen und Sarkophagdeckeln.* Die antiken Sarkophagreliefs 5.4. Berlin.

Kraus, T. (1957) *Aphrodite von Knidos.* Bremen.

(1960) *Hekate. Studien zu Wesen und Bild der Göttin in Kleinasien und Griechenland.* Heidelberg.

Kreeb, M. (1990) 'Hermogenes. Quellen- und Datierungsprobleme', in W. Hoepfner and E.-L. Schwander (eds.), *Hermogenes und die hochhellenistische Architektur.* Mainz am Rhein: 103–13.

Krentz, P. and E. L. Wheeler (1994) *Polyaenus. Stratagems of War.* Chicago.

Krestou, K. (1953–4) 'Artemis Hekate', *Archaiologike Emphemeris*: 188–200.

Krevans, N. (2005) 'The Editor's Toolbox. Strategies for Selection and Presentation in the Milan Epigram Papyrus', in Gutzwiller (ed.): 81–96.

(2007) 'The Arrangement of Epigrams in Collections', in Bing and Bruss (eds.): 141–6.

Kris, E. and O. Kurz (1979) *Legend, Myth, and Magic in the Image of the Artist. A Historical Experiment.* Trans. A Laing. Rev. L. M. Newman. New Haven.

Kroll, J. (1979) 'The Parthenon Frieze as a Votive Relief', *AJA* 83: 349–52.

(1982) 'The Ancient Image of Athena Polias', in *Studies in Athenian Architecture, Sculpture and Topography Presented to Homer A. Thompson.* Hesperia Suppl. 20. Princeton: 65–76.

(2007) 'The Emergence of Ruler Portraiture on Early Hellenistic Coins', in Schultz and von den Hoff (eds.): 113–22.

Krumeich, R. (2004) '"Klassiker" im Gymnasion. Bildnisse attischer Kosmeten der mittleren und späten Kaiserzeit zwischen Rom und griechischer Vergangenheit', in Borg (ed.): 131–55.

(2007) 'Human Achievement and Divine Favor. The Religious Context of Early Hellenistic Portraiture', in Schultz and von den Hoff (eds.): 161–80.

Krumme, M. (1993) 'Das Heiligtum der "Athena beim Palladion" in Athen', *AA*: 213–27.

Kunze, C. (1998) *Der Farnesische Stier und die Dirkegruppe des Apollonios und Tauriskos.* JDAI Ergänzungsheft 30. Berlin.

Kunze, M. (1990) 'Neue Forschungen zum Pergamonaltar', in R. Étienne and M.-T. Le Dinahet (eds.), *L'Espace sacrificiel dans les civilisations méditerranéennes de l'antiquité.* Paris: 135–40.

Kurke, L. (2005) 'Choral Lyric as "Ritualization". Poetic Sacrifice and Poetic Ego in Pindar's Sixth Paian', *ClAnt* 24: 81–130.

Küster, E. (1913) *Die Schlange in der griechischen Kunst und Religion.* Giessen.

Kuttner, A. (2005) 'Cabinet Fit for a Queen. The *Lithika* as Poseidippos' Gem Museum', in Gutzwiller (ed.): 141–63.

Kyrtatas, D. J. (2004) 'The Meaning of Christian Epiphany', *ICS* 29: 205–15.

La Rocca, E. (1994) '*Theoi epiphaneis.* Linguaggio figurativo e culto dinastico da Antioco IV ad Augusto', in K. Rosen (ed.), *Macht und Kultur im Rom der Kaiserzeit.* Bonn: 9–63.

Lacy, L. R. (1990) 'Aktaion and a Lost "Bath of Artemis"', *JHS* 110: 26–42.

Lafond, Y. (2001) 'Lire Pausanias à l'époque des Antonins. Réflexions sur la place de la *Périégèse* dans l'histoire culturelle, religieuse et sociale de la Grèce romaine', in Knoepfler and Piérart (eds.): 387–406.

Lahusen, G. (1982) 'Statuae et imagines', in B. von Freytag, D. Mannsperger and F. Prayon (eds.), *Praestant interna. Festschrift für Ulrich Hausmann.* Tübingen: 101–9.

(1985) 'Funktion und Rezeption des Ahnenbildes', *RM* 92: 261–89.

Laird, A. (1993) 'Sounding out Ecphrasis. Art and Text in Catullus 64,' *JRS* 83: 18–30.

(1997) 'Description and Divinity in Apuleius' *Metamorphoses*', *Groningen Collo-quia on the Ancient Novel* 8: 59–85.

Lamberton, R. and J. J. Keaney (eds.) (1992) *Homer's Ancient Readers*. Princeton.

Lane Fox, R. (1986) *Pagans and Christians*. London.

Lang, B. (1990) 'Buchreligion', in Cancik *et al.* (eds.): vol. II, 143–65.

Langbaum, R. (1983) 'The Epiphanic Mode in Wordsworth and Modern Literature', *New Literary History* 14: 335–58.

Langdon, M. K. (1976) *A Sanctuary of Zeus on Mount Hymmetos*. Princeton.

Lannoy, L. de (1997) 'Le Problème des Philostrate (état de la question)', *ANRW* 2.34.3: 2362–449.

Lapatin, K. D. S. (1996) 'The Ancient Reception of Pheidias' *Athena Parthenos*. The Physical Evidence in Context', in L. Hardwick and S. Ireland (eds.), *The January Conference 1996. The Reception of Classical Texts and Images*. Milton Keynes: 1–20.

(2001) *Chryselephantine Statuary in the Ancient Mediterranean World*. Oxford.

(2005) 'The Statue of Athena and Other Treasures in the Parthenon', in Neils (ed.): 260–91.

Larson, J. (1995) *Greek Heroine Cults*. Madison, WI.

(2001) *Greek Nymphs. Myth, Cult, Lore*. Oxford.

(2007) *Ancient Greek Cults. A Guide*. London.

Lattimore, R. (1962) *Themes in Greek and Latin Epitaphs*. Urbana, IL.

Lau, A. (1996) *Manifest in Flesh. The Epiphany Christology of the Pastoral Epistles*. Wissenschaftliche Untersuchungen zum Neuen Testament 2.86. Tübingen.

Lawrence, M. (1958) 'Season Sarcophagi of Architectural Type', *AJA* 62: 273–95.

(1965) 'The Velletri Sarcophagus', *AJA* 69: 207–22.

Lawton, C. (1995) *Attic Document Reliefs*. Oxford.

Leach, E. W. (1981) 'Metamorphoses of the Acteon Myth in Campanian Painting', *RM* 88: 307–27.

Lefkowitz, M. R. (1981) *The Lives of the Greek Poets*. Baltimore.

(2007) *Women in Greek Myth*. Baltimore.

Lehmann-Hartleben, K. and E. C. Olsen (1942) *Dionysiac Sarcophagi in Baltimore*. New York and Baltimore.

Leipen, N. (1971) *Athena Parthenos. A Reconstruction*. Toronto.

Lenz, L. H. (1975) *Der homerische Aphroditehymnus und die Aristie des Aineias in der Ilias*. Habelts Dissertationsdrucke. Reihe Klassische Philologie 19. Bonn.

Lesher, J. (1992) *Xenophanes of Colophon. Fragments: A Text and Translation with a Commentary*. Toronto, Buffalo and London.

(1999) 'Early Interest in Knowledge', in Long (ed.): 225–49.

Levin, D. M. (ed.) (1997) *Sites of Vision. The Discursive Construction of Sight in the History of Philosophy*. Cambridge, MA.

Lévy, B. and Pernot, L. (eds.) (1997) *Dire l'évidence*. Paris.

Lévy, E. (1967) 'Sondages à Lykosoura et date de Damophon', *BCH* 91: 518–45.

Lévy, E. and J. Marcadé (1972) 'Au Musée de Lycosoura', *BCH* 96: 968–1004.

LiDonnici, L. R. (1995) *The Epidaurian Miracle Inscriptions. Text, Translation and Commentary.* Atlanta, GA.

Liegle, J. (1952) *Der Zeus des Phidias.* Berlin.

Lightfoot, J. L. (ed.) (2003) *Lucian. On the Syrian Goddess.* Oxford.

Lincoln, B. (1999) *Theorizing Myth. Narrative, Ideology, and Scholarship.* Chicago.

Lindberg, D. C. (1976) *Theories of Vision from Al-Kindi to Kepler.* Chicago.

Linders, T. (1972) *Studies in the Treasure Records of Artemis Brauronia found in Athens.* Lund.

(1988) 'The Purposes of Inventories. A Close Reading of the Delian Inventories of the Independence', in D. Knoepfler and J. Tréheux (eds.), *Comptes et inventaires dans la cité grecque.* Neuchâtel: 37–47.

(1992) 'Inscriptions and Orality', *Symbolae Osloenses* 67: 27–40.

Lindner, R. (1984) *Der Raub der Persephone in der antiken Kunst.* Würzburg.

Linfert, A. (1990) 'Die Schule des Polyklet', in H. Beck, P. C. Bol *et al.*, *Polyklet. Der Bildhauer der griechischen Klassik. Ausstellung im Liebieghaus, Museum alter Plastik, Frankfurt am Main.* Mainz: 240–97.

(1995) 'Prunkaltäre', in Wörrle and Zanker (eds.): 131–46.

Lissarrague, F. (1992) '*Graphein.* Écrire et dessiner', in C. Bron and E. Kassapoglou (eds.), *L'Image en jeu. Del'antiquité à Paul Klee.* Yens-sur-Morges: 189–203.

Llewellyn-Jones, L. (2001) 'Sexy Athena. The Dress and Erotic Representation of a Virgin War-Goddess', in Deacy and Villing (eds.): 233–57.

(2003) *Aphrodite's Tortoise. The Veiled Woman of Ancient Greece.* Swansea.

Lloyd, A. C. (1967) 'The Later Neoplatonists', in A. H. Armstrong (ed.), *The Cambridge History of Later Greek and Medieval Philosophy.* Cambridge: 269–325.

Lloyd-Jones, H. (1999) 'The Pride of Halicarnassus', *ZPE* 124: 1–14.

Long, A. A. (ed.) (1999) *The Cambridge Companion to Early Greek Philosophy.* Cambridge.

Longo, V. (1969) *Aretalogie nel mondo greco, I.* Genoa.

Lonsdale, S. H. (1995) '*Homeric Hymn to Apollo.* Prototype and Paradigm of Choral Performance', *Arion* 3.1: 25–40.

Loraux, N. (1991) 'Qu'est-ce qu'une déesse?', in G. Duby and M. Perrot (eds.), *Histoires des femmes*, I. *L'Antiquité.* Paris: 31–62.

(1993) *The Children of Athena.* Trans. C. Levine. Princeton.

(1995) *The Experiences of Tiresias. The Feminine and the Greek Man.* Trans. P. Wissing. Princeton.

Lorenz, T. (1992) 'Die Epiphanie der Dioskuren', in H. Froning, T. Hölscher and H. Mielsch (eds.), *Kotinos. Festschrift für Erika Simon.* Mainz am Rhein: 114–22.

Loucas, I. and E. Loucas (1994) 'The Sacred Laws of Lykosoura', in R. Hägg (ed.): 97–9.

Loucas-Durie, E. (1989) 'Anytos, le parèdre armé de Despoina à Lykosoura', *Kernos* 2: 105–14.

(1991) 'Le Nom de la Thea Despoina', in *Proceedings of the 3rd Conference of Peloponnesian Studies 1987–1988*. Peloponnesiaka Suppl. 13. Athens: 401–19.

Love, I. C. (1972) 'A Preliminary Report of the Excavations at Knidos', *AJA* 76: 61–76.

Lührmann, D. (1975) 'Epiphaneia. Zur Bedeutungsgeschichte eines griechischen Wortes', in G. Jeremias *et al.* (eds.), *Tradition und Glaube. Das frühe Christentum in seiner Umwelt*. Göttingen: 185–99.

Luraghi, N. (2008) *The Ancient Messenians. Constructions of Ethnicity and Memory*. Cambridge.

Lyons, D. (1996) *Gender and Immortality. Heroines in Ancient Greek Myth and Cult*. Princeton.

Ma, J. (1999) *Antiochos III and the Cities of Western Asia Minor*. Oxford.

(2003a) 'Kings', in Erskine (ed.): 177–95.

(2003b) 'Peer Polity Interaction in the Hellenistic Age', *Past & Present* 180: 9–40.

(2006) 'The Two Cultures. Connoisseurship and Civic Honours', *Art History* 29: 325–38.

(2007) 'Hellenistic Honorific Statues and Their Inscriptions', in Newby and Leader-Newby (eds.): 203–20.

MacAlister, S. (1996) *Dreams and Suicides. The Greek Novel from Antiquity to the Byzantine Empire*. London.

Macdonald, W. L. and J. A. Pinto (1995) *Hadrian's Villa and Its Legacy*. New Haven and London.

Mack, R. (2002) 'Facing Down Medusa (An Aetiology of the Gaze)', *Art History* 25.5: 571–604.

Mackey, J. (in press) 'Saving the Appearances. The Phenomenology of Epiphany in Atomist Theology', in Petridou and Platt (eds.).

MacLachlan, B. (1993) *The Age of Grace. Charis in Early Greek Poetry*. Princeton.

Maclean, J. K. B. and E. B. Aitken (2001) *Flavius Philostratus. Heroikos*. Atlanta.

MacLeod, R. (ed.) (2000) *The Library of Alexandria. Centre of Learning in the Ancient World*. London.

MacMullen, R. (1981) *Paganism in the Roman Empire*. New Haven and London.

(1982) 'The Epigraphic Habit in the Roman Empire', *AJPh* 103: 233–46.

Maddoli, G. and V. Saladino (1995) *Pausania. Guida della Grecia. Libro V: L'Elide e Olimpia*. Milan.

Madigan, B. C. (1992) *The Temple of Apollo Bassitas. The Sculpture*. With contributions by F. A. Cooper. Vol. ii of F. A. Cooper.

(1993) 'A Statue in the Temple of Apollo and Bassai', in Palagia and Coulson (eds.): 111–18.

Maffei, S. (1991) 'La σοφία del pittore e del poeta nel proemio delle *Imagines* di Filostrato Maggiore', *Annali della Scuola Normale Superiore di Pisa. Classe di lettere e filosofia*, serie III, 21.3: 591–621.

Magie, D. (1950) *Roman Rule in Asia Minor, to the End of the Third Century after Christ.* 2 vols. Princeton.

Maier, F. G. (1979) 'The Paphian Shrine of Aphrodite and Crete', in *Acts of the International Archaeological Symposium 'The Relations Between Cyprus and Crete, c. 2000–500 BC', 1978.* Nicosia: 228–34.

Malamoud, C. and J.-P. Vernant (eds.) (1986) *Corps des dieux.* Le Temps de la réflexion 7. Paris.

Malkin, I. (1991) 'What is an *Aphidryma*?', *ClAnt* 10: 77–96.

Maltby, P. (2002) *The Visionary Moment. A Postmodern Critique.* New York.

Manakidou, F. (1993) *Beschreibung von Kunstwerken in der hellenistischen Dichtung.* Stuttgart.

Manderscheid, H. (1981) *Die Skulpturenausstattung der kaiserzeitlichen Thermenanlagen.* Berlin.

Manetti, G. (1993) *Theories of the Sign in Classical Antiquity.* Trans. C. Richardson. Bloomington, IN.

Mango, C., M. Vickers and E. D. Francis (1992) 'The Palace of Lausus at Constantinople and Its Collection of Ancient Statues', *Journal of the History of Collections* 4: 89–98.

Manieri, A. (1998) *L'immagine poetica nella teoria degli antichi.* Pisa.
  (1999) 'Colori, suoni e profumi nelle *Imagines.* Principi dell'estetica filostratea', *QUCC* 63.3: 111–21.

Maniura, R. and R. Shepherd (eds.) (2006) *Presence. The Inherence of the Prototype within Images and Other Objects.* London.

Männlein-Robert, I. (2007) 'Epigrams on Art. Voice and Voicelessness in Hellenistic Epigram', in Bing and Bruss (eds.): 251–71.

Mansfield, E. (2007) *Too Beautiful to Picture. Zeuxis, Myth, and Mimesis.* Minneapolis.

Mansfield, J. M. (1985) 'The Robe of Athena and the Panathenaic Peplos.' PhD diss., University of California, Berkeley.

Mantero, T. (1966) *Ricerche sull' Heroikos di Filostrato.* Genoa.

Marquadt, P. A. (1981) 'A Portrait of Hecate', *AJPh* 102: 243–60.

Marrou, H. I. (1956) *A History of Education in Antiquity.* Trans. G. Lamb. London.

Marszal, J. (1998) 'An Epiphany for Athena. The Eastern Pediment of the Old Athena Temple at Athens', in Hartswick and Sturgeon (eds.): 173–80.

Martin, L. (1987) 'Aelius Aristides and the Technology of Oracular Dreams', *Historical Reflections / Réflexions Historiques* 14: 63–72.
  (1991) 'Artemidorus. Dream Theory in Late Antiquity', *Second Century* 8: 97–108.

Martin, L. H. (1995) 'Gods or Ambassadors of God? Barnabas and Paul in Lystra', *NTS* 41: 152–6.

Marvin, M. (1983) 'Freestanding Sculptures from the Baths of Caracalla', *AJA* 87: 347–84.

(2008) *The Language of the Muses. The Dialogue Between Greek and Roman Sculpture.* Los Angeles.

Massenzio, M. (1969) 'Cultura e crisi permanente. La "xenia" dionisiaca', *Studi e Materiali di Storia delle Religioni* 40: 27–113.

Massing, J. M. (1990) *Du texte à l'image. La Calumnie d'Apelle et son iconographie.* Strasbourg.

(2007) 'A Few More Calumnies. Lucian and the Visual Arts', in C. Ligota and L. Panizza (eds.), *Lucian of Samosata Vivus et Redivivus.* Warburg Institute Colloquia 10. London and Turin: 35–53.

Mastronarde, D. (1990) 'Actors on High. The Skene Roof, the Crane, and the Gods in Attic Drama', *ClAnt* 9: 247–94.

(2005) 'The Gods', in J. Gregory (ed.), *A Companion to Greek Tragedy.* Oxford: 321–32.

Matheson, S. B. (1986) 'Polygnotos. An Iliupersis Scene at the Getty Museum', in *Greek Vases in the J. Paul Getty Museum.* Occasional Papers on Antiquities 2, vol. iii. Malibu: 101–14.

(1996) 'The Divine Claudia. Women as Goddesses in Roman Art', in Kleiner and Matheson (eds.): 182–94.

Matz, F. (1956–7) 'An Endymion Sarcophagus Rediscovered', *BMMA* 15: 123–8.

(1958) *Göttererscheinung und Kultbild im minoischen Kreta.* Mainz.

(1969) *Die dionysischen Sarkophage.* Die antiken Sarkophagreliefs 4.3. Berlin.

Maurizio, L. (1993) 'Delphic Narratives. Recontextualizing the Pythia and Her Prophecies.' PhD diss., Princeton University.

(1997) 'Delphic Oracles as Oral Performances. Authenticity and Historical Evidence', *ClAnt* 16.2: 308–34.

Mauss, M. (1950) *The Gift. The Form and Reason for Exchange in Archaic Societies.* London.

Mayor, A. (2000) *The First Fossil Hunters. Paleontology in Greek and Roman Times.* Princeton.

McCann, A. M. (1978) *Roman Sarcophagi in the Metropolitan Museum of Art.* New York.

McClure, L. (2003) *Courtesans at Table. Gender and Greek Literary Culture in Athenaeus.* New York.

McCombie, D. (2002) 'Philostratus, Histoi, *Imagines* 2.28. Ekphrasis and the Web of Illusion', *Ramus* 31: 146–57.

McCracken, G. E. (1949) *Arnobius of Sicca. The Case against the Pagans.* Westminster, MD.

McIntosh Snyder, J. (1981) 'The Web of Song. Weaving Imagery in Homer and the Lyric Poets', *CJ* 76: 193–4.

(1989) *The Woman and the Lyre.* Carbondale.

McNally, S. (1985) 'Ariadne and Others. Images of Sleep in Greek and Early Roman Art', *ClAnt* 4: 152–92.

McNeil, W. (1999) *The Glance of the Eye. Heidegger, Aristotle, and the Ends of Theory.* New York.

Meier, C. A. (1966) 'The Dream in Ancient Greece and Its Use in Temple Cures (Incubation)', in von Grunebaum and Caillois (eds.): 303–19.

 (2003) *Healing Dream and Ritual. Ancient Incubation and Modern Psychotherapy.* Einsiedeln.

Meiggs, R. (1982) *Trees and Timber in the Ancient Mediterranean World.* Oxford.

Meijer, P. A. (2007) *Stoic Theology. Proofs for the Existence of the Cosmic God and of the Traditional Gods.* Delft.

Melville, S. and B. Readings (eds.) (1995) *Vision and Textuality.* London.

Merkelbach, R. (1962) *Roman und Mysterium in der Antike.* Berlin.

 (1995) *Isis regina – Zeus Sarapis. Die griechisch-ägyptische Religion nach den Quellen dargestellt.* Stuttgart and Leipzig.

Messer, W. (1918) *The Dream in Homer and Greek Tragedy.* New York.

Mestre, F. (1990) 'Homère entre Dion Chrysostome et Philostrate', *Anuari de Filologia. Seccio di Studia Graeca et Latina* 13: 89–101.

 (2004) 'Refuting Homer in the *Heroikos* of Philostratus', in Aitken and Maclean (eds.): 127–41.

Mettinger, T. N. D. (1995) *No Graven Image? Israelite Aniconism in Its Ancient Near Eastern Context.* Stockholm.

Metzger, M. (1985) *Königsthron und Gottesthron.* 2 vols. Kevelaer and Neukirchen-Vluyn.

Metzler, D. (1985/6) 'Anikonische Darstellungen', *Visible Religion* 4–5: 96–113.

Meyer, D. (2007) 'The Act of Reading and the Act of Writing in Hellenistic Epigram', in Bing and Bruss (eds.): 187–210.

Meyer, E. (1917) 'Apollonios von Tyana und die Biographie des Philostratos', *Hermes* 52: 371–424.

Michenaud, G. and J. Dierkins (1972) *Les Rêves dans les 'Discours Sacrés' d'Aelius Aristide.* Mons.

Mielsch, H. (1995) 'Die Bibliothek und die Kunstsammlung der Könige von Pergamon', *AA*: 765–79.

Mielsch, H. and H. von Hesberg (1986) *Die heidnische Nekropole unter St. Peter in Rom. Die Mausoleen E-I und Z-Psi.* Atti della Pontificia Accademia romana di archeologia, series 3.16, vol. ii. Rome.

Mikalson, J. D. (1998) *Religion in Hellenistic Athens.* Berkeley and Los Angeles.

 (2006) 'Greek Religion. Continuity and Change in the Hellenistic Period', in G. R. Bugh (ed.), *The Cambridge Companion to the Hellenistic World.* Cambridge: 208–22.

Mikocki, T. (1995) *Sub specie deae. Les impératrices et princesses romaines assimiliées à des déesses: étude iconologique.* Rome.

Miles, G. (2009) 'Reforming the Eyes. Interpreters and Interpretation in the *Vita Apollonii*', in Demoen and Praet (eds.): 129–60.

Millar, F. (1977) *The Emperor in the Roman World*. London.

Miller, A. M. (1979) 'The "Address to the Delian Maidens" in the *Homeric Hymn to Apollo*. Epilogue or Transition?', *TAPA* 109: 173–86.

(1986) *From Delos to Delphi. A Literary Study of the Homeric Hymn to Apollo*. Leiden.

Miller, J. B. F. (2007) '*Convinced That God Had Called Us'. Dreams, Visions, and the Perception of God's Will in Luke-Acts*. Leiden.

Miller, N. K. (1986) 'Arachnologies. The Woman, the Text and the Critic', in N. K. Miller (ed.), *The Poetics of Gender*. New York: 288–90.

Mitchell, M. M. (2004) 'Epiphanic Evolutions in Earliest Christianity', *ICS* 29: 183–204.

Mitchell, W. J. T. (1994) *Picture Theory. Essays on Verbal and Visual Representation*. Chicago.

(2004) *What Do Pictures Want? The Lives and Loves of Images*. Chicago.

Mitropoulou, E. (1977) *Deities and Heroes in the Form of Snakes*. Athens.

Mittag, P. F. (2006) *Antiochos IV Epiphanes. Eine politische Biographie*. Berlin.

Moggi, M. and M. Osanna (2003) *Pausania. Guida della Grecia. Libro VIII: L'Arcadia*. Milan.

Molev, E. A. (2003) 'Bosporos and Chersonesos in the 4th–2nd Centuries BC', in Bilde *et al.* (eds.): 209–15.

Momigliano, A. D. (1972) 'Popular Religious Beliefs and the Later Roman Historians', in G. J. Cuming and D. Baker (eds.), *Popular Belief and Practice*. Cambridge: 1–18.

(1987) 'Ancient Biography and the Study of Religion in the Roman Empire', in M. Détienne *et al.* (eds.), *Poikilia. Études offertes à J.-P. Vernant*. Paris: 33–48.

Montiglio, S. (2005) *Wandering in Ancient Greek Culture*. Chicago.

Morales, H. (1995) 'The Taming of the View. Natural Curiosities in Leukippe and Clitophon', *Groningen Colloquia on the Novel* 6: 39–50.

(1996) 'The Torturer's Apprentice. Parrhasius and the Limits of Art', in Elsner (ed.): 182–209.

(2004) *Vision and Narrative in Achilles Tatius' Leucippe and Clitophon*. Cambridge.

Moreno, P. (1994) *Scultura ellenistica*. 2 vols. Rome.

Moreschini, C. (1994) 'Elio Aristide tra retorica e filosofia', *ANRW* 2.34.2: 1234–47.

Moret, J.-M. (1975) *L'Ilioupersis dans la céramique italiote. Les mythes et leur expression figurée au IVe siècle*. 2 vols. Geneva.

Moretti, L. (1967–2002) *Iscrizioni storiche ellenistiche*. 3 vols. Florence.

Morey, C. R. (1924) *The Sarcophagus of Claudia Antonia Sabina and the Asiatic Sarcophagi*. Princeton.

Morgan, C. (1990) *Athletes and Oracles. The Transformation of Olympia and Delphi in the Eighth Century B.C.* Cambridge.

Morgan, J. R. (2009) 'The Emesan Connection. Philostratus and Heliodorus', in Demoen and Praet (eds.): 263–81.

Morgan, K. A. (2000) *Myth and Philosophy from the Presocratics to Plato*. Cambridge.

Morgan, T. (1998) *Literate Education in the Hellenistic and Roman Worlds*. Cambridge.

Morris, I. (1992) *Death-Ritual and Social Structure in Classical Antiquity*. Cambridge.

Morris, S. P. (1992) *Daidalos and the Origins of Greek Art*. Princeton.

Most, G. W. (1999) 'The Poetics of Early Greek Philosophy', in Long (ed.): 332–62.
   (2005) *Doubting Thomas*. Cambridge, MA.

Müller, F. G. J. M. (1994) *The So-Called Peleus and Thetis Sarcophagus in the Villa Albani*. Amsterdam.

Murray, P. (1981) 'Poetic Inspiration in Early Greece', *JHS* 101: 87–100.
   (2004) 'The Muses and their Arts', in P. Murray and P. Wilson (eds.), *Music and the Muses. The Culture of 'Mousikē' in the Classical Athenian City*. Oxford: 365–89.

Müth, S. (2007) *Eigene Wege. Topographie und Stadtplan von Messene in spätklassisch-hellenistischer Zeit*. Rahden.

Nachtergael, G. (1977) *Les Galates en Grèce et les Sôtéria de Delphes. Recherches d'histoire et d'épigraphie hellénistiques*. Brussels.

Nagy, G. (1983) 'Sēma and Nóēsis. Some Illustrations', *Arethusa* 16: 35–55.
   (1990a) *Greek Mythology and Poetics*. Ithaca.
   (1990b) *Pindar's Homer*. Baltimore.
   (1996) 'Autorité et auteur dans la *Théogonie* hésiodique', in F. Blaise, P. Judet de la Combe and P. Rousseau (eds.), *Le Métier du mythe. Lectures d'Hésiode*. Paris: 41–52.
   (2007) 'Lyric and Greek Myth', in R. D. Woodard (ed.), *The Cambridge Companion to Greek Mythology*. Cambridge: 19–51.

Nead, L. (1992) *The Female Nude*. London and New York.

Neer, R. T. (1995) 'The Lion's Eye. Imitation and Uncertainty in Attic Red Figure', *Representations* 51: 118–53.
   (1998) 'Imitation, Inscription, Antilogic', *Métis* 13: 17–38.
   (2005) *Style and Politics in Athenian Vase-Painting. The Craft of Democracy ca. 530–460 BC*. Cambridge.
   (2010) *Theory of Sculpture. The Emergence of the Classical Style*. Chicago.

Nehamas, A. (1982) 'Plato on Imitation and Poetry in Republic X', in J. Moravcsik and P. Temko (eds.), *Plato on Beauty, Wisdom, and the Arts*. Ottawa: 65–6.

Neils, J. (ed.) (1992) *Goddess and Polis. The Panathenaic Festival in Ancient Athens*. Hanover, NH.
   (ed.) (1996) *Worshipping Athena. Panathenaia and Parthenon*. Madison, WI.
   (ed.) (2005a) *The Parthenon. From Antiquity to the Present*. Cambridge.
   (2005b) '"With Noblest Images on All Sides". The Ionic Frieze of the Parthenon', in Neils (ed.): 199–224.

Nelson, R. S. (ed.) (2000) *Visuality before and beyond the Renaissance*. Cambridge.
   (2003) 'Tourists, Terrorists, and Metaphysical Theatre at Hagia Sophia', in R. S. Nelson and M. Olin (eds.), *Monuments and Memory, Made and Unmade*. Chicago: 59–81.

Nestle, W. (1936) 'Die Horen des Prodikos', *Hermes* 71: 151–70.

Neumann, G. (1979) *Probleme des griechischen Weihreliefs*. Tübingen.

Newby, Z. (2002) 'Reading Programs in Greco-Roman Art. Reflections on the Spada Reliefs', in D. Fredrick (ed.), *The Roman Gaze*. Baltimore: 110–48.
   (2005) *Greek Athletics in the Roman World*. Oxford.
   (2007a) 'Art at the Crossroads? Themes and Styles in Severan Art', in Swain *et al.* (eds.): 201–50.
   (2007b) 'Reading the Allegory of the Archaelaos Relief', in Newby and Leader-Newby (eds.): 156–78.
   (2009) 'Absorption and Erudition in Philostratus' *Imagines*', in Bowie and Elsner (eds.): 322–42.
   (in press) 'In the Guise of Gods and Heroes. Portrait Heads on Mythological Sarcophagi', in J. Elsner and J. Huskinson (eds.), *Life, Death and Representation. New Work on Roman Sarcophagi*. Berlin.

Newby, Z. and R. Leader-Newby (eds.) (2007) *Art and Inscriptions in the Ancient World*. Cambridge.

Newhall, S. (1911) 'Quid de somniis censuerint quoque modo eis usi sint antiqui.' PhD. diss., Harvard University.

Nichols, A. (1987) *The Poetics of Epiphany. Nineteenth-Century Origins of the Modern Literary Moment*. Tuscaloosa and London.

Nick, G. (2002) *Die Athena Parthenos. Studien zum griechischen Kultbild und seiner Rezeption*. Mainz.

Nicosia, S. (1988) 'L'Autobiografia onirica di Elio Aristide', in Guidorizzi (ed.): 173–90.

Nightingale, A. W. (2001) 'On Wandering and Wondering. *Theōria* in Greek Philosophy and Culture', *Arion* 9: 23–58.
   (2004) *Spectacles of Truth in Classical Greek Philosophy. Theōria in its Cultural Context*. Cambridge.
   (2005) 'The Philosopher at the Festival. Plato's Transformation of Traditional *Theōria*', in Elsner and Rutherford (eds.): 151–80.

Nock, A. D. (1932) 'Cremation and Burial in the Roman Empire', *Harvard Theological Review* 25: 321–59.
   (1933) *Conversion. The Old and the New in Religion from Alexander the Great to Augustine of Hippo*. Oxford.
   (1946) 'Sarcophagi and Symbolism. A Review of F. Cumont's *Recherches sur le symbolisme funéraires des Romains*', *AJA* 50: 140–70.
   (1957) Review of Pax (1955), *Gnomon* 29: 229–30.
   (1972) *Essays on Religion and the Ancient World*. 2 vols. Cambridge, MA.

Nora, P. (1996–8) *Realms of Memory. Rethinking the French Past.* Trans. A. Gold-hammer. 3 vols. New York.

Nörenberg, H.-W. (1973) 'Untersuchungen zum Schluss der Περιήγησις τῆς Ἑλλά-δος des Pausanias', *Hermes* 101: 225–52.

Norman, A. F. (1965) *Libanius' Autobiography (Oration 1).* Oxford.

North, J. (1983) 'These He Cannot Take', *JRS* 73: 169–74.

Oakley, J. (2004) *Picturing Death in Classical Athens. The Evidence of the White Lekythoi.* Cambridge.

Obbink, D. (2002) '"All Gods are True" in Epicurus', in Frede and Laks (eds.): 183–221.

(1996) *Philodemus on Piety. Part 1: Critical Text with Commentary.* Oxford.

Oberhelman, S. M. (1977) 'Popular Dream-Interpretation in Ancient Greece and Freudian Psychoanalysis', *Journal of Popular Culture* 11: 680–95.

(1981) 'The Interpretation of Prescriptive Dreams in Ancient Greek Medicine', *Journal of the History of Medicine and Allied Sciences* 36.4: 416–24.

(1987) 'The Diagnostic Dream in Ancient Medical Theory and Practice', *Bulletin of the History of Medicine* 61.1: 47–60.

(1993) 'Dreams in Graeco-Roman Medicine', *ANRW* 2.37.1: 121–56.

Oenbrink, W. (1997) *Das Bild im Bilde. Zur Darstellung von Gotterstatuen und Kultbildern auf griechischen Vasen.* Frankfurt am Main.

Ogden, D. (2001) *Greek and Roman Necromancy.* Princeton and Oxford.

(2004) *Aristomenes of Messene. Legends of Sparta's Nemesis.* Swansea.

(2007) *In Search of the Sorcerer's Apprentice. The Traditional Tales of Lucian's Lover of Lies.* Swansea.

O'Meara, D. J. (1989) *Pythagoras Revived. Mathematics and Philosophy in Late Antiquity.* Oxford.

Omitowoju, R. (2002) *Rape and the Politics of Consent in Classical Athens.* Cambridge.

Osborne, C. (1987) 'The Repudiation of Representation in Plato's *Republic* and its Repercussions', *PCPS* 213 (n.s. 33): 53–73.

Osborne, R. (1985) 'The Erection and Mutilation of the Hermai', *PCPS* 211 (n. s. 31): 47–73.

(1989) 'The Viewing and Obscuring of the Parthenon Frieze', *JHS* 107: 98–105.

(1994) 'Looking on – Greek Style. Does the Sculpted Girl Speak to Women Too?', in I. Morris (ed.), *Classical Greece. Ancient Histories and Modern Archaeologies.* Cambridge: 81–96.

(1996) 'Desiring Women on Athenian Pottery', in Kampen (ed.): 65–80.

(1998) *Archaic and Classical Greek Art.* Oxford.

(1999) 'Inscribing Performance', in Goldhill and Osborne (eds.): 341–58.

(2009) 'The Narratology and Theology of Architectural Sculpture, *or*, What You Can Do with a Chariot but Can't Do with a Satyr on a Greek Temple', in

P. Schultz and R. von den Hoff (eds.), *Structure, Image, Ornament. Architectural Sculpture in the Greek World.* Oxford: 2–12.

Østby, E. (ed.) (2005) *Ancient Arcadia. Papers from the Third International Seminar on Ancient Arcadia, Held at the Norwegian Institute in Athens, 7–10 May 2002.* Athens.

Otto, W. F. (1965) *Dionysus. Myth and Cult.* Trans. R. B. Palmer. Bloomington and Indianapolis.

Overbeck, J. (1868) *Die antiken Schriftquellen zur Geschichte der bildenden Künste bei den Griechen.* Leipzig. Repr. Hildesheim, 1959.

Pache, C. O. (2004) 'Singing Heroes. The Poetics of Hero Cult in the *Heroikos*', in Aitken and Maclean (eds.): 3–24.

Pack, R. (1955) 'Artemidorus and His Waking World', *TAPA* 86: 280–90.

Packer, J. (1998) '*Mire Exaedificavit.* Three Recent Books on Hadrian's Tiburtine Villa', *JRA* 11: 583–96.

Page, D. L. (1955) *Sappho and Alcaeus.* Oxford.

(1981) *Further Greek Epigrams.* Cambridge.

Palagia, O. (1993) *The Pediments of the Parthenon.* Leiden.

(1995) 'Akropolis Museum 581. A Family at the Apaturia?' *Hesperia* 64: 493–501.

(2005) 'Fire from Heaven. Pediments and Acroteria of the Parthenon', in Neils (ed.): 224–59.

Palagia, O. and W. Coulson (eds.) (1993) *Sculpture from Arcadia and Laconia. Proceedings of an International Conference Held at the American School of Classical Studies at Athens, April 10–14, 1992.* Oxbow Monograph 30. Oxford.

Palagia, O. and J. J. Pollitt (eds.) (1996) *Personal Styles in Greek Sculpture.* Yale Classical Studies 30. Cambridge.

Panofsky, E. (1930) *Hercules am Scheidewege und andere antike Bildstoffe in der neueren Kunst.* Leipzig.

Paolitti, J. T. (2006) 'Medici Funerary Monuments in the Duomo of Florence during the Fourteenth Century. A Prologue to "The Early Medici"', *Renaissance Quarterly* 59: 1117–63.

Papalexandrou, N. (2004) 'Reading as Seeing. P.Mil.Vogl. viii 309 and Greek Art', in Acosta-Hughes *et al.* (eds.): 247–58.

Parise Badoni, F. (1990) 'Arianna a Nasso. La rielaborazione di un mito greco in ambiente romano', *DialArch*, ser. 3, 8: 73–89.

Parisinou, E. (2000) *The Light of the Gods. The Role of Light in Archaic and Classical Greek Cult.* London.

Parker, R. (1985) 'Greek States and Greek Oracles', in P. Cartledge and F. D. Harvey (eds.), *Crux. Essays Presented to G. E. M. de Ste. Croix.* London: 298–326.

(1991) 'The *Hymn to Demeter* and the *Homeric Hymns*', *Greece & Rome* 38: 1–17.

(1996) *Athenian Religion. A History.*

(1998) 'Pleasing Thighs. Reciprocity in Greek Religion', in C. Gill *et al.* (eds.): 105–27.

(2004) 'New "Panhellenic" Festivals in Hellenistic Greece', in R. Schlesier and U. Zellmann (eds.), *Mobility and Travel in the Mediterranean from Antiquity to the Middle Ages*. Münster: 9–22.

(2005) *Polytheism and Society at Athens*. Oxford.

Parker, R. and G. Pollock (1981) *Old Mistresses. Women, Art and Ideology*. London.

Parry, H. (1986) 'The *Homeric Hymn to Aphrodite*. Erotic *Ananke*', *Phoenix* 40. 3: 253–64.

Parry, K. (1996) *Depicting the Word. Byzantine Iconophile Thought of the Eighth and Ninth Centuries*. Leiden.

Patillon, M. (ed.) (1997) *Aelius Theon, Progymnasmata*. Paris.

Patton, K. C. (2009) *Religion of the Gods. Ritual, Paradox, and Reflexivity*. Oxford and New York.

Pax, E. (1955)Ἐπιφάνεια. *Ein religionsgeschichtlicher Beitrag zur biblischen Theologie*. Münchener theologische Studien 1.10. Munich.

Payne, M. (in press) 'The Objects of Ecphrasis', in M. Fantuzzi and M. Paschalis (eds.), *Greek and Roman Ekphrasis*. Rethymnon Classical Studies 4.

Pearcy, L. T. (1988) 'Theme, Dream, and Narrative. Reading the *Sacred Tales* of Aelius Aristides', *TAPA* 118: 377–91.

Pease, A. S. (1920) *M. Tulli Ciceronis De divinatione. Liber primus*. Urbana, IL.

Peden, R. G. (1985) 'The Statues in Apuleius' *Metamorphoses* 2.4', *Phoenix* 39: 380–83.

Pelikan, J. J. (1990) *Imago Dei. The Byzantine Apologia for Icons*. New Haven and London.

Pelling, C. (2002) *Plutarch and History. Eighteen Studies*. London.

Pentcheva, B. V. (2006) *Icons and Power. The Mother of God in Byzantium*. Philadelphia.

Penwill, J. L. (1975) 'Slavish Pleasures and Profitless Curiosity. Fall and Redemption in Apuleius' *Metamorphoses*', *Ramus* 4: 49–82.

Perdrizet, P. and G. Lefebvre (1919) *Inscriptiones Graecae Aegypti III*. Paris.

Pérez Jiménez, A. (2001) 'Plutarco *versus* Platón. Espacios místicos en el mito de Tespesio', in Pérez Jiménez and Casadesús Bordoy (eds.): 201–10.

Pérez Jiménez, A. and F. Casadesús Bordoy (eds.) (2001) *Estudios sobre Plutarco. Misticismo y religions mistéricas en la obra de Plutarco (Actas del VII Simposio Español sobre Plutarco, Palma de Mallorca, 2–4 de noviembre de 2000)*. Madrid.

Perkins, J. (1995) *The Suffering Self. Pain and Narrative Representation in the Early Christian Era*. London and New York.

Pernot, L. (1997) *Éloges grecs de Rome. Discours traduit et commentés*. Paris.

Perry, E. E. (2001) 'Iconography and the Dynamics of Patronage. A Sarcophagus from the Family of Herodes Atticus', *Hesperia* 70: 461–92.

(2005) *The Aesthetics of Emulation in the Visual Arts of Ancient Rome*. Cambridge.

Petersen, E. (1907) *Die Burgtempel der Athenaia*. Berlin.

Petrain, D. (2005) 'Gems, Metapoetics, and Value. Greek and Roman Responses to a Third-Century Discourse on Precious Stones', *TAPA* 135: 329–57.

Petridou, G. (2006) 'On Divine Epiphanies. Contextualizing and Conceptualizing Epiphanic Narratives in Greek Literature and Culture (7th C BC – 2nd C AD).' PhD diss., University of Exeter.

(in press a) 'Erotic Epiphanies. Divine Lovers and Aggressors in Greek Literature and Culture', in Petridou and Platt (eds.).

(in press b) 'Peisistratus' *Kathodos*. Epiphany Stratagem and Crisis Management in Hdt 1.60'.

Petridou, G. and V. Platt (eds.) (in press) *Epiphany. Envisioning the Divine in the Ancient World*. Leiden.

Petropoulou, A. (1991) '*Prothysis* and Altar. A Case-Study', in M.-T. Le Dinahet and R. Étienne (eds.), *L'Espace sacrificiel dans les civilisations méditerranéennes de l'antiquité. Actes du colloque tenu à la Maison de l'Orient, Lyon, 4–7 juin 1988*. Paris: 25–31.

Petrovic, A. (2007) 'Inscribed Epigram in Pre-Hellenistic Literary Sources', in Bing and Bruss (eds.): 49–68.

Petrovic, I. (2006) 'Delusions of Grandeur. Homer, Zeus and the Telchines in Callimachus' Reply (*Aitia* Fr. 1) and Iambus 6', *A&A* 52: 16–41.

(2007) *Von den Toren des Hades zu den Hallen des Olymp. Artemiskult bei Theokrit und Kallimachos*. Leiden: 205–24.

(2010) 'The Life Story of a Cult Statue as an Allegory. Kallimachos' Hermes Perpheraios', in J. Mylonopoulos (ed.), *Divine Images and Human Imaginations in Ancient Greece and Rome*. Leiden.

Petrovic, I. and A. Petrovic (2003) 'Stop and Smell the Statues. Callimachus' Epigram 51 Pf. Reconsidered (Four Times)', *MD* 51: 179–208.

Petsalis-Diomidis, A. (2001) ' "Truly beyond Miracles". The Body and Healing Pilgrimage in the Eastern Roman Empire in the Second Century AD.' PhD diss., Courtauld Institute of Art, London.

(2005) 'The Body in Space. Visual Dynamics in Graeco-Roman Healing Pilgrimage', in Elsner and Rutherford (eds.): 183–218.

(2006a) 'Amphiaraos Present. Images and Healing Pilgrimage in Classical Greece', in Maniura and Shepherd (eds.): 205–29.

(2006b) 'Sacred Writing, Sacred Reading. The Function of Aristides' Self-Presentation as Author in the *Sacred Tales*', in B. McGing and J. Mossman (eds.), *The Limits of Ancient Biography*. Swansea, 193–211.

(2008) 'The Body in the Landscape. Aristides' *Corpus* in the Light of the *Sacred Tales*', in Harris and Holmes (eds.): 130–50.

(2010) *Truly beyond Wonders. Aelius Aristides and the Cult of Asklepios*. Oxford.

Pfanner, M. (1979) 'Bemerkungen zur Komposition und Interpretation des Grossen Frieses von Pergamon', *AA*: 46–57.

Pfister, F. (1924) 'Epiphanie', *RE* Supplement 4: 277–323.

(1927) 'Soteria', in *RE* 3A: 1223–5.

Pfrommer, M. (1985) 'Zur Venus Colonna. Ein späthellenistische Redaktion der Knidischen Aphrodite', *IstMitt* 35: 173–80.

Phillimore, J. S. (1912) *In Honor of Apollonius of Tyana*. Oxford.

Phillips, C. R. (1986) 'The Sociology of Religious Knowledge in the Roman Empire to A.D. 284', *ANRW* 2.16.3: 2677–773.

Philonenko, M. (1993) *Le Trône de Dieu*. Tübingen.

Picard, C. (1912) 'Θεοί Ἐπιφανεῖς', in *Xénia. Hommage international à l'Université nationale de Grèce*. Athens: 67–84.

(1922) *Ephèse et Claros. Recherches sur les sanctuaires et les cultes de l'Ionie du nord*. Paris.

(1951) 'Représentations antiques de l'Apologue dit de Prodicos', *CRAI*: 310–22.

(1953) 'Nouvelles remarques sur l'Apologue dit de Prodicos. Héraclès entre le vice et la vertu', *RA* 42: 10–41.

Piccaluga, G. (1980) 'L'olocausta di Patrai', in J. Rudhart *et al.*, *Le Sacrifice dans l'antiquité*. Entretiens sur l'antiquité classique 27. Geneva: 243–88.

Picón, C. A. (1978) 'The Ilissos Temple Reconsidered', *AJA* 82: 47–81.

Pirenne-Delforge, V. (1998) 'La Notion de "panthéon" dans la *Periégèse* de Pausanias', in V. Pirenne-Delforge (ed.), *Les Panthéons des cités grecques des origines à Pausanias*. Kernos Suppl. 8. Paris: 129–48.

(2008) *Retour à la source. Pausanias et la religion grecque*. Kernos Suppl. 20. Paris.

Pirenne-Delforge, V. and G. Pumelle (1997) *Pausanias, Periegesis. Index verborum, listes de fréquence, index nominum*. Liège.

Platt, V. J. (2002) 'Viewing, Desiring, Believing. Confronting the Divine in a Pompeian House', *Art History* 25: 87–112.

(2004) 'Epiphany and Representation in Graeco-Roman Culture. Art, Literature, Religion.' PhD diss., University of Oxford.

(2006) 'Making an Impression. Replication and the Ontology of the Graeco-Roman Seal Stone', *Art History* 29: 233–57.

(2007a) 'Burning Butterflies. Seals, Symbols and the Soul in Antiquity', in L. Gilmour (ed.), *Pagans and Christians. From Antiquity to the Middle Ages*. Oxford: 89–99.

(2007b) 'Honour Takes Wing. Unstable Images and Anxious Orators in the Greek Tradition', in Newby and Leader-Newby (eds.): 247–71.

(2010) 'Art History in the Temple', *Arethusa* 43: 197–213.

(in press a) 'Double Vision. Epiphanies of the Dioscuri in Greece and Rome', in Petridou and Platt (eds.).

(in press b) 'Framing the Dead on Roman Sarcophagi', *RES: Journal of Anthropology and Aesthetics*.

Pointon, M. (1990) *Naked Authority. The Body in Western Painting, 1830–1908*. Cambridge.

Pollitt, J. J. (1974) *The Ancient View of Greek Art*. New Haven and London.

(1986) *Art in the Hellenistic Age*. Cambridge.

(1990a) *The Art of Ancient Greece. Sources and Documents*. Rev. edn. Cambridge.

(1990b) 'The Meaning of Pheidias' Athena Parthenos', in B. Tsakirgis and S. F. Wiltshire (eds.), *The Nashville Athena. A Symposium. The Parthenon: Nashville, Tennessee, May 21 1990*. Nashville: 21–3.

Pomeroy, A. J. (1991) 'Status and Status-Concern in the Greco-Roman Dream Books', *Ancient Society* 22: 51–74.

Pomeroy, S. B. (2002) *Spartan Women*. Oxford.

Poorthuis, M. (2003) 'The Prohibition of Idolatry. Source of Humanity or Source of Violence? Early Jewish and Christian Perspectives on the Prohibition of Images: A Hermeneutic Approach', in R. Burggraeve, J. De Tavernier, D. Pollefeyt and J. Hanssen (eds.), *Desirable God? Our Fascination with Images, Idols and New Deities*. Leuven: 39–60.

Porter, J. I. (1997) 'Aristotle and Specular Regimes. The Theater of Philosophical Discourse', in Levin (ed.): 93–115.

(2001) 'Ideals and Ruins. Pausanias, Longinus, and the Second Sophistic', in Alcock *et al.* (eds.): 63–92.

Porter, P. (1972) *After Martial*. London.

Porter, W. H. (1937) *Plutarch's Life of Aratus*. Dublin and Cork.

Potter, D. (1994) *Prophets and Emperors. Human and Divine Authority from Augustus to Theodosius*. Cambridge, MA.

(2003) 'Hellenistic Religion', in Erskine (ed.): 407–30.

Prag, A. J. N. W. (1972) 'Athena Mancuniensis. Another Copy of the Athena Parthenos', *JHS* 92: 96–114.

(1984) 'New Copies of the Athena Parthenos from the East', in E. Berger (ed.): 182–7.

Prauscello, L. (2006) 'Sculpted Meanings, Talking Statues. Some Observations on Posidippus 142.A–B', *AJPh* 127: 511–23.

Preisshofen, F. (1979) 'Phidias-Daedalus auf dem Schild der Athena Parthenos? Ampelius 8, 10', *JDAI* 89: 50–69.

(1984) 'Zur Funktion des Parthenon nach den schriftlichen Quellen', in E. Berger (ed.): 15–18.

Pretzler, M. (2005) 'Polybios to Pausanias. Arkadian Identity in the Roman Empire', in Østby (ed.): 521–31.

Price, S. (1984a) 'Gods and Emperors. The Greek Language of the Roman Imperial Cult', *JHS* 104: 79–95.

(1984b) *Rituals and Power. The Roman Imperial Cult in Asia Minor*. Cambridge.

(1986) 'The Future of Dreams from Freud to Artemidorus', *Past & Present* 113: 3–37.

(1999) *Religions of the Ancient Greeks*. Cambridge.

Prier R. A. (1989) *Thauma Idesthai. The Phenomenology of Sight and Appearance in Archaic Greek*. Tallahassee.

Prieur, J. (1986) *La Mort dans l'antiquité romaine*. Rennes.

Prinz, F. (1979) *Gründungsmythen und Sagenchronologie*. Munich.

Prioux, E. (2007) *Regards alexandrins. Histoire et théorie des arts dans l'épigramme hellénistique.* Leuven.

Pritchett, W. K. (1979) *The Greek State at War.* Vol. iii. Berkeley.

(1998) *Pausanias Periegetes.* Amsterdam.

(1999) *Pausanias Periegetes, II.* Amsterdam.

Pucci, P. (1977) *Hesiod and the Language of Poetry.* Baltimore.

(1994) 'Gods' Intervention and Epiphany in Sophocles', *AJPh* 115: 15–46.

(1998) *The Song of the Sirens. Essays on Homer.* Lanham, MD.

(2002) 'Theology and Poetics in the Iliad', *Arethusa* 35: 17–34.

Puech, B. (2002) *Orateurs et sophistes grecs dans les inscriptions d'époque impériale.* Paris.

Pugliese-Caratelli, G. (1987) 'Epigrafi di Cos relative al culto di Artemis in Cnido e in Bargylia', *Parola del Passato* 42: 110–23.

Puiggali, J. (1982) 'Dion Chrysostome et Maxime de Tyr', *Annales de la Faculté des Lettres et des Sciences Humaines de l'Université de Dakar* 12: 9–24.

Pulleyn, S. (1997) *Prayer in Greek Religion.* Oxford and New York.

Putnam, M. C. J. (1986) *Artifices of Eternity. Horace's Fourth Book of Odes.* Ithaca, NY, and London.

Pyysiäinen, I. (2002) 'Religion and the Counter-Intuitive', in I. Pyysiäinen and V. Anttonen (eds.), *Current Approaches in the Cognitive Science of Religion.* London and New York: 110–32.

Quet, M.-H. (1993) 'Parler de soi pour louer son dieu. Le cas d'Aelius Aristide', in Baslez *et al.* (eds.): 211–51.

(2001) 'Athéna, inspiratrice onirique d'un orateur "aimé des dieux" au IIe siècle de notre ère', in M. Woronoff, S. Follet and J. Jouanna (eds.), *Dieux, héros et médecins grecs.* Paris: 211–25.

Queyrel, F. (2005) *L'Autel de Pergame. Images et pouvoir en Grèce d'Asie.* Paris.

Quinn, J. C. (2007) 'Herms, Kouroi and the Political Anatomy of Athens', *Greece & Rome* 54. 1: 82–105.

Raubitschek, A. E. (1941) 'Phryne', *RE* 20. 1: 893–907.

(1942) 'An Original Work of Endoios', *AJA* 46: 245–53.

Rausch, H. (1982) *Theoria. Von ihrer sakralen zur philosophischen Bedeutung.* Munich.

Raynor, D. H. (1984) 'Moeragenes and Philostratus. Two views of Apollonius of Tyana', *CQ* 34: 222–6.

Reinhardt, K. (1956) 'Zum homerischen Aphroditehymnus', in *Festschrift Bruno Snell zum 60. Geburtstag.* Munich: 1–14.

Remus, H. (1996) 'Voluntary Association and Networks. Aelius Aristides at the Asclepieion in Pergamum', in J. S. Kloppenborg and S. G. Wilson (eds.), *Voluntary Associations in the Graeco-Roman World.* London and New York: 146–75.

Renberg, G. H. (2003) '"Commanded by the Gods". An Epigraphical Study of Dreams.' PhD diss., Duke University.

Renfrew, C. and J. F. Cherry (eds.) (1986) *Peer Polity Interaction and Socio-Political Change*. Cambridge.

Reynolds, M. (2002) *The Sappho Companion*. London.

Rhomaios, K. A. (1911) 'Arkadikoi ermai', *ArchEph*, 149–59.

Richards, G. C. (1929) 'Timakhidas', in J. U. Powell and E. A. Barber (eds.), *New Chapters in the History of Greek Literature*. 2nd ser. Oxford: 76–82.

Richardson, N. J. (1974) *The Homeric Hymn to Demeter*. Oxford.

Richter, G. M. A. (1966) 'The Pheidian Zeus at Olympia', *Hesperia* 35: 166–70.

Ridgway, B. S. (1970) *The Severe Style in Greek Sculpture*. Princeton.

   (1977) *The Archaic Style in Greek Sculpture*. Princeton.

   (1981) *Fifth Century Styles in Greek Sculpture*. Princeton.

   (1983) 'Painterly and Pictorial in Greek Relief Sculpture', in W. G. Moon (ed.), *Ancient Greek Art and Iconography*. Madison, WI: 193–208.

   (1989) 'Parthenon and Parthenos', in N. Basgelen and M. Lugal (eds.), *Festschrift für Jale Inan*. Istanbul: 295–305.

   (1992) 'Images of Athena on the Acropolis', in Neils (ed.): 119–42.

   (1997) *Fourth-Century Styles in Greek Sculpture*. London.

   (2004) *Second Chance. Greek Sculptural Studies Revisited*. London.

   (2005) '"Periklean" Cult Images and their Media', in J. M. Barringer and J. M. Hurwit (eds.), *Periklean Athens and Its Legacy. Problems and Perspectives*. Austin: 111–18.

Rigsby, K. J. (1996) *Asylia. Territorial Inviolability in the Hellenistic World*. Berkeley and Los Angeles.

Rist, J. M. (2001) 'Plutarch's "Amatorius". A Commentary on Plato's Theories of Love?', *CQ* 51: 557–75.

Robert, C. (1893) 'Sosipolis in Olympia', *AthMitt* 18: 37–45.

   (1897–1919) *Einzelmythen. Die antiken Sarkophagreliefs* 3.1–3. 3 vols. Berlin.

Robert, L. (1937) *Études anatoliennes. Recherches sur les inscriptions grecques de l'Asie Mineure*. Paris.

   (1966) 'Un décret d'Ilion et un papyrus concernant des cultes royaux', in *Essays in Honor of Bradford Welles*. American Studies in Papyrology 1. New Haven: 175–211. Repr. in L. Robert (1990), *Opera minor selecta*. Vol. vii. Amsterdam: 599–635.

Robertson, M. (1975) *A History of Greek Art*. London and Cambridge.

   (1979) 'Two Question-Marks on the Parthenon', in G. Kopcke and M. B. Moore (eds.), *Studies in Classical Art and Archaeology. A Tribute to Peter Heinrich von Blanckenhagen*. Locust Valley, NY: 78–87.

   (1993) 'What is "Hellenistic" about Hellenistic Art?', in Green (ed.): 67–110.

Robertson, N. (1996a) 'Athena and Early Greek Society. Palladion Shrines and Promontory Shrines', in M. Dillon (ed.), *Religion in the Ancient World. New Themes and Approaches*. Amsterdam: 383–475.

   (1996b) 'Athena's Shrines and Festivals', in Neils (ed.): 56–65.

(2001) 'Athena as Weather-Goddess. The *Aigis* in Myth and Ritual', in Deacy and Villing: 29–55.

Rockmore, T. (2004) *On Foundationalism. A Strategy for Metaphysical Realism.* Oxford.

Rogers, G. M. (1991) *The Sacred Identity of Ephesos. Foundation Myths of a Roman City.* London and New York.

Rogge, S. (1995) *Die Attischen Sarkophage. Achill und Hippolytos.* Die antiken Sarkophagreliefs 9.1.1. Berlin.

Rohde, E. (1974) *Der griechische Roman und seine Vorläufer.* 4th edn. Darmstadt.

Romano, I. B. (1980) 'Early Greek Cult Images.' PhD diss., University of Pennsylvania.

(1988) 'Early Greek Cult Images and Cult Practices', in R. Hägg, N. Marinatos and G. C. Nordquist (eds.), *Early Greek Cult Practice. Proceedings of the Fifth International Symposium at the Swedish Institute at Athens, 26–29 June, 1986.* Stockholm: 127–34.

Romm, J. (1992) *The Edges of the Earth in Ancient Thought. Geography, Exploration, and Fiction.* Princeton.

Roosevelt, C. H. (2006) 'Symbolic Door Stelae and Graveside Monuments in Western Anatolia', *AJA* 110: 65–91.

Rosati, G. (1983) *Narciso e Pigmalione. Illusione e spettacolo nelle Metamorfosi di Ovidio.* Florence.

Rostovtzeff, M. (1920) 'Ἐπιφάνειαι', *Klio* 16: 203–6.

Rotondaro, S. (1998) *Il sogno in Platone. Fisiologia di una metafora.* Naples.

Roussel, P. (1924) 'La Fondation des Sôtéria de Delphes', *REA* 26: 97–111.

(1931) 'Le Miracle de Zeus Panamaros', *BCH* 55: 70–116.

Rousselle, A. (2001) 'Images as Education in the Roman Empire', in Too (ed.): 373–403.

Roussos, R. (1999) 'Images of the Female Body in Greek Art of the Fourth Century B.C. and the Female Spectator.' PhD diss., Courtauld Institute of Art, London.

Rouveret, A. (1989) *Histoire et imaginaire de la peinture ancienne. Ve siècle av. J.C.–1er siècle ap. J.-C.* Rome.

Roux, G. (1960) 'Qu'est-ce qu'un *kolossos*?', *REA* 62: 5–40.

Rückert, B. 1998. *Die Herme im öffentlichen und privaten Leben der Griechen. Untersuchungen zum Funktion der griechischen Herme als Grenzmal, Inschriftenträger und Kultbild des Hermes.* Regensburg.

Rudhardt, J. (1992) *Notions fondamentales de la pensée religieuse et actes constitutifs du culte dans la Grèce antique.* 2nd edn. Paris.

(1996) 'Le Préambule de la *Théogonie*. La vocation du poète. Le langage des Muses', in F. Blaise, P. Judet de La Combe and P. Rousseau (eds.), *Le Métier du mythe. Lectures d'Hésiode.* Paris: 25–39.

Russell, D. A. (ed.) (1990a) *Antonine Literature.* Oxford.

(1990b) 'Aristides and the Prose Hymn', in Russell (ed.): 199–220.

(1992) *Dio Chrysostom. Orations VII, XII, XXXVI.* Cambridge.

Russell, D. A. and N. G. Wilson (1981) *Menander Rhetor*. Oxford.

Rusten, J. (2004) 'Living in the Past. Allusive Narratives and Elusive Authorities in the World of the *Heroikos*', in Aitken and Maclean (eds.): 143–58.

Rusyaeva, A. S. (2003) 'The Temple of Achilles on the Island of Leuke in the Black Sea', *Ancient Civilisations from Scythia to Serbia* 9: 1–16.

Rutherford, I. (1995) 'Theoric Crisis. The Dangers of Pilgrimage in Greek Religion and Society', *Studi e Materiali di Storia delle Religioni* 61: 276–92.

(1999) '"To the Land of Zeus". Patterns of Pilgrimage in Aelius Aristides', *Aevum Antiquum* 12: 133–48.

(2000) '*Theōria* and *Darsan*. Pilgrimage and Vision in Greece and India', *CQ* 50: 133–46.

(2001) 'Tourism and the Sacred. Pausanias and the Traditions of Greek Pilgrimage', in Alcock *et al.* (eds.): 40–52.

(2003) 'Pilgrimage in Greco-Roman Egypt. New Perspectives on Graffiti from the Memnonion at Abydos', in R. Matthews and C. Roerner (eds.), *Ancient Perspectives on Egypt*. London: 171–90.

(2009) 'Black Sails to Achilles. Aspects of the Thessalian Pilgrimage in Philostratus' *Heroikos*', in Bowie and Elsner (eds.): 230–47.

(in press) 'Zeus-Amun and the Ram. Egyptian Epiphanies and Greek Perceptions of Them', in Petridou and Platt (eds.).

Ruyt, F. de (1931) 'L'Idée du "bivium" et le symbole pythagoricien de la lettre Y', *Revue Belge de Philologie* 10: 137–44.

Saake, H. (1972) *Sapphostudien. Forschungsgeschichtliche, biographische und literarästhetische Untersuchungen*. Paderborn.

Saïd, S. (1987) 'Deux noms de l'image en grec ancien. Idole et icône', *CRAI*: 309–30.

(ed.) (1991) Ἑλληνισμός. *Quelques jalons pour une histoire de l'identité grecque. Actes du Colloque de Strasbourg, 25–27 octobre 1989*. Leiden.

(2008) 'Aristides' Uses of Myths', in Harris and Holmes (eds.): 51–67.

Salapata, G. (1997) 'Hero Warriors from Corinth and Lakonia', *Hesperia* 66: 245–60.

Saller, R., L. Brink and D. Green (eds.) (2008) *Texts and Artifacts in Context. Studies of Roman, Jewish, and Christian Burials*. Berlin and New York.

Salomon, N. (1997) 'Making a World of Difference. Gender, Asymmetry and the Greek Nude', in A. L. Koloski-Ostrow and C. L. Lyons (eds.), *Naked Truths. Women, Sexuality and Gender in Classical Art and Archaeology*. London: 197–219.

Salzman-Mitchell, P. B. (2005) *A Web of Fantasies. Gaze, Image and Gender in Ovid's Metamorphoses*. Columbus, OH.

(2008) 'A Whole out of Pieces. Pygmalion's Ivory Statue in Ovid's *Metamorphoses*', *Arethusa* 41. 2: 291–311.

Sandbach, F. H. (ed.) (1969) *Plutarch's Moralia*. Vol. xv. *Fragments*. Loeb Classical Library. Cambridge, MA.

(1971) 'Phantasia Katalēptikē, in A. Long (ed.), *Problems in Stoicism.* London: 9–21.

Sansone, D. (2004) 'Heracles at the Y', *JHS* 124: 125–42.

Sarikakis, T. C. (1975) Χιακά Χρονικά 7: 14–27.

Schachter, A. and J. Bingen (eds.) (1992) *Le Sanctuaire grec.* Entretiens sur l'antiquité classique 37. Geneva.

Schauenburg, K. (1977) 'Zu Götterstatuen auf unteritalischen Vasen', *AA*: 285–97.

(1980) 'Porträts auf römischen Sarkophagen', in *Eikones. Studien zum griechischen und römischen Bildnis. Hans Jucker zum sechzigsten Geburtstag gewidmet.* Zwölftes Beiheft zur Halbjahresschrift Antike Kunst. Bern: 153–9.

Scheer, T. S. (1993) *Mythische Vorväter. Zur Bedeutung griechischer Heroenmythen im Selbstverständnis kleinasiatischer Städte.* Munich.

(2000) *Die Gottheit und ihr Bild. Untersuchungen zur Funktion griechischer Kultbilder in Religion und Politik.* Zetemata 105. Munich.

(2003) 'The Past in a Hellenistic Present. Myth and Local Tradition', in Erskine (ed.): 216–31.

Schefold, K. (1937) 'Statuen auf Vasenbildern', *JDAI* 52: 30–75.

(1956) 'Vorbilder römischer Landschaftsmalerei', *Athenische Mitteilungen* 71: 211–31.

(1981) *Die Göttersage in der klassischen und hellenistischen Kunst.* Basel.

Scheid, J. (2003) *An Introduction to Roman Religion.* Trans. J. Lloyd. Bloomington.

Scheid, J. and J. Svenbro (1996) *The Craft of Zeus. Myths of Weaving and Fabric.* Trans. C. Volk. Cambridge, MA.

Schepens, G. and K. Delcroix (1996) 'Ancient Paradoxography. Origins, Evolution, Production and Consumption', in O. Pecere and A. Stramaglia (eds.), *La letteratura di consumo nel mondo greco-latino.* Cassino: 343–460.

Schirren, T. (2005) *Philosophos Bios. Die antike Philosophenbiographie als symbolische Form. Studien zur Vita Apollonii des Philostrat.* Heidelberg.

(2009) 'Irony versus Eulogy. The *Vita Apollonii* as Metabiographical Fiction', in Demoen and Praet (eds.): 161–86.

Schlam, C. (1976) *Cupid and Psyche. Apuleius and the Monuments.* University Park, PA.

(1992) *The Metamorphoses of Apuleius. On Making an Ass of Oneself.* London.

Schmaltz, B. (1997) 'Die Parthenos des Phidias. Zwischen Kult und Repräsentanz', in W. Hoepfner (ed.), *Kult und Kultbauten auf der Akropolis. Internationales Symposion vom 7. bis 9. Juli 1995 in Berlin.* Berlin: 25–30.

Schmid, W. (1887–97) *Der Atticismus in seinen Hauptvertreten.* 4 vols. Stuttgart.

Schmidt, T.-M. (1990) 'Der späte Beginn und der vorzeitige Abbrich der Arbeiten am Pergamonaltar', in B. Andreae (ed.), *Phyromachos-Probleme. Mit einem Anhang zur Datierung des grossen Altares von Pergamon.* RM 31. Berlin: 142–62.

Schmitt-Pantel, P. (1985) 'Banquet et cité grecque', *MÉFRA* 97: 135–58.

Schmitz, T. (1997) *Bildung und Macht. Zur sozialen und politischen Funktion der zweiten Sophistik in der griechischen Welt der Kaiserzeit.* Munich.

(1999) 'Performing History in the Second Sophistic', in M. Zimmermann (ed.), *Geschichtsschreibung und politischer Wandel im 3. Jh. n. Chr.* Stuttgart: 71–92.

Schnapp, A. (1994) 'Are Statues Animated? The Psychology of Statues in Ancient Greece', in C. Renfrew and E. B. W. Zubrow (eds.), *The Ancient Mind. Elements of Cognitive Archaeology.* Cambridge: 40–4.

Schneider-Herrmann, G. (1972) 'Kultstatue im Tempel auf italischen Vasenbildern', *BABesch* 47: 31–42.

Schofield, M. (1986) 'Cicero for and against Divination', *JRS* 76: 47–65.

(1991) *The Stoic Idea of the City.* Cambridge.

Schollmeyer, P. (2001) *Antike Gespanndenkmäler.* Hamburg.

Scholten, J. B. (2000) *The Politics of Plunder. Aitolians and Their Koinon in the Early Hellenistic Era, 279–217 B.C.* Berkeley and Los Angeles.

Schouten, J. (1967) *The Rod and Serpent of Asklepios, Symbol of Medicine.* Amsterdam and New York.

Schrader, H. (1941) 'Das Zeusbild des Phidias in Olympia', *JDAI* 56: 1–71.

Schröder, H. O. (1987) 'Das Odysseusbild des Ailios Aristides', *RhM* 130: 350–6.

Schultz, P. and R. von den Hoff (2007) *Early Hellenistic Portraiture. Image, Style, Context.* Cambridge.

Schweitzer, B. (1925) 'Der bildende Künstler und der Begriff des Künstlerischen in der Antike', *Neue Heidelberger Jahrbücher:* 28–132.

(1934) 'Mimesis und Phantasia', *Philologus* 89: 286–300.

Scott, K. (1928a) 'The Deification of Demetrius Poliorcetes. Part I', *AJPh* 49: 137–66.

(1928b) 'The Deification of Demetrius Poliorcetes. Part II', *AJPh* 49: 217–39.

Seaford, R. (1996) *Euripides. Bacchae.* Warminster.

(2006) *Dionysos.* London.

(in press) 'Some Thoughts on Dionysiac Epiphany. From the Many to the One', in Petridou and Platt (eds.).

Segal, C. P. (1974) 'The *Homeric Hymn to Aphrodite.* A Structuralist Approach', *CW* 67: 205–12.

(1997) *Dionysiac Poetics and Euripides' Bacchae.* Rev. edn. Princeton.

Segre, M. (1927) 'La più antica tradizione sull'invasione gallica', *Historia* 1.4: 18–42.

(1948) 'L'Institution des Nikephoria de Pergame', *Hellenica* 5: 102–28.

Seiler, F. (1992) *Casa degli Amorini dorati (VI 16, 7.38).* Häuser in Pompeji 5. Munich.

Sens, A. (2005) 'The Art of Poetry and the Poetry of Art. The Unity and Poetics of Posidippus' Statue-poems', in Gutzwiller (ed.): 206–2.

Settis, S. (1972) 'Severo Alessandro e i suoi Lari (*SHA, SA* 20.2–3)', *Athenaeum* 50: 237–61.

Shapiro, H. A. (1980) 'Jason's Cloak', *TAPA* 110: 263–86.

(1989) *Art and Cult under the Tyrants in Athens.* Mainz am Rhein.

Sharrock, A. (1991a) 'The Love of Creation', *Ramus* 20.2: 169–82.

(1991b) 'Womanufacture', *JRS* 81: 36–49.

(1996) 'Representing Metamorphosis', in Elsner (ed.): 103–30.

Shaw, G. (1985) 'Theurgy. Rituals of Unification in the Neoplatonism of Iamblichus', *Traditio* 41: 1–28.

(1995) *Theurgy and the Soul. The Neoplatonism of Iamblichus.* University Park, PA.

(1999) 'Neoplatonic Theurgy and Dionysius the Areopagite', *Journal of Early Christian Studies* 7: 573–99.

Shaya, J. (2002) 'The Lindos Stele and the Lost Treasures of Athena. Catalogs, Collections, and Local History.' PhD diss., University of Michigan.

(2005) 'The Greek Temple as Museum. The Case of the Legendary Treasure of Athena from Lindos', *AJA* 109: 432–42.

Sheppard, A. (1982) 'Proclus' Attitude to Theurgy', *CQ* 32: 212–24.

Shumate, N. (1996) *Crisis and Conversion in Apuleius' Metamorphoses.* Ann Arbor.

Sichtermann, K. (1966) *Späte Endymion-Sarkophage. Methodisches zur Interpretation.* Deutsche Beiträge zur Altertumswissenschaft 19. Baden-Baden.

(1992) *Die mythologischen Sarkophage. Apollon, Ares, Bellerophon, Daidalos, Endymion, Ganymed, Giganten, Grazien.* Die antiken Sarkophagreliefs 12.2. Berlin.

Sichtermann, H., and G. Koch (1975) *Griechische Mythen auf römischen Sarkophagen.* Tübingen.

Sidebottom, H. (2002) 'Pausanias. Past, Present, and Closure', *CQ* 52: 494–9.

(2009) 'Philostratus and the Symbolic Roles of the Sophist and Philosopher', in Bowie and Elsner (eds.): 69–99.

Simon, E. (1975) *Pergamon und Hesiod.* Mainz.

(1980) *Die Götter der Griechen.* 2nd edn. Munich.

(1985) 'Hekate in Athen', *Athenische Mitteilungen* 100: 271–84.

Simon, G. (1988) *Le Regard, l'être, et l'apparence dans l'optique de l'antiquité.* Paris.

Sinos, R. H. (1993) 'Divine Selection. Epiphany and Politics in Archaic Greece', in Dougherty and Kurke (eds.): 73–91.

Skinner, M. (1991) 'Aphrodite Garlanded', in F. de Martino (ed.), *Rose di Pieria.* Bari: 77–96.

(2001) 'Ladies' Day at the Art Institute. Theocritus, Herodas, and the Gendered Gaze', in A. Lardinois and L. McClure (eds.), *Making Silence Speak. Women's Voices in Greek Literature and Society.* Princeton and Oxford: 201–22.

Slater, N. (1998) 'Passion and Petrifaction. The Gaze in Apuleius', *CPh* 93: 18–48.

Slater, W. J. (1988) 'The Epiphany of Demosthenes', *Phoenix* 152: 126–30.

Slater, W. J. and D. Summa (2006) 'Crowns at Magnesia', *GRBS* 46: 275–99.

Smelik, K. A. D. and E. A. Hemelrijk (1984) '"Who Knows Not What Monsters Demented Egypt Worships?" Opinions on Egyptian Animal Worship in Antiquity as Part of the Ancient Conception of Egypt', *ANRW* 2.17.4: 1852–2000.

Smith, G. (2000) 'Gaetano Baccani's "Systematization" of the Piazza del Duomo in Florence', *Journal of the Society of Architectural Historians* 59: 454–77.

Smith, J. Z. (1978) 'Towards Interpreting Demonic Powers in Hellenistic and Roman Antiquity', *ANRW* 2.16.1: 425–39.

Smith, M. (1978) *Jesus the Magician*. London.

Smith, P. (1981a) 'Aineidai as Patrons of *Iliad XX* and the *Homeric Hymn to Aphrodite*', *HSCP* 85: 17–58.

  (1981b) *Nursling of Mortality. A Study of the Homeric Hymn to Aphrodite*. Studien zur klassischen Philologie 3. Frankfurt.

Smith, R. R. R. (1988) *Hellenistic Royal Portraits*. Oxford Monographs on Classical Archaeology. Oxford.

  (1991) *Hellenistic Sculpture. A Handbook*. London.

  (1993) 'Kings and Philosophers', in Bulloch *et al.* (eds.): 202–11.

  (1998) 'Cultural Choice and Political Identity in Honorific Portrait Statues in the Greek East in the Second Century AD', *JRS* 68: 56–93.

  (1999) Review of P. Zanker (1995b), *Gnomon* 71.5: 448–57.

Snell, B. B. (1967) '*Vita Activa* and *Vita Contemplativa* in Euripides' *Antiope*', in *Scenes from Greek Drama*. Berkeley: 70–98.

Snowden, F. M., Jr (1991) 'Témoignages iconographiques sur les populations noires dans l'Antiquité gréco-romains', in *L'Image du noire dans l'art occidental*. Tome I: *Des pharaons à la chute de l'Empire romain*. Paris: 133–245.

Solmsen, F. (1940) 'Some Works of Philostratus the Elder', *TAPA* 71: 556–72.

Sophocleous, S. (1985) *Atlas des représentations chypro-archaiques des divinités*. Gothenburg.

Sourvinou-Inwood, C. (1978) 'Persephone and Aphrodite at Locri. A Model for Personality Definitions in Greek Religion', *JHS* 98: 101–21.

  (1991) '*Reading' Greek Culture. Texts and Images, Rituals and Myths*. Oxford.

  (1995) '*Reading' Greek Death. To the End of the Classical Period*. Oxford.

  (2003) *Tragedy and Athenian Religion*. Lanham, MD.

Sowa, C. A. (1984) *Traditional Themes and the Homeric Hymns*. Chicago.

Spawforth, A. J. S. and S. Walker (1985) 'The World of the Panhellenion, I. Athens and Eleusis', *JRS* 75: 78–104.

  (1986) 'The World of the Panhellenion, II. Three Dorian Cities', *JRS* 76: 88–105.

Speyer, W. (1974) 'Zum Bild des Apollonios von Tyana bei Heiden und Christen', *Jahrbuch für Antike und Christentum* 17: 47–63.

  (1975) 'Myrons Kuh in der antiken Literatur und bei Goethe', *Arcadia* 10: 171–9.

  (1980) 'Die Hilfe und Epiphanie einer Gottheit, eines Heroen und eines Heiligen in der Schlacht', in E. Dassmann and K. Suso Frank (eds.), *Pietas. Festschrift für B. Kötting*. Münster (Westfalen): 55–7.

Spivey, N. (1996) *Understanding Greek Sculpture. Ancient Meanings, Modern Readings*. London.

Squire, M. (2009) *Image and Text in the Graeco-Roman World*. Cambridge.

(2010) 'Making Myron's Cow Moo? Ecphrastic Epigram and the Poetics of Simulation', *AJPh* 131: 589–634.

Staab, G. (2002) *Pythagoras in der Spätantike. Studien zu De vita Pythagorica des Iamblichos von Chalkis.* Munich.

Staffieri, G. M. (1976) 'Alcuni puntualizzazioni sul principato teocratico di Olba nella Cilicia Trachea', *Quaderni Ticinesi di Numismatica e Antichità Classiche* 5: 169–68.

(1978) *La monetazione di Olba nella Cilicia Trachea.* Quaderni Ticinesi di Numismatica e Antichità Classiche. Lugano.

Stähler, K. (1978) 'Überlegungen zur architektonischen Gestalt des Pergamonaltares', in *Studien zur Religion und Kultur Kleinasiens. Festschrift für F. K. Dörner.* Études préliminaires sur les religions orientales dans l'Empire romain 61.2. Leiden: 838–67.

Staikos, K. S. (2000) *The Great Libraries. From Antiquity to the Renaissance.* London and New Castle, DE.

Stambaugh, J. E. (1972) *Sarapis under the Early Ptolemies.* Leiden.

Stanley, K. (1976) 'The Role of Aphrodite in Sappho Fr. 1', *GRBS* 17: 305–21.

Stark, I. (1989) 'Religiöse Elemente im antiken Roman', in H. Kuck (ed.), *Der antike Roman.* Berlin: 135–49.

Stehle, E. and A. Day (1996) 'Women Looking at Women. Women's Ritual and Temple Sculpture', in Kampen (ed.): 102–16.

Steiner, D. T. (2001) *Images in Mind. Statues in Archaic and Classical Literature and Thought.* Princeton and Oxford.

Steinleitner, F. (1913) *Die Beichte im Zusammenhang mit der sakralen Rechtspflege in der Antike. Ein Beitrag zur näheren Kenntnis kleinasiatisch-orientalischer Kulte der Kaiserzeit.* Leipzig.

Stemmer, K. (1992) *Casa dell'Ara massima (vi 16, 15–17).* Häuser in Pompeji 6. Munich.

Stephens, S. A. and J. J. Winkler (1995) *Ancient Greek Novels. The Fragments. Introduction, Text, Translation, and Commentary.* Princeton.

Stevens, A. (2002) 'Telling Presences. Narrating Divine Epiphany in Homer and Beyond.' PhD diss., University of Cambridge.

(in press) 'Making Sense of Divine Action in Homer', in Petridou and Platt (eds.).

Stewart, A. (1979) *Attika. Studies in Athenian Sculpture of the Hellenistic Age.* London.

(1986) 'When is a Kouros not an Apollo? The Tenea "Apollo" Revisited', in M. A. del Chiaro (ed.), *Corinthiaca. Studies in Honor of Darrel A. Amyx.* New York: 54–70.

(1990) *Greek Sculpture. An Exploration.* 2 vols. New Haven.

(1993) 'Narration and Allusion in the Hellenistic Baroque', in P. J. Holliday (ed.), *Narrative and Event in Ancient Art.* Cambridge: 130–74.

(1995) 'Rape?', in E. Reeder (ed.), *Pandora. Women in Classical Greece.* Baltimore and Princeton: 65–79.

(1996) 'Reflections', in Kampen (ed.): 136–54.

(1997) *Art, Desire and the Body in Ancient Greece.* Cambridge.

(2000) '*Pergamo Ara Marmorea Magna.* On the Date, Reconstruction, and Functions of the Great Altar of Pergamon', in Grummond and Ridgway (eds.): 32–57.

(2005) 'Posidippus and the Truth in Sculpture', in Gutzwiller (ed.): 183–205.

(2008) 'The Persian and Carthaginian Invasions of 480 b.c.e. and the Beginning of the Classical Style. Part 2, The Finds from Other Sites in Athens, Attica, Elsewhere in Greece, and on Sicily; Part 3, The Severe Style: Motivations and Meaning', *AJA* 112: 581–615.

Stewart, C. (2002) 'Erotic Dreams and Nightmares from Antiquity to the Present', *Journal of the Royal Anthropological Institute* 8 (n.s.): 279–309.

Stewart, P. (2003) *Statues in Roman Society. Representation and Response.* Oxford.

Stiglitz, R. (1967) *Die grossen Göttinen Arkadiens. Der Kultname Megalai Theai und seine Grundlagen.* Vienna.

Stoddard, K. (2004) *The Narrative Voice in the Theogony of Hesiod.* Mnemosyne Suppl. 255. Leiden.

(2005) 'The Muses and the Mortal Narrator: How Gods Relate to Humankind in the *Theogony*', *Helios* 32: 1–28.

Stoneman, R. (1995) 'Riddles in Bronze and Stone. Monuments and their Interpretation in the *Alexander Romance*', *Groningen Colloquia on the Novel* 6: 159–70.

Strocka, V. M. (2000) 'Noch einmal zur Bibliothek von Pergamon', *AA*: 155–65.

Strong, D. (1992) *Roman Art.* 3rd edn. New Haven.

Summers, D. (2003) *Real Spaces. World Art History and the Rise of Western Modernism.* London.

(2007) *Vision, Reflection and Imagination in Western Painting.* Chapel Hill.

Svenbro, J. (1976) *La Parole et le marbre. Aux origines de la poétique grecque.* Lund. Rev. Italian edn: *La parola e il marmo. Alle origini della poetica greca.* Turin, 1984.

(1993) *Phrasikleia. An Anthropology of Reading in Ancient Greece.* Trans. J. Lloyd. Ithaca, NY.

Svoronos, J. N. (1908) *Das Athener Nationalmuseum.* 2 vols. Athens.

Swain, S. (1989) 'Plutarch. Chance, Providence, and History', *AJPh* 110: 272–302.

(1996) *Hellenism and Empire. Language, Classicism and Power in the Greek World, a.d. 50–250.* Oxford.

(1997a) 'Biography and Biographic in the Literature of the Roman Empire', in Swain (ed.): 1–37.

(ed.) (1997b) *Portraits. Biographical Representation in the Greek and Latin Literature of the Roman Empire.* Oxford.

(1999) 'Defending Hellenism. Philostratus, *In Honour of Apollonius*', in M. Edwards, M. Goodman and S. Price (eds.), *Apologetics in the Roman Empire. Pagans, Jews and Christians.* Oxford: 157–96.

(ed.) (2000) *Dio Chrysostom. Politics, Letters and Philosophy.* Oxford.

Swain, S., S. Harrison and J. Elsner (eds.) (2007) *Severan Culture.* Cambridge.

Szarmach, M. (1985) *Maximos von Tyros. Eine literarische Monographie.* Torun.

Takács, S. (2005) 'Divine and Human Feet. Records of Pilgrims Honouring Isis', in Elsner and Rutherford (eds.): 353–69.

Talbert, C. H. (1978) 'Biographies of Philosophers and Rulers as Instruments of Religious Propaganda in Mediterranean Antiquity', *ANRW* 2.16.2: 1619–51.

Tanner, J. (2001) 'Nature, Culture and the Body in Classical Greek Religious Art', *World Archaeology* 33: 257–76.

(2006) *The Invention of Art History in Ancient Greece. Religion, Society and Artistic Rationalisation.* Cambridge.

Taylor, R. (2008) *The Moral Mirror of Roman Art.* Cambridge.

Thalmann, W. G. (1984) *Conventions of Form and Thought in Early Greek Epic Poetry.* Baltimore and London.

Thein, K. (2002) 'Gods and Painters. Philostratus the Elder, Stoic *Phantasia* and the Strategy of Describing', *Ramus* 31: 136–45.

Theissen, G. (1983) *The Miracle Stories of the Early Christian Tradition.* Trans. F. McDonagh. Philadelphia.

Themelis, P. G. (1993) 'Ὁ Δαμοφῶν καὶ ἡ δραστηριότητά του στὴν Ἀρκαδία', in Palagia and Coulson (eds.): 99–109.

(1994) 'Damophon of Messene. New Evidence', in K. A. Sheedy (ed.), *Archaeology in the Peloponnese. New Excavations and Research.* Oxford: 1–37.

(1996) 'Damophon', in Palagia and Pollitt (eds.): 154–85.

(2003) 'Ὁ Δαμοφῶν στὴν Οἰάνθεια', in *Τὸ Γαλαξείδι ἀπὸ τὴν ἀρχαϊότητα ἑὼς σήμερα. Πρακτικὰ τοῦ πρώτου ἐπιστημονικοῦ συνεδρίου (Γαλαξείδι, 29–30 Σεπτεμβρίου 2000).* Athens: 27–33.

Thimmer, D. (1946) 'The Masters of the Pergamene Gigantomachy', *AJA* 50: 345–57.

Thomas, R. (2000) *Herodotus in Context. Ethnography, Science and the Art of Persuasion.* Cambridge.

Thomas, Y. (2004) '*Res Religiosae.* On the Categories of Religion and Commerce in Roman Law', in A. Pottage and M. Mundy (eds.), *Law, Anthropology and the Constitution of the Social. Making Persons and Things.* Cambridge and New York: 40–72.

Thonemann, P. (2007) 'Magnesia and the Greeks of Asia (*I.Magnesia* 16.16), *GRBS* 47: 151–60.

Tigges, W. (ed.) (1999) *Moments of Moment. Aspects of the Literary Epiphany.* Amsterdam and Atlanta, GA.

Todd, S. (2004) 'Revisiting the Herms and the Mysteries', in D. L. Cairns and R. A. Knox (eds.), *Law, Rhetoric, and Comedy in Classical Athens. Essays in Honour of Douglas M. MacDowell.* Swansea: 87–102.

Todisco, L. (1993) *Scultura greca del IV secolo.* Milan.

Tomaselli, S. and R. Porter (eds.) (1986) *Rape. An Historical and Social Enquiry.* Oxford.

Tomlinson, R. A. (1963) 'The Doric Order. Hellenistic Critics and Criticism', *JHS* 83: 133–45.

Too, Y. L. (1996) 'Statues, Mirrors, Gods. Controlling Images in Apuleius', in Elsner (ed.): 133–52.

(ed.) (2001) *Education in Greek and Roman Antiquity.* Leiden, Boston and Cologne.

Too, Y. L. and N. R. Livingstone (eds.) (1988) *Pedagogy and Power. Rhetorics of Classical Learning.* Cambridge.

Torelli, M. (1998) 'L'Asklepieion di Messene, lo scultore Damofonte e Pausania', in G. Capecchi (ed.), *In memoria di Enrico Paribeni.* Rome: 465–83.

Torelli, M. and D. Musti (1991) *Pausania. Guida della Grecia. Libro IV: La Messenia.* Milan.

Toynbee, J. M. C. (1971) *Death and Burial in the Roman World.* Ithaca, NY.

(1977) 'Greek Myth in Roman Stone', *Latomus* 36: 377–412.

Toynbee, J. M. C. and J. B. Ward-Perkins (1956) *The Shrine of St Peter and the Vatican Excavations.* London.

Traill, D. A. (1998) 'Callimachus' Singing Sea (*Hymn* 2.106)', *CPh* 93: 215–22.

Trapp, M. (1990) 'Plato's *Phaedrus* in Second-Century Greek Literature', in Russell (ed.): 141–73.

(1997) *The Philosophical Orations of Maximus of Tyre.* Oxford.

(1999) 'Philosophical Sermons. The "Dialexeis" of Maximus of Tyre', *ANRW* 2.34.3: 1945–76.

(2000) 'Plato in Dio', in Swain (ed.): 213–39.

Travlos, J. (1971) *Pictorial Dictionary of Ancient Athens.* London.

Trendall, A. D. and A. Cambitoglou (1966) 'The Painter of the Birth of Dionysos', in *Mélanges offerts à Kazimierz Michalowski.* Warsaw: 675–99.

(1978) *The Red-Figured Vases of Apulia.* vol. I: *Early and Middle Apulian.* Oxford.

Trendelenburg, A. (1914) *Pausanias in Olympia.* Berlin.

Trimble, J. (2009) *Replicating Women in the Roman Empire.* Cambridge.

Troiani, L. (1988) *Due studi di storiografia e di religione antiche.* Como.

Turcan, R. (1966) *Les Sarcophages romains à représentations dionysiaques. Essai de chronologie et d'histoire religieuse.* Paris.

(1999) *Messages d'outre-tombe. L'iconographie des sarcophages romains.* Paris.

Turkeltaub, D. (2003) 'The Gods' Radiance Manifest. An Examination of the Narrative Pattern Underlying the Homeric Divine Epiphany Scenes.' PhD diss., Cornell University.

(2005) 'The Syntax and Semantics of Homeric Glowing Eyes. *Iliad* 1.200', *AJPh* 126: 157–86.

Turner, S. (2007) 'Lines of Sight. An Encounter with a Classical Attic Grave Stele', *Archaeological Review from Cambridge* 22: 92–106.

(2009) 'Classical Attic Grave Stelai. Gender, Death and the Viewer.' PhD diss., University of Cambridge.

Tylor, E. B. (1871) *Primitive Culture. Researches into the Development of Mythology, Philosophy, Religion, Art, and Custom.* 2 vols. London.

Tzifopoulos, Y. Z. (1991) 'Pausanias as a "Steloskopas". An Epigraphical Commentary of Pausanias' Eliakon A' and B'.' PhD diss., The Ohio State University.

  (1993) 'Mummius' Dedications at Olympia and Pausanias' Attitude to the Romans', *GRBS* 34: 93–100.

Tzortzi, K. (2000) *The Temple of Apollo Epikourios. A Journey Through Time and Space.* Trans. D. Hardy. Athens.

Ugolini, G. (1995) *Untersuchungen zur Figur des Sehers Teiresias.* Tübingen.

Ustinova, Y. (1999) *The Supreme Gods of the Bosporan Kingdom. Celestial Aphrodite and the Most High God.* Leiden.

Valgiglio, E. (1988) *Divinità e religione in Plutarco.* Geneva.

van der Ben, N. (1980) 'De Homerische Aphrodite-hymne I – De Aeneas-passages in de Ilias', *Lampas* 13: 40–77.

  (1986) 'Hymn to Aphrodite 36–291. Notes on the *Pars Epica* of the *Homeric Hymn to Aphrodite*', *Mnemosyne* 39: 1–41.

Van der Stockt, L. (2009) '"Never the Twain shall Meet"? Plutarch and Philostratus' *Life of Apollonius.* Some Themes and Techniques', in Demoen and Praet (eds.): 187–208.

van Dijk, G.-J. (2009) 'The *Odyssey* of Apollonius. An Intertextual Paradigm', in Bowie and Elsner (eds.): 176–202.

van Lieshout, R. G. A. (1980) *Greeks on Dreams.* Utrecht.

van Mal-Maeder, D. (1997) '*Lector, Intende, Laetaberis.* The Enigma of the Last Book of Apuleius' *Metamorphoses*', *Groningen Colloquia on the Novel* 8: 87–118.

van Straten, F. (1976) 'Daikrates' Dream. A Votive Relief from Kos, and Some Other *Kat' Onar* Dedications', *BABesch* 51: 1–38.

  (1981) 'Gifts for the Gods', in Versnel (ed.): 65–151.

  (1992a) 'The Iconography of Epiphany in Classical Greece' (abstract), in Hägg (ed.): 46–7.

  (1992b) 'Votives and Votaries in Greek Sanctuaries', in Schachter and Bingen (eds.): 247–84.

  (1993) 'Images of Gods and Men in a Changing Society. Self-Identity in Hellenistic Religion', in Bulloch *et al.* (eds.): 248–64.

Varner, E. (2006) 'Reading Replications. Roman Rhetoric and Greek Quotations', *Art History* 29: 280–303.

Vasunia, P. (2001) *The Gift of the Nile. Hellenizing Egypt from Aeschylus to Alexander.* Berkeley, Los Angeles and London.

Vermeule, C. C. and M. B. Comstock (1988) *Sculpture in Stone and Bronze. Additions to the Collections of Greek, Etruscan and Roman Art, 1971–1988, in the Museum of Fine Arts, Boston.* Boston.

Vernant, J.-P. (1983) *Myth and Thought among the Greeks.* London and Boston.

  (1985) *La Mort dans les yeux. Figures de l'autre en Grèce ancienne.* Paris.

(1988) *Myth and Society in Ancient Greece*. Trans. J. Lloyd. New York.

(1990a) 'Figuration et image', *Métis* 5: 225–38.

(1990b) *Figures, Idoles, Masques*. Paris.

(1991) *Mortals and Immortals. Collected Essays*. Ed. and trans. F. Zeitlin. Princeton.

(2006) *Myth and Thought among the Greeks*. New edn. Trans. J. Lloyd with J. Fort. Brooklyn, NY.

Versnel, H. S. (ed.) (1981) *Faith, Hope and Worship. Aspects of Religious Mentality in the Ancient World*. Leiden.

(1987) 'What Did Ancient Man See When He Saw a God? Some Reflections on Greco-Roman Epiphany', in C. van der Plas (ed.), *Effigies Dei. Essays on the History of Religions*. Leiden: 42–55.

(1990) *Inconsistencies in Greek and Roman Religion*. Vol. i: *Ter Unus. Isis, Dionysos, Hermes. Three Studies in Henotheism*. Leiden.

(1991) 'Some Reflections on the Relationship Magic–Religion', *Numen* 38: 177–97.

Vestrheim, G. (2002) 'The Poetics of Epiphany in Callimachus' Hymns to Apollo and Pallas', *Eranos* 100: 175–83.

Veyne, P. (1987) 'De Halai en Dalmatie. Un voeu de voyageur et les rêves chez Virgile', in *Poikilia. Études offertes à Jean-Pierre Vernant*. Paris: 381–95.

Vinagre, M. A. (1996) 'Die griechische Terminologie der Traumdeutung', *Mnemosyne* 49: 257–82.

Visscher, F. de (1963) *Le Droit des tombeaux romains*. Milan.

Vlastos, G. (1970) 'Theology and Philosophy in Early Greek Thought', in D. J. Furley and R. E. Allen (eds.), *Studies in Presocratic Philosophy*. Vol. i: *The Beginnings of Philosophy*. London: 92–129. First published in *Philosophical Quarterly* 2 (1952): 97–123.

(1995) *Studies in Greek Philosophy*. Vol. ii: *Socrates, Plato and Their Tradition*. Ed. D. W. Graham. Princeton.

Vollenweider, M.-L. (1958–9) 'Der Traum des Sulla Felix', *Revue Suisse de Numismatique* 39: 22–34.

Vollgraff, W. (1908) 'Praxitèle le jeune', *BCH* 32: 236–58.

von den Hoff, R. (2004) 'Horror and Amazement. Colossal Mythological Statue Groups and the New Rhetoric of Images in Late Second and Early Third Century Rome', in Borg (ed.): 105–29.

von Grunebaum, G. E. and R. Caillois (eds.) (1966) *The Dream and Human Societies*. Berkeley and Los Angeles.

von Reden, S. (1999) 'Re-evaluating Gernet. Value and Greek Myth', in Buxton (ed.): 51–70.

von Rudloff, R. (1999) *Hekate in Ancient Greek Religion*. Victoria, BC.

von Schönborn, C. (1994) *God's Human Face. The Christ-Icon*. Trans. L. Kraugh. San Francisco.

Vout, C. (2006) 'What's in a Beard? Rethinking Hadrian's Hellenism', in Goldhill and Osborne (eds.): 96–123.

(2007) *Power and Eroticism in Imperial Rome.* Cambridge.

Voutiras, E. (1999) 'Opfer für Despoina. Zu Kultsatzung des Heiligtums von Lykosoura *IG* V 2, 514', *Chiron* 29: 233–49.

Wace, A. J. B. (1934) 'The Veil of Despoina', *AJA* 38: 107–11.

Wacht, M. (1998) 'Inkubation', *Reallexikon für Antike und Christentum* 18: cols. 179–265.

Wagenvoort, H. (1956) *Studies in Roman Literature, Culture and Religion.* Leiden.

Wagner, P. (1996) *Icons – Texts – Iconotexts. Essays in Ekphrasis and Intermediality.* Berlin and New York.

Walbank, F. W. (1933) *Aratos of Sicyon.* Cambridge.

(1982) *The Hellenistic World.* Cambridge, MA.

(1984) 'Monarchies and Monarchic Ideas', in F. W. Walbank and A. E. Astin (eds.) *The Cambridge Ancient History.* Vol. vii, part 1: *The Hellenistic World.* 2nd edn. Cambridge: 62–100.

(1987) 'Könige als Götter. Überlegungen zum Herrscherkult von Alexander bis Augustus', *Chiron* 17: 365–82.

Walde, C. (1999) 'Dream Interpretation in a Prosperous Age? Artemidorus, the Greek Interpreter of Dreams', in D. Shulman and G. G. Stroumsa (eds.), *Dream Cultures. Explorations in the Comparative History of Dreaming.* New York and Oxford: 121–42.

(2001) *Antike Traumdeutung und moderne Traumforschung.* Düsseldorf and Zurich.

(2003) Review of Holowchak (2002), *BMCR* 2003.02.01: http://bmcr.brynmawr. edu/2003/2003-02-01.html

(2004) 'Dreams', in *Brill's New Pauly. Encyclopaedia of the Ancient World.* Leiden: 715–19.

Wallace-Hadrill, A. (2008) 'Housing the Dead. The Tomb as House in Roman Italy', in Saller *et al.* (eds.): 39–78.

Wardle, D. (2006) *Cicero on Divination. De Divinatione, Book 1.* Oxford.

Watson, G. (1988) *Phantasia in Classical Thought.* Galway.

(1994) 'The Concept of "Phantasia" from the Late Hellenistic Period to Early Neoplatonism', *ANRW* 2.36.7: 4765–810.

Weaver, J. B. (2004) *Plots of Epiphany. Prison-Escape in Acts of the Apostles.* Berlin.

Webb, P. (1998) 'The Functions of the Sanctuary of Athena and the Pergamon Altar (the Heroon of Telephos) in the Attalid Building Program', in Hartswick and Sturgeon (eds.): 241–54.

Webb, R. (1997a) 'Imagination and the Arousal of the Emotions', in S. Braund and C. Gill (eds.), *The Passions in Roman Literature and Thought.* Cambridge: 112–27.

(1997b) 'Mémoire et imagination. Les limites de l'*enargeia*', in Lévy and Pernot (eds.): 229–48.

(1999) '*Ekphrasis* Ancient and Modern. The Invention of a Genre', *Word and Image* 15: 7–18.

(2006a) 'Fiction, Mimesis and the Performance of the Greek Past in the Second Sophistic', in Konstan (ed.): 27–46.

(2006b) 'The *Imagines* as a Fictional Text. Ekphrasis, *Apatē* and Illusion', in Costantini *et al.* (eds.): 113–36.

Weber, G. (1993) *Dichtung und höfische Gesellschaft. Die Rezeption von Zeitgeschichte am Hof der ersten drei Ptolemäer.* Stuttgart.

(1999) 'Artemidor von Daldis und sein "Publikum"', *Gymnasium* 106: 202–29.

(2000) *Kaiser, Träume und Visionen in Prinzipat und Spätantike.* Stuttgart.

Weinreich, O. (1926) 'Antikes Gottmenschentum', in *Neue Jahrbücher für Wissenschaft und Jungendbildung.* Vol. ii. Leipzig and Berlin: 633–51.

Welles, C. B. (1934) *Royal Correspondence in the Hellenistic Period. A Study in Greek Epigraphy.* New Haven and Prague.

Wendel, C. (1935) *Scholia in Apollonium Rhodium Vetera.* Berlin.

Wesenberg, B. (1985) 'Parthenosgold für den Parthenonbau? Zum Formular der Baurechnungen des Parthenon', *AA*: 49–53.

West, M. L. (1966) *Hesiod. Theogony.* Oxford.

(1970) 'Burning Sappho', *Maia* 22: 307–30.

(1977) 'Balbilla Did Not Save Memnon's Soul', *ZPE* 25: 120.

(1978) *Hesiod. Works and Days.* Oxford.

(2003) 'Iliad and Aithiopis', *CQ* 53: 1–14.

White, H. (1980) 'The Rose of Aphrodite', in H. White (ed.), *Essays in Hellenistic Poetry.* Amsterdam: 17–20.

White, R. J. (1990) *The Interpretation of Dreams. Oneirocritica by Artemidorus. Translation and Commentary.* 2nd edn. Torrance, CA.

Whitmarsh, T. (1998a) 'Reading Power in Roman Greece. The *Paideia* of Dio Chrysostom', in Too and Livingstone (eds.): 192–213.

(1998b) 'The Birth of a Prodigy. Heliodorus and the Genealogy of Hellenism', in R. Hunter (ed.), *Studies in Heliodorus.* Cambridge: 93–124.

(2001a) 'Greece is the World. Exile and Identity in the Second Sophistic', in Goldhill (ed.): 269–305.

(2001b) *Greek Literature and the Roman Empire. The Politics of Imitation.* Oxford.

(2002) 'Written on the Body. Ekphrasis, Perception and Deception in Heliodorus' *Aethiopica*', *Ramus* 31: 111–25.

(2004) 'The Harvest of Wisdom. Landscape, Description, and Identity in the *Heroikos*', in Aitken and Maclean (eds.): 237–49.

(2007) 'Prose Literature and the Severan Dynasty', in Swain *et al.* (eds.): 29–51.

(2009) 'Performing Heroics. Reading and Locating Identity in Philostratus' *Heroicus*', in Bowie and Elsner (eds.): 205–29.

Wiemer, H.-U. (2001) *Rhodische Traditionen in der hellenistischen Historiographie.* Frankfurt am Main.

(2002) *Krieg, Handel und Piraterie. Untersuchungen zur Geschichte des hellenistischen Rhodos*. Berlin.

Wikenhauser, W. (1948) 'Doppelträume', *Biblica* 29: 100–11.

Wilamowitz, U. von (1931) *Der Glaube der Hellenen*. 2 vols. Berlin.

Wildberg, C. (1999–2000) 'Piety as Service, Epiphany as Reciprocity. Two Observations on the Religious Meaning of the Gods in Euripides', *ICS* 24–25: 235–56.

(2002) *Hyperesie und Epiphanie. Ein Versuch über die Bedeutung der Götter in den Dramen des Euripides*. Zetemeta 109. Munich.

Wiles, D. (2007) *Mask and Performance in Greek Tragedy. From Ancient Festival to Modern Experimentation*. Cambridge.

Wilk, S. R. (2000) *Medusa. Solving the Mystery of the Gorgon*. Oxford.

Willcock, M. (1997) 'Neoanalysis', in I. Morris and B. Powell (eds.), *A New Companion to Homer*. Leiden: 174–89.

Willers, D. (1967) 'Zum Hermes Propylaios des Alkamenes', *JDAI* 82: 37–109.

Williamson, G. (2005) 'Mucianus and a Touch of the Miraculous. Pilgrimage and Tourism in Roman Asia Minor', in Elsner and Rutherford (eds.): 219–52.

Winkler, J. J. (1985) *Auctor and Actor. A Narratological Reading of Apuleius'* Golden Ass. Berkeley and Los Angeles.

(1990a) '*Phallos Politikos*. Representing the Body Politic in Athens', *Differences* 2.1: 29–45.

(1990b) *The Constraints of Desire. The Anthropology of Sex and Gender in Ancient Greece*. New York and London.

(2002) 'Double Consciousness in Sappho's Lyrics', in L. K. McClure (ed.), *Sexuality and Gender in the Ancient World. Readings and Sources*. Oxford: 39–71.

Winter, F. E. (2006) *Studies in Hellenistic Architecture*. Toronto.

Wiseman, T. P. (in press) 'Visible Gods, Audible Gods. Epiphany and the Romans', in Petridou and Platt (eds.).

Wohl, V. (2002) *Love among the Ruins. The Erotics of Democracy in Classical Athens*. Princeton.

Wolf, G. (2002) *Schleier und Spiegel. Traditionen des Christusbildes und die Bildkonzepte der Renaissance*. Munich.

Wolfthal, D. (1999) *Images of Rape. The 'Heroic' Tradition and Its Alternatives*. Cambridge.

Wollheim, R. (1980) *Art and Its Objects*. 2nd edn. Cambridge.

Wood, S. (1978) 'Alcestis on Roman Sarcophagi', *AJA* 82: 499–510. Reprinted with a postscript in D'Ambra (ed.) (1993): 84–103.

(2000) 'Mortals, Empresses, and Earth Goddesses. Demeter and Persephone in Public and Private Apotheosis', in Kleiner and Matheson (eds.): 77–100.

Woolf, G. (1994) 'Becoming Roman, Staying Greek. Culture, Identity and the Civilizing Process in the Roman East', *PCPS* 40: 116–43.

Wordelmann, A. (2003) 'Cultural Divides and Dual Realities. A Greco-Roman Context for Acts 14', in T. Penner and C. V. Stichele (eds.), *Contextualizing Acts. Lukan Narrative and Greco-Roman Discourse.* Atlanta, GA: 205–32.

Wörrle, M. (1995) 'Vom tugendsamen Jüngling zum "gestreßten" Euergeten. Überlegungen zum Bürgerbild hellenistischer Ehrendekrete', in Wörrle and Zanker (eds.): 241–50.

Wörrle, M. and P. Zanker (eds.) (1995) *Stadtbild und Bürgerbild im Hellenismus. Kolloquium, München, 24. bis 26. Juni 1993.* Munich.

Wrede, H. (1971) 'Das Mausoleum der Claudia Semne und die bürgerliche Plastik der Kaiserzeit', *RM* 78: 125–66.

   (1981) *Consecratio in formam deorum. Vergöttlichte Privatpersonen in der römischen Kaiserzeit.* Mainz am Rhein.

   (2001) *Senatorische Sarkophage Roms. Der Beitrag des Senatorenstandes zur römischen Kunst der hohen und späten Kaiserzeit.* Mainz am Rhein.

Wu Hung (2009) *The Art of the Yellow Springs. Understanding Chinese Tombs.* London.

Wyler, S. (2006a) 'Images dionysiaques à Rome. À propos d'une fresque augustéenne de Lanuvium', in C. Bonnet, J. Rüpke and P. Scarpi (eds.), *Religions orientales – culti misterici. Neue Perspektiven – nouvelles perspectives – prospettive nuove. Im Rahmen des trilateralen Projektes 'Les religions orientales dans le monde greco-romain'.* Stuttgart: 135–45.

   (2006b) 'Roman Replications of Greek Art at the Villa della Farnesina', *Art History* 29: 213–32.

Yaylalı, A. (1976) *Der Fries des Artemisions von Magnesia am Mäander.* Tübingen.

Zagdoun, M.-A. (2000) *La Philosophie stoïcienne de l'art.* Paris.

Zanker, G. (1987) *Realism in Alexandrian Poetry. A Literature and Its Audience.* London.

   (2003) 'New Light on the Literary Category of "Ecphrastic Epigram" in Antiquity. The New Posidippus (col. x 7 – xi 19 P. Mil. Vogl. viii 309)', *ZPE* 143: 59–62.

   (2004) *Modes of Viewing in Hellenistic Poetry and Art.* Madison, WI.

Zanker, P. (1995a) 'Brüche im Bürgerbild? Zur bürgerlichen Selbstdarstellung in den hellenistischen Städten', in Wörrle and Zanker (eds.): 251–73.

   (1995b) *The Mask of Socrates. The Image of the Intellectual in Antiquity.* Sather Classical Lectures. Berkeley.

   (1999) 'Phädras Trauer und Hippolytos' Bildung. Zu einem Sarkophag im Thermenmuseum', in F. de Angelis and S. Muth (eds.), *Im Spiegel des Mythos. Bilderwelt und Lebenswelt.* Palilia 6. Wiesbaden: 131–42.

Zanker, P. and B. Ewald (2004) *Mit Mythen leben. Die Bilderwelt der römischen Sarkophage.* Munich.

Zeitlin, F. (1986) 'Configurations of Rape in Greek Myth', in Tomaselli and Porter (eds.): 122–51.

(1990) 'The Poetics of Desire. Nature, Art, and Imitation in Longus' *Daphnis and Chloe*', in D. Halperin, J. J. Winkler and F. Zeitlin (eds.), *Before Sexuality. Structures of Erotic Experience in the Ancient Greek World*. Princeton: 417–64.

(2001) 'Visions and Revisions of Homer', in Goldhill (ed.): 195–266.

Ziehen, L. and G. Lippold (1949) 'Palladium', *RE* 18.2: 171–201.

Zimmermann, K. (2000) 'Späthellenistische Kultpraxis in einer karischen Kleinstadt. Eine neue lex sacra aus Bargylia', *Chiron* 30: 451–85.

Ziolkowski, T. (1977) *Disenchanted Images. A Literary Iconology*. Princeton.

Žižek, S. (1989) *The Sublime Object of Ideology*. London.

Züchner, W. (1942) *Griechische Klappspiegel*. Berlin.

Index

Printed in Great Britain
by Amazon

80296987R00285